COMPULSORY PURCHASE AND COMPENSATION

The Law In Scotland

SECOND EDITION

AUSTRALIA
Law Book Co.
Sydney

CANADA and USA
Carswell
Toronto

HONG KONG
Sweet & Maxwell Asia

NEW ZEALAND
Brooker's
Auckland

SINGAPORE and MALAYSIA
Sweet & Maxwell Asia
Singapore and Kuala Lumpur

COMPULSORY PURCHASE AND COMPENSATION

THE LAW IN SCOTLAND

SECOND EDITION

by

Jeremy Rowan Robinson

Emeritus Professor of Planning and Environmental Law,
Aberdeen University
Consultant in Planning and Environmental Law,
Paull & Williamsons, Solicitors

THOMSON
™
W. GREEN

Published in 2003 by

W. Green & Son Ltd
21 Alva Street
Edinburgh EH2 4PS

www.wgreen.co.uk

Typeset by LBJ Typesetting Ltd of Kingsclere
Printed in Great Britain by Creative Print and
Design Wales, Ebbw Vale

No natural forests were destroyed to make this product;
only farmed timber was used and replanted

A CIP catalogue record for this book is available from the British
Library

ISBN 0 414 01468 5

© W. Green & Son Ltd 2003

"Everyone, it seemed, had something bad to say about compulsory purchase law: 'The law is too complex,' say some; 'The powers it confers are inadequate,' say others; 'It's unfair to property owners,' say property owners; 'The procedures are inefficient and slow,' says absolutely everyone. 'Something must be done!' is the cry. Yes, but what?"

Nick Raynsford, Parliamentary Under Secretary of State for the
Environment, Transport and the Regions,
Keynote address to the National Symposium,
Compulsory Purchase: An Appropriate Power for the 21st Century
(1999)

PREFACE

The first edition of this book was published 13 years ago. Deciding when to produce a second edition of a book can be difficult. It has been particularly so in this case given the current interest in the reform of the law relating to compulsory purchase and compensation. Two factors have triggered this interest. First of all, Ministers were under pressure to respond to the very vocal outcry about the effects of the building of a high speed rail link between the Channel Tunnel and London. Secondly, Ministers have been concerned about delays and inefficiencies in bringing land forward to promote urban regeneration.

The outcome was the setting up of the Compulsory Purchase Policy Review Advisory Group (CPPRAG) to look at ways of devising a system of compulsory purchase and compensation which is more efficient, more effective and fairer than that which currently exists. The Group reported in 2000. CPPRAG concluded that the current arrangements are basically sound but went on to recommend quite a large number of changes designed to simplify and speed up the system while making it fairer to those most affected. The report was welcomed by the Minister for Housing, Planning and Regeneration at the DTLR who endorsed many of the recommendations and passed the ball to the Law Commission to consult on proposals for change. At the time of writing, the Law Commission have published two consultation papers, one on compensation and the other on procedure. In the meantime, legislation has now been promoted for England and Wales to implement a proposal to introduce an additional loss payment, beyond market value compensation, for claimants. While this has been going on, an Interdepartmental Working Group has reported on the subject of blight and research has been undertaken into the operation of the Crichel Down rules.

The interest in reform has been felt in Scotland as well. Scotland was represented on CPPRAG and the Executive commissioned a review of the operation of the arrangements for compulsory purchase and compensation in Scotland. This was published in 2001.

It might be thought that a second edition of this book is premature given all this interest in change. After discussion with the publishers, it was decided to proceed for two reasons. First of all, reform is still some years away. The best guess is that the CPPRAG recommendations will not be implemented in England and Wales for a couple of years at least. It remains to be seen whether the Scottish Executive will promote similar reforms in Scotland; but, even if they do, the timescale for implementation will be longer. The opportunity has, however, been taken to draw attention to the principal CPPRAG recommendations at the appropriate points in the text. Secondly, there have been a number of legislative changes and judicial decisions in the 13 years since the first edition appeared to which attention should be drawn. Legislative changes include the Planning and Compensation Act 1991, the Abolition of Feudal Tenure etc. (Scotland) Act 2000, the Title Conditions (Scotland) Bill and the incorporation into domestic law of the European Convention on Human Rights. Judicial decisions of note include those of the House of Lords in *Secretary of State for the Environment v Fletcher*

Estates (Harlescott) Ltd and *Wildtree Hotels Ltd v Harrow London Borough Council* and of the Privy Council in *Director of Buildings and Lands v Shun Fung Ironworks Ltd.*

The primary objective of this book remains as before to describe and explain the procedures governing the compulsory purchase of land and the safeguards, particularly the payment of compensation, which exist to strike an appropriate balance between the interests of the state and those of the individual. As before, the book also goes beyond expropriation to consider the effects on landowners of regulation and blight. For completeness, this edition has gone a step further by introducing a brief explanation of the arrangements whereby utilities acquire rights in land short of ownership.

In writing this second edition, I have tried, as in the first edition, to balance the interests of both practitioners and students. This has meant, not only stating the law, but providing the context for and, in places, commenting on, the law, as well as drawing attention to proposals for change.

I have received assistance from a number of quarters in the preparation of this edition and am pleased to be able to acknowledge this. In particular, I would like to thank Professor Roderick Paisley of the Law School, Aberdeen University, for his helpful comments on Chapter 3 and Paull & Williamsons, Solicitors for allowing me the opportunity to complete the book. I am grateful to the publishers for spiriting an electronic version of the first edition seemingly out of nowhere and to Jennifer Bell and Kathleen Stephen for their magical touch in producing an acceptable final version of the second edition from the depths of my word processor. As always, I am indebted my wife, Yvonne, for her patience.

The law is stated as at February 1, 2003.

Jeremy Rowan Robinson
Aberdeen
February 2003

CONTENTS

TABLE OF CASES

TABLE OF STATUTES OF THE UNITED KINGDOM PARLIAMENT

TABLE OF STATUTES OF THE SCOTTISH PARLIAMENT

TABLE OF PARLIAMENT OF THE UNITED KINGDOM STATUTORY INSTRUMENTS

TABLE OF SCOTTISH STATUTORY INSTRUMENTS

PART 1

COMPULSORY PURCHASE: POWERS AND PROCEDURES

CHAPTER 1

COMPULSORY PURCHASE: POWERS

ORIGINS

From time to time land is required for public purposes. Land may be **1–01** required, for example, to widen a road, to build a school or to install a sewage works. Such land may be, and often is, acquired voluntarily through the normal operation of the market. However, to avoid public purposes being delayed or frustrated by the resistance of a single landowner, land may be acquired compulsorily. "The underlying justification for powers of compulsory purchase," observes Cowie, "is that the loss of private land is offset by the gain to the wider community to which those individuals belong."[1]

The origins of the power to expropriate land probably lie in the sovereignty of the state. The notion that the power has a proprietary core and that, as all land is held ultimately of the Crown, the Crown may resume its original grant is generally discredited.[2] So too is the argument that a social contract exists whereby an individual acquires property under the implied condition that it is to be surrendered at the demand of the state.[3] Erskine says of the power of the state to take private property where required for public purposes:

> "It is another legal limitation or restraint on property, that it must give way to the public necessity or utility. This universal right in the public over property is called by Grotius *dominium eminens*; in virtue of which the supreme power may compel any proprietor to part with what is his own. If, for instance, the public police shall

---

[1] G. S. Cowie, "Background and Concept" in *Compulsory Purchase in Scotland* (1983) *The Law Society of Scotland* Ch. 1.

[2] See Carmen F. Randolph, "The Eminent Domain" (1887) 3 L.Q.R. 314; F. Mann, "Outlines of a History of Expropriation" (1959) 75 L.Q.R. 188; and, generally, the judgements in *Burmah Oil Company (Burma Trading) Ltd. v Lord Advocate*, 1963 S.C. 410; 1964 S.C.(H.L.) 117; 1964 S.L.T. 218.

[3] See above: Although not entering into discussion about the origins of the power of expropriation, both the "Committee on the Acquisition and Valuation of Land for Public Purpose", Scott Committee, Second Report, (1918) HMSO para.8 (Cmnd. 9229) and the "Expert Committee on Compensation and Betterment" Uthwatt Committee, Final Report, (1942) HMSO para.32 (Cmnd. 6386), supported the notion of a social contract in the climate of national emergency following the two World Wars.

require that a highway be carried through the property of a private person, the supreme power may oblige the owner to give up such part of his grounds as is necessary for that purpose; but in this case there must, first, be a necessity or at least an evident utility on the part of the public to justify the exercise of that right; secondly, the persons deprived of their property ought to have a full equivalent for quitting it."[4]

Today, the power of the state to take private property for public purposes is vested in Parliament, and Parliament in turn confers conditional powers of compulsory purchase for specified purposes on various agencies of government and on others. The power to acquire land compulsorily does not, of itself, infringe the European Convention on Human Rights, provided the acquisition is shown to be in the public interest (see p.13).[5] The decision of the House of Lords in *Burmah Oil Co. (Burma Trading) Ltd. v The Lord Advocate*[6] indicates that there remains with the Crown a prerogative power to take or destroy a subject's property in time of War.[7]

DEVELOPMENT

1–02　Cowie, in an interesting description of the early use of compulsory purchase powers in Scotland,[8] suggests that "the Union of the Parliament, the failed Jacobite rebellions and the two revolutions, the agrarian and the industrial, were each partially responsible for stimulating developments which led to the grant of statutory powers of compulsory acquisition." The Union opened up the prospect of trade with the colonies and led to the establishment of harbours and to the conversion of the Clyde into an important navigable waterway. The rebellions resulted in the passage of legislation providing for the expropriation or forfeiture of lands belonging to the disaffected clans. But it was the agrarian and industrial revolutions which first led to the conferment of extensive powers of compulsory purchase.

By the middle of the eighteenth century the movement of population to the towns underlined the need for improved communications. Shortcomings in the statute labour system for maintaining and improving the road network led to the advent of the turnpikes. However, for the bulk transport of raw materials for the new industries attention focused initially on the construction of canals. Construction of the Forth and

---

[4] Erskine, *Institutes*, II, i, 2. See, too, Bell, *Principles*, "the exclusive right of a landowner yields whenever public interest or necessity requires that it should yield."

[5] First Protocol, Article 1.

[6] 1964 S.C. (H.L.) 117; 1964 S.L.T. 218.

[7] But see *Attorney-General v De Keyser's Royal Hotel Ltd.* [1920] A.C. 50 (H.L.) where it was held that a statute providing for conditional compulsory acquisition of land by the Crown was inconsistent with the continuance of a prerogative right of unconditional compulsory acquisition.

[8] G. S. Cowie, "Background and Concept" in *Compulsory Purchase in Scotland*, Chap.1. See too, G. S. Cowie, "Compulsory Acquisition and Compensation—The Background," paper delivered to a Law Society of Scotland seminar in December 1979.

Clyde Canal was authorised by a private Act in 1768 and eventually completed in 1790. The railways, many of which began as canal feeders, soon established themselves as major competitors and between 1812 and 1849, a total of 795 miles of track was laid in Scotland. Competition was fierce and the volume of private legislation required made considerable inroads into parliamentary time. Cowie cites Lord Cockburn in his *Circuit Journeys* in April 1845 as summarising the spirit of the time: "From Edinburgh to Inverness the whole people are mad about railways. The country is an asylum of railway lunatics."[9] Meanwhile, the provision of adequate supplies of water proved particularly problematic and a number of schemes were promoted to improve the position. Notable amongst these was the Act of 1855 which enabled water to be piped from Loch Katrine to the City of Glasgow. Specific powers of compulsory purchase were also conferred on local authorities to whom responsibility for tackling the worst abuses of the industrial revolution was passing. More general powers were contained in the public and general legislation directed at public health, housing and planning which followed in the second half of the nineteenth century and the beginning of the twentieth century.

The acquisition of land for public purposes was envisaged on a large scale in the period of national reconstruction following the end of the First World War. Land would be required for housing, for the development of agriculture and forestry, for reclamation and land drainage, for the provision of an effective and co-ordinated system of transport, for access to natural and mineral resources, for the use of electricity and water power as national sources of energy, for the development of aviation for commercial purposes and for national defence and administration. The first report of the committee dealing with the *Acquisition and Valuation of Land for Public Purposes* (the Scott Committee) emphasised that "Unnecessary delays or prohibitive expenses attaching to the acquisition of land essential for the purposes in question, would be liable to block the whole path of efficient reconstruction, and to stifle at their inception many valuable schemes of productive enterprise."[10]

Similar views were expressed in the final report of the *Expert Committee on Compensation and Betterment* (the Uthwatt Committee) during the Second World War.[11] The simplest and only effective method of coping with the work of post-war reconstruction of towns and cities, concluded the Committee, would be "to confer on the planning authority compulsory powers of purchase, much wider and more simple in operation than under existing legislation, over any land which may be required for planning or other public purposes."[12] Compulsory purchase powers were considered to be the key to positive planning. Subsequent legislation conferred on public authorities wider powers of compulsory purchase than ever before in order to cope with war damage, with the blighted areas of towns and cities, with the redistribution of population through the new town and town development programmes, with the **1–03**

---

[9] See above.
[10] (1918) HMSO para.4 (Cmnd. 8998).
[11] (1942) HMSO paras 6–7 (Cmnd. 6386).
[12] See above, para.144.

programme of nationalisation and with the advance of the welfare state. These powers were widely employed in Scotland to establish the five new towns, to tackle town centre redevelopment and to deal with the legacy of substandard housing resulting from the rapid urbanisation of the nineteenth century. In Glasgow, in particular, the high proportion of one and two-room houses forced housing to the forefront. "The rapid build up of the Nineteenth-Century city meant a rapid accumulation of obsolescent houses in the Twentieth Century. This accumulation has been acute since 1945, bringing a heavy emphasis on slum clearance and the corollaries of high-density new development or overspill beyond the city boundary."[13] The problem was tackled through the designation of 29 comprehensive development areas under the Town and Country Planning (Scotland) Act 1947, supported by a massive programme of land acquisition.

Since the Second World War, both the main political parties have acknowledged the role of compulsory purchase powers in positive planning. The power to acquire land performs an enabling function. However, socialist ideology, as Grant observes, "has viewed public ownership of development land not simply as a key to better planning, but as a desirable end in itself. This is partly a nationalisation argument, but it is also based on the clear financial and planning advantages that public ownership is capable of bringing to the community."[14] Compulsory purchase powers were an important component of the three comprehensive attempts by Labour administrations since the war to recover for the community increases in land values resulting from public sector actions and decisions. The financial provisions of the Town and Country Planning (Scotland) Act 1947, the Land Commission Act 1967 and the Community Land Act 1975 all contained compulsory purchase powers, those in the 1975 Act being particularly extensive. The three attempts ran into very considerable difficulties and were dismantled by the subsequent incoming Conservative administrations. The impact of the compulsory purchase powers was limited.

During the late 1960s and the 1970s attention focussed on the use of compulsory purchase powers to support the road building programme, in particular the motorways. The impact of the road programme was felt not only by those displaced from property along the line of a new road but also by those living alongside it. The environmental impact of the construction and use of a major new road, especially the urban motorways, could be very considerable. The White Paper *Development and Compensation—Putting People First*[15] acknowledged the need to strike a balance between "the overriding duty of the State to ensure that essential developments are undertaken for the benefit of the whole community and the no less compelling need to protect the interests of those whose personal rights or private property may be injured in the process". The White Paper went on to conclude that in recent years this

---

[13] T. Hait, "The Comprehensive Development Area (Oliver and Boyd)", (1968) *University of Glasgow Social and Economic Studies* Occasional Paper No. 9.

[14] M. Grant, *Urban Planning Law* (Sweet & Maxwell, 1982), Second Cumulative Supplement (1989), pp.500–501.

[15] (1972) HMSO para.1 (Cmnd. 5124).

balance in too many cases had been tipped against the interests of the individual and a better deal in the form of improved compensation was required for those who suffered from desirable community developments. This better deal was implemented in the Land Compensation (Scotland) Act 1973. Similar arguments about the need for a better deal have been heard in connection with the proposal for a high speed rail link connecting the Channel Tunnel to London.

To avoid public purposes being delayed or frustrated, compulsory purchase powers continued to be employed during Mrs Thatcher's three administrations notwithstanding that government's commitment to the primacy of the market place. At a public inquiry in 1987 into objections to a compulsory purchase order made by the London Docklands Development Corporation (LDDC), the Corporation's principal surveyor in his evidence on the LDDC's policy on land acquisition stated: "The Corporation has adopted a substantial and increasing programme of Compulsory Purchase Orders (CPOs) to complement and reinforce negotiations for acquisition by agreement with the owners. The Corporation relies on the effective and speedy resolution of its applications for CPOs to ensure regeneration on the scale and pace desired." And Sheffield Development Corporation were given the go ahead for a complex compulsory purchase programme as the key to the revitalisation of the Lower Don Valley having concluded that normal market forces would be unable to assemble the necessary land.[16]

More recently concern has been expressed about the adequacy of **1–04** existing compulsory purchase powers to deal with the regeneration of run down urban areas.[17] In response the DTLR announced an intention in England and Wales to clarify and make more specific the powers under which local authorities can intervene.[18] A contemporary survey of the use of compulsory purchase powers in Scotland showed that, with the exception of road schemes, acquiring authorities make little use of such powers.[19] This was attributed partly to limited need to do so, partly to problems of resourcing and partly to the perception that compulsory purchase procedure is slow and uncertain. The report, however, anticipated some increase in the use of powers by local authorities in the future as a response to the encouragement by government to steer more development to brownfield sites.[20]

---

[16] See too J. Walker, "Revitalisation through redevelopment: the experience of the new towns and UDCs" (1999) "Proceedings of the national symposium on compulsory purchase: An appropriate power for the 21st Century" DETR.

[17] See the discussion in "Fundamental review of the laws and procedures relating to compulsory purchase and compensation" (2000) DETR paras.29–37.

[18] "Compulsory purchase and compensation: delivering a fundamental change" (2001) DTLR para.2.2.

[19] I.H. Murning, Dundas & Wilson and Montagu Evans, "Review of compulsory purchase and land compensation" (2001) *Scottish Executive Central Research Unit* para.4.13. For a contrary view see D. Adams, "The Use of Compulsory Purchase under Planning Legislation" [1996] J.P.L. 275.

[20] The recent I.H. Murning, Dundas & Wilson and Montagu Evans, "Review of Compulsory Purchase and Land Compensation" (2001) SECRU recommended that Scottish Ministers should provide a clear policy statement on the use of compulsory purchase powers (para.6.11(i)).

It seems appropriate to conclude with Davies that: "As long as governments exist, and they will always exist in some form, they and their agencies will need land".[21]

1–05 The loss to the individual from the compulsory purchase of land is justified by the gain to the wider community of which the individual is a part. The history of the development of compulsory purchase powers is one of striving to achieve a balance between retaining adequate safeguards for the interests of the individual on the one hand and the importance of not delaying schemes which are to serve a much needed public purpose on the other.

As already mentioned, it was the agrarian and industrial revolutions which first led to the conferment of extensive powers of compulsory purchase. The harbours, canals and railways which were so much a part of the industrial revolution were constructed and operated by private enterprise. These schemes were generally beyond the resources of a single individual. Promoters would therefore petition for private Act powers from Parliament seeking the benefits of incorporation and the right to expropriate land for the purposes in question so that the schemes could not be held hostage to the whim of a single landowner. Each private Bill was self-contained. It sought compulsory purchase powers in respect of specified land, and made comprehensive provision for the machinery of acquisition and for the assessment and payment of compensation. Before granting such powers, Parliament had to be satisfied that the scheme was of public utility. Furthermore, those whose property rights were to be affected by the proposal had to be given notice and accorded an opportunity of being heard. The massive output of private Acts during the railway building age required a correspondingly large input of parliamentary time.

In order to make more effective use of Parliamentary time a series of Clauses Acts were passed during the middle of the nineteenth century. Clauses Acts contained in one piece of legislation numerous procedural provisions commonly to be found in each individual private Act promoting a particular type of scheme, whether it was a harbour, a water works or a railway. The Clauses Act would be incorporated into each private Act passed subsequently concerned with that type of scheme. This would avoid the need to repeat these provisions in the legislation and enable Parliament to focus more attention on the merits of the scheme proposed.

1–06 The Lands Clauses Acts contain procedural provisions dealing with the acquisition of land and the assessment and payment of compensation. The principal Act is the Lands Clauses Consolidation (Scotland) Act 1845. Section 1 of that Act provides:

"This Act shall apply to every undertaking in Scotland authorised by any Act of Parliament which shall hereafter be passed, and which

---

[21] K. Davies, *Law of Compulsory Purchase and Compensation* (5th ed., Tolley), p.xlvii.

shall authorise the taking of lands for such undertaking, and this Act shall be incorporated with such Act; and all the provisions of this Act, save so far as they shall be expressly varied or expected by any such Act, shall apply to the undertaking authorised thereby so far as the same shall be applicable to such undertaking, and shall, as well as the clauses and provisions of every other Act which shall be incorporated with such Act, form part of such Act, and be construed together therewith as forming one Act."

The 1845 Act does not, of itself, authorise the acquisition of any land. A private Act would still be required to confer the power to acquire particular land. The 1845 Act would then be specifically incorporated into the private Act (referred to as the "special Act")[22] although certain provisions might be expressly excluded.

The provisions of the 1845 Act are grouped under a number of headings including the purchase of lands by agreement, the purchase of lands otherwise than by agreement, the application of compensation, conveyances, and entry on lands. Although the drafting and arrangement of the provisions in the 1845 Act have been the subject of some criticism,[23] and although there has been considerable subsequent amendment, the Act is still the source of much of the law relating to compulsory purchase in Scotland today. There has been no consolidation and amendment of the law such as is to be found in England in the Compulsory Purchase Act 1965. The Compulsory Purchase Policy Review Advisory Group (CPPRAG) recently recommended consolidation, codification and simplification of the legislation south of the border.[24] The need for such change would seem to be even more pressing in Scotland. The detailed provisions of the 1845 Act are examined in later chapters.

Notwithstanding the Lands Clauses Act, private Bill procedure was **1–07** not well-suited to the seemingly unending series of schemes of development which were coming forward in the mid-nineteenth century. As Wraith and Lamb[25] observe: "It was a mode of legislation appropriate to

---

[22] "Special Act" refers to "any Act which shall be hereafter passed, and which shall authorise the taking of lands for the undertaking to which the same relates, and with which this Act shall be so incorporated as aforesaid" (1845 Act, s.2).

[23] For example, in *Bridge of Allan Water Co. v Alexander* (1868) 6 M. 321 the division of the Act into parts was criticised by Lord President Inglis as "not logical or precise but the reverse"; and in *Heriots Trust Governors v Caledonian Railway Co.*, 1915 S.C. (H.L.) 52; (1915) 1 S.L.T. 347 Lord Chancellor Haldane said "The Act is badly drawn. The draftsman seems in more places than one not to have realised clearly the matter of the changes which he was seeking to effect. I think it is idle to find in the various sections a constant and harmonious purpose." See too Lord Dunedin in *Heriot's Trust Governors* and in *Fraser v Caledonian Railway Co.*, 1911 S.C. 145; (1910) 2 S.L.T. 367.

[24] "Fundamental review of the laws and procedures relating to compulsory purchase and compensation" (2000) DETR para.24. See too G. Roots, "Compensation for Compulsory Purchase: Modernising Compensation" in *Proceedings of the National symposium on compulsory purchase: an appropriate power for the 21st Century*, (1999) DETR. In *Compulsory purchase and compensation: a fundamental change* (2001), the DTLR committed itself to working with the Law Commission to introduce clear, unambiguous consolidating legislation.

[25] R. E. Wraith and G. B. Lamb, *Public Inquiries as an Instrument of Government* (George Allen and Unwin, 1971) pp.18 and 19.

a simple society with poor communications, and one which had a high respect for the rights of property, but it was becoming increasingly expensive and time-consuming in the context of a developing country." Provisional order procedure which began to replace private Bill procedure about that time removed from Parliament much of the time-consuming task of scrutinising proposals. Digressing for a moment from the chronology of the attempts to streamline compulsory purchase procedures, it should be noted that private bill procedure was, nonetheless, still being employed on occasion in the second half of the twentieth century as a means of acquiring compulsory purchase powers where provisional order procedure was considered inappropriate.[26] A notable example was the Zetland County Council Bill which became the Zetland County Council Act 1974, and which provided, amongst other things, for the compulsory acquisition of land by order for harbour purposes and for the huge Sullom Voe oil terminal in Shetland.[27] Following devolution, private bills dealing solely with devolved matters can only be introduced into the Scottish Parliament. There they are subject to the procedures described in Chapter 9A of the Standing Orders and in the 'Guidance on Private Bills' produced by the Directorate of Clerking and Reporting. The key to the non-Executive private Bill procedure is the consideration stage by the Private Bill Committee. The procedure is quasi-judicial with the promoter calling witnesses to give evidence who may be cross-examined by those opposing the Bill and with the opponents also giving evidence.

Provisional order procedure was generally more straightforward than private bill procedure. Application for a provisional order was made, not to Parliament, but to a Minister and notice would be given to those most closely affected. The Minister, in the event of objection, would arrange for a public local inquiry to be held by commissioners to consider the proposal and any objection to it. After receiving the report of the commissioners the Minister was empowered to make a provisional order. Such an order was of no effect unless and until it was confirmed by Act of Parliament. The Minister, having made an order, would promote a Provisional Order Confirmation Bill. If, as was usually the case, the Bill was passed without opposition there would be a considerable overall saving of both time and expense. On the other hand, if as occasionally happened the Bill was opposed in Parliament, it would have to go through the equivalent of private Bill procedure and the whole process from petition for a provisional order to eventual enactment would be very time consuming. The Confirmation Act became the "special Act" for the purposes of the Lands Clauses Consolidation (Scotland) Act 1845.

---

[26] Provisional order procedure was inappropriate if the proposed legislation related to matters outside Scotland or raised questions of public policy which were novel and important (Private Legislation Procedure (Scotland) Act 1936, s.2). For a comprehensive reappraisal of the place of private Bill procedure in the twentieth century see Report of the Joint Committee on Private Bill Procedure, session 1987–88, H.L. 97; H.C. 625; (HMSO, July 1988).

[27] The passage of the Bill was described in C.M.G. Himsworth, "The Origins and Legislative History of the Zetland County Council Act 1974," unpublished paper presented to a seminar on Legal Research Related to the Social and Economic Impact of Offshore Oil and Gas, Centre for Petroleum and Mineral Law Studies, University of Dundee, 1979.

Digressing again from the chronology for the sake of completeness, it should be noted that provisional order procedure was still employed from time to time up until devolution by promoters seeking compulsory purchase powers. The procedure to be followed was set out in the Private Legislation Procedure (Scotland) Act 1936.[28] However, following devolution, the procedure no longer applies where a promoter is seeking powers the conferring of which is wholly within the legislative competence of the Scottish Parliament.[29]

Provisional order procedure was also incorporated into public and **1–08** general Acts passed during the second half of the nineteenth century conferring power on local authorities to tackle the abuses of the industrial revolution. With the passage of time, the procedure was refined to reduce delay when possible in implementing schemes.[30] The Public Health (Scotland) Act 1897, for example, made provision for a confirmation Act only in the event of objections to the provisional order. In the absence of objections, the order became final and had the effect of an Act of Parliament.

In 1918 the Scott Committee,[31] looking ahead to the period of national reconstruction which would follow the First World War, drew attention to the "indefensible complexities" of the procedures for acquiring land for public purposes. The committee concluded that: "The need of establishing some simpler, more uniform, less costly, and more expeditious system for the compulsory acquisition of land for any purposes of national importance appears, therefore, to be imperative." The committee's report produced no immediate response but aided the gradual transition in public and general Acts from provisional order to the modern compulsory purchase order which continued up to the end of the Second World War. The effect of the transition was that once Parliament had conferred a general power on, for example, a local authority to acquire land compulsorily for public purposes, the exercise of the power by the authority in a particular case was removed from the scrutiny of Parliament and placed wholly under the control of a Minister. The public and general Act under which the purchase was authorised together with the compulsory purchase order were together treated as the "special Act" for the purposes of the Lands Clauses Consolidation (Scotland) Act 1845.

The Uthwatt Committee in 1942 endorsed the conclusion of the Scott Committee about the need for a "simpler, more uniform, less costly and more expeditious system for the compulsory purchase of land" for public purposes in the aftermath of the Second World War.[32] The somewhat

---

[28] For an interesting example of the use of provisional order procedure prior to devolution see J. Russell and P. Shanks, "The Edinburgh Western Relief Road: By-Pass of Planning Procedures" (1986) 19 S.P.L.P. 73.

[29] Scotland Act 1998, s.125 and Sch.8, para.5.

[30] For a description of the transition from provisional order to compulsory purchase order see G. S. Cowie, "Background and Concept" in *Compulsory Purchase in Scotland* (1983) The Law Society of Scotland Chap. 1.

[31] "First Report of the Committee on the Acquisition and Valuation of Land for Public Purposes" (1918) HMSO (Cmnd. 9229).

[32] "Final Report of the Expert Committee on Compensation and Betterment" (1942) HMSO para.158 (Cmnd. 6386).

draconian measures proposed by the committee were not implemented but in the Acquisition of Land (Authorisation Procedure) (Scotland) Act 1947 a standardised procedure for compulsory purchase was at last introduced. This procedure, which operates today, is considered in detail in Chapters 2 and 3.

The procedure draws on the experience of earlier legislation. Its centrepiece is the compulsory purchase order. The procedure differs slightly according to whether the order is promoted by a local or other authority or by the Scottish Ministers. A local authority seeking to acquire land compulsorily makes such an order which is submitted for confirmation by the Ministers. Notice of the making of the order must be given to those whose interests are being acquired and to the public at large. In the event of an objection by a person whose interest is being acquired a public inquiry must be held. The Scottish Ministers' decision to confirm the order must be notified to those with an interest in the land and to the public at large. There is an opportunity to challenge the validity of the order by way of application to the Court of Session on specified grounds within six weeks of publication of the notice of confirmation. The compulsory acquisition of certain special categories of land (land forming part of a common or open space or held inalienably by the National Trust for Scotland) may still, however, be required to go through an additional parliamentary procedure.[33]

1–09   The 1947 Act not only introduced a standardised compulsory purchase procedure, it incorporated a provision which had appeared in earlier legislation allowing for entry to the land following service of a notice of entry in advance of agreement or on determination of the compensation and in advance of the conveyancing formalities. However, provision for early entry on to the land was not enough in some cases. Acquiring authorities sometimes needed to be able to obtain title to the land speedily. An expedited completion procedure first appeared in the Sixth Schedule to the Town and Country Planning (Scotland) Act 1945. The procedure was restricted in its scope and was subject to ministerial direction. These limitations were gradually removed and the expedited procedure for vesting title in the acquiring authority set out in section 195 of and Schedule 15 to the Town and Country Planning (Scotland) Act 1997 is now widely available.

The Uthwatt Committee was concerned not only with the need for simpler and more uniform acquisition procedures but with the need for much wider compulsory purchase powers to facilitate the task of the public sector in the period of reconstruction following the Second World War. Wide enabling powers were subsequently conferred by the Town and Country Planning (Scotland) Act 1947 on planning authorities to secure the comprehensive development of an area. These powers are now contained in section 189(1) of the Town and Country Planning (Scotland) Act 1997 and empower planning authorities to acquire land compulsorily for development, redevelopment and improvement and for the proper planning of an area.[34] Wide general powers to acquire land

---

[33] See the Scotland Act 1998, s.94 and the Scotland Act 1998 (Transitory and Transitional Provisions) (Orders subject to Special Parliamentary Procedure) Order 1999, SI 1999/1593.

[34] For criticism of the adequacy of these powers to deal with regeneration of run down urban areas, see p.5 above.

compulsorily for the purpose of discharging any of their functions are also conferred on local authorities by section 71 of the Local Government (Scotland) Act 1973 (but see p.18).[35]

More recently, serious concern has been expressed about the length of time taken from the making of a compulsory purchase order to the date of vesting and from the date of vesting to the eventual payment of compensation.[36] CPPRAG acknowledged that long delay and uncertainty can be very unsettling to those directly affected and can be a very real problem for businesses.[37] Their recommendations for speeding up the process were sympathetically received by the DTLR and are currently under consideration.[38] The position in Scotland is awaited.

At the beginning of this section of this chapter it was suggested that the history of the development of compulsory purchase powers has been one of striving to achieve a balance between retaining adequate safeguards for the interests of the individual on the one hand and the importance of not delaying schemes which are to serve a much needed public purpose on the other. Modern compulsory purchase procedure appears to strike a reasonable balance. On occasion, however, it would seem that the dictates of public policy have tipped the balance somewhat against the individual. The New Towns (Scotland) Act 1968, for example, permits the confirming authority to disregard an objection to a compulsory purchase order if he is satisfied that the objection is made on the ground that the acquisition is unnecessary or inexpedient.[39] And the Offshore Petroleum Development (Scotland) Act 1975, which enables the Secretary of State to acquire land for any purposes connected with the exploration for or exploitation of offshore petroleum, contains an expedited compulsory purchase procedure for use where land is required as a matter of urgency under which an inquiry or hearing into objections may be dispensed with.[40]

CONSTRUCTION OF COMPULSORY PURCHASE POWERS

In the search for the appropriate balance between the interests of the **1–10** individual on the one hand and the importance of not delaying schemes which are to serve much needed public purposes on the other, the courts have tended to side with the individual. Indeed the general rule in the

---

[35] The Community Land Act 1975 which was directed at bringing development land into public ownership contained an almost unlimited power to acquire land compulsorily.

[36] City University Business School, "The operation of compulsory purchase orders" (1997) *Department of the Environment*; J. Rowan-Robinson and N. Hutchison, "Compensation for compulsory acquisition of business interests: satisfaction or sacrifice?" (1995) Vol.13(1) *Journal of Property Valuation and Investment* 44.

[37] "Fundamental review of the laws and procedures relating to compulsory purchase and compensation" (2000) DETR Final Report.

[38] "Compulsory purchase and compensation: delivering a fundamental change" (2001) DTLR.

[39] Schedule 3, Pt I, para.4(3). The Community Land Act 1975 contained a similar provision (see s.15 and Sch.4). Although the 1968 Act remains in force, the five Scottish New Town Development Corporations were wound up under the provisions of Part II of the Enterprise and New Towns (Scotland) Act 1990.

[40] The Land Commission Act 1967 contained a similar provision (see s.9 and Sch.2).

interpretation of statutes which interfere with property rights is that they
are subject to restrictive construction.[41] Thus an acquiring authority has
no rights beyond those expressly conferred[42]; it may not, where it is
authorised to acquire land compulsorily for specified purposes, exercise
those powers for a different purpose[43]; and it must act in good faith.[44]

However, in *De Rothschild v Secretary of State for Transport*,[45] the
Court of Appeal firmly rejected the proposition that there were to be
derived from case law special tests which are applicable whenever a
court is considering a challenge to an exercise of compulsory purchase
powers beyond those which are normally applied by the courts in
reviewing the actions and decisions of public bodies. There was no
question that a higher standard falls to be applied by the courts on the
ground that the compulsory acquisition of private property takes place
against the wishes of the owners and occupiers.

This statement needs to be seen in the light of its subsequent
refinement by Laws J in *Chesterfield Properties plc v Secretary of State for
the Environment, Secretary of State for Transport and Stockton-on-Tees
Borough Council.*[46] *De Rothschild,* he said, clearly established that the
ordinary public law principles enunciated in *Wednesbury Corporation v
Minister of Housing and Local Government*[47] apply to compulsory purchase decisions as they do to other statutory discretions. *Wednesbury,*
however, was not a monolithic standard of review. He continued by
saying that, where an administrative decision abrogates or diminishes a
constitutional or fundamental right, *Wednesbury* requires that the
decision-maker provide a substantial justification in the public interest
for doing so. Ownership of land is recognised as a constitutional right.
That, however, means nothing in the absence of a written constitution
unless it is defined by reference to some particular protection which the
law affords to it. He went on:

> "The common law affords such protection by adopting, within
> *Wednesbury,* a variable standard of review. There is no question of
> the court exceeding the principle of reasonableness. It means only
> that reasonableness itself requires in such cases that in ordering the
> priorities which will drive his decision, the decision-maker must give
> a high place to the right in question. He cannot treat it merely as
> something to be taken into account, akin to any other relevant
> consideration; he must recognise it as a value to be kept, unless in
> his judgement there is a greater value that justifies its loss. In many
> arenas of public discretion, the force to be given to all and any

---

[41] P. St J. Langan, *Maxwell on the Interpretation of Statutes* (12th ed., Sweet & Maxwell),
Chap.11.4; S. G. G. Edgar, *Craies on Statute Law* (7th ed., Sweet & Maxwell), Chap.12.3.
And see *Moncrieffe v Perth Harbour Commissioners* (1846) 5 Bell 333.

[42] *Marquess of Breadalbane v West Highland Railway Co.* (1895) 22 R. 307; *Sovmots
Investment Ltd. v Secretary of State for the Environment* [1977] 1 Q.B. 411.

[43] *Municipal Council of Sydney v Campbell* [1925] A.C. 338.

[44] *Michael v Corporation of Edinburgh* (1895) 3 S.L.T. 109.

[45] [1989] J.P.L. 173. See, too, *Singh v Secretary of State for the Environment* (1989) 24
E.G. 128; and, generally, Chap.2, p.40 *et seq.*

[46] [1998] J.P.L. 568.

[47] [1948] 1 K.B. 233.

factors which the decision-maker must confront is neutral in the eye of the law; he may make of each what he will, and the law will not interfere because the weight he attributes to any of them is for him and not the court. But where a constitutional right is involved, the law presumes it to carry substantial force. Only another interest, a public interest, or greater force may override it".[48]

As Purdue observes in his comment on the case, this boils down to a **1–11** requirement that special weight has to be given to the fact that the ownership of land is a constitutional right. So, unlike the normal *Wednesbury* position, the weight to be given to this consideration is not entirely a matter for the decision-maker; the courts could have a role in scrutinising the justification for acquisition to see whether the appropriate weight has been given.

The recognition by Laws J. in *Chesterfield Properties* of ownership as a constitutional right has been reinforced by the incorporation into domestic law of the European Convention on Human Rights. Section 6(1) of the Human Rights Act 1998 provides that it is unlawful for a public authority to act in a way which is incompatible with a Convention right. The relevant right is to be found in Article 1 of the First Protocol to the Convention. This states that:

"Every natural or legal person is entitled to the peaceful enjoyment of his possessions. No one shall be deprived of his possessions except in the public interest and subject to the conditions provided for by law and by the general principles of international law".[49]

Article 1 puts the right to which Laws J. referred on a firmer constitutional footing. However, in considering whether there has been a violation of Article 1, a margin of appreciation is allowed to states. Providing it can be shown that the exercise of compulsory purchase powers was a proportionate response in the circumstances, it will be difficult to argue that there has been an infringement of a Convention right. In *Tesco Stores Ltd v Secretary of State for the Environment, Transport and the Regions and Wycombe District Council*,[50] Sullivan J. held that the Convention and the principle of proportionality add no new dimension to the applicable pre-Convention jurisprudence. As before, it simply requires a compelling case for the acquisition to be shown in the public interest. In *Bexley London Borough Council v Secretary of State for the Environment*[51] Harrison J., after adopting the approach of Sullivan J. in Tesco Stores, observed that it was not necessary for the Secretary of State to set out in some formulaic way the extent to which the scheme being promoted was better than any alternative scheme, the extent of interference with property rights and a conclusion on proportionality following the weighing of these factors. It was sufficient if the relevant conclusions could be determined from reading the decision letter as a whole.

---

[48] pp.579–580.
[49] See too Article 8 of the Convention as respects residential property.
[50] [2001] J.P.L. 106.
[51] [2001] J.P.L. 1442.

The powers of compulsory purchase are conferred on an acquiring authority in furtherance of a particular legislative objective and consequently an agreement in which an authority binds itself not to use those powers will be void.[52] It would appear, though, that there is nothing wrong in an acquiring authority giving an undertaking not to implement the powers conferred by a compulsory purchase order if the owner is prepared to fulfill the purpose for which the land was to be acquired in a rapid and effective manner.[53] However, in *R. v Secretary of State for the Environment, ex p. Leicester City Council*,[54] McCullough J. held that the Secretary of State had not erred in law in refusing to confirm a compulsory purchase order where the acquiring authority had offered undertakings to individual owners of plots of the order land. The undertakings had been to the effect that the authority would not compulsorily acquire the land so long as the owners entered into agreements to make financial contributions towards the construction of roads and sewers. The Secretary of State was not satisfied that the order land was required to be compulsorily purchased for the purposes of redevelopment and improvement. Nor had the Minister erred in his conclusion that if he confirmed the order in these circumstances he would be exercising his power for an improper purpose, namely as a means of inducing the owners to make financial contributions to the development of the land.

---

[52] *Ayr Harbour Trustees v Oswald* (1883) 10 R. (H.L.) 85.
[53] See, for example, *Singh v Secretary of State for the Environment* (1989) 24 E.G. 128.
[54] (1988) 55 P. & C.R. 364.

CHAPTER 2

COMPULSORY PURCHASE: PROCEDURE[1]

The procedure for making and, where appropriate, confirming a com- **2–01**
pulsory purchase order is regulated in most cases by the Acquisition of
Land (Authorisation Procedure) (Scotland) Act 1947.

The 1947 Act procedure was applied to compulsory acquisition by
local authorities under public and general Acts in force at the time of its
commencement[2] and by certain Ministers under specified Acts, and is
usually incorporated with authorising Acts passed subsequently. The
Secretary of State, on the application of a local authority, could also
direct that the 1947 Act procedure should apply to the exercise of a
power to acquire land compulsorily conferred by a local Act in force
prior to April 1, 1946.[3] The 1947 Act procedure may also be applied by
local Acts passed subsequently.

Section 1(1) of the 1947 Act now applies[4] so that the authorisation of
any compulsory purchase of land by a local authority,[5] any statutory
undertakers,[6] by the Scottish Ministers or by another Minister in
connection with a matter reserved by the Scotland Act 1998 shall be
conferred by an order in accordance with the provisions of the first
Schedule to the Act.

The following enactments are specifically excepted from the 1947 Act
procedure[7]:

(i) the Burial Grounds (Scotland) Act 1855;

---

[1] See, generally, The Law Society of Scotland, "Compulsory Acquisition and Compensation", *Stair Memorial Encyclopaedia*, Vol. 5 (Butterworths). Also The Law Society of
Scotland, "Compulsory Purchase in Scotland" (1983).

[2] 1947 Act, s.1(1)(a).

[3] 1947 Act, s.6(1).

[4] As a result of the Community Land Act 1975, s.41 as subsequently re-enacted with
modifications upon the repeal of that Act in the Local Government, Planning and Land
Act 1980, s.120(1).

[5] "Local authority" in relation to Scotland means a council established under the
provisions of the Local Government, etc (Scotland) Act 1994.

[6] "Statutory undertakers" mean: (a) persons authorised by any enactment to carry on
any railway, light railway, tramway, road transport, water transport, canal, inland navigation, dock, harbour, pier or lighthouse undertaking or any undertaking for the supply of
hydraulic power or water; (b) the Post Office, and any other authority, body or undertakers
which by virtue of any enactment are to be treated as statutory undertakers for the
purposes of the Town and Country Planning (Scotland) Act 1997; and (c) any other
authority, body or undertakers specified in an order made by the Scottish Ministers under
this paragraph (Local Government, Planning and Land Act 1980, s.120(3), as amended).

[7] 1947 Act, s.1(4).

    (ii) the Allotments (Scotland) Acts 1892–1950;

    (iii) the Light Railways Acts 1896 and 1912.

In addition, a number of more recent Acts authorising the compulsory acquisition of land prescribe their own procedure. These include the Pipe-lines Act 1962, the Forestry Act 1967 and the New Towns (Scotland) Act 1968.[8] The procedure in such cases is broadly similar to that in the 1947 Act.

The Housing (Scotland) Act 1987, while applying the 1947 Act procedure to the acquisition of land for the provision of housing (s.10(2)), makes a number of modifications to that procedure in its application to land acquisition for the purpose of implementing a housing action area designation (1987 Act, Sch. 8, Pt II, para.5(3)). Provision is also made for an additional procedure to operate alongside the compulsory purchase process for declaring a house to be below the tolerable standard (Land Compensation (Scotland) Act 1963, Sch. 2 as substituted by the 1987 Act, Sch. 23, para.10(2)). Such a declaration has implications for the measure of compensation (see p.189).

What follows is a detailed description of the procedure set out in the First Schedule to the 1947 Act. Reference should be made to the appropriate legislation for the position where an Act prescribes its own procedure or modifies the 1947 Act procedure. It should be noted that the Compulsory Purchase Policy Review Advisory Group (CPPRAG) in their final report[9] identified delay as a major source of dissatisfaction with current compulsory purchase procedures. The Group went on to recommend ways in which the process might be speeded up. At the time of writing, the Minister for Housing, Planning and Regeneration is consulting on proposals for implementing these recommendations in England and Wales.[10] The position in Scotland is awaited.

The First Schedule to the 1947 Act distinguishes between purchases by local authorities and statutory undertakers[11] and purchases by the Scottish or other Ministers. These are considered in turn.

ORDERS MADE BY LOCAL AND OTHER AUTHORITIES

1. Investigating ownership

2–02   Once the decision has been made to acquire land compulsorily, a local authority or statutory undertaker will investigate the ownership position, so that they can compile the schedule of ownership which forms part of a

---

[8] Although the 5 Scottish New Town Development Corporations were wound up under the provisions of the Enterprise and New Towns (Scotland) Act 1990, Part II, the 1968 Act remains in force.

[9] *Fundamental review of the laws and procedures relating to compulsory purchase and compensation: final report,* DETR, 2000. See too City University Business School, *The Operation of Compulsory Purchase Orders,* Department of the Environment, 1996; and J. Rowan Robinson and N. Hutchison, "Compensation for the compulsory acquisition of business interests: satisfaction or sacrifice" (1995) 13(1) *Journal of Property Valuation and Investment* 44.

[10] "Compulsory purchase and compensation: delivering a fundamental change" (2001) DTLR.

[11] The 1947 Act procedure is applied to the compulsory acquisition of land by statutory undertakers by the Local Government, Planning and Land Act 1980, s.120(1).

compulsory purchase order and so that they can serve the required notices (see below). Local authorities have a general power to require the occupier of premises to state the name and address of the owner[12] and some statutes may make their own specific provision in this connection.[13]

A tactic which has sometimes been employed to frustrate the acquiring authority has been to fragment the ownership of land needed for the project thus enormously increasing the burden of investigating ownership.[14] Provision is made for dealing with cases where reasonable inquiry has been made but it has not been practicable to ascertain the name and address of an owner, lessee or occupier of land which will allow the acquiring authority to proceed. The document may be served by addressing it to the 'owner', 'lessee' or 'occupier' of the land and by delivering it to some person on the premises or land. If there is no person on the land to whom it may be delivered, the document or a copy of it may be left on or near the land.[15]

2 The form of the order

A compulsory purchase order made under the First Schedule to the **2–03** 1947 Act must be in the prescribed form and must describe by reference to a map the land to which it applies (paragraph 2). The form which the order must take is prescribed by regulations made by the Scottish Ministers. The current regulations are the Compulsory Purchase of Land (Scotland) Regulations 1976.

The regulations provide a style of the forms which should be closely followed during the compulsory purchase process. Styles of the following forms are provided:

- the form of the compulsory purchase order;
- the form of the newspaper notice of the making of a compulsory purchase order;
- the form of notice to owners, lessees and occupiers of the making of a compulsory purchase order;
- the form of advertisement and notice of confirmation of a compulsory purchase order;
- the form of newspaper notice of the giving of a certificate under Part III of Schedule 1 to the 1947 Act;
- the forms to be employed where a general vesting declaration is used under Schedule 15 of the Town and Country Planning (Scotland) Act 1997.

---

[12] Local Government (Scotland) Act 1973, s.192(5).
[13] See, for example, the Town and Country Planning (Scotland) Act 1997, s.272.
[14] See, for example, the facts in *R v Secretary of State for Transport ex p Blackett* [1992] J.P.L. 1041.
[15] 1947 Act, First Schedule, para.19(4) as amended by the Planning and Compensation Act 1991, Sch.17, para.4.

Of these, the form of the compulsory purchase order bears closer examination. The order is headed with the title of the Act or Acts authorising compulsory purchase. The order commences with the name of the acquiring authority, the precise statutory authority for the compulsory purchase, and the title of the order: for example, "The Donburgh (Union Street) Compulsory Purchase Order 2002." In a letter to the chief executives of all local authorities dated June 28, 1982, the then Secretary of State indicated as regards the reference to the precise statutory authority for an order that the general powers of compulsory acquisition contained in section 71 of the Local Government (Scotland) Act 1973 should only be used in the absence of a more specific power related to the purpose for which the proposed acquisition is to be made. This view would appear to be based on the principle of statutory interpretation that general powers in an Act should not derogate from powers granted specifically in other legislation—*generalia specialibus non derogant.*

There follows a brief description of the purpose for which the land is being acquired. The notes accompanying the form suggest that, where practicable, the words of the relevant Act may be used, but where those words are in general terms covering a range of purposes, the particular purposes for which the land is required should be stated if possible. The point is important because a compulsory purchase order which has been made for one purpose cannot lawfully be confirmed for another purpose or for a purpose additional to that for which it was made.[16]

The land to be acquired is described by reference to an accompanying schedule and map. The schedule is prepared in four columns setting out the number on the map of each plot to be acquired (where more than one plot is being acquired), a short description of the owners and any lessees or occupiers other than for a month or less. The schedule will also show separately any "special category" land being acquired (see below). The colour coding or other method used on the map to identify the land to be acquired must be described; and the map should clearly delineate the boundaries of each plot and should contain sufficient topographical detail to enable the situation of the land to be readily identified and related to the description given in the schedule. The map should state that it is the map referred to in the order, repeating the title of the order.

3. The mining code

2–04   Section 1(3) and the Second Schedule, paragraph 6 to the 1947 Act make provision for the acquiring authority, if they so wish, to incorporate with the legislation authorising the purchase what is generally referred to as the "mining code." If the code is not incorporated the minerals lying under the land being acquired are included in the purchase and the compensation may reflect their development potential. To avoid paying such compensation, the general practice is to incorporate the mining code so that the mineral rights are not acquired by the authority.

---

[16] *Proctor & Gamble Ltd v Secretary of State for the Environment* (1992) 63 P. &.C.R. 317, CA.

To incorporate the mining code, a paragraph in the compulsory purchase order will specifically include section 70 of the Railways Clauses Consolidation (Scotland) Act 1845 and, if considered appropriate, sections 71 to 78 of the 1845 Act in their original form and not as amended by section 15 of the Mines (Working Facilities and Support) Act 1923 with the legislation authorising the acquisition. The terminology of the 1845 Act which refers to railways and railway companies may need to be modified to refer to the land being acquired and to the acquiring authority.

If section 70 of the 1845 Act only is incorporated in the order, the minerals are deemed to be excluded from the acquisition unless expressly conveyed except such as may have to be extracted or used during the construction of the works. The person in right of the minerals may work them subject to obtaining any necessary grant of planning permission.

The incorporation of sections 71 to 78 into the order will however impose some constraint on the winning and working of the minerals. Thirty days notice will have to be given to the acquiring authority of an intention to work mines under or within 40 yards, or such other prescribed distance of the land acquired. The notice is intended to give the authority an opportunity to consider whether such working might damage their interest. If they think it will, they may serve a counter-notice identifying the area which should remain unworked and pay compensation for sterilising the minerals.

4. Special category land

The schedule to the order, in addition to detailing the ownership **2–05** position, will identify any "special category" land which is being acquired. The special categories are listed in section 1(2) of the 1947 Act, as amended.[17] They comprise land forming part of a common or open space[18] or land held inalienably by the National Trust for Scotland.[19] These categories of land were formerly subject to the special provisions set out in Part III of the First Schedule to the 1947 Act. That remains the position with compulsory purchase orders made or to be confirmed by a Minister under powers relating to a reserved matter. For orders made or to be confirmed by the Scottish Ministers the special provisions are to be found, for the time being, in the Scotland Act 1998 (Transitory and Transitional Provisions) (Orders subject to Special Parliamentary Procedure) Order 1999.[20] These different arrangements are considered in turn.

(a) Orders made or to be confirmed under reserved powers: In so far as an order authorises the compulsory purchase of land belonging to and

---

[17] By the Local Government, Planning and Land Act 1980, s.120(2) and the Ancient Monuments and Archaeological Areas Act 1979, Sch.5.

[18] "Open space" is defined as any land laid out as a public garden, or used for the purposes of public recreation, or land being a disused burial ground (1947 Act, s.7(1)). In a consultation paper Land Compensation and Compulsory Purchase Legislation issued in 1989, the Scottish Development Department proposed to amend this definition so that it applies only to land to which the public have clear rights of access and not to land to which the public have access in practice without any legal entitlement (para.35).

[19] For the meaning of this expression see the 1947 Act, s.7(1).

[20] SI 1999/1593.

held inalienably[21] by the National Trust for Scotland, then in addition to the normal procedure Part III provides that the order is to be subject to special parliamentary procedure in any case where an objection has been made by the Trust and has not been withdrawn (paragraph 9).

An order which includes land forming part of a common or open space[22] will also be subject to special parliamentary procedure unless the Minister is satisfied that other land has been or will be given in exchange or that an exchange is unnecessary and certifies accordingly (paragraph 11(1)). Such other land to be given in exchange must not be less in area[23] and must be equally advantageous to the persons, if any, entitled to rights of common or other rights, and to the public; and it must be vested in the persons in whom the order land was vested and subject to the like rights, trusts or incidents (paragraph 11(1)(a)). The Ministers may conclude that an exchange is unnecessary where the order land does not exceed 250 square yards in extent[24] or is required for the widening of an existing road.

Where a Minister proposes to certify that he is satisfied that land has been or will be given in exchange or that an exchange is unnecessary he must, before giving the certificate, direct the acquiring authority to publish notice of his intention to do so and afford an opportunity to all interested persons to make representations and objections (paragraph 11(2)(a)). If he considers it expedient to do so, he may cause a public inquiry to be held. Notice of the giving of a certificate must be published in the prescribed form in one or more local newspapers by the order making authority (para.13).

Special parliamentary procedure is an additional hurdle to which such compulsory purchase orders will be subject and which will follow completion of the 1947 Act procedure. The procedure is set out in the Statutory Orders (Special Procedure) Acts 1945–65 and does not come into operation until the 1947 Act procedure has been completed.[25] A compulsory purchase order subject to special parliamentary procedure will be of no effect until it has been laid before Parliament and has been brought into operation in accordance with the provisions of the Special Procedure Acts. Petitions may be presented against the order within 21 days of the date on which it is laid.[26] A distinction is drawn between petitions of "general objection" and petitions merely of "amendment." Petitions are examined by the Lord Chairman of Committees and the Chairman of Ways and Means who will prepare a report to be laid before both Houses of Parliament. Either House may within 21 days resolve that the order be annulled. If no petitions are presented, the

---

[21] As to the meaning of land "held inalienably," see 1947 Act, s.7(1).

[22] In the consultation paper Land Compensation and Compulsory Purchase Legislation, see above, the Scottish Development Department proposed that the special parliamentary procedure should no longer be required where the purpose of a compulsory purchase order including open space land is the presentation or better management of the open space in question and the Secretary of State (now the Scottish Ministers) certifies that the public's ability to enjoy the open space will not be disadvantaged by the order (para.34).

[23] Unless the persons in whom the land was vested otherwise agree (para.11(1)(a)).

[24] Substituted by the Town and Country Planning (Scotland) Act 1969, s.32(1).

[25] Statutory Orders (Special Procedure) Act 1945, s.2(1).

[26] The manner in which petitions are to be presented is regulated by standing orders of the House of Commons (see Standing Order No. 240).

order comes into operation at the end of that period. Failing that, the petitions are referred to a joint committee of both Houses for consideration. The committee may report the order to both Houses for approval with or without amendments or, where there is a petition of general objection, report that the order be not approved. Where the compulsory purchase order is reported without amendment, it will generally come into operation on the date on which the report is laid before Parliament. Where an order is reported with amendments, it will come into operation as amended on a date to be determined by the Minister. If the Minister does not accept the amendments, he may withdraw the order or, alternatively, submit the order to Parliament by means of a Bill for further consideration. Where the committee report that an order be not approved, it will not take effect unless it is confirmed by Act of Parliament. The joint committee has power to award costs.

(b) Orders made or to be confirmed under devolved powers: Section 94 of the Scotland Act 1998 provides for confirmation of a compulsory purchase order containing special category land by way of an Act of the Scottish Parliament or by way of procedures stipulated in such an Act. At the time of writing, no such special procedure has been stipulated so, in the meantime, an order containing such land is to be subject to the special procedure set out in the Scotland Act 1998 (Transitory and Transitional Provisions) (Orders subject to Special Parliamentary Procedure) Order 1999.

This procedure is an additional hurdle to which such orders will be subject and which will follow completion of the 1947 Act procedure. Public notice of the order is to be given in the Edinburgh Gazette and in a newspaper circulating in the area of the subject land specifying the time within which and the manner in which objections may be made to the order. Where an objection is duly made, the order will not take effect unless it is confirmed, with or without amendment, by an Act of the Scottish Parliament. Such a Bill is to be treated as a Private Bill for the purposes of the Standing Orders of the Parliament.[27] The significance of this is that the stage 2 procedure will be quasi-judicial. The Standing Orders provide for a committee conducting stage 2 of the parliamentary procedure to hold, or arrange for the holding of, an inquiry into the Bill or any of its provisions or any objections.

Where no objection is made in response to the public notice, the Ministers will lay the order before the Parliament. Unless within 40 days the Parliament resolve that the order should be annulled, it will come into operation on such date as will be specified in the order.

5. Notice of the making of the order

The compulsory purchase order requires confirmation from the **2–06** authority specified in the authorising Act as having power to authorise the purchase (referred to as the "confirming authority"). For most purposes, the confirming authority will be the Scottish Ministers. Section 53(2)(c) of the Scotland Act 1998 provides that functions conferred on a

---

[27] See the Scotland Act 1998 (Transitory and Transitional Provisions) (Standing Orders and Parliamentary Publications) Order 1999, c.9, r.9.17.

Minister of the Crown by any pre-commencement enactment, so far as they are exercisable within devolved competence, shall be exercisable by the Scottish Ministers instead of by a Minister of the Crown. However, with orders relating to a matter reserved by Schedule 5 of the Scotland Act 1998, the confirming authority may still be the appropriate Minister of the Crown. References in this chapter to the 'Scottish Ministers' should be taken to include reference to a Minister of the Crown unless the context indicates otherwise.

Before submitting the order for confirmation, the body promoting the order must comply with a twofold notice requirement. First of all, the promoter must serve on every owner, lessee or occupier (except tenants for a month or for a lesser period) of any land comprised in the order, a notice in the prescribed form[28] stating the effect of the order and that it is about to be submitted for confirmation.[29] The notice must also specify the time, not being less than 21 days from the service of the notice, within which, and the manner in which, objections to the order may be made.[30]

In *EON Motors Ltd v Secretary of State for the Environment*[31] it was held that a tenancy granted on terms that the tenant would pay every quarter a rent calculated on the basis of £20 per week was a weekly tenancy so that the tenant company was not entitled to notice of the making of the order even though it had been in occupation for seven years. Sir Douglas Frank Q.C. said that the corresponding requirement to give notice in the English legislation "could not be for the benefit of those who had been tenants for a long time, but for the protection of those who might be entitled to remain for a long period."

The effect of the notice requirement is that there is no question of a proposal being made to expropriate a person's interest in land without their knowledge. This derives from the private legislation procedure of the nineteenth century (above) which required that no Act which touched private property should be passed without notice being given to the landowners concerned.

Section 5(3) of the 1947 Act provides that the notice requirement shall be deemed to be complied with if notice is served on all persons known to the acquiring authority to have an interest in land; service may be effected by sending the notice by registered letter or by recorded delivery[32] or by delivering it to the person or leaving it at that person's

---

[28] See the Compulsory Purchase of Land (Scotland) Regulations 1976, reg.3(c) and Form 3.

[29] The DTLR have proposed that, for England and Wales, the entitlement to notice of the making of an order should be extended to all those who have any private interest in the order land or have a right to occupy it or have a right restrictive of the use of it ("Compulsory purchase and compensation: delivering a fundamental change" (2001) DTLR, para.2.12). Such people would become 'statutory objectors' for the purposes of the objection procedure (see p.27).

[30] 1947 Act, Sch.1, para.3(b).

[31] [1981] J.P.L. 576. See, too, *McMillan v Inverness County Council*, 1949 S.C. 77; 1949 S.L.T. 77 (small landholder with a right of common grazing in the order land not entitled to notice); and *Grimley v Minister of Housing and Local Government* [1971] 2 W.L.R. 449 (person having the benefit of an easement of support over the order land not entitled to notice).

[32] Recorded Delivery Service Act 1962, s.1(1).

proper address.[33] The "proper address" is a reference to the person's last known address or, where the person to be served has furnished an address for service, that address.[34] Service on an incorporated company or body is to be effected by service upon the secretary or clerk of the company or body[35] and the proper address in such a case is the registered or principal office of the company or body.

If the acquiring authority is satisfied after reasonable inquiry that it is not practicable to ascertain the name or address of an owner, lessee or occupier of land, the notice may be served by addressing it to the person by name or by the description of "owner," "lessee" or "occupier" of the land to which it relates (describing it), and by delivering it to some person on the premises to whom it may be delivered, or, if there is no person on the premises or the land to whom it may be delivered, by leaving it or a copy of it on or near the land.[36]

The 1947 Act also requires notice of the making of the order to be **2–07** given to the public at large.[37] This requirement implicitly recognises that there may be people who will be adversely affected by the public acquisition of the land who are not entitled to individual notice. These include, for example, tenants for a month or less who may, nonetheless, have occupied the property for many years, or the proprietors of a servitude right who live or work nearby. Notice must be published for two successive weeks in one or more local newspapers. The form of the notice is prescribed in the Compulsory Purchase of Land (Scotland) Regulations 1976. The notice must state that the order has been made and is about to be submitted for confirmation; it must describe the land in question and the purpose for which it is required; it must name a place locally where the order and map may be inspected; and it must specify the time, not being less than 21 days from the first publication of the notice,[38] within which, and the manner in which, objections to the order may be made.

Having satisfied the requirement to give notice, the body promoting the compulsory purchase order will submit it to the confirming authority for confirmation.

6. Objection

Objections should be sent in writing to the Scottish Ministers or other **2–08** confirming authority at the address given in the notice and within the time specified.[39] There is no special form for objections; a letter is sufficient.

---

[33] 1947 Act, Sch.1, para.19(1).

[34] See above, para.19(3).

[35] See above, para.19(2).

[36] See above, para.19(4) as substituted by Sch.2, para.6 of the Local Government (Miscellaneous Provisions) (Scotland) Act 1981 and subsequently amended by the Planning and Compensation Act 1991, Sch.17, para.4.

[37] See above, para.3(a).

[38] The notice accompanying the prescribed form states that the period of 21 days runs from but does not include the first date of publication.

[39] In *Wilson v City of Glasgow District Council*, unreported, September 17, 1986, Outer House (but see (1987) 21 S.P.L.P. 43) it was held that it was not enough to prove dispatch of an objection; it must reach the Secretary of State. In that case a letter of objection was not received by the Minister.

There are no statutorily prescribed grounds of objection but one or more of the following grounds are commonly employed.

First of all, the objector may attempt to show that there is no need for the scheme for which the land is being acquired. Compulsory acquisition is justified by public necessity; if there is no such necessity, the case for compulsory acquisition collapses. It should be stressed, however, that public authorities do not lightly embark on expropriation. Such an objection is likely to require considerable preparation and will not often succeed. Nonetheless, subject to what follows, the need for the scheme should not be taken for granted.

In some cases, the need for the scheme will have been established prior to the making of the compulsory purchase order thus rendering such an objection pointless. For example, section 200(1) of the Town and Country Planning (Scotland) Act 1997 permits the Scottish Ministers, as confirming authority, to disregard an objection to an order for the compulsory purchase of land for planning purposes where the objection amounts in substance to an objection to the provisions of the development plan defining the proposed use of land. The merits of the development plan will have been open to question at an earlier stage, and provided the plan is not out of date there would seem little point in repeating the exercise.

Similarly, there is little point in questioning the need for a scheme which is being carried forward as a part of established government policy. It will, for example, be too late to object to the government's civil nuclear power programme when land is being acquired for a nuclear power station; and it will be too late to object to the need for a motorway when the land is being purchased for its construction. The ability to question government policy is discussed further in the context of public inquiries (see below).

Secondly, an objector could seek to show that the importance of retaining the land in its existing use should override the purpose for which it is being acquired. Arguments about the importance of continuing the agricultural use of the land, for example, may carry weight and the owner is likely to be well placed to pursue such an objection.

Thirdly, an objector may seek to question the manner in which a scheme is to be implemented. The objector, in such a case, is not questioning the need for the scheme but simply the way in which it is proposed to carry it through. For example, although an objector to a compulsory purchase order might not be able to challenge the need to redevelop the area for which his land is being acquired—the need having been established in the development plan—he might wish to object to the way in which it is proposed to be redeveloped. The objection in such a case is questioning whether the public need for which his land is being acquired will be served or best served by the proposed manner of implementation.

Fourthly, an objector may seek to show that some slight adjustment to the boundary of the land to be acquired or some slight alteration to the manner in which the scheme is to be implemented would substantially reduce the impact of the order on his interest without prejudicing the scheme. An objector is likely to be better able to appreciate the impact of the order on his interest than the promoter. Such an objection can often be resolved by negotiation with the promoter leading, for example, to agreement over some slight alteration to the boundary of the scheme or to the carrying out of accommodation works designed to reduce its impact.

Fifthly, an objector may argue that public acquisition of his land is unnecessary because he is able and willing to implement the purpose for which it is proposed to acquire his land. He may, for example, be ready, perhaps in conjunction with other proprietors, to bring land forward for redevelopment as proposed by the authority. Or the proprietor of a house in a housing action area may object to its compulsory acquisition on the ground that he will undertake to improve or demolish the house, as the case may be.[40]

Such an objection may be inappropriate where the acquisition is with a view to securing some public provision, for example, the building of a secondary school. And it may be contrary to the philosophy of the legislation under which the order is being promoted. For example, the Secretary of State for Scotland, when considering a compulsory purchase order promoted by one of the former new town development corporations under the New Towns (Scotland) Act 1968, could disregard an objection that public acquisition of the land was unnecessary or inexpedient.

Finally, an objector may attempt to argue that there is a better alternative site where the scheme could be implemented. Where such an objection is to be maintained at a subsequent public inquiry, the Scottish Ministers may require that sufficient details of the proposed alternative site are provided to enable it to be identified.[41] The Ministers will then notify any owner of the site of the basis of the objection and allow an opportunity for representations to be made.

It would seem as regards alternative sites that "as long as the objectors **2–09** can put forward a prima facie case, the onus will be on the acquiring authority to rebut that case."[42] In *R. v Secretary of State for the Environment, ex p. Melton Borough Council*[43] a local authority made a compulsory purchase order in respect of land required for the construction of a rear service road to the main shopping street in Melton Mowbray. Two possible routes had been considered by the local authority. The order site necessitated the taking of part of several buildings and part of a supermarket car park. The alternative route was said by the authority to raise planning and legal obstacles although the nature of these obstacles were not very fully explored by the authority's planning officer in his evidence at the subsequent public inquiry. The Secretary of State refused to confirm the order on the basis that he was not satisfied that the alternative route was not viable. The local authority applied for judicial review of the decision. Forbes J. dismissed the

---

[40] But see *Vassily v Secretary of State* [1976] J.P.L. 364.

[41] Compulsory Purchase by Public Authorities (Inquiries Procedure) (Scotland) Rules 1998, r.4(1). Where the question of an alternative site is raised for the first time during a public inquiry, the reporter may adjourn the proceedings in order that the owner of the alternative site may be notified and to allow the acquiring authority to seek further information.

[42] See the comment by M. Purdue on *R. v Secretary of State for the Environment, ex p. Melton Borough Council* [1986] J.P.L. 190.

[43] [1986] J.P.L. 190.

application observing that "[b]ecause it was the acquiring authority's duty to show that the acquisition was necessary it was its duty to lay before the Secretary of State the information necessary to convince him of that fact. If they failed to do so the Secretary of State was fully entitled to say 'I refuse to confirm this order'." There was no obligation on the Minister or his inspector to search around to make good the lacunae in the acquiring authority's case.

Where, however, the Ministers are minded to confirm a compulsory purchase order notwithstanding an objection that there is a more suitable alternative site, it appears that the burden upon them is heavier. In *Prest v Secretary of State for Wales*[44] the Welsh Water Authority made a compulsory purchase order for 30 acres of an estate for the construction of a sewage works. The owner did not agree with the site selected by the water authority and offered a choice of two others. The water authority argued at the inquiry that the construction costs on the order site would be cheaper. The owner subsequently pointed out that the cost of acquisition of the order site would be greater because of its development potential. The Secretary of State's decision confirming the order made no mention of the difference in the cost of acquisition. The Minister's decision was quashed on appeal because in exercising his discretion to confirm the order the Secretary of State had failed to inquire into a vital consideration, namely the respective land values of the two sites. Watkins L.J. described the Minister's role in dealing with a compulsory purchase order as:

> "if not inquisitional, surely investigatory, especially when he was given notice of a relevant matter which might affect his decision by a person likely to be affected by it. He must acquaint himself from the formidable amount of assistance available to him in his department and from public inquiry, with all the information which was indispensable to the making of a just and equitable decision in the making of which he was entrusted with a broad discretionary power. The proper use of a discretionary power was in peril if less than the information essential for its exercise was available to him. If proper use involved him in 'routing around'—see *Rhodes v Minister of Housing and Local Government* [1962] 1 W.L.R. 208 at page 213 . . . he must either cause that to be done or resolve the issue in favour of the landowner."

If an objector succeeds in persuading the confirming authority as to the merits of an alternative site, there is no question of the order being confirmed in respect of that site. All that will happen is that the order for the subject land will not be confirmed and it will be for the promoter to decide whether to bring forward a new compulsory purchase order for the alternative site.

An objection which relates exclusively to matters within the jurisdiction of the Lands Tribunal for Scotland may be disregarded by the confirming authority.[45]

---

[44] [1983] J.P.L. 112.
[45] 1947 Act, First Schedule, para.4(4). The Lands Tribunal for Scotland deals not just with matters of disputed compensation but also, for example, with notices of objection to severance (see p.65 *et seq.*).

Where objection is made to a compulsory purchase order the confirming authority will notify the promoter of the objection and will encourage negotiation with the objector with a view to resolving the matter. If no objection is made, or if all objections so made are withdrawn, the confirming authority may, if they think fit, confirm the order with or without modifications.[46]

7. The right to be heard

In the nineteenth century, the standing orders of both Houses of **2–10** Parliament provided that a person to whom notice of the proposed legislation dealing with the compulsory acquisition of his land had been given was entitled to be heard in support of any objection.[47] This safeguard has been carried through into the 1947 Act. If any objection which has been duly made by an owner, lessee or occupier (except tenants for a month or any period less than a month) (referred to as "statutory objectors")[48] is not withdrawn, the confirming authority must, before reaching a decision on the order, either cause a public inquiry to be held or afford the objector an opportunity of appearing before and being heard by a person appointed for the purpose.[49] In the absence of bad faith on the part of the acquiring authority, the inquiry into objections is to be regarded as conclusive of the matters at issue. There is no opportunity, following a decision to confirm an order, to raise matters which, because of a change of circumstance, might substantially enhance the strength of an objection. Although this could operate harshly on an objector, the principle that the inquiry is conclusive seems to rest on the need for finality in such matters.[50]

It is not altogether clear what the difference is between a public inquiry and a hearing but the implication is that the latter is less formal and less public. The use of a hearing is considered inappropriate for a compulsory purchase order.[51]

Written notice of the intention to cause an inquiry to be held must be given by the Ministers to the acquiring authority, each statutory objector and every other person who has made representations about the order to the Ministers.[52] If the only objections to an order are from third parties (*i.e.* persons other than statutory objectors), the confirming authority is not obliged to hold a public inquiry but may do so at their discretion.

---

[46] See above, para.4(1).

[47] In *Cooper v The Board of Works for Wandsworth Corporation* (1863) 14 C.B. (N.S.) 180 it was held to be a well established common law principle that no man could be deprived of his property without having an opportunity of being heard.

[48] The Compulsory Purchase by Public Authorities (Inquiries Procedure) (Scotland) Rules 1998, r.3(1). Where there is a change of ownership just before the start of a public inquiry, the new owner is not a "statutory objector" but may be heard at the inquiry at the discretion of the reporter (*R. v Secretary of State for the Home Department ex p. Durham City Council* [1995] J.P.L. 38).

[49] 1947 Act, First Schedule, para.4(2). Exceptionally, an Act authorising the compulsory acquisition of land may permit the confirming authority to dispense with an inquiry into some or all objections. See, for example, the Offshore Petroleum Development (Scotland) Act 1975, s.1 and Sch.1.

[50] *R. v Carmarthen District Council, ex p. Blewin* (1990) 59 P. & C.R. 379.

[51] Circular 17/1998, para.24.

[52] The Compulsory Purchase by Public Authorities (Inquiries Procedure) (Scotland) Rules 1998, r.4.

For the objector, the public inquiry will be the focal point of the decision making process. The inquiry has two related purposes. In the context of compulsory purchase, it provides those most closely affected by the order with an opportunity to be heard in defence of their property; and it enables the confirming authority to be better informed about the facts and opinions relevant to the decision they must make.[53]

2–11   Although the inquiry is convened in response to an objection, it would seem that with orders promoted by local authorities and statutory undertakers it is not simply an opportunity to hear the objection. It is not, as with orders promoted by Ministers, a departmental inquiry into objections[54]; it is an investigation conducted independently of the promoter with a view to informing the confirming authority.[55] The confirming authority must be satisfied that there is sufficient evidence regarding the need to acquire the land. As Denning M.R. stated in *Coleen Properties Ltd v Minister of Housing and Local Government*[56]; "I am quite clear that the mere *ipse dixit* of the local council is not sufficient. There must be some evidence to support their assertion." In that case a local authority made a compulsory purchase order in respect of two rows of substandard houses in a clearance area. Included in the order land was a modern building in good condition situated on the corner where the two rows of houses met. The building was required, stated the authority, for the satisfactory development or use of the cleared area. However, at the local inquiry, the authority called no evidence as to the need to acquire the building. The inspector conducting the inquiry concluded that acquisition of the building was not reasonably necessary and recommended that in that respect the order should not be confirmed. The Minister nonetheless confirmed the order. The Court of Appeal, applying the "*Ashbridge* formula,"[57] held that since there was no evidence that the acquisition of the building was reasonably necessary for the development or use of the cleared area the Minister's decision was *ultra vires*. Sachs J. stated:

> "When seeking to deprive a subject of his property and cause him to move himself, his belongings and perhaps his business to another area, the onus lies squarely on the local authority to show by clear and unambiguous evidence that the order sought for should be granted."[58]

---

[53] See, generally, R. E. Wraith and G. B. Lamb, *Public Inquiries as an Instrument of Government* (George Allan and Unwin, 1971). Also the "Report of the Committee on Administrative Tribunals and Inquiries" (1957) HMSO, (Cmnd. 218).

[54] See as regards orders promoted by Ministers *Re Trunk Roads Act 1936* [1939] 2 K.B. 515. Some Acts make it clear that the purpose of an inquiry is simply to hear objections; see, for example, the New Towns (Scotland) Act 1968, s.1 and Sch.1, para.3.

[55] *Magistrates of Ayr v Lord Advocate*, 1950 S.C. 102.

[56] [1971] 1 W.L.R. 433 at p.437. See too *Tesco Stores Ltd v Secretary of State for the Environment, Transport and the Regions and Wycombe District Council* (2000) 80 P. & C.R. 427, *per* Sullivan J. at p.438. But see *Migdal Investments Ltd v Secretary of State* [1976] J.P.L.365.

[57] The formula was spelt out by Lord Denning in *Ashbridge Investments Ltd v Minister of Housing and Local Government* [1965] 1 W.L.R. 1320 and sets out the grounds upon which a court may interfere with a decision by Ministers (see p.40 *et seq.* below).

[58] [1971] 1 W.L.R. 433 at pp.439 and 440.

And in *Prest v Secretary of State for Wales*[59] Watkins L.J. in the Court of Appeal stated that the use of statutory authority for the destruction of proprietary rights "was not to be used unless it was clear that the Secretary of State had allowed these rights to be violated by a decision based upon the right legal principles, adequate evidence and proper consideration of the factor which swayed his mind into confirmation of the order sought." The requirement for the decision-maker to be satisfied with regard to the evidence on the need for the acquisition has been given emphasis by the terms of Article 1 of the First Protocol of the European Convention on Human Rights discussed in Chapter 1. It has been held that it is not a condition precedent of the power to confirm a compulsory purchase order promoted under the planning legislation that the confirming authority must be satisfied that the development will probably be carried out.[60]

The need for the confirming authority's decision to be based on sufficient evidence is sometimes expressed in terms of an "onus" on the acquiring authority to show that the order should be confirmed.[61]

As a first step towards discharging this onus, an acquiring authority is required to provide statutory objectors with a written statement of their reasons for making the order.[62] Unless the statement accompanied the notice of the making of the order, it must be served not later than two weeks after the relevant date.[63] Where the acquiring authority consider that a representation by a government department will be relevant to their case at the inquiry, they must notify the department concerned that an inquiry is to be held and request it to provide a written statement setting out in detail the reasons for the representations (r.5(2)).

Difficulties may be encountered by objectors where the statement of reasons contains a reference to a view expressed by a government department or otherwise indicates that the case for acquisition is founded on national policy. The order land may, for example, be required for the construction of a nuclear power station. Objectors may wish to question the necessity for this only to be told that the need to construct a programme of such stations is a matter of government policy and that the inquiry, while it may examine the reasons for selecting the

---

[59] [1983] J.P.L. 112. See too *Brown v Secretary of State for the Environment* (1978) 40 P. & C.R. 285 *per* Forbes J. at p.291; and *De Rothschild v Secretary of State for Transport* (1989) 57 P. & C.R. 330 *per* Slade L.J. at p.336 and 337.

[60] *Chesterfield Properties plc. v Secretary of State for the Environment* (1998) 76 P. & C.R. 117; *Gala Leisure Ltd v Secretary of State for the Environment, Transport and the Regions and Coventry City Council* (2001) 82 P. & C.R. 118.

[61] See *Brown v Secretary of State for the Environment* (1978) 40 P. & C.R. 285, *per* Forbes J.; *Prest v Secretary of State for Wales* [1983] J.P.L. 112, *per* Watkins L.J.; and *R. v Secretary of State for the Environment, ex p. Melton Borough Council* [1986] J.P.L. 190, *per* Forbes J. But see *Errington v Metropolitan District Railway Co.* (1882) 19 Ch. D. 559, *per* Brett L.J. at p.576; *Company Development (Property) Ltd v Secretary of State for the Environment* [1978] J.P.L. 107; and *De Rothschild v Secretary of State for Transport* [1989] J.P.L. 173, *per* Slade L.J. See, too, *Vassily v Secretary of State* [1976] J.P.L. 364 for an example of a case where the onus was shifted to the objector.

[62] The Compulsory Purchase by Public Authorities (Inquiries Procedure) (Scotland) Rules 1998, r.5(1)(a).

[63] The "relevant date" means the date of the Scottish Ministers' notice to the acquiring authority, to statutory objectors and to others who have made representations about the order of their intention to cause an inquiry to be held (1998 Rules, r.4).

site, will not inquire into the need for nuclear power stations. Although a statutory objector[64] may request that a representative from any government department referred to in the statement of reasons as expressing a view on the proposals contained in the order should be available at the inquiry[65] and although the representative must state the reasons for this view and give evidence and be subject to cross- examination to the same extent as other witnesses, the reporter conducting the inquiry will disallow questions which in his opinion are directed to the merits of government policy.[66] The explanation for the difficulty in which objectors may find themselves is that Ministers and not civil servants are answerable for policy and they, in theory, are accountable to Parliament. In other words, the need to build nuclear power stations will, or should have been, already established at this level. In these circumstances, objectors may find themselves having to advance their objection in isolation from the thing objected to.

2–12   "Policy," as Lord Diplock observed in *Bushell v Secretary of State for the Environment*[67] is a "protean word" and it may sometimes be difficult to distinguish between matters of fact, about which the confirming authority must satisfy themselves that there is sufficient evidence, and matters of government policy, which will not be in issue at the inquiry. In *Bushell* the majority of the House of Lords held that particular methods of traffic forecasting employed to determine motorway construction priorities were an essential element of government policy and were thus unsuitable for investigation by individual inspectors at individual local inquiries.[68]

Public inquiry procedure is governed by the Compulsory Purchase by Public Authorities (Inquiries Procedure) (Scotland) Rules 1998. Additional guidance is provided in Circular 17/1998. The Rules and the guidance are designed to ensure that all the issues can be considered "fairly, thoroughly and consistently but without any unnecessary formality, technicality or delay".[69]

The Ministers will appoint a person to hold the inquiry and to report to them, generally referred to as "the reporter" (1998 Rules, r.3). The Ministers may cause a pre-inquiry meeting to be held where this appears to be desirable (r.7(1)). Such a meeting must be held not later than 16 weeks after the date on which the Ministers gave notice of their intention to hold an inquiry (known as the 'relevant date') and will generally be presided over by the reporter. To maximise the benefit of such a meeting, the acquiring authority will be required to prepare and serve on the Ministers and on the statutory objectors an outline statement of case (r.7(3)). Other parties to the inquiry may also be required to prepare and circulate such a statement (r.7(5)). The outline

---

[64] Or the acquiring authority, a "relevant person" defined in r.3 or the owner of any land proposed as an alternative site (r.18.(1)).

[65] 1998 Rules, r.18(1).

[66] See above r.18(4). The dividing line between questions directed at clarifying government policy which are permitted and questions directed at the merits of government policy which are not will sometimes be difficult to draw.

[67] [1980] 3 W.L.R. 22, HL.

[68] See, too, *Lithgow v Secretary of State for Scotland*, 1973 S.C. 1; 1973 S.L.T. 81.

[69] Circular 17/1998, para.7.

statement should indicate the likely principal lines of arguments and include a list of the documents, so far as these are known, to be put in evidence. The pre-inquiry meeting provides an opportunity to reach agreement on practical arrangements for the inquiry, to clarify the issues to be debated, to identify matters on which the parties are in agreement, and to determine the procedure for production of documents and precognitions. No discussion of the merits of the order will take place at this stage. A note of the matters agreed will be circulated after the meeting. If the Ministers do not convene a pre-inquiry meeting, the reporter may, of his own initiative, decide to do so (r.8).

A full statement of case must be served by the acquiring authority on the Scottish Ministers, the statutory objectors and each relevant person[70] not later than eight weeks from the relevant date or, where a pre-inquiry meeting is held, four weeks from that date (r.9). The statement should include copies of all representations received by the authority in relation to the order. A similar obligation is imposed on statutory objectors (r.10) and may be imposed on other parties to the inquiry (r.11).

Not less than four weeks notice in writing of the date, time and place of the inquiry must be given to the acquiring authority, statutory objectors, all relevant persons and the owner of any land proposed as an alternative site (1947 Act, Fourth Schedule, para.2; and 1998 Rules, r.16(3)). With the agreement of the promoter, all statutory objectors and all relevant persons, a shorter period may be substituted. The intention is that the inquiry should be held within 24 weeks of the relevant date or, where a pre-inquiry meeting is held, within eight weeks of the meeting (r.16(1)). As a matter of practice, notice of the inquiry arrangements are also published in a local newspaper.

At least four weeks before the date fixed for the commencement of **2–13** the inquiry, any party who intends to rely on any documents must provide copies of those documents to the Scottish Ministers and to the parties to the inquiry (r.15). The reporter has discretion to vary the time limit. At least two weeks before the date of the inquiry, or such other date as the reporter may specify, any person intending to give evidence must provide a copy of their precognition to the reporter and to the other parties to the inquiry (r.14). If the precognition exceeds 2,000 words, it must be accompanied by a summary and it is the summary which will be read out at the inquiry. A copy of any document referred to in the precognition must accompany the precognition unless they have already been supplied or arrangements have been made for their inspection.

The reporter may, on the motion of any party to the inquiry or on his own motion, require any person to attend the inquiry to give evidence or to produce any books or documents in his custody or under his control which relate to any matter in question at the inquiry (1947 Act, Fourth Schedule, paras 3 and 5). No person, however, can be compelled to attend an inquiry which is being held more than 10 miles from the place where he resides unless the necessary expenses are paid or tendered to him. Where a government department has made representations relating

---

[70] A person required by the Scottish Ministers to serve a statement of case in terms of rule 11(1) (r.3).

to the order, the acquiring authority, the statutory objectors, any relevant person or the owner of any land proposed as an alternative site may apply to the Scottish Ministers not less than two weeks before the start of the inquiry for a representative of the department to attend.

The acquiring authority, any statutory objectors and any other person who has served a statement of case in terms of rule 11 (above) are entitled to appear at the inquiry (r.17(1)); any other person may appear at the discretion of the reporter conducting the inquiry.[71] Any person entitled or permitted to appear may do so on his own behalf or be represented by counsel or solicitor or by any other person (r.17(3)).

Subject to the provisions of the Inquiries Procedure Rules, the procedure at the inquiry is at the discretion of the reporter (r.19(1)). He will state at the commencement of the inquiry, or before, the procedure which he proposes to adopt (r.19(2)). Generally, the acquiring authority will be heard first and will have the right of final reply; other persons entitled or permitted to appear will be heard in such order as the reporter determines.

The acquiring authority, the statutory objectors and any relevant person are entitled to make opening statements, to call evidence, to cross-examine persons giving evidence (but see p.29) and to make closing statements; any other person appearing at the inquiry may do so only to the extent permitted by the reporter (r.19(4)). The reporter may require evidence to be given on oath (1947 Act, Fourth Schedule, para.4).

Any evidence may be admitted at the discretion of the reporter and he may direct that documents tendered in evidence should be available for inspection by any person entitled or permitted to appear at the inquiry and that facilities be afforded for taking or obtaining copies (r.19(6)). However, the reporter must not require or permit the giving of evidence which would be contrary to the public interest (r.19(6)); neither is he empowered to require any person to produce any book or to answer any question which the person would be entitled, on grounds of privilege or confidentiality, to refuse to produce or answer if the inquiry were a proceeding in a court of law (1947 Act, Fourth Schedule, para.3(b)).

Should any person entitled to appear at the inquiry fail to do so, the reporter may at his discretion nonetheless proceed with the inquiry (r.19(9)). He is entitled to take account of any written submissions received by him before or during the inquiry but must circulate such documents in advance of the inquiry where he considers this to be practicable (r.19(10)).

It is clearly desirable that the reporter should see the land which is the subject of the compulsory purchase order. He may make an unaccompanied inspection of the land before, during or after the inquiry without giving notice of his intention to any person entitled to appear at the inquiry (r.20(1)). He may, and must if so requested by either the acquiring authority or a statutory objector, inspect the land during or after the close of the inquiry in the company of such of the parties to the inquiry as desire to do so; where he intends to make such an inspection, he must announce the date and time of the inspection during the inquiry (r.20(3)).

---

[71] 1947 Act, First Schedule, para.4(3); the 1998 Rules, r.17(2).

8. Post inquiry procedure

After the close of the inquiry, the reporter will prepare his report and **2–14** submit it to the Scottish Ministers. This must include his findings of fact, his conclusions and his recommendations—or his reasons for not making any recommendations (r.21(1)).

Rule 21(2) of the 1998 Inquiries Procedure Rules provides that where the Scottish Ministers: (a) differ from the reporter on a finding of fact, or (b) after the close of the inquiry propose to take into consideration any new evidence (including expert opinion on a matter of fact) or any new issue of fact (not being a matter of government policy) which was not raised at the inquiry and because of this are disposed to disagree with a recommendation made by the reporter, they must not come to a decision at variance with such recommendation without first notifying the acquiring authority and any statutory objector who appeared at the inquiry of their disagreement and the reasons for it. They must then afford those who have been notified an opportunity of making representations in writing within 21 days or (if the Ministers have received new evidence or taken into consideration any new issue of fact not being a matter of government policy) of asking within 21 days for the reopening of the inquiry. Rule 21(3) goes on to provide that, if so requested, the Scottish Ministers must reopen the inquiry; and they may do so in other circumstances if they think fit.[72]

In *Hamilton v Roxburghshire County Council*,[73] for example, the Court held that there had been a breach of the equivalent provision in the 1964 Compulsory Purchase Inquiries Procedure Rules when the Secretary of State sought and obtained information from one party after the close of the inquiry which led him to depart from the recommendation of the reporter without notifying the other parties and giving them an opportunity to make representations.

The corresponding provision in the Planning Inquiries Procedure Rules has provoked considerable litigation.[74] The reference in rule 21(2)(a) to a finding of fact gives rise to some difficulty in distinguishing between fact and opinion.[75] In *Wordie Property Co. Ltd v Secretary of State for Scotland*,[76] for example, where a difference arose as to the amount and the type of shopping space that would be required in Aberdeen in the future, the First Division categorised the former as a matter of fact and the latter as a matter of planning judgment.

---

[72] It would seem that the principles of natural justice impose obligations upon the Scottish Ministers similar to those set out in the procedural rules (see *Lithgow v Secretary of State for Scotland*, 1973 S.C. 1; 1973 S.L.T. 81; *Hibernian Property Co. Ltd v Secretary of State for the Environment* (1973) 27 P. & C.R. 197; and *Fairmount Investments Ltd v Secretary of State for the Environment* [1976] 1 W.L.R. 1255).

[73] 1970 S.C. 248; 1971 S.L.T. 2.

[74] See J. Rowan Robinson, E. Young, M. Purdue and E. Farquharson-Black, *Scottish Planning Law and Procedure* (Scottish Universities Law Institute, 2001), Ch.20.

[75] See, for example, *Lord Luke of Pavenham v Minister of Housing and Local Government* [1968] 1 Q.B. 172, a case turning on the corresponding provision in the English Planning Inquiries Procedure Rules of 1965; also *Pyreford Properties Ltd v Secretary of State for the Environment* (1977) 36 P. & C.R. 28.

[76] 1984 S.L.T. 345. And see the comments on this decision by E. Young at (1983) 10 S.P.L.P. 75.

Difficulties may also arise over the meaning of "new evidence"[77] and "new issue of fact" in the second part of the rule.[78] And the reference in rule 21(2)(b) to "a matter of government policy" raises again the difficulty discussed earlier of distinguishing between matters of policy and matters of fact.[79] In *Lithgow v Secretary of State for Scotland*,[80] for example, where the Minister's decision on the Bishopton bypass was influenced by information on agricultural land values which had not been explored at the inquiry, the Court held that such information was a factor relevant to a decision of policy and there was no obligation to disclose policy factors to objectors.

The confirming authority must notify their decision, with reasons, to the acquiring authority, to the statutory objectors and to any other person, who, having appeared at the inquiry, has asked to be notified of the decision (r.22(1)).[81] If a copy of the reporter's report is not sent with the notification of the decision, the notification must be accompanied by a summary of the reporter's conclusions and recommendations.[82]

Although it would seem that the Ministers' decision letter should not be analysed and picked to pieces "as if each sentence were a subsection in a taxing statute,"[83] it is well established, to use the words of Megaw J. in *Re Poyser and Mills Arbitration*,[84] "that proper, adequate reasons must be given. The reasons that are set out must be reasons which will not only be intelligible but which deal with the substantial points that have been raised."[85]

9. Expenses

2–15   The expenses incurred by the Ministers in relation to the inquiry (including such reasonable sum as the Ministers may determine for the services of the person appointed to hold the inquiry) are to be paid by such of the parties to the inquiry and in such proportions as the

---

[77] See, for example, *Hamilton v Roxburghshire County Council*, 1970 S.C. 248; 1971 S.L.T. 2; *London & Clydeside Properties Ltd v City of Aberdeen District Council*, 1984 S.L.T. 50; and *French Kier Developments Ltd v Secretary of State for the Environment* [1977] 1 All E.R. 296.

[78] See, for example, *Vale Estates (Acton) Ltd v Secretary of State for the Environment* (1970) 69 L.G.R. 543.

[79] See *Bushell v Secretary of State for the Environment* [1981] A.C. 75.

[80] 1973 S.C. 1; 1973 S.L.T. 81.

[81] See, too, the Tribunals and Inquiries Act 1992, s.10(1).

[82] A person entitled to notification of the Scottish Ministers' decision who has not received a copy of the reporter's report may request a copy from the Ministers; the request must be made within the time stipulated in r.22(2).

[83] *De Rothschild v Secretary of State for Transport* [1989] J.P.L. 173, *per* Slade L.J.; *London and Clydeside Properties Ltd v City of Aberdeen District Council*, 1984 S.L.T. 50, *per* Lord Wheatley; *Wordie Property Co. Ltd v Secretary of State for Scotland*, 1984 S.L.T. 345, *per* Lord Grieve; *West Midlands Cooperative Society v Secretary of State for the Environment* [1988] J.P.L. 121, *per* Graham Eyre Q.C.

[84] [1964] 2 Q.B. 467; and see *Givaudan v Minister of Housing and Local Government* [1967] 1 W.L.R. 250, *Westminster City Council v Great Portland Estates plc* [1985] A.C. 661 (H.L), *per* Lord Scarman; *Wordie Property Co. Ltd v Secretary of State for Scotland*, 1984 S.L.T. 345, *per* the Lord President (Lord Emslie).

[85] For a discussion of the considerable litigation which has arisen in connection with decision letters relating to planning appeals see J. Rowan Robinson *et al*, *Scottish Planning Law & Procedure*, Chap.20.

Ministers may order (1947 Act, s.5(1) and Fourth Schedule, para.6(a)).[86] The Ministers may also make orders as to the expenses incurred by the parties to the inquiry and as to the parties by whom such expenses are to be paid (1947 Act, s.5(1) and Fourth Schedule, para.6(b)).[87] The normal practice, where a statutory objector attends or is represented at an inquiry and is successful in his objection so that the Scottish Ministers refuse to confirm the order in respect of his land, is to award him his reasonable expenses. The expenses are paid by the acquiring authority and will include professional fees incurred in pursuing his objection and in attending or being represented at the inquiry. A statutory objector who is partially successful will normally get a partial award of expenses. Statutory objectors who are unsuccessful and third parties (whatever the outcome) are expected to bear their own expenses.[88] Exceptionally, where any party to the inquiry has acted unreasonably an award of expenses may be made against him.

This somewhat restrictive approach to the award of expenses appears to stem from the fear that a more generous policy would encourage objectors, delay much needed public works, and impose a heavier burden on promoters. The consequence of the approach is that statutory objectors must indulge in something of a gamble as it is generally not possible to forecast at the outset what the outcome of an objection will be. As the expense can be considerable this may deter objection.

The decision of the confirming authority may be to confirm the order with or without modifications[89] or to decline to confirm the order. It is not uncommon for an order to be confirmed with modifications directed at the exclusion of identified areas of land. The order may not, however, be modified by the confirming authority so as to authorise the compulsory acquisition of additional land unless all persons interested consent.[90]

If the compulsory purchase order is confirmed, the acquiring authority must, as soon as may be, publish a notice in the prescribed form[91] in one or more local newspapers describing the land, stating that the order has been confirmed and naming a place where a copy of the order, as confirmed, and the order map may be inspected.[92] A similar notice together with a copy of the order as confirmed must be served on all persons who were required to be served with notice of the making of the order (see p.21 above). Amongst other matters, the notice will draw attention to the opportunity for an aggrieved person to question the order by way of an application to the Court of Session (see p.37 below).

Subject to such an application, a compulsory purchase order will become operative on the date on which the notice is first published in the local press.[93]

---

[86] See, too, the Town and Country Planning (Scotland) Act 1997, s.265.

[87] See, too, the Town and Country Planning (Scotland) Act 1997, s.265.

[88] See, generally on expenses, Circular 17/1998, and SDD Circular 6/1990, paras 16–20.

[89] 1947 Act, First Schedule, para.2. See *City of Glasgow District Council v Secretary of State for Scotland*, 1990 S.L.T. 343.

[90] 1947 Act, First Schedule, para.5.

[91] See the Compulsory Purchase of Land (Scotland) Regulations 1976, reg.3(e), Sch.1, Form 5.

[92] 1947 Act, First Schedule, para.6.

[93] 1947 Act, First Schedule, para.16. But see p.19 above as regards orders which are subject to special parliamentary procedure.

PURCHASES BY MINISTERS

2–16 Separate but similar procedural arrangements apply to compulsory purchase orders promoted by the Scottish or other Ministers.[94] These are set out in Part II of the First Schedule to the 1947 Act.

Such an order is first prepared in draft in such form as the Ministers may determine. It must, however, describe by reference to a map the land to which it applies. Notice of the preparation of the order in draft must be given as for the making of an order by a local or other authority. The Ministers must be satisfied that acquisition is justified by the public interest (see p.28). There is the same opportunity to object and a right to be heard in support of an objection.[95] In practice, similar inquiry and post inquiry procedures operate[96] although the order is not confirmed, it is "made" by the Ministers. Notice of the "making" of an order must be given in much the same way as notice of confirmation of an order must be given by a local or other authority. The validity of an order made by Ministers may also be questioned by way of application to the Court of Session.

COMPULSORY ACQUISITION OF STATUTORY UNDERTAKERS' LAND

2–17 Where a compulsory purchase order includes land which has been acquired by statutory undertakers[97] for the purposes of their undertaking, then, if within the period allowed for objection to the order the undertakers make representations to the Scottish Ministers or to their Minister, as appropriate,[98] the Ministers (or Minister) may block the acquisition of that land.[99] Unless the Ministers (or Minister) certify either that the land can be purchased and not replaced without serious detriment to the undertaking or that it can be replaced without serious detriment to the undertaking, the order cannot be confirmed or made, as the case may be, in respect of that land.

Exceptionally, where a compulsory purchase order is promoted under the provisions of Part VIII of the Town and Country Planning (Scotland) Act 1997, the order may be confirmed or made in respect of statutory undertakers' land in the absence of a certificate provided it is confirmed or made by the Scottish Ministers.[1]

---

[94] The Law Commission has proposed that there should be a unified procedure for orders promoted by local authorities and other agencies and by Ministers (Consultation Paper No 169, *Towards a compulsory purchase code: (2) Procedure,* 2002, p.31).

[95] 1947 Act, First Schedule, para.7 (4).

[96] There are, however, no inquiries procedure rules for such inquiries.

[97] For the definition of "statutory undertaker," see n.6 above.

[98] See 1947 Act, s.7(2). See, too, Land Compensation and Compulsory Purchase Legislation, SDD consultation paper, 1989, para.36.

[99] 1947 Act, First Schedule, para.10.

[1] 1997 Act, s.224(7). See, too, Land Compensation and Compulsory Purchase Legislation, *supra,* para.38.

CHALLENGE IN COURT OF SESSION

Any person aggrieved by a compulsory purchase order who desires to **2–18** question its validity[2] may do so by way of application to the Court of Session within six weeks of the date on which notice of its confirmation or making is first published (1947 Act, First Schedule, para.15).[3] The application may be made on one or other or both of the following grounds: (i) that the authorisation granted by the compulsory purchase order is not empowered to be granted; (ii) that the interests of the applicant have been substantially prejudiced by non-compliance with certain statutory requirements.[4]

1. A person aggrieved

As paragraph 15 provides an opportunity to question the validity of a **2–19** compulsory purchase order, it would seem that an acquiring authority is unlikely to be a "person aggrieved" except possibly in so far as they may wish to question any modification made to their order by the confirming authority. In this latter connection, the decision in *Strathclyde Regional Council v Secretary of State for Scotland*[5] is not encouraging. The Second Division held that a regional planning authority was not a "person aggrieved" without the meaning of section 232 of the Town and Country Planning (Scotland) Act 1972 and could not, therefore, challenge the validity of the action by the Secretary of State in modifying the authority's structure plan. A decision by a confirming authority not to confirm an order would be subject, not to a statutory application to quash, but to the general supervisory jurisdiction of the Court of Session.[6]

---

[2] The Law Commission has proposed that the challenge procedure should apply not to the order but to the decision of the confirming authority to confirm or refuse to confirm the order. Earlier stages in the process would be subject to judicial review (Law Commission Consultation Paper No 169, *Towards a compulsory purchase code: (2) Procedure*, 2002, p.39).

[3] For construction of the six week time limit see *Okolo v Secretary of State for the Environment and Kingston upon Hull City Council* [1997] J.P.L. 1005. In *Enterprise Inns plc. v Secretary of State for the Environment, Transport and the Regions and Liverpool City Council* (2001) 81 P. & C.R. 236 it was held that the court had no jurisdiction to entertain an application made before the notice of confirmation of the order was published.

[4] 1947 Act, First Schedule, para.15. A certificate issued under Part II of the First Schedule to the 1947 Act may also be questioned within six weeks on the ground of non-compliance with certain statutory requirements.

[5] 1989 S.C.L.R. 607.

[6] See, for example, *R. v Secretary of State for the Environment, ex p. Melton Borough Council* [1986] J.P.L. 190; *R. v Secretary of State for the Environment, ex p. Leicester County Council* [1987] J.P.L. 787. See, too, *R. v Camden London Borough Council, ex p. Comyn Ching & Co. (London) Ltd* [1984] J.P.L. 661 where Woolf J. held that a resolution by a local authority to make a compulsory purchase order was not encompassed by provision for a statutory application to quash but could be the subject of an application for judicial review. He thought it would be different once the order had been made even though it had not at that stage been confirmed. See, too, *Standard Commercial Property Securities Ltd v Glasgow City Council* 2001 SC 178. In *R. v Secretary of State for the Environment, ex p. Royal Borough of Kensington and Chelsea* [1987] J.P.L. 567 an application for judicial review was granted to an acquiring authority in respect of a decision by an inspector not to admit evidence at a local inquiry vital to the authority's case.

The phrase a "person aggrieved" would encompass owners, lessees and occupiers (except occupiers for a month or less) who are entitled to receipt of notice of the making of the order.[7] However, it is uncertain whether and, if so, to what extent it encompasses other persons generally referred to as "third parties," who may also be concerned about the outcome of the order. It would seem reasonable to suggest that an occupier for a month or less who has resided in the property for a number of years would be regarded as a 'person aggrieved'; but what about local residents? The requirement to give public notice of the making of an order is an acknowledgement that such concern may exist, and Lord Clyde observed in *Martin v Bearsden and Milngavie District Council*[8] that "[a]ppeal against a compulsory purchase order is open under paragraph 15 to 'any person aggrieved', which, while it doubtless does not give an unlimited title for complaint, extends beyond those who had the right to have the order served upon them." But it is clear that the opportunity to question the validity of the order is not available to everyone. The courts will wish to steer a course between those who might fairly be described as having a close interest in the outcome and those who are mere "busybodies."[9]

It has been suggested that in its statutory context a "person aggrieved" should be interpreted "broadly and with reference to the common law rules of title and interest to sue."[10] There is, however, little recent authority in the field of compulsory purchase on the question of title and interest to sue[11] and it is difficult to know how far the evolving case law in the field of town and country planning offers an analogy. In *Simpson v Edinburgh Corporation*[12] a resident in a city square was held to have no title and interest to question the validity of a grant of planning permission to develop other land in the square. He could not show that some legal right conferred on him by the legislation had been contravened. On the other hand, in *Black v Tennent*[13] neighbouring proprietors who had a statutory right to object to the grant of a public house licence and who had unsuccessfully objected were held to have sufficient title to question the validity of the grant of a licence.

The English courts have in recent years adopted a more liberal approach to the interpretation of a "person aggrieved" in the context of

---

[7] See, for example, *McCowan v Secretary of State for Scotland*, 1972 S.C. 93.

[8] 1987 S.L.T. 300.

[9] *Attorney-General of Gambia v N' jie* [1961] A.C. 617, *per* Lord Denning.

[10] *Stair Memorial Encyclopaedia of the Laws of Scotland*, Vol. 1, "Administrative Law", para.315.

[11] In *Standard Commercial Property Securities Ltd v Glasgow City Council*, 2001 S.C. 177, OH, the court held that, although at the date of the decision to promote a compulsory purchase order, the petitioners did not own any property within the site in question, another company within the same group of companies did and the petitioners did own such property at the date of the petition and, in the circumstances, had title and interest to petition for judicial review of the decision.

[12] 1960 S.C. 313; 1961 S.L.T. 17. Also *Bellway Ltd v Strathclyde Regional Council*, 1979 S.C. 92; 1980 S.L.T. 66; and *Reid v Mini-Cabs*, 1966 S.C. 137.

[13] (1889) 1 F. 423. And for recent decisions where a liberal approach has been adopted see *Wilson v I.B.A.*, 1979 S.L.T. 279; and *Scottish Old People's Welfare Council, Petitioner* 1987 S.L.T. 179. See, too, *Lakin Ltd v Secretary of State for Scotland*, 1988 S.L.T. 780; also the report of the Working Party under Lord Dunpark, *Procedure for Judicial Review of Administrative Action*, 1984, para.8.

a statutory application to quash planning decisions. In *Turner v Secretary of State for the Environment*[14] Ackner J. declined to follow the earlier decision of Salmon J. in *Buxton v Minister of Housing and Local Government*[15] and held that a local preservation society, who had been heard at the discretion of the inspector at a local inquiry to consider an application for planning permission for residential development, were entitled to be heard in support of their application to quash the subsequent grant of planning permission by the Secretary of State. Ackner J. said:

> "I see good reason, so long as the grounds of appeal are so restricted, for ensuring that any person who, in the ordinary sense of the word, is aggrieved by the decision, and certainly any person who has attended and made representations at the inquiry, should have the right to establish in the courts that the decision is bad in law because it is ultra vires or for some other good reason."[16]

Evidence of a more liberal approach can also be seen in recent decisions **2–20** of the Scottish courts in the context of using statutory applications to quash planning decisions. In *Strathclyde Regional Council v Secretary of State for Scotland (No 2)*,[17] the regional council challenged the decision of a reporter upholding an appeal against a refusal of planning permission by a district council within its area. The regional council was entitled to, but did not, appear at the public inquiry but submitted written observations instead. The Second Division accepted that the council was 'a person aggrieved'. The phrase, said Lord Justice Clerk Ross, "is apt to include persons who had been given notice of inquiry and who had submitted observations to the inquiry and who would have been entitled to appear at the inquiry". And in *Cumming v Secretary of State for Scotland*[18] the court accepted that a local resident, who had been notified of a planning application and who had had an opportunity to object to the application but had failed to do so, was an aggrieved person for the purposes of challenging the adequacy of the description of the proposed development in the application and in the public advertisement of the application. Lord Murray said:

> "Since the introduction of planning legislation the courts had moved from a strict and legalistic interpretation of the words 'person aggrieved' to a meaning more in accord with ordinary language . . . It would be wrong to give 'person aggrieved' a restrictive interpretation when it was the objective of the planning

---

[14] (1973) 28 P. & C.R. 123. See, too, *Attorney-General of Gambia v N'jie* [1961] A.C. 617; *Maurice v L.C.C.* [1964] 2 Q.B. 362; and *Bizonny v Secretary of State for the Environment* [1976] J.P.L. 306.

[15] [1961] 1 Q.B. 278. It was held in that case that a person aggrieved was someone whose legal rights had been infringed. See, too, *Ex p. Sidebotham* (1880) 14 Ch. D. 458.

[16] (1973) 28 P. & C.R. 123 at p.139.

[17] 1990 S.L.T. 149. See too *North East Fife District Council v Secretary of State for Scotland*, 1992 S.L.T. 373.

[18] 1993 S.L.T. 228. See too *Mackenzie's Trs. v Highland Regional Council*, 1995 S.L.T. 218.

legislation that the public should be made aware of planning proposals and that they should be given an opportunity of making representations about them".[19]

Although public notice is given of the making and confirmation of a compulsory purchase order, it is not clear that the compulsory purchase legislation has the same objective or that the public have the same involvement. In the absence of any recent Scottish decision on the scope of the phrase a "person aggrieved" in the context of paragraph 15 of the First Schedule to the 1947 Act, the position remains uncertain.

2. The statutory grounds of challenge

2–21   Paragraph 15 provides that an application may be made to the Court of Session on the ground that the authorisation of the compulsory purchase order was not within the powers of the legislation or that any requirements of the 1947 Act or of any regulations made under that Act have not been complied with. Section 60 of the Land Compensation (Scotland) Act 1973 provides that the reference to "requirement" is to include reference to any requirements of the Tribunals and Inquiries Act 1992 or of any rules made under, or having effect as made under, that Act.

Notwithstanding the difference in the wording of the two grounds the courts have at times found difficulty in distinguishing between them. There is, said Megaw L.J. in *Gordondale Investments Ltd v Secretary of State for the Environment*,[20] "a real difficulty in seeking to define separate spheres for, or to draw a borderline between, on the one hand, situations in which the order is 'not within the powers of this Act' and, on the other hand, situations in which a 'requirement of this Act has not been complied with'." The distinction will sometimes be important because paragraph 15 goes on to provide that the court may quash an order because of a failure to comply with some requirement of the legislation only if the interests of the applicant have been substantially prejudiced (see p.44 below).

In *McCowan v Secretary of State for Scotland*[21] it was argued for the appellants that a failure to give notice of the making of a compulsory purchase order as required by the legislation enabled the appellant to found upon either of the grounds in paragraph 15. Lord Cameron, whilst reserving his opinion on the point, observed that if an order which is flawed by a failure to comply with the requirements of the Act is one which is not empowered to be granted under the Act, there would seem to be no purpose in presenting a person aggrieved with alternative roads to the quashing of the order.[22] There was, he thought, much to be said for the view that the first alternative in paragraph 15 "relates to an order which in purpose or object is ultra vires the statute under which the authority authorising it purports to act or is ultra vires the authorising authority."

---

[19] See above, pp.232–233.
[20] (1971) 23 P. & C.R. 334.
[21] 1972 S.C. 93.
[22] See, too, *Easter Ross Land Use Committee v Secretary of State for Scotland*, 1970 S.C. 182, *per* the Lord President (Lord Clyde).

However, in some cases it would appear that a failure to comply with a statutory requirement will also mean that the authorisation is not within the powers of the Act. In *Fairmount Investments Ltd v Secretary of State for the Environment*[23] Lord Russell of Killowen concluded that where there had been a departure from the principles of natural justice "it may equally be said that the order is not within the powers of the Act and that a requirement of the Act has not been complied with." In many cases, of course, there will be no doubt that the applicant has been substantially prejudiced; in these cases the distinction will be less significant.

After some initial uncertainty[24] the courts appear to have adopted a broad approach to the scope of the statutory grounds of challenge and have not generally sought to "draw a borderline" between the two. What is generally referred to as the *Ashbridge* formula has now been widely accepted[25] as defining the circumstances in which a court may interfere with the decision of the Secretary of State. In *Ashbridge Investments Ltd v Minister of Housing and Local Government*[26] Denning M.R. said:

"The Court can only interfere on the ground that the Minister has gone outside the powers of the Act or that any requirements of the Act have not been complied with. Under this section it seems to me that the Court can interfere with the Minister's decision if he has acted on no evidence, or if he has come to a conclusion to which on the evidence he could not reasonably come; or if he has given a wrong interpretation to the words of the statute; or if he has taken into consideration matters which he ought not to have taken into account, or vice versa; or has otherwise gone wrong in law. It is identical with the position where the Court has power to interfere with the decision of a lower tribunal which has erred in point of law."

If this statement of the law is correct, it would seem, as Corfield and Carnwath observe, "that little, if any, effect is to be given to the actual words of the statutory provision."[27]

---

[23] [1976] 1 W.L.R. 1255 at p.1263.

[24] In *Smith v East Elloe R.D.C.* [1956] A.C. 736 the majority of the House of Lords (Lords Reid, Morton and Somervell) gave the first ground a narrow interpretation. Viscount Simonds and Lord Radcliffe, on the other hand, gave it a broad construction. See, too, *Hamilton v Secretary of State for Scotland*, 1972 S.C. 72; 1972 S.L.T. 233 *per* Lord Kissen (narrow construction); and *Lithgow v Secretary of State for Scotland*, 1973 S.C. 1; 1973 S.L.T. 81, *per* Lord Dunpark (broad construction).

[25] *Re Lamplugh* (1967) 19 P. & C.R. 125; *Coleen Properties v Minister of Housing and Local Government* [1971] 1 W.L.R. 433; *Gordondale Investments Ltd v Secretary of State for the Environment* (1971) 23 P. & C.R. 334; *Eckersley v Secretary of State for the Environment* (1977) 34 P. & C.R. 124; *Pyrford Properties Ltd v Secretary of State for the Environment* (1977) 36 P. & C.R. 28; *R. v Secretary of State for the Environment, ex p. Ostler* [1977] Q.B. 122, *per* Lord Denning; *De Rothschild v Secretary of State for Transport* [1989] J.P.L. 173; and *Wordie Property Co. Ltd v Secretary of State for Scotland*, 1984 S.L.T. 345, *per* the Lord President (Lord Emslie). See, too, *Seddon Properties Ltd v Secretary of State for the Environment* (1978) 42 P. & CR. 26, *per* Forbes J.

[26] [1965] 1 W.L.R. 1320, a case concerning the statutory grounds of challenge contained in the Housing Act 1957.

[27] Sir Frederick Corfield and R.J.A. Carnwath, *Compulsory Acquisition and Compensation* (Butterworths, 1978) p.55.

In *Associated Provincial Picture Houses Ltd v Wednesbury Corporation*[28] Lord Greene M.R., in a much cited judgment, also sought to define the circumstances in which a court would intervene to review an exercise of discretionary power:

> "The Court is entitled to investigate the action of the local authority with a view to seeing whether they have taken into account matters which they ought not to take into account, or, conversely, have refused to take into account or neglected to take into account matters which they ought to take into account. Once that question is answered in favour of the local authority it may be still possible to say that, although the local authority have kept within the four corners of the matters which they ought to consider, they have nonetheless come to a conclusion so unreasonable that no reasonable authority could ever have come to it."

2–22   In similar vein, Lord Murray, giving judgement for the Inner House in *Thornbank Developments (Galashiels) Ltd v Secretary of State for Scotland and Etterick and Lauderdale District Council,*[29] stated that the proper test to be applied in determining an appeal under the provisions of paragraph 15 of the First Schedule to the 1947 Act was that laid down by Lord President Emslie in *Wordie Property Co Ltd v Secretary of State for Scotland*[30]:

> "[The decision] will be *ultra vires* too, if the Secretary of State has taken into account irrelevant considerations or has failed to take account of relevant and material considerations which ought to have been taken into account. Similarly, it will fall to be quashed on that ground if, where it is one for which a factual basis is required, there is no proper basis in fact to support it".

In that case, it was held that the reporter in his report and the Secretary of State in his decision confirming a compulsory purchase order promoted under the Housing (Scotland) Act 1987 had taken into account an irrelevant consideration, namely that the tenement block in question was an eyesore in a conspicuous position. The power to acquire property designated as a housing action area for demolition was intended to ensure that houses below the tolerable standard should not be inhabited. It was not intended to deal with eyesores. Furthermore, the reference in the reporter's report to "the absence of action by the owners" was a clear error of fact. The report and the Secretary of State's decision had failed to take account of a relevant and material consideration which was that the owner was taking action to redevelop the site. The order was quashed.

In *De Rothschild v Secretary of State for the Environment*[31] the Court of Appeal firmly rejected the argument that there were to be derived from

---

[28] [1948] 1 K.B. 223.
[29] 1991 S.C.L.R. 532.
[30] 1984 S.L.T. 345.
[31] [1989] J.P.L. 173. See, too, *Singh v Secretary of State for the Environment* (1989) 24 E.G. 128.

case law special rules beyond the *Wednesbury/Ashbridge* grounds which applied wherever the court was considering a challenge to a compulsory purchase order. That proposition now needs to be seen in the light of its refinement in *Chesterfield Properties plc v Secretary of State for the Environment*[32] and of the incorporation into domestic law of the European Convention on Human Rights (see the discussion at p.45).

The following provides some indication of the scope of the statutory grounds. Compulsory purchase orders have been successfully challenged on the ground that the statutory basis for an order did not exist,[33] that the substratum of fact required for the exercise of power was lacking,[34] that the confirming authority failed to have regard to a relevant consideration,[35] that the decision on the order was influenced by an irrelevant consideration,[36] that confirmation of the order was in breach of the principles of natural justice[37] and that there was a failure to comply with a procedural requirement.[38] A decision not to confirm a compulsory order was unsuccessfully challenged on the ground of unreasonableness in *City of Glasgow District Council v Secretary of State for Scotland.*[39]

---

[32] [1998] J.P.L. 568. See p.13.
[33] *Sovmots Investments Ltd v Secretary of State for the Environment* [1977] Q.B. 411. For unsuccessful challenges on this ground see *Sharkey and Fitzgerald v Secretary of State for the Environment and South Bucks District Council* [1992] J.P.L. 948; *McMonagle v Secretary of State for Scotland and City of Glasgow Council*, 1993 S.L.T. 807; and *Donnelly v Secretary of State for Scotland*, 1995 G.W.D. 13.704.
[34] *Coleen Properties Ltd v Minister of Housing and Local Government* [1971] 1 W.L.R. 433; *Re Ripon (Highfield) Housing Order* 1938 [1939] 2 K.B. 838; also *R. v Secretary of State for the Environment, ex p. Leicester City Council* [1987] J.P.L. 787. See, too, *Re Lamplugh* (1967) 19 P. & C.R. 125.
[35] *Brown v Secretary of State for the Environment* (1978) 40 P. & C.R. 285 (the existence of an alternative site); *Brinklow and Croft Bros. Ltd v Secretary of State for the Environment* [1976] J.P.L. 299 (relocation of displaced uses); *Prest v Secretary of State for Wales* [1983] J.P.L. 112 (the cost of developing alternative sites); *Sovmots Investments Ltd v Secretary of State for the Environment* [1977] Q.B. 411 (cost of conversion of premises); *R. v Secretary of State for the Environment, ex p. Kensington and Chelsea London Borough Council*, [1987] J.L.P. 567 (housing management consideration); *Thornbank Developments (Galashiels) Ltd v Secretary of State for Scotland and Etterick and Lauderdale District Council*, 1991 S.C.L.R. 532.
[36] *Sydney Municipal Council v Campbell* [1925] A.C. 338 (recovery of betterment); and *Thornbank Developments (Galashiels) Ltd v Secretary of State for Scotland and Etterick and Lauderdale District Council*. See, too, *Hanks v Minister of Housing and Local Government* [1963] 1 Q.B. 999 (planning matters not irrelevant). For an unsuccessful challenge on this ground see *Atlas Investments Ltd v Glasgow District Council*, unreported, Outer House, October 31, 2000 but see (2001) 86 S.P.E.L. 86.
[37] *Fairmount Investments Ltd v Secretary of State for the Environment* (1973) 27 P. & C.R. 197. See, too, *Errington v Minister of Health* [1935] 1 K.B. 249.
[38] *McCowan v Secretary of State for Scotland*, 1972 S.C. 93; *Brown v Minister of Housing and Local Government* [1953] 2 All E.R. 1385 (failure to serve notice of the making of the order on an owner or occupier, cf., *Grimley v Minister of Housing and Local Government* [1971] 2 Q.B. 96); *Richardson v Minister of Housing and Local Government* (1956) 8 P. & C.R. 29 (confirmation of order which should have been subject to special parliamentary procedure); *Hamilton v Roxburghshire County Council*, 1970 S.C. 248; 1971 S.L.T. 2 (obtaining information after an inquiry from one party without notifying the others).
[39] 1990 S.L.T. 343, OH.

3. Substantial prejudice

2–23   An applicant seeking to challenge the validity of a compulsory purchase order on the ground that there has been a failure to comply with a legislative requirement (paragraph 15(1)(b)) must show that he has suffered substantial prejudice as a result of the failure. In *Hibernian Property Co. Ltd v Secretary of State for the Environment*[40] Browne J. said of the corresponding provision in Schedule 3 of the Housing Act 1957:

> "This of course does not mean that the applicant must prove that the decision would have been different if the requirement had been complied with, which would usually be quite impossible. In my view, the loss of a chance of being better off in relation to the proposed order would usually be enough to constitute substantial prejudice."

In that case during the course of a site inspection following an inquiry to hear objections to a compulsory purchase order made under the Housing Act 1957 the inspector questioned occupiers of the premises in the absence of a representative from the applicants. The inspector's recommendation to confirm the order was accepted by the Minister. Browne J. in quashing the order said: "In my judgment the question is not whether the information obtained by the Inspector did in fact prejudice the applicants by contributing to the decision of the Secretary of State to confirm the compulsory purchase order but whether there was a risk that it may have done so."

Thus in *McCowan v Secretary of State for Scotland*[41] a failure to serve notice of the making of a compulsory purchase order on an owner of part of the order land so depriving him of an opportunity of lodging and maintaining an objection was thought by Lord Cameron to be a procedural defect amounting prima facie to substantial prejudice.[42] And in *Paterson v Secretary of State for Scotland*[43] the Court of Session quashed the Secretary of State's decision on a planning appeal because of a failure to make proper findings of fact in Part I of his report as required by the Planning Inquiries Procedure Rules. "I think," said Lord Cameron, "that where, as here, there has been a failure to comply with a fundamental requirement of procedure which goes to the merits of the matter in such an inquiry as this, there is no doubt that an appellant has been substantially prejudiced."[44]

---

[40] (1973) 27 P. & C.R. 197. See, too, *Miller v Weymouth and Melcombe Regis Corporation* (1974) 27 P. & C.R. 468, *per* Kerr J.

[41] 1972 S.C. 93.

[42] See, too, *George v Minister of Housing and Local Government* [1953] 2 All E.R. 1385; *Wilson v Secretary of State* [1973] 1 W.L.R. 1083; and the comment of Lord Clyde in *Martin v Bearsden and Milngavie District Council*, 1987 S.L.T. 300 at p.304 G-H; contrast *George v Secretary of State for the Environment* (1979) 38 P. & C.R. 609; and *McMillan v Inverness-shire County Council*, 1949 S.C. 77; 1949 S.L.T. 77.

[43] 1971 S.C. 1; 1971 S.L.T. (Notes) 2. See, too, *J. & A. Kirkpatrick v Lord Advocate*, 1967 S.C. 165; 1967 S.L.T. (Notes) 27; and *Wordie Property Co. Ltd v Secretary of State for Scotland*, 1984 S.L.T. 345.

[44] For recent planning decisions on the question of substantial prejudice see *Central Regional Council v Secretary of State for Scotland and Strathclyde Regional Council*, 1991 S.C.L.R. 348 (prejudice established); *Mackenzie Trs. v Highland Regional Council*, 1995 S.L.T. 218 (prejudice not established); *Ampliflaire Ltd v Secretary of State for Scotland*, 1998 G.W.D. 8–405 (prejudice not established); and *Stewart Milne Homes Ltd v Secretary of State for Scotland*, 2000 G.W.D. 18–725 (prejudice not established).

If the court considers that the applicant has not been substantially prejudiced by the failure to comply with statutory requirements, it is entitled to disregard the failure.[45] It seems that it is for the applicant to establish that his interests have in fact been substantially prejudiced.[46] The onus may not, however, be particularly heavy. In *Wordie Property Co. Ltd v Secretary of State for Scotland*[47] the Lord President (Lord Emslie) said that a failure by the Minister to give proper and adequate reasons for his decision could not be other than prejudicial to the applicant; and in the same case Lord Cameron observed that "where an applicant has been deprived of the exercise of a right conferred by Parliament, that fact alone would appear to me prima facie to indicate that he has suffered substantial prejudice."

4. Human rights

The Human Rights Act 1998 incorporated into domestic law the European Convention of Human Rights. Section 6(1) provides that it is unlawful for a public authority to act in a way which is incompatible with any Convention right. A person who considers that a public authority has so acted may bring proceedings against the authority, or may rely on Convention rights in any legal proceedings. Convention rights may therefore be raised as an issue in a statutory application to the Court of Session questioning the validity of a compulsory purchase order. **2–24**

The 'Convention rights' are defined in section 1 of the Act. In the context of compulsory purchase, reference has already been made to the First Protocol, Article 1.[48] This provides, *inter alia*, that "no one shall be deprived of his possessions except in the public interest and subject to the conditions provided for by the law and by the general principles of international law" (see p.13).[49] Brief mention has also been made of Article 8 which provides, *inter alia*, that "everyone has the right to respect for his private and family life, his home and his correspondence" (see p.13).

In addition to these substantive rights, the Convention also lays down important procedural safeguards. In particular, Article 6 provides, *inter alia*, that "in the determination of his civil rights and obligations . . . everyone is entitled to a fair and public hearing within a reasonable time

---

[45] *McMillan v Inverness-shire County Council*, 1949 S.C. 77; 1949 S.L.T. 77; *Steele v Minister of Housing and Local Government* (1956) 6 P. & C.R. 386; *Gordondale Investments Ltd v Secretary of State for the Environment* (1971) 23 P. & C.R. 334; *Miller v Weymouth & Melcombe Regis Corporation* (1974) 27 P. & C.R. 468; *Kent County Council v Secretary of State for the Environment* (1977) 33 P. & C.R. 70.

[46] *Gordondale Investments Ltd v Secretary of State for the Environment* (1971) 23 P. & C.R. 334, *per* Lord Denning; *Hibernian Property Co. Ltd v Secretary of State for the Environment* (1973) 27 P. & C.R. 197, *per* Browne J.; *George v Minister of Housing and Local Government* [1953] 2 All E.R. 1385.

[47] 1984 S.L.T. 345.

[48] See generally M. Redman, "Compulsory Purchase, Compensation and Human Rights" [1999] J.P.L. 315.

[49] For unsuccessful applications to quash compulsory purchase orders based on Article 1 of the First Protocol see *Tesco Stores Ltd v Secretary of State for the Environment, Transport and the Regions and Wycombe District Council* [2001] J.P.L. 106; and *Bexley London Borough Council v Secretary of State for the Environment, Transport and the Regions and Another* [2001] J.P.L. 1442.

by an independent and impartial tribunal established by law". An expropriation of a person's right in land would be regarded as a determination of his civil rights. The question is how far the procedures laid down in the 1947 Act provide for a fair and public hearing by an independent and impartial tribunal.

In attempting to answer this question, a distinction should be drawn between compulsory purchase orders promoted otherwise than by the Scottish Ministers or by a Minister of the Crown in respect of a reserved matter and orders promoted by the Scottish Ministers or by a Minister of the Crown. In the former case, for example, an order promoted by a local authority, the provision for confirmation of the order by the Scottish Ministers, the requirement for a hearing (generally a public inquiry) by a person appointed by the Ministers in the event of objection to the order by a statutory objector and the opportunity for a person aggrieved to question its validity before the Court of Session would together seem to meet the requirements of Article 6. In the field of town and country planning considerable interest has focused on whether planning procedures are Article 6 compliant in the context of third party objectors to planning applications who have no right of appeal against a grant of planning permission. There must be considerable doubt whether a third party objector to a compulsory purchase order would be regarded as a "victim" for the purposes of a claim under section 6(1) of the 1998 Act that a public authority had acted in a way which was incompatible with Convention rights (1998 Act, s.7(4)). A "victim" is a person who is directly affected by the act or omission in issue.[50] With the possible exception of a tenant for a month or less who has occupied the subject premises for some time or the proprietor of a servitude right over the subject premises, it must be doubtful whether a third party could show the necessary direct effect (see p.23).

On the face of it, the position is different where an order is promoted by the Scottish Ministers or by a Minister of the Crown. As the Ministers promote the order, appoint the person to conduct an inquiry into any objections and then decide whether to make their own order, there would seem to be a strong argument for saying that statutory objectors would not at that stage have had the benefit of a fair and public hearing by an independent and impartial tribunal. This argument was raised in what is widely referred to as the *"Alconbury"* case. The *Alconbury* case involved three separate appeals which were heard together.[51] One case involved a planning application which had been called-in for a decision by the Secretary of State; the second involved the "recovery" of two planning appeals from an inspector by the Minister; and the third involved an improvement scheme at a road junction with a compulsory purchase order and related roads orders made by the Minister. In other words, the Minister had such a close interest in the decisions in each

---

[50] For a discussion of the meaning of the word 'victim' see D. Hart, "The Impact of the European Convention on Human Rights on Planning and Environmental Law" [2000] J.P.L. 117.

[51] *R. v Secretary of State for the Environment, Transport and the Regions, ex p. Holding Barnes plc; R. v Secretary of State for the Environment, Transport and the Regions, ex p. Alconbury Developments Ltd;* and *R. v Secretary of State for the Environment, Transport and the Regions, ex p. Legal and General Society Ltd* [2001] J.P.L. 920, HL.

case that it was difficult to see that he could be regarded as independent and impartial.

The question in issue before the House of Lords was whether the processes by which such decisions are taken, including the opportunity to appeal to the court, are compatible with Article 6(1) of the Convention. A similar question had arisen before the Court of Session in *County Properties Ltd v The Scottish Ministers*[52] and the Lord Advocate intervened before the House of Lords to support the case advanced on behalf of the Secretary of State.

The Divisional Court in *Alconbury* had concluded that "what is objectionable in terms of Article 6(1) is that [the Minister] should be the judge in his own cause where his policy is in play". In view of the restricted jurisdiction of the court on a statutory appeal, the court had concluded that Article 6 prevents the Minister from being both a policy maker and a decision-taker.

The House of Lords concluded that it was hardly surprising that the **2–25** Minister was not independent and impartial within the meaning of Article 6(1). There was nothing sinister or unusual about the decision-making process. Such decisions were of an administrative rather than a judicial nature and the Minister was accountable for them to Parliament and the electorate. The question was whether the requirements of Article 6(1) were satisfied by the right to have a decision reviewed by the courts. The Divisional Court had concluded that the restricted power of review did not satisfy the requirements. On this point their Lordships disagreed. Although the court had to have 'full jurisdiction', that meant, said Lord Clyde, "full jurisdiction in the context of the case". This would depend on a number of considerations such as the subject matter of the dispute, the nature of the decision of the public authority which is in question, the procedure for review of the decision by a body acting independently of the authority concerned and the scope of that review.[53] In this context, their Lordships held that the courts would have 'full jurisdiction' to review the decisions in question and that the procedures were Article 6 compliant. Subsequently, the Inner House in *County Properties* followed the decision of the House of Lords in *Alconbury* and dismissed the petition for judicial review.

Although subsequent litigation on Article 6 in the field of town and country planning has focused on whether a court would have full jurisdiction to review a decision in the context of the particular case,[54] the general position with the 1947 Act procedure would seem to be that the provision for a public inquiry into objections by statutory objectors coupled with the scope of review by the court through the statutory right of appeal should be sufficient to comply with the requirements of Article 6.

5. The six-week time period for challenge

Paragraph 15 of the First Schedule to the 1947 Act provides that an **2–26** application to the Court of Session by a person aggrieved by a compulsory purchase order must be made within a period of six weeks

---

[52] 2000 S.L.T. 965.

[53] Both Lords Hoffman and Clyde referred with approval to the Opinion of Mr Nicolas Bratza in *Bryan v United Kingdom* (1995) 21 E.H.R.R. 342 at p.354.

[54] See M. Purdue, "Human Rights and Planning" (2002) S.L.T. Articles 195.

from the date on which notice of the confirmation or making of the order was first published. In *Griffiths v Secretary of State for the Environment*[55] the House of Lords held that the date actions were taken by the Secretary of State for the purpose of challenge under section 245(1) of the Town and Country Planning Act 1971 was the date a letter conveying the decision was date stamped and that time ran from that date and not when the decision was received. Paragraph 16 of the First Schedule to the 1947 Act goes on to provide that, subject to the provisions of paragraph 15, a compulsory purchase order shall "not . . . be questioned in any legal proceedings whatsoever." Whether the provision in paragraph 16 is effective to exclude the jurisdiction of the court after the six week time period has elapsed is a question which has caused considerable difficulty and it is not possible to reconcile all the decisions in this field.[56]

Underlying this question is the policy of Parliament that it is necessary to strike a balance on the one hand between the dictates of justice that those affected by a compulsory purchase order should have an opportunity, where appropriate, to question its validity and on the other hand the dictates of administration that there should be finality and certainty regarding the order so that schemes of much needed public works may proceed.

In *Smith v East Elloe Rural District Council*[57] the majority of the House of Lords held that the words used in the corresponding ouster clause in paragraph 16 of the English Act of 1946 were wide enough to cover any kind of challenge which an aggrieved person may think fit to make. In that case the appellant brought an action against the local authority more than six weeks after notice of confirmation of a compulsory purchase order on the ground that the order had been made and confirmed wrongfully and in bad faith. Lord Radcliffe said:

> "I do not see how it is possible to treat the provisions of paragraphs 15 and 16 of Part IV of Schedule 1 of the Act as containing anything less than a complete statutory code for regulating the extent to which, and the conditions under which, courts of law might be resorted to for the purpose of questioning the validity of a compulsory purchase order within the protection of the Act."[58]

Subsequently, in *Anisminic Ltd v Foreign Compensation Commission*[59] the House of Lords held that an ouster clause which provided that a determination by the Commission should "not be called into question in any court of law" would not protect a determination made without jurisdiction and which was thus a nullity.[60]

---

[55] [1983] 2 A.C. 51.
[56] For a helpful review of these decisions see E. Young, "Procedural Defects and Ouster Clauses" [1988] J.P.L. 301.
[57] [1956] A.C. 736.
[58] See above p.768.
[59] [1969] 2 A.C. 147.
[60] Lord Reid in that case was critical of the decision in *Smith* as there had been little consideration given to the question whether an ouster clause was effective where nullity was in issue.

The decisions in *Smith* and *Anisminic* were considered by the Court of Session in *Hamilton v Secretary of State for Scotland*[61] where the pursuers sought to reduce a compulsory purchase order outside the six week time period as being illegal and *ultra vires* because the proceedings had been contrary to the requirements of natural justice. Lord Kissen, in holding that the jurisdiction of the court was ousted by paragraph 16 of the Scottish Act, distinguished *Anisminic* on the ground that, unlike paragraphs 15 and 16 of the 1947 Act, there was no provision of any kind in the Foreign Compensation Act 1950 for an application to the court to test questions of nullity. In the 1947 Act "there is provision for quashing at least some kinds of null orders. I cannot see how it can be said, on the basis of *Anisminic*, that, as pursuer's counsel maintained, one kind of nullity can be remedied by the application of said paragraph 15 but all other kinds can be remedied by ordinary proceedings in the Court."

The decisions in *Smith* and *Anisminic* were further considered in *R. v Secretary of State for the Environment, ex p. Ostler*[62] where a road scheme order and a compulsory purchase order were challenged outside the six week period on the grounds of want of natural justice and bad faith verging on fraud. The Court of Appeal, following *Smith* and distinguishing *Anisminic*, held that their jurisdiction was ousted on the expiry of the six week time period. *Anisminic* was distinguished on the ground that the section in the Foreign Compensation Act 1950 provided for a complete ouster of the court's jurisdiction whereas in *Smith* (as in *Ostler*) the court had power to inquire into all matters raised provided application was made within six weeks. It was, said Lord Denning, more like a limitation period than a complete ouster. *Anisminic* was further distinguished on the grounds that the decision of the Foreign Compensation Commission was that of a judicial body whereas in *Ostler* the order was in the nature of an administrative decision; that in *Anisminic* the Commission had acted outside its jurisdiction whereas in *Ostler* the decisions in question had been within the jurisdiction of the Minister; and that the policy of the legislature was that there should be certainty with compulsory purchase orders on the expiry of the six-week period. **2–27**

In *McDaid v Clydebank District Council*,[63] however, the First Division of the Court of Session held that an ouster clause in section 85(10) of what was then the Town and Country Planning (Scotland) Act 1972 did not exclude the court's jurisdiction in respect of an enforcement notice which had not been served as required by the Act and was therefore a nullity. In that case the planning authority had failed to serve enforcement notices on the landowners, although their identities were known to the authority, with the result that the owners did not become aware of

[61] 1972 S.C. 72; 1972 S.L.T. 233. See too *Lithgow v Secretary of State for Scotland*, 1973 S.C. 1; 1973 S.L.T. 81.

[62] [1977] Q.B. 122. See too *Cartwright v Minister of Housing and Local Government* (1967) 65 L.G.R. 384; *Routh v Reading Corporation* (1970) 217 E.G. 1337; *Westminster City Council v Secretary of State for the Environment* [1984] J.P.L. 27; and *R. v Secretary of State for the Environment, ex p. Kent* [1988] J.P.L. 706; [1990] J.P.L 124 CA.

[63] 1984 S.L.T. 162. And see comment by Colin T. Reid in 1984 S.P.L.P. 74. See too *R. v Greenwich London Borough Council, ex p. Patel* (1985) 84 L.G.R. 241 where the Court of Appeal upheld the effect of the ouster clause in the corresponding provision of the English planning legislation.

the notices until the time for lodging an appeal against them with the Secretary of State had passed.

Section 85(10) of the 1972 Act (see now section 134 of the 1997 Act) provided that the validity of an enforcement notice is not to be questioned on certain specified grounds except by way of an appeal to the Secretary of State. There was no provision in the 1972 Act corresponding to paragraphs 15 and 16 of the First Schedule to the 1947 Act which would allow the validity of a notice to be questioned on specified grounds and within a specified time period on application to the Court of Session. In one sense, therefore, the provision in s.85(10) was equivalent to an absolute ouster clause and thus regarded the decision in *McDaid* may be reconciled with *Smith, Hamilton* and *Ostler*.[64] The decision, however, also indicates that an enforcement notice which is not properly served is a nullity and is not as a result protected by the ouster clause. The reasoning in *McDaid* has been described as "impeccably that of *Anisminic* to which the court made approving reference."[65]

The decision in *McDaid* was considered by the Outer House in *Martin v Bearsden and Milngavie District Council*.[66] In that case a local authority failed to serve notice of the making of a compulsory purchase order on the owner of land included in the order. The land was subsequently vested in the authority. Some years later, the owners, still unaware of the order, disposed of part of the order land to the petitioners. Thereafter the petitioners learned of the existence of the order and applied for judicial review seeking its reduction and damages. The district council, as statutory successors to the order making authority, relied on the ouster clause in paragraph 16 of the First Schedule to the 1947 Act which precludes the jurisdiction of the court after the six week period.

Lord Clyde, in concluding that the application for judicial review was rendered incompetent by paragraph 16, accepted the submission of the local authority that there was "a valid and significant difference" between the provisions of the 1972 Act in issue in *McDaid* and paragraphs 15 and 16 of the First Schedule to the 1947 Act. Although both made provision for recourse to the Secretary of State against the action of the authority, the 1972 Act had no provision corresponding to paragraph 15 which allowed for an application to the Court of Session. In the context of the time limited provision in paragraph 15, Lord Clyde held that the provision for the exclusion of legal proceedings in paragraph 16 takes on a significance which the ouster provision in issue in *McDaid* did not have. "It cannot," he said, "be affirmed that paragraph 16 was not intended to cover an order which was open to attack on grounds of nullity."

McDaid was further distinguished on the ground that the requirement in the 1947 Act for the public advertisement of the making of a compulsory purchase order in addition to the serving of notice on those with an interest in the land could attract interest from persons who had not had any notice served upon them. The reference to "any person

---

[64] To which decisions the court made no reference.
[65] "The Exclusion of Judicial Review" (1984) S.L.T. (News) 297.
[66] 1987 S.L.T. 300. See too *Pollock v Secretary of State for Scotland and Pilmuir Waste Disposal Ltd*, 1992 S.C.L.R. 972.

aggrieved" in paragraph 15 extended beyond those entitled to notice of the making of the order. In the context of the 1972 Act, where those who were to be served with a copy of the enforcement notice and those who had a right of appeal were so closely linked, the reasoning which was adopted in *McDaid* was more readily applicable than in the context of the 1947 Act. Furthermore, in *McDaid* service was of the essence. Section 84 of the 1972 Act (now section 127 of the 1997 Act) empowered a planning authority to serve an enforcement notice; without service there is no notice. A compulsory purchase order, on the other hand, is a means of authorising a compulsory purchase by a local authority. It requires to be made, and then submitted and confirmed by the confirming authority. Prior to submission, notice must be advertised and served on certain persons. "The omission of service in that context," said Lord Clyde, "does not seem to me to be of the same gravity as the omission to serve an enforcement notice."

Although, therefore, the position remains somewhat uncertain, the indications are that paragraph 16 is effective to oust the jurisdiction of the court after the six week period even where the order is alleged to be a nullity.

6. Powers of the court

Until final determination of an application under paragraph 15 of the First Schedule to the 1947 Act, the court may by interim order suspend the operation of the compulsory purchase order or of any provision contained in it, either generally or in so far as it affects any property of the applicant.[67] If satisfied that one or other or both of the statutory grounds have been made out, the court in its discretion may quash the compulsory purchase order or any provision contained in it, either generally or in so far as it affects any property of the applicant.[68]

POWER TO EXTINGUISH PUBLIC RIGHTS OF WAY

Where land is acquired or proposed to be acquired by a body possessing **2–28** compulsory purchase powers to which the 1947 Act applies and there subsists over any part of the land a public right of way (not being a right enjoyable by vehicular traffic), the Scottish Ministers may take steps to extinguish that right of way.[69] The Ministers must be satisfied either that a suitable alternative right of way has been or will be provided or that such alternative provision is not required. The date from which the right is extinguished will be specified in the order and must not be earlier than:

---

[67] 1947 Act, First Schedule, para.15(1)(a). The power to make an interim order applies also with regard to a challenge of a certificate made under Part III of the First Schedule.

[68] 1947 Act, First Schedule, para.15(1)(b). This power applies also to certificates made under Part III of the First Schedule.

[69] 1947 Act, s.3. Section 3 has no application if the provisions of the Town and Country Planning (Scotland) Act 1997, Part IX apply (1947 Act, s.3(5), as amended). Nor does it have any effect in relation to land acquired or proposed to be acquired by the Civil Aviation Authority under section 42 of the Civil Aviation Act 1982.

    (i) the date of the making of the order;

   (ii) where the acquiring authority take possession before the acquisition is completed, the date of possession;

  (iii) where the acquiring authority do not take possession in advance of acquisition, the date of acquisition.

The Ministers must publish notice stating the effect of the proposed order and allow an opportunity (not less than 21 days from the publication of the notice) for objection. If an objection, duly made, is not withdrawn, a public local inquiry must be arranged.[70]

No such order is to be made with regard to a right of way over land on, over or under which there is any apparatus belonging to statutory undertakers unless the undertakers consent to the making of the order. Consent must not be unreasonably refused. Such consent may be conditional upon suitable safeguards being included in the order for the protection of the undertakers.[71]

---

[70] See above, ss. 3(2) and (3).
[71] See above, s.3(4).

CHAPTER 3

COMPULSORY PURCHASE: ACQUIRING TITLE

Once a compulsory purchase order has been made or confirmed, the **3–01**
acquiring authority will wish to take steps to implement the order.
Implementation may not follow immediately upon confirmation but it
should be noted that the power to acquire land compulsorily conferred
by an order cannot be exercised after the expiration of a period of three
years from the date on which the order becomes operative.[1] The
operative date of an order is the date on which notice of the making or
confirmation (as appropriate) of the order is first published, although
some other period may be prescribed in the order.[2]

The serving of a notice to treat (below) is sufficient exercise of the
power.[3] In *Advance Ground Rents Ltd v Middlesborough Council,*[4] the
Lands Tribunal held that a failure by the acquiring authority to serve a
notice to treat on a mortgagee until after the expiration of the three year
period meant that the notice was invalid and the authority had lost their
opportunity to rectify the omission. On the other hand, in *Westminster
City Council v Quereshi*[5] it was held that the requirement to exercise the
powers of compulsory purchase within three years did not require that
all acts necessary to vest title had to be completed within that period. An
acquiring authority intending to use the general vesting declaration
procedure rather than a notice to treat (see below) must notify certain

---

[1] 1845 Act, s.116. Section 116 refers to a period of three years from the passing of the
Special Act. In the case of a compulsory purchase order made or confirmed under the 1947
Act procedure, the order together with the authorising Act are deemed to be the Special
Act (1947 Act, Second Schedule, para.1(a)). See the 1947 Act, First Schedule, para.17 for
the operative date where an order is subject to special parliamentary procedure. Note also
that under para.15(1)(a) of the First Schedule, the Court of Session may, in the event of a
challenge to the validity of the order, suspend its operation until the final determination of
the proceedings. See p.59 as regards interests omitted to be purchased. CPPRAG
recommended that, because of the hardship that can be caused by delay and uncertainty,
owners and occupiers should be able to take the initiative before the end of the three year
period and serve a notice on the acquiring authority requiring it to treat for the acquisition
of the order land (*Fundamental review of the laws and procedures relating to compulsory
purchase and compensation: final report,* DETR, 2000, para.56). This recommendation was
not accepted for England (*Compulsory Purchase Policy Response,* ODPM, 2002,
para.11(iii)). The government have, however, proposed shortening the period for serving a
notice to treat (or general vesting declaration) for England from 3 years to 18 months
(*Compulsory Purchase Response Document,* ODPM, 2002, para.12(iii)).
[2] 1947 Act, First Schedule, para.16.
[3] *Grice v Dudley Corporation* [1958] 1 Ch. 329. See, too, *Edinburgh & Glasgow Railway
Co. v Monklands Railway Co.* (1850) 12 D. 1304; 13 D. 145.
[4] (1986) 280 E.G. 1015. And see *Fagan v Metropolitan Borough of Knowsley* (1983) 46 P.
& C.R. 226 L.T.; reversed (1985) 50 P. & C.R 363, CA.
[5] (1990) 60 P. & C.R. 380.

particulars before such a declaration can be issued. In that case, notices of these particulars were served under section 3 of the Compulsory Purchase (Vesting Declarations) Act 1981 (corresponding to Schedule 15, paragraph 2 of the Town and Country Planning (Scotland) 1997 Act) within three years of the operative date of the compulsory purchase orders. Although the general vesting declarations were executed after the expiration of the period of three years, it was held that the compulsory purchase orders were operative and effective as a result of the section 3 notices.

The acquiring authority may, as a preliminary step towards implementation, on giving not less than three nor more than 14 days notice to the owner or occupiers, enter on the order land for the purposes of surveying and taking levels, of probing or boring to establish the nature of the soil and of setting out the line of the works (1845 Act, s.83).[6] The authority must compensate the owner or occupier for any resulting damage.

There are two ways in which an acquiring authority may proceed to exercise the powers conferred by the order.[7] They may serve what is commonly referred to as a "notice to treat" or they may execute a general vesting declaration. The advantages and disadvantages of the two procedures are summarised later in this Chapter. As a matter of practice, the general vesting declaration is extensively used in Scotland in preference to the notice to treat. From this point of view, the treatment of the notice to treat in this chapter may seem disproportionate. The explanation for this is simply that the notice to treat procedure has been in existence for very much longer than the vesting declaration and has been the subject of considerable judicial scrutiny. There is, therefore, a lot more to say about the law relating to the notice to treat than there is about the general vesting declaration. Furthermore, as the vesting declaration operates as a deemed notice to treat it would seem sensible to deal with the notice to treat first. The two procedures are now examined in turn.

NOTICE TO TREAT

3–02 Section 17 of the 1845 Act makes provision for the service of a notice to treat where the promoters wish to acquire any of the order land. It provides that promoters shall give notice of their intention to implement the order to all persons with an interest in the land.[8] The notice will describe the land to be acquired[9] and state that the promoters are willing

---

[6] This is not treated as entry on the land for the purposes of establishing the valuation date or the date from which interest on compensation is calculated (*Courage Ltd v Kingswood District Council* (1978) 35 P. & C.R. 436).

[7] The acquiring authority may, of course, decide to hold these powers in reserve and proceed to purchase the necessary land by agreement in the normal way.

[8] The acquiring authority may serve separate notices at different times in respect of different parts of the same parcel of land provided all the notices are served within the period of three years (*Coats v Caledonian Railway Co.* (1904) 6 F. 1042).

[9] *Coats v Caledonian Railway Co., supra.* In *Rush v Fife Regional Council*, unreported, November 5, 1993, Extra Division, see case note at (1994) 42 S.P.E.L. 30, the Inner House held that, while it was necessary at least that the lands which were acquired should be identifiable, to require the acquiring authority to state the particulars with the degree of precision required in a heritable title was asking too much. It is helpful if rights such as servitudes are given some specification.

to treat for its purchase and for compensation (hence "notice to treat"). Service may be effected in accordance with the provisions of paragraph 19 of the First Schedule to the 1947 Act.[10] The recipients are required to give particulars of their interest in the land and of their claim for compensation. There is no prescribed form of notice.[11]

1. Parties to be served

Section 17 requires the notice to be given "to all the parties interested **3–03** in such lands, or to the parties enabled by this or the special Act to sell and convey the same, or their rights and interests therein." In any given case there may, of course, be a number of persons with separate interests in the land.[12] The position of the more important of them is now considered:

(1) The owner or owners: In Scotland, reference to the owner is reference, at the time of writing, to the proprietor of the *dominium utile*.[13] The proprietor of the *dominium utile* is entitled to notice to treat. The Abolition of Feudal Tenure etc. (Scotland) Act 2000 provides that, on the appointed day, the estate of *dominium utile* will cease to exist as a feudal estate but shall forthwith become the ownership of the land (s.2).

The reference to the proprietor is not, of course, confined to an individual. The word "owner" is defined in section 3 of the 1845 as meaning "any person or corporation, or trustee or others, who under this or the special Act would be enabled to sell or convey lands to the promoters of the undertaking". An interest in land may be owned by a person on his own behalf or as a trustee on behalf of others. Furthermore, an interest may be owned by two or more persons either jointly or in common.

(2) Persons having a qualified interest: The person enjoying possession and use of the land being acquired may have no more than a qualified interest in the land. He may, for example, be an heir of entail subject to a prohibition against disposing of the entailed estate (it should be noted that the Abolition of Feudal Tenure etc. (Scotland) Act 2000 provides that land which immediately before the appointed day is held under an entail will be disentailed on that day (s.50)); or he may be a liferenter having possession and use of the land only during his life. The acquiring authority will wish to acquire such qualified interests. In the

---

[10] 1947 Act, Second Schedule, para.5. These provisions have effectively superseded those of section 18 of the 1845 Act in practice. See, too, *Shepherd v Corporation of Norwich* (1885) 30 Ch. D. 553; and *Fagan v Knowlsley Metropolitan Borough Council* [1986] J.P.L. 355.

[11] *Coats v Caledonian Railway Co.* (1904) 6 F. 1042; *Renton v North British Railway Co.* (1845) 8 D. 247.

[12] See generally: D. M. Walker, *Principles of Scottish Private Law* (4th ed., Clarendon Press) Book V, Vol. III; W. M.; Gloag and R. C. Henderson, *Introduction to the Law of Scotland* (11th ed., W. Green & Son Ltd, 2001) Chap. 36, 40 and 41. For a detailed exposition see W. M. Gordon, *Scottish Land Law* (2nd ed., W. Green & Son Ltd 1999); J. M. Halliday, *Conveyancing Law and Practice in Scotland* (2nd ed., W. Green & Son Ltd, 1996). Practical problems can arise with a party having an option to acquire land. An option is not a real right but if it appears in the title as a pre-emption or reversion in the form of a real burden, acquiring authorities will often serve a notice on such a person.

[13] *Heriot's Trust v Caledonian Railway Co.*, 1915 S.C. (H.L.) 52; 1915 1 S.L.T. 347, *per* Lord Dunedin.

nineteenth century the nature of the qualification sometimes inhibited the ability to sell. Section 7 of the 1845 Act facilitated the acquisition of such interests by enabling parties with a qualified interest to sell and convey their interest to the authority.[14] Many of these inhibitions on sale have been removed by subsequent legislation[15] so that section 7 is now of little practical significance. A person having a qualified interest will be entitled to a notice to treat.

(3) Lessees: Where the order land is subject to a lease the acquiring authority may simply acquire the landlord's interest and allow the lease to expire by effluxion of time or following the service of a notice to quit. Where, however, the authority are unable to wait for the lease to run its course, they will have to acquire the interest of the lessee and the lessee will be entitled to notice to treat and to compensation for the loss consequent on the expropriation of the residue of his term.

Where, however, the tenant has no greater interest in the land than as a tenant for a year or from year to year (referred to as a "short tenant") such an interest will not be acquired. The acquiring authority may terminate such a tenancy and the tenant will be entitled under section 114 of the 1845 Act to compensation for any consequent loss (see p.254).

Where part only of land the subject of a lease is to be acquired, section 112 of the 1845 Act makes provision for apportionment of the rent.

3–04   **(4) Heritable creditors:** A heritable creditor has an interest in land and is entitled to a notice to treat.[16] Section 99 of the 1845 Act makes provision for redemption of a heritable security by the acquiring authority.[17] The authority may purchase or redeem the interest of the creditor and pay the creditor the principal and interest due on the security together with any expenses and charges and six months additional interest. Thereupon, the holder of the security is to convey his interest to the authority. Alternatively, the authority may give notice in writing to the heritable creditor that they will pay off the principal and interest at the end of a period of six months. At the expiration of that period, on payment by the authority of the principal and interest together with any expenses and charges, the creditor will convey and discharge to the authority his interest in the land comprised in the security.

If any land subject to such a security is of less value than the principal, interest and expenses secured, the value of the land or the compensation to be paid for it is to be settled in the normal way by agreement between

---

[14] Section 9 of the 1845 Act made provision for the assessment of compensation in such cases and for the compensation to be paid into a bank.

[15] See, for example, the Entail Amendment Act 1914, the Trusts (Scotland) Act 1921, the Bankruptcy (Scotland) Act 1985 and, now, the Abolition of Feudal Tenure (Scotland) Act 2000, Schs 12 and 13.

[16] See *Martin v London, Cheltenham etc. Railway Co.* (1863) 1 L.R. Eq. 145; reversed (1866) 1 L.R. Ch.501.

[17] See on this *Shewu, Shewu and Richmond upon Thames London Borough Council v London Borough of Hackney* [2000] J.P.L. 498. It is common practice for heritable securities to contain a provision that the debtor will inform the creditor in the event of receipt of any notice of the making of a compulsory purchase order. The security may also provide for the creditor to carry on negotiations with the acquiring authority and for the assignation to the creditor of any compensation.

the parties or, failing agreement, by reference to the Lands Tribunal for Scotland. The amount determined upon is then to be paid by the authority to the holder of the security in satisfaction of his claim so far as it will go, and upon payment, the holder will, at the authority's expense, dispone and assign his debt, so far as it has been paid, and his security and interest in the land to the authority. The party entitled to the land under burden of the security will thereupon cease to be interested in or have any right to it (1845 Act, s.101).[18]

If part only of land the subject of a heritable security is being acquired and the part being acquired is of less value than the outstanding principal, interest and costs secured on the land as a whole, and the holder of the security does not regard the remainder of the land as a sufficient security for the sum due, the value of the part being acquired together with compensation for severance, if any (see Chapter 11), is to be determined by agreement between the parties or, failing agreement, by reference to the Lands Tribunal for Scotland. The amount so determined is then to be paid by the authority to the heritable creditor in satisfaction of the debt, so far as it will go. The creditor will then convey or discharge to the authority his interest in the land and the party entitled to the land under burden of the security will thereupon cease to be interested in or have any right to it. A memorandum of what has been paid, signed by the heritable creditor, will be endorsed on the heritable security and a copy of the memorandum is to be furnished by the authority (if required) to the party entitled to the land under burden of the security (1845 Act, s.103).[19]

(5) Servitudes and real burdens: Where the order land is the subject of a servitude or real burden, the person having the right of enforcement is not entitled to a notice to treat.[20] The effect of the existence of a servitude or real burden right on the carrying out of the works for which the order land has been authorised to be acquired is not entirely clear but it is thought that it cannot impede the works.[21] The position will be clarified by the Title Conditions (Scotland) Act 2003. This states that, except in so far as the terms of the compulsory purchase order or the consequent conveyance provide otherwise, on registration of the conveyance (as defined) any real burden or servitude over the land will be extinguished (s.106(1)).[22] Without prejudice to the generality of the exception, the Act goes on to say that the order or conveyance may specifically provide for the variation of any real burdens or servitudes or

---

[18] See section 102 of the 1845 Act for the arrangements for depositing money in a bank where it is refused on tender by the creditor.

[19] Provision is made for depositing the money in a bank where it is refused on tender (s.104), for early payment of the sum secured (s.105) and for compensation for loss of interest (s.106).

[20] *Thicknesse v Lancaster Canal Co.* (1838) 4 M. & W. 472; *Grimley v Minister of Housing and Local Government* [1971] 2 Q.B. 96.

[21] Some enabling Acts make specific provision to this effect; see, for example, the Town and Country Planning (Scotland) Act 1997, s.194. See, too, *Largs Hydropathic Ltd v Largs Town Council*, 1967 S.C. 1. In *Town Council of Oban v Callander and Oban Railway Co.* (1892) 19 R. 912 Lord President Robertson went so far as to say that "when land is taken by a railway company it is taken absolutely, with a resulting extinction of all servitudes".

[22] See s.107 for the extinction of real burdens and servitudes where land is acquired by agreement.

for the extinction of part of them or for their extinction only in relation to certain parts of the burdened property or in respect of the enforcement rights of owners of certain of the benefited properties (s.106(2)). Interference with a real burden or servitude entitles the proprietor of the benefited property to claim compensation for injurious affection[23] under section 61 of the 1845 Act or under section 6 of the Railways Clauses Consolidation (Scotland) Act 1845.[24] The Title Conditions (Scotland) Act will confer an express entitlement to compensation in the event of the extinguishment of a personal real burden (as defined) (s.106(4)).

3–05   **(6) The superior:** Section 2 of the Abolition of Feudal Tenure etc (Scotland) Act 2000 abolishes the estate of superiority with effect from the appointed day.[25] Until then, consideration needs to be given to the position of the superior. In *Campbell's Trustees v London and North-Eastern Railway Co.*[26] Lord President Clyde said that "under the Lands Clauses Act, the undertaker purchases and acquires a title only to the lands 'taken and used' for the purpose of his statutory undertaking. He neither 'takes' nor 'uses' any estate of superiority which may be in those lands, and he has therefore neither right nor obligation to acquire any such." And in *Heriot's Trust v Caledonian Railway Co.*[27] Lord Dunedin said:

> "The exact extent of the lands to be acquired is usually left to the judgment of the promoters. The lands are to be taken from the owners thereof, and the method of taking is regulated by the provisions of the Lands Clauses Act, which is incorporated in the Special Act. 'Owner' in Scotland is the proprietor of the *dominium utile*, that is to say, the vassal, and not the superior. Consequently, the superior never receives a notice to treat."

The 1845 Act provides for the taking of land from the owner but deals separately with the burdens affecting the land so taken. In *Heriot's Trust*, Lord Dunedin went on to say that:

> "the radical error which has pervaded the mind of the draftsman of the Act is that one of these burdens on the property is the superiority, whereas, if you had asked a Scottish lawyer of the eighteenth century if the superiority was a burden on the *dominium utile* he would have infallibly have answered that, so far from that being the case, the *dominium utile* was rather of the nature of a burden on the superior's title."

Similarly, it would seem that the rights of a creditor in a ground annual are not acquired but are treated as a burden on the *dominium utile*.[28]

---

[23] See Chap. 11 and 14.

[24] As applied by the 1947 Act, Second Schedule, para.1. See *Clark v School Board for London* (1874) 9 L.R. Ch. 120; *School Board of Edinburgh v Simpson* (1906) 13 S.L.T. 910.

[25] The appointed day is November 28, 2004.

[26] 1930 S.C. 182; 1930 S.L.T. 128.

[27] 1915 S.C. (H.L.) 52; (1915) 1 S.L.T. 347.

[28] *Campbell's Trustees v London and North-Eastern Railway Co.*, 1930 S.C. 182; 1930 S.L.T. 128; *Blythswood Friendly Society v Glasgow District Council*, 1976 S.L.T. (Lands Tr.) 29.

However, the compulsory acquisition of the owner's land may none-theless constitute in the words of Lord President Clyde "a serious invasion of any estate of superiority therein, and also of the rights of the creditor in any ground annual payable furth thereof."[29] The effect of the acquisition on the relationship between superior and vassal is considered below (p.72). At this stage attention is simply drawn to sections 107 to 111 of the 1845 Act which made provision for the continued payment or discharge of certain incumbrances on the land in the nature of recurring money payments including feu duties and ground annuals and which conferred an entitlement to compensation upon discharge. These pro-visions of the 1845 Act must now be read in conjunction with section 6 of the Land Tenure Reform (Scotland) Act 1974 which has to some extent superseded them. Section 6 provides that where land is acquired by an authority possessing compulsory purchase powers the authority is to redeem such recurring payments as feu duties and ground annuals.[30] They must also be read in conjunction with the provisions of the Abolition of Feudal Tenure etc. (Scotland) Act 2000 which provides for the extinction of feu duties and ground annuals.[31]

2. Interest omitted to be purchased

If, after the acquiring authority have taken possession of any land **3–06** which they have been authorised to acquire, it appears that through "mistake or inadvertency" there is a right or interest in that land which they have failed to purchase or pay compensation for, section 117 of the 1845 Act provides that the authority may remain in undisturbed possession of the land. They must, however, within six months of receipt of notice of a claim which they do not dispute, purchase or pay compensation for such right or interest. Where the authority dispute the claim,[32] time runs from the date on which the claim is established by law. It makes no difference that the period of three years allowed for the exercise of the power conferred by the order has expired (see p.64). The compensation is to be assessed according to the value of the right or interest at the time the authority took possession and without regard to any improvements carried out by the authority; but the claimant is entitled to compensation for any profits or interest which would have accrued to him during the period that the authority have been in possession.

Section 117 of the 1845 Act is of no avail if the authority did not, prior to the expiration of the period allowed for the exercise of power conferred by the order, intend to acquire the right or interest which they have omitted to purchase.[33]

3. The land to be acquired

Service of the notice to treat is the first step in the actual acquisition **3–07** of the order land. It is appropriate at this stage to consider briefly what is meant by "land." It is clear from section 3 of the 1845 Act that land is

---

[29] *Campbell's Trustees, supra* at p.193.

[30] See s.6(4) as regards redemption on the acquisition of land by general vesting declaration.

[31] See ss.7 and 56.

[32] Section 119 of the 1845 Act makes provision regarding the expenses of litigation in this connection.

[33] *Davidson's Trustees v Caledonian Railway Co.* (1894) 21 R. 1060.

not confined simply to the physical surface but extends to "houses, lands, tenements and heritage, of any description or tenure." Thus the general rule in the sale and purchase of heritage that the subjects of sale include all corporeal heritable property[34] applies so that the acquisition will include fixtures. "Fixtures" have been defined as anything "annexed to the land that is fastened to or connected with it, not in mere juxtaposition to the soil."[35]

Furthermore, it is also implied that rights of property in land extend *a caelo usque ad centrum*[36] so that compulsory acquisition will give the acquiring authority not merely a right to the surface of the land but to everything above and beneath it. However, certain minerals, *i.e.* gold, silver and lead are *regalia minora* and do not pass by implication; petroleum and natural gas belong to the Crown and coal to British Coal. And to avoid paying compensation reflecting, for the most part, the development potential of other minerals, it is common practice, as explained in Chapter 2 (see p.18), to incorporate the "mining code" into the legislation authorising the purchase so that mineral rights are not acquired.

The 1947 Act (s.7(1)) states that "land" in relation to compulsory purchase under any Act is to include any definition of that word in that Act. In other words, it will also be necessary to have regard to any specific definition of the term in the authorising Act. For example, section 235 of the Local Government (Scotland) Act 1973 defines land as including "land covered with water and any interest right or servitude in or over land."[37] The reference is to an existing right or servitude.[38] Section 110(2) of the Roads (Scotland) Act 1984 provides that any power to acquire land under that Act will include power to acquire a servitude right by the creation of a new right. And section 190(3) of the Town and Country Planning (Scotland) Act 1997 gives the Scottish Ministers powers to acquire compulsorily a new servitude or other right by the grant of a new right; but section 189 of the Act confers no such powers on local authorities.[39] Not all authorising Acts provide a definition of land and in such a case the general position described above applies.

4. Effect of notice to treat

3–08   As Deas comments "dicta are to be found in the reports, with regard to the effect of the notice to treat in constituting a completed contract of sale, which are not altogether easy to reconcile."[40] For example, in *Campbell v Edinburgh and Glasgow Railway Co.*,[41] Lord Curriehill stated

---

[34] Trees are heritable until cut; and cultivated crops are heritable until harvested (see *Chalmer's Trustees v Dick's Trustees*, 1909 S.C. 761).

[35] *Brand's Trustees v Brand's Trustees* (1876) 3 R. (H.L.) 16.

[36] Stair II, iii, 75; Ersk. II, vi, 1–5.

[37] See, too, the Town and Country Planning (Scotland) Act 1997, s.277(1); Housing (Scotland) Act 1987, s.338(1).

[38] *Sovmots Investments Ltd v Secretary of State for the Environment* [1977] Q.B. 411.

[39] The definition of "land" in s.277(1) includes "any servitude or right in or over land" but this would seem to be a reference to an existing servitude or right.

[40] F. Deas, *The Law of Railways Applicable to Scotland* (revised by J. Ferguson, W. Green & Son Ltd, 1897) p.163.

[41] (1855) 17 D. 613. See, too, *Heron v Espie* (1856) 18 D. 917, *per* Lord Justice-Clerk Hope at p.922.

that "The moment the respondents serve the notices, the purchase is complete, from which neither party can resile;" and in *Ayr Harbour Trustees v Oswald*[42] Lord Blackburn said, "The notice to take had the effect of a purchase by the trustees absolutely of the piece of ground." The theory that a landowner's consent to expropriation is "vicariously given" by Parliament,[43] was very clearly accepted by the Scottish courts. In *Forth & Clyde Junction Railway Co. v Ewing*, for example, Lord Justice-Clerk Inglis said "The Special Act is substantially an offer of the land by the landowner to the company, and notice by the company of their intention to take the land is an acceptance of the offer."[44] In *Corporation of Edinburgh v Lorimer*[45] Lord Anderson summarised the position when he said that although it was "perhaps not strictly accurate to describe the legal result [of a notice to treat] as a sale, in respect that delivery does not follow until a later stage," the true view seemed to be "that service of a notice to treat establishes a contract between the parties whereby they are mutually bound to carry to completion a transaction of sale. Under the contract the right of the landowner is to be paid the price or compensation; the right of the promoters on payment of the price or compensation is to obtain delivery of the subjects along with title thereto."

More recently, however, in *Birmingham Corporation v West Midland Baptist (Trust) Association (Inc.)*[46] the speeches in the House of Lords appear to indicate something of a shift in attitude to the notice to treat. In the words of one commentator,[47] their Lordships "expressed the effect of a notice to treat in a much lower key" than had many of their predecessors. Lord Morris of Borth-y-Gest declared, for example:

> "A notice to treat does not establish the relation of vendor and purchaser between the acquiring authority and the owner. It does not transfer either the legal or the equitable interest to the acquiring authority. It informs the owner that the land is to be taken and informs him that the acquiring authority are ready to negotiate with him as to the price of the land . . . It makes a demand for particulars of estates and interest and of claims."

Lord Donovan also stressed that the notice to treat did not operate to transfer any kind of equitable title to the land and pointed out that it did not even deprive the owner of power to alienate the property in question.

In effect, therefore, their Lordships viewed the notice to treat as little more than notification of an intention to take the land from the owner.[48]

---

[42] (1883) 10 R (H.L.) 85.

[43] F. A. Mann, "Outlines of a History of Expropriation" (1959) 75 L.Q.R. 188.

[44] (1864) 2 M. 684 at p.693. Also *Campbell v Edinburgh and Glasgow Railway Co.* (1855) 17 D. 613, *per* Lord Curriehill. See, too, *Mackenzie v Inverness and Aberdeen Junction Railway Co.* (1866) 4 M. 810, *per* Lord President McNeil at p.817.

[45] (1914) 2 S.L.T. 225.

[46] [1970] A.C. 874.

[47] F. A. Mann, "The Relevant Date for the Assessment of Compensation" (1969) 85 L.Q.R. 516.

[48] See too *Simpson Motor Sales (London) Ltd v Hendon* [1963] 1 Ch. 57 *per* Upjohn L.J. at p.82; *Rush v Fife Regional Council*, Extra Division, unreported, November 5, 1993, but see case note at (1994) 42 S.P.E.L. 30; and *R v Northumbrian Water Ltd, ex p. Able UK Ltd* (1996) 72 P. & C.R. 95 *per* Carnwath J.

While the effect of service of a notice to treat remains in some respects uncertain (see Chapter 5), there is little doubt that it has the following significance:

1. it determines the land to be taken (but see "counter-notice" below);

2. it enables either party to insist on having compensation determined (p.71 below) and the transaction completed;

3. it enables the acquiring authority to take possession of the land after service of notice of entry (p.70 below);

4. the owner cannot by altering the land or creating more interests in it increase the burden of compensation on the acquiring authority.

3–09   The decision in *City of Glasgow Union Railway Co. v McEwen & Co.*[49] illustrates this last point. At the date of the notice to treat (October 1868), the subject land was occupied by *McEwen & Co.* The company had been in occupation under a written lease for three years which had expired at Whitsunday 1868. They had subsequently continued in occupation without any written title of possession. In February 1869, the company obtained a further three year lease, with the commencement of the term backdated to Whitsunday 1868. The First Division rejected the company's claim for compensation as it had not obtained a written lease until after the date of the notice to treat.

The common law position is enlarged upon as regards compulsory acquisitions to which the 1947 Act applies by paragraph 7 of the Second Schedule to that Act. Paragraph 7 provides that in assessing compensation no account is to be taken of:

"any interest in land, or any enhancement of the value of any interest in land by reason of any building erected, work done, or improvement or alteration made, whether on the land purchased or in any other land with which the claimant is or was at the time of the erection, doing or making of the building, works, improvement or alteration directly or indirectly concerned if . . . the creation of the interest, the erection of the building, the doing of the work, the making of the improvement or alteration, as the case may be, was not reasonably necessary and was undertaken with a view to obtaining compensation or increased compensation."

It should be noted that paragraph 7 is not confined to interests, etc. created solely since the date of the notice to treat, but would appear to be capable of applying to anything done prior to that date if it "was not reasonably necessary and was undertaken with a view to obtaining compensation or increased compensation." This does not, however, preclude an owner from continuing to manage and even to deal in his

---

[49] (1870) 8 M. 747. See, too, *In re Marylebone Improvement Act* (1871) 12 L.R. Eq. 389; *Mercer v Liverpool etc. Railway Co.* [1904] A.C. 461.

property either before or after the date of the notice to treat, for example, by assigning his interest[50] or by granting a short tenancy to ensure continuity of income pending the taking of possession by the acquiring authority.

There is some doubt whether the interests to be acquired are fixed as at the date of the notice to treat (see Chapter 5).

5. Withdrawal or abandonment of the notice to treat

One effect of the service of the notice to treat, as mentioned above, is **3–10** that it enables either party to insist on having compensation determined and the transaction completed. Once served, the notice cannot be withdrawn except in the following circumstances.

Section 39(1) of the Land Compensation (Scotland) Act 1963 provides that the acquiring authority may at any time within six weeks of receipt from a claimant of his notice of claim withdraw a notice to treat. Where the claimant has failed to deliver such a notice, or an adequate notice[51] so that the amount of compensation has to be referred to the Lands Tribunal for Scotland for determination, the period of six weeks runs from the date when compensation has been finally determined (1963 Act, s.39(2)).[52] In *R. v Northumbrian Water Ltd ex p Able UK Ltd*,[53] a notice to treat and notice of entry had been served in 1992 and entry was taken in 1993. A valuable certificate of appropriate alternative development (see p.146) was issued in 1994. Thereafter a notice of claim was served by the claimant on the acquiring authority in response to the notice to treat. The authority responded within six weeks with a letter announcing the withdrawal of the notice to treat. The claimant argued that there was no right to withdraw the notice to treat after possession had been taken. Carnwath J held that the statutory right to withdraw was not limited by entry.

The acquiring authority is liable to pay compensation to the person served with the notice to treat for any loss or expenses occasioned by the giving and withdrawal of the notice (1963 Act, s.39(3)). Where no proper claim for compensation has been delivered by the claimant, the liability does not extend to any loss or expenses incurred after the time when, in the tribunal's opinion, such notice of claim should have been delivered. In default of agreement, the amount of any loss or expenses will be determined by the tribunal (1963 Act, s.39(4)).

A notice to treat may also be withdrawn in response to a notice of objection to severance (see p.65).

It used to be the case that, once a notice to treat had been served, the order would remain operative indefinitely unless the acquiring authority evinced an intention to abandon the rights given by the notice (see below). In the absence of any action to follow up the notice to treat,

---

[50] *Caledonian Railway Co. v Barr's Trustees* (1871) 9 S.L.R. 49. See, too, *Landlink Two Ltd v Sevenoaks District Council* (1986) 51 P. & C.R. 100.
[51] See *Trustees for Methodist Church Purposes v North Tyneside Metropolitan Borough Council* (1979) 250 E.G. 647.
[52] A claim is not finally determined until the time within which it may be challenged in the Court of Session has expired (1963 Act, s.39(6)).
[53] (1996) 72 P. & C.R. 95.

owners and occupiers of the order land faced very considerable uncertainty. Following a recommendation from the Royal Institution of Chartered Surveyors, the Planning and Compensation Act 1991 now provides that a notice to treat will cease to have effect after three years, or such longer period as may be agreed, unless certain specified circumstances have occurred (s.78). The circumstances are:

    (a) the compensation has been agreed or awarded or has been paid or paid into a bank;

    (b) a general vesting declaration has been executed;

    (c) the acquiring authority have taken possession of the notice land; or

    (d) the question of compensation has been referred to the Lands Tribunal for Scotland (s.78(1)).

Where a notice to treat ceases to have effect in this way, the acquiring authority must give notice to those upon whom it was served and shall be liable to pay compensation to any person entitled to such a notice for any loss and expenses occasioned to him by the giving of notice to treat and its ceasing to have effect (s.78(3)).[54]

When an acquiring authority evince an intention to abandon the rights given by a notice to treat, the person upon whom it has been served will be entitled to treat the rights as abandoned. The question of abandonment is likely to arise only in exceptional circumstances following the introduction of the three year time limit for acting on the notice to treat (above). The concept was established in the case of *Grice v Dudley Corporation*.[55] A compulsory purchase order for road widening and for the erection of a market hall was confirmed and a notice to treat was served in 1939. Negotiations over compensation lapsed on the outbreak of the Second World War. After the war several new improvement schemes were considered by the council although no final decision was made. In 1954, the council raised the question of acquiring the order land at its 1939 price when the notice to treat had been served and threatened to pay that sum into court and acquire title by execution of a deed poll. The plaintiffs, the executors of the claimant, sought a declaration that the notice to treat was no longer valid and effective as the council's plans did not include road widening or the erection of a market hall. Upjohn J. held that the fact that the council were attempting to acquire land for purposes substantially different from

---

    [54] It seems that section 78 of the 1991 Act may not have gone far enough. Because of the hardship that can still be caused by delay and uncertainty over the date on which possession is to be taken, CPPRAG considered that a norm of one year should be sufficient for acquiring authorities to follow up on a notice to treat or a vesting declaration (*Fundamental review of the laws and procedures relating to compulsory purchase and compensation: final report*, DETR, 2000, para.55). The government have opted for a period of eighteen months for England (*Compulsory Purchase Response Document*, ODPM, 2002, para.12(iii)).

    [55] [1958] 1 Ch. 329. See, too, *Simpson Motor Sales (London) Ltd v Hendon Corporation* [1964] A.C. 1088; and *Corporation of Edinburgh v Lorimer*, 1914 2 S.L.T. 225.

those set out in the compulsory purchase order amounted to abandonment of the order and thus an abandonment of the rights under the notice to treat. The council's action was not consistent with the general principle that statutory powers should be exercised for the purpose for which they were conferred.

It would seem that unexplained delay may amount to an intention to abandon the rights given by a notice to treat. In *Grice*, Upjohn J. said:

> "the promoter exercising statutory powers must proceed to enforce his notice in what, in all the circumstances of the case, is a reasonable period. If he sleeps on his rights he will be barred if his delay is not explained."

In *Simpson Motor Sales (London) Ltd v Hendon Corporation*[56] Lord Evershed, giving judgment for the House of Lords, fully accepted as correct Upjohn J.'s analysis of the law in *Grice*.

COUNTER-NOTICE

1. House, building or manufactory

A notice to treat may be directed at part only of a "house, building or **3–11** manufactory, or of a park or garden belonging to a house." However, no person is required to sell part only if they are willing and able to sell the whole unless the Lands Tribunal for Scotland determines that, in the case of a house, building or manufactory, the part can be taken without material detriment to the remainder or that, in the case of a park or garden, it can be taken without seriously affecting the amenity or convenience of the house.[57] In determining questions of material detriment or the effect on the amenity or convenience of a house the tribunal is to take into account not only the effect of severance but also the use to be made of the part proposed to be acquired; and where the part is to be acquired for works or other purposes extending to other land, the tribunal is to have regard to the effect of the whole of the works and the use to be made of the other land.[58]

When a counter-notice is served it is open to the acquiring authority to agree to acquire the whole or to abandon the purchase altogether.[59] If the authority persist with their intention to take part only, they must satisfy the tribunal that the part may be taken without material detriment to or seriously affecting the amenity or convenience of the remainder, as the case may be.[60] The contention that there can be no

---

[56] [1964] A.C. 1088.

[57] 1947 Act, Second Schedule, para.4, substituting for s.90 of the 1845 Act. Where part only of a tenement is acquired, care will need to be taken to ensure that appropriate rights of access, support, drainage and so on are granted or reserved depending on the circumstances.

[58] Land Compensation (Scotland) Act 1973, s.54(1).

[59] A notice of objection to severance must therefore be served prior to entry being taken so that the acquiring authority can elect whether or not to continue with the scheme (*Glasshouse Properties Ltd v Secretary of State for Transport* (1993) 66 P. & C.R. 285, LT).

[60] The decision in *McIlroy v Strathclyde Regional Council*, unreported, June 8, 1994, Lands Tribunal for Scotland, indicates that the onus of satisfying the tribunal rests on the acquiring authority.

material detriment unless some severance is caused for which compensation is not an adequate remedy has been rejected;[61] if that was the case,
the provision would rarely, if ever, come into play.

In *Ravenseft Properties Ltd v London Borough of Hillingdon*[62] it was
held that the test for material detriment was whether, on part being
taken, the remainder would be less useful or less valuable in some
significant degree.[63] In *McMillan v Strathclyde Regional Council*[64] the
Lands Tribunal for Scotland, applying the test in *Ravenseft*, concluded
that the remainder of the land would be no less useful or less valuable
than would have been the case if the compulsory purchase order had not
been promoted. The regional council compulsorily acquired part of the
front garden of a bungalow for road widening, the effect of which would
be to bring the heel of the footpath to be constructed alongside the road
to a point some 15 feet from the nearest part of the front wall of the
bungalow—the existing road being at present some 31 feet away.
Notwithstanding the anticipated increase in noise and loss of privacy, the
tribunal found that under the terms of the disposition of the bungalow,
the owners were required, if called upon by the local authority, to form a
roadway and footpath not materially different to that constructed as a
result of the compulsory purchase order. In *McIlroy v Strathclyde
Regional Council*[65] it was submitted that, for a notice of objection to
severance to be successful, the physical effect must be serious. The
tribunal concluded that the legislation did not intend the test to be so
demanding. On the other hand, "the detriment must be more than slight.
It must be substantial and to some extent the question must be one of
what is reasonable". The correct approach was whether the severance
would "affect, not a particular person, but the generalised concept of a
purchaser as reflected in 'the market'". In other words, the assessment
was intended to be objective rather than the subjective opinion of the
owner or any other person.

The word "house" has been given a wide meaning. In *Ravenseft* it was
held to extend to a building which was used for business purposes and
was not restricted to mere dwelling-houses; and it has been held that
land which is part of the curtilage is to be treated as part of the house.[66]

In *McMillan* the Lands Tribunal for Scotland found it unnecessary to
distinguish between material detriment and serious injury to amenity or
convenience. The former would seem to be the more onerous test.

There is no prescribed form of counter-notice and no time limit is
prescribed for its service[67] although it seems likely that it should be
served before the acquiring authority have taken steps to follow up the
notice to treat.

---

[61] *Ravenseft Properties Ltd v London Borough of Hillingdon* (1968) 206 E.G. 1255.
[62] *ibid.*
[63] See, too, *Caledonian Railway Co. v Turcan* (1897) 35 S.L.R. 404.
[64] 1984 S.L.T. (Lands Tr.) 25. In that case the counter-notice was served in response to a
general vesting declaration made under the Town and Country Planning (Scotland) Act
1972, what was then the Sch.24, para.20. See too *McIlroy v Strathclyde Regional Council*,
unreported, June 8, 1994, (Lands Tr).
[65] See above.
[66] *Caledonian Railway Co. v Turcan* (1897) 35 S.L.R. 404; and see, generally, F. Deas,
The Law of Railways Applicable to Scotland, *supra*, p.199 *et seq.*
[67] Contrast the position where a counter-notice is to be served in response to a general
vesting declaration (see p.76 below).

2. Intersected lands

Section 91 of the 1845 Act provides that if any lands, not situated in a **3–12** town or built upon, are so cut through and divided by the works as to leave either on both sides or on one side, a parcel of land less than half an acre, and the owner has no other adjoining land with which the parcel may be merged, the owner may require the promoter to acquire the parcel. Where the intersected land can be merged with an owner's adjoining land, the cost of effecting the merger is to be borne by the promoter. The provision is a hang-over from the railway building era when intersection of land was not uncommon. Road building gives rise to the same sort of problem for landowners.

Section 92 of the 1845 Act deals with the situation where an owner has no adjoining land with which the severed portions may be merged and the severed portions are together less than half an acre or the cost of linking them, for example, by a bridge or underpass exceeds their value. In that case, notwithstanding the wishes of the owner, the promoter may insist on acquiring the intersected land.

3. Agricultural land

Helpful as the provisions of sections 91 and 92 may be, they do not **3–13** assist the owner or tenant of an agricultural unit, the continuing viability of which is threatened by severance arising, for example, from a motorway being taken through the unit. This situation is dealt with in sections 49 to 52 of the Land Compensation (Scotland) Act 1973.

Section 49 of the 1973 Act provides that where an acquiring authority serve a notice to treat in respect of any agricultural land on a person (whether in occupation or not) having a greater interest in the land than as a tenant for a year or from year to year and the person has such an interest in other agricultural land in the same agricultural unit, the person (referred to as "the claimant") may serve a counter-notice on the authority claiming that the other land is not reasonably capable of being farmed either by itself or in conjunction with other land.[68] The counter-notice must be served within two months of the date of service of the notice to treat. In *Johnson v North Yorkshire County Council*,[69] the Lands Tribunal held a counter-notice served under the corresponding English provision to be invalid. In that case some two per cent of the claimant's farm land was being acquired for a gypsy caravan site. The claimant required the purchase of the whole of the land on the ground that the risk of vandalism, theft and trespass resulting from the proposed use of the land to be acquired would adversely affect the viability of their farming enterprise. The claimant had a bank loan secured on the subject land and there was a need to maintain the value of the security subjects. The Tribunal held that it was reasonable to consider the nature and degree of the effect of taking the order land and its use as a gypsy site on the notice land. However, it was not satisfied that the effect of the use

---

[68] This provision also has effect where a notice to treat is deemed to be served under the provisions of ss.88–99 of the Town and Country Planning (Scotland) Act 1997 (purchase notice) (1973 Act, s.49(5)).

[69] (1993) 65 P. & C.R. 65, LT.

would be such as to render the notice land incapable of being farmed. The claimant's personal circumstances were not relevant to the decision. There was no basis for reading the section as though the relevant test was whether the notice land was not reasonably capable of being farmed by the present owner and occupier.

"Agricultural unit" is defined as land occupied as a unit for agricultural purposes, including any dwelling-house or other building occupied by the same person for the purpose of farming the land.[70] "Other relevant land" means land comprised in the same agricultural unit as the land to which the notice to treat relates, being land in which the claimant does not having a greater interest than as tenant for a year or from year to year; the term also includes land comprised in any other agricultural unit occupied by the claimant on the date of service of the notice to treat in which he has a greater interest than as a tenant for a year or from year to year (1973 Act, s.49(3)). A copy of the counter-notice must also be served within the same period on any other person having an interest in the land to which the counter-notice relates.

Should the acquiring authority serve a separate notice to treat in respect of the other agricultural land in the same unit in which the claimant has a greater interest than as a tenant for a year or from year to year, it is to be assumed that the other land is not available to him for the purpose of making up a viable economic farming unit. The same applies where a notice to treat is served in respect of any of the "other relevant land" (1973 Act, s.49(4)).

If the acquiring authority have not accepted the counter-notice as valid within two months of the date of its service either party may within a further period of two months refer it to the Lands Tribunal for Scotland (1973 Act, s.50(1)). The tribunal will determine whether the counter-notice is justified and declare it to be valid or invalid accordingly. Where a counter-notice is accepted as or declared to be valid, the acquiring authority are deemed to be authorised to acquire compulsorily the claimant's interest in the land to which it relates and to have served a notice to treat on the same date as the original notice to treat (1973 Act, s.50(2)).

A counter-notice may be withdrawn at any time before the compensation which follows from the deemed notice to treat has been determined by the Lands Tribunal for Scotland or within six weeks of such compensation being so determined (1973 Act, s.50(3)).

Where a counter-notice is withdrawn the deemed notice to treat is also considered to be withdrawn.[71]

Where as a result of the operation of the counter-notice provision, the acquiring authority become, or will become, entitled to a lease but not to the interest of the lessor, they must offer to renounce the lease to the lessor on such terms as the authority consider reasonable (1973 Act, s.50(6)). Failing agreement as to what terms are reasonable, the question

---

[70] 1973 Act, s.80(1) applying s.196(1) of the Town and Country Planning (Scotland) Act 1972 (see now the 1997 Act, s.122).

[71] The power conferred by s.39 of the Land Compensation (Scotland) Act 1963 to withdraw a notice to treat is not exercisable in the case of a notice to treat deemed to have been served under s.50 of the Land Compensation (Scotland) Act 1973 (see s.50(4)).

is to be determined by the Lands Tribunal for Scotland.[72] Any terms as to renunciation contained in the lease are to be disregarded for the purposes of this provision.

Section 51 of the 1973 Act makes similar provision for service of a **3–14** counter-notice where the acquiring authority have served notice of entry on the person in occupation of an agricultural holding,[73] being a person having no greater interest in the holding than as tenant for a year or from year to year (referred to as "the claimant") and the notice relates to part only of the holding. The claimant may, within two months of the service of the notice of entry, serve a counter-notice on the authority claiming that the remainder of the holding is not reasonably capable of being farmed, either by itself or in conjunction with other relevant land, as a separate agricultural unit and electing to treat the notice of entry as relating to the entire holding. A copy of the counter-notice is also to be served on the landlord of the holding.

"Other relevant land" in this case refers to land comprised in the same agricultural unit[74] as the agricultural holding; and also to land comprised in any other agricultural unit occupied by the claimant on the date of service of the notice of entry, being land in respect of which the claimant has a greater interest than as a tenant for a year or from year to year (1973 Act, s.51(3)).

If the acquiring authority have served a notice to treat in respect of land in the agricultural holding, other than that to which the notice of entry relates, or in respect of the other relevant land (above), that other land is not to be considered as available for the purpose of determining whether the remainder of the holding is reasonably capable of being farmed (1973 Act, s.51(4)).

If the acquiring authority do not, within two months of the date of service of the counter-notice, accept it as valid, the question may be referred to the Lands Tribunal for Scotland for determination (1973 Act, s.52(1)).

Where a counter-notice is accepted or declared to be valid, then if within 12 months the claimant has given up possession of every part of the agricultural holding to the acquiring authority, the notice of entry is to be deemed to have extended to the part of the holding to which it did not relate and the authority are to be deemed to have taken possession of that part on the day before the expiration of the year of the tenancy which is current when the counter-notice is accepted or declared (1973 Act, s.52(2)).

Where the claimant has given up possession of an agricultural holding to the acquiring authority in such circumstances but the authority have not been authorised to acquire the landlord's interest in, or in any of, the part of the holding to which the notice of entry did not relate (referred to as "the land not subject to compulsory purchase"), the authority must immediately give up possession of the land to the landlord and he must

---

[72] Where the lessor refuses to accept any sum payable to him resulting from such an arrangement, provision is made for payment into a bank (1973 Act, s.50(7)).

[73] "Agricultural holding" has the meaning given to it in s.1 of what is now the Agricultural Holdings (Scotland) Act 1991 (1973 Act, s.80(1)).

[74] 1973 Act, s.80(1).

take possession (1973 Act, s.52(3)(b)). The tenancy is to be treated as terminated on the date on which the acquiring authority acquired possession of the holding (1973 Act, s.52(3)(c)); and the acquiring authority take the place of the claimant as regards any rights or liabilities arising on or out of the termination of the tenancy (1973 Act, s.52(3)(d)). Any disagreement over any payment to be made in respect of any such right or liability will be determined by the Lands Tribunal for Scotland.

NOTICE OF ENTRY

3–15 Having served a notice to treat, the acquiring authority will wish to take possession of the order land. They may do this in advance of the conveyance of the land to them and even in advance of the compensation being determined. Sections 83 to 89 of the 1845 Act make detailed provisions for entry on the land. Section 83 provides that an acquiring authority shall not, except with the consent of the owners or occupiers of land, take possession until they have paid compensation to everyone having an interest in the land.[75] Section 84 enables entry to be taken before payment and without consent on depositing in a bank by way of security a sum equivalent to the compensation claimed or to the amount determined by an independent valuer and delivering, if required, to those with an interest in the land a bond for a sum equal to that deposited for payment of the compensation eventually determined together with interest from the date of entry to the date of payment.

Although the procedure under sections 83–89 is still available, the provisions have now been overtaken by the much simpler arrangements set out in paragraph 3 of Schedule 2 to the 1947 Act. An acquiring authority may at any time after serving notice to treat and after serving on the owner, lessee and occupier of the land not less than 14 days' notice[76] take possession of the order land or so much of it as is specified in the notice of entry. Research indicates that in England and Wales notice of entry is often served at the same time as the notice to treat.[77] Most acquiring authorities give significantly longer than the minimum period of notice[78]; if they do not and notice to treat and notice of entry are served together, then owners and occupiers can face considerable hardship.[79]

---

[75] Entry may be taken for the purpose of surveying, etc. the land on giving not less than three nor more than 14 days' notice (see p.54).

[76] The provisions for the serving of notices set out in paragraph 19 of the First Schedule to the 1947 Act apply to service of a notice of entry (1947 Act, Second Schedule, para.(2)).

[77] City University Business School, *The Operation of Compulsory Purchase Orders*, Department of the Environment, 1996.

[78] *ibid.*

[79] See J Rowan-Robinson and N Hutchison, "Compensation for compulsory acquisition of business interests: satisfaction or sacrifice?" (1995) 13(1) *Journal of Property Valuation and Investment* 44. The government have proposed extending the minimum period for England from two weeks to one month and imposing a time limit on the validity of the notice of one month (*Compulsory Purchase Response Document*, ODPM, 2002, para.12(iii)).

The consent of the owner, lessee and occupier is not required for entry; nor is compliance with sections 83–88 of the 1845 Act. The acquiring authority must, however, in due course compensate those with an interest in the land[80] together with interest from the date of actual entry[81] to the date of payment.[82] Where an occupant fails to remove on the expiry of notice of entry, the acquiring authority may petition the sheriff for possession under section 89 of the 1845 Act.

In *Chilton v Telford Corporation*[83] possession of the order land was taken by the acquiring authority in several parcels. The question in issue was whether for valuation purposes there was a single date when possession was taken of the first parcel or whether there were several dates, one for each parcel. The Court of Appeal held that first entry on any part of the land described in the notice constituted entry on the whole. It would seem that if an authority wish to take entry in stages they may do so with a succession of notices of entry each limited to the particular stage.

COMPENSATION

One effect of the service of the notice to treat is that it enables either **3–16** party to insist on having the compensation determined. The notice to treat requires those with a compensation interest to provide particulars of their claim. The provision of such particulars will be the first step towards settlement of the compensation. The particulars should give details of the compensation claimed, distinguishing the amount under separate heads and showing how the amount under each head is claimed. Failure to deliver adequate particulars to enable the acquiring authority to make a proper offer of compensation may result in a reference to the Lands Tribunal for Scotland and an award of expenses against the claimant (see p.292).[84] At any time within six weeks after the delivery of such particulars, the acquiring authority may withdraw the notice to treat (see p.63).

An application to the Lands Tribunal for Scotland for the determination of any question of disputed compensation may not be made before the expiration of 30 days from the date of service of the notice to treat (see p.289).[85] It is not clear that there is any time limit for a reference.[86]

CONVEYANCING

Where, following service of a notice to treat, compensation has been **3–17** agreed or determined, the person able to convey the land must do so when required by the acquiring authority. The conveyance will be in the

---

[80] *Glasgow Corporation v The Friendly Bar Ltd*, 1971 S.C. 71; 1971 S.L.T. 174.

[81] *Friendly Bar Ltd v Glasgow Corporation*, 1975 S.L.T. (Lands Tr.) 18.

[82] The rate of interest is prescribed by regulations made under the Land Compensation (Scotland) Act 1963, s.40 (see p. 281).

[83] [1987] 1 W.L.R. 872.

[84] Land Compensation (Scotland) Act 1963, s.11.

[85] Lands Tribunal for Scotland Rules 1971, r.11(3).

[86] Contrast the position with the execution of a general vesting declaration (p.77). In *Hillingdon London Borough Council v ARC Ltd* [1998] R.V.R. 242 it was held that a reference to the (English) Lands Tribunal following the service of a notice to treat was subject to limitation in accordance with s.9(1) of the Limitation Act 1980.

statutory form provided for in section 80 and Schedule A to the 1845 Act.[87] Where, however, land is being taken from someone who is unable or unwilling to convey it or who cannot be traced, title may be acquired under section 74 of the 1845 Act by expeding an instrument under the hand of a notary public. If, as is often the case in Scotland, a general vesting declaration is being employed in lieu of a notice to treat,[88] title will vest in the acquiring authority not under the 1845 Act but under the provisions of section 195 and Schedule 15 to the Town and Country Planning (Scotland) Act 1997. The provisions of Schedule 15 are considered in detail in the next section of this chapter.[89] For completeness, it should be said that there is nothing to prevent title being acquired by way of a disposition in common form. As Welsh points out[90] "the legislation providing for these statutory methods of taking title is permissive and not mandatory." However, as Welsh goes on to observe, "the benefits which attach to the statutory methods are such that one or other of them is invariably utilised." The use of the statutory conveyance and the notarial instrument for acquiring title are now considered briefly in turn.

1. Statutory conveyance

3–18   Section 80 of the 1845 Act provides that the conveyance of the land to be acquired may be effected by using the form of conveyance set out in Schedule A to the Act or a form as near to it as the circumstances will admit.[91] The section states that the conveyance, being duly executed and registered:

> "shall give and constitute a good and undoubted right and complete and valid title in all time coming to the promoters of the undertaking, and their successors and assigns, to the premises therein described, any law or custom to the contrary notwithstanding."

For some time there has been considerable uncertainty about the nature of the relationship, if any, created between the acquiring authority and

---

[87] As amended, from the appointed day, by the Abolition of Feudal Tenure etc. (Scotland) Act 2000, Sch.12.

[88] It is not necessary to agree or determine compensation in advance of the execution of a general vesting declaration.

[89] Where servitudes or real conditions are affected by compulsory acquisition, it has been common practice to reconstitute reciprocal rights and real burdens by a new deed of conditions after the acquisition. In this way the effect of compulsory acquisition is put beyond doubt.

[90] G. Welsh, "'Taking Title' in Compulsory Purchase in Scotland" (1983) 6 *The Law Society of Scotland* 6.9.

[91] Section 80 has been amended, from the appointed day, by the Abolition of Feudal Tenure etc. (Scotland) Act 2000, Sch.12. For a discussion of the style see G. Welsh, above; also see the "Compulsory Acquisition and Compensation" 5 *Stair Memorial Encyclopaedia of the Laws of Scotland* 84.

the superior by a Schedule A conveyance.[92] That uncertainty will be removed by the Abolition of Feudal Tenure etc. (Scotland) Act 2000 with effect from the appointed day. The Act abolishes the feudal system of land tenure and the estate of superiority will cease to exist on that date.

2. Notarial instrument

Where a seller refuses or is unable validly to convey his interest in the **3–19** land to the acquiring authority or fails or neglects to make out a title to the land, or cannot be traced, the authority may deposit the compensation, as agreed or determined, in a bank to the account of the seller as provided in sections 75 and 76 of the 1845 Act and may thereafter expede an instrument under the hands of a notary public. Once it is duly stamped with the appropriate stamp duty, the instrument will have effect to vest the seller's right and interest in the acquiring authority.[93] Upon registration, the instrument will have the same effect as a statutory conveyance.[94]

No style is provided in the 1845 Act but the instrument should describe the land being acquired and recite the circumstances in which the compensation has come to be deposited in the bank and the names of the party or parties to whose credit the deposit has been made.[95]

GENERAL VESTING DECLARATION

The notice to treat and notice of entry procedure just described enables **3–20** an acquiring authority to gain entry to the land in the shortest possible time. Having served notice of the making or confirmation of the compulsory purchase order, as appropriate, the authority may serve a notice to treat together with a notice of entry and take entry after 14 days. This may be important where, for example, the authority is working to a deadline for handing over the site to a contractor for commencement of the work for which the land is being acquired. However, the title to the land may not follow for some considerable time; compensation must first be agreed or determined so that where the authority need to acquire title in the shortest possible time, for example, in order to grant a building lease or to sell the land on for the carrying out of the work,

---

[92] See on this *Duke of Argyle v London, Midland and Scottish Railway*, 1931 S.C. 309 *per* Lord President Clyde at pp.319–320. Also R. Paisley, "Various Aspects of Reform and Abolition of the Feudal System of Landholding in Scotland" (1987) *Department of Conveyancing and Professional Practice, Research Report, Aberdeen University*. Part of the uncertainty was attributable to the apparent conflict between s.80 of the 1845 Act which appeared to extinguish the feudal relationship and s.126 which appeared to continue it, at least for certain purposes. For a possible explanation of the provision in s.126, see R. Paisley, above, citing *Macfarlane v Monklands Railway Co.* (1864) 2 M. 519, *per* Lord Justice-Clerk Inglis at pp.529–531. Section 126 has been abolished from the appointed day by the Abolition of Feudal Tenure etc (Scotland) Act 2000, Schs 12 and 13.

[93] There would appear to be some overlap between the provisions of ss.74 and 76 of the 1845 Act.

[94] 1845 Act, ss.74 and 76.

[95] See above.

the general vesting declaration procedure is to be preferred. At the end of the period specified in the declaration (see below) the title to the land, together with the right of entry, vest in the acquiring authority. The general vesting declaration procedure is also administratively more convenient where there are a considerable number of interests in the order land to be acquired or where owners are hard to trace. For these reasons the general vesting declaration procedure is widely employed in Scotland. In *Apostolic Church Trustees v Glasgow District Council*[96] the Lands Tribunal for Scotland commented:

> ". . . that when the United Kingdom Parliament first introduced the . . . expedited procedure for completion of compulsory purchase it may never have intended this procedure to be used unless it was urgently necessary for local planning authorities to obtain immediate entry to land and title thereto—before it was possible to do so under the ordinary procedures. The expedited procedure, when first introduced, may thus not have been intended to be used (as it is now most frequently used in Scottish urban areas) in cases where immediate physical entry is neither desired nor intended to avoid the administrative difficulties which may be involved from multiple conveyances of Scottish tenement property."

Research suggests that the preference for the general vesting declaration is less clear cut in England and Wales with the notice to treat procedure predominating for highways and utility compulsory purchase orders but the general vesting declaration being preferred for housing and planning acquisitions.[97] What follows is a discussion of the general vesting declaration procedure.

The provisions governing the procedure are contained in Schedule 15 to the Town and Country Planning (Scotland) Act 1997 but they are not confined to orders promoted under that legislation. It appears that a general vesting declaration may be employed in connection with orders made or confirmed under the 1947 Act procedure or under any other procedure.[98] The vesting declaration procedure may not be used in respect of an interest in land which is already the subject of a notice to treat.

Before making a general vesting declaration with respect to any land[99] which is subject to a compulsory purchase order, the acquiring authority must include an indication of their intention to use the vesting declaration procedure in the notice of the making or confirmation of the order required to be published or served by paragraph 6 of the First Schedule to the 1947 Act[1] or in a notice given subsequently.[2] The indication must

---

[96] 1977 S.L.T. (Lands Tr.) 24.

[97] City University Business School, *The Operation of Compulsory Purchase Orders,* Department of the Environment, 1996.

[98] 1997 Act, Sch.15, paras 2(1) and 6(a).

[99] It is not necessary that all the order land should be the subject of a declaration; and there may be several general vesting declarations executed at different times in respect of different parts of the order land.

[1] Or required to be published or served under other procedures.

[2] The requirements relating to publication and service of a notice of making or confirmation of a compulsory purchase order apply equally to a notice given subsequently (1997 Act, Sch.15, para.2(2)).

contain a statement of the effect of paragraphs 1–8 of Schedule 15[3] together with an invitation to those entitled to claim compensation to give information to the acquiring authority in the prescribed form[4] with regard to their name and address and the land in question.

A general vesting declaration may not be executed before the end of a period of two months, beginning with the date of the first publication[5] of the notice containing the indication of the intention to use the procedure, unless every occupier of the land specified in the declaration consents in writing to a shorter period (Schedule 15, paragraph 3(2)).

Having executed the declaration,[6] the acquiring authority must serve a notice in the prescribed form[7] specifying the land and stating the effect of the declaration on every occupier of any of the land specified (other than land in which there subsists a short tenancy or a long tenancy which is about to expire—see below) and on every other person who has given information to the authority with respect of any of that land in response to their (the authority's) invitation (above) (Schedule 15, paragraph 4). The declaration will state the period at the end of which it is to take effect, which must be a date not less than 28 days after the date on which service of these notices has been completed.[8]

The effect of a general vesting declaration is threefold. First of all, at **3–21** the end of the period specified in the declaration the specified land, together with the right to enter on and take possession of it, vests in the acquiring authority as if the authority had expeded a notarial instrument under the provisions of the 1845 Act (see above).[9] This would seem to be reinforced by paragraph 37 of Schedule 15 which provides that at the end of the period specified in the declaration, it is to be recorded in the General Register of Sasines or, as the case may be, registered in the Land Register of Scotland and, once recorded, it will have effect as a conveyance registered in accordance with section 80 of the 1845 Act (see above). It should be noted that recording a general vesting declaration is not a precondition of vesting; the effect of recording is simply to confer a real right.

Secondly, the provisions of the 1845 Act, s.6 of the Railways Clauses Consolidation (Scotland) Act 1845 (both as incorporated by the Second Schedule to the 1947 Act) and the Land Compensation (Scotland) Acts of 1963 and 1973 apply as if on the date on which the declaration was made a notice to treat had been served. Either party may accordingly

---

[3] See Forms 8 and 9 in Schedule 1 to the Compulsory Purchase of Land (Scotland) Regulations 1976.

[4] See above, Form 10.

[5] It is not clear why Schedule 15 refers to "first" publication as there is no requirement for second or subsequent publication.

[6] For the form of the general vesting declaration see the 1976 Regulations, Schedule 1, Form 7.

[7] See above, Form 11.

[8] See note to Form 7. A certificate by the acquiring authority that the service of notices required by para.4 was completed on a date specified in the certificate will be conclusive evidence of the fact so stated (1997 Act, Sch.15, para.5).

[9] As regards possession of the documents of title see the 1997 Act, Sch.15, para.35. The provisions of Sch.15, para.32 dealing with the apportionment of feu duty, ground annuals or other charges now need to be read in the light of the Abolition of Feudal Tenure etc. (Scotland) Act 2000, ss.7 and 56.

insist on having compensation determined. However, the power conferred by section 39 of the Land Compensation (Scotland) Act 1963 to withdraw a notice to treat (p.63 above) is not exercisable where a general vesting declaration has been employed (Schedule 15, paragraph 18); the interests in respect of which a notice to treat is deemed to have been served have already vested in the acquiring authority.

Thirdly, it fixes the date for valuing the interest acquired (see Chapter 5). In *Mrs Annie R. Renfrew's Trustees v Glasgow Corporation*[10] the claimants, who had been allowed to remain in possession of a public house after vesting and were still continuing to trade at the date of the eventual hearing before the Lands Tribunal for Scotland to determine compensation, argued that the date of valuation was the date of the assessment by the tribunal. The tribunal concluded that in the light of the speeches in *Birmingham Corporation v West Midland Baptist (Trust) Association (Inc.)*[11] (see Chapter 5) the valuation date where the expedited completion procedure is employed is the date of vesting.

The general vesting declaration applies to the interest of a lessee for a term of years unexpired[12] but has no effect as regards any person entitled to a short tenancy or a long tenancy which is about to expire. These terms are defined in paragraph 38 of Schedule 15. A "short tenancy" means a tenancy for a year or from year to year or a lesser interest; a "long tenancy which is about to expire" means a tenancy granted for an interest greater than a short tenancy, but having at the date of the declaration a period still to run which is not longer than what is referred to as the "specified period". The "specified period" is a period, longer than one year, specified in the declaration in relation to the land in which the tenancy subsists.[13] The right to enter and take possession of the land specified in a general vesting declaration will be subject to any short tenancies or long tenancies which are about to expire.

3–22   Where such tenancies exist, the acquiring authority may be content, having acquired the landlord's interest, to let them expire in the normal way at the end of their term. Alternatively, if they are unable to wait that long before taking entry, they must first serve a notice to treat in respect of the tenancy followed by a notice of entry stating that at the end of such period as is specified in the notice (not being less than 14 days from the date of service) they intend to enter upon and take possession of the land. This is an exception to the general rule that a short tenant is not entitled to a notice to treat but service of such a notice does not alter the basis of compensation (see Chapter 12).[14]

Schedule 15 makes its own provision (paragraphs 19 to 29) for service of a counter-notice objecting to severance where a general vesting declaration comprises part only of a house, building or factory, or of a park or garden belonging to a house and requiring the acquisition of the whole of the interest. In this case, however, the counter-notice must be

[10] 1972 S.L.T. (Lands Tr.) 2. See, too, *Ware v Edinburgh District Council*, 1976 S.L.T. (Lands Tr.) 21.

[11] [1970] A.C. 874.

[12] For the apportionment of rent see the 1997 Act, Sch.15, para.33.

[13] 1997 Act, Sch.15, para.38(1) and (2).

[14] *Smith and Waverley Tailoring Co. v Edinburgh District Council (No. 2)*, 1977 S.L.T. (Lands Tr.) 29.

served not later than 28 days from the date of service of the notice stating the effect of the declaration (see p.75).[15] Where a counter-notice is served, the interest will not vest in the authority and the authority may not enter and take possession of the land until the notice has been disposed of under the provisions of the Schedule.

Within three months of receipt of a counter-notice, the acquiring authority must either serve a notice withdrawing the deemed notice to treat in respect of the land proposed to be severed, serve notice that the general vesting declaration is to have effect as if the whole of the land had been included in the declaration, or refer the counter-notice to the Lands Tribunal for Scotland for determination. The tribunal's powers as regards disposal of the notice are much the same as for the disposal of a counter-notice served in response to a notice to treat (see p.65 above).

The provisions of ss.49 and 50 of the Land Compensation (Scotland) Act 1973 apply as regards the severance of agricultural land by a general vesting declaration (1973 Act, s.49(5)).

Where land vests in the acquiring authority following execution of a general vesting declaration the authority must pay the like compensation, together with interest, as they would have paid had they taken possession of the land following service of a notice of entry under the 1947 Act, Sch.15, para.30.[16]

In *Hussain v Oldham Metropolitan Borough Council*[17] the corresponding provision in the English legislation was taken to mean that compensation, including compensation for disturbance, is to be calculated as if steps had been taken to obtain actual physical entry at the date of divestiture. In *Park Automobile Co. Ltd v Strathclyde Regional Council*[18] the Lands Tribunal for Scotland reserved its opinion on the decision in *Hussain*. Such an interpretation where the former owner was left in occupation following divestiture would appear to undermine the principle that compensation should reflect the actual loss sustained; it would also seem to undermine the related duty to mitigate that loss. The tribunal doubted whether paragraph 30 of Schedule 24 of what was then the 1972 Act was really intended to effect such a fundamental alteration in the law. The concept of deemed physical entry was "more likely to have been introduced to fix the valuation date for the heritage and not for consequential loss or the interrelated duty to minimise that loss when occasion offers; for this can only occur subsequently" (see Chapter 10).

Paragraph 36 of Schedule 15 imposes a time limit of six years for **3–23** referring questions of disputed compensation to the Lands Tribunal for Scotland following execution of a general vesting declaration. The six year time limit runs from the date at which the person claiming compensation, or a person from whom he derives title, first knew or could reasonably be expected to have known of the vesting of the interest.[19] In *Apostolic Church Trustees v Glasgow District Council*

---

[15] But see para.29.

[16] Paras 9–14 of Schedule 15 make provision for the recovery of overpaid compensation.

[17] (1981) 259 E.G. 56.

[18] 1984 S.L.T. (Lands Tr.) 14; [1983] R.V.R. 108.

[19] And see para.36(2). No such time limit appears to operate for the notice to treat procedure.

(No.2)[20] the reference to the tribunal was made more than 11 years after vesting. The tribunal held that the onus was on the authority to show that an owner knew, or could reasonably be expected to have known of the vesting of his interest more than six years before the date of the reference and that in the particular circumstances of the case the onus had not been discharged. In *Lawrence Garvey v Clydebank District Council*,[21] on the other hand, where the reference was almost 12 years after the date of vesting, the tribunal concluded in the circumstances that the claimants had been aware of the vesting and that it had no jurisdiction to deal with the matter.

The consequence of failing to meet the six year time limit for a reference was first considered by the Lands Tribunal for Scotland in *Apostolic Church Trustees*. In that case the tribunal held that the time bar provisions did not extinguish the actual claim for compensation or cause it to prescribe but merely limited the time within which a statutory reference could be made. It was still open to the parties to agree to a voluntary reference to the tribunal. Subsequently, a similar question came before the Second Division in *The Royal Bank of Scotland plc v Clydebank District Council.*[22] The case involved a petition for judicial review for declarator that, although a reference was time barred, the claimant had not lost the right to payment of compensation and the local authority was under an obligation to pay an amount assessed on a reasonable basis. The court rejected the petition. Lord Justice-Clerk Ross said that, as it was no longer possible to go to the Lands Tribunal, the respondents were under no obligation to pay compensation unless compensation was agreed between the parties. As the respondents could not be forced to reach an agreement, it followed that the petitioner no longer had an enforceable claim for compensation. Lord McCluskey professed to be unable to understand the notion of an obligation to pay whatever, if anything, may in future be agreed, in the absence of any obligation to reach agreement; and Lord Clyde observed that the effect of what was then paragraph 36 of Schedule 24 to the 1972 Act was not to destroy the basic right to compensation but the right became an imperfect one, being unenforceable because it depended upon the voluntary agreement of both parties for the quantification of the amount of compensation.[23] Lord Clyde considered that this conclusion was not inconsistent with the decision of the Lands Tribunal for Scotland in *Apostolic Church Trustees*.

In *Smith and Waverley Tailoring Co. v Edinburgh District Council*[24] the tribunal held that the corresponding time bar in Schedule 6 to the Town and Country Planning (Scotland) Act 1945 was intended to refer only to statutory references. The time bar provision was "enacted within the context of statutory references and procedures which is all the draftsman can therefore have had in mind".

---

[20] 1978 S.L.T. (Lands Tr.) 17.

[21] Unreported, April 24, 1987, Lands Tribunal for Scotland.

[22] 1992 S.L.T. 356.

[23] In *Co-operative Wholesale Society v Chester le Street District Council* (1997) 73 P. & C.R. 111 the Lands Tribunal held that it was possible to waive the statutory time limit either expressly or by conduct.

[24] 1976 S.L.T. (Lands Tr.) 19.

In *Smith and Waverley Tailoring Co.* the tribunal questioned why Parliament should have singled out expedited procedure cases for such arbitrary treatment. In such cases, owners are more likely to be left undisturbed for long periods and are less likely therefore to be alerted to the need to make an actual reference to the tribunal before the six year period has expired, particularly if compensation negotiations are in progress.

SURPLUS LAND

Where land acquired by, or under the shadow of, compulsory purchase **3–24** becomes surplus to requirements, no right of reversion or resumption operates for the benefit of the original owner unless express provision to that effect exists in the enabling Act. Nonetheless, as Bingham L.J. observed in *R. v Commission for the New Towns, ex p. Tomkins*:[25]

> "When land is compulsorily purchased the coercive power of the state is used to deprive a citizen of his property against his will. He is obliged to take its assessed value whether he wants it or not. This exercise is justified by the public intention to develop the land in the wider interest of the community of which the citizen is a part. If, however, that intention is not for any reason fulfilled, and the land becomes available for disposal, common fairness demands that the former owner should have a preferential claim to buy back the land which he had been compelled to sell, provided he is able and willing to pay the full market price at the time of repurchase."

The 1845 Act, ss.12–127[26] sets out special provisions governing the sale of superfluous lands which require that, unless the lands are situated in a town or built upon, they are to be offered first to the owner of the lands from which they were severed or, failing that, to adjoining owners. Otherwise, the lands are to be disposed of in the most advantageous manner or, in default, they will vest in the owners of adjoining land.

These provisions, however, have very limited application today because with compulsory purchase orders to which the 1947 Act applies, sections 120–125 of the 1845 Act are specifically excepted from incorporation with the legislation under which the purchase is authorised.[27] Furthermore, it should be noted that section 73 of the Local Government (Scotland) Act 1973 confers wide powers on local authorities to appropriate land which is no longer needed for the purpose for which it was acquired for other local government purposes.[28]

The original owner, subject to the very limited application of the provisions in the 1845 Act, therefore, has no statutory rights in respect of surplus land. Nevertheless, following the row in the early 1950s over the

---

[25] (1988) 58 P. & C.R. 57.

[26] As amended from the appointed day by the Abolition of Feudal Tenure etc (Scotland) Act 2000.

[27] 1947 Act, Second Schedule, para.2(a).

[28] See, too, the Town and Country Planning (Scotland) Act 1997, Part VIII.

unsatisfactory way in which Crichel Down, compulsorily acquired as a wartime bombing range, was subsequently disposed of by the Ministry of Agriculture when it became surplus to requirements, informal guidelines on disposal were introduced. Government departments which had acquired but now had no further use for agricultural land were to offer it first to the original owner at current market value. The guidelines did not apply to non-agricultural land. However, as a result of dissatisfaction in 1980 over the way in which the disposal of land no longer required for the extension of the British Library was handled, the guidelines were revised and extended to non-agricultural land.

The revised guidelines, entitled the "Crichel Down Rules," are set out in Part III of the memorandum accompanying SDD Circular 21/1984. They apply to all land and buildings surplus to requirements but originally acquired by a government department by or under the shadow of compulsory acquisition or in response to a blight notice served under Part V, Chapter II of the Town and Country Planning (Scotland) Act 1997. They do not, however, apply to the disposal of land acquired under the Small Landholders (Scotland) Acts 1886–1931; such land is governed by its own provisions.

The general rule under the guidelines is that land, the character of which has not been materially changed[29] since the original acquisition by the government, and which becomes surplus to requirements within a prescribed period,[30] will be offered first to the former owner at its current market value.[31] "Former owner" includes a person to whom the land would have devolved under the original owner's will or intestacy.

There are, inevitably, a number of exceptions to the general rule. These include cases where the Scottish Ministers specifically authorise disposal to another government department or agency, or in exceptional cases, to a local authority or other public body; where the disposal is in execution of government policy transferring certain functions to the private sector; where disposal would fragment a site and substantially reduce its market value or prejudice its prospects of development; and where disposal would be inconsistent with the purpose of its original acquisition.

Although the rules apply only to surplus government land, the general principles are commended to local authorities disposing of land which is surplus to their requirements.

Recent research undertaken for the Department of the Environment, Transport and the Regions showed anecdotal evidence of widespread failure to apply the Rules.[32] Criticism was levelled at the advisory status of the Rules, the lack of clear procedures and the absence of mechanisms for accountability and dispute resolution. The result, suggested the research, has been inconsistent application of the Rules by governmental and other agencies. The Department of Transport, Local Government

---

[29] "Material change" will be very much a matter of fact and degree but a useful guide will be the level of expenditure required to restore the land to its former use.

[30] The "prescribed period" is a reference to agricultural land acquired since the beginning of 1935 and to other land which becomes surplus within 25 years of its acquisition.

[31] But see *R. v Commission for the New Towns, ex p. Tomkins* (1988) 58 P. & C.R. 57.

[32] The Operation of the Crichel Down Rules (2000) DETR.

and the Regions has responded to the criticism with a proposal to put the Rules on a statutory footing in England and to provide a dispute resolution mechanism.[33]

---

[33] "Compulsory purchase and compensation: delivering a fundamental change" (2001) DTLR, para.5.3.

PART 2

COMPENSATION FOR COMPULSORY ACQUISITION

CHAPTER 4

COMPENSATION: INTRODUCTORY MATTERS

THE ENTITLEMENT TO COMPENSATION

4-01 In many countries throughout the world the entitlement to compensation for the expropriation of land is enshrined in the constitution.[1] The Fifth Amendment to the Constitution of the United States of America, for example, provides "nor shall private property be taken for public use without just compensation". There is, however, no such constitutional guarantee of compensation in Britain. Indeed, as with compulsory purchase powers, the entitlement to compensation for the last 150 years has depended upon statutory authority.[2] "No owners of lands expropriated by statute for public purposes," said Lord Parmoor in *Sisters of Charity of Rockingham v The King*, "is entitled to compensation, either for the value of the land taken, or for damage, on the ground that his land is injuriously affected unless he can establish a statutory right."[3]

Nonetheless, institutional writers such as Mackenzie and Erskine, in their discussion of the doctrine of *dominium eminens*, conclude that justice requires compensation for loss inflicted on a subject for the benefit of the community.[4] Erskine, for example, states that where private property rights have to give way to the demands of "public necessity or utility . . . the persons deprived of their property ought to have a full equivalent for quitting it".[5] As Lord President Clyde observed in *Burmah Oil Company (Burma Trading) Ltd v Lord Advocate*[6]: "our law, being based upon equitable considerations, has always looked askance at confiscation, and has always leaned towards compensating individuals where property is taken from them for the benefit of others".

---

[1] See F. Mann, "Outline of a History of Expropriation" (1959) 75 L.Q.R. 188.

[2] Note, however, that in *Burmah Oil Company (Burma Trading) Ltd v Lord Advocate*, 1964 S.C. (HL.) 117, the House of Lords held that compensation was payable for the taking or destruction of a subject's property by the Crown in the exercise of its prerogative power in time of war.

[3] [1922] 2 A.C. 315 at p.322.

[4] Sir George MacKenzie, *Jus Regium*, Vol.II, p.452; Erskine, *An Institute of the Law of Scotland*, II, i, 2.

[5] See above II, i, 2.

[6] 1963 S.C. 410 at p.449. It is interesting to note that the decision of the House of Lords on the award of compensation in this case was immediately overridden by the passing of the War Damages Act 1965, thus indicating where the real *dominium* lay.

The Human Rights Act 1998 also requires legislation to be interpreted, so far as possible, in conformity with the European Convention on Human Rights. Mention was made in Chapter 1 of Article 1 of the First Protocol to the Convention which provides that "every natural and legal person is entitled to the peaceful enjoyment of his possessions. No one shall be deprived of his possessions except in the public interest and subject to the conditions provided for by law and the general principles of international law". Although Article 1 makes no specific mention of compensation, the taking of property without compensation is likely to be treated as justifiable only in exceptional circumstances.[7]

Although, therefore, a claimant must be able to point to statutory authority to support a claim, "there is a natural leaning in favour of compensation in the construction of a statute".[8] For example, in *Wells v London, Tilbury and Southend Railway Co.*[9] a railway company obtained private Act powers which, *inter alia*, extinguished certain footways across their railway. In the course of his judgment Bramwell L.J. said on the issue of compensation:

> "The legislature, in an Act providing for the execution of public works, never takes away the slightest private right without providing compensation for it, and the general recital that it is expedient that the works should be done is never supposed to mean that in order to carry them out a man is to be deprived of his private rights without compensation."[10]

Again, in *Attorney-General v Horner*,[11] where the point in issue was whether Paving Acts took away the rights of an owner of a market franchise, Brett M.R. said on the question whether the Act provided for expropriation without compensation "it is a proper rule of construction not to construe an Act of Parliament as interfering with or injuring persons' rights without compensation, unless one is obliged so to construe it.[12] And Salter J. in *Newcastle Breweries Ltd v The King*[13] referred to "an established rule that a statute will not be read as authorising the taking of a subject's goods without payment unless an intention to do so be clearly expressed".[14] There is now a line of cases which supports the judicial presumption that an intention to take away the property of a subject without giving him a legal right to compensation for the loss of it is not to be imputed to the legislature unless that

---

[7] *James v United Kingdom* (1987) 8 E.H.R.R. 123. See too M Redman, "Compulsory Purchase, Compensation and Human Rights" [1999] J.P.L. 315; also, "Towards a Compulsory Purchase Code: (1) Compensation—A Consultative Report" 165 Law Commission Consultation Paper, para.2.20.

[8] Lord Hodson in *Burmah Oil Company (Burma Trading) Ltd v Lord Advocate*, 1964 S.C. (H.L.) 117 at p.154.

[9] [1877] 5 Ch.126.

[10] See above at p.130.

[11] (1884) 14 Q.B.D. 245.

[12] See above at p.257.

[13] [1920] 1 K.B. 854.

[14] See above at p.866.

intention is expressed in unequivocal terms.[15] In other words, the courts have developed what has been described as a "liability rule" to protect private property rights in land[16]; the state may destroy the initial entitlement to the property but only on the payment of an objectively determined value; the loss resulting from expropriation does not lie where it falls but is shared amongst all the citizens of the state.

It is, of course, open to the legislature to make explicit provision in an Act of Parliament for the taking of property without compensation.[17] For example, in *Re a Petition of Right*[18] the Court of Appeal decided, *inter alia*, that the effect of certain regulations made under the Defence of the Realm Act 1914 was to enable the Crown to take land without paying compensation. This decision was followed by Lord Anderson in the Outer House in *The Moffat Hydropathic Co. Ltd v Lord Advocate*,[19] a case involving the interpretation of the same legislation.

4–02   A more explicit example of the legislature providing other than for a "full equivalent" for the compulsory acquisition of land is to be found in section 45 of the Planning (Listed Buildings and Conservation Areas)(Scotland) Act 1997. The section provides that where a planning authority propose to acquire compulsorily a listed building, they may, if they are satisfied that the building has deliberately been allowed to fall into disrepair, apply to the Scottish Ministers for a direction that only minimum compensation be paid. If such a direction is issued, any development potential which the land may have is disregarded in assessing compensation and the landowner in such a case will receive considerably less than a "full equivalent". A further example is to be found in section 17 and Schedule 2 to the Land Compensation (Scotland) Act 1963, as substituted by s339(2) and Schedule 23, paragraph 10 of the Housing (Scotland) Act 1987 (see Chapter 9). This provides that, where property being compulsorily acquired under specified powers comprises a house below a prescribed standard of fitness, compensation is not to exceed the value of the site of the house as a cleared site available for development. In many cases, this, too, will result in a claimant receiving less than a "full equivalent" of the loss.

The focus of the discussion so far has been on the question of the entitlement to compensation in the circumstances of the expropriation of property rights by the state; and it is with the consequences of the expropriation of property rights in land that this book is very largely concerned. However, private property rights in land may have to give

---

[15] *Burmah Oil Company (Burma Trading) Ltd v Lord Advocate, supra; Tiverton and North Devon Railway Co. v Loosemore* (1884) A.C. 480; *Colonial Sugar Refining Co. Ltd v Melbourne Harbour Trust Commissioners* [1927] A.C. 343; *Bond v Nottingham Corporation* [1960] Ch.429; *Belfast Corporation v O.D. Cars Ltd*. [1960] A.C. 490; and *Westminster Bank Ltd v Minister of Housing and Local Government* [1971] A.C. 508.

[16] G. Calabresi and P. Melamed, "Property Rules, Liability Rules, and Inalienability: One View of the Cathedral," 85 Harv. L. R. 1089.

[17] Such provision would, however, require adequate justification on the grounds of interest to comply with Article 1 of the First Protocol of the European Convention on Human Rights (*James v United Kingdom* (1987) 8 E.H.R.R. 123).

[18] [1915] 3 K.B. 649. See, too, *Musselburgh Real Estate Co. v Magistrates of Musselburgh* (1905) 7 F. 113, HL.

[19] (1919) 1 S.L.T. 82. See, too, *Sheffield City Council v Yorkshire Water Services Ltd*, Independent Law Reports, May 18, 1990.

way to the demands of "public necessity or utility" in circumstances which fall short of a physical taking of the land. For example, a landowner may, as a result of a refusal of planning permission, be denied the opportunity to develop his land because it is in the wider public interest to preserve the continuation of the existing use; or the value of the land may be very substantially diminished by the construction and use on neighbouring land of much needed public works such as a motorway or airport. To determine the entitlement to compensation simply on the question whether or not there has been a taking of the land is to ignore the consequences of other forms of state intervention. Michelman[20] poses the question of "when to compensate" in broader terms:

"When a social decision to redirect economic resources entails painfully obvious opportunity costs, how shall these costs ultimately be distributed among all the members of society? Shall they be permitted to remain where they fall initially or shall the government, by paying compensation, make explicit attempts to distribute these in accordance with decisions made by whatever process fashions the tax structure, or perhaps according to some other principle? Shall the losses be left with the individuals on whom they happen first to fall, or shall they be socialised?"

He goes on to argue that a clear statement of the purposes of compensation practice is desirable in a form which shows how to state with precision the variables which ought to determine entitlements to compensation. However, as Farrier and McAuslan observe,[21] there has not been in the United Kingdom "a questioning of the basic assumptions or philosophy of compensation law nor any real consideration given to the relationship between compensation and development and attitudes thereto". The legislative development of compensation practice has been piecemeal; for the rest, it has been left to the courts to work out compensation entitlements in this broader area with little assistance from Parliament.

Having dealt in general terms with the entitlement to compensation for the expropriation of private property rights in land, it is appropriate now to consider the specific entitlement upon which, for the most part claims for compensation are founded. Compulsory purchase today is carried on very largely by public bodies acting under the authority of powers conferred by public and general Acts.[22] These Acts do not themselves make specific provision regarding the entitlement to compensation.[23] Instead, reliance is placed upon the provisions of the Lands

---

[20] F. Michelman, "Property, Utility and Fairness: Comments on the Ethical Foundations of 'Just Compensation' Law" 80 Harv. L. Rev 1165.

[21] D. Farrier and P. McAuslan, *"Compensation, Participation and Compulsory Acquisition of Homes"* in *Compensation for Compulsory Purchase: A Comparative Study*, (J. F. Garner ed., United Kingdom National Committee of Comparative Law, London, 1975).

[22] Compulsory purchase powers are occasionally conferred by private and local Acts. For a notable example see the Zetland County Council Act 1974, s.24.

[23] They may, however, make provision dealing with specific aspects of compensation. See, for example, the Roads (Scotland) Act 1984, ss.106 and 116.

Clauses Consolidation (Scotland) Act 1845, as amended, which are applied in two ways. First of all, section 1 of that Act provides that:

> "This Act shall apply to every undertaking in Scotland authorised by any Act of Parliament which shall hereafter be passed, and which shall authorise the taking of lands for such undertaking, and this Act shall be incorporated with such an Act; and all the provisions of this Act, save so far as they shall be expressly varied or excepted by any such Act, shall apply to the undertaking authorised thereby."

Strictly, that would seem to be sufficient. However, perhaps with a view to avoiding any possibility of confusion over variations and exceptions, section 1(3) and the Second Schedule to the Acquisition of Land (Authorisation Procedure) (Scotland) Act 1947 also specifically apply the provisions of the Lands Clauses Act for the purposes of any compulsory purchase covered by the 1947 Act[24] but subject to the express variations and exceptions mentioned.

4–03   Curiously, the Lands Clauses Consolidation (Scotland) Act 1845 confers no specific entitlement to compensation except for the interests of certain lessees; but it is clearly phrased on the assumption that compensation will be paid. Section 17, for example, requires the promoters to serve a notice to treat on all persons having an interest in the land to be acquired otherwise than by agreement stating that they are willing to treat for the purchase thereof and for compensation for any damage caused by the execution of the works. Section 20 provides that disputes over "the value of such lands or of any interests therein, or as to the compensation to be made in respect thereof" may be referred to arbitration.[25] Section 36 provides that any party entitled to compensation exceeding £50 may have the amount determined by a jury.[26] And section 48 requires the jury in such cases to state separately the sums of money due for the purchase of the land and for severance and other injurious affection. The closest the 1845 Act comes to conferring a specific entitlement to compensation is section 61 and this is the provision upon which most claims are founded. Section 61 provides that in estimating the purchase money or compensation to be paid:

> "regard shall be had not only to the value of the land to be purchased or taken by the promoters of the undertaking, but also to the damage, if any, to be sustained by the owner of the lands by reason of the severing of the lands taken from the other lands of such owner, or otherwise injuriously affecting such land by the exercise of the powers of this or the special Act, or any other Act incorporated therewith."

---

[24] The provisions of the 1947 Act are applied, for example, to compulsory purchase orders promoted under the Town and Country Planning (Scotland) Act 1997, s.189 and the Local Government (Scotland) Act 1973, s.71.

[25] The Acquisition of Land (Assessment of Compensation) Act 1919 provided for the resolution of disputes over compensation by official arbiters in place of juries; the power to refer a dispute over quantum to a private arbiter remained. Private arbitration and the official arbiters were replaced by the Lands Tribunal for Scotland in 1971.

[26] See above.

The Railways Clauses Consolidation (Scotland) Act 1845 is more specific.[27] Section 6 provides that:

> "The Company shall make to the owner and occupier of and all other parties interested in any lands taken or used for the purposes of the railway or injuriously affected by the construction thereof, full compensation for the value of the lands so taken or used, and for all damage sustained by such owners, occupiers, and other parties by reason of the exercise as regards such lands of the powers of this, or the Special Act, or any Act incorporated therewith, vested in the Company."

Section 6 of the Railways Clauses Act is incorporated with the enactment under which any compulsory purchase, to which the provisions of the 1947 Act apply, is authorised[28] and, therefore, confers a specific statutory entitlement to compensation.

The interpretation of section 6 has, however, given rise to some difficulty in practice, at least as regards claims for injurious affection (see Chapter 14). In view of the judicial presumption to which reference was made earlier that a statute will not be read as authorising the taking of property without compensation unless that intention is clearly expressed, the provisions of the Lands Clauses Act of 1845, and in particular section 61, have generally been accepted by the courts as conferring an entitlement to compensation.[29] In *Lanarkshire and Dumbartonshire Railway Co. v Thomas Main*,[30] for example, Lord Kinnear said:

> "it is a well-settled rule in the construction of the Lands Clauses Act that when lands have been taken in the exercise of powers of compulsory purchase, the owner or occupier as the case may be, is entitled not only to the market value of his interest but to full compensation for all loss which he may sustain by being deprived of his land."[31]

And in *Venables v Department of Agriculture for Scotland*[32] Lord Justice-Clerk Alness accepted that the principle to be derived from the 1845 Act was that "the person dispossessed should get compensation for all loss occasioned to him by reason of his dispossession".[33]

---

[27] See *Royal Bank of Scotland v Glasgow District Council*, 1992 S.L.T. 356 *per* Lord McClusky.

[28] 1947 Act, s.1(3) and Second Schedule, para.1.

[29] The (English) Law Commission has proposed that a new compensation code should begin with a simple statement that those interested in the subject land are entitled to compensation (*Towards a Compulsory Purchase Code: (1) Compensation*, Law Commission Consultation Paper No 165, para.4.2). Note that the entitlement to compensation for a tenant having no greater interest in land than as a tenant for a year or from year to year rests upon s.114 of the 1845 Act (see p.255 below).

[30] (1895) 22 R. 912.

[31] See above at p.919.

[32] 1932 S.C. 573.

[33] See above at p.581.

THE MEASURE OF COMPENSATION FOR COMPULSORY PURCHASE

1. The concept of compensation

4–04   As mentioned above, section 61 of the 1845 Act provides that in
estimating the compensation to be paid regard is to be had to the value
of the land to be acquired and to any damage sustained by severance or
other injurious affection. "Severance" occurs when the physical taking of
part of a parcel of land depreciates the value of the remaining land.
"Other injurious affection" is a reference to depreciation in the value of
the remaining land caused by the construction and use of the works for
which the part was taken. Section 61, therefore, specifies the two heads
under which compensation may be claimed[34]; but it says nothing about
the measure or yardstick to be applied in assessing the compensation.
The result of the "unusually open texture"[35] of the legislation was that,
until 1919 (see below), the measure of compensation was left to the
arbiters or juries to determine "with a freedom which might have
amazed even the compiler of a continental code".

The question "what should be the measure of compensation" depends
upon the objective which compensating a claimant is intended to
achieve. Objectives vary. Michelman, in a wide ranging article,[36] develops
two models of compensation designed to achieve different objectives,
one derived from classical utilitarianism and the other, the fairness
model derived from the "justice as fairness" approach of John Rawls.[37]
Michelman's main concern was with the question "when to compensate". However, Bell, in an article based on research into the compensation implications of a number of major road schemes for agricultural
interests,[38] considers how the objectives of these two models might be
reflected in the measure of compensation. Bell suggests that the
objective of the utilitarian approach would be to maximise social welfare.
His research indicates that in view of the time, trouble and expense
being invested in lengthy negotiations with landowners, the greater net
benefit would be likely to be achieved by a measure of compensation
which provides claimants with a small balance of advantage thus
encouraging less objection and speedier settlements.

An interesting example of a utilitarian approach to compensation is
provided by Cullingworth who cites the Minister of Transport in a
memorandum in 1958 to the Minister of Housing and Local Government as stating that his department "could not be more strongly in
favour" of a Bill providing for an increase in the measure of compensation for compulsory acquisition because of the difficulties faced by his

---

[34] See also s.114 of the 1845 Act as regards the heads of claim for a tenant having no
greater interest in the land than as a tenant for a year or from year to year.
[35] See W. A. Elliott, "The Scope for 'General Principle' Legislation" (1977) *Proceedings
of the 5th Commonwealth Law Conference*.
[36] F. Michelman, "Property, Utility, and Fairness: Comments on the Ethical Foundations of 'Just Compensation' Law," 80 Harv. L. R. 1165.
[37] J. Rawls, "Justice as Fairness," 67 Phil. Rev. 164 (1958).
[38] M. Bell, "Taking Justice Seriously: Rawls', Utilitarianism and Land Compensation"
(1980) 3 *Urban Law and Policy* 23.

department in time-consuming procedures for compulsory acquisition at unattractive rates of compensation.[39]

Bell suggests that this small balance of advantage might be assessed by reference to the optimum point on a claimant's satisfaction curve. On the data available he estimated that this would point to an addition of some 30 per cent to the market value of a holding.

A "Rawlsian" approach to compensation would view matters from a different perspective. Rawls suggested that the principles of justice for the basic structure of society should be those principles "that free and rational persons concerned to further their own interests would accept in an initial position of equality as defining the fundamental terms of their association".[40] Bell hypothesised that Rawls' rational men, who had no idea whether they would be faced with the prospect of the expropriation of their land, would select a measure of fairness which would ensure that the worst affected group would end up marginally better off. He considered that the compensation decisions of the lay juries prior to 1919 (see below) exhibited some of the characteristics of a Rawlsian approach to compensation and on this basis concluded that such a measure might add at least 10 per cent to the market price.

Atiyah makes a distinction in the context of compensation for accidents between that which is intended to provide a financial equivalent for what has been lost and that which is intended as a substitute or solace for what has been lost.[41] The former is generally taken to refer to the lump sum required to leave the claimant as well off but no better off than he or she would be without the change in their expectations. This would seem to be another way of expressing the basic measure of damages for breach of contract[42] and delict[43] which is that there should be *restitutio in integrum*. Compensation for compulsory purchase based on equivalence might typically reflect the price which the claimant could have expected to have obtained for the property on a sale in the open market together with other consequential loss.

Compensation which is granted as a substitute or solace for what has **4–05** been lost would seem to comprehend rather more intangible loss, something that cannot be replaced, something other than patrimonial loss. "Solatium" is sometimes included as an element in an award of damages in Scotland. It is a payment made in cases of personal injury in

---

[39] J. B. Cullingworth, "Environmental Planning" (1980) IV HMSO 185. A somewhat similar response was made by Mrs Thatcher in response to a parliamentary question from Sir Michael McNair (HC Deb., July 19, 1990, col. 1167). See, too, P. McAuslan, *Ideologies of Planning Law* (Pergamon Press, 1980), Chap.4.

[40] J Rawls, *A Theory of Justice* (Harvard University Press, 1971), p.22.

[41] P. Cane, *Atiyah's Accidents: Compensation and the Law* (6th ed., Butterworths), Chap.18.

[42] W. M. Gloag, *The Law of Contract in Scotland* (2nd ed., W. Green & Son Ltd, Edinburgh, 2001); W. W. McBryde, *The Law of Contract in Scotland* (2nd ed., W. Green & Son Ltd, Edinburgh, 2000), paras 22–88.

[43] *Admiralty Commissioners v S. S. Susquehanna* [1926] A.C. 655, cited with approval in a number of Scottish decisions; for example, *Hutchison v Davidson*, 1945 S.C. 295; *The Trustees of the Clyde Navigation v The Bowring Steamship Co.*, 1929 S.C. 715. See also *Livingstone v Rawyards Coal Co.* (1880) 7 R. (H.L.) 1 *per* Lord Blackburn at p.7.

recognition of pain or suffering.[44] Solatium has been replaced as an element of damages in case of death by a rather more broadly based award reflecting distress and anxiety, grief and sorrow and loss of non-patrimonial benefit.[45] Although solatium and the loss of society award may be distinguished[46] they are both concerned with intangible loss and may fairly be said to be represented by Atiyah's description of compensation as a substitute or solace. Solatium as an element in an award of compensation for compulsory purchase might provide recompense for the individual value which people commonly ascribe to heritable property in excess of its market value.[47] This is sometimes referred to as "householder's surplus" and reflects loss of ties with the area, friendships made, and so on—items which are difficult to value. Both the utilitarian and fairness models of compensation would be likely to make some allowance, although for different reasons, for the subjective expectations of the claimants. Some support for the provision of an allowance for loss of householder's surplus in compulsory purchase compensation was given in the report of the commission on the third London airport[48] and in the report of the Urban Motorways Committee.[49] The latter commented that:

"it will not be sufficient to assume that in the case of those who have to move the cost of compensation or rehousing fully reflects the burden that is put upon them. Many individuals are attached to their particular house or their particular neighbourhood and would not freely move simply for the market value of their property. They suffer an additional loss—sometimes called loss of householder's surplus—which is real for them but for practical purposes very difficult to value in specific cases."[50]

The consequence of the committee's report for the measure of compensation for compulsory purchase is discussed below.

Knetsch goes somewhat further and questions whether there might not be some advantage in terms of both efficiency and equity in a measure of compensation the objective of which would be to enable a

---

[44] As to the nature of solatium as an element in an award of damages see *Traynor's Executors v Bairds and Scottish Steel Ltd*, 1957 S.C. 311; *McCallum v Paterson*, 1968 S.C. 280; *Dingwall v Walter Alexander and Sons (Midland) Ltd*, 1981 S.L.T. 313; and, generally, D. M. Walker, *The Law of Delict in Scotland* (2nd ed. revised, W. Green & Son Ltd, Edinburgh) Chap.14.

[45] Damages (Scotland) Act 1976, s.1(4) as amended by the Damages (Scotland) Act 1993, s.1(1).

[46] *Dingwall v Walter Alexander and Sons (Midland) Ltd*, 1981 S.L.T. 313.

[47] See D. Farrier and P. McAuslan, *supra*; also J. L. Knetsch, *Property Rights and Compensation* (Butterworths & Co. (Canada) Ltd, 1983) Chap.4, and P. McAuslan, *Ideologies of Planning Law* (Pergamon Press, 1980) Chap.4.

[48] HMSO, 1971.

[49] Department of the Environment, HMSO, 1972.

[50] See above, paras 12, 18–19. See too the arguments for an additional allowance in non-residential cases of compulsory acquisition (*Compensation for Compulsory Acquisition*, RICS, 1995, para.1.16) and for commercial cases of compulsory acquisition (Compulsory Purchase Policy Review Advisory Group, *Fundamental review of the laws and procedures relating to compulsory purchase and compensation: final report*, DETR, 2000, para.97).

claimant to participate in the social worth of the scheme for which the land is acquired.[51] Such an approach would be concerned not so much with measurement of loss but with redistribution of profit but then, as one commentator has argued,[52] why should a landowner be expected to sell at a price less than that which represents the true value of the land to the purchaser and the community? The Sheaf Committee considered the possibility of encouraging the voluntary sale of land to local authorities by allowing payment of a price which gave the landowner part of the equity estimated to arise on its subsequent development.[53]

This could be achieved by basing the price on a residual valuation, the method commonly employed by developers to determine the offer price for development land. A developer begins his calculations by estimating the selling price of the development, for example, houses. From this is deducted the anticipated development costs, cost of finance, marketing expenses, overheads, any contingency allowance and the developer's profit margin.[54] The residue is the maximum price which may be offered for the land in question. The Sheaf Committee rejected this as a measure of compensation. "Payments on such a basis," concluded the committee, "would be bound in themselves, if made on an extensive scale, to inflate the market value of the land." Furthermore, the committee recognised that there would be cases where local authorities would have to continue to acquire land at a price which excluded any element of value due to the scheme underlying the acquisition so that "a dual valuation standard would emerge". This, they felt, would be inequitable as between one landowner and another.

2. The measure of compensation pre-1919

In the absence of any guidance in the 1845 Act as to the objectives of **4–06** the legislation or the measure to be adopted, it was inevitable that the courts should be called upon to interpret the intention of the legislature. Perhaps not surprisingly their decisions appear to have been influenced by principles derived from the measurement of damages at common law, in particular the principle of *restitutio in integrum*.[55] In *Stebbing v The Metropolitan Board of Works*,[56] an early decision which turned on the construction of the English Lands Clauses Act, Lush J. observed that:

> "The Act did not intend to put the owner of the land in a better position than he would have been in if the land had not been taken from him. What the legislature intended to give is full compensation

---

[51] J. L. Knetsch, *supra*, Chap.5.

[52] W. D. Jones, "The Impact of Public Works on Farming: A Case Study Relating to a Reservoir and Power Station in North Wales," (1972) 23 *Journal of Agricultural Economics* 12.

[53] Report of the Working Party on Local Authority/Private Enterprise Partnership Schemes, (1972) HMSO, paras 94–96 and Annex K.

[54] See J. Rowan-Robinson and M. G. Lloyd, *Land Development and the Infrastructure Lottery* (T. & T. Clark, 1988) Chap.6.

[55] See, for example, *Ricket v Metropolitan Railway Co.* (1865) 34 L.J.Q.B. 257, *per* Erle C.J.; and *Palatine Graphic Arts Co. Ltd v Liverpool City Council* [1986] 2 W.L.R. 285, *per* Glidewell L.J.

[56] (1870) L.R. 6 Q.B. 37.

and indemnity to the persons from whom land is taken for the loss of the land."[57]

In that case, the claimant based his claim, not on the existing use value of the three parcels of land in question as burial grounds—which to all intents and purposes was nil—but on their social worth to the purchaser and to the community for the laying out of a street and for the erection of buildings. The Court of Queen's Bench rejected this basis of assessment. Cockburn C.J. said:

> "When Parliament gives compulsory powers, and provides that compensation shall be made to the person from whom property is taken, for the loss that he sustains, it is intended that he shall be compensated to the extent of his loss; and that his loss shall be tested by what was the value of the thing to him, not by what will be its value to the persons acquiring it."[58]

In other words, the courts rejected the social worth of the scheme as the basis of assessment and opted for the measure of equivalence. The measure of compensation, said Lord Watson in *Commissioners of Inland Revenue v Glasgow and South Western Rail Co.*[59] is "an equivalent for that which the railway company take and acquire and which the proprietor gives up to them". "Value to the owner" was affirmed as the measure of compensation for compulsory purchase in numerous subsequent cases.[60]

The "open-texture" of the legislation has, nonetheless, enabled the courts with some ingenuity to ensure that within the constraints of "value to the owner" a claimant was fully compensated for all loss consequent on the compulsory acquisition of the land. The first head of claim under section 61 of the 1845 Act was held to encompass not only the value of the land itself, but all consequential loss commonly referred to as "disturbance". As the Lord Chancellor, Lord Halisbury, said in *Glasgow and South Western Rail Co.*[61]:

> "what the jury have to ascertain is the value of the land. In treating of that value, the value under the circumstances to the person who is compelled to sell (because the statute compels him to do so) may be naturally and properly and justly taken into account, and when such phrases as 'damages for loss of business' or 'compensation for the goodwill' taken from the person, are used in a loose and general sense, they are not inaccurate for the purpose of giving verbal expression to what everybody understands as a matter of business, but in strictness the thing which is to be ascertained is the price to

---

[57] See above, p.46.
[58] See above, p.42.
[59] (1887) 14 R. (H.L.) 33 at p.35.
[60] See, for example, *Corrie v McDermott* [1914] A.C. 1056; *Cedar Rapids Manufacturing and Power Co. v Lacoste* [1914] A.C. 569; *Re Lucas and Chesterfield Gas and Water Board* [1909] 1 K.B. 16; *Fraser v City of Fraserville* [1917] A.C. 187.
[61] (1887) 14 R. (H.L.) 33, p.34. See, too, *Jubb v Hull Dock Co.* (1846), L.R. 9 Q.B. 443.

be paid for the land—the land with all the potentialities of it, with all the actual use of it by the person who holds it, is to be considered by those who have to assess the compensation."

And in *Lanarkshire and Dumbartonshire Railway Co. v Thomas Main*,[62] Lord Kinnear considered it to be well-settled that a claimant was entitled "not only to the market value of his interest but to full compensation for all the loss which he may sustain by being deprived of his land".

The decision in *Thomas Main* also illustrates that, as with the assessment of damages at common law,[63] the courts did not adopt rigid rules in valuing land but were prepared to consider in the circumstances of each case what would best achieve, if not restitution, then a financial equivalent which was the next best thing. In *Thomas Main*[64] compensation was assessed, not on the market value of the land taken, but on the basis of the cost of equivalent reinstatement, an approach which Lord President Clyde described in *McEwing & Sons Ltd v The County Council of the County of Renfrew*[65] as "indeed a typical case of a common practice under the 1845 Act of using reinstatement value, instead of market value, to fix the compensation".

Early decisions by the courts on the measure of compensation for **4–07** injurious affection, the second head of claim under section 61 of the 1845 Act where land has been compulsorily acquired, suggest that here, too, they were concerned with a financial equivalent. However, it would seem that the measure of compensation was the whole of the depreciation in the value of the remaining land resulting from the taking of land and from the construction and use of the works. It was immaterial that the loss would not have been actionable in the absence of statutory authority. In *Cowper Essex v Acton Local Board*,[66] for example, the House of Lords held that the injurious effects on the remaining land of the construction and use of a sewage works on the land taken were not too remote even though no nuisance might be caused. In other words, the measure of compensation in this respect was somewhat more generous than the measure of damages for nuisance (see Chapter 11).

However, while the courts, in the relatively few cases that came before them, were asserting the principle of equivalence, it would seem that the great majority of disputed claims were being settled at first instance according to a yardstick which has been described as more akin to a "Rawlsian" measure of compensation.[67] Under the 1845 Act, claims not exceeding £50 were to be settled by the sheriff unless both parties agreed

---

[62] (1895) 22 R. 912, p.919.

[63] See, for example, *Hutchison v Davidson*, 1945 S.C. 395.

[64] See, too, *Corporation of Edinburgh v North British Railway,* unreported, but noted in H. Parrish, *Cripps on Compulsory Acquisition of Land* (11th ed., Stevens and Sons Ltd, London,) para.4–016. Also *Streatham Estates Co. v Public Works Commrs.* (1888) 4 T.L.R. 766.

[65] 1960 S.C. 53, p.63.

[66] (1889) 14 A.C. 153. See, too, *Re Stockport, Timperley and Altringham Railway Co.* (1864) 33 L.J.Q.B. 251; and *Buccleuch (Duke) v Metropolitan Board of Works* (1872) L.R. 5 H.L. 418.

[67] M. Bell, "Taking Justice Seriously: Rawls' Utilitarianism and Land Compensation" (1980) 3 *Urban Law and Policy* 23.

to refer the claim to arbitration: claims exceeding £50 could be dealt with either by arbitration or before the sheriff and in the latter case the parties could petition the sheriff to summon a jury.[68] The universal practice of juries and arbiters was to award an additional sum over and above the price for the land as an acknowledgement of the compulsory nature of the acquisition.[69] In England and Wales this additional sum was usually of the order of 10 per cent of the price for the land; but in Scotland in some cases of agricultural land it seems that this allowance approached 100 per cent. The Wharncliffe Committee, appointed by the House of Lords in 1845 to consider and report on the expediency of establishing some principle of compensation for lands compulsorily acquired for the construction of railways, was of the opinion that "a very high percentage, amounting to not less than 50 per cent upon the original value, ought to be given in compensation for the compulsion only to which the seller is bound to submit".[70] Furthermore, in assessing the prospective value of the land "merely hypothetical and often highly speculative elements of value which had no real existence have crept into awards as if they were actual; while elements of remote future value have too often been inadequately discounted, and valued as if there were a readily available market".[71] It would seem that awards by arbiters and juries were much influenced by the fact that the promoters were often railway companies where profit rather than the direct interest of the state was the motivation.

3. The Acquisition of Land (Assessment of Compensation) Act 1919

4–08   Anticipating a major programme of public works in the aftermath of the First World War, a committee (the Scott Committee) was appointed in 1917 "To consider and report upon the defects in the existing system of law and practice involved in the acquisition and valuation of land for public purposes, and to recommend any changes that may be desirable in the public interest". In their second report, the committee reflected the changing climate of opinion on the measure of compensation:

> "In our opinion, no landowner can, having regard to the fact that he holds his property subject to the right of the state to expropriate his interest for public purposes, be entitled to a higher price when in the public interest such expropriation takes place, than the fair market value apart from compensation for injurious affection, etc."[72]

---

[68] See ss.20, 21 and 36.

[69] For a discussion of this practice see F. Deas, *The Law of Railways Applicable to Scotland*, (revised edition by J. Ferguson, W. Green & Son Ltd, 1897), pp.292–299. In *Oswald v Ayr Harbour Trustees* (1883) 10 R. 472 Lord Young observed that "In the case of land compulsorily taken, the compulsion is an element of price none the less that experienced arbiters generally or invariably estimate it separately—usually by adding a percentage".

[70] Cited in F. Deas, *The Law of Railways Applicable to Scotland, supra*, p.297n(a). See, too, the "Second Report of the Committee Dealing with the Law and Practice relating to the Acquisition and Valuation of Land for Public Purposes" (The Scott Committee) (1918) HMSO, para.9 (Cmnd. 9229).

[71] The Scott Committee, *supra*, para.8.

[72] See above.

Many of the recommendations of the report were given effect in the Acquisition of Land (Assessment of Compensation) Act 1919. The object of the Act was to dispense with the "extravagant, dilatory, and cumbrous" procedures of the 1845 Act and "to provide machinery by which in case of dispute, a price that is fair and reasonable may be fixed, and fixed without unnecessary expense or avoidable delay".[73] In order to introduce realism into awards and to curb excesses, the Act did away with recourse to juries and arbiters and substituted a panel of official arbiters having special knowledge in the valuation of land to settle disputes over compensation.[74]

The central provision, however, was a set of six "rules" to be observed by the official arbiters in assessing compensation for the value of land compulsorily acquired. The position regarding compensation for injurious affection was left unchanged. Rule (1) abolished the payment of the additional 10 per cent by providing that "No allowance shall be made on account of the acquisition being compulsory". Rule (2) provided that the basic measure of compensation was to be "the amount which the land if sold in the open market by a willing seller might be expected to realise". The overall purpose was still to assess the owner's loss but that part of it reflected in the value of the land was now to be assessed under rule (2). In other words, so that there should be no doubt, the measure was now expressly defined as the objective "value to a willing seller" rather than the more subjective "value to the owner," a definition which, in the view of Scott L.J. in *Horn v Sunderland Corporation* was, more than any other provision, "likely to check exaggerated prices for the land sold".[75] The assessment was to be made from the point of view of a hypothetical willing seller on the open market criterion rather than that of the unwilling actual owner. Rules (3) and (4) imposed some qualification on the factors which could be taken into account in assessing the value which a willing seller might be expected to realise for his land in the open market. Rule (5) reaffirmed the use of equivalent reinstatement as the measure of compensation in cases where there was no general demand or market for the land. Rule (6) safeguarded the right to compensation for disturbance (see Chapter 10).

The 1919 Act rules gave statutory expression to equivalence as the measure of compensation for the value of land compulsorily acquired. The principle underlying this statutory measure is best expressed in what is generally regarded as the leading case on both sides of the border— *Horn v Sunderland Corporation*.[76] In that case agricultural land was compulsorily acquired and the claimant argued, successfully, that the land had development potential and it was so valued. He further claimed compensation for disturbance to his agricultural operation. This was disallowed by the court on the ground that valuation of the land for building purposes implied a willingness to bear the agricultural disturbance. Scott L.J. outlining the purpose of compensation said:

> "what it gives to the owner compelled to sell is compensation—the right to be put, so far as money can do it, in the same position as if

---

[73] H. C. Deb., Vol 114, cols. 2275 & 2276 (April 10, 1919), Sir Gordon Hewart.

[74] Acquisition of Land (Assessment of Compensation) Act 1919, s.1.

[75] [1941] 2 K.B. 26, p.40.

[76] See above.

his land had not been taken from him. In other words, he gains the right to receive a money payment not less than the loss imposed on him in the public interest, but on the other hand no greater."[77]

and later stated:

"The statutory compensation cannot and must not exceed the owner's total loss, for, if it does, it will put an unfair burden upon the public authority or other promoters, who on public grounds have been given the power of compulsory acquisition, and it will transgress the principle of equivalence which is at the root of statutory compensation, which lays it down that the owner shall be paid neither less nor more than his loss."[78]

The dicta of Scott L.J. have been cited with approval in a number of decisions by the Court of Session and by the Lands Tribunal for Scotland.[79]

4. Post-war reconstruction

4–09   The prospect of the massive programme of reconstruction to be carried out at the end of the Second World War placed the measure of compensation for compulsory purchase under scrutiny again. A committee (the Uthwatt Committee) was appointed to look at the whole question of the payment of compensation and the recovery of betterment (the appreciation in land values resulting from public policies and proposals) in respect of the public control of the use of land and to advise, as a matter of urgency, what steps should be taken to prevent the work of reconstruction being prejudiced.[80] The committee made an interim recommendation that because of the effect of the war on land values, compensation on the public acquisition of land should, for a temporary period, be based on the values prevailing at the last date when there was an undisturbed market in land. This recommendation was given effect in the Town and Country Planning (Scotland) Act 1945[81] which provided that in assessing compensation under the 1919 Act rules,

---

[77] See above, p.42.

[78] See above, p.49.

[79] See *D. M. Hoey Ltd v Glasgow Corporation*, 1972 S.C. 200, *per* Lord Justice-Clerk Grant at p.204; *Odeon Associated Theatres v Corporation of Glasgow*, 1974 S.L.T. 109, *per* Lord Kissen at p.114 and Lord Fraser at p.115; *Prestwick Hotels v Glasgow Corporation*, 1975 S.C. 105, *per* Lord President Emslie at p.108; *Miller v Edinburgh Corporation*, 1978 S.C. 1, *per* Lord Justice-Clerk Wheatley at p.6 and Lord Mulligan at p.12; *Smith v Strathclyde Regional Council*, 1982 S.L.T. (Lands Tr.) 2. For a modern restatement of the principle see *Director of Buildings and Lands v Shun Fung Ironworks Ltd* [1995] A.C. 111, *per* Lord Nicholls at p.125. Lord Nicholls stated that a claimant was entitled "to be compensated fairly and fully for his loss".

[80] "The Expert Committee on Compensation and Betterment Final Report" (1942) HMSO (Cmnd. 6386).

[81] Section 53. In *Powner and Powner v Leeds Corporation* [1953] E.G.D. 99, the Lands Tribunal observed of the operation of the corresponding provision of the English legislation in that case "put bluntly and with some reluctance, the claimants, by virtue of subsection (3) are denied compensation for the factual loss and can only be awarded something much less".

the value of any interest in land was to be ascertained by reference to the prices current at March 31, 1939. Provision was made for the payment in certain cases of an owner-occupier supplement.

This provision was subsequently repealed by the Town and Country Planning (Scotland) Act 1947 which introduced comprehensive planning control and which gave effect to the decision of the post-war Labour government to appropriate development value in land to the state. The intention was that land should change hands at the value attributable to its existing use. The 1919 Act rules were accordingly modified so that only planning permission for those limited categories of development listed in the Third Schedule to the Act could be taken into account in the assessment of compensation on compulsory acquisition.[82]

The incoming Conservative government in 1951 was committed to repealing the financial provisions of the 1947 legislation and restoring development value in land to the landowner. The difficult question was whether development value should also be reflected in the measure of compensation for compulsory purchase. Whilst considerations of equity suggested that it should, the government were concerned that, with the advent of comprehensive planning control, public authorities would now be faced, if the measure of compensation reflected development value, with paying a price inflated by their own policies, decisions and proposals. In the event, it was decided that compensation on the public acquisition of land should be restricted to existing use value plus any "unexpended balance of established development value" together with interest.[83]

This dual price system was a clear departure from the principle of equivalence and, not surprisingly, it was short-lived. The passage of time merely served to emphasise the discrimination between those who sold land in the open market and those who sold under compulsion to public authorities. The Franks Committee in its report in 1957 commented:

"One final point of great importance needs to be made. The evidence which we have received shows that much of the dissatisfaction with the procedures relating to land arises from the basis of compensation. It is claimed that objections to compulsory purchase would be far fewer if compensation were always assessed at not less than market value. It is not part of our terms of reference to consider and make recommendations upon the basis of compensation. But we cannot emphasise too strongly the extent to which the financial considerations affect the matters with which we have to deal. Whatever changes in procedure are made, dissatisfaction is, because of this, bound to remain."[84]

As a result of increasing discontent, development value was restored as an element in the assessment of compensation by the Town and Country Planning (Scotland) Act 1959.[85]

---

[82] Sections 47 and 48.

[83] Town and Country Planning (Scotland) Act 1954, s.32; and see generally on this J. B. Cullingworth, *Environmental Planning*, Vol. 10; Land Values, Compensation and Betterment (HMSO, 1980). For an explanation of the "unexpended balance of established development value" see Chap.13.

[84] "The Report of the Committee on Tribunals and Inquiries" (1957) HMSO, para.278 (Cmnd. 218).

[85] Section 1.

However, the introduction of detailed planning control meant that development value was no longer "the simple function of the forces of undisturbed demand and supply which it was in a less complicated age".[86] The 1959 Act accordingly set out a complex framework for determining what planning permission(s) could be taken into account or assumed in assessing the prospective value of the land acquired.[87] The purpose of the framework of permissions and assumptions is to place the claimant as nearly as possible in the position he or she would have been on a sale of the property in the open market (see Chapter 7). In other words, it strives to maintain the analogy which was central to rule (2) of the 1919 Act.

The 1959 Act also introduced additional provisions to be taken into account by those responsible for resolving disputed claims. To counteract criticism that the return of development value to the landowner would impede much needed schemes by imposing an unduly heavy burden of compensation on public authorities, provision was made in the 1959 Act for the recoupment by public authorities of some of the betterment generated by their schemes.[88] Any increase in the value of the land acquired due to the scheme underlying the acquisition was to be ignored in the assessment of compensation. And any increase as a result of the scheme in the value of contiguous or adjacent land held by the same landowner was to be set off against the compensation for the land taken. As betterment is treated somewhat differently on the sale of land in the open market, those provisions would seem to depart from the analogy created by rule (2) of the 1919 Act and to have implications for the principle of equivalence. This is discussed more fully in Chapter 8.

The statutory provisions governing the assessment of compensation for compulsory purchase were subsequently re-enacted in slightly modified form in the Land Compensation (Scotland) Act 1963.

5. "Putting People First"

4–10   During the late 1960s there were clear indications that the pendulum of public opinion, which in time of national emergency had supported a restrictive approach to the assessment of compensation, was now swinging back again. "The complaint made about the present basis [of compensation]," said the Chartered Land Societies Committee in a memorandum in 1968, "is that it produces compensation which is in some cases inadequate. This is precisely the reverse of the complaint made against the interpretation of the Lands Clauses Acts before the 1919 amendments, namely, that the compensation awarded was in many cases excessive."[89] This groundswell of "complaint" would seem to have been generated by the increasing use of compulsory powers to support major schemes of public works such as the programme of urban motorways.

---

[86] See *Compensation for Compulsory Acquisition and Planning Restrictions*, Chartered Land Societies Committee, 1968, para.17.

[87] Part 1.

[88] s.9; and see on this J. B. Cullingworth, *Environmental Planning*, Volume 10: Land Values, Compensation and Betterment, *supra*. The legislation also made provision for compensating "worsement" generated by such schemes—see Chapter 8.

[89] *Compensation for Compulsory Acquisition and Planning Restrictions*, para.16.

A series of influential reports[90] focussed attention on perceived inadequacies in the compensation code. The Commission on the Third London Airport[91] and the Urban Motorways Committee,[92] for example, both recognised that when people's homes are acquired for public developments, the occupiers who are obliged to uproot themselves suffer a loss over and above that represented by the market value of the property plus disturbance. This loss, which was referred to earlier as "householder's surplus," reflects personal upset and inconvenience, loss of social ties with the area and so on. The Urban Motorways Committee recommended that some extra payment should be made "in recognition of the real personal disturbance that is inflicted on [residential occupiers] when they are required to move".[93] Other reports, such as those from the Chartered Land Societies Committee and from JUSTICE highlighted amongst other matters, some of the illogicalities in the provision of compensation for injurious affection. These are discussed in detail in Chapter 14.

The government's response to this growing concern about inadequacies in the compensation code was contained in a White Paper, *Development and Compensation—Putting People First*.[94] This stated that:

> "The Government believe the time has come when all concerned with development must aim to achieve a better balance between provision for the community as a whole and the mitigation of harmful effects on the individual citizen. In recent years this balance in too many cases has been tipped against the interests of the individual. A better deal is now required for those who suffer from desirable community developments.
>
> The Government is determined to provide this better deal."[95]

Whilst reaffirming their intention to retain market value as the basis of compensation, the government announced that they were adopting the recommendation of the Urban Motorways Committee to make a lump sum payment to residential occupiers to reflect the special hardship caused by the loss of a home. Provision for "home loss" payments was subsequently made by sections 27 to 30 of the Land Compensation (Scotland) Act 1973 (see Chapter 12).

Farrier and McAuslan suggest that the objective of the home loss payment was "to provide for solace compensation in addition to the equivalency compensation based on the market value of the property". They go on to conclude, however, that, as the payment bears no

---

[90] See *Compensation for Compulsory Acquisition and Planning Restrictions, supra; Compensation for Compulsory Acquisition and Remedies for Planning Restrictions together with a Supplemental Report*, JUSTICE (Stevens, 1973); the *Report of the Commission on the Third London Airport* (HMSO, 1971); *Report of the Urban Motorways Committee: New Roads in Towns*, Department of the Environment (HMSO, 1972).

[91] HMSO, 1971.

[92] HMSO, 1972.

[93] See above, paras 12.18–19.

[94] (1972) HMSO (Cmnd. 5124).

[95] See above, para.5.

relationship at all to the value placed by an occupier on his or her home, it bears some of the hallmarks of a utilitarian approach to compensation. "The conclusion may reasonably be that this payment is being held as a sugar-plum to tempt people to give up their homes quickly and without dispute, thus helping to save on administrative costs."[96] It nonetheless marks some slight shift in the measure of compensation back towards the pre-1919 position.

The pendulum of opinion is continuing to swing in favour of more generous compensation. In a report published in 1989 entitled *Compensation for Compulsory Acquisition* the Royal Institution of Chartered Surveyors concluded that the time had come to pay an additional allowance in all cases of compulsory acquisition in recognition that the claimant is an unwilling seller and that, if he is an occupier, he suffers social and psychological upset for which financial equivalence makes no allowance.[97] The payment, said the Institution, should not be limited to occupiers. Publication of the report coincided with massive and strident opposition to a proposal by British Rail to build a high speed rail link through Kent from the Channel Tunnel to Kings Cross. The government's response was to produce a consultation paper seeking views on proposals to amend the law on land compensation.[98] The paper proposed no change in the fundamental principle that compensation for the compulsory purchase of land should be based on the open market value of the land disregarding any effect on that value of the proposal giving rise to the compulsory purchase. It did, however, invite comments on whether some further provision, apart from the home loss payment, would be appropriate for owner-occupiers who are displaced as a result of compulsory purchase.[99] In the event, the government decided not to enlarge the scope of the supplement but simply to increase its amount and availability to residential occupants. This was given effect in Part IV of the Planning and Compensation Act 1991.

4–11   Subsequently, the new Labour administration in 1998 commissioned a fundamental review of the laws and procedures relating to compulsory purchase and compensation. The review was conducted by the Compulsory Purchase Policy Review Advisory Group (CPPRAG). Amongst other things, CPPRAG briefly considered whether there might be any justification for moving away from the principle of equivalence as the measure of compensation. Given the return of a number of the utilities to the private sector during the 1980s and 1990s and their focus on the pursuit of profit as well as the public good, it was fitting to consider whether the time was ripe for a return to the more generous approach to compensation of the pre 1919 days. The Group concluded that equivalence remained the appropriate measure but the question was whether the current arrangements actually achieved that.[1] It went on to say that

---

[96] D. Farrier and P. McAuslan, "Compensation, Participation and the Compulsory Acquisition of 'Homes" in *Compensation for Compulsory Purchase: A Comparative Study, supra.* See, too, P. McAuslan, *The Ideologies of Planning Law, supra,* Chap.4.

[97] paras 2.12–2.13.

[98] Land Compensation and Compulsory Purchase Legislation, Scottish Development Department, 1989.

[99] See above, paras 3 and 8.

[1] "Fundamental review of the laws and procedures relating to compulsory purchase and compensation: final report" (2000) DETR, para.78.

market value compensation provided the most satisfactory means of achieving equivalence (paragraph 81) but it made a number of recommendations about the way in which the present compensation provisions could be improved. These are referred to at the appropriate points in this book. It also recommended the introduction of a business loss payment similar to the supplement paid to residential occupants (paragraph 97).

The Department of Transport, Local Government and the Regions responded to the CPPRAG report in a paper published in 2001.[2] It accepted the need to consolidate, codify and simplify the compensation legislation operating in England and adopted most of the detailed proposals, including an additional payment in recognition of the compulsory nature of the purchase (paragraph 3.17). This was followed by Law Commission Consultation Paper No 165[3] which set out proposals for codifying, consolidating and updating the compensation provisions in England, including suggestions for taking forward most of the matters raised in the CPPRAG report. Amongst other things, it proposed an express statutory statement of the general objective of the compensation code in the following form:

> "The right to compensation shall be a right to an amount (not less than nil), assessed in accordance with the principle of fair compensation, having regard to the following matters (as defined below): market value of the subject land; disturbance; injury to retained land (severance or injurious affection, less betterment); (where applicable) equivalent reinstatement."[4]

It remains to be seen whether similar reforms will be promoted in Scotland.

This review of the evolution of the law relating to compensation shows that, although there is nothing sacrosanct about market value as the measure of compensation (a different measure was employed pre-1919 and other measures have not been tried), it has proved to be resilient. It was introduced in the climate of national emergency following the First World War and was reinforced in the aftermath of the Second World War. That climate changed from the 1960s onwards and so did the rhetoric. The talk was no longer about the evils of over-generous compensation but about the importance of securing a fair deal for claimants. Nonetheless, market value still survives as the basic building block in achieving equivalence for claimants. However, the advent of the home loss payment, its enlargement in 1991 and the proposal now for an additional loss payment in all cases of compulsory acquisition is a timely reminder that the exercise of compulsory powers gives rise to disruption and hardship for those whose interests are expropriated. In the absence of a national emergency, it is arguable that Rule 1 of the Land Compensation Act rules, which states that "No allowance shall be made on account of the acquisition being compulsory", has had its day.

---

[2] "Compulsory purchase and compensation: delivering a fundamental change" (2001) DTLR.

[3] *Towards a compulsory purchase code: (1) compensation,* 2002.

[4] See above, Proposal 2.

While it is sometimes said that the objective of compensation is to secure equivalence for the claimant, it would seem that, like the principle of *restitutio in integrum* in damages claims, equivalence was initially a very generalised concept. It gave the courts flexibility to respond in whatever way seemed best in the circumstances for ensuring that a claimant was compensated for all loss. With the passage of time that flexibility has increasingly been replaced by detailed statutory provisions which prescribe how certain important elements in a claim for compensation are to be assessed. These have reflected changing perceptions in the distributive goals of society. The ability to apply general principles to the circumstances of a claim has been reduced.[5] The principle of equivalence is now largely, although not wholly, enshrined in statutory rules, the central provision of which is that the value of land shall be taken to be the amount which the land if sold by a willing seller in the open market might be expected to realise. Subsequent chapters examine these provisions and the extent to which they are capable of providing claimants with a financial equivalent of their loss. In the meantime, the Law Commission's proposal to include a statement of the objective of 'fair compensation' in a new compensation code, if enacted, may serve as a reminder to those engaged in negotiations that, in applying the rules, the goal is to compensate for all loss.

---

[5] It has not, however, been entirely eliminated. See, for example, the decision of the House of Lords in *Birmingham Corporation v West Midland Baptist (Trust) Association (Incorporated)* [1969] 3 All E.R. 172; and that of the Lands Tribunal for Scotland in *Smith v Strathclyde Regional Council*, 1982 S.L.T. (Lands Tr.) 2. See also, E. Young and J. Rowan-Robinson, "Disturbance Compensation: Flexibility and the Principle of Equivalence", 1984 J.R. 133. The Chartered Land Societies Committee in their Report in 1968 commented "it may perhaps be considered in retrospect that if the 1919 reforms had been confined to the appointment of the panel of official arbitrators, the precursors of the Lands Tribunal, many of the difficulties examined in this memorandum would have been avoided". In rather similar vein see the conclusion of B. Denyer-Green, "Agricultural Compensation: The Injustice of Market Value in Severance Cases" [1980] J.P.L. 505.

CHAPTER 5

THE DATE FOR FIXING AND VALUING INTERESTS[1]

Compulsory purchase procedures and the settlement of compensation **5–01**
for the interests in land that are being acquired in response to a notice to
treat or deemed notice to treat may be spread over a considerable period
of time. During that period the nature and extent of those interests and
the value of those interests may change. It will not be possible to assess
compensation until the point in time at which the interests are to be
taken as fixed and the date at which they are to be valued may have been
determined. The choice of one date rather than another may decide who
is to be compensated and for what and may have important consequences for the level of compensation.

Until the decision in *Birmingham Corporation v West Midland Baptist
(Trust) Association (Inc.)*,[2] the position appeared to be that the date of
service of the notice to treat was the key date for fixing both interests
and values in land. However, in *Birmingham Corporation* the House of
Lords rejected that date as the appropriate point in time for valuing
interests. As a result of that decision the date at which interests are to be
valued, generally referred to as the "valuation date," is now clear.
Unfortunately, however, the position regarding the date at which
interests in land are to be taken as fixed is now somewhat confused.[3] The
relevant dates are considered in more detail below.

THE VALUATION DATE[4]

In *Penny v Penny*[5] Sir William Page Wood V.C. said: "[t]he scheme of **5–02**
the Act [*i.e.* the Lands Clauses Consolidation Act 1845] I take to be this:
that every man's interest shall be valued, *rebus sic stantibus*, just as it

---

[1] See, generally, E. Young and J. Rowan-Robinson, "Compensation for Compulsory
Purchase: Equivalence and the Date for Fixing Interests" [1986] J.P.L. 727.

[2] [1970] A.C. 874.

[3] The Compulsory Purchase Policy Review Advisory Group (CPPRAG) recommended
that the uncertainty should be removed ("Fundamental review of the laws and procedures
relating to compulsory purchase and compensation: final report" (2000) DETR, para.85).
This recommendation was taken up by the DTLR (*Compulsory purchase and compensation: delivering a fundamental change*, 2001, para.3.5). See too the Law Commission
Consultation Paper No 165, "Towards a compulsory purchase code: (1) Compensation",
2002, para.5.78.

[4] See, generally, E. Young and J. Rowan-Robinson, "Compulsory Purchase and the
Valuation Date" (1985) S.L.T. 205.

[5] (1868) L.R. 5 Eq. 227.

occurs at the very moment when the notice to treat was given." That sentence, as Salmon L.J. remarked in *Birmingham Corporation*, was accepted for a hundred years as "holy writ".[6] It was endorsed by the courts,[7] adopted by the textbook writers[8] and consistently acted upon in practice.

Its application during a time of inflation in land values and in other costs such as has existed since the Second World War gave rise to very considerable injustice. Matters eventually came to a head in the *Birmingham Corporation* case. The corporation compulsorily acquired 981 acres of the City of Birmingham, including the chapel owned by the claimants, for a major scheme of redevelopment. It was accepted that the compensation for the chapel was to be based on the reasonable cost of equivalent reinstatement (see p.181). At the date of the deemed notice to treat in August 1947 the cost of reinstatement would have been £50,025. However, the corporation were not in a position to allocate a new site for the chapel until an advanced stage in the scheme of redevelopment and it was agreed that the earliest date at which building on the new site might reasonably have begun was the end of April 1961. By that time the cost of equivalent reinstatement had risen to £89,575.

The corporation contended that the general rule of law, supported by authority, was that interests were to be valued as at the date of the notice to treat, a contention that was accepted by the Lands Tribunal. The contention was subsequently rejected by the Court of Appeal and by the House of Lords.

Lord Reid and Lord Morris of Borth-y-Gest in the House of Lords both concluded that the decision in *Penny v Penny* did not support the proposition advanced by the corporation. In *Penny* an executor held a house on trust to permit the testator's sons to have the house at a low rent so long as they carried on the family business there. At the date of the notice to treat the sons were still carrying on the business. The executor argued that the effect of the notice to treat, followed by the taking of possession, would be to terminate the carrying on of the business, thus giving him the right to sell the leasehold interests, and that his interest as executor should be compensated accordingly. That argument was rejected. The essence of the decision was that compensation should be awarded having regard to the interests of the claimants as they existed at the date of the notice to treat and the remarks of Page Wood V.C. in *Penny* were, said their Lordships, to be construed in that context. They were not authority for the proposition that interests were to be valued at the date of the notice to treat. As Lord Morris observed: "what justification can there be for making an out-of-date valuation?"[9]

Having disposed of the date of the notice to treat their Lordships had then, of necessity, to select an alternative valuation date. It was clear that some flexibility was required as no one date would secure equivalence for the claimant on all occasions. In the words of Lord Reid:

---

[6] [1968] 2 Q.B. 188 at p.213.

[7] See, for example, *Horn v Sunderland Corporation* [1941] 2 K.B. 26; *Hull and Humber Investment Co. Ltd v Hull Corporation* [1965] 2 Q.B. 145; *Newham London Borough Council v Benjamin* [1968] 1 W.L.R. 694.

[8] H. Parrish, *Cripps on Compulsory Acquisition of Land* (11th ed., Stevens and Sons Ltd), para.2–058.

[9] [1970] A.C. 874 at p.903.

"No stage can be singled out as the date of expropriation in every case. Sometimes possession is taken before compensation is assessed. Then it would seem logical to fix the market value of the land as at that date and to take actual or consequential losses as they occurred then or thereafter, provided that the dispossessed owner acted reasonably. But if compensation is assessed before possession is taken, taking the date of assessment can I think be justified because then either party can sue for specific performance and the promoters obtain a right to the land, as if there had been a contract of sale at that date. In cases under rule 5 I have already said that that rule appears to point to assessment of the cost of reinstatement at the date when that became reasonably practicable."[10]

Thus, where compensation is assessed on the basis of equivalent reinstatement, the valuation date is the date when reinstatement might reasonably have begun. Although the observations of their Lordships on the position where compensation is assessed on the open market value of the land being acquired might be regarded as *obiter*, they provide, as Slade L.J. said in *Washington Development Corporation v Bamlings (Washington) Ltd*,[11] "authoritative guidance" on the position and have been followed in practice. The valuation date in such a case is either the date when the acquiring authority take possession of the property or, if earlier, the date on which compensation is agreed by the parties or determined by the appropriate tribunal.[12]

In *Birmingham Corporation* it was not necessary for the House of Lords to consider precisely when possession is taken or when compensation is "assessed"; nor did their Lordships have to consider the position where, instead of proceeding by way of notice to treat, an acquiring authority conclude a sale by agreement thus displacing the need to use a notice to treat or choose to employ the alternative procedure of making a general vesting declaration in respect of the land. These matters are now considered in turn.

1. When is possession taken?

After service of a notice to treat, an acquiring authority may serve a **5–03** notice of entry (see p.70) on the owner, lessee and occupier and after fourteen days enter on and take possession of the land.[13] The notice of entry is, however, merely permissive. Possession does not automatically follow upon expiry of the period of notice. In *Friendly Bar Ltd v Glasgow*

---

[10] See above at p.899. Lord Wilberforce agreed with the speech of Lord Reid and Lord Morris stated the relevant principle in very similar terms. Lord Donovan in his speech appeared to suggest a slightly different approach, but see the construction put upon this by Slade L.J. in *Washington Development Corporation v Bamlings (Washington) Ltd.* (1985) 273 E.G. 980. Lord Upjohn agreed with the speeches of Lords Reid, Morris and Donovan.

[11] (1985) 273 E.G. 980. But see *Miller and Partners Ltd v Edinburgh Corporation*, 1978 S.C. 1, *per* the Lord Justice-Clerk (Lord Wheatley) at p.7.

[12] See, too, *W. & S. (Long Eaton) Ltd v Derbyshire County Council* (1975) 31 P. & C.R. 99; and *Miller and Partners Ltd v Edinburgh Corporation*, 1978 S.C. 1.

[13] The Acquisition of Land (Authorisation Procedure) (Scotland) Act 1947, second Schedule, para.3(1).

Corporation[14] the claimants' public house was compulsorily acquired by the corporation and a notice to treat was served on June 19, 1969. The notice was accompanied by a notice of entry which stated that the corporation intended to take entry on August 1, 1969. In fact, possession of the public house was not taken until March 8, 1971. The tribunal concluded that a notice containing a date of intended entry could not be equated to the taking of possession. The legal effect of giving notice was merely to give a *jus possidendi*. Possession, observed the tribunal,[15] "requires actual holding or detention coupled with the animus to possess in order to clothe the physical fact of possession with its legal consequences". The valuation date was not August 1, 1969, as contended by the landowners, but the date of actual dispossession, *i.e.* March 8, 1971.[16]

A further illustration is provided by the decision in *Courage Ltd v Kingswood District Council*.[17] An acquiring authority served a notice to treat and a notice of entry on April 28, 1972 in respect of about 0.9 of an acre of vacant land, formerly an orchard. In July 1972, two workmen from the council under the supervision of a works superintendent entered the land, cleared a large area of overgrown grass and weeds, grubbed up a hedge and dug five trial bores. Subsequently a survey was concluded to establish levels and further site clearance work was carried out. A shed to provide shelter and storage was also placed on the land. In February, the owner attached a padlock to the gate to the land, a key to the padlock being passed to the council on February 21. The question in issue was whether possession had been taken in July 1972, in which case the compensation would be £22,500, or February 1973, in which case it would be £33,500. The tribunal held that July 1972 was the appropriate date. What had been done by the council was all part and parcel of the works for which the council required the land and was consistent with having taken possession.[18] Taking possession, said Douglas Frank Q.C. "must mean or include the doing of acts only consistent with ownership or the right to ownership unless done under some other power." Section 11(3) of the English Compulsory Purchase Act 1965, which permits access on notice for the purpose of taking levels and making test bores, was not a sufficient warrant for what had been done in this case.

In *Chilton v Telford Development Corporation*[19] the acquiring authority took possession of some 67.87 acres of farmland, following service of a notice to treat and notice of entry under the New Towns Act 1961 and the Compulsory Purchase Act 1965, in eight separate parcels between June 1978 and October 1980. The question in issue was whether

---

[14] 1975 S.L.T. (Lands Tr.) 18.

[15] Citing J. Rankine, *The Law of Land-Ownership in Scotland* (4th ed., W. Green & Son 1909), p.3.

[16] See, too, *Buckingham Street Investments Ltd v Greater London Council* (1975) 31 P. & C.R. 453 in which the Lands Tribunal said there must be "some overt act on the part of the acquiring authority." *cf., Harris v Birkenhead Corporation* [1976] 1 W.L.R. 279.

[17] (1978) 35 P. & C.R. 436. See, too, *Pandit v Leicester City Council* [1989] J.P.L. 621.

[18] Entry on property for some purpose unrelated to the acquiring authority's purchase of the land will not be treated as taking possession for compensation purposes (*West v Exeter City Council* (1974) 230 E.G. 1447; *Otterspool Investments Ltd v Merseyside County Council* (1984) 270 E.G. 46).

[19] [1988] J.P.L. 37.

possession was taken on a single date, namely the date on which possession of the first parcel was taken, or on several dates, namely the dates on which possession was taken of the several parcels. The Court of Appeal held that where notice of entry has been given in respect of the whole land, taking possession of part in pursuance of the notice is to be treated as taking possession of the whole. The valuation date for the whole land was accordingly the date of entry on the first parcel of the land. It would appear that the acquiring authority could avoid this outcome by simply serving a notice of entry in respect of each separate parcel as and when possession is required.

It would seem that the onus, in the event of a dispute as to whether possession has been taken, rests with the acquiring authority to establish that their actions amount to taking possession.[20]

The ability to take possession following service of a notice of entry means that acquiring authorities are well-placed to choose a valuation date advantageous to them. As the Lord Justice-Clerk (Lord Wheatley) pointed out in *Miller and Partners Ltd v Edinburgh Corporation*[21]: "In a period of rising values the acquiring authority can at any time before the final award bring forward the date of assessment by taking possession of the land." Apart from seeking to expedite the making of an award by the Lands Tribunal for Scotland, a claimant, however, has little unilateral control over the valuation date and could not, for example, act to anticipate a reduced award of compensation in a time of declining values. Lord Wheatley expressed the view that this inequality might "call for consideration in future legislation".

2. Date of assessment

Where the acquiring authority have not taken possession of the land **5–04** then, in the absence of agreement on compensation, the valuation date is the "date of assessment" of compensation.[22] In *Corporation of Hull Trinity House v County Council of Humberside*[23] the Lands Tribunal observed that the date of assessment could be one of three dates, namely, the date of the reference to the tribunal, the date or dates of the hearing, or the date of the decision. The tribunal concluded that the date of decision was inappropriate because, in practice, it would be impossible to assess values at the date of the decision unless the decision was given on the day of, or within a few days of, the hearing. There were also disadvantages in adopting the date of the hearing (although, as the parties were agreed, that date was taken as the date of assessment) because at the time of the hearing values might have changed and changed quite substantially between the lodging of documents under the Lands Tribunal rules and that date. On grounds of both justice and convenience, the tribunal considered there was much to be said for the date of reference. It would enable either party to fix the date of assessment thus going some way towards meeting the inequality referred

---

[20] *Burson v Wantage Rural District Council* (1973) 27 P. & C.R. 556.
[21] 1978 S.C. 1.
[22] *Birmingham Corporation v West Midlands Baptist (Trust) Association (Inc.)* [1970] A.C. 874.
[23] (1975) 29 P. & C.R. 243.

to in *Miller* (above). Furthermore, valuations and comparables would not have to be altered right up to the time of, or during the course of, the hearing.

In *W. & S. (Long Eaton) Ltd v Derbyshire County Council*[24] Buckley L.J., giving judgment for the Court of Appeal, acknowledged the convenience of adopting the date of reference as the date of assessment but concluded that it was inconsistent with the decision in *Birmingham Corporation* that the time for measuring the compensation does not arrive until the owner is physically dispossessed of his property, or the title to it passes in law or equity to the acquiring authority. Notwithstanding possible anomalies, the court held that the date of assessment was the date of the award which in practical terms meant the last day of the hearing before the Land Tribunal. The court added, however, that: "if in a particular case the tribunal were to think it likely that values had changed materially since the hearing and before the award was promulgated, further evidence could be heard and, if thought desirable, arrangements could be made for the award to follow almost immediately after the further hearing". In *Miller & Partners Ltd v Edinburgh Corporation*,[25] the Second Division had to consider the position when considerable time elapsed between the hearing of evidence as to values and the date of the final award, time during which values might vary substantially one way or another. The Lord Justice-Clerk (Lord Wheatley) concluded that a full reading of the speeches in *Birmingham Corporation* disclosed that where, as in this case, possession had not been taken, the valuation date "is the date at which according to law either party can sue for specific performance as if there had been a contract of sale at that date". In a case like the one under consideration in which the issue of compensation had been remitted to arbitration that date is the date of the arbiter's final award. Assessment at that date was not impracticable. Should a material change in values occur between the date of the hearing and the date of the arbiter's final award, arbitration proceedings are sufficiently flexible to allow a proper assessment as at the date of the final award. In Lord Milligan's view it was only at the date of the final award that the claimant's real loss could be quantified and the principle of equivalence satisfied.

In *Hoveringham Gravels Ltd v Chiltern District Council*,[26] where a case was referred back to the Lands Tribunal by the Court of Appeal to determine the amount of compensation to which the court had held the claimants entitled, the claimants argued that in assessing values regard should be had not to the values prevailing at the previous hearing but to those prevailing at the time of the determination of the matters remitted. The Lands Tribunal held that it would be wrong to extend the appropriate date merely because of an appeal. Such a course would produce anomalies; in particular, it might affect a decision whether or not to appeal. A claimant, for example, might be deterred in a falling market, because he would run the risk of the payment of a penalty

---

[24] (1976) 31 P. & C.R. 99.
[25] 1978 S.C. 1. It should be noted that the case was decided by the Second Division in November 1973.
[26] (1978) 39 P. & C.R. 414.

arising from reduced values. The decision in *W. S. (Long Eaton) Ltd* on which the claimants relied could be distinguished as the effect of an appeal to the Court of Appeal did not arise in that case.

3. Sale by agreement in the absence of a notice to treat

In *Washington Development Corporation v Bamlings (Washington)* **5–05** *Ltd*.[27] the claimants and the corporation, as is not uncommon, entered into a written agreement for the sale and purchase of the claimants' property comprised in a confirmed compulsory purchase order. The agreement provided that the price was to be agreed with the district valuer or, failing agreement, to be settled by the Lands Tribunal as if the necessary steps for acquiring such interest compulsorily had been taken under the New Towns Act 1965 and a notice to treat had been served on the date of the written agreement. No notice to treat had been or was subsequently served in respect of the claimants' interest. Possession of the property was taken piecemeal by the corporation in six parcels spread over a period from June 1975 to April 1980. The corporation contended that the valuation date was, in respect of the entirety of the land, the date of the agreement. The claimants argued that the proper date was, in respect of each of the several parcels of land, the date on which the corporation took possession.

Slade L.J., giving judgment for the Court of Appeal, stated that in view of the wording of the agreement the proper approach was to ask what would have been the valuation date if the necessary steps to acquire the interest compulsorily had been taken under the legislation and a notice to treat had been served on the date of the agreement. In the light of that approach it was clear from the decision in *Birmingham Corporation* that the date of the agreement (the date of the notional notice to treat) was not the proper date for ascertaining values. The proper date would be the date when the price was agreed between the parties or, in default, assessed by the tribunal or, if earlier, the date when possession was taken. In the circumstances of the case, the valuation date was the date when the corporation took possession of the several parcels of land.

4. General vesting declaration

An acquiring authority may, instead of proceeding by way of notice to **5–06** treat, make use of the general vesting declaration procedure (see p.73). The procedure is set out in section 195 of and Schedule 15 to the Town and Country Planning (Scotland) Act 1997. The effect is that "at the end of the period specified in a general vesting declaration, the land specified in the declaration, together with the right to enter upon and take possession of it, shall vest in the acquiring authority".[28] Once the acquiring authority are vested in the land they cannot withdraw and, on the other hand, it is open to the claimant to adjust and settle compensation at that stage.

The question of the appropriate valuation date where the procedure for expedited completion is employed arose in *Mrs Annie R. Renfrew's*

---

[27] (1985) 273 E.G. 980.
[28] Town and Country Planning (Scotland) Act 1997, Sch.15, para.7.

Trustees v Glasgow Corporation.[29] In that case a public house and three
tenement houses in Glasgow were included in an area the subject of a
confirmed compulsory purchase order. The order provided for expedited
completion of title and, following execution of a declaration of vesting
under paragraph 3 of the sixth Schedule to the Town and Country
Planning (Scotland) Act 1945,[30] a notice of title was recorded on January
12, 1966. The claimants were allowed to remain in possession of the
public house and were continuing to trade at the date of the hearing
before the Lands Tribunal for Scotland. The claimants argued that the
valuation date should be the date of the assessment of the compensation
by the tribunal. The corporation contended that the appropriate date
was January 12, 1966 when the title vested in them. The tribunal
concluded that, read in conjunction with the speeches in *Birmingham
Corporation* the valuation date, where the expedited completion procedure is employed, is the date of vesting—in that case January 12,
1966.[31]

In a period of rising property values use of the general vesting
declaration procedure has the advantage to the acquiring authority that
prices are fixed at the date of vesting and any subsequent increase in
property values is ignored. Having vested the property in themselves, the
authority may then lease it back to the former owner until such time as it
is actually required. In the meantime the claimant's compensation may
be dissipated in rental payments. The claimant may face other hardship
where a general vesting declaration is employed.[32] In particular, as was
argued in *Renfrew's Trustees*, in a period of rapid inflation of property
values, compensation measured at the date of vesting rather than at the
date of assessment or possession which may follow sometime later is
unlikely to be a realistic measure of the claimant's loss at the time he is
required to move. Because of such difficulties the Royal Institution of
Chartered Surveyors have recommended that where the vesting declaration procedure is used, the valuation date should be the date on which
possession is taken by the acquiring authority.[33] However, whilst acknowledging the hardship, the Lands Tribunal for Scotland in *Renfrew's
Trustees* pointed out that in such cases a claimant is in a position to
compel the acquiring authority to settle the compensation at the time of
vesting and if claimants choose to continue in occupation it may be
assumed that this is because it suits their purpose to do so.

THE DATE FOR FIXING INTERESTS

5–07 Interests in land are not static. The nature and extent of an interest may
change over time, existing interests may be transferred or extinguished,
and new interests may be created. It is sometimes important for the

---

[29] 1972 S.L.T. (Lands Tr.) 2. See, too, *Khan v Glasgow District Council*, 1977 S.L.T.
(Lands Tr.) 35. Also *Hussain v Oldham Metropolitan Borough Council* (1981) 259 E.G. 56;
Birrell Ltd v City of Edinburgh District Council, 1982 S.C. 75, HL; 1982 S.L.T. 363, HL.

[30] As incorporated in the eleventh Schedule to the Town and Country Planning
(Scotland) Act 1947.

[31] In the unlikely event that compensation is agreed or determined prior to the date of
vesting, the earlier date would be the valuation date.

[32] See B. Denyer-Green, "Compensation: Date of Assessment under a General Vesting
Declaration" (1982) 132 N.LJ. 697; also a letter by T. J. Templeman, published at (1982)
261 E.G. 107.

[33] *Compensation for Compulsory Acquisition*, 1989, para.6.38.

purposes of assessing compensation to determine the point in time at
which interests are to be taken as fixed.

1. The traditional approach

As indicated earlier, the traditional, although not invariable (see **5–08**
below), approach has been that the notice to treat fixes the interests to
be compensated.[34] As Lord Pearson observed in *Rugby Joint Water Board
v Shaw Fox*,[35] there could be drawn from the decisions in *Penny v Penny*
(above) and *Re Morgan and London and North-Western Railway Co*.[36]
"the principle that the nature of the claimant's interest is to be
ascertained at the time of (or immediately before or immediately after)
the service of the notice to treat". The traditional approach would
appear to derive from the view taken in early decisions of the general
effect of the notice to treat. In Chapter 3, reference was made to
statements made in a number of nineteenth century Scottish cases that
the notice to treat created a relationship similar in effect to that of a
contract between the acquiring authority and the landowner.[37]

The consequence of adopting the traditional approach may be illustrated by reference to the decision of an official arbiter in *Jennings v
Edinburgh Corporation*.[38] The claimant was the owner of a shop let on a
twenty one year lease. The lease made provision for rent reviews at
seven and fourteen years. At the date of the deemed notice to treat, the
first review was still a year away. However, when the owner's interest
subsequently vested in the corporation, the date for the first review had
passed and the right of review had not been exercised. The owner
argued, nonetheless, that compensation should be assessed on the basis
that her interest and that of the tenant were fixed at the date of the
notice to treat and that their respective interests should be valued
reflecting the possibility of a rent review occurring in a year's time. The
arbiter accepted this argument.[39]

In *Birmingham Corporation* their Lordships, as one commentator
said,[40] "expressed the effect of a notice to treat in a much lower key"
than had many of their predecessors (see Chapter 3). They appeared to
view the notice to treat as little more than notification of an intention to
take land from the owner.[41] As Lord Morris of Borth-y-Gest declared:

---

[34] H. Parrish, *Cripps on Compulsory Acquisition of Land, supra*, para.2–059.

[35] [1973] A.C. 202. See, too, the view expressed by Lord Hodson.

[36] [1896] 2 Q.B. 469.

[37] *Ayr Harbour Trustees v Oswald* (1883) 8 A.C. 623; 10 R. 85, HL *per* Lord Blackburn;
Forth and Clyde Junction Railway Co. v Ewing (1864) 2 M. 684, *per* Lord Justice-Clerk
Inglis; *Campbell v Edinburgh & Glasgow Railway Co.* (1855)17 D. 613 *per* Lord Curriehill;
Heron v Espie (1856) 18 D. 917, *per* Lord Justice-Clerk Hope; and *Mackenzie v Inverness
and Aberdeen Junction Railway Co.* (1866) 4 M. 810, *per* Lord President McNeil.

[38] Ref. No. 2/1967.

[39] See, too, *Square Grip Reinforcement Co. (London) Ltd v Rowton Houses Ltd.* [1967]
Ch. 877.

[40] F. A. Mann, "The Relevant Date for the Assessment of Compensation" (1969) 85
L.Q.R. 516.

[41] It, nonetheless, still determines the land to be taken and it generally entitles either
party to insist on completion of the transaction. Furthermore, the owner cannot increase
the burden of compensation on the acquiring authority by creating new interests (see
Chapter 3).

"A notice to treat does not establish the relation of vendor and purchaser between the acquiring authority and the owner. It does not transfer either the legal or the equitable interest to the acquiring authority. It informs the owner that the land is to be taken and informs him that the acquiring authority are ready to negotiate with him as to the price of the land. . . . It makes a demand for particulars of estates and interest and of claims."

Influenced by dicta in *Birmingham Corporation*, the Lands Tribunal has in several cases held that interests are to be considered as they stand, not at the date of the notice to treat, but at the valuation date. It is not clear, therefore, whether the traditional approach that the notice to treat fixes the interests for the purpose of assessing compensation has survived. It is not possible to reconcile the various decisions and dicta on this point and the position remains uncertain. These decisions and dicta are explored in more detail below.

2. Non-traditional approaches

5–09   Even before the decision in *Birmingham Corporation*, there are several cases which suggest that interests in land were not invariably taken as fixed by the notice to treat. In *R. v Kennedy*[42] a lease had 25 years to run at the date of service of the notice to treat. Under the terms of the lease the landlord was entitled to regain possession on giving three months' notice. Following receipt of the notice to treat the landlord terminated the lease on giving the appropriate notice. The tenant claimed the value of the residue of the lease as at the date of the notice to treat. This was rejected by the court on the ground that no claim had been submitted prior to the notice to quit. The lessee's claim was limited to the balance of the three months' period of notice remaining at the time of actual expropriation. As Davies points out,[43] by determining the case on this basis the court evaded the issue of whether the notice to treat fixed the claimant's interest. However, in *Banham v London Borough of Hackney*[44] (below) the President of the Lands Tribunal regarded the decision in *Kennedy* as being inconsistent with the view that interests are fixed as at the date of the notice to treat. "It is true," he said, "that the court did not go on to say 'The owner's interest too must be valued as it was at the date of entry' but I find it difficult to understand why this should not follow."

In *Holloway v Dover Corporation*[45] a leasehold interest still had five and a half years to run at the date of the deemed notice to treat. No further procedural steps were taken by the acquiring authority and the lease expired before possession was taken. It was held in the Court of Appeal that it would have been open to the lessees to invoke the statutory procedures and claim compensation at any time after the date of the notice to treat; they had not done so but had continued instead in

---

[42] (1893) 1 Q.B. 533.
[43] K. Davies, *Law of Compulsory Purchase and Compensation* (5th ed., Tolley, 1994), p.120.
[44] (1970) 22 P. & C.R. 922.
[45] [1960] 1 W.L.R. 604.

full enjoyment of the premises; no interest had in fact been compulsorily acquired from them and they were not entitled to compulsory purchase compensation. Lord Evershed M.R. commented: "I am at any rate comforted that this conclusion, I think, accords with plain common sense." Again, as Davies points out,[46] the court avoided direct consideration of the question whether the claimants' interest should be treated as fixed at the date of the notice to treat.

In *Soper and Soper v Doncaster Corporation*[47] the claimants were the lessees under a five year lease due to expire in January 1963. Notice to treat was served in August 1962 and notice of entry in September 1963. Since the claimants had enjoyed the full benefit of their lease, the Lands Tribunal awarded a nominal sum of £1 on account of the acquisition of their interest plus disturbance. *Holloway* was distinguished on the ground that in *Soper* the claimants had responded to the notice to treat by submitting a claim before the expiry of the lease.

The decisions in *Kennedy*, *Holloway* and *Soper* all predate that of the House of Lords in *Birmingham Corporation*. However, in a number of cases since *Birmingham Corporation* the Lands Tribunal, influenced by dicta in that case, have moved away from the traditional approach that the date of the notice to treat fixes the interests to be valued. In *Banham v London Borough of Hackney*[48] an acquiring authority rehoused a tenant between the date of the notice to treat and the date of valuation. The owner claimed compensation based on vacant possession. The President of the Lands Tribunal (Sir Michael Rowe Q.C.) concluded that in the light of the decision in Kennedy and of the speeches of Lords Reid, Donovan and Morris of Borth-y-Gest in *Birmingham Corporation* it seemed "impossible to say that the interests in land compulsorily acquired are immutably fixed by the service of the notice to treat". The true view, he continued, "would seem to be that interests as well as values must be taken as at the date of valuation or entry unless the owner has done something which so altered the interests as to increase the burden of compensation on the acquiring authority". The interests were accordingly valued as at the date of entry.

In *Bradford Property Trust Ltd v Hertfordshire County Council*[49] the tribunal (Douglas Frank Q.C.), while expressing agreement with what had been said by Sir Michael Rowe in *Banham*, reached a slightly different conclusion. The tenants of two houses being compulsorily acquired by the county council were rehoused by the local housing authority between the date of the notice to treat and the date of the notice of entry. The tribunal held that interests subsisting at the date of the notice to treat should be valued as they stood at the date of the notice of entry (*i.e.* no longer encumbered by tenancies), a conclusion which resembles that reached in *Soper*.[50] On the other hand, in *Midland's Bank Trust Co. Ltd (Executors) v London Borough of Lewisham*,[51] the

---

[46] K. Davies, *Law of Compulsory Purchase and Compensation, supra*, p.120.
[47] (1964) 16 P. & C.R. 53.
[48] (1970) 22 P. & C.R. 922.
[49] (1973) 27 P. & C.R. 228.
[50] See, too, *Metcalfe v Basildon Development Corporation* (1974) 28 P. & C.R. 307.
[51] (1975) 30 P. & C.R. 268.

tribunal found it impossible to accept that what had to be valued were the interests subsisting at the date of the notice to treat by reference to prices prevailing at the date of entry. "Our conclusion is that valuation at the time of entry can only be a sensible exercise or principle if the interests are to be taken as they exist on that date".

Acquiring authorities who had incurred the expense of re-housing tenants between the date of the notice to treat and the date of entry were, not surprisingly, aggrieved at being faced with claims for compensation from owners based on vacant possession value. This anomaly has been resolved by section 46 of the Land Compensation (Scotland) Act 1973 which broadly provides that in assessing compensation no account is to be taken of any change in the value of an interest caused by the re-housing of a tenant.

Support for the traditional approach that the notice to treat fixes the interests to be valued still, however, persists. In *Lyle v Bexley London Borough Council*,[52] for example, where the tenants of two houses were re-housed by the acquiring authority between the date of the notice to treat and the date of entry, the Lands Tribunal held that the owner was "deemed to be selling the actual interest he enjoyed at the date of the notice to treat, for which he receives the value attaching to that interest at the date the acquiring authority took possession". In other words, compensation was assessed on the basis of tenanted occupation. And in *Runcorn Association Football Club v Runcorn and Warrington Development Corporation*[53] the Lands Tribunal also took the view that the material date for determining the extent of the tenants' interest was the date of the notice to treat. In that case notice to treat was served in respect of a leasehold interest with more than two years to run. When the acquiring authority served notice of entry less than a year of the lease remained unexpired. The acquiring authority argued that compensation fell to be assessed under section 20 of the Compulsory Purchase Act 1965 which makes special provision with regard to compensation for tenancies for a year or less or from year to year. Given their finding on the material date, the tribunal concluded that section 20 had no application in this case.

In the light of the decisions considered above, one may readily sympathise with the Lands Tribunal member in *Metcalfe* who commented somewhat plaintively: "Having heard the arguments, I find it is very difficult now to reconcile all the recent cases dealing with the alteration of interests between the date of the notice to treat and the date of entry." The difficulty remains unresolved but it may be suggested that the approach which appears to accord best with the principle of equivalence will normally result from a rule that interests subsisting at the date of the notice to treat should be valued according to their nature or extent at the valuation date.[54]

---

[52] [1972] R.V.R. 318; 223 E.G. 687.

[53] (1982) 54 P. & C.R. 183.

[54] CPPRAG, *supra*, came to the same conclusion (para.85) and their recommendation for clarification of the position was taken up by the DTLR in *Compulsory purchase and compensation: delivering a fundamental change*, 2001, para.3.5. See too, "Towards a compulsory purchase code: (1) Compensation" (2002) *Law Commission Consultation Paper No 165* para.5.78.

INTERESTS IN LAND AND "THE SCHEME"

There is a well-established rule that any increase or decrease in the value   **5–10**
of an interest which is due to the scheme underlying the acquisition is to
be ignored in assessing compensation (see Chapter 8).[55] It is important,
therefore, to distinguish between a change in the nature of an interest
and a change in its value. For example, if, as in *Banham* (above), the
acquiring authority rehouse a tenant between the date of the notice to
treat and the date of valuation so that the owner gives vacant possession
on entry, does this result in a change in the nature of the owner's interest
or in a change in its value? If it is the latter, the effect on value is to be
ignored in assessing compensation.

The distinction is not always easy to see. In *J. & D. Littlejohn v City of
Glasgow*[56] a flat was vacated by the tenant after the date of the notice to
treat but before possession was taken by the acquiring authority. The
evidence before the official arbiter was to the effect that the tenant had
moved out because of the impending acquisition; had it not been for that
she would have remained. The arbiter decided that as vacant possession
was the direct consequence of the scheme of acquisition, the effect of the
scheme should be ignored and the interest in the property should be
valued as though the tenant had remained in occupation. In other words,
the arbiter appeared to treat the change as a change in the value of the
interest and one which, therefore, fell to be ignored under the rule in
*Pointe Gourde Quarrying and Transport Co. v Sub-Intendent of Crown
Lands* (see Chapter 8 for a discussion of this rule).

However, in *Rugby Joint Water Board v Shaw-Fox*[57] the House of Lords
treated a similar change as a change in the nature of the interest. The
water board had obtained planning permission in respect of a large part
of a farm for use as a reservoir. As a result of the permission the tenant
lost his security of tenure because the owner was placed in a position
whereby he could serve a notice to quit which could not be contested. A
notice to treat was subsequently served on the landlord who claimed
compensation on the basis that his interest was subject to an unprotected
tenancy. The water board contested this on the ground that their scheme
had altered the landlord's interest and increased its value. In other
words, this was an increase in value due to the scheme underlying the
acquisition which falls to be ignored under the rule in *Pointe Gourde*.
The House of Lords (Lord Simon dissenting) disagreed with the water
board, holding that the rule in *Pointe Gourde* applied not to the
ascertainment of the interests to be valued but to the value of the
interests when ascertained. The change in this case had been to the
interest to be ascertained. "[The] reversion to an unprotected tenancy,"
said Lord Pearson, "is a different interest from a reversion to a
protected tenancy."[58] The landlord's interest was accordingly valued as
subject to an unprotected tenancy.

---

[55] Land Compensation (Scotland) Act 1963, s.13; *Pointe Gourde Quarrying and Transport
Co. v Sub-Intendent of Crown Lands* [1947] A.C. 565.

[56] Decision of an Official Arbiter ref. No. 6/1969.

[57] [1973] A.C. 202 approving the decision of the Court of Appeal in *Minister of Transport
v Pettitt* (1969) 67 L.G.R. 449.

[58] See above at p.216.

Section 44 of the Land Compensation (Scotland) Act 1973 has been introduced to overcome the sort of hardship experienced by the agricultural tenant in *Shaw-Fox*. It applies where an authority, acting under legislation providing for the acquisition or taking of possession of land compulsorily, acquire the interest of the landlord or the tenant in, or take possession of, all or part of an agricultural holding. In assessing the compensation payable to the landlord and the tenant, there is to be disregarded any right of the landlord to serve a notice to quit and any notice to quit already served which would not be or would not have been effective but for the reference in the Agricultural Holdings (Scotland) Act 1991 to the land being required (s.25(2)(c)) or used (s.26(1)(e)) by an acquiring authority. There is also to be disregarded any entitlement of the landlord to resume land in the holding by virtue of a stipulation in the lease and any notice already given as a result of a stipulation in the lease which would not be or would not have been effective but for the power to resume the land because it is required by the acquiring authority.[59] Should the tenant have quitted all or part of the holding by reason of such a notice to quit or should land in the holding have been resumed by virtue of such a stipulation, it is to be assumed that that has not happened.

The tenant's compensation, assessed under section 44 of the 1973 Act, is to be reduced by an amount equal to any reorganisation payment which the acquiring authority are liable to make under section 56 of the Agricultural Holdings (Scotland) Act 1991; but if the resulting compensation is less than it would otherwise have been, it is to be increased by the amount of the deficiency (see p.278).

Similar provision is made in respect of crofters, landholders, and statutory small tenants.[60]

5–11   The decision in *Shaw-Fox* was subsequently applied by the Lands Tribunal in *Metcalfe v Basildon Corporation*.[61] A statutory tenant in occupation of residential premises at the date of the notice to treat was re-housed by the acquiring authority five days before possession. The first question in issue was whether the owner's interest should be valued on the basis of vacant possession or subject to the statutory tenancy. The tribunal, following the guide given in *Banham* and *Bradford Property Trust Ltd.* (above), concluded that interests as well as values must be taken as at the date of valuation so that the owner's interest was valued on the basis of vacant possession. The question then arose whether the resulting difference in the level of compensation for the owner's interest was an increase in value due to the acquiring authority's scheme which fell to be disregarded under the rule in *Pointe Gourde*. The tribunal concluded that, although the increment was entirely due to the scheme, the rule in *Pointe Gourde* had no application since it related to the value of an interest when ascertained rather than to the ascertainment of what

---

[59] See, for example, *Anderson v Moray District Council*, 1978 S.L.T. (Lands Tr.) 37; *Dawson v Norwich City Council* (1979) 250 E.G. 1297.

[60] Land Compensation (Scotland) Act 1973, s.45.

[61] (1974) 28 P. & C.R. 307. See, too, *Midland Bank Trust Co. Ltd (Executors) v London Borough of Lewisham* (1975) 30 P. & C.R. 268; and *Abbey Homesteads Ltd v Northants CC* (1992) 32 R V R 110, CA.

is the interest to be valued. The effect of the decision in *Shaw-Fox*, said the tribunal, had been "to remove from the ambit of the *Pointe Gourde* principle any increment stemming from the event, or even the possibility of the enlargement of an interest or the removal of an encumbrance". The right to receive this sort of "windfall" profit was subsequently removed by section 46 of the Land Compensation (Scotland) Act 1973 (above).

In *Murray Bookmakers Ltd v Glasgow District Council*[62] a lease provided that upon compulsory acquisition of the premises it would automatically terminate. A claim for compensation by the tenant following the compulsory acquisition of the premises was rejected by the Lands Tribunal for Scotland. The effective cause of the elimination of the tenant's interest at the date of the general vesting declaration was not the declaration, said the tribunal, but the private agreement between the parties to the lease without which the reversion would not have occurred. The landlords were entitled to full vacant possession value.

INCREASING THE BURDEN OF COMPENSATION

There may be an appreciable delay, perhaps a matter of years, between **5–12** the date of service of a notice to treat and eventual taking of possession by the acquiring authority. In the meantime, the owner may wish to deal with existing interests in the ordinary course of the management of the land. The service of the notice to treat does not prevent this.[63] However, it appears to be the case that, whatever may be the appropriate date for fixing the interests to be compensated, interests created or works carried out after service of the notice to treat will, if they go beyond what is necessary for the owner's continued enjoyment of the land and will add to the burden of compensation on the acquiring authority, be disregarded in the assessment of compensation.[64] In *City of Glasgow Union Railway Co. v James McEwen & Co.*[65] the railway company gave notice to *McEwen & Co.* of its intention to take their land under statutory powers. At the date of the notice, *McEwen & Co.*, who had been tenants of the land under a three year lease which had expired earlier that year, were in occupation of the land without any written title of possession. Shortly after service of the notice, the owner of the land granted a further lease to *McEwen & Co.* for a term of three years. A claim for compensation by *McEwen & Co.* in respect of their three year term was rejected by the court: "When the respondents obtained the only lease they have, they did so with such knowledge of what was going on as to preclude them from altering the state of matters, to the prejudice of the suspenders."

The underlying principle appears to have been slightly extended by statute. Section 1(3) and paragraph 7 of the Second Schedule to the Acquisition of Land (Authorisation Procedure) (Scotland) Act 1947, under which most compulsory acquisitions proceed, provides:

---

[62] 1979 S.L.T. (Lands Tr.) 8.
[63] *Cardiff Corporation v Cook* [1923] 2 Ch. 115.
[64] *Mercer v Liverpool, St Helens and South Lancashire Rly Co.* [1903] 1 K.B. 652 *per* Matthew L.J. at p.667; affirmed [1904] A.C. 461, HL.
[65] (1870) 8 M. 747.

"The arbiter shall not take into account any interest in land, or any enhancement of the value of any interest in land by reason of any building erected, work done, or improvement or alteration made, whether on the land purchased or on any other land with which the claimant is, or was at the time of the erection, doing or making of the building, works, improvement or alteration directly or indirectly concerned, if the arbiter is satisfied that the creation of the interest, the erection of the building, the doing of the work, the making of the improvement or alteration, as the case may be, was not reasonably necessary and was undertaken with a view to obtaining compensation or increased compensation."

The provision does not appear to be confined solely to interests, etc., created after the date of the notice to treat.

RISK OF DAMAGE TO PROPERTY[66]

5–13 In *Phoenix Assurance Co. v Spooner*[67] buildings were destroyed by fire after the date of the notice to treat but before the acquiring authority had taken possession of the property. The court held that the authority were bound to pay the value of the subjects as at the date of the notice to treat, that being the date of valuation. The loss resulting from the fire accordingly fell on the acquiring authority.

In *Birmingham Corporation* the House of Lords held that *Phoenix* had been wrongly decided. Lord Reid said:

"It seems to me to be wrong that the risk should pass as at the notice to treat although the promoters or acquiring authority then acquire no right or interest in the property: it would mean that the owner though still in full control would cease to have any duty to preserve the property or any incentive to insure it. It does not at all follow from the fact that [after service of a notice to treat] the owner cannot act so as to increase the burden on the promoters, that the burden on the promoters may not be diminished by events later than the notice to treat."

The position now is that the risk of damage or destruction of property which is the subject of a compulsory purchase order, and the responsibility for insurance, remains with the owner until entry or determination of compensation, whichever is the earlier.[68] Where a general vesting declaration is employed, the relevant date at which the risk passes will be the date of vesting unless, which is unlikely, compensation is agreed or determined prior to vesting.

This may be illustrated by the decision in *Otterspool Investments Ltd v Merseyside County Council.*[69] A notice to treat together with a notice of

---

[66] See, generally, J. Rowan-Robinson & E. Young, "Compulsory Acquisition, Compensation and Risk of Damage to Property" (1985) 30 J.L.S. 312.

[67] [1905] 2 K.B. 753.

[68] *Socratous v Camden London Borough* (1974) 233 E.G. 161; and *Lewars v Greater London Council* (1981) 43 P. & C.R. 129.

[69] (1984) 270 E.G. 46. See *Simpson v Stoke-on-Trent City Council* (1982) 44 P. & C.R. 226 for an illustration of the difficult position in which an owner may now find himself.

entry was served in 1973 in respect of a property comprising three flats. The acquiring authority did not, in the event, take possession until October 1982. In the meantime, the condition of the premises deteriorated. In July 1981 they were occupied by squatters. They were subsequently damaged severely in the "Toxteth riots" and, as a result, the building authority had them demolished in August 1981 because of their dangerous condition. The Lands Tribunal observed that until the claimants relinquished possession it was in their own interests to continue to maintain the premises and to insure against damage. They could, if they had so wished, have had compensation settled at an earlier date by referring the matter to the tribunal. As it was, at the date of entry the owners were entitled to compensation of £300, being the value of the property as a cleared site.

Where, however, damage to property is found to be caused by the scheme underlying the acquisition any decrease in value falls to be ignored under section 13 of the Land Compensation (Scotland) Act 1963 and the rule in *Pointe Gourde* (see Chapter 8). Thus in *Macdonald v Midlothian County Council*,[70] where the value of the subject property was depressed by some £300 because of the derelict condition of property on either side which had been acquired under the scheme and left vacant, the tribunal held that the depreciation was to be ignored in valuing the subject property because it was depreciation resulting from the scheme underlying the acquisition.

In *Gately v Central Lancashire New Town Development Corporation*[71] compensation was claimed in respect of a house and garage which had been left "standing alone amidst rubble and desolation" in an area cleared by the acquiring authority. While still occupied, the property suffered damage from vandalism. The Lands Tribunal held the acquiring authority responsible for 50 per cent of the diminution in value resulting from the vandalism, this being the reduction in value entirely due to the scheme underlying the acquisition. The authority, said the tribunal, were not entitled, because of the manner in which the scheme was implemented, to increase the risk of vandalism borne by the owner. In the same case it was held that damage to the claimant's garage during the course of the demolition by the acquiring authority of adjoining property was a loss which was entirely attributable to the scheme and one which should, therefore, be borne by the authority.[72] It does not, however, automatically follow that the *Pointe Gourde* principle will operate merely because property being compulsorily acquired has been left empty and has been vandalised. The vandalism may be due to a claimant's failure to take reasonable steps for the protection of this property.[73]

---

[70] 1975 S.L.T. (Lands Tr.) 24. See, too, *Kirby and Shaw v Bury County Borough Council* (1973) 228 E.G. 537.

[71] (1984) 48 P. & C.R. 339. See too *Blackadder v Grampian Regional Council*, unreported, Lands Tribunal for Scotland, March 18, 1992.

[72] In the alternative, the tribunal held that the acquiring authority could not take advantage of a state of affairs they had themselves produced (*New Zealand Shipping Co. Ltd v Société des Ateliers et Chantiers de France* [1919] A.C. 1 *per* Lord Finlay; also *Robinson v Stoke-on-Trent City Council* (1980) 256 E.G. 393.

[73] See *Arrow v London Borough of Bexley* (1977) 35 P. & C.R. 237; and *Lewars v Greater London Council* (1981) 43 P. & C.R. 129. See, too, R. Carnwath, "Vandalism and 'The Scheme" [1974] R.V.R. 562. For an illustration of the difficult position in which a claimant may find himself see *Simpson v Stoke-on-Trent City Council* (1982) 44 P. & C.R. 226.

THE DATE FOR DETERMINING THE PLANNING STATUS OF THE LAND

5–14   The value of land in the open market will depend in many cases upon its planning status. This status may alter over the period of the compulsory acquisition. In valuing land for compensation purposes it may, therefore, be important to know at what date its planning status is to be determined.

Sections 22 to 24 of the Land Compensation (Scotland) Act 1963 provide that certain assumptions may be made about the planning status of land being valued for the purposes of compensation and give some indication of the relevant date for the purposes of the assumptions (see Chapter 7). These assumptions are stated to be in addition to any planning permissions in existence at the date of the notice to treat which have not yet been implemented (1963 Act, s.22(2)).

Section 23(1) of the 1963 Act states that, if on the date of service of the notice to treat there is not in force planning permission for the purpose for which the land is being acquired, it is to be assumed that planning permission would be granted such as would permit development of the land for those purposes. And section 24 broadly provides that planning permission may be assumed for development which accords with the provisions of the "current development plan". The "current development plan" refers to the development plan in the form in which that plan is in force on the date of service of the notice to treat.[74]

Section 22(3) of the 1963 Act makes it clear that nothing in sections 23 and 24 of that Act is to be construed as requiring it to be assumed that planning permission would necessarily be refused for development other than that for which permission is to be assumed. Inevitably, however, such a prospect is likely to be subject to some discount for uncertainty. The 1963 Act accordingly provides a mechanism whereby a claimant may seek to upgrade that "hope value" to a certainty. In specified circumstances a claimant (or the acquiring authority) may apply to the planning authority for a certificate of appropriate alternative development (see Chapter 7) stating the classes of development which in the applicant's opinion would be appropriate for the land in question if it were not being purchased by the acquiring authority.

For a while there was some uncertainty about the relevant date for determining what, if any, alternative development would have been appropriate. In *Jelson Ltd v Minister of Housing and Local Government*[75] Lord Denning held that, as a matter of statutory construction of the English equivalent of section 25 of the 1963 Act, the planning authority must form an opinion as to what planning permission might reasonably have been expected to be granted at the date when the interest in land was proposed to be acquired. The Act stipulated that the date of the proposal was the date of the actual or deemed notice to treat or of the offer of purchase (see below). However, in *Robert Hitchins Builders Ltd v Secretary of State for the Environment*[76] Sir Douglas Frank Q.C.

---

[74] 1963 Act, s.45 (1).

[75] [1970] 1 Q.B. 243.

[76] (1979) 37 P. & C.R. 140. Applying the dictum of Lord Macnaghton in *Bwllfa & Merthyr Dare Steam Collieries (1891) Ltd v Pontypridd Waterworks Co.* [1903] A.C. 426 at p.431. See, too, an appeal decision by the Secretary of State for the Environment under reference APP/5193/D83/13 and PLUP 2/5193/B/1862 reported at (1984) 272 E.G. 659.

considered that, having regard to the scheme of the Act, the relevant date for applying planning policies[77] "should as nearly as possible coincide with the date of the assessment of compensation". He accordingly quashed two decisions made by the Secretary of State on appeals against certificates of appropriate alternative development on the ground that he should have regard to the planning policies at the time of his decisions and not at some antecedent date. Subsequently, in *Fox v Secretary of State for the Environment*[78] Roch J declined to follow *Hitchins* and reverted to the position in *Jelson*. He held that the English equivalent of section 25(3)(4) required the planning authority to look back, on a literal reading, to the moment immediately after the application for the certificate is made as well as to what might happen in the future. The matter was finally laid to rest by the English Court of Appeal in *Secretary of State for the Environment v Fletcher Estates (Harlscott) Ltd*[79] in which Buxton LJ, giving judgement for the court, held that the issue had been concluded as a matter of authority by the decision in *Jelson*.[80]

The relevant date for considering physical factors is to be determined by reference to section 30(2) of the 1963 Act. Regard must be had to the state of the subject land and the area in which it is situated at whichever of the three following dates is appropriate: (1) Where an interest in land is being compulsorily acquired, the date of the publication of notice of the making of the compulsory purchase order[81]; or (2) Where an interest in land is being acquired as a result of the service of a purchase notice[82] or a blight notice,[83] the date on which the notice to treat is deemed to have been served; or (3) Where an interest in land is being acquired as a result of a written offer to negotiate, the date of that offer.[84]

It follows that, in determining what, if any, alternative development would be appropriate, no distinction is made between the relevant date for applying planning policies and the relevant date for considering physical factors. As Roch J. observed in *Fox,* it is more 'elegant' that both factors should be looked at at the same date. However, the Compulsory Purchase Policy Review Advisory Group, in its Final Report, commented that this aspect of the judgement in *Fletcher* warrants further review.[85]

---

[77] Distinguishing *Jelson Ltd v Minister of Housing and Local Government* [1970] 1 Q.B. 243.

[78] (1991) 40 E.G. 116. Roch J was influenced by the judgement of Lord Dunpark dealing with the relevant date in *Grampian Regional Council v Secretary of State for Scotland*, 1984 S.L.T. 212.

[79] [1998] 4 All E.R. 838, CA.

[80] The decision of Roch J in *Fox* was referred to with approval; the decision in *Hitchins* was disapproved.

[81] See appeal decision noted at [1987] J.P.L. 659.

[82] See p.304. See, too, the appeal decision noted at [1987] J.P.L. 660.

[83] See p.328.

[84] See *Jelson Ltd v Minister of Housing and Local Government* [1970] 1 Q.B. 243. Also *Grampian Regional Council v Secretary of State for Scotland*, 1984 S.L.T. 1212; *Fox v Secretary of State for the Environment* (1991) 62 P & C.R. 459 *per* Roch J. at p.475; and *Fletcher Estates (Harlscott) Ltd v Secretary of State for the Environment* [1998] 4 All E.R. 838, CA.

[85] "Fundamental review of the laws and procedures relating to compulsory purchase and compensation" (2000) DETR, para.113.

CHAPTER 6

MARKET VALUE

6–01 As mentioned in Chapter 4, most claims for compensation for compulsory purchase are founded upon section 61 of the 1845 Act. This provides that in estimating the purchase money or compensation regard is to be had both to the value of the land being acquired and to any damage to retained land caused by severance or other injurious affection. In Chapters 6 to 10 aspects of the first head of claim—the purchase price for the land—are examined; severance and other injurious affection are considered in Chapter 11.

Except in cases where land is devoted to a purpose for which there is no general demand or market (see Chapter 9), the measure of the purchase price for the land is its market value,[1] together with compensation for other consequential loss. This measure derives from a recommendation of the Scott Committee in 1918.[2] The committee considered that the absence of a statutorily prescribed standard of value was allowing what they regarded as excessively high settlements of compensation. They recommended that the standard should be "the market value as between a willing seller and a willing buyer".

Although "market value" may appear to be a self-explanatory expression, it has had to be statutorily defined because, as the Sheaf Committee commented[3]:

> "it has to be ascertained in circumstances where there is in fact no market (because the acquiring authority has stepped in with compulsory powers). There must be rules for ensuring that 'market value' in the technical sense assigned to it in the compensation code is aligned with what the market would have paid in a normal transaction."

The theory underlying the standard, as the Chartered Land Societies Committee observed, is that:

> "the dispossessed owner could go out into the market and purchase with his compensation money a property roughly similar to that

---

[1] Land Compensation (Scotland) Act 1963, s.12(2). But see the discussion in Chap.9 of "cleared site value" as the measure of compensation for residential property below the tolerable standard.

[2] Cmnd. 9229, para.8.

[3] "Report of Working Party on Local Authority/Private Enterprise Partnership Schemes" (1972) HMSO Annex K.

which had been acquired, any incidental loss or expense being met from the proceeds of the disturbance claim."[4]

It must be doubtful, however, as the Committee also observed, whether the Scott Committee anticipated that the concept of market value in the post-Second World War planned economy would prove to be "something very different from the simple function of the forces of undisturbed demand and supply which it was in a less complicated age". In particular, the introduction of a comprehensive system of planning control has introduced considerable complexity into the assessment of the purchase price for the land. This has been further aggravated by the ability of public authorities to recoup from a claimant some of the increase in land values resulting from their schemes. Both factors reflect on the ability of a dispossessed owner to purchase with his compensation money "a property roughly similar to that which had been acquired". Because of this complexity it would seem appropriate to divide the discussion of the purchase price for the land into five separate headings:

(1) market value;

(2) development potential;

(3) disregarding the scheme;

(4) special values;

(5) disturbance.

This chapter is concerned with the first of these headings—market value.

RULE (2)[5]

The statutorily prescribed standard of value recommended by the Scott **6–02** Committee is now contained in section 12(2) of the Land Compensation (Scotland) Act 1963 (the 1963 Act). This provides that:

"The value of land shall, subject as hereinafter provided, be taken to be the amount which the land if sold in the open market by a willing seller might be expected to realise."

In *Oswald v Ayr Harbour Trust* in 1883,[6] Lord Young observed that; "In the case of land compulsorily taken, the compulsion is an element of price". However, a price to be ascertained by reference to the amount which the land might be expected to realise on a sale in the open market

---

[4] "Compensation for Compulsory Acquisition and Planning Restrictions" (1968) para.18.
[5] See generally on rule (2) W. A. Leach, "Market Value Under Rule (2): A Fresh Appraisal I-VII" (1975) 231 E.G. 459, 1003, 1095, 1237, and 1547; also "Compensation for Compulsory Acquisition" (1995) *Royal Institution of Chartered Surveyors* 1.17–1.29.
[6] (1883) 10 R. 472.

would now seem to exclude any element of solatium (see Chapter 4). To be doubly sure, section 12(1) specifically provides that in assessing compensation: "No allowance shall be made on account of the acquisition being compulsory."[7]

The term "open market" is not defined in the Act. However, in *Inland Revenue Commissioners v Clay* and *Inland Revenue Commissioners v Buchanan*, an estate duty case turning on a similarly worded provision, Swinfen-Eady L.J. stated that:

> "A value, ascertained by reference to the amount obtainable in an open market shows an intention to include every possible purchaser . . . the section means such amount as the land might be expected to realise if offered under conditions enabling every person desirous of purchasing to come in and make an offer."[8]

This does not necessarily imply a sale by auction or roup. "A sale takes place in open market," said Lord Johnson in *Glass v Inland Revenue Commissioners*, "if the subject is put on the market and the best offer taken, however made."[9] What is envisaged is the price which might be amicably negotiated at arm's length between willing parties with no necessity or anxiety on either side.[10] Subject to what is said below about rules (3) and (4) the proper basis of compensation under rule (2) is that which yields the greatest price for the land. In *Robertson's Trustees v Glasgow Corporation*,[11] for example, a local authority proposed to acquire a block of tenement property owned by trustees comprising a public house, shops, a store, and a number of dwelling-houses, some of which were subject to controlled tenancies. The trustees argued that each unit in the tenement, with the exception of the controlled dwellings should be valued separately. The local authority maintained that the property should be valued as a whole. The trustees' basis of valuation produced the higher figure. The court held that the trustees' approach was the correct one:

> "where compensation is being assessed under section 12(2), then, if on a sale in the open market the land or property might be expected

---

[7] In "Compensation for Compulsory Acquisition", *supra*, the RICS conclude that the time has come to pay an additional allowance in all cases of compulsory acquisition in recognition of the compulsion and that the claimant is usually an unwilling seller. And see p.100.

[8] [1914] 3 K.B. 466 at p.475. In *Priestman Colliers Ltd v Northern District Valuation Board* [1950] 2 K.B. 395 it was held that "open market" does not contemplate a purely hypothetical market to be regarded as exempt from restrictions imposed by law. Valuation of this "expectation" will be according to the methods normally employed by valuers. See W. Britton, K. Davies and T. Johnson, *Modern Methods of Valuation* (8th ed., Estates Gazette Ltd, 1989); A. Baum, *Statutory Valuations*, (3rd ed., London International Thompson Business, 1997); R Hayward (ed.), *Valuation: Principles into Practice* (5th ed., Estates Gazette Ltd, 2000); and A Bawm, D Mackmin and N Nunnington, *The Income Approach to Property Valuation* (4th ed., London International Thomson Business, 1997). See also *Encyclopaedia of Compulsory Purchase and Compensation*, para.2–1061.

[9] 1915 S.C. 449; 1915 S.L.T. 297.

[10] *Edmonstone v Central Regional Council*, 1985 S.L.T. (Lands Tr.) 57; *Glass, supra*.

[11] 1967 S.C. 124; 1967 S.L.T. 240. See, too, *Mrs Fulton's Trustees v Glasgow Corporation*, 1976 S.L.T. (Lands Tr.) 14; and *Carter v Windsor and Maidenhead Royal Borough Council*, unreported, but see (1988) E.G.C.S. 84.

to realise a greater *cumulo* price if sold in reasonable and natural
lots or sub units than if it were sold as a *unum quid*, it is that greater
price that is the basis of compensation."

Rule (2) introduces a hypothetical "willing seller" into the valuation
exercise.[12] In other words, any disinclination by the claimant to part with
the land is not to influence the assessment of compensation; neither is it
to be assumed that the claimant is compelled by circumstances to sell his
land for anything he can get. A willing seller, said Pickford L.J. in *Clay*:

"means one who is prepared to sell, provided a fair price is obtained
under all the circumstances of the case. I do not think it means only
a seller who is prepared to sell at any price and on any terms, and
who is actually at the time wishing to sell. In other words, I do not
think it means an anxious seller."[13]

And in *Robertson's Trustees* Lord Justice-Clerk Grant said "We have to
assume a hypothetical sale by a willing seller . . . in the open market.
One cannot assume that in such a sale the seller will act without due
regard to his own interests."[14]

The reference in rule (2) to the amount which land might be
"expected" to realise refers to "the expectations of properly qualified
persons who have taken pains to inform themselves of all the particulars
ascertainable about the property and its capabilities, the demand for it,
and the likely buyers".[15] Market value is not, of course, a precise
measure. It is an approximation. As Ungoed-Thomas J. aptly observed:
"It has been established time and again in these courts, as it was in our
case, that there is range of price, in some circumstances wide, which
competent valuers would recognise as the price which 'property would
fetch if sold in the open market'."[16]

RESTRICTIONS

From what has been said so far, it will be clear that statutory valuation **6–03**
involves "something of the hypothetical and unreal".[17] The valuer is to
assume a sale in the open market by a willing seller. The land which is

---

[12] One consequence of assuming a hypothetical owner would seem to be that in assessing
the value of the land the actual owner may be included as a possible bidder. Although no
mention is made of a "willing buyer" in rule (2) (*i.e.* one not acting under compulsion),
this would seem to be implied; see the Expert Committee, "Compensation and Betterment: Final Report," (1942) HMSO 185 (Cmnd. 6386); see also the RICS discussion
paper, *supra*.
[13] [1914] 3 K.B. 466 at p.478. And see *Glass v Commissioners of Inland Revenue*, 1915
S.C. 449; 1915 S.L.T. 297.
[14] 1967 S.C. 124; 1967 S.L.T. 240.
[15] *Inland Revenue Commissioners v Clay; Inland Revenue Commissioners v Buchanan*
[1914] 3 K.B. 466, *per* Swinfen-Eady L.J. at p.475 commenting on a similar provision in the
Finance (1909–1910) Act 1910, s.25.
[16] In *re Hayes' Will Trusts* [1971] 1 W.L.R. 758 at p.768. See also *Inland Revenue
Commissioners v Clay* [1914] 3 K.B. 466, *per* Swinfen Eady L.J. at p.475; *Church Cottage
Investments Ltd v Hillingdon London Borough Council* (1990) 9015 E.G. 51.
[17] Lord Johnston in *Glass, supra*.

notionally being sold is, however, to be valued subject to all its restrictions. As Lord Dunedin stated in *Corrie v MacDermott*:

> "The value which has to be assessed is the value to the old owner who parts with his property, not the value to the new owner who takes it over. If, therefore, the old owner holds the property subject to restrictions, it is a necessary point of inquiry how far these restrictions affect the value."[18]

Thus, in *Abbey Homesteads (Developments) Ltd v Northamptonshire County Council*[19] it was held that compensation should be assessed having regard to restrictions on use imposed by an agreement under section 52 of the Town and Country Planning Act 1971; and in *Stokes v Cambridge Corporation*[20] the compensation for land with development potential reflected the price a purchaser would have expected to pay to secure a satisfactory access to the land. In *Odeon Associated Theatres Ltd v Glasgow Corporation*[21] a derelict cinema was compulsorily acquired by Glasgow Corporation. The claimants, who were the landlords of the premises, claimed that in assessing compensation account should be taken of the rent of £3,500 which they received from a lease of the property. The local authority contended that the lease should be disregarded on the ground that it was in favour of a holding company. The holding company would have ensured that the claimants, as a wholly owned subsidiary company, would not have been permitted to sell the property to a third party subject to the lease. The claimants' interest in the lease was not, therefore, marketable and should be disregarded in assessing compensation. The claimants contended that for the purposes of rule (2), the attitude of the holding company to the claimants' interest passing to a third party had to be ignored. The statutory hypothesis of a "willing seller" and an "open market" meant that the fact that the landlords were likely to be restricted by the attitude of the holding company was irrelevant to the valuation exercise.

The Second Division of the Court of Session disagreed with the claimants. The correct approach was to estimate the value of the claimants' interest on the open market subject to the existing lease to the holding company but on the basis that the rent and the tenants' other obligations would be exigible only if the purchaser were a subsidiary of the holding company and that they would cease to be exigible if the purchaser were an outside third party. Assessment on that basis would, it seemed to Lord Fraser "give effect to the realities of the situation so far as one can give effect to them in relation to a hypothetical sale on the open market".[22] As Lord Kissen observed "if the appellants' argument is

---

[18] [1914] A.C. 1056 at p.1062.

[19] (1986) 278 E.G. 1249. Subsequently, in *Abbey Homesteads (Developments) Ltd v Northamptonshire County Council* (1991) 61 P. & C.R. 295 the Lands Tribunal held that the imposition of the restrictive covenant in the s.52 agreement was part of the scheme underlying the acquisition and that the diminution in value, accordingly, fell to be disregarded under the rule in *Pointe Gourde Quarrying and Transport Co. v Sub-intendent of Crown Lands* [1947] A.C. 565.

[20] (1961) 13 P. & C.R. 77.

[21] 1974 S.C.81; 1974 S.L.T. 109.

[22] See above.

correct they would be entitled to payment of a sum as compensation which they could not have obtained if they had tried to sell the subject voluntarily in the open market".[23]

A further illustration is provided by the decision in *Edinburgh Corporation v North British Railway*.[24] A strip of land in West Princes Street Gardens, Edinburgh, was compulsorily acquired from Edinburgh Corporation by the railway company for the construction of a railway. The terms on which the gardens were held by the corporation precluded any building on or alienation of the land and required them to be available for all time as a public garden. The railway company accordingly argued that they were worth nothing. The corporation, on the other hand, contended that compensation should reflect the cost of providing another strip of exactly the same quality. As this could only be done by taking a strip of Princes Street itself, the cost of doing so should be the measure of compensation. The arbiter held both views to be wrong. In view of the restriction, compensation could not be measured by the value of unrestricted land in a similar position; on the other hand, the strip was of value to the corporation as part of a public garden and the value of the garden would be diminished by its loss. This diminution in value was the measure of compensation.

POTENTIALITIES AND RULE (3)

The analogy which rule (2) seeks to create with a sale by a willing seller **6–04** in the open market means that not only is the land to be valued subject to any restrictions but also with the benefit of all its potentialities. "So far as rule (2) is concerned," said Lord President Clyde in *McEwing and Sons Ltd v Renfrewshire County Council*, "the value of land is not restricted to its actual use at the time it is taken. Its potentialities must be taken into account, for these would obviously enter into the market price."[25] The extent to which they will enter into the market price will depend very largely upon what assumptions may be made about the planning status of the land (see Chapter 7) and upon the extent to which the potentialities arise from the scheme underlying the acquisition (see Chapter 8).

Under the Lands Clauses Act such potentialities could encompass any special suitability or adaptability which the land might have for a particular purpose by reason of its location, its configuration or its surroundings. This could include any special suitability or adaptability which the land might have for the purposes of the acquiring authority although such potential could be taken into account only as a possibility and not as realised.[26]

---

[23] See above.

[24] Unreported, but referred to in *Corrie v MacDermott* [1914] A.C. 1056.

[25] 1960 S.C. 53; 1960 S.L.T. 140. See, too, *Commissioners of Inland Revenue v Glasgow & South-Western Rail Co.* (1887) 14 R. (H.L.) 33, *per* Lord Chancellor Halsbury at p.34; *Sri Raja v Revenue Divisional Officer, Vizagapatam* [1939] 2 All E.R. 317, *per* Lord Romer at pp.321–322.

[26] See *Gough v The Aspatria, Silloth and District Joint Water Board* [1904] 1 K.B. 417; In re Lucas and Chesterfield Gas and Water Board [1909] 1 K.B. 16; *Glass v Commissioners of Inland Revenue*, 1915 S.C. 449; *Sri Raja v Revenue Divisional Officer, Vizagapatam* [1939] 2 All E.R. 317. See also *Countess Ossalinsky v Manchester Corporation*, unreported but referred to in *Gough, supra*.

However, the ability to take into account such potentialities has been somewhat curtailed by section 12(3) of the 1963 Act,[27] as amended by the Planning and Compensation Act 1991.[28] This provides that in assessing compensation:

> "The special suitability or adaptability of the land for any purpose shall not be taken into account if that purpose is a purpose to which it could be applied only in pursuance of statutory powers, or for which there is no market apart from the requirements of any authority possessing compulsory purchase powers."

The effect of the 1991 Act amendment has been to narrow the scope of the rule. It is now directed at two situations:

(1) First of all, it provides that, in assessing compensation, no account is to be taken of any value due to the special suitability or adaptability of the land for any purpose to which it could be applied only in pursuance of statutory powers.

(2) Secondly, it also directs that no account is to be taken of any value arising from the special suitability or adaptability of the land for any purpose for which there is no market apart from the requirements of any authority possessing compulsory purchase powers.

These situations are considered below. The 1991 Act amendment removed a third situation in which the rule operated. This provided that no account was to be taken of any value which the land might have because of its special suitability or adaptability for a purpose for which there was no market apart from the special needs of a particular purchaser. That part of the rule had been aptly described as "the unsure progeny of a footnote in the report of the Scott Committee".[29] The Committee had expressed some concern about the effect of the decision of the English Court of Appeal in *Inland Revenue Commissioners v Clay* and *Inland Revenue Commissioners v Buchanan*[30] which involved the valuation of land for estate duty purposes. The subject house adjoined a nursing home, the trustees of which wanted to extend their premises. The value of the house to the nursing home because of its location exceeded its value in the market as a private residence. The court held that "a value to be ascertained by reference to the amount obtainable in an open market shows an intention to include every possible purchaser" including the trustees of the nursing home. The Scott Committee expressed the view that the price realised in that case was not the market value as between a willing buyer and a willing seller but was solely due to the necessities of the adjoining owner.[31] The intention of that part of rule

---

[27] See generally on rule (3) Q.F., "Compulsory Acquisition: Special Suitability for a Purpose, I–III" (1975) 232 E.G. 1101, 1169 and 1327; and A. Baum, "Marriage value and rule (3)" (1981) 260 E.G. 999.

[28] See s.79 and Sch.17, para.5.

[29] J Kekwick, "On Rule (3)" (1955) *Chartered Surveyor* 15.

[30] [1914] 3 K.B. 466.

[31] (1918) Cd.9229, footnote to para.10.

(3) would seem to have been to eliminate any value arising from such potentiality where there was only one person in the market. It came into play typically where the land acquired was the key to the development of other land. However, tribunals and the courts were reluctant to apply the rule in practice. They seemed to be, as one commentator observed, "motivated by the view that the rule is a restriction placed upon the generally accepted 'fair' measure of compensation afforded by rule (2). They therefore seem to perceive their duty to be the circumnavigation of the rule whenever possible".[32] Not surprisingly, there was pressure for change and in a letter from the Scottish Development Department to the Convention of Scottish Local Authorities dated August 13, 1980, the Department stated:

> "It is now felt that there is no justification for modifying the market value where the land has special suitability to the needs of a particular purchaser and it is proposed to amend the provision accordingly."

This was eventually achieved by the 1991 Act which repealed the 'special purchaser' part of the rule.

The two situations in which rule (3) still applies come into operation **6–05** where land has a quality which makes it specially suitable or adaptable for any purpose.[33] In *Batchelor v Kent County Council*[34] the land comprised in the compulsory purchase order provided the most suitable access to other development land but it was not the only land across which access could be taken. Rule (3) was held not to apply. In the Court of Appeal, Mann LJ concluded that, although a special suitability could be found where land has a positional advantage for the purpose in hand, "most suitable does not correspond with specially suitable".

The two limbs of rule (3) are now considered in turn.

(i)   Land has a special suitability or adaptability for a purpose to which it could be applied only in pursuance of statutory powers: This part of rule (3) would seem to be directed at eliminating the basis of value permitted by the Privy Council in *Cedar Rapids Manufacturing and Power Co v Lacoste.*[35] In that case the purpose for which the land was specially suited, in the absence of the actual acquisition, was as part of a water power development, a purpose which could only be achieved if appropriate statutory powers were granted. The Privy Council concluded that if the land was put up for auction, "there was a probability of a purchaser who was looking out for special advantages being content to give this enhanced value in the hope that he would get the other powers and acquire the other rights which were necessary for a realised scheme". The compensation should accordingly reflect this enhanced value.

---

[32] T.J. Templeman (1981) 260 E.G. 1171. In both *Dicconson Holdings Ltd v St Helen's Metropolitan Borough Council* (1978) 249 E.G. 1075, 1178 and *Chapman, Lowry and Puttick v Chichester District Council* (1984) 269 E.G. 955, for example, the Lands Tribunal was concerned that the application of rule (3) would deny the claimants equivalence.
[33] *Batchelor v Kent County Council* [1990] 14 E.G. 129.
[34] See above.
[35] [1914] A.C. 569.

This part of rule (3) is designed to eliminate this enhanced value when assessing compensation. For example, in *Livesey v Central Electricity Generating Board*[36] agricultural land was acquired as the site for a power station. The claimant based his claim on the special suitability of the land as the site for a power station. The Lands Tribunal held that as statutory powers were required to use the land as a power station, rule (3) applied to eliminate that potentiality. On the other hand, in *Allan v Banff and Buchan District Council*[37] the Lands Tribunal for Scotland declined to accept that rule (3) applied to eliminate value attributable to the special suitability or adaptability of the land in question for the extraction of sand and gravel and for the disposal of waste. These were not purposes to which it could be applied only in pursuance of statutory powers. There would have existed a market for the subject land which would have extended to contractors in the private sector. More questionable is the decision of an official arbiter in *Trustees of Young v Central Land Board*.[38] Land was acquired for new town purposes within the designated area of East Kilbride New Town. A claim was lodged based on the value of the land for new town purposes. That basis of claim was rightly rejected by the arbiter (see Chapter 8) but on the ground that rule (3) operated to exclude any potentiality due to the special suitability of the land for new town purposes, that being a purpose to which the land could be put only in pursuance of statutory powers. It is not, however, clear from the decision whether the land had a quality or some physical attribute which made it specially suitable for new town purposes, thus bringing rule (3) into operation.

However, the decision of the House of Lords in *Hertfordshire County Council v Ozanne*[39] makes it clear that the use of the word 'only' means that this part of the rule only applies where statutory powers are a legal requirement for the purpose in question. Lord Mackay of Clashfern giving judgement for the House said "the statutory powers in question must be powers enabling a person entitled to use the land to apply it to the purpose in question and since the purpose in question is one to which the land could be applied *only* in pursuance of the statutory powers the statutory powers must be necessary to enable such person to use the land for that purpose. I do not see how statutory powers not related to the use of the land acquired could form a basis for the application of this part of the rule".

In that case, the acquiring authority argued that the land in question had an enhanced value over the agricultural value only in respect of its special suitability or adaptability for the purpose of providing a road realignment which would enable development to proceed. To use the land for the realignment, it was necessary to stop up part of the existing road and as the road was a public road, such stopping-up required the exercise of statutory powers. The House concluded that statutory powers conferred on the Secretary of State to order the stopping-up of a

---

[36] (1965) E.G.D. 205. See, too, *Hertfordshire County Council v Ozanne* (1991) 13 E.G. 157.

[37] Unreported, June 29, 1993, Lands Tribunal for Scotland.

[38] Ref. No. 11–18/1955.

[39] (1991) 13 E.G. 157

highway on land being acquired could not form the basis of the application of this part of the rule to the land acquired. "I consider", continued Lord Mackay, "that statutory powers conferred upon the Secretary of State to order the stopping-up of a highway on land which is not part of the land being acquired could not form the basis of the application of this part of the rule to the land acquired." If the argument of the acquiring authority was to prevail, it would bring within the compass of the rule a purpose to which a piece of land could be put only after obtaining some particular statutory consent such as a planning permission. To exclude any value attached to such a consent would clearly be absurd.

It should be noted, as the Uthwatt Committee pointed out, that, if the purpose is one which may also be achieved in the absence of statutory powers, its effect on value may properly be taken into account.

(ii) Land has a special suitability or adaptability for a purpose for which there is no market apart from the requirements of any authority possessing compulsory purchase powers: No account shall be taken of the special suitability or adaptability of the land for a purpose for which there is no market apart from the requirements of any authority possessing compulsory purchase powers.

This part of rule (3) was added during the passage through Parliament of the Acquisition of Land (Assessment of Compensation) Bill (which became the Act of 1919). Its object, notes the Royal Institution of Chartered Surveyors (RICS)[40] was to ensure that when a public authority was purchasing land under compulsory powers the value should be determined by reference to the private demand for the land without regard to the fact that a public body was in the market.

However, as the Uthwatt Committee pointed out, this part of the rule fails to achieve its object:

> "it is directed to excluding special adaptability 'for a purpose for which there is no market' apart from the requirements of public authorities, rather than to excluding enhancement of value by reason of any demand by public authorities, whether or not competitive."[41]

The committee expressed the view that any increased value due to public **6–06** demand for land should be excluded in assessing the compensation payable on acquisition and went on to recommend that this part of rule (3) should be recast so as to achieve its objective. The RICS commented that the Uthwatt proposals "are too wide at a time when public authorities are increasingly competing for land which is equally suitable for private or public purposes".

CPPRAG considered how far it was appropriate for the restrictions in rule (3) to continue to apply in situations where the newly privatised utilities, operating principally on a profit-making basis, retain com-

---

[40] See "Compensation for Compulsory Acquisition" (1995) RICS 1.33.
[41] Expert Committee, "Compensation and Betterment: Final Report" (1942) HMSO 187 (Cmnd. 6386).

pulsory purchase powers and where compulsory purchase orders are being promoted by local authorities acting in partnership with developers to achieve a profit-making development.[42] Their conclusion was that the reform of rule (3) was bound up with the reform of the rule that the effects of the scheme should be disregarded in assessing compensation (see Chapter 8) and that both should be reviewed together.[43] A subsequent review by the Law Commission concluded that the judicial rule in *Pointe Gourde Quarrying and Transport Co. v Subintendent of Crown Lands*[44] had expanded to fill the place of rule (3). The scope of the rule had been further cut back by the Planning and Compensation Act 1991 (see p.128) to the point where it now served little remaining purpose and could be repealed.[45]

RULE (4)

6–07   Section 12(4) of the 1963 Act provides that:

> "Where the value of the land is increased by reason of the use thereof or of any premises thereon in a manner which could be restrained by any court, or is contrary to law, or is detrimental to the health of the occupants of the premises or to the public health, the amount of that increase shall not be taken into account."

Rule (4) is concerned with cases where a proportion of the market value results from what may loosely be termed an "unlawful" use. The rule provides that the value attributable to that use is to be disregarded in assessing compensation.

In *Hughes v Doncaster Metropolitan Borough Council*[46] the House of Lords held that rule (4) applies to the assessment of compensation generally, including any element referable to disturbance.

Just what activities are covered by rule (4) is a little uncertain, although this is not a matter which seems to have given rise to much difficulty in practice. The rule is derived from the report of the Scott Committee who recommended that "no enhancement of market value should be taken into account which arises from the use of the premises in question in a manner contrary to sanitary laws and regulations".[47]

---

[42] See "Fundamental review of the laws and procedures relating to compulsory purchase and compensation: final report" (2000) DETR 100. See too "Compensation for Compulsory Acquisition" (1995) RICS 1.36–1.37. The Scottish review of compulsory purchase and compensation recommended that privatised utilities should obtain a "public interest certificate" if they wish to benefit from the application of rule (3) (I Murning, Dundas & Wilson, and Montagu Evans, *Review of Compulsory Purchase and Land Compensation* (2001) *Scottish Executive Central Research Unit* 6.15).

[43] At the time of writing, the matter is being considered in England by the Law Commission (see "Towards a compulsory purchase code: (1) compensation", (2002) *Law Commission Consultation Paper No 165* Part VI).

[44] [1947] A.C. 565.

[45] "Towards a compulsory purchase code: (1) compensation" (2002) *Consultation Paper No 165*, Appendix 5, A93–A97.

[46] (1991) 61 P. & C.R. 355, HL.

[47] (1918) HMSO para.11 (Cmnd. 9229).

What the committee appeared to have in mind was any value resulting from the use of premises which were overcrowded, unfit or which constituted a statutory nuisance. This sort of situation is now partly covered by section 17 of and Schedule 2 to the 1963 Act, as substituted by section 339(2) of and Schedule 23, paragraph 10 to the Housing (Scotland) Act 1987, which broadly provide that in assessing compensation for the compulsory purchase of residential property which is below what is called the "tolerable standard" the assumption is that the property has no value and compensation is based on the value of the land as a cleared site (see Chapter 9). These provisions and rule (4) would appear to overlap. It should be noted that, where the value of land is increased by a use which is detrimental to the health of the occupants of the premises or to the public health, that use does not have to be capable of restraint at law to bring rule (4) into operation.

Whether a particular use of land is one which could be restrained by a court, for example, as a nuisance, is a question to which it will not always be possible to give a precise answer. Where the matter is in doubt, it would seem, as Corfield and Carnwath suggest,[48] that the likelihood of restraint should be taken into account.

A use of land which is being carried on without planning permission but which is immune from enforcement action is not to be treated as 'contrary to law' for the purposes of rule (4).[49] Such a use would attract value on a sale in the open market and it would be inequitable to deprive the owner of such value on a compulsory purchase of the land.

---

[48] Sir Frederick Corfield and R. J. A. Carnwath, *Compulsory Acquisition and Compensation* (Butterworths, 1978), p.180.

[49] *Hughes v Doncaster Metropolitan Borough Council* (1991) 61 P. & C.R. 355, HL. And see now the Town and Country Planning (Scotland) Act 1997, s.150(2) which provides that, for the purposes of that Act, if no enforcement action may be taken in respect of a use or operation because the time for taking action has expired, the use or operation is lawful.

CHAPTER 7

DEVELOPMENT POTENTIAL

INTRODUCTION

7–01 In Chapter 6 it was pointed out that the value of land "sold in the open market by a willing seller"[1] is not to be measured solely by reference to the use to which it is being put at the time it is compulsorily acquired; account may also be taken of the potential which it may have for some other more profitable use.[2] As Lord Romer observed in *Sri Raja v Revenue Divisional Officer, Vizagapatam*:

> "No authority, indeed, is required for this proposition. It is a self-evident one. No one can suppose, in the case of land which is certain, or even likely, to be used in the immediate or reasonably near future for building purposes, but which at the valuation date is waste land, or is being used for agricultural purposes, that the owner, however willing a vendor, will be content to sell the land for its value as waste or agricultural land, as the case may be. It is plain that in ascertaining its value the possibility of its being used for building purposes would have to be taken into account."[3]

However, to realise the development potential of land in the real world, a landowner would have to abandon the existing use and incur any consequential disturbance; it is implicit in the realisation of such potential that disturbance may occur. If, therefore, land is valued on the basis of its potentiality for some other more profitable use, there should not be included in that value an element for disturbance, otherwise the claimant will receive more than his actual loss.[4] In such circumstances, as Cripps states: "the land has two values; (i) existing use value plus disturbance; (ii) potential value. The claimant is entitled to whichever is the higher".[5]

---

[1] Land Compensation (Scotland) Act 1963, s.12(2).

[2] *McEwing v County Council for the Council of Renfrew*, 1960 S.C. 53; 1960 S.L.T. 140, *per* Lord President Clyde; see also *Commissioners of Inland Revenue v Glasgow and South Western Rail Co.* (1887) 14 R. 33, HL *per* Lord Chancellor Halsbury. But note the operation of rule (3) (see Chapter 6).

[3] [1939] 2 All E.R. 317.

[4] *Horn v Sunderland Corporation* [1941] 2 K.B. 26; and see *D. M. Hoey Ltd v Glasgow Corporation*, 1972 S.C. 200. Compensation for disturbance is discussed in Chapter 10.

[5] H. Parrish, *Cripps on Compulsory Acquisition of Land* (11th ed., Stevens and Sons Ltd, London), para. 4–217.

Before the introduction of planning control the assessment of the development potential of land was simply a valuation problem. Now, however, this potential depends to a very considerable extent upon the obtaining of planning permission. Planning permission is required for the development of land.[6] In some situations a purchaser may, of course, be willing to speculate on the prospect of obtaining such permission but where this occurs, any value attributable to the development potential of the land is likely to be subject to a discount because of uncertainty.

Planning permission alone, though, is not enough to create development value. As Denning M.R. observed in *Camrose (Viscount) v Basingstoke Corporation* "it is not planning permission by itself which increases value. It is planning permission coupled with demand".[7] Thus, in *Bromilow v Greater Manchester Council*[8] the English Lands Tribunal held that a claimant, who was entitled to assume planning permission for the development of land for offices, could not obtain development value as there would be no demand for the land for that development. The site was in an area in which industrial use predominated; there was a large engineering works 50 yards away and an unattractive and obnoxious smelling bone factory 100 yards away. Because of this the tribunal concluded that there would be no demand for the land for development for offices.

On a sale in the open market, either the vendor or purchaser may test the development potential of land by submitting one or more planning applications. Where land is being acquired by a public authority, however, such an approach is likely to prove unhelpful because any application will probably be refused on the ground that the land is required for public purposes. If a claimant is to be placed in as good a position as on a sale in the open market, some alternative mechanism is required for establishing the planning position of land which is being compulsorily acquired. Such a mechanism is provided in sections 22–24 and Part IV of the 1963 Act, as amended by the Planning and Compensation Act 1991.

Section 22(1) provides that for the purpose of assessing compensation such one or more of the assumptions[9] as to planning permission mentioned in sections 23 and 24 as are applicable to the land being acquired,[10] or any part of it, shall be made in ascertaining its value.[11]

There are six assumptions (see below). Their object, as Leach states, "is that, once it has been established that any one or more of them may be made, there should be certainty in respect of permission for the relevant development or developments so that valuations can be made as

---

[6] Town and Country Planning (Scotland) Act 1997, s.28(1).
[7] [1966] 1 W.L.R. 1100.
[8] (1975) 29 P. & C.R. 517.
[9] Whether the assumptions are to be treated as cumulative or alternative for the purposes of calculating development value will depend on the physical circumstances in any particular case.
[10] The assumptions apply only to the land being acquired; the development potential of any retained land may be tested by the submission of one or more planning applications in the normal way.
[11] Section 22(3A) of the 1963 Act, added by the Planning and Compensation Act 1991, Sch.17, para.7, provides that regard is to be had to any contrary opinion expressed in relation to that land in a certificate of appropriate alternative development (see p.146).

if on facts and not on mere possibilities".[12] The assumptions, therefore, go some way towards relieving valuers and tribunals of the task of having to determine the planning position.

Section 22(2) goes on to provide that any planning permission which is to be assumed in accordance with the provisions of those sections is in addition to any planning permission which may be in force at the date of the notice to treat. This includes permissions granted by development order.[13] It is immaterial whether the permission in question, which relates to the land in question taken by itself or in respect of an area including that land, is conditional or unconditional or is full or in outline.[14] Such planning permissions will, however, only assist a claimant if they are valuable.[15] A personal or time limited permission, for example, may be taken into account but is unlikely to add much value.[16]

The six assumptions in sections 23 and 24 are divided between those which are derived from the development plan (s.24) and those which are not (s.23). The assumptions are now considered in turn under these two headings.

ASSUMPTIONS DERIVED FROM THE DEVELOPMENT PLAN

7–02 Section 24 of the 1963 Act provides that for the purposes of assessing compensation certain assumptions may be made about the grant of planning permission for development which accords with the provisions of the development plan in the form in which that plan is in force at the date of the notice to treat.[17] The development plan is prepared by the appropriate planning authority(ies) and sets out policies and proposals for the development and use of land in the plan area. The plan is prepared in two tiers and provisions for the preparation of each tier are contained in Part II of the Town and Country Planning (Scotland) Act 1997.[18] The first tier

---

[12] W. A. Leach, "Compulsory Purchase Valuation: The Six Assumptions of Planning Permission" [1973] J.P.L. 454 and 527.

[13] See Town and Country Planning (General Permitted Development) (Scotland) Order 1992, Sch.1, Art. 3.

[14] An outline planning permission means a planning permission for the carrying out of building or other operations which is granted subject to a condition requiring subsequent approval to be obtained from the planning authority for one or more reserved matters.

[15] See, for example, *J. Davy Ltd v London Borough of Hammersmith* (1975) 30 P. & C.R. 469; *Bromilow v Greater Manchester Council* (1975) 31 P. & C.R. 398; and *David Bell v Glasgow Corporation*, decision of an Official Arbiter Ref. No. 2/1969.

[16] But see *McArdle v Glasgow Corporation*, 1972 S.C. 41. See too *Wilson v West Sussex County Council* [1963] 2 Q.B. 764; *Waverley District Council v Secretary of State for the Environment* [1982] J.P.L. 105; and *Williamson and Stevens (Executors of Walter Williamson deceased) v Cambridgeshire County Council* [1977] J.P.L. 529. Cf, *East Suffolk County Council v Secretary of State for the Environment* (1972) 70 L.G.R. 595.

[17] Land Compensation (Scotland) Act 1963, s.45(1).

[18] Provision for two-tier development plans was first introduced in Scotland in the Town and Country Planning (Scotland) Act 1969. Before that, development plans were prepared as a single comprehensive document. These "old style" plans will remain in force (although they can no longer be amended) until they are superseded by local plans. In the meantime, the "old style" development plan and any approved structure plan will together make up the development plan for an area, although in cases of conflict between the two, the latter will for most purposes prevail (Town and Country Planning (Scotland) Act 1997, Sch.1).

comprises the structure plan.[19] This is prepared for each local authority area by the relevant planning authority. Where structure plan areas have been designated covering the area of more than one authority,[20] the structure plan is prepared by the relevant planning authorities working jointly. The structure plan is a written statement setting out strategic policies and proposals. The second tier comprises one or more local plans. These are prepared by each planning authority and comprise a map and written statement setting out detailed proposals for the development and use of land in the plan area. Of the two tiers, the local plans are likely to be more specific about the identification of land for development and will, consequently, have a more pronounced effect on value.

There are four assumptions and it will be necessary to consider which, if any, are applicable in the circumstances of any particular case.

(1) If the land acquired or any part of it consists of or forms part of a site allocated in the current[21] development plan for a particular purpose, it is to be assumed that planning permission would be granted for the development of the land for that purpose (s.24(1)).[22] For example, the land may be defined in the development plan as the site for a school, a hospital or a road. In view of the nature of these purposes, this assumption is not often of much value to a claimant. If the land is shown in the development plan as subject to comprehensive development then, regardless of whether it is allocated for a particular purpose, the appropriate assumption is that in s.24(4) (see below).

(2) If the land acquired or any part of it consists of or forms part of an area allocated in the current development plan primarily for a specified use, for example, residential, industrial or commercial, it is to be assumed that planning permission would be granted for the development of all or part of the land, as the case may be, for that use (s.24(2)). Such development must, however, be development for which planning permission might reasonably have been expected to be granted assuming no part of the land was to be acquired for public purposes (s.24(2)(b) and (7)).[23] If the land is shown in the development plan as subject to comprehensive development then, regardless of whether it is allocated primarily for a specified use, the appropriate assumption is that in s.24(4) (see below).

The phrase "development for which planning permission might reasonably have been expected to be granted" has given rise to some difficulty in practice. In *Menzies Motors Ltd v Stirling District Council*[24] Lord Cameron observed that this phrase is "not one of hypothetical

---

[19] In the *Review of Strategic Planning*, SEDD, 2002, the Scottish Executive announced their intention to remove the requirement for planning authorities to prepare structure plans except for the four major city regions.

[20] See the Designation of Structure Plan Areas (Scotland) Order 1995.

[21] See 1963 Act, s.45 (1). And see *City of Aberdeen District Council v Skean Dhu plc*, 1991 (Lands Tr.) S.L.T. 22.

[22] The wording suggests that the assumption applies to the whole of the land acquired even if only part is so allocated.

[23] See, for example, *Richardson Developments Ltd v Stoke Corporation* (1971) 22 P. & C.R. 958.

[24] 1977 S.C. 33.

assumption but is directed to the factual probabilities of a particular situation in relation to a particular site. What is 'reasonable' in a particular case one would necessarily think was a question primarily of fact and circumstance".

7–03   The operation of the phrase may be illustrated by the decision in *Margate Corporation v Devotwill Investments Ltd.*[25] The claimants owned a piece of land fronting on to a main road which was allocated in the development plan for residential use. A planning application for residential development was refused because part of the land was required for a bypass scheme and development was considered to be premature until the details were finalised. The claimants subsequently served a purchase notice which was accepted. The claimants lodged a claim for compensation based on an assumed planning permission for immediate residential development comprising 20 houses with access to the main road. The corporation argued for compensation based on an assumed planning permission for immediate residential development for nine houses with permission for a further 11 houses deferred pending some resolution of the problem of traffic congestion on the main road. The Lands Tribunal reached their decision on the basis that no land of the claimants would be taken for the bypass so that it could not have been built on the line proposed. They concluded, however, that since there would still have been an urgent need for traffic relief, it had to be assumed that a bypass would have been constructed on some other line thus enabling the immediate development of the land in question for residential purposes. The House of Lords held that the tribunal had erred as a matter of law in assuming that there would inevitably be a bypass on some other line. The possibility of the construction of a bypass elsewhere was a matter which could not rest on an assumption but on an examination of all the relevant factors. The case was remitted to the Lands Tribunal to reconsider what planning permission might reasonably have been expected to be granted in all the circumstances.

The case highlights a practical problem where land is being acquired by a roads authority. It is necessary to disregard, in assessing development potential, any value attributable to the road improvement scheme for which the land is being acquired (see Chapter 8). The need for the road improvement scheme will, however, still exist and in order to establish the development potential of the land the practice has been to consider in all the circumstances what, if any, alternative scheme the authority would have been most likely to pursue if they had not acquired the subject land. Such speculation is unsatisfactory and it is now provided that in assessing such potential it is to be assumed that no alternative scheme would be undertaken to meet the same, or substantially the same, need. Section 22(5)(6) of the 1963 Act[26] provides that—in determining whether planning permission might reasonably have been expected to be granted—it is to be assumed in assessing compensation, where land is being acquired for or in connection with providing, altering or improving a public road or such a use or use in that connection is

---

[25] [1970] 3 All E.R. 864, HL. See, too, *City of Aberdeen District Council v Skean Dhu plc*, 1991 S.L.T. (Lands Tr.) 22.

[26] Added by the Planning and Compensation Act 1991, s.74.

being considered by the roads authority, that, if the land were not to be so used, no road would be provided, altered or improved to meet the need or substantially the same need for which it is being acquired.[27]

A further illustration of the difficulties to which the phrase "development for which planning permission might reasonably have been expected to be granted" has given rise is provided by the decision of the Lands Tribunal for Scotland in *James Miller and Partners Ltd v Lothian Regional Council*.[28] The case concerned a small plot of land allocated in the development plan, along with other surrounding land, for residential purposes. The plot was acquired by the regional council as sewerage authority for the provision of a pumping station to service the claimant's housing scheme on the surrounding land. The regional council argued, on a voluntary reference to the Lands Tribunal, that a pumping station was required for residential development and that without it planning permission could not reasonably have been expected to be granted and compensation should be assessed accordingly. The Lands Tribunal, however, concluded that further inquiry was needed to establish whether planning permission for housing would be allowed over all or any part of the land assuming no part of it was to be acquired for a pumping station. After further inquiry the conclusion was that the pumping station would have been sited elsewhere and that permission for residential development would have been likely to be granted but with a restricted access and with part of the land being set aside for the planting of a tree belt.[29]

Although the planning assumption in section 24(2) of the 1963 Act is **7–04** designed to place a claimant as nearly as possible in the position in which he would have found himself on a sale in the open market, it in fact places a claimant in a position of slight advantage. As the Lands Tribunal for Scotland observed in *James Miller and Partners Ltd*: "a situation in which planning permission for housing might reasonably have been expected (without having been obtained) might still cause a valuer to make some discount from value to reflect the possibility of a refusal. However, section 24(2) also directs 'it shall be assumed that planning permission would be granted' in these circumstances—so the assumption becomes absolute affecting value".

It is, of course, conceivable that inquiry may show that the development is not one for which planning permission might reasonably have been expected to be granted. As Leach comments "it is well known that where an area is allocated to a use in a development plan permission for development for that use would not necessarily be granted for every plot of land within that area".[30] Thus, in *Provincial Properties (London) Ltd v Caterham and Warlingham Urban District Council*[31] the claimants owned

---

[27] This provision does not sit entirely happily with the approach adopted by the courts in determining the position under the certificate of appropriate alternative development procedure (*Secretary of State for the Environment v Fletcher Estates (Harlscott) Ltd* [1998] 4 All E.R. 838, CA (see p.153 below). The Law Commission have proposed that the 'cancellation assumption' adopted in *Fletcher* should apply also to the planning assumptions in s.24 (Consultation Paper No 165, 2002, para.7.37).

[28] 1981 S.L.T. (Lands Tr.) 3.

[29] 1984 S.L.T. (Lands Tr.) 2.

[30] W. A. Leach, "Compulsory Purchase Valuation: The Six Assumptions of Planning Permission" [1973] J.P.L. 454 and 527.

[31] [1972] 1 Q.B. 453.

an estate consisting of a house together with grounds of over six acres along the top of a ridge. The estate was allocated for residential development in the development plan. Whilst planning permission was granted for residential development on some of the land, permission was repeatedly refused both by the local planning authority and by the Minister on appeal for the development of the land at the top of the ridge because of the harmful effect which such development would have on the visual amenity of the surrounding area. A purchase notice was subsequently served and confirmed. The claimants argued that compensation should be assessed on the basis that planning permission could be assumed, in accordance with the provisions of the development plan, for residential purposes. The English Court of Appeal concluded that on the evidence planning permission could not reasonably have been expected to be granted so that the condition upon which the assumption rested had not been fulfilled. Similarly, in *O'Donnell v Edinburgh District Council*,[32] the Lands Tribunal for Scotland concluded on the evidence that, with changes in planning policy, planning permission for industrial use (the allocation in the current development plan) would be unlikely to be granted so that the assumption in section 24(2) of the 1963 Act could not be made.

The likelihood or otherwise of planning permission being sought and implemented would seem to be irrelevant for the purposes of making the assumption contained in section 24(2).[33] The subsection provides that if the preconditions are satisfied the assumption is to be made. However, the assumed planning permission will not, of itself, increase the value of the land[34] and the likelihood of demand for the land with that permission will clearly be relevant to the assessment of value.

7–05   (3) If the land acquired or any part of it consists of, or forms part of, an area allocated in the current development plan primarily for a range of two or more specified uses, for example, residential and commercial, or commercial and industrial, it is to be assumed that planning permission would be granted for the development of all or part of the land, as the case may be, for any one of the range of uses (s.24(3)). As with the preceding subsection, such development must, however, be development for which planning permission might reasonably have been expected to be granted assuming no part of the land was to be acquired for public purposes (s.24(3)(b) and (7)). The comments made regarding the corresponding provision in section 24(2) apply equally to this subsection. If the land is shown in the development plan as subject to comprehensive development then the appropriate assumption is that in section 24(4) (see below).

[32] 1980 S.L.T. (Lands Tr.) 13. See, too, *City of Aberdeen District Council v Skean Dhu plc*, 1991 S.L.T. (Lands Tr.) 22.

[33] *Sutton v Secretary of State for the Environment* [1984] J.P.L. 647.

[34] *Bromilow v Greater Manchester Council* (1975) 31 P. & C.R. 398; *J. Davy Ltd v London Borough of Hammersmith* (1975) 30 P. & C.R. 469; and *David Bell v Glasgow Corporation*, decision of an Official Arbiter Ref. No. 2/1969.

(4) If the land acquired or any part of it is allocated in the current development plan for comprehensive development,[35] it is to be assumed that planning permission would be granted for the development of all or any part of the land, as the case may be, for any one of the planned range of uses shown in the development plan for the area, whether or not the use is indicated in the plan for the land acquired (s.24(4) and (5)).[36] However, such development must be development for which planning permission might, in the circumstances mentioned below, reasonably have been expected to be granted assuming no part of the land was to be acquired for public purposes (s.24(4) and (7)). The comments made earlier regarding the corresponding provision in section 24(2) apply equally to this subsection.

The circumstances referred to above are those that would have existed if: (i) the area in question had not been allocated in the development plan as one for comprehensive development and no particulars or proposals relating to the area had been comprised in the plan (s.24(4)(a)); and (ii) in a case where, at the date of the service of the notice to treat, land in that area has already been developed or redeveloped in accordance with the plan, no land in that area had been so developed on or before that date (s.24(5)(b)).

In *Menzies Motors v Stirling District Council*[37] the claimants attempted to distinguish the reference to a reasonable expectation of a grant of planning permission in section 24(4) from the corresponding provisions in s.24(2) and (3). The absence of the conjunction "and" immediately preceding the provision in section 24(4), it was argued, meant that it was unnecessary to establish that planning permission might reasonably have been expected; it could be assumed. The Second Division rejected this argument. The absence of the conjunction has no significance; "expectation" is a prerequisite in the circumstances specified.

Section 24(6) goes on to provide that in respect of any of the assumptions as to planning permission which may be derived from the development plan (see s.24(2) to (4) above), it is also to be assumed that the permission would be subject to such conditions, if any, as might reasonably have been expected to be imposed in the circumstances mentioned in the relevant subsection; furthermore, if the development plan indicates that any such planning permission would be granted only at a future time then it is to be assumed that the grant of planning permission would be postponed to that time.

The planning assumptions in section 24 have been criticised as anachronistic. They were introduced at a time when development plans

---

[35] The reference in the 1963 Act to an area allocated for comprehensive development is presumably a reference to what used to be referred to as a "comprehensive development area" and is now referred to as an "action area" (see Town and Country Planning (Scotland) Act 1997, s.11(6)). It used to be the case that a planning authority were required to indicate in their structure plan any part of their area selected for comprehensive treatment; a local plan then had to be prepared for any such area. This is no longer the case and what is now an "action area" can be promoted in a local plan without any prior notation in the structure plan.

[36] See *McArdle v Glasgow Corporation*, 1972 S.C. 41; *Menzies Motors Ltd v Stirling District Council*, 1977 S.C. 33. For the definition of "the planned range of uses" see the 1963 Act, s.24(5).

[37] 1977 S.C. 33. See, too, *Camrose (Viscount) v Basingstoke Corporation* [1966] 1 W.L.R. 1100.

tended to be more site specific than they are now. Nowadays there is as much or more reliance on the policies set out in the written statement which forms part of the plan. The problem is compounded by the fact that planning authorities have experienced very considerable difficulty in keeping development plans up-to-date and relevant. Because of these problems, CPPRAG recommended that the corresponding assumptions in the English legislation should be replaced by a simplified version of the certificate of appropriate alternative development procedure (see below).[38]

ASSUMPTIONS NOT DERIVED FROM THE DEVELOPMENT PLAN

7–06 In assessing compensation for the compulsory acquisition of land there are three assumptions that may be made as to the grant of planning permission which are not derived directly from the development plan (s.23). These are:

> (i) that planning permission would be granted for the development of the land in accordance with the proposals of the acquiring authority;
>
> (ii) that planning permission would be granted for development of any class specified in Schedule 11 of the Town and Country Planning (Scotland) Act 1997; and
>
> (iii) that planning permission would be granted for the development or classes of development stated in a certificate of appropriate alternative development.

These assumptions are considered in turn.

1. Development in accordance with proposals of the acquiring authority

Section 23(1) of the 1963 Act provides that where land is being taken to implement development proposals of the acquiring authority on all or part of the land and planning permission for that development is not in force at the date of the service of the notice to treat,[39] it is to be assumed that planning permission would be granted such as would permit the development of the land, or part as the case may be, in accordance with the proposals of the acquiring authority. Unlike the assumptions as to planning permission in section 24(2) to (4) where it is necessary to show that the development is one for which planning permission might reasonably have been expected to be granted, section 23 (1) simply provides that planning permission is to be assumed for development in accordance with the proposals of the acquiring authority.

---

[38] "Fundamental review of the laws and procedures relating to compulsory purchase and compensation" (2000) DETR 110. See too, "Towards a compulsory purchase code: (1) compensation" (2002) *Law Commission Consultation Paper No 165* 118–120.

[39] No account, however, is to be taken of any planning permission which does not run with the land (1963 Act, s.23(2)).

At first sight it might appear that this assumption entitles a claimant to participate in the social worth of the scheme; compensation would seem to be based on value to the purchaser. However, such a proposition was disposed of in *Myers v Milton Keynes Development Corporation*.[40] The claimant in that case owned a 323-acre estate in an area designated as a new town. At the date of valuation, the new town master plan designated the estate for residential development 10 years hence. The Lands Tribunal concluded that the operation of the corresponding assumption in the (English) Land Compensation Act 1961 conflicted with the so-called *Pointe Gourde* principle which states that "compensation for the compulsory acquisition of land cannot include an increase in value which is entirely due to the scheme underlying the acquisition".[41] The Court of Appeal disagreed. Denning M.R. explained the relationship between these two provisions in this way:

"In valuing the estate, you are to disregard the effect of the scheme, but you are to assume the availability of planning permission. This is best explained by taking an imaginary instance. A scheme is proposed for building a motorway across Dartmoor with a service station every five miles. Suppose that land is taken on which a service station is to be built as soon as possible. In assessing compensation, you are to disregard any increase due to the proposed motorway, or service station . . . you are to assume that he would have been granted planning permission for a service station . . . And you are to value that land with that permission in the setting in which it would have been if there had been no scheme. If it would have been a good site for a service station, there would be a great increase in value. If it would have been in an inaccessible spot on the wild moor, there would be little, if any, increase in value, because there would be no demand for it."

A further illustration is provided by the decision of the official arbiter in *W. M. Leggat v East Kilbride Development Corporation*.[42] The development corporation had compulsorily acquired 130 acres of farmland for industrial development in accordance with the new town master plan. The claimant was accordingly entitled to assume planning permission for the industrial development of land. However, it was necessary to consider whether in the absence of the new town there would have been any demand for industrial development. On the facts of the case, the arbiter concluded that there would have been no such demand and compensation was assessed on the existing use value of the land for agriculture.

It is apparent, said Lord Denning in *Myers*:

"that the valuation has to be done in an imaginary state of affairs in which there is no scheme. The valuer must cast aside his knowledge

[40] [1974] 1 W.L.R. 696. And see W. A. Leach, "The Milton Keynes Case" (1974) 230 E.G. 281.
[41] *Pointe Gourde Quarrying and Transport Co. v Sub-Intendent of Crown Lands* [1947] A.C. 565.
[42] Ref. No. 2/1961.

of what has in fact happened in the past eight years due to the scheme. He must ignore the development which will in all probability take place in the future 10 years owing to the scheme. Instead, he must let his imagination take flight to the clouds. He must conjure up a land of make-believe, where there has not been, nor will be, a brave new town: but where there is to be supposed the old order of things continuing."

The effect of the assumption in section 23(1) is that the valuer may, as one commentator observed,[43] find himself assessing the value of a greenfield site with a positive planning permission to be assumed but with an inadequate system of roads and services and little or no infrastructure. In such circumstances, he will need to quantify the cost of providing these and compare the result with the dead-ripe value of the land. This may or may not produce a positive development value.

CPPRAG considered that the corresponding assumption in the English legislation would no longer be required if planning assumptions were to be based on a simplified version of the certificate of appropriate alternative development procedure (see below).[44]

2. Schedule 11 development

7–07   Section 23(3) of the 1963 Act[45] provides that planning permission is to be assumed in respect of the land acquired or any part of it:

(i) for any development of a class specified in what is now paragraph 1 of Schedule 11 to the Town and Country Planning (Scotland) Act 1997;

(ii) for any development of a class specified in paragraph 2 of the said Schedule 11.

To understand this assumption it is necessary to go back to the Town and Country Planning (Scotland) Act 1947. Under the 1947 Act a development charge was payable where a grant of planning permission for new development unlocked development value. However, it was considered unreasonable that the development charge should apply to certain categories of development closely related to the existing use of the land. To avoid the development charge, these categories of development were classified in the Third Schedule to the 1947 Act as "Development not constituting new development". Their value remained with the landowner and was, accordingly, taken into account in assessing compensation for compulsory purchase.

Perhaps more importantly, a failure to realise the value of certain of these categories of development as a result of a refusal of planning

---

[43] M. Clark, "'Valuation Aspects of Land Taken Under a Scheme—1' in Compensation for Compulsory Purchase" (1975) *Journal of Planning and Environment Law Occasional Paper.*

[44] "Fundamental review of the laws and procedures relating to compulsory purchase and compensation: final report" (2000) DETR, para.111.

[45] As substituted by the Planning and Compensation Act 1991, s.60 and Sch.12, para.1.

permission or the imposition of onerous conditions rendered the land-owner eligible for compensation from the planning authority. This arrangement continued with occasional modification until 1991. Because of the effect which the threat of a compensation claim might have on planning decisions for such development and because of the potential for abuse, the entitlement to compensation following an adverse decision was removed by section 60(2) of the Planning and Compensation Act 1991. At the same time, the categories of "Development not constituting new development" were reduced to two.[46] These are set out in what is now paragraphs 1 and 2 of Schedule 11 to the Town and Country Planning (Scotland) Act 1997. The value of the development described in these paragraphs is still treated as belonging to the landowner and it is to be assumed in assessing compensation for compulsory acquisition that planning permission would be granted for such development.[47]

The categories of development set out in paragraphs 1 and 2 of Schedule 11 are as follows:

1. The carrying out of:

   (a) the rebuilding, as often as occasion may require, of any building which was in existence on July 1, 1948, or of any building which was in existence before that date but was destroyed or demolished after January 7, 1937, including the making good of war damage sustained by any such building;

   (b) the rebuilding, as often as occasion may require, of any building erected after July 1, 1948 which was in existence at the date by reference to which the Schedule falls to be applied (referred to as the 'material date')[48];

   (c) works for the maintenance, improvement or other altera-tion of any building, being works which:

   • affect only the interior of the building, or do not materially affect the external appearance of the building, and

   • are works for making good war damage.

2. The use as two or more separate dwellinghouses of any building which at a material date was used as a single dwellinghouse.

There is a proviso to paragraph 1. The cubic content[49] of the original building[50] must not be exceeded by more than one-tenth or 1750 cubic feet (whichever is the greater) in the case of a dwelling-house and in any other case by more than one-tenth.

Given the relatively minor nature of these categories of development, the assumption in section 23(3) of the 1963 Act is unlikely to give much

---

[46] Planning and Compensation Act 1991, Sch.12, para.32.
[47] 1963 Act, s.23(3).
[48] Town and Country Planning (Scotland) Act 1997, Sch.11, para.5.
[49] Measured externally (1997 Act, Sch.11, para.1).
[50] As defined in the 1997 Act, Sch.11, para.6.

assistance to a claimant. CPPRAG recommended that the corresponding provision in the English legislation should be repealed and replaced by a simplified version of the certificate of appropriate alternative development procedure (see below).[51]

3. Development referred to in a certificate of appropriate alternative developments[52]

7–08   Section 23(5) of the 1963 Act provides that where a certificate of appropriate alternative development (CAAD) is issued under Part IV of the Act, planning permission is to be assumed[53] for the development or classes of development which, according to the certificate, would have been granted permission if the land was not being acquired for public purposes. If the certificate indicates that such permission would have been subject to specified conditions or would have been granted only at some specified future time, those constraints are also to be assumed.[54]

The certificate procedure may assist a claimant in cases where the statutory assumptions, particularly those arising from the development plan, are of little or no value. For example, the development plan may be out of date and simply show the land in question as "white land" where the existing uses are expected to remain undisturbed, notwithstanding that development has recently been permitted nearby.

Section 22(3) of the 1963 Act makes it clear that the statutory assumptions as to planning permission are not necessarily exhaustive. In attempting to establish that land has development value a claimant may base his claim upon the prospect that some other planning permission would be likely to have been granted but for the compulsory acquisition of the land.[55] However, such a claim for what is generally referred to as "hope value" will be subject to some discount for uncertainty. This is, inevitably, a speculative area which will involve valuers and the Lands Tribunal in arguments about planning policies and proposals. Section 25 of the 1963 Act gives the claimant an opportunity, by way of an application for a CAAD, to dispose of this uncertainty. The intention is that arguments about the hypothetical planning position of the land should be settled before an appropriate forum and in advance of the negotiations over compensation. If a "positive" certificate of appropriate alternative development (see below) is granted (sometimes referred to as

---

[51] "Fundamental review of the laws and procedures relating to compulsory purchase and compensation: final report" (2000) DETR para.110.

[52] See generally in connection with such certificates, W. A. Leach, "Compensation on Compulsory Purchase: Section 17 Certificates" [1985] J.P.L. 291.

[53] For all or part of the land as the case may be.

[54] See, for example, SDD appeal decision (ref. P/ACC/GC/1&2) in which a certificate was issued stating that planning permission would have been granted for a residential or open space development on the relevant land but subject to a density restriction and to a condition which would have reserved for subsequent approval by the planning authority details of layout, siting, design, external appearance, means of access and landscaping. See too the D. of E. appeal decision noted at [1971] J.P.L. 48.

[55] It should be noted, however, that s.22 (3A) (substituted by the Planning and Compensation Act 1991, Schedule 17, para.7(2) for the proviso to s.22(3) of the 1963 Act) requires account to be taken of any contrary opinion expressed in a CAAD. It would seem, therefore, that a claimant should not lightly embark on the certificate procedure; an adverse decision may well prejudice any subsequent claim for "hope value" under s.22(3).

a "valuable" certificate), planning permission is to be assumed for valuation purposes for the development or classes of development referred to in the certificate (s.23(5)). The object of the procedure, as Lord Macdonald observed in *Grampian Regional Council v Secretary of State for Scotland*[56] "is to remove the hardship which a landowner might sustain in comparison with similar landowners who are able to develop their land profitably outwith the shadow of compulsory acquisition".

Section 25(1) of the 1963 Act, as substituted by section 75(1) of the Planning and Compensation Act 1991, provides that where an interest in land is proposed to be acquired[57] by an authority possessing compulsory purchase powers, either the claimant or the acquiring authority may apply to the planning authority for a CAAD. Where, however, a notice to treat has been served or agreement has been reached for the sale of the land to the acquiring authority and the amount of the compensation has been referred to the Lands Tribunal for Scotland to determine, no application for a certificate may be made without the consent of the other party or without leave of the tribunal.

There is no prescribed form of application for a certificate but it must **7–09** be in writing and must include a plan or map sufficient to identify the land to which it relates.[58] The application is to specify what class or classes of development[59] would, in the applicant's opinion, be appropriate for the land in question if it were not being acquired for public purposes; it must also specify the time at which such development would be appropriate (s.25(3)(a)). The applicant must state the grounds for holding that opinion (s.25(3)(b)). The application is to be accompanied by a statement specifying the date on which a copy of the application has been or will be served on the other party (s.25(3)(c)).

On receipt of an application, the planning authority must (not sooner than 21 days from the date on which a copy of the application was served on the other party (s.25(4)), but not later than two months from the date of receipt of the application or such extra period as may be agreed in writing)[60] issue to the applicant a certificate stating one of two things; either:

> (a) that, in their opinion, planning permission would have been granted for development of one or more classes specified in the

---

[56] 1984 S.L.T. 212.

[57] Leach argues that an application cannot be made where the interest has already been acquired, for example, by way of general vesting declaration (see W. A. Leach, "Compensation on Compulsory Purchase: Section 17 Certificates" [1985] J.P.L. 291). This argument was rejected by the Secretary of State in SDD appeal decision (ref. P/AAC/TC/3); the use of the words "proposed to be acquired" in s.25 (1) is explained, it was said, by the fact that at the date of the deemed notice to treat the words reflect the status of the acquiring authority. See, too, *Young v Lothian Regional Council*, unreported, May 9, 1990, Lands Tribunal for Scotland.

[58] The Land Compensation (Scotland) Development Order 1975, reg.3(1).

[59] The reference to "class" and "classes" is not linked in any way to the Town and Country Planning (Use Classes) (Scotland) Order 1997. It simply means that all development may be classified in one way or another (*Sutton v Secretary of State for the Environment* [1984] J.P.L. 647; *Essex Construction Co. Ltd v Minister of Housing and Local Government* [1968] R.V.R. 818).

[60] The 1975 Order, reg.3(2).

certificate (whether specified in the application or not) and for any development for which the land is to be acquired,[61] but would not have been granted for any other development (a "valuable" or "positive" certificate)[62]; and the certificate may indicate that any permission would have been subject to specified conditions or granted at a specified future time;[63] or

(b) that, in their opinion, planning permission would have been granted for any development for which the land is to be acquired, but would not have been granted for any other development (a "nil" or "negative" certificate)).[64]

It should be noted that the test for a valuable certificate is what planning permission "would have been granted". This test was first introduced in the Community Land Act 1975. Prior to that it was only necessary to state the purpose or purposes for which planning permission "might reasonably have been expected". The present test would seem to be more stringent.

If the planning authority fail to issue a certificate within the prescribed time, the applicant may lodge an appeal (see below) against a deemed "nil" certificate (s.26(4)).[65]

Establishing the relevant date for determining what, if any, alternative development would have been appropriate may be important. For a while it was unclear whether the relevant date for considering physical factors and the relevant date for considering planning policy were the same. The relevant date for considering physical factors falls to be determined by reference to s.30(2) of the 1963 Act. Thus, regard should be had to the state of the subject land at whichever of the three following dates is appropriate:

(i) where an interest in land is being compulsorily acquired, the date of publication of notice of the making of the compulsory purchase order[66]; or

(ii) where an interest in land is being acquired as a result of the service of a purchase notice[67] or a blight notice,[68] the date on which the notice to treat is deemed to have been served; or

(iii) where an interest in land is being acquired as a result of a written offer to negotiate, the date of that offer.[69]

---

[61] Development is "development for which the land is to be acquired" if the land is to be acquired for purposes which involve the carrying out of proposals of the acquiring authority for that development.

[62] 1963 Act, s.25(4)(a), as substituted by the Planning and Compensation Act 1991, s.75(2).

[63] 1963 Act, s.25(5).

[64] 1963 Act, s.25(4)(b), as substituted by the Planning and Compensation Act 1991, s.75(2).

[65] The two month period for issuing a certificate may be extended by agreement of the parties in writing (1963 Act, s.26(4)).

[66] See appeal decision noted at [1987] J.P.L. 659.

[67] See the Town and Country Planning (Scotland) Act 1997, ss.88–99. And see appeal decision noted at [1987] J.P.L. 660.

[68] See the Town and Country Planning (Scotland) Act 1997, ss.100–122.

[69] See *Jelson Ltd v Minister of Housing and Local Government* [1970] 1 Q.B. 243. Also *Grampian Regional Council v Secretary of State for Scotland*, 1984 S.L.T. 212.

As explained in Chapter 5 (see p.120), for a while there was some **7–10** uncertainty about the relevant date for considering planning policy. In *Jelson Ltd v Minister of Housing and Local Government*[70] it was held that, as a matter of construction of the English equivalent of section 25, the planning authority must form an opinion as to what planning permission "might reasonably have been expected to be granted" at the date when the interest in land was proposed to be acquired, and that was the date of the actual or deemed notice to treat or of the offer of purchase. However, in *Robert Hitchins Builders Ltd v Secretary of State for the Environment*[71] it was held that the relevant date for applying planning policies "should as nearly as possibly coincide with the date of assessment of compensation". The result of applying this decision was that a distinction had to be made between the relevant date for applying planning policies and the relevant date for considering physical factors (see below). Subsequently, in *Fox v Secretary of State for the Environment*[72] the court declined to follow *Hitchins* and reverted to the position in *Jelson*. The uncertainty was finally resolved by the English Court of Appeal in *Secretary of State for the Environment v Fletcher Estates (Harlscott) Ltd*[73] in which it was held that the issue had been determined as a matter of authority by the decision in *Jelson*.[74] That being so, the relevant dates for considering physical factors and for considering planning policy are the same.

In determining whether planning permission for any particular class of development would have been granted in respect of any land, the planning authority must disregard the prospect of the land being acquired by any authority possessing compulsory purchase powers.[75] Furthermore, the planning authority must not rule out that class of development simply because it would have involved development of the land contrary to the provisions of the development plan (s.25(7)).[76] To treat the provisions of the development plan as conclusive of the issue would defeat many applications because the development plan may simply allocate the land for the purpose for which it is being acquired. However, it does not follow that the development plan provisions should be ignored. The provisions may be taken into account as a material but not a conclusive factor.[77] Thus in *Skelmersdale Development Corporation v Secretary of State for the Environment*[78] Griffith J. considered that it was perfectly proper for a local planning authority, in determining what alternative development should be specified in a certificate for land in a

[70] [1970] 1 Q.B. 243.

[71] (1979) 37 P. & C.R. 140.

[72] (1991) 40 E.G. 116.

[73] [1998] 4 All E.R. 838, CA.

[74] CPPRAG, in its final report, commented that this aspect of the judgement in *Fletcher Estates* warrants further review ("Fundamental review of the laws and procedures relating to compulsory purchase and compensation" (2000) DETR, para.113).

[75] *Grampian Regional Council v Secretary of State for Scotland*, 1984 S.L.T. 212, HL. And see ss.23(5) and 25(3)(a) of the 1963 Act (both as amended).

[76] See appeal decision noted at [1987] J.P.L. 660.

[77] See SDD appeal decisions ref. P/AAC/GC/4; P/AAC/LD/1; P/AAC/FA/1. Also *Skelmersdale Development Corporation v Secretary of State for the Environment* [1980] J.P.L. 322; and the appeal decisions noted at [1987] J.P.L. 659, 660.

[78] [1980] J.P.L. 322. See, too, the appeal decision noted at [1987] J.P.L. 659.

new town, to have regard to the operative master plan for the new town. A decision on an application for a certificate may be consistent with the provisions of the development plan but that does not mean that it was reached solely because of the plan.[79]

If the planning authority issue a certificate otherwise than for the class or classes of development specified in the application or contrary to representations in writing made to them by either the claimant or the acquiring authority, the certificate must include their reasons for so doing.[80] On issuing a CAAD to either of the parties directly concerned, the planning authority must serve a copy of the certificate on the other party (s.25(9)).

Section 26 of the 1963 Act makes provision for an appeal to the Scottish Ministers against a certificate. The certificate must give particulars of the manner in which and the time in which an appeal may be made.[81] An appeal may be made either by the claimant or by the acquiring authority and notice of the appeal must be lodged in writing with the Scottish Ministers within one month of the date of the receipt of the certificate or of the expiry of the period for issuing the certificate.[82] Copy of the notice of appeal must be given by the appellant to the other party and to the planning authority to whom the application was made.[83] Within one month of giving notice of appeal, or within such longer period as the Scottish Ministers may allow, the appellant must furnish the Ministers with a copy of the application to the planning authority and the certificate (if any) together with a statement of the grounds of appeal.[84] Failure to furnish the Ministers with these documents within the time prescribed will result in the appeal being treated as withdrawn.[85]

7–11   On an appeal against a certificate, the Scottish Ministers are to deal with the matter as if the application for a certificate had been made to them in the first instance.[86] They may confirm the certificate, vary it, or cancel it and issue a different certificate in its place (s.26(2)). However, before determining an appeal, the Ministers must afford the claimant and the acquiring authority an opportunity of appearing before and being heard by a person appointed by them for the purpose.[87]

---

[79] *Bell v Lord Advocate*, 1968 S.C. 14. See, too, *Skelmersdale Development Corporation, supra.*

[80] The 1975 Order, reg.3(3).

[81] The 1975 Order, reg.3(3). Failure to do so will vitiate the certificate (*London and Clydeside Estates Ltd v Aberdeen District Council*, 1980 S.C. (H.L.) 1; 1980 S.L.T. 81).

[82] The 1975 Order, reg.4(1). Note that the period for issuing the certificate may be extended by the parties by agreement in writing in which case the time for lodging an appeal runs from the expiry of the extended period.

[83] The 1975 Order, reg.4(2).

[84] The 1975 Order, reg.4(3).

[85] The 1975 Order, reg.4(4).

[86] See *Maidstone Borough Council v Secretary of State for the Environment and Kent County Council* (1995) 69 P. & C.R. 1; also appeal decision noted at [1987] J.P.L. 660.

[87] The 1963 Act, s.26(3). The hearing is generally in the form of a public local inquiry. The normal practice in such inquiries was for each party to bear the expenses which they themselves incurred unless one party could be shown to have acted unreasonably, vexatiously or frivolously. However, s.25(9A) of the 1963 Act, added by s.75(3) of the Planning and Compensation Act 1991, now provides that the expenses of an appeal where any of the issues are determined in favour of the appellant shall be taken into account in the assessment of compensation.

The certificate procedure is a fictional exercise related to the assessment of compensation and not a factual exercise in planning.[88] Its sole purpose, as Lord Bridge observed in *Grampian Regional Council v Secretary of State for Scotland*,[89] is "to provide a basis for determining the development value, if any, to be taken into account in assessing compensation payable on compulsory acquisition".[90] This may be illustrated by the decision in *Grampian Regional Council*.[91] Developers applied for, and were granted, planning permission for the layout of a new suburb of Aberdeen. Plans accompanying the application earmarked two sites for schools and in due course Grampian Regional Council, as education authority, offered to purchase the two sites from the developers in order to construct a primary and secondary school. The offers were accepted, the price to be determined as for a compulsory acquisition. The developers considered that had it not been for the proposals of the education authority, the two sites would have had development potential and this should be reflected in the price. However, no assistance could be derived from the assumptions in the development plan as the plan was out of date. The developers accordingly applied to the planning authority pursuant to section 25 of the 1963 Act for a CAAD. The planning authority issued a "nil" certificate stating that in their opinion planning permission would not have been granted for any development other than that proposed to be carried out by the education authority. On appeal by the developers, the Secretary of State substituted "valuable" certificates to the effect that planning permission would have been granted in respect of the primary school site for residential development and in respect of the secondary school site for residential or commercial development, in each case subject to conditions.

The planning authority and the education authority applied unsuccessfully under section 29 of the 1963 Act (see below) to the Inner House, and from there to the House of Lords, to have the Minister's decision quashed on the ground that it was not within the powers of the Act. The authorities argued that, although in determining an application for a certificate the planning authority were obliged to ignore the actual proposal by the education authority to buy the two sites, the underlying requirement to devote those sites to the needs of public education remained and afforded a complete answer to the claims for "valuable" certificates. This argument was rejected. To accept it, said Lord Bridge, would "defeat the essential purpose of the procedure for obtaining certificates of appropriate alternative development, as part of the overall

---

[88] In *South Lanarkshire Council v Lord Advocate*, 2002 S.C. 88, IH the Lord President, Lord Rodger, referred to the exercise as entering "the realm of the counterfactual" (p.92).

[89] 1984 S.L.T. 212, HL.

[90] However, as with the other planning assumptions, a valuable certificate will not, of itself, enhance the value of the land; demand must also be shown (*Bromilow v Greater Manchester Council* (1975) 31 P. & C.R. 398; *J Davy Ltd v London Borough of Hammersmith* (1975) 30 P. & C.R. 469; and *David Bell v Glasgow Corporation*, decision of an Official Arbiter, Ref. No. 2/1969).

[91] 1984 S.L.T. 212, HL. See too SDD appeal decisions ref. P/AAC/GA/4; and P/AAC/GA/3&5; also the appeal decision noted at [1987] J.P.L. 660.

scheme of the Act to secure the payment of fair compensation to landowners who were expropriated . . . Assuming," he continued, "that every compulsory purchase of land could be justified by reference to the public purpose for which the land was required, to allow reliance on that public requirement to determine the question raised by an application under section 25 would lead to the issue of a negative certificate in every case".[92]

Although the acquiring authority must ignore the proposed acquisition and the underlying requirement to buy the subject land, does this mean it is still open to the authority to argue that, if the underlying need cannot be met elsewhere, development of the subject land would not be appropriate? This argument was advanced by Lothian Regional Council in an appeal to the Secretary of State against the issuing of a valuable certificate by the West Lothian District Council as planning authority in respect of land being acquired by the region for a primary school.[93] If, as is required, it is to be assumed that the subject land was not being acquired for the construction of the school, it was difficult, argued the regional council, to see how it could be regarded as appropriate for residential development.[94] There was no alternative site upon which the school could be constructed and in the absence of a school it would be inappropriate to permit residential development. The Secretary of State concluded that the 1963 Act did not require and was not intended to require the planning authority, or the Minister on appeal, to consider where the school would have been located if it were not to go on the subject land. In the hypothetical situation imposed by section 25(3) of the Act, it was enough to assume that a school site would be provided to serve the residential area and it was not necessary to point to a site either identified in the development plan or which was otherwise feasible to justify a certificate for residential use of the subject land.

7–12   The argument advanced by the regional council in this case would seem to be similar to that put forward by the regional council in *Grampian*, although presented in a different way. It is not really surprising, therefore, that the Secretary of State should have reached the conclusion he did. Nonetheless, this approach departs from the analogy which the certificate procedure is attempting to make with the open market. In a market situation, planning permission would only be likely to be granted if it could be shown that an impediment to development, for example an educational or a sewerage capacity constraint, could be met elsewhere. It is one thing to assume that the subject land is not to be acquired; it is quite another to assume that the purpose for which the subject land is being acquired can be met elsewhere. The ability to assume a solution would seem to place the claimant at an advantage and does not square with the test applied in *James Miller and Partners Ltd* for a section 24 assumption, namely that it is "development for which

---

[92] See, too, *Scunthorpe Borough Council v Secretary of State for the Environment* [1977] J.P.L. 653.

[93] Ref. P/AAC/LD/1.

[94] For a similar argument see *James Miller & Partners Ltd v Lothian Regional Council*, 1981 S.L.T. (Lands Tr.) 3, a case turning on section 24 of the 1963 Act, where, in the absence of the public acquisition of land for a sewage pumping station, it was argued that residential development could not take place (see p.139).

planning permission might reasonably have been expected to be granted" (p.139).

In the situations discussed so far, all that was necessary was to disregard the proposal to acquire the subject land and the underlying requirement for which the land was being acquired. The matter is less straightforward where the subject land forms part of a wider scheme of public works. Leach, commenting on the operation of the corresponding English legislation, suggested that the assumption that the subject land is not being acquired for public purposes may "cause either the whole scheme to fail, to be carried out wholly on other land, or carried out with modifications with or without the addition of fresh land, or the problem to be overcome in some other manner . . . to the extent that the scheme would go ahead it would have to be taken into account in deciding what developments of the relevant land would be permitted in that setting".[95] The question is what assumption is to be made about the position.

This point arose in the context of an application for a CAAD for land being acquired for the construction of the Perth Western Bypass. The applicant appealed to the Secretary of State against a "nil" certificate issued by the planning authority. On appeal, the planning authority argued, *inter alia*, that, in considering what development, if any, would have been appropriate on the subject land were it not being acquired for the road scheme, it was necessary to consider the likely effect on the scheme of the assumed non-availability of the subject land. The planning potential of the subject land should be judged on the basis of that effect. The Secretary of State in his decision letter[96] accepted that it was in order for him to consider the possibility of an alternative line for the bypass and the effect which such an alternative line might have had on the development potential of the ground being acquired.[97]

Because of the difficulty of assessing how the need for road improvements would have been met, if at all, in the absence of the land being acquired, it is now to be assumed in assessing development potential for compensation purposes that no public road would be constructed to meet the need or substantially the same need.[98] This provision applies to the certificate procedure in the same way it applies to the planning assumptions in section 24 (p.138).

Reference was made earlier, in the context of the assumption in section 23(1) (p.143), to the problem of determining what might have happened had the acquiring authority's scheme not been promoted. Lord Denning in *Myers* referred to the need for the valuer to "conjure up a land of make-believe". The valuers problems have been alleviated somewhat so far as a certificate application is concerned by the decision of the House of Lords in *Secretary of State for the Environment v Fletcher Estates (Harlscott) Ltd.*[99] In that case, Lord Hope, giving judgement for

---

[95] W.A. Leach, "Compensation on Compulsory Purchase: Section 17 Certificates" [1985] J.P.L. 291.

[96] Ref. P/AAC/TC/3. See, too, *Young v Lothian Regional Council*, 1992 S.L.T. (Lands Tr.) 17.

[97] See *Margate Corporation v Devotwill Investments Ltd* [1970] 3 All E.R. 864, HL. See too R. J. Yuille and N Howells, "Section 17 of the Land Compensation Act—Adventures in the Land of Make Belief" [1990] J.P.L. 3; also letter at [1990] J.P.L. 202.

[98] 1963 Act, s.22(5)—(7), added by the Planning and Compensation Act 1991, s.74.

[99] (2000) 80 P. & C.R. 95.

the House, stated that the key words "if it were not proposed to be acquired" in the English equivalent of section 17(4) of the 1963 Act are drafted in the present conditional. It followed that no assumption had to be made as to what may or may not have happened in the past. The assumption to be made was that the scheme for which the land is to be acquired, together with the underlying proposal which may appear in the planning documents, are cancelled as at the relevant date.

7–13   Although those key words do not appear in section 17(4) of the 1963 Act, it is clear that the certificate procedure in Scotland also operates on the basis that the subject land is not proposed to be acquired[1] so that the guidance in *Fletcher* applies also in Scotland.[2] The valuer, therefore, has to consider in the light of planning policy and the physical factors at the relevant date what alternative development would have been appropriate on the assumption that the proposal underlying the acquisition is cancelled at that date.

The application of the "cancellation assumption" in *Fletcher* was considered by the Inner House in *South Lanarkshire Council v Lord Advocate*.[3] In that case, an application for the certificate of appropriate alternative development followed the deemed confirmation of a purchase notice. The application was for, *inter alia*, non-food retail development. At the time of the deemed notice to treat (the "relevant date" for determining the planning position), the Secretary of State had before him two applications for planning permissions for non-food retail development in the Gorbals area of Glasgow. The certificate application came before the Secretary of State following a deemed refusal by the planning authority and a public inquiry was held. The reporter conducting the certificate inquiry heard evidence with regard to the two planning applications. The reporter concluded that the certificate site would have been "at the front of the queue" in the no scheme world. He accordingly recommended that a "valuable" certificate should be issued specifying, amongst other alternative classes of development, non-food retail, a recommendation which the Scottish Ministers (who had taken over from the Secretary of State) adopted. The local authority challenged the certificate on the ground that the reporter had erred in considering the Gorbals application at all. The cancellation assumption required the Ministers to assume that the deemed compulsory acquisition and proposal to construct an extension to the M74 (which in this case underlay the deemed acquisition) were cancelled at the relevant date. The Council argued that it was also necessary to ignore the two Gorbals applications since they had been made before the relevant date in the context of the grant of planning permission for the M74 extension. As the assumption was that the M74 proposal was no longer extant, it should follow that the two applications were also eliminated. The Lord President, Lord Rodger, giving judgement for the Inner House held that argument to be misconceived. What had to be assumed was that the acquisition scheme and the underlying proposal were cancelled on the

---

[1] See the 1963 Act, s.17(3)(a) and *Grampian Regional Council v Secretary of State for Scotland*.

[2] *South Lanarkshire Council v Lord Advocate*, 2002 S.C. 88, IH.

[3] 2002 S.C. 88.

relevant date, not that they had never existed prior to that date. On that basis, the Gorbals applications formed part of the planning landscape which the reporter and the Scottish Ministers had to take into account in determining the application for the certificate in the light of the cancellation assumption. The reporter and the Scottish Ministers had to consider how a non-food retail proposal would have fared on the certificate site in that situation. If it would have succeeded, then the certificate should reflect that; on the other hand, if the other applications would have been preferred and the certificate proposal would have failed, then the certificate should equally reflect that.

In considering what classes of alternative development would have been appropriate, regard may properly be paid not only to the possibility of development on the subject land but also to the prospect of its development as a part of a larger area, whether or not that larger area is under the control of the applicant.[4] The likelihood of such permission being sought or implemented is irrelevant; the legislation presupposes that an application will be made.[5]

Whether or not any permission which may be assumed under section 23(5) of the 1963 Act as a result of the issuing of a valuable CAAD will in fact increase the value of the land is a matter for the claimant and the acquiring authority to determine, or failing agreement for the Lands Tribunal to decide.[6] In *David Bell v Corporation of Glasgow*[7] an official arbiter rejected the view that demand as well as permission could be assumed and concluded in the circumstances of that case that there would have been no demand for certain of the activities referred to in the CAAD.

Section 29 of the 1963 Act provides that any person aggrieved by a decision of the Scottish Ministers on an appeal under section 26 or the planning authority may, within six weeks of the date of the decision, question its validity by way of application to the Court of Session on the grounds that it is not within the powers of the Act or that any procedural requirements have not been complied with.

CPPRAG recommended that a simplified and updated version of the certificate procedure was essential as a means of identifying the planning assumptions for the purposes of valuing the land for compulsory purchase compensation in order to minimise delays and to prevent an increase in the number of referrals to the Lands Tribunal.[8]

The cost of obtaining a CAAD, including expenses incurred in connection with any appeal under section 26 where any of the issues on appeal are determined in the claimant's favour, is an expense that may be recovered as part of the claim for compensation.[9]

---

[4] *Sutton v Secretary of State for the Environment* [1984] J.P.L. 647.

[5] See above. The likelihood of the permission being implemented may well be relevant to the question of demand.

[6] See *Bromilow v Greater Manchester Council* (1975) 31 P. & C.R. 398; *J. Davy Ltd v London Borough of Hammersmith* (1975) 30 P. & C.R. 469; and *David Bell v Glasgow Corporation,* decision of an Official Arbiter, Ref. No. 2/1969.

[7] Ref. No. 2/1969. See, too, *Young v Lothian Regional Council,* 1992 S.L.T. (Lands Tr.) 17.

[8] "Fundamental review of the laws and procedures relating to compulsory purchase and compensation: final report" (2000) DETR para. 116.

[9] Section 25(9A) of the 1963 Act added by the Planning and Compensation Act 1991, s.75(3) partly reversing the decision in *Hull and Humber Investment Co. Ltd v Hull Corporation* [1965] 2 Q.B. 145.

7–14 Cases sometimes arise where land is acquired for a particular form of development and compensation is assessed accordingly but, in the light of changed circumstances, it is subsequently decided to use the land for an alternative form of development. The effect of the grant of planning permission for the alternative development may be to increase the value of the land above that on which the original award of compensation was based. Where an increase in value occurs in this way, it seems reasonable that the original owner of the land should be in a position to benefit. Part V of the Land Compensation (Scotland) Act 1963 makes provision for such benefit.[10]

Section 31 of the 1963 Act provides for the payment of additional compensation where an interest in land is compulsorily acquired or is sold to an authority possessing compulsory purchase powers and, before the end of the period of ten years beginning with the date of completion, a planning decision is made granting permission for the carrying out of additional development on the land.[11] The additional compensation is payable in response to a claim[12] where the original compensation or price is less than it would have been if the permission had been in force at the date of the notice to treat. The additional compensation is assessed under the provisions of Part III of the 1963 Act[13] and is equal to the difference. Provision is made for claims by successors in title (s.31(4)).

No additional compensation is payable in respect of a planning decision relating to land acquired:

(a) under ss.142 or 143 of the Local Government, Planning and Land Act 1980 (acquisitions by urban development corporations and by roads authorities in connection with urban development areas)[14];

(b) under the New Towns (Scotland) Act 1968 (acquisitions by development corporations and by roads authorities in connection with new town areas)[15]; or

(c) where the compulsory purchase order included a direction under section 45(1) of the Planning (Listed Buildings and Conservation Areas) (Scotland) Act 1997 (minimum compensation in case of listed building deliberately left derelict).

---

[10] Added by the Planning and Compensation Act 1991, s.77 and Sch.16. The provisions revive in modified form Part V of the 1963 Act repealed by the Land Commission Act 1967.

[11] "Additional Development" is defined in s.37(1) of the 1963 Act, added by s.77 and Sch.16 to the 1991 Act.

[12] As to who may claim, see s.31(1) (4) and the Third Schedule to the 1963 Act added by s.77 and Sch.17 to the 1991 Act.

[13] And see paras.1–3 of the Third Schedule to the 1961 Act.

[14] No such areas have been designated in Scotland.

[15] The Enterprise and New Towns (Scotland) Act 1990, Part II, provided for the winding up and dissolution of the new town development corporations in Scotland.

The additional compensation will carry interest at the rate prescribed under section 31 of the 1963 Act from the date of the planning decision until payment.

To facilitate the making of a claim under section 31, the person entitled may give the acquiring authority an address for service (s.32(1)). The acquiring authority must then give notice to the person in the event of the making of a planning decision which would trigger a s.31 claim (s.32(2)).

A section 31 claim will be of no effect if it is made more than six months after the date of the notice referred to in section 32(2) or, if no address for service has been given, six months after the date of the planning decision(s.32(4)). If there is an appeal against the planning decision time runs from the date of the decision on appeal.

Where the acquiring authority cease to be entitled to the whole or part of the land in question, the authority must arrange with the planning authority to give notice to them of any planning decision so that they (the acquiring authority) will in turn be able to give notice under section 32(2) (s.32(6)(7)).

The provisions in section 31 and 32 are applied to any planning permission granted or deemed to be granted in the circumstances mentioned in column 1 of the Table as if the planning decision granting that permission had been made on the date shown in column 2 (s.33(1)):

Planning permission	Date of decision
Permission granted by a development order	When development is initiated
Permission granted by the adoption or approval of a simplified planning zone scheme	When the scheme is approved or adopted
Permission granted by an order designating an enterprise zone	When the designation takes effect
Permission deemed to be granted by a direction under section 57 of the Town and Country Planning (Scotland) Act 1997	When the direction is given
Permission deemed to be granted by a planning authority	The occurrence of the event in consequence of which the permission is deemed to be granted

Where, in such a case, the development is proposed to be carried out by the acquiring authority, or by some other person who has notified the acquiring authority, the authority must give notice of the proposal to any person who has left an address for service under section 32(1) so that a claim for additional compensation under section 31 may be made (s.33)(2)). However, such a claim will be of no effect if made more than six months after the date of a notice given under section 32(2). If no such address for service has been left with the acquiring authority, the six month period will run from the date shown in column 2 of the Table (s.33(4)).

The provisions of sections 31 and 32 are applied by section 34 to additional development initiated by or on behalf of the Crown or initiated in right of the Crown interest in the land. A Crown interest refers to an interest belonging to the Queen in right of the Crown or belonging to a government department or held in trust for her Majesty for the purposes of a government department (s.34(7)).

The form of any notice to be given under Part V may be prescribed by regulations made by the Scottish Ministers (s.36(1)).

CHAPTER 8

DISREGARDING THE SCHEME

INTRODUCTION

Actions or decisions of government bodies may affect the value of land. **8–01**
The Uthwatt Committee referred to an increase in the value of land
from such actions or decisions as "betterment",[1] a decrease in value is
generally referred to either as "worsenment," "injurious affection" or
"blight." The purpose of this chapter is to consider whether, and if so to
what extent, such increases or decreases may be reflected in compensation for the compulsory acquisition of land.[2]

In Chapter 7 it was pointed out that in assessing the market value of
the land account may be taken of the potential which it may have for
some other more profitable use and the way in which such potential may
be established for compensation purposes was examined. It is important
to bear in mind, however, that what is being compensated is the
claimant's loss and the claimant cannot, as Denyer-Green observes, "add
to this by taking advantage of the statutory purchaser's needs and
requirements which might give the land in the purchaser's hands a
higher value".[3] In assessing the potential of the land the claimant must
disregard any increase in value which is due to the scheme for which it is
being acquired; that is the value of the land to the purchaser.[4]

Thus, in *Fraser v City of Fraserville*,[5] part of a river including a
waterfall, was acquired from the claimant for a hydroelectric scheme.
The intention was to construct a dam on other land higher up the river

---

[1] "Expert Committee on Compensation and Betterment: Final Report" (1942) HMSO
(Cmnd. 6386).
[2] For a comprehensive review of the development of the law in this field see Law
Commission Consultation, "Towards a Compulsory Purchase Code: (1) Compensation"
(2002) *Paper No 165* App.5.
[3] B. Denyer-Green, "The Pointe Gourde Principle" (1978) 8 Kingston L.R. 101. And see
Penny v Penny (1868) L.R. 5 Eq. 227; *Stebbing v Metropolitan Board of Works* (1870) L.R. 6
Q.B. 37. One aspect of this has already been seen in the discussion of rule (3) in Chapter
5. Rule (3) provides that, in assessing compensation, no account is to be taken of certain
potential which land may have because of its special suitability or adaptability. As to the
interrelation of rule (3), see comment at p.132.
[4] If, however, the premium value was pre-existent to the acquisition and does not
depend upon the acquiring authority's scheme, that value may be taken into account (see
Wards Construction (Medway) Ltd v Barclays Bank plc and Kent County Council (1994) 68
P. & C.R. 391; and *Allan v Banff and Buchan District Council*, unreported, June 29, 1993,
Lands Tribunal for Scotland).
[5] [1917] A.C. 187.

with a view to increasing the flow of water over the waterfall at certain times so as to generate power. The claimant argued that compensation should reflect the value of the waterfall to those promoting the electricity generating scheme. The Judicial Committee of the Privy Council rejected this approach and held that any increase in the value of the land to the acquiring authority as a result of its scheme was to be ignored. Lord Buckmaster said:

> "the value to be ascertained is the value to the seller of the property in its actual condition at the time of expropriation with all its existing advantages and with all its possibilities excluding any advantage due to the carrying out of the scheme for which the property is compulsorily acquired. The question of what is the scheme being a question of fact for the arbitrator in each case."[6]

Considerable difficulty, however, arises where the subject land is just one part of a much wider area of land being acquired for the scheme of development and the development or prospect of development of the other land in implementation of the scheme enhances or depreciates the value of the land being acquired. Consider as a relatively straightforward example, the facts in *MacDonald* v *Midlothian County Council*.[7] Mac-Donald's house was compulsorily purchased as part of a redevelopment scheme in Kirknewton, a scheme involving the improvement of some houses, the demolition and rebuilding of others and the improvement and realignment of certain roads. The Lands Tribunal for Scotland found that the result of improvements already carried out in the area under the scheme was to put up the value which a willing seller would have been likely to have obtained for MacDonald's property in the open market by some £1,660. Similarly, the presence of houses on either side of MacDonald's which had been acquired under the scheme for redevelopment but which had been vandalised in the interim would have depressed the value of MacDonald's property in the open market by about £300. For reasons which will be explained shortly, these effects on value resulting from the scheme were disregarded in the assessment of compensation. The point to be made at this stage is that the adjustment in value, although caused by the redevelopment scheme, would have been reflected in a sale of the house by a willing seller in the open market.

In *MacDonald* the adjustments were to the existing use value of the land but such adjustments may also be made to the potential which the land has for some other use. A local authority scheme for the development of a greenfield site for residential purposes may increase the value of other greenfield sites in the vicinity due to expectations about their future allocation for similar purposes.

The question is, given the analogy with a sale by a willing seller in the open market which rule (2) strives to achieve, should these adjustments

---

[6] In 1919, Parliament, as explained in Chapter 4, substituted a hypothetical willing seller for the actual seller in an effort to achieve a more objective measure of compensation (s.2 of the Acquisition of Land (Assessment of Compensation) Act 1919) but it did not otherwise alter the basis of compensation.

[7] 1975 S.L.T. (Lands Tr.) 24.

in value be reflected in compensation when the land is acquired for the scheme? If not, why not?

In *South-Eastern Railway Co. v London County Council*[8] in 1915, the Court of Appeal held that in the absence of specific statutory authority no adjustment was to be made to the compensation for land taken for a road improvement scheme to reflect the appreciation in the value of other neighbouring land belonging to the claimants resulting from the scheme. Eve J. at first instance pinpointed the difficulty of adjusting compensation on account of betterment. It would unfairly discriminate between a landowner whose land was compulsorily acquired and a neighbour whose land was not acquired but was similarly increased in value as a result of the scheme. It would, he said:

> "bring about some startling results; the most obvious one being that it would upset all uniformity of value, in as much as the value of the identical piece of land in the hands of one vendor might be assessed at many times its value in the hands of another, and this, not from any intrinsic distinction, but by reason solely of extraneous considerations. Moreover, it would be calculated to work injustice in that a vendor compelled to sell, and who the legislature intended should be compensated for being compelled to sell, might have to accept from the undertakers a price far less than he would have obtained from any other purchaser, and out of all proportion to the true value of the land had it been ascertained without reference to the fortuitous circumstances of his also being interested in the contiguous land."[9]

Similarly, in *Walker's Trustees v Caledonian Railway Company*[10] the trustees claimed compensation for the depreciation in the value of their premises caused by the adverse effects, on their access, of the construction of a railway. The railway company argued that, in assessing compensation, the beneficial effects on the value of the premises from the location of a railway station in the immediate neighbourhood should be taken into account. In the Court of Session, Lord Young rejected the railway company's argument. "This contention is," he said, "admittedly novel, and I content myself with saying that it is in my opinion inadmissible."[11]

THE POINTE GOURDE PRINCIPLE

However, the decision of the Judicial Committee of the Privy Council in **8–02** *Pointe Gourde Quarrying and Transport Co. Ltd v Sub-Intendent of Crown Lands*[12] in 1947 is widely regarded as authority for the proposition that

---

[8] [1915] 2 Ch. 252.
[9] See above at p.259.
[10] (1881) 8 R. 405.
[11] Although the case went to the House of Lords this particular line of argument was not pursued.
[12] [1947] A.C. 565.

compensation should be adjusted to account for betterment arising from the scheme. The facts of the case were that the Crown compulsorily acquired the company's stone quarry in Trinidad for use in the construction of a nearby naval base. The ordinance under which the compensation was assessed followed closely the provisions of the Acquisition of Land (Assessment of Compensation) Act 1919. The total claim for the quarry as a going concern amounted to $101,000. Of this, $15,000 represented additional value reflecting the increased profits which an operator of the quarry could have expected to make selling stone for the construction of the nearby naval base had it not been expropriated by the Crown. The point at issue was whether the item of $15,000 was allowable in law as a part of the compensation. Much of the argument centred on whether the item was excluded by the local equivalent of rule (3). The court held that it was not.[13] However, Lord MacDermott, giving judgment for the court, went on to say:

> "But it does not follow that this part of the award can stand. It is well settled that compensation for the compulsory acquisition of land cannot include an increase in value which is entirely due to the scheme underlying the acquisition."

The court held that the sum of $15,000 represented an increase in value due to the scheme and it was disallowed. As authority for his statement, Lord MacDermott cited dicta by Eve J. in *South Eastern Railway* and by Lord Buckmaster in *Fraser*. However, in the former case, the increase in the value of the remaining land caused by the scheme was not set off against the compensation; and the latter was concerned with excluding value to the purchaser.

Different views have been expressed about the correctness of the decision in *Pointe Gourde*. Davies, for example, regards the decision as correct but for the wrong reason.[14] There was, he argues, a blatant inconsistency in the claim. "There could be no market for the *land* among persons who (as such) wanted the *stone*, any more than there can be a market for shop premises among persons who (as such) want the goods sold by retail in such a shop. A man who wishes to eat sausages does not buy the butcher's shop; and a man who buys the butcher's shop does not do so in order to eat the sausages." However, Davies regards the formulation of the *ratio decidendi* of the decision as exceptionable. There was, he says, "no 'increase in value' to be disregarded, merely an unwarranted increase in the amount claimed". Denyer-Green, on the other hand, argues that the decision was incorrect.[15] "There was," he

---

[13] As the Law Commission point out, the court adopted a narrow interpretation of rule (3) and expanded the judicial rule in *Pointe Gourde* to fill its place. For a discussion of the inter-relation between rule (3) and the *Pointe Gourde* rule see *Waters v Welsh Development Agency* [2002] J.P.L. 1481, CA *per* Carnwath L J. The scope of rule (3) was further cut back by the Planning and Compensation Act 1991 to the point where, in the Law Commission's view, it now has little remaining purpose and could be repealed (Consultation Paper, "Towards a compulsory purchase code: (1) compensation" (2002) *No 165* App.5, A93–A97).

[14] Keith Davies, "The Pointe Gourde Rule" (1975) *The Conveyancer and Property Lawyer* p.414.

[15] B. Denyer-Green, "The Pointe Gourde Principle" (1978) 8 *Kingston Law Review* 101 and 184.

says, "some ground for considering the extra sum as representing an increase in value, for there can be a market for the land among persons who wish to quarry and sell the stone". However, he criticises the *ratio decidendi* of the decision because it appears to apply the rule excluding an increase in value due to the scheme so as to exclude betterment value caused by competition among persons desirous of selling stone to the naval base, two quite different things.[16]

Whatever view is taken about the correctness of the decision, it is important because, as Denyer-Green observes, "for the first time betterment to market value caused by the scheme of the acquiring authority was disregarded for the purpose of assessing compensation for the land taken".[17] The converse of the decision is that worsenment, the depreciation in the value of land resulting from the scheme underlying the acquisition, should also be brought into account so as to increase the compensation.[18] In *Jelson Ltd v Blaby District Council*[19] Lord Denning accepted that the *Pointe Gourde* principle applies not only to appreciation in value but also to depreciation in value. And in the Privy Council decision in *Melwood Units Property Ltd v Commissioner of Main Roads,*[20] Lord Russell of Killowen held that "In their Lordships' opinion it is a part of the common law deriving as a matter of principle from the nature of compensation for resumption or compulsory acquisition, that neither relevantly attributable appreciation nor depreciation in value is to be regarded in the assessment of land compensation".[21]

STATUTORY EXPRESSION OF THE POINTE GOURDE PRINCIPLE

The proposition that the effects of betterment or worsenment due to the **8–03** scheme on the value of land being acquired should be disregarded in assessing compensation was subsequently given statutory expression.[22]

---

[16] And see the Law Commission Consultation, "Towards a Compulsory Purchase Code: (1) Compensation" (2002) *Paper No 165* App.5. Also the decision in *Waters v Welsh Development Agency* [2002] J.P.L. 1481, CA *per* Carnwath L J.

[17] B. Denyer-Green, "Recapture of Betterment" (1980) 255 E.G. 615.

[18] In *Blackadder v Grampian Regional Council,* unreported, March 18, 1992, Lands Tribunal for Scotland, the tribunal held that, although the scheme underlying the acquisition was a factor contributing to the risk of damage to the subject property, the real reason for the property being damaged was that the claimant had left it empty in such circumstances that it might be regarded as derelict and abandoned. The claimant therefore had to bear the loss due to the damage to the property; it was not regarded as a depreciation in value due to the scheme.

[19] [1978] 1 All E.R. 548.

[20] [1979] A.C. 426. See, too, W. A. Leach, "Pointe Gourde Principle" (1979) 250 E.G. 966.

[21] For decisions of the Lands Tribunal for Scotland where the *Pointe Gourde* principle has been considered see *MacDonald v Midlothian County Council*, 1975 S.L.T. (Lands Tr.) 24; *Mrs Fulton's Trustees v Glasgow Corporation*, 1976 S.L.T. (Lands Tr.) 14; *Hugh MacDonald's Representatives v Sutherland District Council*, 1977 S.L.T. (Lands Tr.) 7; *Spence v Lanarkshire County Council*, 1976 S.L.T. (Lands Tr.) 2; *Gray v Glasgow District Council*, 1980 S.L.T. (Lands Tr.) 7; *Barr v Highland* Regional Council, unreported, April 24, 1987, Lands Tribunal for Scotland.

[22] In *Waters v Welsh Development Agency* [2002] J.P.L. 1481, CA Carnwath L J. stated that the corresponding provision in the English and Welsh legislation could not be seen "as simply an exercise in clarification of the established rule". The section both enunciated and extended the judicial rule.

Section 13 of the Land Compensation (Scotland) Act 1963, as amended, now provides that no account is to be taken of any increase or decrease in the value of land which is attributable to the scheme as defined in Schedule 1.

To explain section 13 it is necessary to go back to the Town and Country Planning (Scotland) Act 1954 which introduced a dual price system in land (see Chapter 4). While private sales were to be at market value, compensation on the compulsory acquisition of land was to be restricted to existing use value plus any "unexpended balance of established development value" together with a sum representing interest. This dual price system was a clear departure from the principle of equivalence and it provoked considerable unease. "The dual price system," notes Cullingworth, "was inherently unstable, and disquiet about its operation rapidly mounted—from the land professions, from organisations of land-owners, from local authorities, from government departments, and from government back-benchers."[23] Eventually, the government felt compelled to alter the arrangements. The obvious solution was to restore market value as the measure of compensation. However, fears were expressed about the increased cost which would fall upon public authorities in acquiring land, one of the principal reasons for the introduction of the dual price system in the first place. "It was thought," says Cullingworth, "that this would expose the Government to the criticism of impeding municipal development, which would be particularly embarrassing in relation to slum clearance in Glasgow and other congested urban areas. Moreover, a Bill which increased the level of compensation for compulsory acquisition but made no attempt to deal with the problem of betterment would be likely to revive public interest in the whole question of the taxation of land values."[24] The upshot was that market value was restored as the measure of compensation by the Town and Country Planning (Scotland) Act 1959 and limited provision was made in the Act to enable public authorities to recover betterment generated by their schemes by way of deduction from the compensation payable. No account was to be taken in assessing compensation of increases (and decreases) in value due to the scheme as defined. This was thought to be in line with practice recognised by the Privy Council in *Pointe Gourde*.[25] The provision in the 1959 Act is now to be found in section 13 of the 1963 Act, as amended.

Section 13 is a complex provision.[26] In *Camrose (Viscount) v Basingstoke Corporation*[27] Russell L.J. observed of the corresponding English provision: "The drafting of this section appears to me to be calculated to postpone as long as possible comprehension of its purport." The section needs to be read in conjunction with Schedule 1 to the 1963

---

[23] J. B. Cullingworth, *Environmental Planning* (1980) HMSO Vol.10, p.195. See, too, *Report of the Committee on Administrative Tribunals and Inquiries* (1957) HMSO, para.278 (Cmnd. 218).

[24] J. B. Cullingworth, *supra*, p.95.

[25] See above at p.205 citing the "Notes on clauses".

[26] In *Waters v Welsh Development Agency* [2002] J.P.L. 1481, CA Carnwath LJ observed of the corresponding English and Welsh provision that "there can be few stronger candidates on the statute book for urgent reform".

[27] [1966] 1 W.L.R. 1100.

Act. Part I of Schedule 1 is divided into two columns. The left hand column lists six different circumstances in which land may be earmarked for acquisition for public purposes. The characteristic of each circumstance is that the land in question ("the relevant land")[28] forms part only of a wider area earmarked for a scheme of works. The right hand column delimits the extent of the scheme in the six different circumstances. Section 13 provides that in assessing compensation for the acquisition of "the relevant interest"[29] in one of the six circumstances listed, no account is to be taken of an increase or decrease in the value of that interest which is attributable to development under the corresponding scheme as defined. Any reference to development of any land is to be construed as including a reference to the clearing of that land.[30] Like the *Pointe Gourde* principle, section 13 modifies the effect of rule (2) by providing that in certain cases actual or prospective development is to be disregarded.

The six circumstances and the corresponding scheme are as follows: **8–04**

Case 1: A single compulsory purchase order or special Act quite often authorises the acquisition of a number of different parcels of land with a number of different interests. In assessing the value of any one of the interests authorised to be acquired by the order or Act ("the relevant interest") it may be found that the development or prospect of development for the purposes of the scheme of any of the other land authorised to be acquired[31] has increased or decreased the value of that interest. No account is to be taken of that increase or decrease in value. The extent of the scheme is defined by the land authorised to be acquired by the order or Act but excluding the relevant land.

Case 2: In assessing the value of the relevant interest in land forming part of an action area or comprehensive development area,[32] no account is to be taken of any increase or decrease in the value of that interest which is attributable to the development or redevelopment, or the prospect of development or redevelopment, of any of the other land in accordance with the scheme for the action area or comprehensive development

---

[28] In s.45 of the 1963 Act "the relevant land" is defined as the land in which "the relevant interest" subsists; and "the relevant interest" is defined as the interest acquired in pursuance of the appropriate notice to treat.

[29] See above.

[30] Section 13(3) of the 1963 Act. And see *Davy v Leeds Corporation* [1964] 1 W.L.R. 1218; affirmed [1965] 1 W.L.R. 445.

[31] This refers to the aggregate of the land authorised to be acquired by the compulsory purchase order or the special Act (s.13(3)(a)). In respect of land authorised by any Act to be acquired for defence purposes, see s.13(3)(b).

[32] The Town and Country Planning (Scotland) Act 1972 required authorities to indicate in their structure plan any part of their area selected for comprehensive treatment by means of development, redevelopment or improvement (referred to as 'action areas', replacing the earlier 'comprehensive development areas'). A local plan then had to be prepared for the action area. This provision has been repealed and the position now is that an action area can be promoted in a local plan without any prior notation in the structure plan.

area. The extent of the scheme is defined by the action area or comprehensive development area but excludes the relevant land.

Cases 3–4A: Provision very similar to that for action areas is made in respect of land:

- which at the date of the notice to treat formed part of an area designated as the site of a new town (Case 3)[33] or as an extension of a site of a new town (Case 3A)[34];

- forming part of an area to which a town development scheme under Part II of the Housing and Town Development (Scotland) Act 1957 relates, being a scheme which is in operation at the date of the notice to treat (Case 4);

- forming part of an area designated as an urban development area by an order under section 134 of the Local Government, Planning and Land Act 1980 (Case 4A).[35]

It should be noted that section 13 does not apply if the development or prospect of development giving rise to the adjustment in value would have been likely to be carried out:

- as regards Case 1, if the acquiring authority had not acquired and did not propose to acquire any of the land authorised to be acquired; and

- as regards Cases 2, 3, 3A and 4A, if the area or areas referred to had not been so defined or designated; and

- as regards Case 4, if the scheme had not come into operation.[36]

8–05   Section 47 of the Land Compensation (Scotland) Act 1973 could operate to enlarge the scope of Cases 3 and 3A in certain circumstances. The section provides that, where the Scottish Ministers have made a draft order under section 1 of the New Towns (Scotland) Act 1968 designating any area as the site of a new town or as an extension of the site of a new town so as to provide housing or other facilities required because of the carrying out of a particular public development,[37] they may before the order is finalised give a direction specifying that

---

[33] Designated under the New Towns (Scotland) Act 1968 (see Sch.9, para.5). And see the 1963 Act, ss.13(2) and (2A) and Sch.1, Pt II. Section 13(2A) was added by the Local Government, Planning and Land Act 1980, Sch.25, Pt IV, para.9(2)(b)(3). The new town development corporations in Scotland were wound up and dissolved during the 1990s under the provisions of Part II of the Enterprise and New Towns (Scotland) Act 1990.

[34] Inserted by the New Towns Act 1966, Schedule, Part II, para.4. See, too, s.13(2A) and Sch.1, Pt II of the 1963 Act.

[35] Inserted by the Local Government, Planning and Land Act 1980, s.145(1). And see s.13(2A) of and Sch.1, Pt III to the 1963 Act. No such order has yet been made in respect of any area in Scotland. Pt III of Schedule 1 was added to the 1963 Act by the Local Government, Planning and Land Act 1980, s.145(4). For a case turning on Case 4A see *Waters v Welsh Development Agency* [2002] J.P.L. 1481, CA.

[36] Section 13(1)(a) and (b) of the 1963 Act (as amended by the Local Government, Planning and Land Act 1980, s.145(5)(a) and Schedule 25, Part IV, paras.9(2)(a) and (3)).

[37] See s.47(6) of the 1973 Act.

development for the purposes of the section. The effect of such a direction is that in applying section 13 of the 1963 Act to Cases 3 and 3A there is also to be disregarded in the assessment of compensation any increase or decrease in the value of the relevant interest which is attributable to the carrying out or the prospect of the public development specified. It has been suggested that this provision was introduced at a time when it was thought that the third London airport would be located at Maplin and that a new town would be required to deal with the development the airport would generate.[38] No such direction appears to have been made in Scotland.

Cases 3–4A have little practical relevance today, partly because the new town development corporations were wound up and dissolved under the provisions of Part II of the Enterprise and New Towns (Scotland) Act 1990, partly because the provisions of Part II of the Housing and Town Development (Scotland) Act 1957 have little continuing relevance and partly because no urban development areas have been designated in Scotland.

An illustration of the way in which section 13 and Schedule 1 may operate is provided by the decision of an official arbiter in *Mrs Leckie's Trustees v East Kilbride Development Corporation*,[39] a case turning on the earlier provision in section 9 of the Town and Country Planning (Scotland) Act 1959. The Railway Tavern in East Kilbride was compulsorily purchased for the purposes of a new town. The construction of the new town had begun in the late 1940s and the influx of people into the area had resulted over the years in a considerable increase in the profitability of the tavern. In valuing the premises for compensation, the arbiter took the view that the profitability had been much inflated by the scheme and that in so far as this increase in profitability was reflected in the market value of the premises it should be disregarded.

A further illustration is provided by *Davy v Leeds Corporation*[40] which turned on the corresponding provision in the English legislation. The appellants were owners of back-to-back houses in Leeds. The area in which these houses were situated was designated a clearance area by the city council under the provisions of Part III of the Housing Act 1957. A compulsory purchase order was subsequently made and confirmed for the acquisition of land in 13 clearance areas, including the one in question, together with other land for clearance and redevelopment. As the appellants' houses were unfit for human habitation compensation was assessed on the value of the appellants' land as sites cleared of buildings and available for development in an area zoned for residential development (see Chapter 9). The appellants argued that, in assessing compensation regard should be had to the fact that instead of buying a site with bad housing around it, a purchaser in the open market would be buying a site in an area which was bound to be cleared and available for development. The House of Lords held that under Case 1 it was necessary to disregard the development, including the clearance, of any of the land authorised to be acquired because such clearance would not

---

[38] [1985] J.P.L. 78.
[39] Ref. No. 10/1961.
[40] [1965] 1 W.L.R. 445.

have been likely to have occurred in the absence of the council's scheme. In other words, the fact that the surrounding houses had been authorised for acquisition and would be cleared in accordance with the clearance area designation was to be disregarded. Viscount Dilhorne, referring to the dictum of Lord MacDermott in *Pointe Gourde,* observed that it seemed to him that Parliament "has given statutory expression to the principle which Lord MacDermott stated was well settled."[41]

THE RELATIONSHIP BETWEEN THE POINTE GOURDE PRINCIPLE AND
SECTION 13

8–06 For a while, however, the relationship between the *Pointe Gourde* principle and its statutory expression was not altogether clear.[42] In *Camrose (Viscount) v Basingstoke Corporation,*[43] for example, some 550 acres of land were acquired under the Town Development Act 1952 for the expansion of Basingstoke. At issue, *inter alia,* was the interpretation of section 6 and Schedule 1, Case 4 of the English Land Compensation Act 1961. In defining the extent of the development, the effect of which on the value of the relevant interest is to be disregarded, Case 4 specifically excludes development of the "relevant land".[44] The claimant argued that although no regard could be paid to the effect on the value of the "relevant land" of the prospect of development of other land in the course of the town development scheme, the prospect of the development of the "relevant land" itself under the scheme was not covered by this exclusion. The section, therefore, implied permitted regard to be had to any increase in value due to the development of the relevant land itself under the town development scheme. The Court of Appeal held that the *Pointe Gourde* principle was left untouched by the statutory provision and that the increase in value claimed which was due to the scheme should be disregarded.

The decision in *Camrose* was subsequently followed in *Wilson v Liverpool City Council.*[45] The city council wished to acquire some 391 acres of land for housing development. 305 acres were acquired by agreement but the remaining 86 acres, of which the claimant owned 74 acres, were the subject of a compulsory purchase order. The claimant acknowledged that any increase in the value of his land attributable to the development of any of the other land authorised to be acquired by the compulsory purchase order had to be disregarded under section 6 of and Part I of Schedule 1 to the English Land Compensation Act of 1961. However, he argued, these provisions were exhaustive. There was no requirement to disregard any increase in the value of his land attributable to the prospect of the development of the 305 acres which had not been compulsorily acquired. The Court of Appeal, applying the decision

[41] See above, p.453.
[42] See *Halliwell and Halliwell v Skelmersdale Development Corporation* (1965) 16 P. & C.R. 305; and *Kaye v Basingstoke Corporation* (1968) 20 P. & C.R. 417.
[43] [1966] 1 W.L.R. 1100.
[44] So indeed do the other Cases.
[45] [1971] 1 W.L.R. 302.

in *Camrose* rejected that argument. Lord Denning said: "It is suggested that that provision[46] contains a code which defines exhaustively the increases which are *not* to be taken into account: so that any other increase is to be taken into account: and, accordingly, there is no room for the *Pointe Gourde* principle. But this court has rejected that argument."

IDENTIFYING THE SCHEME

It is clear, therefore, that section 13 of and Schedule 1 to the 1963 Act **8–07** and the *Pointe Gourde* principle operate concurrently[47] and this may lead to some difficulty in identifying the scheme, the effects of which on value are to be ignored. In *Wilson*, the claimant argued that the *Pointe Gourde* principle could only apply where the scheme is precise and definite and is made known to all the world. Denning M.R. disagreed. "A scheme," he observed, "is a progressive thing. It starts vague and known to few. It becomes more precise and better known as time goes on. Eventually it becomes precise and definite, and known to all. Correspondingly, its impact has a progressive effect because it is so vague and uncertain. As it becomes more precise and better known, so its impact increases until it has an important effect. It is this increase, whether big or small, which is to be disregarded at the time when value is to be assessed."[48] In the same case, Widgery L.J. said "It would I think be a great mistake if we tended to focus our attention on the word 'scheme' as though it had some magic of its own"; and later "It is for the tribunal of fact to consider just what activities—past, present or future—are properly to be regarded as the scheme within the meaning of this proposition."[49] In *Bolton Metropolitan Borough Council v Tudor Properties Ltd*,[50] Mummery LJ, giving judgement for the Court of Appeal, stated that "the identification of the underlying scheme involves the application of a legal principle to available material in order to arrive at a factual conclusion".

Within these broad guidelines identification of the scheme would seem to turn, as the Lands Tribunal for Scotland observed in *Mrs Fulton's Trustees v Glasgow Corporation*,[51] very largely on the facts and circumstances of each case. In that case the tribunal held that the scheme underlying the compulsory acquisition could be traced back beyond the designation of the comprehensive development area in 1972 to the written statement accompanying the quinquennial review of the development plan submitted in 1960. The statement contained proposals which were sufficiently precise and sufficiently public to constitute an identifiable scheme. In *Bird & Bird v Wakefield Metropolitan District Council*[52] the Court of Appeal held that it was not necessary for the

[46] s.6 of and Sch.1, Pt I to the 1961 Act.
[47] *Sprinz v Kingston upon Hull City Council* (1975) 30 P. & C.R. 273.
[48] [1971] 1 W.L.R. 302 at p.309.
[49] See above. at p.310. And see *Fraser v City of Fraserville* [1917] A.C. 187, *per* Lord Buckmaster at p.194; and *Waters v Welsh Development Agency* [2002] J.P.L. 1481, CA *per* Carnwath L.J. at pp.1493–1495.
[50] (2000) 80 P. & C.R. 537.
[51] 1976 S.L.T. (Lands Tr.) 14.
[52] (1978) 248 E.G. 499.

scheme to provide for compulsory acquisition; it was enough that it underlay the acquisition.[53]

In *MacDonald v Midlothian County Council*,[54] the Lands Tribunal for Scotland rejected the claimants' contention that the proposed road realignment for which his house was being acquired was the scheme. The scheme comprised the housing redevelopment being undertaken in that part of Kirknewton involving both the improvement of existing houses and the building of new ones. The road realignment was incidental to the overall redevelopment. In *Cronin and Taylor v Swansea City Council*[55] the Lands Tribunal held that the scheme underlying the acquisition included the whole town centre development dating from 1947 of which the relevant comprehensive development area merely formed the latest phase. In that case the tribunal went on to observe that they were obliged under *Pointe Gourde* to disregard an increase in value *entirely* due to the scheme underlying the acquisition. They could, therefore, have regard to any enhancement in value due to the activity of bodies other than the local authority acting in exercise of compulsory powers, so far as such enhancement was not entirely due to the scheme.

In *Bell v Newcastle-upon-Tyne City Council*[56] the Lands Tribunal considered that the scheme included at least six comprehensive development areas within the city centre submitted to the Minister between 1962 to 1966 and all originating from a planning report in 1961. In that case the member concluded:

> "I am therefore satisfied on the evidence that the Burns First Report was a scheme of works with a clear starting point in time in 1961, sufficiently precise to enable an interested party to find out its proposals which were not to be greatly changed as each succeeding CDA came into being and was implemented. I find it in no way surprising that separate CDAs were necessary for a scheme extending to more than 200 acres of mainly built-up land in the centre of the City for administrative convenience, programming and financial considerations; but that did not make each CDA a fundamentally separate 'scheme'."

On the other hand, in *Sprinz v Kingston upon Hull City Council*[57] the tribunal held that the application for planning permission for development in that case was an entirely fresh project. Provision by the council for dealing with overspill was not, on the evidence, a continuing process coming under one scheme. And in *Bolton Metropolitan Borough Council v Tudor Properties Ltd*[57a] the Court of Appeal declined to disturb the decision of the Lands Tribunal that, in the circumstances of that case, the scheme to be disregarded in assessing compensation was the narrower of the two schemes canvassed by the parties.

---

[53] See too *Abbey Homesteads (Developments) Ltd v Northamptonshire County Council* (1991) 61 P. & C.R. 295, LT.

[54] 1975 S.L.T. (Lands Tr.) 24.

[55] (1972) 24 P. & C.R. 382.

[56] [1971] R.V.R. 209. See, too, *North-Eastern Housing Association Ltd v Newcastle upon-Tyne City Council* (1972) 25 P. & C.R. 178.

[57] (1975) 34 P. & C.R. 77.

[57a] (2000) 80 P. & C.R. 537.

In *Jelson Ltd v Blaby District Council*[58] the Court of Appeal accepted that there could be a scheme underlying an acquisition triggered by a purchase notice so that under *Pointe Gourde* any depreciation in value resulting from the scheme had to be ignored in assessing compensation. In that case a planning application for a substantial residential development had been granted subject to the reservation of a strip for a proposed public road, the line of which was shown in the development plan. The houses were built. In the meantime, the proposal for the road was abandoned. A subsequent planning application to build houses on the reserved strip was refused because of the adverse effect such development might have on the new houses on either side of the strip. A purchase notice was served and confirmed. In awarding compensation based on the development potential of the strip, the Lands Tribunal adopted a causal approach to the identification of the scheme. It was the road scheme which underlay or was the foundation of the purchase notice and its confirmation, a view with which the Court of Appeal concurred. On the other hand, in *Birmingham District Council v Morris and Jacombs*,[59] another purchase notice case, the Court of Appeal declined to accept that a condition on a planning permission for residential development requiring a strip of land to be reserved for vehicular access to the development could constitute a scheme. The value of the strip as an access was not due to any scheme of the local authority but simply to a condition on the planning permission.

VALUING IN THE "NO SCHEME" WORLD

Having identified the scheme it is then necessary to determine what **8–08** would have happened but for the scheme and to consider whether the scheme has, by comparison with the position in the "no scheme" world, resulted in an increase or decrease in the value of the subject land. Visualising the circumstances that would have prevailed in the "no scheme" world is for the valuer, as one commentator observed "perhaps the most difficult of the preliminaries to valuation with which he is confronted, for although he will study whatever evidence is available to him, in the end it must be inevitably a matter of conjecture."[60] Lord Denning in *Myers v Milton Keynes Development Corporation*[61] expressed the valuer's predicament in more graphic but possibly less helpful terms:

> "It is apparent, therefore," he said, "that the valuation has to be done in an imaginary state of affairs in which there is no scheme.

---

[58] [1977] 1 W.L.R. 1020.

[59] (1976) 33 P. & C.R. 27. See, too, *Lawlor v London Borough of Hounslow* [1981] J.P.L. 203.

[60] Maurice Clark, " 'Valuation Aspects of Land Taken Under a Scheme—1' in Compensation for Compulsory Purchase", (1975) *Journal of Planning and Environmental Law Occasional Paper* (Sweet and Maxwell). See, too, T. J. Nardecchia, " 'Valuation aspects of Land Taken Under a Scheme—2' in Compensation for Compulsory Purchase" (1975) *Journal of Planning and Environmental Law Occasional Paper* (Sweet and Maxwell); and A. Baum, "Pointe Gourde: The Valuation Problems" [1981] J.P.L. 726.

[61] [1974] 1 W.L.R. 696.

The valuer must cast aside his knowledge of what has happened in the past eight years due to the scheme. He must ignore the developments which will in all probability take place in the future ten years owing to the scheme. Instead, he must let his imagination take flight to the clouds. He must conjure up a land of make-believe, where there has not been, nor will be, a brave new town but where there is to be supposed the old order of things continuing."[62]

The sort of exercise that valuers and the Lands Tribunal for Scotland may have to engage in is well illustrated in *Mrs Fulton's Trustees v Glasgow Corporation*.[63] In that case the tribunal was called upon to determine what would probably have occurred to the relevant part of Govan in the "no scheme" world. The scene in Govan at the date of valuation 15 years after its designation for comprehensive development was one of dereliction and devastation. In support of their argument that the scheme had depressed values, the claimants cited certain streets in Paisley, where residential property had been gradually rehabilitated by owners and occupiers over a period of years, as an illustration of what would probably have happened in Govan in the absence of the local authority scheme. The tribunal rejected this comparison. Their view, on the evidence, was that dereliction as well as bad layout was the cause of the original designation of Govan for comprehensive development and selected clearance would probably have occurred in the area notwithstanding the change of emphasis towards rehabilitation of property in the housing legislation in the intervening years. There was evidence of closing and demolition orders being issued in respect of property all around the relevant land both before and after the designation of the area for comprehensive development. As the claimants' property was below the tolerable standard, action by the local housing authority would have been likely and discretionary improvement grants would probably not have been available in the circumstances. "Our general conclusion," said the tribunal, "is that background conditions in Govan coupled with the ordinary operation of housing legislation would probably have deterred private investors from purchasing the reference subjects, either for the purpose of improvement or in the hope of obtaining vacant possession of some of the houses for resale." This view of the "no scheme" world enabled the tribunal to determine that the local authority's scheme had done little to detract from the market value of the tenement properties in question to the private investor purchaser. There had, in other words, been no depreciation due to the scheme.

In *Hugh MacDonald's Representatives v Sutherland District Council*,[64] on the other hand, the Lands Tribunal for Scotland concluded on the evidence of that case that in the "no scheme" world the subject property would have had potential for improvement with grant aid and arrived at

---

[62] See above at p.704.
[63] 1976 S.L.T. (Lands Tr.) 14. See, too, *Domestic Hire Co. Ltd v Basildon Development Corporation* (1969) 21 P. & C.R. 299; *Collins v Basildon Development Corporation* (1969) 21 P. & C.R. 318; *Barr v Highland Regional Council*, unreported, April 24, 1987, Lands Tribunal for Scotland; and *Young v Lothian Regional Council* 1992 S.L.T. (Lands Tr.) 18.
[64] 1977 S.L.T. (Lands Tr.) 7.

a market value, based on comparisons with other cottages in the vicinity which had been sold, somewhat above that calculated by the acquiring authority.

In *Abbey Homesteads (Developments) Ltd v Northamptonshire County Council*,[65] the subject land was compulsorily acquired for a school. It was subject to a restrictive covenant (a planning agreement) reserving the land for school purposes. Glidewell LJ, giving judgement for the Court of Appeal, said that the Lands Tribunal had been entitled to accept the claimants' hypothesis that in the "no scheme" world a situation would be reached in which a potential purchaser of the subject land would be entitled to say that there was a very good chance that the restrictive covenant would be discharged and that chance would be reflected in the purchase price. There would be an expectation in the no scheme world that, since the authority had either purchased an alternative site or had not purchased the subject land, they were no longer seeking to acquire the subject land for a school.

In *North-Eastern Housing Association Ltd v Newcastle-upon-Tyne City Council*,[66] what was in issue was an appreciation in value due to the scheme. The subject premises, a 70 year old inter-terrace dwelling extensively altered and extended for use as offices, was valued for compensation purposes by reference to the prices obtained on the sale of four comparable properties in the open market. The council argued that there had been an increase in the prices paid in those transactions due to the scarcity of office property created by the council's comprehensive development scheme. The tribunal agreed that no account should be taken of this increase since the acquisitions by the acquiring authority which had resulted in the scarcity of office property was a manifestation of the comprehensive development scheme in action.

In *MacDonald* the Lands Tribunal for Scotland found that there was both an appreciation and a depreciation in the value of the subject property to be disregarded. The tribunal found that the result of improvements already carried out in the area under the scheme was to put up the value which a willing seller would have been likely to have obtained for MacDonald's property in the open market by some £1,660. Similarly, the presence of houses on either side of MacDonald's which had been acquired under the scheme for redevelopment but which had been vandalised in the interim would have depressed the value of MacDonald's property in the open market by about £300.[67]

It may, of course, be the case at the end of the day that, as in *Mrs Fulton's Trustees,* the value of the land on a notional sale in the open market in the "no scheme" world will not be substantially different from its value having regard to the scheme.[68]

The difficulty in determining what would have happened but for the scheme may be contrasted with the much simpler exercise of determin-

---

[65] (1992) 26 E.G. 140.

[66] (1972) 25 P. & C.R. 178.

[67] This would seem to depart from the general rule that the risk of damage does not pass to the acquiring authority until the date of valuation (see Ch.5). See J. Rowan Robinson and E Young, "Compulsory Acquisition, Compensation and Risk of Damage to Property" (1985) 30 J.L.S. 312; and R. Carnwath, "Vandalism and 'the Scheme" [1974] R.V.R. 562.

[68] See *Barr v Highland Regional Council*, unreported, April 24, 1987, Lands Tribunal for Scotland.

ing, for the purposes of a certificate of appropriate alternative development, what alternative development would have been appropriate if the
subject land were not proposed to be acquired. The "cancellation
assumption" introduced in *Secretary of State for the Environment v
Fletcher Estates (Harlscott) Ltd*[69] simplifies the exercise considerably (see
p.153).

COMMENT ON THE OPERATION OF THE PRINCIPLE AND ITS
STATUTORY EXPRESSION

8–09 In *Wilson* Widgery L.J. commented that "the purpose of the so-called
Pointe Gourde rule is to prevent the acquisition of the land being at a
price which is inflated by the very project or scheme which gives rise to
the acquisition".[70] This would seem also to underlie its statutory
expression in section 13 of and Schedule 1 to the 1963 Act. In a
memorandum presented by the then Minister of Housing and Local
Government to the Cabinet in October 1957, when the Cabinet were
considering the restoration of market value as the measure of compensation for compulsory acquisition, the Minister said:

> "But we must pause and see what it would involve. Take the case of
> agricultural land which acquires building value through the pro-
> vision, at public expense, of roads and sewers and water supply. If it
> is then agreed that the land is suitable for building, its value may be
> increased from (say) £50 an acre to as much as £1,000 an acre, or
> even more in areas where, as a result of planning restrictions,
> building land is in short supply. If that land is then needed for any
> public purpose, the public—whether as taxpayer or as ratepayer—in
> effect has to pay twice."[71]

As Cullingworth observes "unearned increment on the scale indicated
was hard to defend, and had considerable political implications".[72]

However, there are doubts about whether the *Pointe Gourde* principle
is either just or sound.[73] That it is not just may be illustrated by reference
to the decision in *Wilson*. In applying the *Pointe Gourde* principle, the
tribunal, with the subsequent approval of the Court of Appeal, made
their valuation by taking note of some comparable land next door to the
subject land which had been sold not long before for £6,700 an acre. It
had been sold by a private owner to a private developer at its dead-ripe
value. That value was an enhanced value because the seller and the
purchaser knew that the corporation would install sewage works and so

---

[69] (2000) 80 P. & C.R. 95.
[70] [1971] 1 W.L.R. 302 at p.310.
[71] Cited in J. B. Cullingworth, "Environmental Planning" (1980) HMSO Vol.4, p.180.
[72] See above. See, too, "Second Report of the Committee Dealing with the Law and
Practice relating to the Acquisition and Valuation of Land for Public Purposes" (1918)
HMSO, para.32 (Cmnd. 9229); and "Final Report of the Expert Committee on Compensation and Betterment" (1942) HMSO, para.188 (Cmnd. 6386).
[73] See for example, Keith Davies, *Law of Compulsory Purchase and Compensation* (5th
ed., Tolley), paras 7.4–7.20.

forth of which the developers could take advantage. Making all allowances, and deducting the enhancement in value due to the scheme, the tribunal valued the comparable subject land at £4,615 per acre. It seems hardly just that the betterment should accrue (subject possibly to taxation) to the neighbouring landowner selling in the open market but not to the landowner whose land is being compulsorily acquired.

Similar criticism may be levelled at the statutory expression of the *Pointe Gourde* principle in section 13 of and Schedule 1 to the 1963 Act. In *Mrs Leckie's Trustees v East Kilbride Development Corporation,* for example, the increased profitability of the public house due to the development over the years of the new town which would have been reflected in the value of the premises on a sale in the open market was disregarded on the compulsory sale of the premises to the development corporation. And in *North-Eastern Housing Association Ltd* the solicitor for the claimants pointed out that they had had to purchase their office premises in the "real" open market as affected by the acquiring authority's incursions but were now liable to be expropriated at a hypothetical but lower price presumed to represent the value of the premises in a hypothetically unaffected market.[74]

The criticism that the rule is not sound follows from the way in which it can come into conflict with the basic measure of compensation: "the amount which the land if sold in the open market by a willing seller might be expected to realise" (rule (2)). It is abundantly clear that in *Wilson, Mrs Leckie's Trustees* and *North-Eastern Housing Association Ltd* the claimants did not receive in compensation what they could have expected on a sale of their property in the open market. There is no way in which the dispossessed owners could have gone out into the market and purchased with their compensation money a property roughly similar to that which had been acquired unless they were prepared to move to similar property in an area wholly unaffected by the scheme. Furthermore, the awards would appear to transgress the principle of equivalence which requires that claimants should be paid neither more nor less than their loss.[75] There would seem to be much to be said for Davies' comment that "in so far as the *Pointe Gourde* rule coincides with the willing seller rule . . . it is redundant. In so far as it conflicts with that rule it is mischievous".[76]

The Law Commission have recently conducted a comprehensive review of the origins and development of the rule and of the problems of its operation in practice.[77] They found that the need for such a rule rested on two grounds. First of all, it protected an acquiring authority

---

[74] See, too, *Kaye v Basingstoke Development Corporation* [1968] R.V.R. 744. Also T. J. Nardecchia, " 'The Valuation Aspects of Land Taken Under a Scheme—2' in Compensation for Compulsory Purchase" (1975) Journal of Planning and Environmental Law Occasional Paper (Sweet and Maxwell). It should be noted that the principle and its statutory expression may, in some cases, operate to the benefit of a claimant by requiring a decrease in value due to the scheme to be disregarded.

[75] *Horn v Sunderland Corporation* [1941] 2 K.B. 26.

[76] Keith Davies, "The Pointe Gourde Rule" (1975) *The Conveyancer and Property Lawyer* 414.

[77] "Towards a Compulsory Purchase Code: (1) Compensation" (2002) *Consultation Paper No 165* Chaps 6 and 7 and App.5.

from having to pay a price inflated by its own regeneration activities. Secondly, it protected the authority from having to pay a price inflated by its own special location requirements.[78] In addition to its divergence on occasion from the principle of equivalence,[79] the Commission identified two principal problems with the operation of the rule. It was necessary to construct a hypothetical 'no-scheme world' which could involve a speculative exercise in re-writing history; and the wider the 'scheme', the more potential there was for unfairness between those whose land was acquired and those in the same area who retain their land.[80]

If the effects of the scheme are to be disregarded (and this, as CPPRAG pointed out, raises a fundamental policy issue),[81] the Law Commission invited responses to a suggestion that the existing statutory and judicial versions of the rule should be replaced by a new formulation. The formulation would disregard "changes in value attributable to the prospect of, or the carrying out of, the project[82] for which the authority is authorised to acquire the land".[83] Such a formulation would tie the valuation exercise more narrowly to any change resulting from the project for which the acquisition is authorised. The Commission acknowledged, however, that an acquiring authority might need on occasion to justify its acquisition of land by reference to a project extending beyond the boundary of the particular compulsory purchase order. In that case, it would be open to the authority to contend for a wider scheme and to define its nature and extent in the order. The Commission further suggested that the 'cancellation assumption' established in *Fletcher Estates (Harlscott) Ltd v Secretary of State for the Environment*[84] (see p.153 above) should be applied.[85]

The objective of the reforms would be to produce a rule which would be clear and coherent. It should, said the Commission harking back to earlier judicial comments, "leave valuers and the Tribunal with their feet on the ground in the real world, rather than force them to make unrealistic flights into a world of make-believe".[86]

DEPRECIATION DUE TO THE PROSPECT OF COMPULSORY ACQUISITION

8–10 In *Jelson Ltd v Blaby District Council*,[87] referred to earlier in this chapter, Lord Denning in the Court of Appeal concluded that the depreciation in the value of the strip of land caused by its earmarking in the develop-

---

[78] See above paras 6.39 and 7.7(i).

[79] See above paras 6.42–6.43.

[80] See above para.6.9.

[81] "Fundamental review of the laws and procedures relating to compulsory purchase and compensation: final report" (2000) DETR para.102.

[82] The Commission rejected the word 'scheme' as being accompanied by too much historical 'baggage'.

[83] Consultation Paper No 165, *supra*, para.6.29.

[84] (2000) 80 P. & C.R. 95.

[85] Consultation Paper No 165, *supra*, para.7.19.

[86] See above, para.7.8.

[87] [1977] 1 W.L.R. 1020.

ment plan for a proposed public road, later abandoned, had to be disregarded in assessing compensation both as a result of the *Pointe Gourde* principle and because of section 9 of the Land Compensation Act 1961.[88] The Scottish equivalent of section 9 is to be found in section 16 of the Land Compensation (Scotland) Act 1963. It provides that:

"No account shall be taken of any depreciation of the value of the relevant interest which is attributable to the fact that (whether by way of allocation or other particulars contained in the current development plan,[89] or by any other means[90]) an indication has been given that the relevant land is, or is likely, to be acquired by an authority possessing compulsory purchase powers."

Although there may be circumstances where the *Pointe Gourde* principle and section 16 overlap, the latter appears to be directed at a narrower and rather more specific cause of depreciation. The fact that land is to be compulsorily acquired will have an adverse effect on its market value but, if the analogy with a sale by a willing seller in the open market is to be sustained, the blighting effect of the compulsory purchase must be ignored. This illustrates what Davies describes as "a paradox which lies at the heart of the law of compulsory purchase of land . . . to say that compulsory purchase compensation is to be assessed at 'market value' is to say that a state of affairs is to be visualised in terms of its direct opposite".[91] Any assessment of compensation based on the value which the land might be expected to realise if sold in the open market must necessarily disregard any depreciation in value due to the prospect of the compulsory acquisition of land. That would seem to be implicit in rule (2). Presumably for the avoidance of doubt, section 16 of the 1963 Act specifically requires such depreciation to be disregarded. Thus, for example, if a house is earmarked in a local authority plan for demolition to make way for a road improvement, the depressing effect on value resulting from the earmarking will be ignored in assessing compensation upon its eventual acquisition.

Section 16 would appear to extend not only to depreciation in the value of the land put to its existing use[92] but also to "depreciation" resulting from a failure to realise development value.[93] For example, in *Trocette Property Co. Ltd v Greater London Council*[94] the claimants were lessees under a long lease of a disused cinema. The lease was due to expire in 1984. Planning permission for redevelopment of the site for a

---

[88] See too *Abbey Homesteads (Developments) Ltd v Northamptonshire County Council* (1991) 61 P. & C.R. 295.

[89] For the meaning of the "current development plan" see s.45(1).

[90] For an example of depreciation in value attributable to an indication "by any other means" that land is likely to be acquired see *London Borough of Hackney v MacFarlane* (1970) 21 P. & C.R. 342.

[91] Keith Davies, *Law of Compulsory Purchase and Compensation, supra*, p.129.

[92] See by way of example *Sukmanski v Edmonton Borough Council* (1961) 12 P. & C.R. 299. Also *Spence v Lanarkshire County Council*, 1976 S.L.T. (Lands Tr.) 2 (depreciation held not to be attributable to such an indication).

[93] *Grampian Regional Council v Secretary of State for Scotland*, 1984 S.L.T. 212, HL.

[94] (1974) 28 P. & C.R. 408. But see *Davy v London Borough of Hammersmith* (1975) 30 P. & C.R. 469.

supermarket, shops and a bowling centre was granted in 1963. Before embarking on such a scheme, the lessees sought early renewal of the lease. Renewal seemed likely until the county council as highway authority produced a plan for a new road which would affect the cinema site at which point negotiations were broken off. To bring matters to a head, the lessees then applied for planning permission for the erection of a shop on the site. As anticipated, this was refused on the ground that the application was premature because of the road proposal and Trocette thereupon served a purchase notice which was accepted. Trocette's claim for compensation was based on the "marriage value" of the freehold and leasehold interests, *i.e.* there would have been little prospect of development unless both interests merged and the sum of the merged interests would be greater than the value of each continuing separately. The council argued that a prospective assignee would offer nothing for marriage value because the lessor had actually broken off negotiations. Trocette responded that the negotiations had been broken off as a result of an indication that the compulsory acquisition of their leasehold interest was likely and that under section 9 of the (English) Land Compensation Act 1961 no account was to be taken of any depreciation in the value of their interest resulting from that indication. The majority of the Court of Appeal agreed that section 9 applied and marriage value was allowed. Megaw L.J. observed that the phrase "attributable to" in section 9 of the Act of 1961 is deliberately used to ensure greater scope for flexibility in its application than would have been achieved by other phrases such as "caused by".[95]

A similar view was taken in *Jelson Ltd v Blaby District Council*.[96] As mentioned earlier, a purchase notice was served following a refusal of planning permission for development of a strip of land which had been reserved for a proposed road but which proposal was subsequently abandoned. The district council argued that the compensation should reflect the fact that the strip had no development potential. The claimants argued that had it not been for the public road proposal, permission for residential development of the strip could have been anticipated at the outset. The refusal of permission was due to an indication that the land was to be acquired by an authority possessing compulsory purchase powers and under section 9 of the 1961 Act no account should be taken of the resulting depreciation in value. The Court of Appeal, following the flexible construction of the words "attributable to" applied in *Trocette,* found for the claimants.

Both the Lands Tribunal and the Court of Appeal accepted in *Jelson* that the link between the scheme and the loss of value was sufficiently direct notwithstanding that the road scheme had been abandoned some years before the deemed compulsory acquisition took effect. Nonetheless, it is at least arguable that it was stretching the elastic of section 9 of the 1961 Act overmuch to suggest that there was depreciation in value attributable to an indication that the land was to be compulsorily acquired. As Davies points out, the disputed strip was no longer "indicated" for compulsory acquisition. This was the very reason why the

---

[95] See above, p.417.
[96] 34 P. & C.R. 77.

purchase notice was used.[97] The claimants' remedy lay in invoking the purchase notice procedure in connection with the initial reservation of the strip for the road scheme.[98]

---

[97] Keith Davies, *Law of Compulsory Purchase and Compensation, supra*, p.133.

[98] The Law Commission have proposed that the landowners position should continue to be protected. They favour a wide rule requiring any diminution in value or reduced profits caused by the project itself or any advance 'indication' of the project to be disregarded. They note that it would be logical to link such a provision to the statutory blight provisions (see Chapter 14) ("Towards a Compulsory Purchase Code: (1) Compensation" (2002) *Consultation Paper No 165*, para.7.27).

CHAPTER 9

SPECIAL VALUES

9–01 In Chapter 4 it was pointed out that the courts initially measured compensation for compulsory purchase by the extent of the loss to the claimant. Since the Acquisition of Land (Assessment of Compensation) Act 1919, Parliament has provided that the extent of that loss is to be assessed by reference to the "amount which the land if sold in the open market by a willing seller might be expected to realise" together with disturbance and severance and other injurious affection, if appropriate. However, that measure is of no assistance where, as occasionally happens, land is devoted to a purpose for which there is no general demand or market. In these circumstances some alternative way of assessing the loss is required. This was recognised in the 1919 Act which provided for compensation in such cases to be calculated on the basis of the reasonable cost of equivalent reinstatement, a provision which has been repeated in the Land Compensation (Scotland) Act 1963.

There are also circumstances in which Parliament, for whatever reasons of policy, has decreed that compensation is to be measured by reference to some standard other than the market value of the land. For example, section 45 of the Planning (Listed Buildings and Conservation Areas) (Scotland) Act 1997 provides that where a direction for minimum compensation is made in connection with the compulsory acquisition of a listed building which has been deliberately allowed by the proprietor to fall into disrepair so as to justify its demolition, the compensation is to be assessed on the assumption that planning permission would not be granted for any development or redevelopment of the site of the building and that listed building consent would not be granted for any works for the demolition, alteration or extension of the building other than development or works necessary for restoring it to, and maintaining it in, a proper state of repair.

Such a direction is very uncommon. Rather more common, however, is the compulsory acquisition of houses that are below what the Housing (Scotland) Act 1987 defines as the "tolerable standard". The compensation provisions in such cases operate broadly on the assumption that such buildings have no value; the maximum compensation payable, subject to certain supplements, is the value of the land as a cleared site, what is generally referred to as "restricted value".

This chapter examines these cases where a claimant's loss is measured by reference, not to the market value of land, but to equivalent reinstatement value or to the restricted value.

CPPRAG focused attention on a further situation in which consideration might be given to some measure of compensation other than market value. That is where an acquiring authority seek to exercise compulsory purchase powers in an area where there has been a collapse of the property market and where owners may be in a position of negative equity.[1] CPPRAG considered that there should be some means of helping such owner-occupiers to overcome the almost inevitable funding gap between the market value compensation for the property taken and the price of any reasonably similar house elsewhere. The prospect of transferring debt to the replacement property and 'like for like' replacement schemes were considered. The DTLR, in their response, announced an intention to broaden the scope for using replacement grants to alleviate such hardship in England.[2]

EQUIVALENT REINSTATEMENT

The assessment of compensation for the value of land prior to 1919 was **9–02** not based on rigid rules but on what would best achieve restitution for a claimant. In some cases, the cost of equivalent reinstatement was considered a more appropriate measure than market value.[3] For example, in *Lanarkshire and Dumbartonshire Railway Co. v Thomas Main*,[4] the claimant had spent considerable sums of money on preparing garden ground for the growing of fruit trees. Before he could put the ground to use, part of it was compulsorily acquired for the construction of a railway. As other land contiguous to the remainder of the garden was available to the claimant, the arbiter awarded compensation on the basis of the cost of reinstatement on this contiguous land. The Court of Session confirmed this approach to the assessment of compensation in the circumstances of that case. In *McEwing and Sons Ltd v The County Council of the County of Renfrew,* Lord President Clyde commented that the decision in *Main* was "indeed a typical case of a common practice under the 1845 Act of using reinstatement value, instead of market value, to fix the compensation".[5] This method was used generally in cases where it was considered that the income derived, or probably to be derived, from the land would not constitute a fair basis for assessing the value to the owner.[6] The Scott Committee, in their report in 1918,[7] recognised that compensation based on the value which a willing seller would realise for property in the open market would not provide a just

---

[1] "Fundamental review of the laws and procedures relating to compulsory purchase and compensation: final report" (2000) DETR paras 162–174.

[2] "Compulsory purchase and compensation: delivering a fundamental change" (2001) DTLR paras 3.29–3.36.

[3] This would seem to have been a reflection of the approach of the courts to awards of damages at common law for loss of heritable property. See, for example, *Gibson v Fairie* (1918) 1 S.L.T. 404; and, for a more recent example, *Hutchison v Davidson*, 1945 S.C. 395.

[4] (1895) 22 R. 912. But see *Corporation of Edinburgh v North British Railway* unreported, but cited in H. Parrish, *Cripps on Compulsory Acquisition of Land* (11th ed., Sweet and Maxwell, London), para.4–016.

[5] 1960 S.C. 53 at p.63. See too *A & B Taxis Ltd v Secretary of State for Air* [1922] 2 K.B. 328, *per* Banks L.J. at p.336.

[6] "Compulsory Acquisition and Planning Restrictions" (1968) *Chartered Land Societies Committee* para.21.

[7] The Second Report of the Committee, "Dealing with the Law and Practice relating to the Acquisition and Valuation of Land for Public Purposes" (1918) HMSO (Cmnd. 9229).

measure of compensation for property for which there was no general demand. Examples of such property are churches or chapels, schools, cemeteries, theatres, hospitals and clubs. The owner in such a case, says Cripps, "cannot be placed in as favourable a position as he was before the exercise of compulsory purchase powers, unless such a sum is assessed as will enable him to replace the premises or lands taken by premises or lands which would be to him of the same value".[8] The Scott Committee accordingly recommended that where property was used for a purpose for which there was no general demand, compensation should be assessed not on the fictional basis of a notional sale in the open market but on the factual basis of equivalent reinstatement.[9] This recommendation was given effect in the Acquisition of Land (Assessment of Compensation) Act 1919 and was re-enacted as rule (5) in section 12 of the Land Compensation (Scotland) Act 1963.

Rule (5) provides that:

"Where land is, and but for the compulsory acquisition would continue to be, devoted to a purpose of such a nature that there is no general demand or market for land for that purpose, the compensation may, if the [Lands Tribunal for Scotland] is satisfied that reinstatement in some other place is bona fide intended, be assessed on the basis of the reasonable cost of equivalent reinstatement."

In *Sparks and Others (Trustees of East Hunslet Liberal Club) v Leeds City Council*[10] the English Lands Tribunal spelt out the essentials of a rule (5) claim under the corresponding English provision[11]:

"There are four essentials in rule (5) to be satisfied by the claimants, on whom is the burden of proof:

(i) that the subject land is devoted to the purpose, and but for the compulsory acquisition would continue to be so devoted;

(ii) that the purpose is one for which there is no general demand or market for the land;

(iii) the bona fide intention to reinstate on another site; and

(iv) these conditions being satisfied, that the tribunal's reasonable discretion should be exercised in their favour."

The onus is on the claimant to demonstrate that these pre-requisites are satisfied in any case.[12] The four "essentials" are now considered in turn.[13]

---

[8] *Cripps on Compulsory Acquisition of Land, supra*, para.4–047.
[9] Para.12.
[10] (1977) 244 E.G. 56.
[11] Land Compensation Act 1961, s.5(5).
[12] *Wilkinson v Middlesborough Borough Council* (1981) 45 P. & C.R. 142 *per* Sir David Cairns.
[13] See, generally, on rule (5) W. A. Leach, "Equivalent Reinstatement" (1980) 253 E.G. 1331; (1980) 254 E.G. 107, 277 and 391.

1. Devoted to a purpose

A distinction is to be made between land which is "devoted to a **9–03** purpose" and land which is simply "used for a purpose". The former introduces a conception of intention.[14] Thus in *Trustees of the Central Methodist Church, Todmorden v Todmorden Corporation*[15] rule (5) was held to be inapplicable where surplus church premises were leased to a local authority for use for their school meals service. The purpose was not one to which the premises had deliberately and voluntarily been put by the claimants.

However, in *Aston Charities Trust Ltd v Stepney Corporation*,[16] rule (5) was applied notwithstanding that the charitable and religious work carried on by the claimants in the premises had been curtailed by war damage and most of the premises had been let for other purposes. A distinction was drawn between the *de facto* use of the premises at the date of the notice to treat and the intended purpose which had been temporarily disrupted.

The date of the notice to treat is the date at which it must be shown that premises are devoted to a purpose for which there is no general demand or market.[17] In *Zoar Independent Church Trustees v Rochester Corporation*[18] church premises were vested in trustees for the purposes of worship by Protestant dissenters. In the early 1960s, the trustees, faced with a dwindling congregation, sought to raise money to move the centre of worship elsewhere by submitting a planning application for a change of use of the premises for community purposes. Permission was refused and in 1964 a purchase notice was served and accepted. In the meantime, because of lack of funds the premises remained as a centre of worship although there were no more than 12 and the pastor in the congregation. The structure fell into disrepair and in 1966 the roof fell in and the building ceased to function as a church. The Lands Tribunal concluded that there was no likelihood of the premises continuing to be devoted to the purpose of worship in view of the declining congregation. The Court of Appeal, however, held that at the date of the deemed notice to treat (*i.e.* the date on which the purchase notice was accepted) the premises were devoted to the purpose of worship and that because of lack of funds it appeared that they would continue to be devoted to that purpose indefinitely. "Devoted," said Buckley L.J. "does not signify that land must be committed to that use for any particular length of time, definite or indefinite." He went on to add that the probable duration of the continuance of use was a matter which might affect the tribunal's decision on whether to exercise its discretion to apply rule (5).

Not only must land be shown to be devoted to such a purpose at the appropriate date, but it must be shown that devotion to that purpose

---

[14] *Aston Charities Trust v Stepney Corporation* [1952] 2 Q.B. 642.

[15] (1959) 11 P. & C.R. 32.

[16] [1952] 2 Q.B. 642, CA. See too *Kolbe House Society v Department of Transport* (1994) 68 P. & C.R. 569.

[17] But note that compensation falls to be assessed by reference to the date when reinstatement of the premises first becomes reasonably practicable (*Birmingham Corporation v West Midlands Baptist (Trust) Association (Inc.)* [1963] 3 W.L.R. 398, HL).

[18] [1974] 3 W.L.R. 417.

Compulsory Purchase and Compensation

would have continued but for the compulsory acquisition. In *Zoar Independent Church Trustees* Russell L.J. observed "The requirement of continuity of devotion is not directed to perpetuity; I regard it as sufficiently complied with if it appears that at the time of the notice to treat it is then intended by the owners of the site to continue to devote it to the relevant purpose with no future time limit." In *Trustees of the Nonentities Society v Kidderminster Borough*[19] the necessary continuity was held to have been established notwithstanding an earlier threat by the trustees to terminate the purpose to which the premises were devoted, in that case a theatre, because of financial difficulties. The evidence showed that the threatened closure was intended as a shock tactic to generate support for the theatre and that there had been a clear intention to continue the use but for the acquisition.

2. No general demand or market

9–04   The second "essential" has given rise to some difficulty in practice. In *Harrison and Hetherington Ltd v Cumbria County Council*,[20] for example, the subject of the claim was a livestock auction mart in Carlisle. Evidence was given to the effect that since 1957 there had been no more than 18 transactions in England and Wales relating to the 16 marts and that "a kind of equilibrium had been reached" in the supply of marts to meet the needs of the community. Lord Fraser of Tullybelton, giving judgment for the House of Lords, held that the word "land" where it appeared the second time in rule (5) referred to the land in general and not the subject land. Accordingly the first requirement of rule (5) was not satisfied merely by showing demand for the subject land. As Waller L.J. observed in *Wilkinson v Middlesborough Borough Council*,[21] "it is not sufficient that there should be demand for the land in question but that there must be a general demand, *i.e.* a demand not only for that land but for other land elsewhere for the same purpose." In *Harrison and Hetherington* the evidence showed that there was no market for land devoted to the purpose of a livestock mart; that was the inevitable inference from the very small number of transactions in land devoted to that purpose. There could not be a market, said Lord Fraser, unless both supply and demand existed. There could, however, be a general demand[22] although there was no supply and the issue to be decided was whether a general demand existed for land devoted to that purpose. Although there was no evidence of a present general demand, the Lands Tribunal had considered that it was enough that a latent demand could be inferred in the event of a profitable mart being offered for sale. Lord Fraser rejected that argument on two grounds. First of all, rule (5) by using the word "is" requires a presently existing general demand. Secondly, there was no evidence of a general demand but only a special demand which would arise in particular circumstances. The first require-

---

[19] (1970) 22 P. & C.R. 224.
[20] (1985) 50 P. & C.R. 396. See too *Kolbe House Society v Department of Transport* (1994) 68 P. & C.R. 569; and *Nicholls v Highways Agency* (2000) 24 E.G. 167.
[21] (1982) 45 P. & C.R. 142. And see *Vaughan (Viscount) v Cardiganshire Water Board* (1963) 185 E.G. 949.
[22] The word "general" in rule (5) was held to qualify only "demand" and not "market".

ment of rule (5) was satisfied and, the other requirements being satisfied, compensation could be assessed on the basis of equivalent reinstatement if the tribunal, in their discretion, thought fit.

It is not entirely clear whether, as Leach argues,[23] the benefit of rule (5) is related to the precise purpose of the evicted owner or whether, in considering the application of the rule, account is to be taken of any other purpose for which the land may be suitable. In *Bathgate Football Club v Burgh of Bathgate*[24] the club claimed compensation amounting to £3,650 being the reasonable cost of equivalent reinstatement following the compulsory purchase of their football ground. The arbiter rejected the claim and awarded £1,351 being the open market value of the ground under rule (2) as a "sports ground". It was, he said, the general rather than the specific purpose for which the property is devoted which is relevant for the purpose of rule (5). On the other hand, in *Trustees of the Manchester Homeopathic Clinic v Manchester Corporation*[25] the Lands Tribunal held that it would be wrong to approach the question in terms of the Use Classes Order. In that case, the premises in question were purpose built for consultation and treatment in homeopathy but could, with 'insignificant' changes be made suitable for use generally for medical consultation, diagnosis and the limited treatment of ailments. It was in respect of that slightly wider purpose that the question of a general demand or market had to be considered. Leach, however, argues that the possibility of disposing of the premises as a general medical clinic was not relevant to the question whether the land was devoted to a purpose for which there was no general demand or market; rather it was a factor to be taken into account in the exercise of the tribunal's discretion on the application of rule (5). Leach's argument finds support in the more recent decision of the Lands Tribunal in *Kolbe House Society v Department of Transport.*[26] The tribunal rejected the argument that a home run by a charity for the relief of Poles and other refugees from central Europe should be regarded as an 'old peoples' home' for the purpose of determining the existence of a general demand or market. The two purposes were different.

The fact that premises devoted to a particular purpose do not come onto the market in the ordinary way does not preclude the existence of a general demand or market for the land for that purpose. In *Wilkinson v Middlesborough Borough Council*[27] the Court of Appeal upheld the decision of the Lands Tribunal that the normal method of disposal of veterinary practices in an area by taking partners into the firm pointed to the existence of a market even though the practices were not bought or sold in the open market.

In *Kolbe House* the Lands Tribunal had to consider the geographical area to which the evidence of a general demand or market had to relate.[28] Assuming it was necessary to consider the wider purpose of

---

[23] W. A. Leach, "Equivalent Reinstatement" (1980) 254 E.G. 107.
[24] Decision by an Official Arbiter Ref. No. 6/1932.
[25] (1970) 22 P. & C.R. 241.
[26] (1994) 68 P. & C.R. 569, Lands Tr.
[27] (1981) 45 P. & C.R. 1422.
[28] See too *Wilkinson.*

residential care homes for the elderly people of Ealing, the tribunal did not envisage "the market for land for a residential care home for the elderly people living in the Ealing district extending much beyond the boundaries of the borough". This was on the assumption that the purpose to which the land was devoted was restricted to providing accommodation for the elderly people of Ealing. The appropriate area of search was subsequently raised as an issue in *Prielipp v Secretary of State for the Environment, Transport and the Regions.*[29] The case in involved a rule (5) claim for the reinstatement of a riding school and the claimants, relying on the decision in Kolbe House, argued that the appropriate area was the catchment area of the riding school. However the Lands Tribunal, distinguishing the decision in *Kolbe House,* concluded on the evidence that there was nothing to prevent the proprietors of the riding school operating outwith their present area and there was nothing in the purpose to which the land was devoted which required evidence of general demand or market to be confined to the catchment area of the school. A commercial riding school could be established in virtually any location.

3. *Bona fide* intention to reinstate

9–05   In *Zoar,* the Court of Appeal were called upon to consider whether there was a *bona fide* intention to reinstate as required by rule (5). After the roof of the existing building had fallen in and it had ceased to function as a church, one of the church trustees bought property and temporarily established a new church with similar purposes to Zoar. The congregation at the new church included one member from Zoar. The trustees of Zoar, as prospective purchasers of that property, were subsequently granted planning permission for a new church at that site. The Lands Tribunal concluded that there could be no *bona fide* intention to reinstate because the new premises had effectively attracted a different congregation. However, the Court of Appeal, Lawton L.J. dissenting, held that it was the purpose and not the congregation that had to be reinstated and the evidence showed a sufficient intention to reinstate the purpose which the former chapel served. Furthermore, the fact that the realisation of the intention to reinstate was dependent upon the receipt of compensation assessed under rule (5) did not, in Lord Russell's view, "deprive the intention of any necessary quality".[30]

A similar situation arose in *Trustees of the Nonentities Society v Kidderminster Borough Council*[31] where a theatre was acquired for highway purposes. Although there was an intention to reinstate the

[29] [2002] R.V.R. 169, Lands Tr.
[30] See, too, *Sparks and Others (Trustees of East Hunslet Liberal Club) v Leeds City Council* (1977) 244 E.G. 56; and *Trustees of the Nonentities Society v Kidderminster Borough Council* (1970) 22 P. & C.R. 224. But see *Festiniog Railway Co. v Central Electricity Generating Board* (1962) 13 P. & C.R. 248, *per* Harman L.J. The Royal Institution of Chartered Surveyors recommended that it be made clear by legislation that reinstatement can be *bona fide* intended although it is conditional upon an award under rule (5) (*Compensation for Compulsory Acquisition*, 1995, para.1.49). They also suggest that the Lands Tribunal should be given power to direct that the whole or part of the sum awarded should be retained and paid as and when reinstatement takes place (para.1.46).
[31] (1970) 22 P. & C.R. 224.

purpose elsewhere, the intention was to be implemented by a new trust. The acquiring authority argued that, in the circumstances, the present trustees could not be said to have an intention to reinstate. The Lands Tribunal held that as the new theatre was designed to fulfil the purpose of the old there was a sufficient intention to reinstate. It was the purpose, not the trust, which had to be reinstated.

In *Edgehill Light Railway Co. v Secretary of State for War,*[32] however, the Lands Tribunal were not satisfied that reinstatement was *bona fide* intended, the only indication to that effect being a resolution passed by the company on the advice of counsel in pursuing their rule (5) claim. By contrast, in *Trustees of the Nonentities Society,* a threat by the trust to close the theatre was regarded in the light of the evidence as simply a shock tactic designed to generate financial support for the theatre and did not of itself show an intention not to reinstate.

4. The tribunal's discretion

Even where a claimant satisfies the first three "essentials" for a rule **9–06** (5) claim, an award is at the discretion of the tribunal. Rule (5) states that compensation *may* be assessed on the basis of the reasonable cost of equivalent reinstatement.[33] In *Festiniog Railway Co. v Central Electricity Generating Board*[34] Harman L.J. observed that "reinstatement is usually resorted to in cases where the displaced undertaking was some non-productive enterprise such as a church or a hospital which was not intended to make a profit but to perform some public service to the community which could not equally well be performed in another situation". He went on to say that: "There are, however, cases in the books which show that reinstatement may be applied to a commercial concern." In *Festiniog,* the tribunal declined to exercise its discretion to award rule (5) compensation in respect of the compulsory purchase of part of a light railway line, notwithstanding that the claim satisfied the other requirements of rule (5). Equivalent reinstatement would have involved a diversion of the line costing £180,000. The tribunal concluded that this would have imposed a heavy burden of compensation upon the acquiring authority, particularly bearing in mind that the claimants were conducting what was essentially a business venture and the cost of reinstatement would far exceed the total value of the assets of the railway company. The decision was upheld by the Court of Appeal, Ormerod L.J. observing that "if the undertaking in question is a business undertaking, then the question of the relation between the cost of reinstatement and the value of the undertaking is relevant and may be paramount in considering the question of reasonableness."

In *Sparks and Others (Trustees of East Hunslet Liberal Club) v Leeds City Council,*[35] on the other hand, the tribunal exercised its discretion in favour of the claimant and awarded rule (5) compensation of £97,832;

---

[32] (1956) 6 P. & C.R. 211.
[33] But see the Land Compensation (Scotland) Act 1973, s.42 which entitles a person with an interest in a dwelling which has been specially adapted for a disabled person to elect to have compensation assessed on the basis of equivalent reinstatement.
[34] (1962) 13 P. & C.R. 248.
[35] (1977) 244 E.G. 56.

compensation assessed under rules (2) and (6) would have amounted to £9,000. The social purpose of the club was contrasted with the commercial venture carried on in the *Festiniog* case.

The decision in *Festiniog* raises the question whether the measure of compensation in such cases can truly be said to reflect equivalence. How, as the Scott Committee acknowledged in 1918,[36] can rule (2) provide a satisfactory measure in a case where it is acknowledged that the land is devoted to a purpose for which there is no general demand or market? It is difficult to see that the purpose of compensation in such cases can be said to be the placing of the claimant in as favourable a position as he was in before the exercise of compulsory purchase powers. This would seem to have been acknowledged by Lord Pearson in *Festiniog*. The governing consideration, he said, "for deciding to apply or not to apply the reinstatement basis of assessment must be to consider whether it would produce a measure of compensation which would be just as between the claimant and the authority". That is a different measure from equivalence.

5. Equivalent Reinstatement

9–07   Where the four "essentials" referred to in *Sparks and Others (Trustees of East Hunslet Liberal Club)* are satisfied, compensation is to be assessed on the basis of the reasonable cost of equivalent reinstatement. Difficulties can arise in determining what is reasonable. As Davies observes "The replacement of monumental Victorian architecture by a modern functional construction often makes it difficult to decide on what is in truth 'equivalent' or comparable."[37] In similar vein, JUSTICE commented "One significant effect of the application of this rule is that owners could find themselves in possession of property more valuable than that which had been taken from them. This seems to be unavoidable, since to provide otherwise would make the rule either impossible or extremely difficult to apply."[38] However, as Leach points out,[39] what is being reinstated under rule (5) is the "purpose"; the question to be asked is what accommodation is required "to continue the purpose as effectively both in scale and manner as it would have been continued if it had not been disturbed by the acquisition ... but allowing for any previous change in scale or manner attributable to pending acquisition". This would suggest that the replacement building need not necessarily be comparable in size and quality with the one which has been compulsorily acquired.

The point arose in *Trustees of Zetland Lodge of Freemasons v The Tamar Bridge Joint Committee*.[40] The acquiring authority argued that the requirement of rule (5) in respect of a masonic hall would be satisfied by a new purpose built hall with an equivalent number of smaller rooms. This argument was rejected by the Lands Tribunal in the circumstances

---

[36] Cmnd. 9229, para.12.

[37] *Law of Compulsory Purchase and Compensation* (5th ed., Tolley), para.7.48.

[38] *Compensation for Compulsory Acquisition and Remedies for Planning Restrictions together with a Supplemental Report* (1973) Stevens para.12.

[39] W. A. Leach, "Equivalent Reinstatement" (1980) 265 E.G. 277.

[40] (1961) 12 P. & C.R. 326.

of the case but the tribunal commented that had the smaller rooms simply eliminated wasted height or passage space that would have been a factor for consideration. In *Trustees of Old Dagenham Methodist Church v Dagenham Borough Council*,[41] the question in issue was whether the cost of enhanced facilities at the new premises, in this case car parking space, could properly form part of a rule (5) claim. The tribunal held that it could as the cost of reinstatement had been increased by a requirement of the planning permission. Where, however, the cost of reinstatement is increased through choice by the claimant, that increase may not be reflected in the claim for compensation. It is well established that claimants must minimise, not maximise, their loss.[42]

ACQUISITION OF HOUSES BELOW THE TOLERABLE STANDARD

1. Introduction

Special provision is made where the land being acquired comprises a **9–08** house which in the opinion of the acquiring authority does not meet the tolerable standard.[43] The compensation is not to exceed the value of the site of the house as a cleared site available for development.

The explanation for this provision lies in the slum clearance programmes of the late nineteenth century.[44] A royal commission set up in 1884 to look into worsening slum conditions concluded that the normal compensation arrangements for the acquisition of unfit houses put a premium on neglect. As a consequence, the Housing of the Working Classes Act 1890 provided that compensation for the acquisition of a house that was unfit and not reasonably capable of being made fit was to be assessed on the value of the land and any materials from the buildings.

Progress with slum clearance remained slow and Cullingworth states that by "1919 the Government had become satisfied that no solution to the slum problem could be achieved unless the cost of closing property was in some way reasonably commensurate with the value of the land".[45] The Housing, Town Planning, Etc. (Scotland) Act 1919 accordingly provided that compensation for an unfit house, whether reasonably capable of repair or not, was to be the value of the land as a cleared site and this continued as the basis of compensation in subsequent slum clearance legislation. Owners of slum dwellings were to receive no compensation beyond the value of the site, a provision which "no doubt owed a good deal in its origin to moral indignation at slum landlordism".[46]

Because of the hardship which this basis of compensation sometimes imposed on owners of slum property, provision was subsequently made

---

[41] (1961) 179 E.G. 295.
[42] See, for example, *Park Automobile Co. Ltd v Strathclyde Regional Council*, 1984 S.L.T. (Lands Tr.) 14.
[43] Defined in the Housing (Scotland) Act 1987, s.86.
[44] See J. B. Cullingworth, *Environmental Planning*, (1980) HMSO Vol. 4, App.A.
[45] See above, p.423.
[46] See above, p.450.

for certain supplementary payments. The Housing (Scotland) Act 1935 introduced well-maintained payments "to encourage owners of substandard houses to maintain them for as long as they stood".[47] More problematic was the position of owner-occupiers of slum property who because of housing shortages had been compelled to buy substandard housing but had nonetheless paid a substantial sum reflecting the scarcity value of housing and who still had substantial mortgage commitments. For them, cleared site value could represent considerable hardship. In England, the Slum Clearance (Compensation) Act 1956 addressed this problem by providing that an owner-occupier living in an unfit house purchased between the outbreak of the Second World War and the end of 1955 would on compulsory acquisition of the house at any time in the subsequent ten years receive in compensation the amount that would have been received had the house not been declared unfit. No change was made to the position in Scotland at that time.

Subsequently, the White Paper, "The Older Houses in Scotland: A Plan for Action"[48] commented that a factor "which has been delaying progress with clearance is the compensation which is payable when an unfit house is acquired by a local authority. Many owners who object to clearance proposals do so because they are dissatisfied with the compensation they will get if their house is classified as unfit." The government proposed to introduce a supplement for owner-occupiers who had owned their houses for two years equivalent to the amount by which the market value of the house exceeds the value derived under the existing statutory framework. This supplement was introduced in the Housing (Scotland) Act 1969. The arrangements in England for the payment of an owner-occupier supplement which had operated since 1956 were brought into line in the Housing Act 1969.

These concessions have not satisfied everyone. The Chartered Land Societies Committee, in a memorandum to the Ministry of Housing and Local Government in 1968, recommended on the grounds of simplicity and equity that the cleared site value basis of compensation for unfit houses "should be abolished and that the normal rules governing the assessment of compensation should apply to such houses".[49] And the Royal Institution of Chartered Surveyors commented that "in spite of the steps that have been taken to mitigate the harshness of this rule, it still causes serious inequities and the Institution has for a long time considered that there is no longer justification for retaining this basis of compensation for unfit dwellings".[50] Furthermore, dissatisfaction with the level of compensation may give rise to more sustained opposition to the compulsory purchase.

The government acknowledged that site value compensation could give rise to anomalies and indicated their intention to introduce legislation to provide for full market value compensation to all owners.[51]

---

[47] See above, p.425.

[48] (1968) HMSO (Cmnd. 3598).

[49] "Compensation for Compulsory Acquisition and Planning Restrictions" (1968) para.47.

[50] "Compensation for Compulsory Acquisition" (1989) para.23. See, too, B. Denyer Green, "Unfit Houses—The Injustice of Bare Site Value to Owner-Occupiers" (January 8, 1981) N.L.J. p.30.

[51] H. C. Deb, Vol. 107, col. 394, December 15, 1986; May 23, 1988 Hansard, Vol. 134, Written answer, col. 60.

This was achieved for England and Wales by the Local Government and Housing Act 1989.[52] No change has yet been made for Scotland.

What follows is a detailed explanation of this basis of compensation as it operates at present.

2. Compensation not to exceed cleared site value

The provisions governing the assessment of compensation for the **9–09** compulsory acquisition of houses below the tolerable standard are to be found in section 17 of and Schedule 2 to the Land Compensation (Scotland) Act 1963 as substituted by section 339(2) and Schedule 23, paragraph 10 of the Housing (Scotland) Act 1987. They apply to the compulsory acquisition of such a house under the following legislation:

(i) an acquisition under Part VIII of the Town and Country Planning (Scotland) Act 1997 or sections 42–47 of the Planning (Listed Buildings and Conservation Areas) (Scotland) Act 1997;

(ii) an acquisition under section 13 of the Housing and Town Development (Scotland) Act 1957;

(iii) an acquisition pursuant to Part V of the Town and Country Planning (Scotland) Act 1997 or sections 28–33 of the Planning (Listed Buildings and Conservation Areas) (Scotland) Act 1997;

(iv) an acquisition of land within the area designated by an order under section 1 of the New Towns (Scotland) Act 1968 as the site of a new town[53];

(v) an acquisition by a development corporation or a local roads authority or the Scottish Ministers under the New Towns (Scotland) Act 1968 or under any enactment as applied by any provision of that Act[54];

(vi) an acquisition by means of an order under section 141 of the Local Government, Planning and Land Act 1980 vesting land in an urban development corporation[55]; and

(vii) an acquisition by such a corporation under section 142 of that Act.[56]

Broadly, Schedule 2 of the 1963 Act, as substituted, applies to such acquisitions the provisions relating to cleared site value, owner-occupier supplement and well-maintained payments which apply to the com-

---

[52] Section 194(4) and Schedule 12.

[53] The new town development corporations in Scotland have been wound up and dissolved under the provisions of the Enterprise and New Towns (Scotland) Act 1990, Part II.

[54] See above.

[55] No urban development corporations have been established in Scotland.

[56] Land Compensation (Scotland) Act 1963, Sch.2 as substituted by the Housing (Scotland) Act 1987, Sch.23, para.10.

pulsory acquisition of houses below the tolerable standard under Part IV of or Schedule 8 to the Housing (Scotland) Act 1987. Curiously, the provisions are not applied to the acquisition of houses below the tolerable standard under the Roads (Scotland) Act 1984.

Where an order declaring that a house does not meet the tolerable standard has been confirmed by the Scottish Ministers either before or concurrently with the confirmation of the related compulsory purchase order,[57] the provisions of Schedule 8, paragraphs 12(2) and (3) of the Housing (Scotland) Act 1987 apply. Schedule 8, paragraph 12(2) provides that compensation shall not exceed the value, at the time when the valuation is made, of the site of the house as a cleared site[58] available for development in accordance with the requirements of the building regulations for the time being in force in the district.[59] In other words, the claimant receives the lesser of two bases of compensation, cleared site value or market value. Where, for example, because of scarcity, the market value of the house exceeds the value of the land as a cleared site, the latter is the basis of compensation. Where, on the other hand, the market value of the land encumbered with the building is less than the value of the land as a cleared site, the former is the measure. Two valuations of the subjects will therefore be required. However, provided the person entitled to the relevant interest was in occupation of the house on the date of the making of the compulsory purchase order and continues to be entitled to the relevant interest at the date of the service of the notice to treat, the amount of compensation is not in any event to be less than the gross annual value of the dwelling.[60] The reference to compensation is a reference to the compensation payable in respect of the purchase exclusive of any compensation for disturbance or for severance or for injurious affection.[61]

Before submitting an order declaring that a house does not meet the tolerable standard to the Scottish Ministers for confirmation,[62] the acquiring authority must serve notice on the owner, the superior (if

---

[57] With blight notices, purchase notices and notices served under section 11 of the New Towns (Scotland) Act 1968, the order must be made before the date on which the notice to treat is deemed to have been served and is subsequently confirmed by the Scottish Ministers (1963 Act, Sch.2, para.2(1)(b) as substituted by the 1987 Act, Sch.23, para.10).

[58] In *Hugh MacDonald's Representatives v Sutherland District Council*, 1977 S.L.T. (Lands Tr.) 7, the Lands Tribunal for Scotland held that the words "as a cleared site" which appeared in earlier legislation required an assumption to be made that the site had already been cleared of buildings down to ground level and, accordingly, no further deduction was to be made for demolition. See, too, *Gray v Glasgow District Council*, 1980 S.L.T. (Lands Tr.) 7.

[59] The site may, of course, be too small to permit rebuilding in accordance with the building regulations and may, therefore, have no more than a nominal value.

[60] Land Compensation (Scotland) Act 1963, Sch.2, para.3(1) and (2), as substituted by the Housing (Scotland) Act 1987, Sch.23, para.10. In calculating the amount of compensation for the purposes of para.3(2) of Sch.2 of the 1963 Act, account is to be taken of any well-maintained payment paid under the 1987 Act, s.305 (see p.198) but no account is to be taken of such part of the compensation as is attributable to disturbance, severance or injurious affection. The gross annual value of the dwelling is to be determined in accordance with the provisions of the 1963 Act, Sch.2, para.3(4); and see now the Abolition of Domestic Rates Etc. (Scotland) Act 1987, s.5(3).

[61] Housing (Scotland) Act 1987, Sch.8, para.12(3).

[62] The order is to be in such form as may be prescribed by regulations made under the Housing (Scotland) Act 1987, s.330.

reasonably ascertainable)[63] and any heritable creditor stating the effect of the order and specifying the time within which, and the manner in which, objection may be made.[64] Before reaching a decision on the order, the Ministers must consider any such objection and, if either the objector or the acquiring authority so request, must make provision for a hearing. It should be noted that there is no subsequent opportunity to object to site value compensation and this is sometimes a cause of considerable hardship in practice where an owner does not appreciate the compensation implications of such an order.

In calculating both the market value of the property in question and **9–10** the cleared site value, the valuation must be made in the normal way under rule (2) having regard to any potential for improvement but ignoring any appreciation or depreciation in value due to the compulsory acquisition and to the scheme behind it.[65] For example, in *Spence v Lanarkshire County Council*,[66] a demolition order was placed on a dwelling, part of a tenement block, below the tolerable standard. Later, and quite separately, the whole tenement was compulsorily acquired by the local authority to make way for a car park. The value of the dwelling was depreciated as a result of its designation for demolition but as the demolition order was not made in pursuance of the scheme behind the acquisition, that depreciation was to be taken into account; in other words, a purchaser in the open market would have known that there was no prospect of the renovation of the property with an improvement grant. At the valuation date, the only value was in the site itself. The most likely use of the site in the circumstances would be for private housing. The site was valued on that basis taking account of the demolition costs and the liability for ground burdens and the resulting figure was divided between the proprietors of the tenement to arrive at the claimant's share. In *Hugh MacDonald's Representatives v Sutherland District*[67] the premises in question, one of a row of fishermen's houses in Golspie, were acquired compulsorily following the declaration of the row as a housing treatment area to be dealt with by way of demolition. The tribunal considered that in the absence of the scheme an improvement grant would probably have been available and, notwithstanding the cost, the premises would have had a value in the market to a person interested in the shell of the cottage for improvement of £700. The alternative valuation as a cleared site available for development, assuming under section 23(3) of the 1963 Act that planning permission would be granted to rebuild a dwelling on the site, was £300. In view of the cleared site value ceiling, compensation was awarded at the lower figure.

In *Davy v Leeds Corporation*[68] the claimants owned back-to-back houses in Leeds in an area zoned in the development plan for residential

---

[63] Section 2 of the Abolition of Feudal Tenure etc (Scotland) Act 2000 abolishes the estate of superiority with effect from the appointed day.
[64] 1963 Act, Sch.2, para.2(2), as substituted by the Housing (Scotland) Act 1987, Sch.23, para.10.
[65] 1963 Act, s.13; *Pointe Gourde Quarrying and Transport Co. v Sub-Intendent of Crown Lands* [1947] A.C. 556.
[66] 1976 S.L.T. (Lands Tr.) 2.
[67] 1977 S.L.T. (Lands Tr.) 7. See, too, *Gray v Glasgow District Council*, 1980 S.L.T. (Lands Tr.) 7; and *O'Donnell v Edinburgh Corporation*, 1980 S.L.T. (Lands Tr.) 13.
[68] [1965] 1 W.L.R. 445, HL.

development. The corporation declared the area to be a clearance area and decided to acquire the houses compulsorily. There were 12 other clearance areas in the immediate neighbourhood. In valuing their land as sites cleared of buildings and available for development in an area zoned for residential development, the claimants argued that a willing purchaser would have regard to the fact that all the other buildings in the clearance areas would be cleared away and this would be reflected in the value of their land. The House of Lords concluded that in the absence of the corporation's scheme there was no prospect of clearance and that any increase in value as a result of the clearance by the corporation was to be ignored as an increase in value due to the scheme.

Special provision is made where a house is compulsorily acquired at restricted value and on the date of the order the house is occupied in whole or in part as a private dwelling by a person who throughout the relevant period[69] holds an interest in the house which is subject to a heritable security or charge or is party to an agreement to purchase the house by instalments. Any party to the security, charge or agreement may apply to the sheriff who, after giving other parties an opportunity to be heard, may make an order discharging or modifying any outstanding liabilities of the occupier arising from the security, charge or agreement.[70] The order may be subject to terms and conditions including conditions with respect to the payment of money. In determining what order, if any, to make the sheriff is to have regard in particular, in the case of a heritable security or charge, to whether the heritable creditor or person having the benefit of the charge acted reasonably in advancing the principal sum on the terms of the security or charge.[71] He will be deemed to have acted unreasonably if, at the time when the security or charge was created, he knew or ought to have known that the terms of the security or charge did not afford sufficient security for the principal sum advanced. Regard will also be had, where the security or charge secures a sum representing all or part of the purchase price for the interest, to whether the purchase price was excessive.[72]

In the case of an agreement to purchase by instalments the sheriff will have regard in particular to how far the aggregate of the amount already paid by way of principal together with so much, if any, of the compensation in respect of the compulsory purchase as falls to be paid by the seller represents a fair price for the purchase.[73]

3. Owner-occupier supplement

9–11   Section 308 of the Housing (Scotland) Act 1987 provides that where a house has been compulsorily acquired at restricted value:

(i) so that a local housing authority may carry out works required by an improvement order[74];

---

[69] This is the period from the date of the making of the compulsory purchase order to the date of the notice to treat or deemed notice to treat (or if the purchase is effected without service of a notice to treat, the date of completion of that purchase) or, if earlier, to the date of the death of the person (1987 Act, s.309 (4)).
[70] 1987 Act, s.309(2).
[71] 1987 Act, s.309(3).
[72] 1987 Act, s.309 (3)(a).
[73] 1987 Act, s.309(3)(b).
[74] 1987 Act, s.88.

(ii) so that a local housing authority may secure that a house which could be the subject of a closing or demolition order remains in use as housing accommodation[75];

(iii) in, adjoining or surrounded by an area in respect of which a draft resolution has been made declaring it to be a housing action area for demolition, improvement or demolition and improvement; and[76]

(iv) in pursuance of an order made under Schedule 2, paragraph 2(1) of the Land Compensation (Scotland) Act 1963, as substituted by Schedule 23, paragraph 10 of the Housing (Scotland) Act 1987,[77]

then, subject to the following pre-condition being satisfied, the acquiring authority will make a supplementary payment to the claimant equal to the difference between the full compulsory purchase value and the restricted value. The full compulsory purchase value of the interest being acquired must, of course, be greater than the restricted value for any supplement to be paid.[78] Any question as to such value is to be determined by the Lands Tribunal for Scotland. The "full compulsory purchase value" in relation to an interest in a house means the compensation which would be payable in respect of the compulsory purchase of that interest if the house was not being dealt with as below the tolerable standard.[79] "Restricted value" refers to compensation not exceeding the value of the site as a cleared site available for development.[80]

The pre-condition to be satisfied is that on the relevant date and throughout the qualifying period the house must have been occupied as a private dwelling, and the person so occupying the house (or, if during that period it was so occupied by two or more persons in succession, each of those persons) must have been a person entitled to an interest[81] in that house or a member of the family[82] of a person so entitled.[83]

The "relevant date" varies according to the purpose for which the house is being acquired. Where a local housing authority determine to acquire a house which could be the subject of a closing or demolition order so as to secure that it remains in use as housing accommodation the relevant date is the date on which the authority serve notice under section 121 of the 1987 Act of their determination to purchase the house. If the house is comprised in an area declared by a final resolution

---

[75] 1987 Act, s.121.
[76] 1987 Act, Sch.8, para.5.
[77] See p.191 above.
[78] 1987 Act, s.308(1)(b).
[79] 1987 Act, s.311(2).
[80] 1987 Act, s.311(2).
[81] "Interest" does not include the interest of a tenant for a year or any less period or of a statutory tenant within the meaning of the Rent (Scotland) Act 1984 or of a statutory assured tenant within the meaning of the Housing (Scotland) Act 1988 (1987 Act, s.311(2) as amended by the Housing (Scotland) Act 1988, s.72 and Sch.9, para.18).
[82] Defined in the 1987 Act, s.338 applying the definition in s.83 as amended by the Housing (Scotland) Act 2001, s.108.
[83] 1987 Act, s.308(1)(a).

under Part IV of the 1987 Act to be a housing action area, the relevant date is the date when the notice of that resolution was published and served. If the house was declared not to meet the tolerable standard by an order under Schedule 2, paragraph 2(1) of the Land Compensation (Scotland) Act 1963,[84] it is the date when the order was made. And where a local housing authority purchase the house in order to carry out works required by an improvement order it is the date when the order was served.[85]

The "qualifying period" means the period of two years ending with the relevant date.[86] Where, however, that date is earlier than July 31, 1970, it means the period beginning with August 1, 1968, and ending with the relevant date.

Where an interest was acquired by a person on or after August 1, 1968 but less than two years before the relevant date as defined above and a supplementary payment would have been made had the qualifying period been a period beginning with the acquisition and ending with the relevant date, the authority concerned will nonetheless make such a payment provided the following conditions are satisfied. The authority must be satisfied that the first owner, before acquiring the interest, made all reasonable inquiries to ascertain whether any of the events by reference to which the "relevant date" is defined (above) were likely to occur within two years of the acquisition and had no reason to believe that it was likely; and the person entitled to the interest at the date when the house is purchased must be the first owner or a member of that person's family.[87]

9–12   Determining whether the pre-condition referred to above has been satisfied has given rise to considerable difficulty. Questions of entitlement have been referred in practice to the Lands Tribunal both north and south of the border to determine although it is not altogether clear that such matters are within their jurisdiction. In *Hugh MacDonald's Representatives v Sutherland District Council*,[88] the Lands Tribunal for Scotland was prepared to adopt a pragmatic approach: "A reference to the tribunal in a compulsory purchase case requires us to determine the total compensation due, and it would be cumbersome if the question of entitlement had to be referred to another forum".[89]

The interpretation of "continuity of occupation" during the qualifying period has proved to be the most troublesome aspect of the pre-condition. Where there has been a break in continuity during the course of a single occupation, tribunals appear to have been slow to disqualify a claimant. Thus in *Manzur Hussain v Tameside Metropolitan Borough Council*[90] the qualifying period ran from July 5, 1976, to July 4, 1978.

---

[84] As substituted by the 1987 Act, Sch.23, para.10.

[85] 1987 Act, s.311(1).

[86] 1987 Act, s.311(1).

[87] 1987 Act, s.308(3). For the definition of "family" see s.338 applying s.83 as amended by the Housing (Scotland) Act 2001, s.108.

[88] 1977 S.L.T. (Lands Tr.) 7.

[89] The tribunal commented that the question of entitlement may have to be otherwise determined where a supplementary payment follows a closing or demolition order. See *Spence v Lanarkshire County Council*, 1976 S.L.T. (Lands Tr.) 2.

[90] [1982] J.P.L. 252. See, too, *Abdul Aziz v Tameside Metropolitan Borough Council* [1982] J.P.L. 252.

The claimant was in occupation at the beginning of the qualifying period and until he went to Pakistan in August 1977 because his mother was ill. During his absence, his wife moved temporarily to another house and he therefore arranged for a couple to live in as caretakers. On his return to England in December 1977, there was some delay in securing alternative accommodation for the caretakers but he and his wife resumed occupation of the house in February 1978 and remained there until the end of the qualifying period. The tribunal concluded that occupation included occupation enjoyed vicariously through furniture and caretakers and constructively through control of the subject premises so that the claimant was entitled to the supplementary payment. In *Begum Bibi v Blackburn Borough Council*[91] the qualifying period ran from February 8, 1983 to February 7, 1985. In February 1984 the claimant took her children on holiday to Pakistan. During her absence the house was damaged by fire. Delay on the part of the insurers meant that repairs could not be effected for some time and on her return to England she lived first of all with friends and subsequently in a local authority house. She nonetheless kept her furniture in the damaged house, visited it regularly to keep an eye on it and intended to return there once necessary repairs had been carried out. She was still waiting for a settlement from the insurers at the end of the qualifying period. The tribunal held she was entitled to a supplementary payment. The fact that the house was damaged by fire did not alter the character of the occupation. The claimant continued in occupation through her furniture and her intention to return.[92]

The legislation expressly contemplates successive owner-occupation during the qualifying period. It is, however, unrealistic to expect that a purchaser will always take up residence on the day the vendor leaves so that there is no break in occupation. Nonetheless, in this respect tribunals appear to have interpreted "continuity of occupation" more strictly. Thus in *Reeve v Hartlepool Borough Council*[93] claims for supplementary payments in respect of six houses were rejected. Each house had changed hands during the qualifying period and in each case there was a period of delay between the vendor leaving the house and the claimant taking up residential occupation ranging from 5 weeks to 10 months. In each case, void periods had been allowed by the rating authority. The fact that in three cases there was no gap between the date on which the vendor vacated the house and the claimant began to occupy it for the purposes of repair and improvement was not sufficient. It did not give the occupation the necessary residential quality.

A similar approach was adopted in *Laundon v Hartlepool Borough Council.*[94] In that case there was a break of one month between the vendor vacating the house and the purchaser taking up residence. The purchaser had nonetheless bought furniture from the vendor which remained after the latter had moved out and during the break of one

---

[91] [1988] J.P.L. 418. See too *Samrai v Sandwell MBC* (1993) 66 P. & C.R. 494.
[92] *cf., Westerman v St Helens Metropolitan Borough Council* (1983) 46 P. & C.R. 236 where the owner was considered unlikely to return.
[93] (1975) 30 P. & C.R. 517.
[94] [1978] 2 All E.R. 307, CA.

month the purchaser was engaged in decorating the house. The Court of Appeal declined to accept that the mere presence of furniture in the house constituted occupation of the house as a private dwelling. The court went on to indicate, however, that where the gap between successive residential occupiers was of the order of no more than a week or ten days, the *de minimis* rule would apply. Such a gap would be too insignificant to destroy the quality of occupation as a private dwelling.

A rather more sympathetic view was taken by the Lands Tribunal for Scotland in *Hugh MacDonald's Representatives v Sutherland District Council*.[95] The house in question was occupied originally during the qualifying period by the claimant's brother who was ill. The claimant, herself, stayed at the house every two or three months during her brother's illness. Her sister, who lived nearby, called to see him nearly every day and the sister's husband, who worked together with the brother on the fishings, kept belongings at the house and continued to do so after the brother's death. The claimant kept her furniture in the house throughout the qualifying period even though for part of the period her main residence was a furnished let elsewhere. Following her brother's death, the claimant continued to keep her furniture in the house and to reside there from time to time until eventually moving in permanently.

The acquiring authority's contention, that in order to qualify for the supplementary payment the claimant or her sister should have moved in immediately following the brother's death, was rejected by the tribunal. The tribunal concluded that it was not directed by the legislation to consider whether the relevant occupation was by a qualifying person as her sole or main residence. There was sufficient evidence to establish that during the qualifying period the house was occupied as a private dwelling in the general sense required by the legislation. The supplementary payment was designed to offset the restricted compensation. "As such it should be liberally construed in the spirit of the Statute so as to enable displaced householders to receive the full market value of their houses which is the normal measure of compensation."

It is not essential that the owner-occupier should occupy the whole house provided the rest of the house is, nonetheless, occupied for residential purposes, for example, by a tenant.[96] Neither is it necessary to show that all the normal incidents of residential occupation are carried on in order to establish the residential quality of the occupation.[97]

4. Well-maintained payments

9–13 Section 305 of the Housing (Scotland) Act 1987, as applied by Schedule 2 of the Land Compensation (Scotland) Act 1963,[98] provides that, where an acquiring authority are satisfied that a house which is being acquired and which does not meet the tolerable standard has been well-maintained, they shall make a payment in respect of the house calculated in accordance with section 306. However, no such payment

---

[95] 1977 S.L.T. (Lands Tr.) 7.

[96] *Hunter v Manchester City Council* (1975) 30 P. & C.R. 58.

[97] *Patel v Leicester City Council* (1981) 259 E.G. 985 (meals not taken on the premises).

[98] As substituted by the 1987 Act, Sch.23, para.10.

will be made where an owner-occupier's supplement is to be paid under section 308 (above).[99] Both payments together, when added to the compensation for the acquisition of the interest, would give a claimant more than he would have received if the house had not been below the tolerable standard and thus more than his actual loss.

Where the house is occupied by the owner the well-maintained payment is made to him; otherwise it is paid to the person or persons liable to repair and maintain the house and if there is more than one such person it will be shared in such portions as the acquiring authority consider to be equitable in the circumstances.[1] Where, however, any other person satisfies the authority that the good maintenance of the house is attributable to a material extent to work carried out by him or at his expense, the payment may be made in whole or in part to him.

The acquiring authority will give notice whether or not they propose to make a well-maintained payment and such notice will accompany the notice of the making of the compulsory purchase order.[2] Any person aggrieved by a notice which states that no such payment is to be made, may within 21 days of the service of the notice, refer the matter to the Scottish Ministers. The Ministers may arrange for an inspection of the house and, if they think it appropriate to do so, direct the authority to make such a payment.[3]

The amount of the well-maintained payment will be equal to the rateable value of the house multiplied by a multiplier prescribed from time to time by an order made by the Scottish Ministers.[4] The payment is not in any case to exceed the amount, if any, by which the full compulsory purchase value of the house[5] exceeds the restricted value.[6] Any dispute as to value is to be determined, in default of agreement, by the Lands Tribunal for Scotland.

---

[99] 1987 Act, s.306(5).

[1] 1987 Act, s.305(2).

[2] 1987 Act, s.305(3).

[3] 1987 Act, s.305(4).

[4] 1987 Act, s.306(2). As regards the calculation of the rateable value following the Abolition of Domestic Rates Etc. (Scotland) Act 1987, see s.5(3) of that Act, as amended by the Local Government Finance Act 1988, Sch.12, para.17(3). The multiplier is at present 12.7 (Housing (Payment for Well Maintained Houses) (Scotland) Order 1983).

[5] Defined in the 1987 Act, s.311(2).

[6] See above.

CHAPTER 10

DISTURBANCE

THE ENTITLEMENT TO DISTURBANCE COMPENSATION

10–01 Where an interest in land is compulsorily acquired the person dispossessed may incur losses as a consequence of the acquisition in addition to the value of the land itself. He may incur fees and other costs in finding and taking alternative accommodation, removal expenses, costs in adapting the new premises so that they are suitable for use, loss of goodwill, and so on, all as a direct result of the acquisition. These items, generally referred to as "disturbance," may form a substantial part of a dispossessed person's loss, in some cases more than the value of the land itself. If the person is to receive the financial equivalent of his loss he must be compensated for disturbance.

A claimant must, as mentioned in an earlier chapter, be able to point to statutory authority to support his claim (see Chapter 4). The only specific statutory reference to compensation for disturbance is to be found in rule (6) of section 12 of the 1963 Act. This provides: "The provisions of rule (2) shall not affect the assessment of compensation for disturbance or any other matter not directly based on the value of land".

Rule (6) is not, however, an authority for the payment of compensation. In *Horn v Sunderland Corporation*[1] Greene M.R. observed "Now rule (6) does not confer a right to claim compensation for disturbance. It merely leaves unaffected the right which the owner would before the Act of 1919 have had in a proper case to claim that the compensation should be increased on the ground that he had been disturbed."[2] It is, therefore, necessary to refer back to the 1845 Act and the interpretation placed upon it by the courts to find the authority for disturbance compensation. Although, in the words of Lord Kinnear in *Lanarkshire and Dumbartonshire Railway Co. v Thomas Main*[3] "it is a well-settled rule in the construction of the Lands Clauses Act that when lands have been taken in the exercise of powers of compulsory purchase, the owner or occupier, as the case may be, is entitled not only to the market value of his interest but to full compensation for all the loss which he may sustain by being deprived of his land," there is some uncertainty as to the provision in which this entitlement is to be found. One line of judicial authority suggests that it is to be found by implication in sections 48 and 61 as part

---

[1] [1941] 2 K.B. 26.
[2] pp.33–34.
[3] (1895) 22 R. 912 at p.919.

of the value of the land to the person dispossessed. A more recent line of authority suggests that a claim for consequential loss exists separately to the value of the land taken. These two lines of authority are now considered in turn.

In *Horn*, Scott L.J. stated that "the judicial eye which has discerned that right in the Act must inevitably have found it in . . . the fair purchase price for the land taken."[4] In other words, as sections 48 and 61 of the Act only recognise two components in a compensation claim, *i.e.* the value of the land to be purchased or taken and damage arising from injurious affection, disturbance must inevitably form part of the value of the land. "Such compensation," says Cripps,[5] "may flow from an application of the principle that the basis on which compensation for lands taken is the value of the lands to the owner." Authority for this is to be found in *Commissioners of Inland Revenue v Glasgow and South-Western Railway Co.*[6] In that case the question at issue was whether a jury's separate award under section 48 of the 1845 Act of £9,500 for loss of business following the compulsory acquisition of business premises was to be regarded as part of the "consideration for the sale" of those premises for the purposes of charging *ad valorem* duty under the Stamp Act 1870. Lord Chancellor Halsbury explained the position in this way:

> "The two things—and the only two things—which are within the ambit and contemplation of the statute are the value of the lands and such damage as may arise to other lands held therewith by reason of the particular land which is being taken from them . . . It is admitted therefore impliedly that the only thing which the jury had here to assess was the value of the land. . . In treating of that value, the value under the circumstances to the person who is compelled to sell (because the statute compels him to do so) may be naturally and properly and justly taken into account, and when such phrases as 'damages for loss of business,' or 'compensation for the goodwill' taken from the person, are used in a loose and general sense, they are not inaccurate for the purpose of giving verbal expression to what everybody understands as a matter of business, but in strictness the thing which is to be ascertained is the price to be paid for the land—the land with all the potentialities of it, with all the actual use of it by the person who holds it, is to be considered by those who have to assess the compensation."[7]

In other words, the price to be paid for the land on a compulsory purchase is to include not only its market value but also any personal

[4] [1941] 2 K.B. 26 at p.43.
[5] H. Parrish, *Cripps on Compulsory Acquisition of Land* (11th ed., Stevens and Sons Ltd) para.4–215.
[6] (1887) 14 R. (H.L.) 33.
[7] pp.33 and 34. See, too, *Birmingham City Corporation v West Midland Baptist (Trust) Association Inc.* [1970] A.C. 874 *per* Lord Reid at p.893; *Woolfson v Strathclyde Regional Council;* 1978 S.C. (HL) 90; *Palatine Graphic Arts Co. Ltd v Liverpool City Council* [1986] Q.B. 335, *per* Glidewell L.J. at p.341; and *Hughes v Doncaster Metropolitan Borough Council* [1991] 1 All E.R. 295 *per* Lord Bridge at pp.299–301. See, also, *Jubb v Hull Dock Co.* (1845) 9 Q.B. 443.

loss imposed on the owner by the forced sale, otherwise the claimant will not be fully compensated.

Recent endorsement of the view that a disturbance claim forms part of the value of the land to the seller is to be found in the decision of the House of Lords in *Hughes v Doncaster Metropolitan Borough Council*.[8] Lord Bridge of Harwich, giving judgement for the Court, said "[i]t is well-settled law that whatever compensation is payable to an owner on the compulsory acquisition of his land in respect of disturbance is an element in assessing the value of the land to him, not a distinct and independent head of compensation". In that case the site in question was used by the claimants as merchants dealing in scrap metal and rags. No planning permission had ever been obtained for the use. The site was compulsorily acquired by the local authority. In assessing compensation the authority argued that rule (4) of the 1961 Act applied to eliminate any value attributable to such use as the use was "contrary to law".[9] The claimants argued that rule (4) applied only to the market value of the land acquired and not to the assessment of compensation for disturbance. That being so, they were entitled to a sum in compensation for the loss of the goodwill of the scrap metal and rag merchant's business. Lord Bridge rejected the claimant's argument on this point:

> "[A]lthough compensation in respect of the market value of land acquired and compensation for disturbance must in practice be separately assessed, the courts have consistently adhered to the principle, both before and after the present rules were introduced by the Act of 1919, that the two elements are inseparable parts of a single whole in that together they make up 'the value of the land' to the owner, which unless he retains other land depreciated by severance or injurious affection, was the only compensation which the 1845 code awarded him".[10]

10–02 A similar conclusion was arrived at in *McArdle v Glasgow Corporation*.[11] In 1956 a publican obtained planning permission to use a dwelling as an extension to his public house, subject to the condition that the permission was limited to the period expiring on December 31, 1967. He converted the dwelling into a lounge bar and it was used as such by him and after his death by his widow until 1965 when the whole premises were acquired compulsorily by the local authority. In a claim for compensation by the widow the authority conceded that by reason of sections 22(1) and 24(4) of the 1963 Act it had to be assumed in assessing the value of the premises under rule (2) that permission for the change of use of the dwelling had been granted without limit of time (see Chapter 7), but they contended that that assumption did not fall to be made in assessing compensation for disturbance. The First Division,

---

[8] [1991] 1 All E.R. 295.

[9] The acquiring authority was successful on this point.

[10] See too *Director of Buildings and Lands v Shun Fung Ironworks Ltd* [1995] 1 All E.R. 846 *per* Lord Nicholls of Birkenhead at pp.851–852.

[11] 1972 S.C. 41. See, too, *Woolfson v Strathclyde Regional Council*, 1978 S.C. (H.L.) 90 *per* Lord Keith at p.96.

affirming the decision of the Lands Tribunal for Scotland, held that the assumption applied to the assessment of compensation for disturbance, as well as to the value of the premises, as disturbance was an element in the total value of the "relevant interest". Lord President Clyde said "[t]he distinction which the acquiring authority seek to make between a disturbance claim and a claim for the value of the land is thus a false distinction. They are both elements in the value of the relevant interest within the meaning of that phrase in this series of Acts of Parliament."[12]

Rule (6) in section 12 of the 1963 Act could be interpreted as lending support for the view that disturbance is to be treated as part of the value of the land to the owner. Rule (6) would seem to be intended to preserve the entitlement to disturbance in the face of rule (2). Rule (2) provides that compensation for the value of the land shall be assessed by reference to the amount which a notional willing seller, not the actual owner, might be expected to realise on a sale in the open market. That hypothesis leaves no grounds for assuming that a claim for disturbance is involved as part of the value of the land. It is, therefore, necessary to spell out in rule (6) that that hypothesis is not to be taken as affecting the entitlement to disturbance.

Rule (6) might alternatively be construed as simply clarifying that the changes introduced following the Scott Committee report in 1918 left unaffected the entitlement to disturbance[13] and this would seem to be the view taken by the Second Division in *Venables v Department of Agriculture for Scotland*[14] where the statutory authority for a disturbance claim was considered to rest on a somewhat different footing. At issue was the authority for a claim by a tenant for personal loss resulting from dispossession following the compulsory acquisition by the department of a deer forest let for sporting purposes under a 99 year lease. While commenting that the 1845 Act "seems to me to throw little light on the problem," Lord Justice-Clerk Alness concluded that the loss was recoverable. "The sound principle would seem to be that the person dispossessed should get compensation for all loss occasioned to him by reason of his dispossession."[15] In reaching this conclusion he was influenced to a considerable extent by his reading of sections 17, 19, 71 and 114 of the 1845 Act which, he said, plainly contemplated that compensation is payable in respect of damage sustained by the evicted person in addition to compensation for the value of the lands.

It is doubtful whether these sections provide any clearer general authority for a disturbance claim than the legal fiction referred to in *Glasgow and South-Western Railway Co.* (to which, incidentally, no reference was made in *Venables*) that it is to be regarded as part of the value of the land. Sections 17 and 19 refer to compensation for damage sustained by reason of the execution of the works. Although this is a form of consequential loss, it seems more likely to be directed at injurious affection than disturbance. Sections 71 and 114 both include references to what is generally understood as disturbance but are limited

---

[12] 1972 S.C. 41 at p.48.
[13] Scott, L.J. in *Horn, supra* at p.41 suggested it served both purposes.
[14] 1932 S.C. 573; 1932 S.L.T. 411.
[15] See above at p.581.

to specified classes of claimant, the former to life-renters and the latter to yearly tenants.

The implied authority for disturbance referred to in *Venables* received some support from the Lands Tribunal for Scotland in *Park Automobile Company Ltd v Strathclyde Regional Council.*[16] In that case the claimants' garage premises were acquired for road widening. The premises were vested in the acquiring authority by general vesting declaration in May 1975 although the claimants were allowed to continue in occupation. Compensation under rule (2) for the value of the land was determined by the tribunal in July that year but the claimants expressly reserved their right to make a later claim for disturbance. It is common practice to reserve the position on disturbance until the extent of the consequential loss is apparent. Where a general vesting declaration is employed there is, however, a time limit of six years from the date of divestiture within which such claims must be made.[17] The claimants, who were still in occupation of the premises upon the expiry of the time limit, submitted a notional disturbance claim to safeguard their position and the issue before the tribunal (which is not relevant to the present discussion) was the amount of the claim.[18]

The tribunal, however, felt obliged to register "serious reservations" about the position agreed between the parties that the disturbance compensation should be assessed at the date of divestiture when the heritage fell to be valued.[19] Such a position might seem to follow from the decisions in *Glasgow and South-Western Railway Co.* and *McArdle* which treated disturbance as part of the value of the land. The tribunal, however, were conscious that the use of the general vesting declaration procedure (widely employed in Scotland) meant that divestiture would precede actual disturbance or dispossession sometimes by a long period. Assessing disturbance in such cases with any degree of accuracy or regard for the principle of equivalence before actual dispossession took place was difficult. The question of how and when disturbance compensation should be assessed could, therefore, be very important. The tribunal, accordingly, felt that their failure to comment on the position taken by the parties over the date for assessing disturbance might be construed in subsequent cases as agreement with a position about which they entertained considerable doubts. The tribunal went on to express the view that, while compensation for disturbance is part of the global sum of purchase money or compensation, disturbance compensation must relate to actual loss sustained or still expected to be sustained as at the date of assessment and not to some hypothetical loss "valued" at some anterior date. The distinction drawn by the tribunal between the appropriate dates for valuing the heritage and the consequential loss was much influenced by the basis for disturbance compensation adopted in *Venables.*

---

[16] 1984 S.L.T. (Lands Tr.) 14; [1983] R.V.R. 108.

[17] Town and Country Planning (Scotland) Act 1997, Sch.15, para.36(1).

[18] The claimants could, alternatively, have referred the claim to the tribunal before the expiry of the time limit and then, as sometimes happens, sisted the claim until the position became clearer.

[19] See E. Young and J. Rowan Robinson, "Disturbance Compensation: Flexibility and the Principle of Equivalence", 1984 J.R. 133.

The present position may be summarised by saying that while there is **10–03** no doubt that the entitlement to disturbance compensation derives from the 1845 Act, some uncertainty remains about the precise authority. However, whatever view is taken of the authority for disturbance, the result is essentially the same[20] with disturbance compensation and compensation for the market value of the land being aggregated (together with injurious affection compensation where appropriate) to form the total price at which the land is conveyed to the acquiring authority.

The Chartered Lands Societies Committee in a memorandum in 1968[21] observed "it may be thought somewhat surprising that a right of such importance should still depend on decisions by judges whose 'judicial eye' (to use Lord Justice Scott's expression) 'discerned' such a right in a statute of 1845 which made no express reference to it". They went on to recommend that "the time has come to put the right to compensation for consequential loss on a firm independent statutory foundation". There is, however, a risk that a detailed statutory provision might unduly inhibit claims for consequential loss. With this in mind, CPPRAG recommended that the principle of compensation for disturbance should be expressed in primary legislation but in a way that would retain the flexibility and common sense approach which have been established in case law.[22]

It should be noted that rule (6) in section 12 of the 1963 Act refers not only to disturbance but also to "any other matter not directly based on the value of the land". In *Lee (Judge) v Minister of Transport*[23] Lord Denning considered that disturbance in the corresponding provision in the English legislation referred to the right to receive compensation for the personal loss sustained by reason of having to vacate the premises; other matters not directly based on the value of the land were held in that case to include professional fees incurred in the preparation of the claim for compensation.[24]

In *McLaren's Discretionary Trustee v Secretary of State for Scotland*[25] the Lands Tribunal for Scotland declined to accept the argument that "any other matter" was confined to expenditure incurred in preparing a claim. Although there was a tendency now to refer to any claim under rule (6) not directly based on the value of land as a "disturbance claim," "disturbance" in its narrower sense referred to the disturbance of an occupier upon dispossession.[26] To give "any other matter" such a limited interpretation did not square with the reference in *Lanarkshire and Dumbartonshire Railway Co.* to "full compensation for all loss". The

---

[20] The decisions in *McArdle* and *Park* indicate that there may, exceptionally, be cases where the result may not be the same.

[21] "Compensation for Compulsory Acquisition and Planning Restrictions," paras 43 and 44.

[22] *Fundamental review of the laws and procedures relating to compulsory purchase and compensation: final report*, para.138.

[23] [1966] 1 Q.B. 111.

[24] See, too, *London County Council v Tobin* [1959] 1 W.L.R. 354; and *Redfield Hardware Ltd v Bristol Corporation* (1963) 15 P. & C.R. 47.

[25] 1987 S.L.T. (Lands Tr.) 25.

[26] See, too, *Hull and Humber Investment Co. Ltd v Hull Corporation* [1965] 2 Q.B. 145, *per* Pearson L.J. at p.161.

tribunal instanced the decisions in *Smith v Strathclyde Regional Council*[27] and *City of Aberdeen District Council v Sim*[28] on pre-notice to treat expenses (see below) as examples of a wider interpretation of "any other matter". The object of rule (6) was to preserve the entitlement to compensation for all consequential loss. In *McLaren* the tribunal held that a sum to compensate for the future maintenance or removal of accommodation works was not to be treated as consequential loss for the purposes of rule (6) but as an item of injurious affection.

THE RULE (6) CLAIM MUST BE CONSISTENT

10–04 As what is commonly referred to generically, and will for convenience be referred to hereafter, as a "rule (6) claim" or a "disturbance claim" goes to build up the global sum of purchase money or compensation, all heads of claim, whether under rules (2) or (6), must, as the Lands Tribunal for Scotland observed in *Park Automobile Co. Ltd*, be interrelated and not duplicatory otherwise the claimant will receive more than the financial equivalent of his loss. Where, for example, land which is being compulsorily acquired has potential beyond its present use which can only be realised by disturbing the present use, the claimant is entitled, if he chooses, to compensation assessed on the potential value of the land but may not in those circumstances also claim disturbance compensation otherwise he will receive more than his real loss. As Cripps points out,[29] the land in such a case has two values to the claimant: (i) the existing use value and a right to compensation for disturbance; and (ii) the potential value. The claimant is entitled to whichever is the higher.

Thus in *Horn v Sunderland Corporation*[30] the Court of Appeal held[31] that the claimant could not in Cripps' words[32] "claim that the land for the purposes of valuation be treated as building land and for purposes of disturbance as agricultural land, those claims being inconsistent with one another".[33]

Similarly, in *Prestwick Hotels Ltd v Glasgow Corporation*,[34] the First Division held that the claimants were not entitled to relocation expenses where compensation had been awarded on the basis of the total extinguishment of the business. The claimants carried on the business of a licensed hotel in premises which they owned. The hotel was com-

---

[27] 1982 S.L.T. (Lands Tr.) 2.

[28] 1983 S.L.T. 250.

[29] *Cripps on Compulsory Acquisition of Land*, paras 4–217 and 4–228.

[30] [1941] 2 K.B. 26. See, too, *Mizen Bros. v Mitcham U.D.C.*, unreported, July 19, 1929, D.C. cited with approval in *Horn*.

[31] Goddard L.J. dissenting.

[32] Para.4–217.

[33] For a criticism of the decision in *Horn* see M. Horton and J. Trustram Eve, "Compensation and Valuation Matters" in (1991) *The Planning Balance in the 1990s Journal of Planning and Environment Law Occasional* Paper No. 18.

[34] 1975 S.C. 105. See too *Mallick v Liverpool City Council* (2000) 79 P. & C.R. 1, CA where it was held that a claim for loss of future profits was incompatible with compensation based on the total extinguishment of the business.

pulsorily acquired as part of a comprehensive development scheme. Although the claimants intended to carry on their business elsewhere, the arbiter considered the circumstances were such that compensation should be awarded on the basis that the business, including the entire goodwill, was being extinguished. He proposed also to award compensation in respect of the costs to be incurred by the claimants in professional fees and personal outlays in searching for, locating and acquiring another hotel as a going concern. On appeal the court held that compensation awarded on the basis of the total extinguishment of the business would represent the full price for the premises and the business as a going concern, thus putting the claimants in a financial position equivalent to the position they would have been in if their land had not been taken. To give them an additional sum representing relocation costs would result in the total compensation being greater than the measure of the whole loss suffered. Relocation costs could only arise if there was something to relocate. In this case there had been a notional transfer of the entire business to the acquiring authority so there was nothing to relocate.

On the other hand, in *D. M. Hoey Ltd v Glasgow Corporation*[35] where the question of consistency was raised, the Second Division held that the claimants were entitled to disturbance compensation in addition to the agreed value of retail premises. The level of profits made by the claimants in the four years preceding compulsory acquisition had been unduly low. The value of the premises for business purposes was based on the anticipated level of profits which could be made. The authority argued that the compensation was based therefore on the potential value of the premises and that, on the strength of the decision in *Horn*, the owner was being inconsistent in claiming disturbance as well. This argument was rejected on the ground that the local authority were confusing the distinction between economic and uneconomic use with the distinction between existing use and potential use. In this case there was no question of a change in the existing use and the disturbance claim was allowed.

THE LIMITS OF A DISTURBANCE CLAIM

Subject to what is said below in connection with remoteness, a person **10–05** who receives and is entitled to receive a notice to treat may lodge a rule (6) claim in respect of all consequential loss. In *Venables v Department of Agriculture for Scotland*[36] Lord Justice-Clerk Alness referred to the claimant's right to "all consequential loss occasioned by his dispossession". Persons having no greater interest in land than as a tenant for a year or from year to year are not entitled to receive a notice to treat and

---

[35] 1972 S.C. 200. And in *Palatine Graphic Arts Co. Ltd v Liverpool City Council* (1986) 42 P. & C.R. 308 the Court of Appeal held that although compensation for compulsory acquisition was not to exceed the actual loss sustained, this did not mean that regional development grant payable on relocation had to be deducted from the disturbance claim.

[36] 1932 S.C. 573 at p.591. See, too, *Lanarkshire and Dumbartonshire Railway Co. v Thomas Main* (1895) 22 R. 912, *per* Lord Kinnear at p.919.

have no entitlement to rule (6) compensation.[37] If, however, such a person is required to give up possession before the expiration of their term or interest, they are entitled to compensation for any loss or injury they may sustain.[38]

A disturbance claim is made once and for all in respect of all consequential loss both present and prospective as at the date of assessment.[39] Although the content of a disturbance claim will depend very much on the particular circumstances of each case, it may sometimes be possible to trace the consequences of dispossession through a seemingly endless series of events. In such cases the courts and tribunals have had to define the limits of a disturbance claim. The object of compensation, like damages, is to put the claimant, so far as money can do it, in the same position as he would have been in had the dispossession not occurred.[40] It is not surprising, therefore, that in defining these limits recourse has been had to concepts derived from the law relating to damages. Concepts such as causation, remoteness and mitigation have all been applied to disturbance claims to determine the limits of loss occasioned by dispossession.[41] The defining and refining of these limits are described in McGregor on *Damages*[42] as producing the most difficult problems in the whole field of damages. The same comment appears to apply equally to the application of these limits to the assessment of disturbance compensation.

Disentangling questions of causation from remoteness of loss and questions of remoteness from mitigation may not be easy. Causation is concerned with the question whether the acquisition of the land by the acquiring authority caused the claimant's loss. If this question is answered in the claimant's favour, it is then necessary to consider whether the law protects the claimant from the particular loss which has been suffered or whether it is too remote. As Lord Wright commented in *Liesbosch Dredger v S. S. Edison*[43] "[t]he law cannot take account of everything that follows a wrongful act; it regards some subsequent matters as outside the scope of its selection, because 'it were infinite for the law to judge the cause of causes' or consequences of consequences." And in *Director of Buildings and Lands v Shun Fung Ironworks Ltd*,[44] Lord Nicholls of Birkenhead observed that "the adverse consequences to

[37] *Newham London Borough Council v Benjamin* [1968] 1 W.L.R. 694.

[38] The 1845 Act, s.114. Where, however, the acquiring authority purchase the landlord's interest and simply allow the tenant's interest to expire following the service of a notice to quit, the tenant may be entitled to a disturbance payment under ss.34 and 35 of the Land Compensation (Scotland) Act 1973 (see Chapter 12).

[39] Agreement may sometimes be reached in practice to defer certain aspects of a claim for disturbance until the extent of loss is clearer.

[40] *Ricket v Metropolitan Railway Co.* (1865) 34 L.J.Q.B. 257, *per* Erle C.J. at p.261; *Palatine Graphic Arts Co. Ltd v Liverpool City Council* [1986] Q.B. 335, *per* Glidewell L.J. at pp.342 and 343.

[41] See *Director of Buildings and Lands v Shun Fung Ironworks Ltd* [1995] 1 All E.R. 846 *per* Lord Nicholls of Birkenhead on pp.852–853. For a useful discussion of the application of these concepts to disturbance see P. H. Clarke, "Remoteness of Loss in Disturbance Compensation" [1977] J.P.L. 138; and E. Young, "Remoteness, Impecuniosity and Disturbance" [1981] J.P.L. 707.

[42] Harvey McGregor, *McGregor on Damages* (16th ed., Sweet & Maxwell Ltd) para.107.

[43] [1933] A.C. 449 at p.460.

[44] [1995] 1 All E.R. 846.

a claimant whose land is taken may extend outwards and onwards a very long way, but fairness does not require that the acquiring authority shall be responsible ad infinitum". Finally, the question must be asked whether the claimant has taken all reasonable steps to mitigate the loss to him consequent upon the acquisition. There will, of course, be cases where these distinctions, particularly that between causation and remoteness, are more theoretical than real. Nonetheless, they provide a framework within which some of the decisions in this complex area may be considered.

1. Causation

In *Shun Fung* Lord Nicholls of Birkenhead stated that "a prerequisite **10–06** to an award of compensation is that there must be a causal connection between the resumption or acquisition and the loss in question". In *McGhee v National Coal Board*[45] Lord Reid commented that the legal concept of causation "is not based on logic or philosophy. It is based on the practical way in which the ordinary man's mind works in the everyday affairs of life."[46] Whether a loss may be said to be caused by an acquiring authority will depend on the particular circumstances of a case. The onus is upon the claimant to establish by evidence all the items of his disturbance claim.[47]

Consequential loss may take many different forms[48]; indeed, it is probable, as Davies remarks,[49] that the categories of disturbance are never closed. Nevertheless, grouping decisions in this field under a number of separate headings may help to give some indication of, to borrow Lord Reid's words, the practical way in which the test of causation has been applied in the everyday operation of the compensation code. The exercise may also give some idea of the possible scope of a disturbance claim.

Increased operating costs

In *J. Bibby and Sons Ltd v Merseyside County Council*[50] the Court of **10–07** Appeal accepted that increased operating costs consequent on the removal to new premises could form the subject of a disturbance claim provided there was no alternative to incurring them and provided also that no benefit was derived by the claimant as a result of the extra operational costs which made it worthwhile to incur them. In that case the court refused to interfere with the finding of the Lands Tribunal that the claimants had failed to satisfy the second proviso. And in *Easton v Islington Corporation*,[51] a claim for increased outgoings at the new premises in the form of increased rent and rates was disallowed on the

---

[45] 1973 S.C. (H.L) 37.
[46] See above at p.53.
[47] *Campbell Douglas and Co. Ltd v Hamilton District Council*, 1984 S.L.T. (Lands Tr.) 44; *Bede Distributors Ltd v Newcastle-upon-Tyne Corporation* (1973) 26 P. & C.R. 298.
[48] For a useful discussion of the different forms of consequential loss see W. A. Leach, *Disturbance on Compulsory Purchase* (3rd ed., Estates Gazette Ltd) with supplement.
[49] K. Davies, *Law of Compulsory Purchase and Compensation* (5th ed., Tolley) p.206.
[50] (1979) 251 E.G. 757.
[51] (1952) 3 P. & C.R. 145.

same basis. As Cripps says, "loss therefore can only be the reasonable consequence of the taking of the land if the increased rent or other expenses of the new premises are unproductive to the claimant."[52] Duplicate operating costs incurred while a business is transferred from one set of premises to another would be recoverable in an appropriate case.[53]

Fees and expenses

10–08   The expense of obtaining professional advice in preparing and negotiating the compensation claim is generally accepted as a direct consequence of dispossession[54]; so also are professional fees incurred in searching for and acquiring alternative accommodation.[55] The costs incurred in securing the issue of a certificate of appropriate alternative development, including pursuing a successful appeal to the Scottish Ministers, must also be taken into account.[56] Claimants, themselves, are likely to devote considerable time to protecting their interests during the period of dispossession and it would seem that the cost of this time may be a proper item of claim.[57]

Interest and charges

10–09   In *Service Welding Ltd v Tyne and Wear County Council*[58] the Court of Appeal disallowed bank interest and charges on an overdraft for financing the capital progressively laid out in the preparation of the site to which the claimant was intending to remove and the building of a factory. The interest and charges were regarded as part of the price for the factory.[59] The court considered that a person selling a factory on the open market would include interest charges incurred during construction as part of the cost. Bridge L.J. said:

> "What the authorities . . . very clearly establish, however, is that when an occupier, whether residential or business, does, in conse-

[52] *Cripps on Compulsory Acquisition of Land*, para.4–232. And see *Rought (W.) Ltd. v West Suffolk County Council* [1955] 2 Q.B. 338; *Ratter v Manchester Corporation* (1974) 28 P. & C.R. 443.

[53] For example, see *Mogridge (W.J.) (Bristol 1937) Ltd v Bristol Corporation* (1956) 8 P. & C.R. 78; *Sloan v Edinburgh District Council* 1988 S.L.T. (Lands Tr.) 25.

[54] *London County Council v Tobin* [1959] 1 W.L.R. 354.

[55] *Harvey v Crawley Development Corporation* [1957] 1 Q.B. 485. In that case professional fees incurred in abortive negotiations over alternative accommodation were also allowed. And in *Smith v Strathclyde Regional Council*, 1982 S.L.T. (Lands Tr.) 2 professional fees incurred in connection with an abortive scheme to preserve part of the subject premises were allowed.

[56] The Land Compensation (Scotland) Act 1963, s.9A added by the Planning and Compensation Act 1991, s.75(3).

[57] See, for example, *D. B. Thomas and Son Ltd v Greater London Council* (1982) 262 E.G. 991 and 1086; *Smith v Birmingham Corporation* (1974) 29 P. & C.R. 265.

[58] (1979) 250 E.G. 1291.

[59] CPPRAG noted that the cost of a loan to buy replacement premises is different from the purchase price of the premises themselves and claimants could be left out of pocket if they are not compensated for the cost of interest charged on such a loan ("Fundamental review of the laws and procedures relating to compulsory purchase and compensation: final report", (2000) DETR para.155).

quence of disturbance, rehouse himself in alternative accommodation, *prima facie* he is not entitled to recover by way of compensation for disturbance or otherwise, any part of the purchase price which he pays for the alternative accommodation to which he removes, whether that accommodation is better or worse than, or equivalent to, the property from which he is being evicted. The reason for that is that there is a presumption in law, albeit a rebuttable presumption, that the purchase price paid for the new premises is something for which the claimant has received value for money."

A similar view was taken by the Lands Tribunal with regard to a claim for bank charges and interest on bridging finance in *D. B. Thomas and Son Ltd v Greater London Council.*[60]

In *Sloan v Edinburgh District Council*,[61] on the other hand, compensation for additional interest and rates was awarded by the Lands Tribunal for Scotland. The claimants wished to buy another house and decided to sell their existing house. They were, however, unable to sell the existing house as it was discovered that the local authority were going to include it in a housing action area and that demolition was a possibility. They nonetheless proceeded to buy the alternative house on the assumption that the authority would buy the existing house. Negotiations with the authority over the existing house were protracted and the claimants were left in the position of incurring two sets of loan interest and rates over a prolonged period. Eventually, the claimants served a blight notice which was accepted and lodged a claim for the additional interest and rates paid over a period of two and a half years. The claim was referred to the Lands Tribunal for Scotland for determination. The tribunal concluded that the payments were entirely due to the authority's scheme of acquisition and should be compensated.[62]

Adaptations

The cost of carrying out adaptations to new premises to make them **10–10** suitable for use by the claimants has been allowed by the Lands Tribunal.[63] However, in the light of the comments by Bridge L.J. in *Service Welding Ltd, supra,* it would seem that where the adaptations are reflected in the value of the premises, the claimant will be presumed to have obtained value for money and the cost would not form part of the disturbance claim.[64]

---

[60] (1982) 262 E.G. 991 and 1086. See, too, *Simpson v Stoke-on-Trent City Council* (1982) 263 E.G. 673; and *Emslie and Simpson Ltd v Aberdeen District Council*, 1995 S.L.T. 355. Contrast *Roberts v Greater London Council* (1949) 229 E.G. 975. And see, generally, *Service Welding Ltd, supra.*

[61] 1988 S.L.T. (Lands Tr.) 25.

[62] See, too, *Cole v Southwark London Borough Council* (1979) 251 E.G. 477.

[63] *Powner and Powner v Leeds Corporation* (1953) 4 P. & C.R. 167. See, too, *Tamplin's Brewery Ltd v County Borough of Brighton* (1971) 22 P. & C.R. 746. This would seem to include the cost of reinstating fixtures if their value has not been reflected in the market value of the land taken (*Nicholls v Highways Agency* (2000) 24 E.G. 167, Lands Tr.).

[64] See *Bresgall and Sons Ltd v London Borough of Hackney* (1976) 32 P. & C.R. 442; and *Smith v Birmingham Corporation* (1974) 29 P. & C.R. 265.

Removal costs

10–11   Losses incurred through the necessity of removing to alternative premises are a common item in a disturbance claim. These may include the loss of trade fixtures to a tenant,[65] loss on the forced sale of equipment,[66] actual removal costs, adaptations to carpets, curtains and blinds,[67] re-installation of cooker and telephone,[68] notification of change of address, and depreciation of machinery caused by its unseating, removal and reseating.[69]

Loss of profits

10–12   In *McEwing and Sons Ltd v Renfrew County Council*[70] the claimants, a firm of builders, in addition to claiming for the market value of the subject land with the benefit of planning permission for residential development, claimed for the loss of future profits they would have enjoyed if they had been left to erect and sell houses on the subject land. The First Division rejected the claim on the ground that the profitability of the land was reflected in the compensation for the value of the land. As Lord Moulton aptly observed in *Pastoral Finance Association Ltd v Minister (New South Wales)*[71] "no man would pay for land in addition to its market value the capitalised value of the savings and additional profits which he would hope to make by the use of it".[72] It would seem, therefore, as Cripps says,[73] that there is no right to claim for disturbance of land in relation to its potentiality. An owner can only be disturbed from an actuality.

However, it appears that, if a business is so disrupted by dispossession that it has to discontinue all or part of its operations for a period, a claim for temporary loss of anticipated profits may be competent.[74] To borrow Cripps' phraseology, the claimant in these circumstances may be said to be disturbed from an "actuality".

---

[65] *Evans v Glasgow District Council*, 1978 S.L.T. (Lands Tr.) 5. The case concerned a disturbance payment under the Land Compensation (Scotland) Act 1973, ss.34 and 35. However, the measure of the payment is essentially the same as for disturbance compensation (see Ch.12).

[66] *Venables v Department of Agriculture for Scotland*, 1932 S.C. 573; 1932 S.L.T. 411.

[67] See, for example, *Harvey v Crawley Development Corporation* [1957] 1 Q.B. 485. In *Allen v Doncaster Metropolitan Borough Council* (1997) 73 P. & C.R. 98 the Lands Tribunal allowed the cost of new curtains.

[68] *Bryce v Motherwell District Council* [1980] R.V.R. 282.

[69] *Mogridge, W.J. (Bristol 1937) v Bristol Corporation* (1956) 8 P. & C.R. 78.

[70] 1960 S.C. 53.

[71] [1914] A.C. 1083 at p.1088. In *Mallick v Liverpool City Council* (2000) 79 P. & C.R. 1, CA it was held that a claim for loss of future profits was incompatible with compensation assessed on the basis of the total extinguishment of the business.

[72] See, too, *Collins v Feltham U.D.C.* [1937] 4 All E.R. 189; *George Wimpey and Co. Ltd v Middlesex County Council* [1938] 3 All E.R. 781; *Watson v Secretary of State for Air* [1954] 3 All E.R. 582.

[73] *Cripps on Compulsory Acquisition of Land*, para.4–228.

[74] See, for example, *West Suffolk County Council v W. Rought Ltd* [1957] A.C. 403; *Evans v Glasgow District Council*, 1978 S.L.T. (Lands Tr.) 5; *Bede Distributors Ltd v Newcastle-upon-Tyne Corporation* (1973) 26 P. & C.R. 298; *Smith v Birmingham Corporation* (1974) 29 P. & C.R. 265; *Bailey v Derby Corporation* [1965] 1 W.L.R. 213. And see the comments of Lord Sorn in *McEwing and Sons Ltd, supra* at p.67. In *Bissett v Secretary of State for Scotland*, unreported, January 23, 1991, Lands Tribunal for Scotland, a claim for loss of profits was treated as part of a claim for injurious affection rather than disturbance.

In *Emslie and Simpson Ltd v City of Aberdeen District Council*[75] shop premises were acquired for a city centre redevelopment scheme. The tenants included in their claim an item of £54,000 for loss of profits in the years prior to vesting, resulting from the blighting effect of the impending acquisition. The acquiring authority resisted the claim on the ground that this was not a loss caused by the dispossession of the claimant.[76] They were losses due to the blight caused by the underlying scheme over a period of years and would have been no different even if they had not been displaced. Although it was accepted that compensation for disturbance may include reimbursement of expenditure incurred in anticipation of dispossession, that was not the same as compensating for losses caused by the overall blighting effect of the scheme of acquisition. The First Division accepted the acquiring authority's argument and rejected this item of claim.

Loss of goodwill

Goodwill has been defined as "the possibility of the continuance of a business connection".[77] This possibility may depend on the personality and ability of the owner, upon the reputation of the business or upon the location of the premises in which the business is carried on. The value of the possibility rests upon an objective assessment of the performance of the business and of its prospects.   **10–13**

Goodwill arising by virtue of the location of the premises, as for example with a public house where the goodwill may simply represent the habit of customers resorting to the premises, passes as part of the value of the land.[78] Apart from this, goodwill is a personal asset and does not pass to the acquiring authority with the land and remains with the trader. The loss or diminution in the value of the goodwill upon compulsory acquisition may be the subject of a rule (6) claim. The extent of loss or diminution will depend on the character of the business. In *Prestwick Hotels Ltd v Glasgow Corporation,*[79] for example, the Court of Session accepted that the claimants, who carried on the business of licensed hoteliers, were unlikely to find other premises near enough to their present site to enable them to move any of their goodwill to the new premises. In the circumstances, the claimants were entitled to compensation for the total extinguishment of the goodwill. On the other hand in *London County Council v Tobin,*[80] where an opticians business was relocated, it was accepted that there had been no more than a

---

[75] 1994 S.C.L.R. 69. In *Director of Buildings and Lands v Shung Fung Ironworks Ltd* [1995] 1 All E.R. 846 the Privy Council held that loss due to the threat of dispossession may be claimed. *Shun Fung* can be distinguished from *Emslie and Simpson* on the ground that the loss claimed was confined to the consequences of the threat of acquisition rather than to the general blighting effects of the acquiring authority's scheme.

[76] The argument by the claimant for a broader construction of the word "dispossession" was rejected by the First Division (see J. Rowan Robinson and N. Hutchison, "The Principle of Equivalence and the Limits of Disturbance Compensation" [1994] J.P.L. 320).

[77] *Cripps on Compulsory Acquisition of Land*, para.4–234.

[78] But see *Park Automobile Co. Ltd v City of Glasgow Corporation* (1975) 30 P. & C.R. 491, a case concerning a filling station.

[79] 1975 S.C. 105.

[80] [1959] 1 W.L.R. 354.

partial loss of goodwill.[81] It may be that a wholesale business taking orders from a wide area would suffer very little or no loss of goodwill on relocation.

Pre-notice to treat expenses

10–14   An area which has given rise to some uncertainty in the past has been the competence of a claim for consequential loss arising prior to the date of the notice to treat or the deemed notice to treat. In a line of cases[82] culminating in *M. Bloom (Kosher) v Tower Hamlets London Borough Council*,[83] the English Lands Tribunal declined to allow costs incurred in anticipation of dispossession as part of the disturbance claim. In *Bloom* the claimant's factory was compulsorily acquired as part of a clearance scheme under the Housing Act 1967. Knowing of the forthcoming clearance area declaration and of the compulsory purchase order, the claimants sought and obtained alternative premises and moved into them before the date of the notice to treat. In doing so, they incurred professional fees, capital expenditure on alterations to machinery, losses on non-transferable plant and machinery and the cost of alterations to the new premises.

The claim for these expenses was rejected by the tribunal. "As a matter of causation or remoteness or indeed as a matter of meaningful English language," said the tribunal member, "I cannot accept that a loss is consequent upon an acquisition if it is incurred before there is an acquisition".[84]

The question whether the cost of taking action in anticipation of dispossession might be recovered as part of the disturbance claim was answered in quite a different way by the Lands Tribunal for Scotland in *Smith v Strathclyde Regional Council*.[85] The claimant in *Smith* was the owner of a public house in Hamilton. In 1971 the local authority wrote to say that part of the premises would need to be demolished for a road realignment scheme. Negotiations were opened to buy necessary land. The claimant initially took the view that the whole building would have to be demolished but the local authority suggested that part could be retained and adapted. Detailed discussions took place between the authority and the claimant's advisers about alternative schemes of adaptation. In the meantime, compulsory purchase orders were promoted and confirmed for the land and notice to treat was deemed to have been served in 1973. The discussions about the adaptation of the remainder of the building came to nothing and it was eventually

[81] And see *R. v Scard* (1894) 10 T.L.R. 545; *Remnant v London County Council* (1952) 3 P. & C.R. 185; and *John Line and Sons Ltd v Newcastle-upon-Tyne Corporation* (1956) 6 P. & C.R. 466.
[82] *Webb v Stockport Corporation* (1962) 13 P. & C.R. 339; *Widden v Kensington and Chelsea Royal London Borough* [1970] R.V.R. 160; *Bostock, Chater and Son v Chelmsford Borough Council* (1973) 26 P. & C.R. 321; and *Walter, Brett Park v South Glamorgan County Council* (1976) 238 E.G. 733.
[83] (1978) 35 P. & C.R. 423.
[84] The decision would seem to accord with the general position at common law where damages cannot be given on account of any loss before the cause of action arises (MacGregor, *Damages*, Chap.9).
[85] 1982 S.L.T. (Lands Tr.) 2.

demolished in 1976. The claimant included an item in his disturbance claim for the professional fees incurred prior to the date of the deemed notice to treat in the abortive negotiations over adapting the rump of the premises. This item was rejected by the acquiring authority on the basis of the decision in *Bloom*.

The tribunal declined to follow *Bloom*. Founding strongly on the principle of equivalence referred to by Lord Justice-Clerk Alness in *Venables* and by Lord Justice Scott in *Horn v Sunderland Corporation,* the tribunal concluded that the consequences of dispossession had to be viewed in a causal rather than a strictly temporal sense and they upheld the claim.[86]

The decision in *Smith* was subsequently approved by the Court of Session in *Aberdeen District Council v Sim*[87] where solicitor's fees incurred by the claimants in acquiring alternative accommodation some five years prior to the date of the deemed notice to treat were allowed as part of the disturbance claim, and followed in England by the Court of Appeal in *Prasad v Wolverhampton Borough Council*[88] where a disturbance payment was allowed in respect of loss incurred in moving out of a house prior to the date of the notice to treat.[89] Stephenson L.J., with whom Fox L.J. and Kerr L.J. agreed, cited the decision in *Smith* at some length because "it exactly expresses better than I can my opinion of the authorities and the principle to be drawn from them and applied to costs and loss incurred in obtaining alternative accommodation to that which is threatened with compulsory acquisition".

In *Director of Buildings and Lands v Shun Fung Ironworks Ltd*[90] news **10–15** of the prospect of resumption (the Hong Kong equivalent of compulsory acquisition) of the claimants' industrial premises for a new town resulted in the 'slow asphyxiation' of their business. Customers became unwilling to enter into long-term contracts; and the claimants, themselves, decided they could not enter into contracts of more than 6 months duration. As a consequence, the claimants suffered substantial loss of profits. The Privy Council had to consider whether a loss occurring before resumption could be regarded for compensation purposes as a loss caused by the resumption. The court held, by a majority, that losses incurred in anticipation of resumption and because of the threat which resumption presented are to be regarded as losses caused by the resumption as much as losses arising after resumption. *Sim* and *Prassad* were considered to have been correctly decided.

The decisions in *Smith, Sim, Prasad* and *Shun Fung,* nonetheless, place a claimant in an anomalous position in that expenses incurred at an early stage in a scheme of acquisition will not be recoverable unless a notice to treat or deemed notice to treat is subsequently served. They also raise difficult questions about how far back the consequences of dispossession

---

[86] See, too, the decisions of the official arbiters in *Mrs Leckie's Trustees v East Kilbride Development Corporation*, ref. 10/1961; and *Duthie v Glasgow Corporation*, ref. 9/1965.
[87] 1983 S.L.T. 250; 1982 R.V.R. 251.
[88] [1983] Ch. 333.
[89] See, too, *Campbell Douglas and Co. Ltd v Hamilton District Council*, 1984 S.L.T. (Lands Tr.) 44; *Park Automobile Co. Ltd v Strathclyde Regional Council*, 1984 S.L.T. (Lands Tr.) 14; and *Sloan v Edinburgh District Council*, 1988 S.L.T. (Lands Tr.) 25.
[90] [1995] 1 All E.R. 846.

may be traced, a matter which now falls to be determined in the light of the test of remoteness (below)[91] and about the extent to which a claimant may be expected to take steps prior to the notice to treat to mitigate loss (below). The decision sacrifices certainty for principle but in the circumstances that would seem more equitable.[92] In *Shun Fung* Lord Nicholls of Birkenhead addressed the question of uncertainty:

> "Their Lordships have in mind that, at the outset of a shadow period, there may be no certainty that resumption will take place. As time passes, and the scheme proceeds, the likelihood of resumption increases, until the Governor makes a resumption order. At that stage, but not before, there is a legal commitment. Their Lordships can see no sound reason for attempting to draw a spurious line somewhere along this penumbra of gradually darkening shadow. One of the conditions for compensation is that the loss must have been reasonably incurred. If a reasonable person would have continued to trade normally the landowner cannot claim compensation for losses incurred by his refusal to accept any more orders. He cannot simply let his business run down, and then seek to recover compensation for his losses. The less certain the prospect of resumption, the greater will be the burden of showing that he acted reasonably in running down his business and that the losses were caused by the prospect of resumption."

CPPRAG, however, felt that the appropriate date from which losses and costs can be claimed should be precisely defined in statute and the majority on the Group recommended the date on which the compulsory purchase order becomes operative.[93] The DTLR in their response opted for the date on which the acquiring authority notify those affected of the making of the CPO as the date from which appropriate losses can be reimbursed and as the date from which such claimants have a duty to mitigate their losses.[94]

2. Remoteness of loss

10–16   Having established that an acquiring authority's action has caused a particular loss, it is then necessary to consider whether the loss may be recovered as part of the disturbance claim. Some losses may be too remote and, therefore, beyond recovery.

---

[91] See *Sim* and *Smith, supra.*

[92] For comment on the question of pre-notice to treat expenses see E. Young and J. Rowan-Robinson, "Disturbance Compensation: Flexibility and the Principle of Equivalence," 1984 J.R. 133; W. A. Leach, "Disturbance—the 'Prasad' case" (1983) 267 E.G. 669; B. Denyer-Green, "Disturbance before notice to treat," (1983) *Chartered Surveyor Weekly* p.661; Fraser P. Davidson, "Compensation for Disturbance: Opening Pandora's Box," 1983 S.P.L.P. 45; "Compensation for Compulsory Acquisition" (1995) *Royal Institution of Chartered Surveyors*, paras 4.9–4.12; N. Macleod, "Compensation for Disturbance on Compulsory Acquisition" [1989] J.P.L. 891; and letters at (1981) 257 E.G. 663; (1983) 265 E.G. 744; and (1983) 266 E.G.7.

[93] "Fundamental review of the laws and procedures relating to compulsory purchase and compensation: final report" (2000) DETR para.140.

[94] *Compulsory purchase and compensation: delivering a fundamental change,* (2001) para.3.8.

The test for remoteness in disturbance cases which has been widely adopted[95] is that laid down by Romer L.J. in *Harvey v Crawley Development Corporation.*[96] Influenced in particular by the decision in *Venables,* he stated:

> "any loss sustained by a dispossessed owner (at all events one who occupies his house) which flows from a compulsory acquisition may properly be regarded as the subject of compensation for disturbance, provided, first, that it is not too remote and, secondly, that it is the natural[97] and reasonable consequence of the dispossession of the owner."[98]

It is not altogether clear from this statement whether there are two separate tests or whether the two tests referred to by Romer L.J. are simply the opposite sides of the same coin. In *J. Bibby and Sons Ltd v Merseyside County Council,*[99] Megaw L.J., after referring to the passage in Romer L.J.'s judgment, said "I do not find it necessary to pause here to consider whether there are, as the law has now developed, separate considerations relating to being 'too remote', on the one hand, and being not 'the natural and reasonable consequence,' on the other hand. It may be that those two have now merged."[1] The decisions in this field do not appear to show any clear separation between them. In *Director of Buildings and Lands v Shun Fung Ironworks Ltd*[2] Lord Nicholls of Birkenhead appeared to suggest that a flexible approach should be adopted in determining whether a loss was too remote. He said:

> "The familiar and perennial difficulty lies in attempting to formulate clear practical guidance on the criteria by which remoteness is to be judged in the infinitely different sets of circumstances which arise. The overriding principle of fairness is comprehensive, but it suffers from the drawback of being imprecise, even vague, in practical terms. The tools used by lawyers are concepts of chains of causation and intervening events and the like. 'Reasonably foreseeable', 'not unlikely', 'probable', 'natural' are among the descriptions which are or have been used in particular contexts. Even the much maligned epithet 'direct' may still have its uses as a limiting factor in some situations".

The operation of the test of remoteness may be illustrated by reference to two different questions which have arisen in connection

---

[95] See, for example, *Sim* and *Smith, supra.*

[96] [1957] 1 Q.B. 485.

[97] In *Evans v Glasgow District Council*, 1978 S.L.T. (Lands Tr.) 5 the Lands Tribunal for Scotland commented that "natural" in damages cases was interpreted as "according to the ordinary course of things" which may, said the tribunal, include reasonable human conduct (*S.S. Baron Vernon v S.S. Meta Gamma*, 1928 S.C. (H.L.) 21; 1928 S.L.T. 117, *per* Lord Haldane L.C. at p.118; *Steel v Glasgow Iron and Steel Co.*, 1944 S.C. 273; 1945 S.L.T. 70, *per* Lord Justice-Clerk Cooper at p.74).

[98] Page 494. Denning LJ. at p.492 applied a somewhat different test of remoteness: "all damage directly consequent on the taking of the house under statutory powers".

[99] (1979) 39 P. & C.R. 53.

[1] See above at p.65.

[2] [1995] 1 All E.R. 846 at p.853.

with disturbance. The first concerns the categories of claimant who may be disturbed; the second concerns the circumstances of the claimant and their effect on the disturbance claim.

Who may be disturbed

10–17   A person who receives and is entitled to receive a notice to treat (see Chapter 3) may claim compensation for any consequential loss. However, it would seem that such person must be in occupation. This requirement appears to derive from what the Lands Tribunal for Scotland in *McLaren's Discretionary Trustee v Secretary of State for Scotland*[3] described as a narrow view of disturbance as the loss caused to an occupier on dispossession.[4] There are dicta to support this view. In *Venables* Lord Justice-Clerk Alness referred to "compensation for all loss occasioned to him by reason of his dispossession;" in *McArdle* Lord President Clyde referred to "a right to compensation for his enforced removal and the disturbance which this entails to him;" and in *Woolfson v Strathclyde Regional Council*[5] Lord Wheatley in the Second Division stated "compensation for disturbance is payable to the occupier of the premises".[6]

Thus in *Roberts v Coventry Corporation*,[7] an owner of land who was also the principal shareholder of the company which occupied the land was unable to claim for the depreciation in the value of her shares which she claimed was the consequence of the compulsory acquisition of the land.[8] "I am content," said Lord Goddard C.J., "to put my judgment on the short ground that the damage is far too remote for the appellant to be able to claim compensation in respect of it."[9]

The requirement that a claimant had to be in occupation resulted in an inability to recover losses which in the ordinary sense of the words could be said to be the natural and reasonable consequence of the compulsory acquisition. In particular, a landlord who was not in occupation could recover professional expenses incurred in preparing and negotiating his claim for the value of his interest in the land acquired (these being treated as other matters not directly based on the value of the land) but he was unable to recover the costs of reinvestment. In *Harvey* Denning L.J. said:

> "Supposing a man did not occupy a house himself but simply owned it as an investment. His compensation would be the value of the house. If he chose to put the money into stocks and shares, he could not claim the brokerage as compensation. That would be much too remote. It would not be the consequence of the compulsory

---

[3] 1987 S.L.T. (Lands Tr.) 25.

[4] See p.205 above.

[5] 1977 S.C. 84; 1977 S.L.T. 60.

[6] See, too, Romer L.J. in *Harvey* at p.494; and Davies L.J. in *Lee (Judge) v Minister of Transport* [1966] 1 Q.B. 111 at p.122.

[7] [1947] 1 All E.R. 308.

[8] A somewhat similar argument was advanced, *inter alia*, before the House of Lords by the claimant in *Woolfson* (1978 S.C. (H.L.) 90; 1978 S.L.T. 59) with equal lack of success.

[9] [1947] 1 All E.R. 308 at p.309.

acquisition but the result of his own choice in putting the money into stocks and shares instead of putting it on deposit at the bank. If he chose to buy another house as an investment, he would not get the solicitors' costs on the purchase. These costs would be the result of his own choice of investment and not the result of the compulsory acquisition."

This may be an equitable conclusion in the sort of circumstances which applied in *Prestwick Hotels Ltd v Glasgow Corporation*[10] (see above) where reference was made to this passage in Lord Denning's judgment.[11] In that case an award of compensation was based on the total extinguishment of the business and a claim for expenses incurred in the reinstatement of the business was rejected.

It was, however, difficult to see what difference there was in principle between a person who invested his savings in a house from which he derived a regular income and who would, as a result of the compulsory acquisition of the house, have to consider incurring the costs of investing in another house and a person who occupied a house who would have to consider incurring the costs of finding another house to occupy. As Mann stated,[12] it was hard to see why such costs are not recoverable "so long as the act of reinvestment is a natural and reasonable step for the investor to take and one which he would not have taken but for the acquisition." As long ago as 1918 the Scott Committee recommended that "where the claimant can prove that, acting reasonably, he is put to special expense for reinvestment, the cost of a single reinvestment should be allowed as an item of claim".[13]

The government accepted the inequity of the position and the Planning and Compensation Act 1991, s.79 and Sch.17, para.6 added a new section 17A to the Land Compensation (Scotland) Act 1963. Section 17A provides that where the acquiring authority acquire an interest of a person who is not then in occupation of the land and that person incurs incidental charges or expenses in acquiring an interest in other land in the United Kingdom, the charges or expenses are to be taken into account in assessing that person's compensation as they would be taken into account if the person were in occupation of the land. The incidental charges or expenses incurred in acquiring the interest in other land must, however, be incurred within the period of one year beginning with the date of entry.

CPPRAG noted that the 1991 Act amendment is limited to 'incidental charges and expenses' and that an investment owner may well incur other losses corresponding to disturbance which cannot be claimed under section 17A. They concluded that it was for the legislator to decide whether, if a general statutory entitlement to disturbance com-

---

[10] 1975 S.C. 105.

[11] Lord President Emslie at p.109.

[12] M. Mann, "Adequacy of the Law of Disturbance to meet Actual Losses" in *Compensation for Compulsory Purchase* (1975) Journal of Planning and Environment Law Occasional Paper, also N. Macleod, "Compensation for Disturbance on Compulsory Acquisition" [1989] J.P.L. 891.

[13] "Second Report of the Committee dealing with the Law and Practice relating to the Acquisition and Valuation of Land for Public Purposes" (HMSO) para.17 (Cmnd. 9229).

pensation is to be introduced, explicit reference should be made to the position of investment owners.[14]

There was until 1973 a further difficulty over the question who may be disturbed, although this difficulty has also now been corrected. This was highlighted in the decision of the Lands Tribunal for Scotland in *Lander Equipment Co. v Glasgow Corporation*.[15] The corporation compulsorily acquired premises which included a ground floor shop. The shop premises were owned by a husband and wife partnership under the name Lander Equipment Co. The occupier of the shop was a limited company, Bothwell Electric Supplies (Glasgow) Ltd, the entire share capital of which was held by the husband and wife. The husband and wife were compensated for the value of their interest in the shop as landlords but received nothing for disturbance as they were not legally in occupation, notwithstanding their plea that the company was merely their *alter ego*. Unfortunately, the company as occupier was also unable to claim disturbance as there was no lease between the company and the partnership so the company had no interest in the premises entitling it to receive a notice to treat. As the tribunal commented, "[i]n considering this part of the claim the Tribunal is dealing with a region of valuation in which the application of the law as it exists is not infrequently regarded as giving rise to unfortunate results."

10–18   The decision in *Lander* highlights a not uncommon situation in which a claimant does not occupy the heritable property which is being acquired but nonetheless has such a commanding interest in the occupation of the property as to be the person who is really adversely affected by the disturbance. There have been instances where, in connection with a compensation claim, courts and tribunals have been prepared to "lift the corporate veil" of a limited company in order to expose the *alter ego* underneath.[16] However, the decision of the House of Lords in *Woolfson v Strathclyde Regional Council*[17] suggests that the courts will be slow to deny the legal effects of incorporation[18] and that it will only be appropriate to lift the corporate veil where special circumstances exist indicating that a company is a mere facade concealing the true facts.

In *Woolfson* a company, M. & L. Campbell Ltd, traded as a shop from five premises, three of which were owned by Mr Woolfson and two by Solfred Holdings Ltd (a company all the shares in which were owned by Mr and Mrs Woolfson). Mr Woolfson owned 999 shares of the 1,000 issued shares in Campbell Ltd, the remaining share being owned by his wife. The premises were compulsorily acquired by Glasgow Corporation. As Campbell Ltd never occupied the premises under a formal lease it

---

[14] "Fundamental review of the laws and procedures relating to compulsory purchase and compensation: final report" (2000) DETR para.153.

[15] 1973 S.L.T. (Lands Tr.) 8. See, too, *Taylor v Greater London Council* (1973) 25 P. & C.R. 451.

[16] *Smith, Stone and Knight Ltd v Birmingham Corporation* [1939] 4 All E.R. 116; *D.H.N. Food Distributors Ltd v London Borough of Tower Hamlets* [1976] 3 All E.R. 462; *Wharvesto Ltd v Cheshire County Council* (1984) 270 E.G. 149.

[17] 1978 S.C. (H.L.) 90; 1978 S.L.T. 59.

[18] *Salomon v A. Salomon and Co. Ltd* [1877] A.C. 22. And see B. C. Cunningham, "Lifting the Veil: An English–Scottish Contrast" (1977) 22 J.L.S. 52.

was, when displaced, a tenant at will with no entitlement to rule (6) compensation. Before the Lands Tribunal for Scotland it was argued that the business carried on in the premises was truly that of the claimants (Mr Woolfson and Solfred Holdings Ltd) which Campbell Ltd conducted impliedly as their agents.[19] The claimants were the true occupiers of the premises and entitled as such to disturbance compensation amounting to £95,469. The tribunal held, after considering the circumstances, that there were no special factors concerning the relationship between the claimants and the company which justified denying the legal effects of incorporation and the claim was rejected.[20] On appeal to the Court of Session, Mr Woolfson pursued a different line of argument to the effect that he, Campbell Ltd and Solfred Holdings Ltd should all be treated as a single entity embodied in himself,[21] thus entitling him to disturbance compensation. This argument, too, was rejected both by the Second Division[22] and on appeal to the House of Lords,[23] Lord Justice-Clerk Wheatley commenting that if someone decided "so to organise things to produce what he considered the best way of securing his own interests, then he must accept the consequences of that policy, however unfortunate for him that may be".

An occupier in the sort of situation described in *Lander* and *Woolfson* may, nonetheless, be entitled under section 114 of the 1845 Act to compensation for "any loss or injury they may sustain" if they are required to give up possession before the expiration of their term (see Ch.12). If, however, the acquiring authority purchase the landlord's interest and bring the tenant's interest to an end through the service of a notice to quit, the occupier faces similar consequential loss but until 1973 had no *right* to any redress under the compulsory purchase code, although he might receive a "disturbance payment" at the *discretion* of the acquiring authority.[24] JUSTICE in a report in 1973 commented of such a payment: "if justice requires that it be paid, it should be paid as of right".[25] Sections 33 and 34 of the Land Compensation (Scotland) Act 1973 now provide for the making of "disturbance payments" as of right to displaced occupiers without compensatable interests (see Ch.12) and these should overcome in many cases the sort of hardship encountered in *Lander* and *Woolfson*.

The circumstances of the claimant

As Mann pointed out,[26] a person's age, health and financial position **10–19** can each in reality affect his ability to mount a response to a compulsory acquisition and the question arises whether in considering what are the

---

[19] Reliance being placed on the decision in *Smith, Stone and Knight Ltd v Birmingham Corporation, supra.*

[20] 1976 S.L.T. (Lands Tr.) 5.

[21] Reliance being placed on the decision in *D.H.N. Food Distributors Ltd v London Borough of Tower Hamlets, supra.*

[22] 1977 S.C. 84; 1977 S.L.T. 60.

[23] 1978 S.C. (H.L) 90; 1978 S.L.T. 59.

[24] Land Compensation (Scotland) Act 1963, s.38.

[25] "Compensation for Compulsory Acquisition and Remedies for Planning Restrictions together with a Supplemental Report" (1973) Stevens, para.113.

[26] M. Mann, "Adequacy of the Law of Disturbance to meet Actual Losses," *supra;* and N. Macleod, "Compensation for Disturbance on Compulsory Acquisition" [1989] J.P.L. 891.

natural and reasonable consequences of dispossession the acquiring authority must, as in personal injury cases, take the claimant as they find him.

In *Evans v Glasgow District Council*[27] the claimant carried on a printer's business in premises occupied under a yearly tenancy in Ballater Street, Glasgow. The premises were compulsorily acquired and, in due course, the claimant transferred his business elsewhere. The business did not prosper in its new location and was disposed of some two years later. The claimant sought a disturbance payment under sections 34 and 35 of the Land Compensation (Scotland) Act 1973 which included an item of £14,512 for temporary loss of profits. Although a disturbance payment under the 1973 Act is quite distinct from disturbance compensation under rule (6) (see Chap.12), the First Division held in *Glasgow Corporation v Anderson*[28] that such a claim could properly include "all reasonable expenses, reasonably incurred as the direct and natural consequence of, and in, the compulsory removing, in addition to the expenses strictly referrable to 'the removal' itself."[29] In *Evans* the Lands Tribunal for Scotland concluded that in assessing such payments the test of remoteness laid down in *Harvey* and in *Anderson* should be applied.

The claim for loss of profits in *Evans* was attributed in part to lack of capital which made it difficult for the claimant to adapt his business to the new premises. The tribunal after hearing evidence was not altogether satisfied that the lack of capital had contributed to the loss of profits but, in so far as it had, the tribunal considered that this was not a consequence of the displacement, any more than it would be regarded as consequential in a claim for damages. In reaching this conclusion, the tribunal was influenced by the decision of the House of Lords in *Liesbosch Dredger v S. S. Edison*.[30]

In that case, the *Liesbosch Dredger* was sunk as a result of the negligence of the master of the steamship *Edison*. The dredger had been engaged on a contract which provided for heavy penalties in the event of delay. For want of funds, the owners of the dredger were unable to buy a replacement and, therefore, had to hire one to complete the contract. In an action for damages, the owners of the dredger were awarded its market value but were unable to recover the cost of hiring a second dredger to complete the contract. The House of Lords held that that cost arose from the claimants' own impecuniosity, a matter which was not traceable to the respondents' acts and which was, as a result, outside the legal purview of the consequences of those acts.[31]

---

[27] 1978 S.L.T. (Lands Tr.) 5.

[28] 1976 S.L.T. 225.

[29] Although *Glasgow Corporation* was concerned with a claim under s.35(1)(a) of the 1973 Act, the Lands Tribunal for Scotland considered in *Evans* that the same broad approach applied to a claim under s.35(1)(b).

[30] [1933] A.C. 449.

[31] In recent years the courts seem to have circumvented a rigorous application of the decision in the field of damages. See, for example, *Martindale v Duncan* [1973] 1 W.L.R. 574; *Dodd Properties v Canterbury City Council* [1980] 1 W.L.R. 433; *Bunclark v Hertfordshire County Council* (1977) 243 E.G. 381 and 455; *Perry v Sidney Phillips and Son* (1982) 263 E.G. 888.

The decision in the *Liesbosch Dredger* was subsequently applied by the Lands Tribunal for Scotland in *Bryce v Motherwell District Council.*[32] Mr Bryce was displaced from his council house and had to move to another in circumstances which qualified him for a disturbance payment. Being a man of limited means, he found he could not, after spending money on carpets, blinds, and so on, afford the cost of immediately reinstalling the telephone at his new house. The telephone was finally reinstalled some two years after the move, by which time the installation cost had risen from £32.40 to £48. The local authority refused to pay the difference and the tribunal, when the matter came before it, held that it was the claimant's own admitted impecuniosity which had caused the delay and led to the increased cost. The increase "was not reasonably incurred as a direct and natural consequence of, and in, his compulsory removing".

A similar approach was taken by the Court of Appeal in *Bailey v Derby Corporation*[33] with regard to loss resulting from the poor state of health of the claimant. A builder's yard and workshop were compulsorily acquired. Ill health, not the result of the expropriation but an "unhappy coincidence," prevented him from re-establishing his business on another site. He sought compensation based on the total extinguishment of his business, a basis of assessment which would have produced an award considerably in excess of disturbance compensation based on relocation of the business in alternative premises. This approach was rejected on the ground that the corporation were not acquiring the business; this was not a loss flowing from the acquisition.[34] Lord Denning said of the claim:

> "I am quite clear in this case that the loss which is the 'natural and reasonable consequence' of the acquisition is the cost of removal and the loss of profits immediately and directly consequent on his having to move. In so far as any loss is due, not to the acquisition, but to the state of health of the claimant, that seems to me to be an extraneous and independent matter which must be put on one side. It should not be taken into account in assessing the compensation. It is comparable to the impecuniosity mentioned in the *Edison*."[35]

It would seem from the decisions in *Bailey, Bryce* and *Evans* that the **10–20** application of the test of remoteness laid down by Romer L.J. in *Harvey* does not involve the acquiring authority taking the claimant as they find him. Loss resulting on expropriation as a result of the particular financial

---

[32] [1980] R.V.R. 282. See too *Emslie and Simpson Ltd. v Aberdeen District Council*, unreported, August 12, 1992, Lands Tribunal for Scotland, where interest incurred on additional borrowings was disallowed by the Lands Tribunal for Scotland as part of the disturbance claim because it was due to the claimant's impecuniosity and therefore too remote.

[33] [1965] 1 All E.R. 443.

[34] Contrast the decision in *Bede Distributors Ltd. v Newcastle-upon-Tyne Corporation* (1973) 26 P. & C.R. 298 in which the Lands Tribunal held it was not unreasonable for a company without liquidity to go into liquidation instead of removing to an alternative site (see *'Mitigation'* below). See too the decision in *Knott Mill Carpets v Stretford Borough Council* (1973) 26 P & C.R. 129.

[35] See above at p.445.

or physical circumstances of the claimant are not treated as the "natural and reasonable consequence" of the acquisition.

It has been argued that this does not accord well with the principle of equivalence. Young in an interesting discussion of the *Bryce* decision points out that "a person who is forced, as a result of action taken in the interests of the community at large, to leave the property he occupies has a right to expect that he will be left no worse off than he was prior to the dispossession. *Bryce* appears to show that if the *Liesbosch* principle is applied, such expectations may not be fulfilled where the claimant is short of money".[36] And JUSTICE, in a comment on the decision in *Bailey,* recommended that "the personal circumstances of the claimant, such as age and state of health, be taken fully into account" in assessing compensation for disturbance.[37]

The position of some claimants has now been eased following the introduction of section 43 of the Land Compensation (Scotland) Act 1973. This provides that disturbance compensation for a person carrying on a trade or business on land which is or forms part of a hereditament the annual value of which does not exceed a prescribed amount,[38] who is required in consequence of the compulsory acquisition of the land to give up possession and who on the date of giving up possession has attained the age of 60, shall be assessed on the basis of the total extinguishment of the business. The person must not have disposed of the goodwill of the trade or business and must undertake that he will not dispose of the goodwill and that he will not, within such area and for such period of time as the acquiring authority may require, directly or indirectly engage in or have an interest in any other similar trade or business. Compensation so assessed will usually be more generous than compensation based on the cost of transferring the business elsewhere.[39]

To meet the concerns that remain over the way in which the personal circumstances of a claimant have been dealt with under the law, the Law Commission, in its recent Consultation Paper on the reform of the compensation code, has proposed that any general statutory entitlement to disturbance compensation (see p.205 above) should expressly allow the personal circumstances of the claimant to be taken into account.[40]

---

[36] E. Young, "Remoteness, Impecuniosity and Disturbance" [1981] J.P.L. 707.

[37] *Compensation for Compulsory Acquisition and Remedies for Planning Restrictions together with a Supplemental Report* (1973) Stevens paras 41 and 42. See also M. Mann, "Adequacy of the Law of Disturbance to meet Actual Losses," *supra;* and N. Macleod, "Compensation for Disturbance on Compulsory Acquisition" [1989] J.P.L. 891.

[38] This is the amount prescribed for the purposes of section 100(3)(a) of the Town and Country Planning (Scotland) Act 1997 (interests qualifying for protection under the planning blight provisions). At the time of writing the amount prescribed is £24,725 (see the Town and Country Planning (Limit of Annual Value) (Scotland) Order 2001, SSI 2001/164). For the definitions of "annual value" and "hereditament" see the 1997 Act, s.122.

[39] Where a person has disposed of the goodwill of part of a trade or business, the provisions may nonetheless operate on the remainder.

[40] "Towards a Compulsory Purchase Code: (1) Compensation" (2002) *Consultation Paper No 165* para.4.59.

3. **Mitigation**

It may not be enough to show that the loss is the natural and **10–21**
reasonable consequence of dispossession. Claimants are also under a
duty to mitigate their loss. This derives from the well-established
principle in the law of damages that:

> "the plaintiff must take all reasonable steps to mitigate the loss
> consequent upon the defendant's wrong and cannot recover
> damages for any such loss which he could thus have avoided but has
> failed, through unreasonable action or inaction, to avoid. Put
> shortly, the plaintiff cannot recover for avoidable loss."[41]

This principle also applies to disturbance. In *Service Welding Ltd v Tyne
and Wear County Council*[42] Bridge L.J. said:

> "It is clear, however, that where as here a business occupier is in a
> position to find alternative accommodation in which to carry on his
> business and prevent its extinction, he is under a duty to mitigate his
> disturbance compensation by removing his business to the alterna-
> tive accommodation."[43]

And in *Director of Buildings and Lands v Shun Fung Ironworks Ltd*[44]
Lord Nicholls of Birkenhead said:

> "Fairness requires that claims for compensation should satisfy a
> further, third[45] condition in all cases. The law expects those who
> claim recompense to behave reasonably. If a reasonable person in
> the position of the claimant would have taken steps to reduce or
> eliminate the loss, and the claimant failed to do so, he cannot fairly
> expect to be compensated for the loss or the unreasonable part of it.
> Likewise if a reasonable person in the position of the claimant
> would not have incurred, or would not incur, the expenditure being
> claimed, fairness does not require that the authority should be
> responsible for such expenditure."

Indeed, as the Lands Tribunal for Scotland pointed out in *Smith,*
compulsory purchase cases differ from delict in that pending loss, prior
to the acquisition, can often be seen from afar; so anticipatory action to
mitigate loss becomes more feasible.

---

[41] McGregor, *Damages*, para.285. And see *British Westinghouse Co. v Underground Railway* [1912] A.C. 673, *per* Viscount Haldane L.C. at p.689; and *Pomphrey v Cuthbertson Ltd*, 1951 S.C. 147, *per* Lord Patrick at p.162; D. M. Walker, *The Law of Damages in Scotland* (W. Green & Son, 1955) pp.168–181; W. M. Gloag, *The Law of Contract* (2nd ed., W. Green & Son, Edinburgh) p.688; W. W. McBryde, *The Law of Contract in Scotland* (2nd ed., W. Green & Son, Edinburgh, 2001), Chap.22.4.

[42] (1979) 38 P. & C.R. 352.

[43] See above at p.357.

[44] [1995] 1 All E.R. 846 at p.853.

[45] The first two conditions to be satisfied are that there must be a causal connection between the acquisition and the loss and the loss must not be too remote.

An illustration of the duty to mitigate loss is provided by the decision in *Park Automobile Co. Ltd v Strathclyde Regional Council.*[46] A garage and petrol station was compulsorily acquired and the premises vested in the acquiring authority in May 1975. The claimant company, anticipating dispossession, had purchased an alternative property assisted by an advance payment of compensation from the authority. However, the claimants were allowed by the acquiring authority to remain in occupation as tenants of the original premises and for business reasons they chose to do this and they continued to trade profitably. Subsequently, as the local authority showed no signs of requiring possession of the garage, the claimants sold their alternative premises. The six year time bar from the date of divestiture for referring disputed claims for compensation to the Lands Tribunal for Scotland[47] eventually compelled the claimants to lodge a claim for anticipated disturbance although at that time the loss had not actually arisen. The claim was based on the notional total extinguishment of the business as at the date of vesting. The tribunal considered that the claimants were not entitled to absolve themselves from all duty to find alternative accommodation by choosing to stay on. That was not minimising but maximising the authority's liability for compensation. The claimants could have relocated the business at the date of vesting. It was a business decision to stay where they were. That was not mitigating their loss; it was a decision not to do so. They could not, therefore, claim for more than they would have obtained had they taken reasonable steps to relocate.

The duty to mitigate loss would seem to be no more than a duty to act reasonably in the circumstances.[48] What is reasonable is a question of fact depending on the circumstances in each case.[49] The onus appears to be upon the acquiring authority to demonstrate that the claimant has not acted reasonably.[50] In *Millar v Strathclyde Regional Council*[51] the Lands Tribunal for Scotland had to consider whether the claimant's decision not to relocate his business was a reasonable one in all the circumstances. The claimant had made no attempt to find suitable alternative property. After examining possible alternatives put forward by the acquiring authority, the tribunal concluded that there were no suitable alternative premises available at the date of displacement and the claimant had not acted unreasonably and was entitled to compensation on the basis of the extinguishment of the business.

[46] 1984 S.L.T. (Lands Tr.) 14. See, too, *J. Shulman (Tailors) Ltd v Greater London Council* (1966) 17 P. & C.R. 244; *Simpson v Stoke-on-Trent City Council* (1982) 263 E.G. 673; *Thomas and Son Ltd v Greater London Council* (1982) 262 E.G. 991 and 1086; *Clifford v Glasgow District Council*, unreported, October 31, 1986, Lands Tribunal for Scotland; *Sloan v Edinburgh District Council*, 1988 S.L.T. (Lands Tr.) 25.
[47] Town and Country Planning (Scotland) Act 1997, Sch.15, para.36(1).
[48] *Director of Buildings and Lands v Shun Fung Ironworks Ltd* [1995] 1 All E.R. 846 *per* Lord Nicholls of Birkenhead at p.853; *Millar v Strathclyde Regional Council*, 1988 S.L.T. (Lands Tr.) 9; *MacLeod v Strathclyde Regional Council*, unreported, May 18, 1987, Lands Tribunal for Scotland.
[49] *Payzu Ltd v Saunders* [1919] 2 K.B. 581.
[50] *MacLeod v Strathclyde Regional Council, supra; Millar v Strathclyde Regional Council, supra; Lindon Print Ltd v West Midlands County Council* [1987] EGLR 200, LT. And see *MacGregor on Damages*, para.299.
[51] 1988 S.L.T. (Lands Tr.) 9. See too *Mallick v Liverpool City Council* (2000) 79 P. & C.R. 1, CA.

The duty to mitigate loss does not, however, require a claimant to subject himself to unreasonable commercial risks especially if lacking the financial means to do so. In *MacLeod v Strathclyde Regional Council*[52] the Lands Tribunal for Scotland concluded that the claimant, who had carried on a business retailing, servicing, repairing and reconditioning Hoover equipment, was entitled to compensation based on the total extinguishment of the business. Alternative premises were available in a good retail position but the evidence showed that it would be economically hazardous to move to such a position paying either a retail rent or a retail purchase price, with appropriate rates, when the requirement was for a workshop with no more than a limited retail facility.[53] And in *Bede Distributors Ltd v Newcastle-upon-Tyne Corporation*[54] the Lands Tribunal held that it was not unreasonable for a company without liquidity to go into liquidation instead of removing.[55]

The question whether compensation should be assessed on the basis of **10–22** the relocation of the business or on the basis of its total extinguishment can give rise to difficulties in practice. In *Shun Fung*, Lord Nicholls of Birkenhead said "[I]t all depends on how a reasonable businessman, using his own money, would behave in the circumstances".[56] In that case, unusually, the cost of extinguishment would have been substantially less than relocation. The acquiring authority argued that, as a matter of law, the claimant could not be awarded a larger sum on a relocation basis than its maximum entitlement on an extinguishment basis. The Judicial Committee of the Privy Council held that there was no rule that a claimant could never be entitled to compensation on a relocation basis if that exceeded the amount of compensation payable on an extinguishment basis. If a reasonable business man, using his own money, would consider it worthwhile incurring expenditure in relocating to new premises and continuing his business there because of its potential rather than accepting the present value of the business, the tribunal assessing compensation was entitled to employ the relocation basis to assess compensation. However, the greater the disparity between extinguishment and relocation compensation, the greater the need to examine the basis of the claim. The Court went on to lay down three tests to be applied to relocation claims:

> (i) Can the business be relocated, or has it effectively been extinguished? For example, a suitable site may not exist so that relocation is not possible; or the new business may not have retained sufficient attributes of the old business sensibly to be regarded as the old business on a new site. In *Shun Fung* the Court could see no ground for departing from the view of the

---

[52] unreported, May 18, 1987, Lands Tribunal for Scotland.
[53] See, too, *Knott Mill Carpets Ltd v Stretford Borough Council* (1973) 26 P. & C.R. 129.
[54] (1973) 26 P. & C.R. 298.
[55] A claimant is not precluded from claiming compensation on an extinguishment basis simply because it ceased trading between the date on which the compulsory purchase order was confirmed and the date on which the acquiring authority took possession (*Glossop Sectional Buildings v Sheffield Development Corporation* (1994) 40 E.G. 132).
[56] See generally R. Turrall-Clarke, "Rail/Road schemes: business relocation" (1995) 34 E.G. 68.

Lands Tribunal that, as a matter of fact and degree, there would be no continuity between the old business and the new business so that the relocation claim failed.

(ii) Does the claimant intend to relocate? The claimant must have reached a firm decision to relocate his business and must be reasonably assured that he will be able to do so. Compensation cannot be assessed on a relocation basis, said the Court, unless the claimant has moved his business or intends to do so. However, a claimant will not lack the necessary intention simply because relocation is dependent on the receipt of adequate compensation.

(iii) Would a reasonable business man relocate the business?[57] The acquiring authority cannot be expected to be responsible for expenses which no reasonable businessman would incur. In *Shun Fung* it was held that that a reasonable businessman would not have relocated to the new site because by ordinary commercial standards the return on the investment to set up the new works was far short of the return an investor would expect relative to the risks. The relocation claim accordingly failed on that ground also.

Unlike the test for remoteness (above), it seems from the decisions in *MacLeod* and *Bede* that in considering whether a claimant has discharged his duty to mitigate his loss, account may be taken of his financial circumstances. This is in line with the law of damages. In *Clippens Oil Co. Ltd v Edinburgh and District Water Trustees*[58] Lord Collins said "in my opinion the wrongdoer must take his victim *talem qualem,* and if the position of the latter is aggravated because he is without the means of mitigating it, so much the worse for the wrongdoer, who has got to be answerable for the consequences flowing from his tortuous act".[59] It is important to note that Lord Collins, here, was dealing not with the measure of damage but with the victim's duty to minimise damage.[60] It is, therefore, necessary as Young observes "to draw a distinction between, on the one hand, a loss which is too remote because it was *caused* by the victim's lack of means and, on the other hand, a loss which the victim was unable to *mitigate* because of his lack of means."[61]

---

[57] The Law Commission noted that this test is more precise, and possibly more restrictive, than that applied in other cases. The Commission proposed a test of 'reasonableness', rather than one tied to 'the reasonable businessman' ("Towards a Compulsory Purchase Code: (1) Compensation" (2002) *Law Commission Consultation Paper No 165,* para.4.33).

[58] 1907 S.C. (H.L) 9.

[59] See above at p.14.

[60] See the comment by Lord Wright in *Liesbosch Dredger v S.S. Edison* [1933] A.C. 449 at p.461.

[61] E. Young, "Remoteness, Impecuniosity and Disturbance" [1981] J.P.L. 707. R. G. Lawson in "The Status of the Edison" (1974) 124 N.L.J. 240 comments that "the distinction between a separate loss caused by straightened means, and one which is simply a loss not abated . . . is superficial at best, for each is, at bottom, a case of damage arising where ample funds would have dictated otherwise".

The corollary of the duty to take all reasonable steps to mitigate loss is that where a claimant takes such steps, he can recover for loss incurred in so doing. This would seem to be so, even if the steps prove to be abortive or the resulting loss is greater than it would have been if the mitigating steps had not been taken.[62] In the words of Lord Collins in *Clippens Oil Co*: "I think the wrongdoer is not entitled to criticise the course honestly taken by the injured person on the advice of his experts, even though it should appear by the light of after events that another course might have saved loss." In *Evans v Glasgow District Council,*[63] for example, the Lands Tribunal for Scotland, in dealing with a claim for temporary loss of profits, considered the claimant's conduct in seeking to carry on the family business in new premises to have been reasonable, even though the business failed at the end of the day. And in *Smith v Strathclyde Regional Council*[64] the tribunal allowed as part of the disturbance claim professional fees incurred in abortive plans to retain and shore up part of a public house, the whole of which was eventually acquired. On the other hand, in *Simpson v Stoke-on-Trent City Council*[65] the Lands Tribunal disallowed interest on a bridging loan as part of a disturbance claim. The claimant had not acted reasonably in taking out the loan to buy another house. The need for a loan could have been avoided by referring the compensation claim for the value of the land to the tribunal for determination and taking a 90 per cent advance payment on the compensation (see Chap.12).

[62] McGregor, *Damages*, para.286.
[63] 1978 S.L.T. (Lands Tr.) 5.
[64] 1982 S.L.T. (Lands Tr.) 2.
[65] (1982) 263 E.G. 673. See, too, *Thomas v Greater London Council* (1982) 262 E.G. 991 and 1086.

CHAPTER 11

REMAINING LAND

11–01 It will sometimes be the case that an acquiring authority will only take part of a parcel of land in which an interest subsists. The scheme of public works for which the part has been acquired may affect the value of the remaining land. It may enhance its value by opening up the prospect of development for some more profitable use; or it may reduce its value because of nuisance arising from the scheme. The actual physical severance of the part taken may also give rise to some reduction in the profitability in continuing the existing use of the remaining land which is reflected in its value. The question is whether such increase or decrease in the value of the remaining land should be taken into account in assessing compensation. This chapter is given over to consideration of this question. It is divided into two parts. The first part examines the extent to which an enhancement in the value of the remaining land may be set-off against the compensation for the land taken. The second part considers whether depreciation in the value of the remaining land may form part of the overall claim for compensation arising from the compulsory acquisition.

SET-OFF

11–02 In the absence of any express statutory provision, the courts have not been prepared to countenance the suggestion that an increase in the value of remaining land resulting from the scheme of the acquiring authority should be set-off against compensation for the land taken. In *South-Eastern Railway Co. v London County Council,*[1] referred to in Chapter 8, Eve J. spelt out the objection to set-off. It would, he said:

> "upset all uniformity of value, inasmuch as the value of the identical piece of land in the hands of one vendor might be assessed at many times its value in the hands of another, and this, not from any intrinsic distinction, but by reason solely of extraneous considerations. Moreover, it would be calculated to work injustice in that a vendor compelled to sell, and who the legislature intended should be compensated for being compelled to sell, might have to accept from the undertakers a price far less than he would have obtained from any other purchaser, and out of all proportion to the true

---

[1] [1915] 2 Ch. 252.

value of the land had it been ascertained without reference to the fortuitous circumstances of his also being interested in the contiguous land."[2]

Neither have the courts been prepared to imply such a provision in dealing with claims for compensation for injurious affection to land no part of which has been the subject of compulsory acquisition (see Ch.14). In *Senior v Metropolitan Railway Co.*[3] Wilde B. said "if the company were entitled to set-off the benefit derived from proximity to the station, one individual would be made to pay something for that, whereas his neighbour would pay nothing. It is the first time such an idea has been brought forward, and I see no reason for giving countenance to it." A similar argument was subsequently rejected by the Court of Session in *Walker's Trustees v Caledonian Railway Co.*[4]

There Lord Young said "[t]he third question regards the contention of the complainers that they are entitled to set the benefits which they have conferred on the respondents' property against the damage which they have done to that property of a character entitling them to compensation under the statute. This contention is admittedly novel, and I content myself with saying that it is in my opinion inadmissable."[5]

Over the years, however, express provision for set-off has appeared in specific legislation. Such provision first appeared in the General Turnpike Act for Scotland 1831,[6] section 64 of which provided that in assessing compensation for land taken for making or improving roads, the assessing authority was to take into consideration "all the circumstances of the case and particularly the advantages arising to the proprietors and occupiers by new or altered roads". Other provisions for set-off subsequently appeared in Acts such as the Artisans Dwellings Act 1879, the Light Railways Act 1896, the Development and Road Improvement Funds Act 1909, the Restriction of Ribbon Development Act 1935, the Housing (Scotland) Act 1966 and the Roads (Scotland) Act 1970. The Metropolitan Management Act 1858 adopted a rather different approach by making no provision for compensation for depreciation resulting from the public works apparently on the ground that the depreciation would effectively be compensated for by the benefit arising from the works.[7]

The possibility of introducing a general set-off provision into compensation legislation was considered by both the Scott[8] and Uthwatt[9] Committees. The former, although advocating the recovery of better-

---

[2] See above, p.259.

[3] (1863) 32 L.J. Ex.Ch. 225. See, too, *Eagle v Charing Cross Railway Co.* (1867) L.R. 2 C.P. 638.

[4] (1881) 8 R. 405.

[5] This particular point was not pursued in the subsequent appeal to the House of Lords.

[6] Referred to in the "Final Report of the Expert Committee on Compensation and Betterment" (1942) HMSO para.265 (Cmnd. 6386).

[7] "Second Report of the Committee Dealing with the Law and Practice relating to the Acquisition and Valuation of Land for Public Purposes" (1918) HMSO App.3 (Cmnd. 9229).

[8] See above.

[9] "The Final Report of the Expert Committee on Compensation and Betterment", *supra*.

ment by promoters, rejected set-off in favour of an alternative approach based upon scheduled betterment areas. The Uthwatt Committee, while acknowledging the principle of set-off to be equitable, drew attention to two perceived defects.[10] First of all, it could only be collected from landowners from whom land had been acquired for the scheme. It was thus "very much a hit and miss method of recovery and is unfair as between one owner and another." Secondly, the maximum amount which can be collected is the actual cost to the promoter of the particular parcels of land which are being acquired. In view of these imperfections, the committee concluded that the balance of advantage was against this method of collecting betterment. They advocated instead recovery by way of a periodic levy on increases in annual site values. However, if that was not accepted, they recommended the introduction of a general provision for setting off betterment against compensation on the basis that "something is better than nothing".

A general provision for set-off was subsequently introduced in the Town and Country Planning (Scotland) Act 1959[11] when the government abandoned the dual price system and restored market value in land as the measure of compensation for compulsory purchase (see Ch.4). In introducing the provision the government were clearly influenced by the extent to which express provision for set-off was made in specific Acts. As Cullingworth observes "[t]he honourable ancestry of set-off was clearly an important factor in this decision."[12] Section 9 of and Schedule 1 to the 1959 Act were subsequently replaced by sections 14 and 15 of and Schedule 1 to the Land Compensation (Scotland) Act 1963 (below).

Express provision for set-off may, however, still be encountered in specific public and general Acts which incorporate their own compensation arrangements. For example, section 110 of the Roads (Scotland) Act 1984 makes special provision for compensation including set-off in respect of the acquisition of land for the construction and improvement of roads[13]; and section 10 of and Schedule 1 to the Housing (Scotland) Act 1987, which make special provision for compensation where land is acquired for the provision of housing, provides that:

> "The Lands Tribunal shall (except as provided in section 15(1) of the Land Compensation (Scotland) Act 1963) have regard to, and make an allowance in respect of, any increased value which, in their opinion, will be given to other premises of the same owner by the demolition by the local authority of any buildings."

And express set-off provisions may also be found in private and local Acts, the Zetland County Council Act 1974, providing for the acquisition of land in connection with the construction of the Sullom Voe oil terminal, being a notable example.

11–03   Section 14 of the 1963 Act[14] provides that where, on the date of service of the notice to treat, the person from whom land is being

---

[10] See above, para.285.

[11] s.9 and Sch.1.

[12] J. B. Cullingworth, *Environmental Planning* (1980) HMSO Vol. IV, p.207.

[13] In *Bisset v Secretary of State for Scotland*, 1994 S.L.T. (Lands Tr.) 12 it was held that for set off to apply the betterment must be quantified.

[14] Which is expressed to be subject to the provisions of s.15 (see below).

acquired is also entitled in the same capacity to contiguous or adjacent land,[15] there is to be deducted from the compensation for the land acquired any increase in the value of the contiguous or adjacent land which, in the circumstances described, is attributable to and which would not have occurred but for the scheme as defined. The circumstances in which land may be earmarked for acquisition for public purposes are described in column 1, Part I of Schedule 1 to the 1963 Act; and the scheme for the purposes of each such circumstance is defined in column 2. These are set out in detail at pages 165 and 166 above.[16] It would seem that it is only when those circumstances apply that a set-off is to be made[17]; there is no judicial authority corresponding to the *Pointe Gourde* principle[18] which allows for the recovery of betterment in this way in other circumstances.[19] In other words, the definition of "the scheme" for the purposes of the remaining land will in some cases be narrower than it is for the land taken (see Ch.8).

Section 14 is not to apply to an acquisition under a "corresponding enactment"[20] or a private or local Act which makes separate provision for set-off.[21]

It should be stressed that for the set-off provisions to apply it must be shown that the increase in the value of the remaining land would not have occurred but for the scheme. In *James Miller and Partners Ltd v Lothian Regional Council (No. 2)*[22] the claimants owned some 40 acres of land allocated in the development plan for residential development. Planning permission was granted in accordance with the allocation. The plans attached to the grants of planning permission earmarked a small part of the site (0.42 of an acre) for a sewage pumping station. In due course, the regional council as sewerage authority, in discharge of their duty under section 1 of the Sewerage (Scotland) Act 1968, acquired the site in order to construct the pumping station. The parties disagreed over the price and the matter came before the Lands Tribunal for Scotland by voluntary reference. The council argued that they were entitled under section 14 of the 1963 Act to set-off the value of the pumping station land against any increase in the value of the claimant's adjoining land due to the construction of the pumping station. The presence of the pumping station, they argued, enabled the residential development to

---

[15] A person is entitled to two interests in land in the same capacity in the circumstances set out in s.45(5) of the 1963 Act.

[16] The definition of the scheme in column 2 in each case is modified by the omission of the words "other than the relevant land" (s.14(2)).

[17] *South-Eastern Railway Co. v London County Council* [1915] 2 Ch. 252.

[18] See also *Camrose (Viscount) v Basingstoke Corporation* [1966] 1 W.L.R. 1100; and *Wilson v Liverpool City Council* [1971] 1 W.L.R. 302.

[19] But see *Melwood Units Property Ltd v Commissioner of Main Roads* [1979] A.C. 426 as regards *depreciation* in the value of the remaining land.

[20] See 1963 Act, s.15(7) as amended by the Roads (Scotland) Act 1984, Sch.11 and by the Housing (Scotland) Act 1987, Sch.23.

[21] Section 15(5) of the 1963 Act. Section 15(6) provides that where any such local Act includes a provision restricting the assessment of the increase in value by reference to existing use, the Act is to have effect as if it did not include that provision.

[22] 1984 S.L.T. (Lands Tr.) 2. See, too, *Laing Homes Ltd v Eastleigh Borough Council* (1979) 250 E.G. 350 and 459; and *Young v Lothian Regional Council*, unreported, May 9, 1990, Lands Tr.

proceed and consequently raised the value of the adjoining land by over
£150,000, thus effectively extinguishing any compensation for the land
taken. The question the tribunal had to answer was whether the
claimant's housing scheme would still have been likely to have been
carried out if the authority had not acquired the subject land for a
pumping station. Their conclusion was that the authority would have
been able to provide and would have been likely in terms of their
statutory duty to provide a sewage disposal unit on other land so that the
residential development could have proceeded. Accordingly, there was
no set-off to be made.

In their interpretation of the somewhat differently worded set-off
provision in what was section 222(6) of the Highways Act 1959 (now
section 261 of the Highways Act 1980) the Lands Tribunal have taken a
fairly strict view of what is meant by benefit to remaining land attributable
to the purpose for which the land is acquired. In *Cooke v Secretary of State
for the Environment*[23] farmland was compulsorily acquired for a road
improvement. The acquiring authority sought to deduct from the compensation for the land taken the sum of £4,200 (net) paid by the contractors
for the right to tip surplus soil from the roadworks onto the claimant's
land. The tribunal held that the set-off provision did not apply since the
true purpose of the acquisition was the establishment of a road and the
retained land had benefitted, not from the construction of the road, but
from the dumping of soil which was purely incidental to the construction
of the road. The tribunal member went on to say that he thought the
purpose of section 222(6) of the 1959 Act was to set-off any value which
the land would have, particularly for development purposes, by reason of
having a new or improved access to it.

11–04   In *Portsmouth Roman Catholic Diocesan Trustees v Hampshire County
Council*[24] land at Winchester was acquired for a distributor road. The
question before the Lands Tribunal was whether the value of the
planning permission for development of the claimant's remaining land
which was a virtual certainty upon completion of the road should be set-
off against the compensation for the land taken. The tribunal concluded
that the grant of a planning permission was not the kind of benefit to
which it was required to have regard under section 222(6) of the 1959
Act. "The kind of benefit to which the tribunal is required to have
regard," said the tribunal member, "is, in my opinion, one which is
directly referable to the purpose for which the land is authorised to be
acquired, such as where the coming of the road will provide access to the
retained land of a new or improved kind (including the creation of a
frontage to a widened highway), which benefit increases the value of that
land. It appears to me that the grant of planning permission by the local
planning authority in respect of the green land was an indirect effect of
the purpose for which the land taken was acquired; it was too remote."[25]
A different view was taken in *Leicester City Council v Leicestershire
County Council.*[26] In that case the claimant argued that the decision in

[23] (1973) 27 P. & C.R. 234.
[24] (1980) 253 E.G. 1236 and 1347.
[25] See also *Lorbright Ltd v Staffordshire County Council* (1979) 254 E.G. 53. But see the
letter from W. A. Leach at (1980) 254 E.G. 1730.
[26] (1995) 32 E.G. 74. See too *Cotswold Trailer Parks Ltd v Secretary of State for the
Environment* (1972) 27 P. & C.R. 219.

Portsmouth meant that the effect (in terms of enhanced value) of any planning permission in expectation of the relevant road provision did not count as a benefit to the retained land. Only benefits directly attributable to the road provision, such as improved access or the creation of a frontage, could be considered in terms of set off. The tribunal rejected the claimant's argument. In *Leicester* land was acquired for the construction of a link road. This was "the purpose for which the land is authorised to be acquired". The value of land retained by the claimant was benefited by that purpose. Planning permission had been issued for the development of the retained land but the development was restricted until enhanced highway capacity was made available. The purpose for which the land was acquired was to provide that enhanced capacity. The retained land benefited from this and the tribunal applied the set off provision in section 261(1)(a) of the Highways Act 1980. The decision in *Portsmouth* was distinguished on the facts.

Where the enhancement in the value of the remaining land exceeds the compensation for the land taken there is no provision for recovery of the excess. This is one of the imperfections of this method of recovering betterment to which the Uthwatt Committee referred (see above). For example, in *Cotswold Trailer Parks Ltd v Secretary of State for the Environment*[27] a small piece of land forming part of a site with permission for the erection of a motel was acquired for a road scheme. The severance of the small piece of land in no way prejudiced the motel proposal but in the absence of the road scheme some improvement would have been required to the existing road network to enable it to proceed. Because of the road scheme this was no longer necessary. The benefit accruing to the remaining land as a result of the scheme was far in excess of the value of the land taken so the compensation awarded was nil.

When it operates, the set-off provision is, as the Uthwatt Committee observed "unfair as between one owner and another".[28] Why should two landowners, both of whom own land which has benefited from a scheme of public works, be treated differently solely because of the coincidence that one of them has had part of his land acquired for the scheme? CPPRAG accepted that there was an issue of equity and recommended that the set off provision should apply only to the amount payable for severance or injurious affection.[29] The government agreed that this would accord more closely with the spirit of equivalence[30] and the recommendation has been taken up by the Law Commission.[31]

The provision can also cause hardship in practice. Bell cites the example of bypass schemes with small areas of remaining farmland between the village and the bypass being assessed for increased hope

---

[27] (1974) 27 P. & C.R. 219.

[28] "Final Report of the Expert Committee on Compensation and Betterment", *supra*, para.285.

[29] "Fundamental review of the laws and procedures relating to compuslory purchase and compensation: final report" (2000) DETR para.124.

[30] "Compulsory purchase and compensation: delivering a fundamental change" (2001) DTLR para.3.40.

[31] "Towards a compulsory purchase code: (1) compensation" *Consultation Paper No 165*, p.63.

value because of the apparent improvement in their prospect of development. Such increased hope value may be set-off against compensation at the date for valuing the land being taken notwithstanding that the owner may have no intention of realising the potential or may subsequently be unable to obtain planning permission. Betterment, suggests Bell, should not be levied until it arises.[32]

Section 15 of the 1963 Act complements section 14. Its object is to avoid the possibility of betterment to remaining land arising from a scheme being set-off twice against compensation. The section applies to a subsequent acquisition where the interest acquired is the same as the interest previously taken into account[33] or is an interest deriving from that interest (s.15(3)).

The section is directed at two different circumstances. First of all, where remaining land which has been the subject of set-off is, itself, subsequently acquired in whole or in part for the scheme, section 15 provides that, in assessing compensation, the increase in value due to the scheme is *not* to be left out of account by virtue of section 13 or taken into account by virtue of section 14. Secondly, where remaining land which has been the subject of compensation for injurious affection is, itself, subsequently acquired in whole or in part for the scheme, then, in assessing compensation, the decrease in value due to the scheme is not to be left out of account by virtue of section 13. Section 15 applies even if the subsequent acquisition is by agreement (s.15(4)).

INJURIOUS AFFECTION

11–05 As mentioned earlier, the compulsory acquisition of part only of land in which an interest subsists may result in harm to what remains. The construction and use on the land taken, perhaps in conjunction with other land, of major public works such as roads, airports, urban redevelopment schemes, sewage works and so on will in many cases cause intentional harm to the remaining land. These activities are ostensibly promoted in the public interest. To what extent are private rights expected to yield to the public interest? Activities which seriously disturb a person in the enjoyment of his land may be the subject of reparation or restraint as a nuisance; such activities are considered to be an infringement of a person's right to the comfortable enjoyment of heritable property.[34] Are major schemes of public works open to restraint at common law at the suit of the disturbed neighbour?

The plea of "public interest" is not, of itself, a sufficient answer to an action at common law.[35] It has, however, long been established that where an activity is authorised expressly or by implication by an Act of Parliament, or by an instrument of delegated legislation, then, subject to what is said below, the body carrying on the activity will be immune from

---

[32] M. Bell, "Agricultural Compensation: The Way Forward" [1979] J.P.L. 577.
[33] Although the subsequent acquisition need not extend to the whole of the land in which that interest previously subsisted (s.15(3)(a)).
[34] Bell, *Principles*, para.974.
[35] *Duke of Buccleuch v Cowan* (1866) 5 M. 214.

an action at common law.[36] The Act authorising the activity does not usually confer an express immunity: rather it is the inevitable consequence of the authorisation.[37]

However, for anything done in excess of or contrary to such authorisation, the common law remedy remains.[38] Furthermore, certain consequences may not flow inevitably from the authorisation. The Act may merely authorise something to be done in respect of which nuisance is not a necessary incident.[39] If, as Deas states[40] "the cause of the injury is not the necessary result of the execution of the works authorised by the statute, but is the result of the negligent or improper manner in which they have been constructed, the only remedy is by action".

Thus, for example, in *Ogston v Aberdeen District Tramways*[41] a tramway company who, following a snowstorm, were in the habit of clearing snow off their tracks and piling it at the side of the rails to the considerable inconvenience of horse traffic were held unable to rely on the defence of statutory authority to an action for interdict as it was not shown that the nuisance complained of was in any sense necessary for the efficient carrying out of the purposes for which the respondents had been incorporated by the legislature. On the other hand, in *Edinburgh and District Water Trustees v Sommerville*[42] the trustees were able to rely on the defence of statutory authority to an action for damages resulting from the discharge of contaminated water from their reservoir down a water course. It could not be shown that by reasonable precautions—"such precautions as men skilled in the management of water-works acting prudently but not possessing supernatural foreknowledge might be expected to take"[43]—the trustees could have prevented the injury to the respondents. It would seem, therefore, that a statute authorising the execution of certain works which would constitute a cause of action if not so authorised, protects anyone not acting negligently from liability for injury caused by the execution of the authorised works.

Certain activities may be excluded by the authorising statute. For example, section 107 of the Railways Clauses Consolidation (Scotland) Act 1845 provides that "[e]very locomotive steam engine to be used on

---

[36] *R. v Pease* (1832), 4 B. & Ad. 30; *Caledonian Railway Co. v Ogilvy* (1856) 2 Macq. 229, *per* Lord Chancellor Cranworth at p.236; *Vaughan v Taff Vale Railway Co.* (1868) 5 H. & N. 679; *Hammersmith City Railway Co. v Brand* (1869) L.W. 4 (H.L.) 171; *City of Glasgow Union Railway Co. v Hunter* (1870) 8 M. (H.L.) 156; *Lord Blantyre and Others v Clyde Navigation Trustees* (1871) 9 M. (H.L.) 6; *Muir v Caledonian Railway Co.* (1890) 17 R. 1020; *Allen v Gulf Oil Refining Ltd.* [1981] 1 All E.R. 353.

[37] *Hammersmith and City Railway Co. v Brand* (1869) L.R. 4 (H.L.) 171; *Allen v Gulf Oil Refining Ltd* [1981] 1 All E.R. 353.

[38] *Caledonian Railway Co. v Colt* (1860) 3 Macq. 833.

[39] *Metropolitan Asylum District v Hill* (1881) 6 App.Cas. 193; *Lord Advocate v North British Railway Co.* (1894) 2 S.L.T. 71; *Pentland v Henderson* (1855) 17 D. 542; *Colt v Caledonian Railway Co.* (1869) 21 D. 1108; *Ogston v Aberdeen District* Tramways (1869) 24 R. (H.L.) 8; *Rapier v London Tramways Co.* [1893] 2 Ch. 588; *Edinburgh and District Water Trustees v Sommerville* (1906) 8 F. (H.L.) 25. See, too, David M. Walker, *The Law of Delict in Scotland* (2nd ed., W. Green & Son, Edinburgh), revised, pp.328–331.

[40] F. Deas, *The Law of Railways Applicable to Scotland* (William Green & Son, 1897) revised by James Ferguson, p.307.

[41] (1896) 24 R. (H.L.) 8.

[42] (1906) 8 F. (H.L.) 25.

[43] See above *per* Lord Macnaghten at p.31.

the railways shall, if it uses coal or other similar fuel emitting smoke, be constructed on the principle of consuming and so as to consume its own smoke". Statutory authority would be unlikely in such circumstances to provide a defence to an action for excessive disturbance caused by smoke from passing trains.

11–06   Where a body carrying out a scheme of public works is rendered immune by statutory authority from an action at common law in respect of the consequences of the scheme, it is reasonable to expect that Parliament will make provision for compensation in lieu. Reference is generally made in this regard to the provisions of the Lands Clauses Consolidation (Scotland) Act 1845. Section 48 of the Act requires a jury to deliver their verdict separately for the sum to be paid for the land taken:

> "and for the sum to be paid by way of compensation for the damage, if any, to be sustained by the owner of the lands by reason of severing of the lands taken from the other lands of such owner, or otherwise injuriously affecting such lands."

And section 61 provides that, in estimating the purchase money or compensation to be paid:

> "regard shall be had not only to the value of the land to be purchased or taken by the promoters of the undertaking, but also to the damage, if any, to be sustained by the owner of the lands by reason of the severing of the lands taken from the other lands of such owner, or otherwise injuriously affecting such land."

Although neither section constitutes a specific direction to compensate for injury to remaining land, the Act recognises such loss as a separate head of claim and, given the judicial presumption that an intention to take away the property of a subject without giving him a legal right to compensation for the loss of it is not to be imputed to the legislature unless that intention is expressed in unequivocal terms (see page 83), that would seem to be sufficient.

In *Royal Bank of Scotland v Glasgow District Council*[44] Lord McClusky regarded section 6 of the Railways Clauses Consolidation (Scotland) Act 1845 as providing a more specific, if somewhat indirect, authority. This provides that full compensation for all damage sustained shall be made to the owner and occupier of any lands taken. Section 6 is incorporated with the enactment under which any compulsory purchase, to which the provisions of the Acquisition of Land (Authorisation Procedure) (Scotland) Act 1947 apply, is authorised.

The term "severance" used in sections 48 and 61 of the Lands Clauses Act 1845 refers to the harm caused to the remaining land by the physical loss of the land taken. The most notable cases of severance arise from the construction of major roads through farm land. The result may be to separate the farm buildings from the farm land and to require the

---

[44] 1992 S.L.T. 356.

reorganisation of the farm enterprise, if it is to continue, along with the rearrangement of access, land drainage, fencing and so on. Severance may, of course, also affect industrial, commercial or residential property.

If the harm resulting from severance is particularly severe, a proprietor may prefer, instead of claiming compensation, to serve a notice objecting to the severance. The statutory provisions governing the service of such a notice are to be found partly in the Acquisition of Land (Authorisation Procedure) (Scotland) Act 1947,[45] partly in the Town and Country Planning (Scotland) Act 1997,[46] partly in the Lands Clauses Consolidation (Scotland) Act 1845[47] and partly in the Land Compensation (Scotland) Act 1973.[48] These provisions, which vary according to the nature of the land affected and the procedure adopted for acquiring title, are explained in Chapter 3.

"Other injurious affection" in sections 48 and 61 refers to the adverse effect on the remaining land arising from the construction and use of the works for which the land was acquired. For example, the construction and bringing into use of a major road may render an access to property very much less convenient, may spoil a good view and result in loss of privacy and may give rise to noise, fumes and disturbance from lights at night-time from traffic using the road.

These adverse effects may be just as serious for proprietors who have **11–07** had no land taken as they are for those who have had part of their land acquired for the scheme. Other injurious affection does not discriminate between those who have had their land taken and those who have not. The entitlement to compensation, however, differs. The position of a proprietor who has had no land taken for the scheme is discussed in Chapter 14.

The reference in the 1845 Act to severance and *other* injurious affection indicates that severance is to be treated simply as one form, albeit a somewhat specialised form, of injurious affection. The requirements to be satisfied are the same for both.

In addition to the general provisions for injurious affection compensation in sections 48 and 61, the 1845 Act makes certain special provisions. Section 113 specifically provides that where part only of lands comprised in a lease or missive of lease for a term of years unexpired is acquired, the lessee is entitled to compensation for damage to his interest arising from severance or "otherwise by reason of the execution of the works".[49] And section 114 makes special provision for a person having no greater interest in land than as a tenant for a year or from year to year. Such a person has no compensatable interest for the purposes of sections 48 and 61 (see Ch.12). Where such a person is required to give up possession of

---

[45] s.1(3), Sch.2, para.4 (amended by the Land Compensation (Scotland) Act 1973, s.63(3)).

[46] s.195, Sch.15, paras 19–29 (where a general vesting declaration is employed).

[47] ss.91 and 92.

[48] ss.49–54.

[49] It is not clear whether the words "by reason of the execution of the works" are intended to limit the extent of a claim for injurious affection in such cases by excluding damage arising from the *use* of the works. Cripps suggests that the corresponding provision in the (English) Lands Clauses Act does not exclude the application of the general provisions in that Act relating to injurious affection (para.4–250).

part of the land in which he has an interest before the expiration of his term, he is entitled to compensation for, *inter alia,* the damage done by severance or other injurious affection.

Section 103 of the 1845 Act deals with the position where part only of land subject to a heritable security is acquired. If the value of the land acquired is less than the sums outstanding under the security and the holder of the security considers that the remaining land does not provide a sufficient safeguard for such sums, the value of the part acquired and the compensation to be paid in respect of severance or otherwise are to be settled by agreement between the lender and the borrower on the one hand and the acquiring authority on the other, or, failing agreement, by the Lands Tribunal for Scotland; and the amount of such value or compensation is to be paid to the lender in satisfaction, so far as adequate, of the sums outstanding. Sections 109 and 111 make provision for apportioning a feu duty or ground annual (by agreement or in default by the sheriff) where part only of land subject to such a burden is acquired. Section 6(3) of the Land Tenure Reform (Scotland) Act 1974 provides for the redemption of the amount of feu duty or ground annual apportioned to the land acquired.[50] These provisions must now be read in conjunction with the provisions of the Abolition of Feudal Tenure etc (Scotland) Act 2000 which provides, from the appointed day, for the extinction of feu duties and ground annuals.[51]

1. Lands held therewith

11–08   Section 48 of the 1845 Act, which sets out the way in which juries were to deliver their verdict following an inquiry into the amount of compensation to be paid, begins "[w]here such inquiry shall relate to the value of lands to be purchased, and also to compensation claimed for injury done or to be done to the *lands held therewith*." The phrase in italics has been taken to mean that to succeed in a claim for compensation for injurious affection, the claimant must show that the land affected was held together with the land which has been acquired. In *Caledonian Railway Co. v Lockhart*[52] Lord Chancellor Campbell observed in this connection: "[t]he right to compensation depends on 'cause and effect', not on 'distance or proximity'."

This is well illustrated by the decision in *Holt v Gas Light and Coke Co.*[53] There the plaintiffs, a volunteer corps, had leased land on which they had constructed a rifle range. They had also of necessity to have control of the land beyond the butts in order to operate the range safely. They had secured a verbal agreement regarding the use of the marsh land immediately behind the butts and a lease of the marsh meadows beyond. The defendants compulsorily acquired part of the marsh meadows for the construction of a road to their plant. The formation and bringing into use of the road rendered it impossible to use the range. In addition to compensation for the land taken the plaintiffs

---

[50] Section 6(4) of the 1974 Act deals with the position where land, the subject of such a burden, is acquired by a general vesting declaration.

[51] See ss.7 and 56.

[52] (1860) 3 Macq. 808.

[53] (1872) L.R. 7 Q.B. 728.

sought compensation for severance and other injurious affection reflecting the closure of the rifle range. The defendants argued that there was no actual severance of land from the rifle range; the plaintiffs' interest in the intervening marsh land governed by the verbal agreement was little more than precarious. The court held that although the land taken and the remaining land were separated by the intervening marsh land, they were held together for the purposes of the legislation. The land so taken was, said Cockburn C.J., "held at the same time and for a common purpose, and was connected with the land which has been left".[54]

It would seem, therefore, that contiguity is not the test. In *Cowper Essex v Acton Local Board*[55] Lord Watson in the House of Lords said "I cannot assent to the argument that there can be no severance within the meaning of the Act unless the part taken and the parts left were in actual contiguity." In that case land taken for the construction of a sewage works was separated from other building land belonging to the claimant which would be adversely affected by the works. Lord Watson went on to say "where several pieces of land owned by the same person are, though not adjoining, so near to each other and so situated that the possession and control of each gives an enhanced value to all of them, they are lands held together within the meaning of the Lands Clauses Consolidation Act 1845, sections 49 and 63."[56]

Reservations may, therefore, be expressed about the judgments of Lord Justice-Clerk Moncrieff and Lord Young in *Nisbet-Hamilton v The Commissioners of Northern Lighthouses*[57] in which both appeared to be of the opinion that proximity was the test for a claim for injurious affection.[58]

Where a claimant is unable to satisfy this test, it may still be possible to claim compensation in respect of injurious affection on the same basis as a claim where no land has been taken (see Ch.14).

Where, however, the claim for the land taken is based on its value for a purpose which could only be realised by reducing the value of the remaining land, the claimant is effectively acknowledging that the remaining land is not "held together" with the land taken and such reduction in value could not form the subject of a claim for injurious affection. A claim for injurious affection must, in other words, be consistent with the claim for the land taken,[59] otherwise the claimant will be compensated for more than his real loss. There is, however, nothing inconsistent about a claim for injurious affection in respect of remaining

---

[54] See above, p.735. Lush J. in the same case said "I think it means lands connected together in use as regards the purpose for which the owner has applied them" (p.740).

[55] (1889) 14 App.Cas. 153.

[56] Corresponding to ss.48 and 61 of the Lands Clauses Consolidation (Scotland) Act 1845. In *City of Glasgow Union Railway Co. v Hunter* (1870) 8 M. (H.L.) 156 it was held that the mere fact that the two parcels of land were held under the same title was not sufficient to support a claim for injurious affection. And see *Oppenheimer v Minister of Transport* [1942] 1 K.B. 242.

[57] (1886) 13 R. 710.

[58] But see the dissenting judgement of Lord Rutherfurd Clark.

[59] H. Parrish, *Cripps on Compulsory Acquisition of Land* (11th ed., Stevens & Sons Ltd.) para.4–257. See too *Hoddom and Kinmount Estates v Secretary of State for Scotland* (1992) 22 E.G. 118, (Lands Tr.).

land where the property acquired is valued as a cleared site because it is below the tolerable standard.[60]

2. Measure of Loss

11–09   Although injurious affection compensation is referred to separately in the 1845 Act from compensation for the value of the land taken, it is nonetheless just one element of the overall price[61] and is measured by the depreciation in the value of the remaining land.[62] Mere personal inconvenience is not, therefore, a matter for compensation unless the inconvenience to owners and occupiers is such as would be reflected in the value of the land. In *Caledonian Railway Co. v Ogilvy*[63] the claimants, in addition to a claim for the acquisition of land for the construction of a railway through part of an estate, sought compensation for "very material injury done to the place as a residence and deterioration to the amenity and value of the house and policy by the railway crossing the approach to the lodge and gate on the level immediately in front of and within a few yards of the gate". This part of the claim was rejected by the House of Lords partly because it did not constitute an injury to remaining land. "[A]ll attempts at arguing that this is damage to the estate is a mere play upon words," said Lord Chancellor Cranworth. "It is no damage at all to the estate, except that the owner of that estate would oftener have a right of action from time to time than any other person, inasmuch as he would traverse the spot oftener than other people would traverse it."[64]

As mentioned at the beginning of this chapter, compensation for "other injurious affection" may be viewed to an extent as a substitute for a nuisance action. It would seem, however, that a claim for "other injurious affection" under the Lands Clauses Act may be made in respect of *any* depreciation in the value of the remaining land resulting from the construction or use of the works for which the land was acquired—regardless of whether the cause of the depreciation could have founded an action at common law in the absence of the statutory authority for the works.[65] This is a matter upon which initially there was

---

[60] Housing (Scotland) Act 1987, s.95(3) and Sch.8, Pt 111, para.12(3); and see generally Ch.9. See, too, *Palmer and Harvey Ltd v Ipswich Corporation* (1953) 4 P. & C.R. 5.

[61] *Oswald v Ayr Harbour Trustees* (1883) 10 R. 472, *per* Lord Young at p.489. See too *Bisset v Secretary of State for Scotland*, 1994 S.L.T. (Lands Tr.) 12; and *Hoddom and Kinmount Estates v Secretary of State for Scotland* (1992) 22 E.G. 118, (Lands Tr.).

[62] H. Parrish, *Cripps on Compulsory Acquisition of Land*, supra, 4–276. See, too, *Re Stockport, Timperley, and Altrincham Railway Co.* (1864) 33 L.J. Q.B. 251; *Cowper Essex v Acton Local Board* (1889) 14 App.Cas. 153; *Buccleuch (Duke) v Metropolitan Board of Works* (1872) L.W. 5 H.L. 418.

[63] (1852) 2 Macq. 229 overruling *Scottish Central Railway Co. v Cowan's Hospital* (1850) 12 D. 999. See too *Bisset v Secretary of State for Scotland*, 1994 S.L.T. (Lands Tr.) 12. Diminution in market value may include diminution in rental value caused by temporary effects (*Wildtree Hotels Ltd v Harrow London Borough Council* (2001) 81 P. & C.R. DG9).

[64] See above at p.603. See, too, *Nisbet-Hamilton v The Commissioners of Northern Lighthouses* (1886) 13 R. 710.

[65] *Re Stockport, Timperley and Altrincham Railway Co.* (1864) 33 L.J.Q.B. 251; *Cowper Essex v Acton Local Board* (1889) 14 App.Cas. 153, HL; *Buccleuch (Duke) v Metropolitan Board of Works* (1872) L.R. 5 418, HL; *Caledonian Railway Co. v Walker's Trustees* (1881) 8 R. 405, *per* Lord Ordinary Curriehill at p.410. Contrast the position of a claimant for injurious affection where no land has been taken (*Penny v South-Eastern Railway Co.* (1857) 7 E. & B. 660; *Hammersmith and City Railway Co. v Brand* (1869) L.R. 4 171, HL; and *City of Glasgow Union Railway Co. v Hunter* (1870) 8 M. 156, HL; and see Chap.14).

some uncertainty. In *Caledonian Railway Co. v Ogilvy*,[66] referred to above, a claim for injurious affection was lodged in respect of the inconvenience to the estate caused by the construction and use of a level crossing on a public highway giving access to the estate. In the House of Lords, Lord Chancellor Cranworth asserted "the construction that is put upon this expression, 'injuriously affected', in the clauses in the Act of Parliament which gives compensation for injuriously affecting lands, certainly does not entitle the owner of lands which he alleges to be injuriously affected, to any compensation in respect of any act which, if done by the Railway Company without the authority of Parliament, would not have entitled him to bring an action against them."[67] And in *Nisbet-Hamilton v The Commissioners of Northern Lighthouses*[68] Lord Justice-Clerk Moncrieff observed: "it is a rule that has been laid down frequently—that a use of property which could not be made the subject of action or interdict apart from the acquisition of compulsory powers, will not be a ground of compensation in estimating the amount due from the use of the powers".

In other words, the view initially taken was that a claim for "other injurious affection" was coextensive with an action for nuisance. There had to be *damnum cum injuria.* While that seems still to be the position for a claim for compensation for injurious affection where no land has been taken (see Chapter 14), it is no longer the position as regards a claim for "other injurious affection" under sections 48 or 61 of the Lands Clauses Act.

In his dissenting judgement in *Nisbet-Hamilton* Lord Rutherfurd Clark relied on the decision in *Re Stockport, Timperley and Altrincham Railway Co.*[69] which had drawn a distinction between claims for injurious affection where land had been taken and claims in cases where no land had been taken. In that case compensation was awarded for depreciation arising from the risk of fire to a cotton mill from the use of a railway where it passed over ground acquired from the mill. It was argued by the railway company that exposing property to damage by fire was not actionable *per se*; neither would a fire which occurred without negligence give rise to any liability. No claim to compensation could arise in respect of an activity sanctioned by Parliament for which no action could have been maintained in the absence of Parliament's sanction. In his judgement for the claimants, Crompton J. held that that rule did not apply where the mischief complained of is caused by what is done on the land taken.

> "Where, however, the mischief is caused by what is done on the land taken, the party seeking compensation has a right to say, 'it is by the Act of Parliament, and the Act of Parliament only, that you have done the acts which have caused the damage; without the Act of Parliament, everything you have done, and are about to do, in making and using the railway, would have been illegal and action-

---

[66] (1852) 2 Macq. 600.
[67] See above, p.602.
[68] (1886) 13 R. 710 at p.719.
[69] (1864) 33 L.J. Q.B. 251.

able, and is, therefore, matter for compensation according to the rule in question'."[70]

The judgement of Crompton J. was subsequently approved unanimously by the House of Lords in *Cowper Essex v Acton Local Board.*[71] Part of the claimant's land was acquired for a sewage works. There was evidence that the existence of the sewage works, even if conducted so as not to create a nuisance, depreciated the value of the claimant's remaining land for building purposes. Their Lordships confirmed the distinction made by Crompton J. and held that the damage in this case was not too remote even though no nuisance might be caused.[72]

The scope of a claim for injurious affection compensation under sections 48 or 61 of the 1845 Act is not, therefore, coextensive with a nuisance action and may include the full consequential loss in so far as it is reflected in depreciation in the value of the remaining land. Although the list of activities which may be recognised by the law as a nuisance is open-ended,[73] there are some activities which in the ordinary sense of the words could be said to disturb a person in the enjoyment of his property and which may depress the value of the property but which will not be regarded as a nuisance. Loss of a good view and loss of privacy are examples.[74] These may nonetheless form part of a claim for "other injurious affection" under sections 48 or 61. In other words *damnum* alone would appear to be sufficient to support such a claim.

11–10   In the *Stockport* case Crompton J. referred to the mischief "caused by what is done on the land taken". For many years the position was that a claim for compensation for "other injurious affection" was limited to the mischief caused by what was done on the land taken from the claimant; it could not encompass any injury caused by what was being done on other land acquired by the promoter. Thus in *City of Glasgow Union Railway Co. v Hunter,*[75] where a parcel of land was acquired from the claimant for the construction of a railway, compensation was claimed under section 48 of the 1845 Act for depreciation in the value of the remaining land arising from the use of the railway. The claim under section 48 was rejected as the land taken was not held together with the land retained (see above). Lord Chelmsford pointed out that "[a]s no part of the property of the respondent has been injured by anything done on his land over which the railway runs, his right to compensation for damage appears to me to be precisely the same as if none of his land had been taken by the company."[76]

---

[70] See above at p.253.

[71] (1889) 14 App.Cas. 153, HL.

[72] Lord Chancellor Halsbury and Lords Watson and Bramwell considered that the distinction had already been settled by the decision of the House of Lords in *Buccleuch (Duke) v Metropolitan Board of Works* (1872) L.R. 5 418, HL. The difficulty with that decision is that although their Lordships agreed on the result, they did not appear to arrive at that result upon the same general construction of the provisions of the Act.

[73] See John Rankine, *The Law of Landownership in Scotland* (4th ed., W. Green & Son, Edinburgh) pp.384–412; also David M. Walker, *The Law of Delict in Scotland, supra,* pp.955–974.

[74] *Penny v South-Eastern Railway Co.* (1857) 7 E. & B. 660; *Caledonian Railway Co. v Walker's Trustees* (1881) 8 R. 405, *per* Lord Ordinary Curriehill at p.410.

[75] (1870) 8 M. 156, HL.

[76] See above at p.163.

More recently, in *Edwards v Minister of Transport*[77] some 302 square
yards of land were compulsorily acquired from a householder for the
construction of a trunk road. The householder claimed compensation on
the basis of the injurious affection to his house from the annoyance
caused by traffic on the new road. The Court of Appeal held he was
entitled to compensation for injurious affection only in respect of that
attributable to traffic on the small plots of land acquired from him.[78]

The decision of the House of Lords in *Buccleuch (Duke) v Metropolitan Board of Works*[79] might, at first sight, appear to depart from this
position. The claimant was the lessee of a large house with grounds
running down to the Thames. There was a causeway and landing place
belonging to the house which provided access to and from the river. The
causeway and landing place were acquired to make way for the Victoria
Embankment which was constructed between the garden and the river.
The claimant sought compensation not only for the loss of the causeway
and landing place but also for depreciation resulting from the conversion
of the land between the house and the river into a highway and the
consequent public use of it. In the light of the discussion above, one
might have expected the claim for injurious affection to have been
limited to mischief arising on the small bit of land taken for the scheme.
However, their Lordships unanimously agreed that compensation was
due for the proximity of the embankment and all the consequences of its
use as a public highway. The grounds upon which this conclusion was
arrived at are not clear but the explanation for the decision may lie in
the judgement of Lord Cairns who held that the claimant was entitled to
the whole loss because of the acquisition of his rights as riparian owner
to the undisturbed flow of the river along the whole frontage of the
property.[80] If that is the explanation, the decision is consistent with those
discussed above.

The result of these decisions, as Cripps observes, was that "no
compensation is payable in respect of what is done on lands other than
those taken from the claimant".[81] The decision in *Edwards* provoked
considerable dissatisfaction[82] and the government agreed to introduce
amending legislation.[83] Section 41 of the Land Compensation (Scotland)
Act 1973 now provides that where land is acquired from any person for
the purpose of works which are to be situated partly on that land and
partly elsewhere, compensation for a claim for injurious affection under

---

[77] [1964] 1 All E.R. 483.

[78] See, too, *R. v Mountford, ex p. London United Tramways (1901) Ltd* [1906] 2 K.B. 814;
Horton v Colwyn Bay and Colwyn Bay U.D.C. [1908] 1 K.B. 327; *Sisters of Charity of
Rockingham v R.* [1922] 2 A.C. 315. It would seem that the claim for "other injurious
affection" in *Ogilvy* might equally have been rejected on this ground.

[79] (1872) L.R. 5 418, HL. The decision in this case much influenced three of the
judgments in the House of Lords in *Cowper Essex v Acton Local Board, supra.*

[80] This was the explanation of the decision advanced in *Edwards, supra.*

[81] H. Parrish, *Cripps on Compulsory Acquisition of Land, supra*, para.4–263.

[82] JUSTICE, *Compensation for Compulsory Acquisition and Remedies for Planning
Restrictions together with a Supplemental Report* (Stevens & Sons Ltd, 1973) para.54;
Chartered Lands Societies Committee, "Compensation for Compulsory Acquisition and
Planning Restrictions" (1968) s.5.

[83] Cmnd. 5124, para.29.

sections 48 or 61 of the 1845 Act[84] is to be assessed by reference to the whole of the works and not only the part situated on the land acquired or taken from him.

In *Hoddom and Kinmount Estates v Secretary of State for Scotland*[85] the Lands Tribunal for Scotland observed that the tests for disturbance compensation set out by Lord Justice Clerk Alness in *Venables v Department of Agriculture for Scotland*[86] and by Romer LJ in *Harvey v Crawley Development Corporation*[87] applied equally to a claim for severance and other injurious affection (see p.217 above). In other words, any loss sustained by the dispossessed owner may be recovered "provided, first, that it is not too remote and, secondly, that it is the natural and reasonable consequence of the dispossession of the owner".[88] In that case farm land was compulsorily acquired for a road scheme. A claim for severance and injurious affection under section 61 of the 1845 Act was lodged reflecting additional loss arising from the failure to secure the allocation of a milk quota for the farm. On the facts the tribunal held that the loss would not have been incurred but for the happening of an extraneous event (the introduction of the milk quota system) completely unconnected with the compulsory acquisition. The loss was not a reasonably forseeable consequence of the compulsory acquisition. It was too remote a consequence of the severance for the claimants to be entitled to compensation.

It would seem that the measure of compensation based upon land as an investment rather than as a factor of production may cause hardship to farmers faced with severance, particularly where the market value of the retained land remains high. As Hamilton states, "the severance may cause greater damage to the profitability of working the land than it does to the value of the land itself.'[89] This may be illustrated by the decision in *Cooke v Secretary of State for the Environment*.[90]

11–11   A farm already severed by the A40 trunk road, found the effects of severance considerably aggravated by the carrying out of improvements to that road in the form of the construction of a large roundabout and a new dual carriageway. As a result of the improvement it was no longer possible to drive cattle across the road, the farmhouse was severed from the land, all the farm buildings with the exception of a modern corn store had to be demolished as they were located on the land acquired, and the area of the farm was reduced by nine acres. The claimants based their claim for severance on the amount required to reinstate the farm as

---

[84] Section 41 of the 1973 Act applies also to claims for severance and other injurious affection under section 114 of the 1845 Act by a person who has no greater interest in land than as a tenant for a year or from year to year.

[85] (1992) 22 E.G. 118, (Lands Tr.). See too *Bisset v Secretary of State for Scotland*, 1994 S.L.T. (Lands Tr.) 12.

[86] 1932 S.C. 573.

[87] [1957] 1 Q.B. 485.

[88] See above at p.494.

[89] R. N. D. Hamilton, "Compensation for Compulsory Acquisition of Agricultural Land" (1980) RICS para.39. See, too, M. Bell, "Compensation: Can money do it?" (1978) *Chartered Surveyor Rural Quarterly No.6*, p.3; M. Bell, "Agricultural Compensation: The Way Forward" [1979] J.P.L. 577; and B. Denyer-Green, "Agricultural Compensation: The Injustice of Market Value in Severance Cases" [1980] J.P.L. 505.

[90] (1973) 27 P. & C.R. 234.

a working holding and included a substantial proportion of the cost of the new buildings, the whole cost of constructing a concrete farmyard and a new farm road and an outfall sewer, the cost of transporting stock across the A40 and the capitalised cost of travelling by car to the site of the new farm buildings. The whole claim, including the value of the land taken was assessed at £19,373. The tribunal considered that the basis of the claim was misconceived. Compensation for severance was to be measured by the depreciation in the market value of the land not taken. They awarded £3,376 for the land taken and £3,048 for severance.[91]

CPPRAG acknowledged the hardship that could result in the sort of situation that occurred in *Cooke* where market value compensation did not reflect the cost of providing replacement buildings. They recommended that for cases where loss is directly attributable to the scheme and cannot properly be compensated for on the basis of open market value for the land taken plus severance and injurious affection, provision should be made to allow for compensation for the loss of an agricultural building to be based on the reasonable cost of providing a replacement building.[92] The government, however, saw this as a matter that could more appropriately be dealt with as an item in the disturbance claim,[93] a conclusion with which the Law Commission agrees.[94]

Some of the consequences of severance may be recoverable under the heading of disturbance (see Chap.10)[95]; but if the expense has been taken into account in the valuation of the remaining land for a severance claim, it cannot also form part of a disturbance claim. In *McLaren's Discretionary Trustee v Secretary of State for Scotland*,[96] the Lands Tribunal for Scotland were asked to decide whether the cost of meeting the future maintenance and renewal of accommodation works (see below) was an item of injurious affection to the retained land or of disturbance. The tribunal decided that as the accommodation works were intended to mitigate what would otherwise be a much larger claim for injurious affection, and as they became fixtures and thus a part of the owner's property, what was being valued was a proprietary interest in land. "So in calculating the claimant's overall loss in the present case, it was not unfair to do so under Rule 2 by reference to the overall diminution in the value of the retained land—provided this is estimated

---

[91] For a possible approach to assessing depreciation in the value of remaining land which will reflect decreased profitability see R. N. D. Hamilton, "Compensation for Compulsory Acquisition of Agricultural Land", *supra*, para.39. In *Compensation for Compulsory Acquisition* (1995), paras 2.6–2.11, the Royal Institution of Chartered Surveyors recommended that the Lands Tribunal should be given a discretion to award an additional sum in such cases over and above the compensation otherwise payable.

[92] "Fundamental review of the laws and procedures relating to compulsory purchase and compensation: final report" (2000) DETR para.127.

[93] "Compulsory purchase and compensation: delivering a fundamental change" (2001) DTLR para.3.39.

[94] "Towards a compulsory purchase code: (1) compensation" *Consultation Paper No 165* paras 4.63–4.64.

[95] See H. Parrish, *Cripps on Compulsory Acquisition of Land, supra*, para.4–283; and R. N. D. Hamilton, "Compensation for Compulsory Acquisition of Agricultural Land", *supra*, para.44.

[96] 1987 S.L.T. (Lands Tr.) 25. See too *Bisset v Secretary of State for Scotland*, 1994 S.L.T. (Lands Tr.) 12.

by taking into account the likely future expenditure involved to provide a guide to the amount by which notional purchasers in the market would be likely to lower their offers."

Subject to what is said below, compensation for injurious affection is assessed on a "before and after" basis. This involves calculating the difference between the market value of the land not taken before severance and other injurious affection and the value after that date. There would seem to be some flexibility in approach to the calculation of this sum.[97]

In *Cuthbert v Secretary of State for the Environment*[98] the Lands Tribunal suggested that a valuer should assume that immediately before the date of valuation a notional purchaser had agreed to buy the whole estate at a particular price; that at the date of valuation he was told of the intended acquisition of part of the estate and the agreement to purchase became void; and that immediately after the date of valuation he made a fresh bid for the estate less the land being acquired. The Lands Tribunal for Scotland, however, declined to follow this approach in *McLaren's Discretionary Trustee*,[99] a case which turned on the compensation payable to cover the future costs of maintaining and renewing accommodation works (see above) on retained land. The tribunal considered that it would be unfair in the circumstances to assess compensation for injurious affection by reference to the test adopted in *Cuthbert*. The hypothetical purchaser might well shrug off such a relatively minor expenditure when bidding for a large sporting estate. "While there may be other possible valuation approaches, the Tribunal prefer, therefore, a more down to earth approach involving a build-up of various items of injurious affection (on a 'before and after valuation') to those specified parts of the retained land which the accommodation works were actually designed to serve."

The Royal Institution of Chartered Surveyors in a discussion paper raised two questions about valuation for injurious affection:[1] 1. Should the land taken be valued as severed or as part of the whole? 2. Is severance compensation payable only in respect of the land retained by the claimant or in respect of the land taken and the land retained?

11–12   The decision of the Lands Tribunal in *Abbey Homesteads Group Ltd v Secretary of State for Transport*[2] suggests that the land taken should be valued as severed[3] and that severance compensation is payable only in respect of the land retained.[4] This, as the RICS point out, may result in a claimant receiving compensation for less than the full loss suffered.[5] In the *Abbey Homesteads* case some farmland was acquired for the con-

[97] *Executors of J. R. Bullock, deceased v Minister of Transport* [1969] R.V.R. 442.
[98] (1979) 252 E.G. 1178.
[99] 1987 S.L.T. (Lands Tr.) 25.
[1] "Compensation for Compulsory Purchase: Revisions to the Law on Severance and Injurious Affection Where Land is Taken" (1983) paras 7–11.
[2] (1982) 263 E.G. 983. See, too, *A.D.P.&E. Farmers v Department of Transport* (1988) 8818 E.G. 80; 8819 E.G. 147; and 8820 E.G. 104.
[3] But see H. Parrish, *Cripps on Compulsory Acquisition of Land, supra*, para.4–279 for a contrary view.
[4] *Hoveringham Gravels Ltd v Chiltern District Council* (1979) 252 E.G. 815.
[5] See W. A. Leach, "Market Value Under Rule (2): A Fresh Appraisal" (1974) 231 E.G. 907; G. S. Sams, "Severance and the Land Taken" (1982) 1 *Journal of Valuation* 9.

struction of the Witney Bypass. The claimants argued that, because the land taken had no development potential on its own but only in conjunction with the retained land, it was right to value the entirety of the land and apportion its value to the several parts. In other words, they advocated assessing the totality of the loss and apportioning it to the relevant statutory provisions. The Lands Tribunal held that as a matter of law a separate assessment of compensation was required for the land taken, although in making that separate assessment regard could be taken of any value attributable to the prospect of "marrying" the land taken with the land retained. The overall compensation for the land taken and for the damage to the land retained was not to be ascertained by deducting the value of what was left to the owner after the acquisition from the aggregate value of the entirety immediately prior to the acquisition. CPRAG recommended that the opportunity should be taken in legislation to confer discretion on the Lands Tribunal on the approach to be adopted according to the circumstances.[6]

Prospective value may sometimes be an important element in a claim for injurious affection. In assessing compensation for injurious affection a claimant may, in the words of Cockburn C.J. in *R. v Brown,*[7] "take into account not only the present purpose to which the land is applied, but also any other more beneficial purpose to which in the course of events at no remote period it may be applied, just as an owner might do if he were bargaining with a purchaser in the market."[8] Thus in *Ripley v Great Northern Railway Co.,*[9] where the railway company acquired land from the claimant on which cotton mills would probably have been built, it was held that compensation for severance was properly awarded on the basis of the profits which might have been derived from supplying water to the mills from a reservoir built by the claimant on land remaining in his ownership.

In assessing the development potential of the remaining land, no assistance may be obtained from the statutory planning assumptions set out in sections 22 to 24 of the Land Compensation (Scotland) Act 1963 (see Chap.7). These apply only to the "relevant land" (ss.22(1) and 45(2)). Furthermore, the procedure for applying for a certificate of appropriate alternative development (see Chap.7) would seem to be available only in respect of the land acquired.[10] A claimant may, however, test the development potential of the remaining land by applying for planning permission in the normal way.

In assessing the value of the remaining land "before" severance, the effect of the scheme underlying the acquisition must be ignored.[11] In

---

[6] "Fundamental review of the laws and procedures relating to compulsory purchase and compensation: final report" (2000) DETR para.129. And see the Law Commission Consultation Paper No 165, 2002, p.64.

[7] (1867) L.R. 2 Q.B. 630.

[8] See above at p.631. And see *Bolton Metropolitan Council v Waterworth* (1981) 259 E.G. 625.

[9] (1875) 10 Ch.App. 435.

[10] A certificate granted in respect of land acquired may, however, be persuasive as to the development potential of the land retained (*Abbey Homesteads Group Ltd v Secretary of State for Transport* (1982) 263 E.G. 983; and *A.D.P.& E. Farmers v Department of Transport* (1988) 8818 E.G. 80; 8819 E.G. 147; and 8820 E.G. 104).

[11] *Pointe Gourde Quarrying and Transport Co. Ltd v Sub-Intendent of Crown Lands* [1947] A.C. 565.

Clark v Wareham and Purbeck Rural District Council[12] 2.69 acres of land were acquired for the construction of a new sewage works. The claimant sought compensation for depreciation in the value of his remaining land resulting from the scheme. The claim was based on the difference in the value of the remaining land having regard to the actual state of affairs (the "with scheme world") and the state of affairs that would have existed in the absence of the scheme underlying the acquisition (the "no scheme world"). The Lands Tribunal agreed with the claimant that the correct yardstick for measuring injury from injurious affection was the difference between the value of the remaining land in the "with scheme world" and its value in the "no scheme world" but disagreed that there would have been any difference in value in the circumstances of the case.

Although, as indicated at the beginning of this chapter, it is not possible in the absence of an express statutory provision to set-off any increase in the value of the remaining land due to the scheme against the compensation for the land taken, it would seem that any such increase should be set-off against the compensation for injurious affection. In *George Wimpey and Co. Ltd v Middlesex County Council*[13] land was acquired from the claimants for open space purposes. Adjoining land belonging to the claimants was damaged by the loss of access to a main road. However, in assessing compensation for this damage, the court held that account should be taken of the increase in the value of the adjoining land resulting from the provision of open space.

It is common practice for an acquiring authority to undertake with the agreement of the claimant what are generally termed "accommodation works" designed to mitigate the damage to remaining land by injurious affection.[14] Such works often take the form of fencing, walling, drainage, screening, planting and the provision of alternative forms of access. These works must be taken into account when assessing compensation for injurious affection. The cost of future maintenance and renewal of accommodation works may be a factor in formulating a claim for injurious affection.[15] Account should also be taken of any steps to mitigate the injurious effect of public works carried out in accordance with the provisions of Part II of the Land Compensation (Scotland) Act 1973. CPPRAG expressed sympathy with the problems faced by claimants in securing agreement to, and satisfactory completion of, accommodation works because these are generally undertaken by the contractor responsible for the construction of the scheme rather than by the acquiring authority. The Group recommended that acquiring authorities should take greater responsibility for ensuring the undertaking and completion of such works,[16] a recommendation that is being taken up by the government.[17]

---

[12] (1972) 25 P. & C.R. 423. See, too, *Melwood Units Property Ltd v Commissioner of Main Roads* [1979] A.C. 426.

[13] [1938] 3 All E.R. 781.

[14] Any such agreement must, however, be consistent with the purpose for which the land is acquired (*Ayr Harbour Trustees v Oswald* (1883) 8 App.Cas. 623).

[15] *McLaren's Discretionary Trustee v Secretary of State for Scotland*, 1987 S.L.T. (Lands Tr.) 25.

[16] "Fundamental review of the law and procedures relating to compulsory purchase and compensation: final report" (2000) DETR paras 144–145.

[17] "Compulsory purchase and compensation: delivering a fundamental change" (2001) DTLR para.3.49.

The claim for injurious affection should embrace all damage both present and prospective.[18] In *Croft v London and North-Western Railway*[19] Cockburn C.J. said in the context of a claim under the (English) Lands Clauses Act:

> "The statute provides that compensation, in respect of land taken, and in respect of land injuriously affected, shall at once and, as it appears to me, for all be settled; and there is no provision whatever for any further damage presenting itself, not contemplated by the parties at the time of compensation by the jury, or not entered upon before the jury. I think if the Act of Parliament had intended that the inquiry should be renewed from time to time, if that, which at the time of the first inquiry might more or less be speculative, should be afterwards realised, there certainly would have been some provision in some of the statutes."[20]

In determining a claim for damage for severance the Lands Tribunal **11–13** have applied the general principle that applies to the assessment of damages at common law established in *Bwlfa and Merthyr Dare Steam Collieries (1891) Ltd v Pontypridd Waterworks Company*[21] to the effect that in assessing damages it is unnecessary to speculate on what might be the measure of loss if at the time of the trial the true loss has become a fact.[22]

Because of the difficulty in formulating a claim in respect of future or contingent damage, the Uthwatt Committee recommended that a claim for injurious affection should be deferred until the authorised works have been completed and in operation for an appreciable time.[23] "Facts are better than predictions" was their view.[24] Although there is no requirement to defer a claim, agreement is sometimes reached in practice to reserve certain aspects of a claim for injurious affection until the impact of the scheme of works is clearer.[25] Subject to that, it would seem that no further claim may be made in respect of damage arising later which could be foreseen at the date of valuation.

---

[18] *Sisters of Charity of Rockingham v R.* [1922] 2 A.C. 315; *Caledonian Railway Co. v Lockhart* (1860) 3 Macq. 808, *per* Lord Chancellor Campbell, 813; *Croft v London and North-Western Railway Co.* (1863)32 L.J.Q.B. 113; *North British Railway Co. v Hay* (1852) 14 D. 832; *Abercrombie v Lothian Regional Council*, unreported, October 21, 1986, Lands Tribunal for Scotland.

[19] (1863) 32 LJ. Q.B. 113.

[20] See above at pp.119 and 120.

[21] [1903] A.C. 426.

[22] See *Bolton Metropolitan Borough Council v Waterworth* (1978) 251 E.G. 963 and 1071; and (1981) 259 E.G. 625; also *A.D.P.& E. Farmers v Department of Transport* (1988) 8818 E.G. 80; 8819 E.G. 147; and 8820 E.G. 104.

[23] "Final Report of the Expert Committee on Compensation and Betterment" (1942) HMSO para.211 (Cmnd. 6386).

[24] See, too, "Compensation for Compulsory Purchase: Revisions to the Law on Severance and Injurious Affection Where Land is Taken," (1983) *Royal Institution of Chartered Surveyors Discussion Paper*, paras 12–17.

[25] See R. N. D. Hamilton, "Compensation for Compulsory Acquisition of Agricultural Land", *supra*, para.42.

CONCLUSION

11–14 "In our opinion," said the Scott Committee, "the principle of Betterment, *i.e.*, the principle that persons whose property has clearly been
increased in market value by an improvement should specially contribute
to the cost of such an improvement, and the principle of Injurious
Affection, *i.e.*, the principle that persons whose properties are damaged
by the construction or user of the promoters' works shall be entitled to
receive compensation, are correlative."[26] It would seem logical, therefore, to treat them as such. However, with the exception of section 13 of
the 1963 Act (see Ch.8), Parliament has not treated betterment and
injurious affection as correlative. It will be apparent from this chapter
that set-off and "other injurious affection" are concerned broadly with
converse positions; yet the general provision for compensating injurious
affection has been available since 1845, while the general provision for
recovering betterment accruing to remaining land was not introduced
until 1959.

There is, furthermore, an important difference in the operation of the
provisions for recovering betterment and compensating injurious affection. The latter is measured by the full loss to the remaining land arising
from the scheme[27]; the former, as the Uthwatt Committee observed,[28] is
measured by the cost to the public authority of the part of the land
acquired.[29]

As mentioned earlier, the Uthwatt Committee also regarded set-off as
unfair in principle "between one owner and another". It discriminates
against a person whose land is being compulsorily acquired. The increase
in the value of the land left is set-off against the compensation for the
land taken. A neighbour who has had no land taken for the scheme
enjoys the full benefit of any betterment that accrues.[30]

Compensation for "other injurious affection" may also be regarded as
unfair between one owner and another although the advantage is
reversed. The injurious effects of a scheme do not discriminate between
those who have had land taken and those who have not. Yet the
entitlement to compensation differs (see Ch.14); and a person who has
land acquired may be compensated more generously for these effects
than one who has not. In *Buccleuch* Mr Justice Hannen sought to
explain the distinction on the ground that the landowner who has had
land acquired for the scheme "was possessed of something without
which the proposed public purpose could not be accomplished".[31] Whilst

---

[26] "Second Report of the Committee Dealing with the Law and Practice relating to the
Acquisition and Valuation of Land for Public Purposes" (1918) HMSO para.32 (Cmnd.
9229).

[27] *Stockport, Timperley and Altrincham Railway Co.* (1864) 33 L.J.Q.B. 251; *Cowper Essex
v Acton Local Board* (1889) 14 App.Cas. 153.

[28] *Final Report of the Expert Committee on Compensation and Betterment* (1942) HMSO
para.285 (Cmnd. 6386).

[29] There also appears to be a further difference in that set-off and injurious affection
may not necessarily arise in respect of the same land. Section 14 of the 1963 Act refers to
set-off in the context of "contiguous or adjacent" land. Injurious affection is concerned
with land "held together" with the land taken.

[30] Subject to prevailing fiscal policy.

[31] (1872) L.R. 5 H.L. 418 at p.445.

this may be a ground for awarding some special element in the compensation for the land taken, it has very little to do with injury to the land retained.

For these reasons the present arrangements for recovering betterment and compensating "other injurious affection" may be regarded as both illogical and confusing.[32] The law relating to compensation for compulsory purchase would be much simpler if these elements of gain and loss were removed from the legislation; they are not a direct consequence of compulsory acquisition. There would seem to be something to be said for a separate code of legislation which treated like cases alike rather than making artificial distinctions because of the coincidence that a person has had land acquired for the scheme.

---

[32] These criticisms are not directed at compensation for severance which is part of the consequential loss arising from compulsory acquisition.

CHAPTER 12

COMPENSATION: OTHER MATTERS

SHORT TENANCIES

12–01 Section 114 of the 1845 Act is a self-contained provision dealing with the interests of short tenants. A "short tenant" is one who has no greater interest in land than as a tenant for a year or from year to year. Because such tenancies are short, the acquiring authority may content themselves with persuading the landlord to serve a notice to quit or with purchasing the landlord's interest and giving such a notice themselves. If a tenant's interest simply expires in this way there is no entitlement to compensation under the compulsory purchase legislation[1] as there has been no compulsory acquisition or compulsory extinguishment of the interest. It merely terminates under the contractual terms of the tenancy.

Where, however, the acquiring authority require early possession they may be unable to wait for the contractual arrangements to run their course. In that event, having served a notice of entry,[2] they may enter on the land and extinguish the tenant's interest and pay compensation under section 114 for the extinguishment of that interest.

Subject to what is said below about the general vesting declaration procedure, short tenants are not entitled to a notice to treat under section 17 of the 1845 Act as that interest is not being acquired but simply extinguished. As was said in *Greenwood Tyre Services Ltd v Manchester Corporation*,[3] "this procedure did not involve the acquisition of an interest in land; a short tenancy did not become *acquired*, it became simply *snuffed out* by entry". However, as a matter of practice, acquiring authorities may serve such a notice to announce their intention to take the land or to clarify particulars of interests which may not be known to them. Service of a notice to treat on a short tenant in these circumstances does not alter the basis of compensation.[4]

Where a general vesting declaration has been executed in respect of any land, short tenancies are excluded from the deemed notice to treat and divestiture provisions. The right of entry which arises upon vesting is not exercisable in respect of any land in which a short tenancy subsists.[5]

---

[1] But note the right of a person served with notice to quit an agricultural holding to opt in prescribed circumstances for notice of entry compensation (1973 Act, s.55); see p.279.

[2] Acquisition of Land (Authorisation Procedure) (Scotland) Act 1947, Sch.2, para.3.

[3] (1971) 23 P. & C.R. 246.

[4] *Newham London Borough Council v Benjamin* [1968] 1 W.L.R. 694.

[5] Town and Country Planning (Scotland) Act 1997, Sch.15, para.8. And see *Anderson v Moray District Council*, 1978 S.L.T. (Lands Tr.) 37.

The authority must first serve a notice to treat on such tenants followed by a notice of entry before possession can be taken. This is an exception to the general rule that a short tenant is not entitled to a notice to treat but here, too, service of such a notice does not alter the basis of compensation.[6]

Section 114 provides that a short tenant will be entitled upon extinguishment of his tenancy to compensation:

(i) for the value of his unexpired term;

(ii) for any just allowance which ought to be made to him by an incoming tenant;

(iii) for any loss or injury he may sustain;

(iv) where part only of the land is required, compensation for damage arising from severance and other injurious affection.

In *Greenwood Tyre Services Ltd*, it was held that for a periodic tenancy the "unexpired term" was the period which would have elapsed from the date on which the acquiring authority actually took possession until a notice to quit deemed to have been given on that date would have expired. And in *Smith and Waverley Tailoring Co.* the Lands Tribunal for Scotland concluded that, where a general vesting declaration had been executed, what was then Schedule 24, paragraph 8(b) of the Town and Country Planning (Scotland) Act 1972[7] indicated that a short tenancy subsisting at the date of divestiture automatically terminated at its next term date without a formal notice to quit. In that case, although the claimants continued in occupation after that date they did so at the will of the acquiring authority who could displace them at any time. They accordingly had no extant claim under section 114 in respect of an unexpired term on their eventual displacement.

Compensation falls to be assessed under section 114 when the tenant is required to give up possession.[8]

A number of points may be made regarding the assessment of compensation. First of all, a person with a short tenancy of business premises with a rateable value not exceeding the prescribed amount[9] who is over the age of 60 and who does not wish to relocate the business is entitled, subject to giving certain undertakings (see page 224), to have compensation assessed on the basis of the total extinguishment of the business (1973 Act, s.43).

Secondly, in *Lynch v Glasgow Corporation*[10] Lord President Kinross thought it doubtful whether regard could be had in assessing compensation under section 114 to the prospect of the renewal of the tenancy

---

[6] *Smith and Waverley Tailoring Co. v Edinburgh District Council (No. 2)*, 1977 S.L.T. (Lands Tr.) 29, a case which involved the expedited vesting procedure contained in Schedule 6 to the Town and Country Planning (Scotland) Act 1945.

[7] See now the 1997 Act, Sch.15, para.8(b).

[8] *Newham London Borough Council v Benjamin* [1968] 1 W.L.R. 694, *per* Lord Denning at p.700.

[9] See the Land Compensation (Scotland) Act 1973, s.43(2).

[10] (1903) 5 F. 1174; 11 S.L.T. 263.

which the tenant may have had prior to displacement as a result of the acquiring authority's action. However, section 44 of the 1973 Act, reversing the effect of the decision of the House of Lords in *Rugby Joint Water Board v Shaw-Fox*[11] provides that no account is to be taken of the consequence of the acquiring authority's scheme on the nature of the interest being extinguished. Thus, as Gill says, "there is to be disregarded the vulnerability of the tenant to removal by notice to quit by virtue of section 22(2)(b) or section 24(1)(e) of the Agricultural Holdings (Scotland) Act 1991 or to resumption under a clause in the lease".[12]

In *Anderson v Moray District Council*[13] the yearly tenant of an agricultural holding was displaced to make way for council house development. In assessing the value of the unexpired term the tribunal had to estimate how long, having regard to the tenant's circumstances and the security of tenure afforded by the Agricultural Holdings Act, the tenant might remain in possession had the local authority not needed the land for council housing. The tribunal concluded on the evidence that in the absence of the local authority requirement, the land was near ripe for residential development. Provided the landlord had first obtained planning permission to develop the land for that purpose, he would have been able to terminate the tenancy not less than one year and not more than two years from the term date and what was then section 25(2)(c) of the Agricultural Holdings (Scotland) Act 1949 would then operate to dispense with the consent of the Land Court. The unexpired term was accordingly taken to be two years.

The reference to any just allowance and to all loss or injury in section 114 would seem to encompass the sort of matters that may be the subject of a disturbance claim under rule (6) (see Chap.10).[14] The whole claim must, however, be consistent within itself so that any claim for loss or injury must be based on the unexpired term.[15] It may be that loss incurred in anticipation of displacement is now recoverable.[16]

As regards severance and other injurious affection, the English Lands Tribunal in *Warlock v Sodbury Rural District Council*[17] held that compensation was not recoverable by a person in possession under a short tenancy in respect of other land held under a separate tenancy. That has now been changed as a result of the Planning and Compensation Act 1991 which amended section 114[18] so that, rather than referring to "in his tenancy", it now refers simply to damage done to him "by severing" lands held by him. Section 41 of the 1973 Act, reversing the effect of the decision in *Edwards v Minister of Transport*,[19] now provides that compen-

---

[11] [1973] A.C. 203.

[12] B. Gill, *The Law of Agricultural Holdings in Scotland* (3rd ed., W. Green & Son, 1997) para.32.03. For the position of crofters, landholders and statutory small tenants see the 1973 Act, s.45.

[13] 1978 S.L.T. (Lands Tr.) 37.

[14] For an illustration of the sort of items that might be comprised in such a claim see *Anderson v Moray District Council*, 1978 S.L.T. (Lands Tr.) 37.

[15] See *Greenwood Tyre Services Ltd v Manchester Corporation* (1971) 23 P. & C.R. 246.

[16] *Smith v Strathclyde Regional Council*, 1982 S.L.T. (Lands Tr.) 2; *Aberdeen District Council v Sim*, 1983 S.L.T. 250.

[17] (1961) 12 P. & C.R. 315.

[18] See Sch.17, para.1.

[19] [1964] 2 Q.B. 134.

sation for injurious affection will have regard to the whole of the work and not only the part situated on the land from which the tenant has been displaced.

HOME LOSS PAYMENTS

Sections 27 to 30 of the 1973 Act make provision for home loss **12–02** payments. The object of such payments is to make some recompense for the personal upset and distress which people suffer when they are compulsorily displaced from their homes. As Lord Widgery C.J. observed, the purpose of the payment is "to make some compensation to a man for the loss of his home as opposed to the loss of any interest he might have in the particular dwelling which he formerly occupied".[20] The provisions stem from a recommendation in the report of the Urban Motorways Committee that an additional head of compensation should be payable to the occupiers of dwellings in recognition of the real personal disturbance that is inflicted on them when they are required to move.[21] In the White Paper *Development and Compensation—Putting People First*,[22] the government acknowledged that "the principle of a lump sum payment of this sort, quite independent of the payment for the interest acquired" was right.

Section 27(1) provides that a person will be entitled to a home loss payment from the appropriate authority[23] where he is displaced from a dwelling on any land in consequence of:

(i) the compulsory acquisition of an interest in the dwelling;

(ii) the making, passing or acceptance of:

- demolition or closing order under Part VI of the Housing (Scotland) Act 1987 or an order under section 88 of that Act;
- a resolution under section 125 of the 1987 Act;
- an undertaking accepted under section 117(2)(a) of the 1987 Act; or
- a final resolution under Part I of Schedule 8 to the 1987 Act (s.36(1)(b))[24];

[20] *R. v Corby District Council, ex p. McLean* [1975] 1 W.L.R. 735 at p.736.

[21] *New Roads in Towns*, (1972) HMSO *Department of the Environment* paras 12.18–19. See, too, the discussion of consumer surplus in the *Final Report of the Commission on the Third London Airport* (1968–71) HMSO 1971. P. McAuslan, *The Ideologies of Planning Law* (Pergamon Press, 1980) views the carrot of more compensation in this and other provisions of the 1973 Act as very much a utilitarian measure designed to lessen opposition and objection to public works and so speed up development (see Chap.4).

[22] (1972) HMSO para.36 (Cmnd. 5124).

[23] *i.e.* the body responsible for displacement—see s.27(1) as amended by the Housing Act 1974, s.130 and Sch.13, para.42(1)(b); the Housing (Financial Provisions) (Scotland) Act 1978, Sch.2, para.12(a)(ii); and the Housing (Scotland) Act 1986, s.20(2)(b).

[24] See the 1973 Act, s.27(7), as amended first by the Housing (Scotland) Act 1974, Sch.3, para.48, and then by the Housing (Scotland) Act 1987, s.339 and Sch.23, para.19.

(iii) the carrying out of any improvement to the dwelling[25] or of redevelopment on the land[26] where the land has previously been acquired by an authority possessing compulsory purchase powers or appropriated by a local authority and is for the time being held by the authority for the purposes for which it was acquired or appropriated[27];

(iv) the carrying out of any improvement to the dwelling or of redevelopment on the land by a housing association which has previously acquired the land and at the date of displacement is registered[28];

(v) a requirement to remove from the building containing the dwelling as a result of action being taken in respect of a dangerous building under section 13 of the Building (Scotland) Act 1959 or any other enactment which requires the demolition of the building on account of its condition;[29]

(vi) an order for recovery of possession of the dwelling under section 16(2) of the Housing (Scotland) Act 2001 on the ground set out in paragraph 10 to Schedule 2.[30]

12–03   A person is not to be treated as displaced from a dwelling in consequence of the carrying out of any improvement to it or of a requirement to remove under section 13 of the Building (Scotland) Act 1957 unless he is permanently displaced from it (s.27(3A)).[31] Nor is a person to be treated as displaced from a dwelling in consequence of the compulsory acquisition of an interest if he gives up occupation of it before the date on which the acquiring authority were authorised to acquire the interest (s.27(3)). Apart from that, a person is entitled to a payment, whether or not he has been required by the authority to give up his occupation of the dwelling. Section 27(6) makes it clear that a

---

[25] See the Housing Act 1974, s.130 and Sch.13, para.42(1)(a).

[26] "Improvement" includes alteration and enlargement and "redevelopment" includes a change of use (s.27(7A) added by the Housing Act 1974, s.130 and Sch.13, para.42). In *R v Corby District Council, ex p. McLean* [1975] 1 W.L.R. 735 it was held that the carrying out of redevelopment in the corresponding provision in the English legislation would include the act of demolition which preceded the substitution of new buildings which were to come under a redevelopment scheme. The applicant was accordingly treated as displaced in consequence of the carrying out of redevelopment and thus entitled to a home loss payment. In *Greater London Council v Holmes* [1986] 1 All E.R. 739 the Court of Appeal held that in the circumstances of that case displacement to make way for demolition and clearance of property as an essential step in the sale and redevelopment of the land was displacement as a result of "redevelopment". See, too, *Follows v Peabody Trust* (1983) 10 H.L.R. 62.

[27] "Purposes for which it was required" refers to the broad and general purposes for which the authority acquired the land rather than the precise scheme envisaged at the time of acquisition (*Greater London Council v Holmes* [1986] 1 All E.R. 739).

[28] Substituted by the Housing Rents and Subsidies (Scotland) Act 1975, Sch.3, para.9(1).

[29] Added by the Housing (Financial Provisions) (Scotland) Act 1978, Sch.2, para.12(a)(i). From the date on which it comes into force the Buildings (Scotland) Act 2003 will replace the Act of 1959.

[30] Housing (Scotland) Act 2001, Sch.10, para.3 replacing s.48(2) and Sch.3, Part I, para.10 to the Housing (Scotland) Act 1987, s.15(2).

[31] Added by the Housing Act 1974, s.130, Sch.13, para.42(2).

tenant is entitled to a payment where the authority acquire the landlord's interest by agreement, provided he does not give up occupation before the date of the agreement.

The exclusion of home loss payments in cases where the acquisition follows the service of a blight notice cases has been removed.[32]

To qualify for a home loss payment, it used to be necessary for a person to show he had been in occupation of the dwelling for a period of five years preceding displacement. This qualifying period has now been reduced to a period of one year preceding displacement providing the claimant can show that:

(a) he has been in occupation of the dwelling or a substantial part of it, as his only or main residence; and

(b) he has been in such occupation by virtue of an interest or right to which section 27 applies (below).[33]

A person who has satisfied these requirements for less than the full qualifying period may count any immediately preceding period during which he has satisfied the requirements in another dwelling or in other dwellings. Account may also be taken of any immediately preceding period during which the claimant was resident in the dwelling as his only or main residence without satisfying the requirements but some other person or persons have satisfied those conditions.[34]

Where the claimant has successively occupied different rooms in the same building,[35] s.27(2) has effect as if these rooms constituted the same dwelling (s.29(5)).

The interests or rights to which section 27 applies are:

(i) any interest in the dwelling;

(ii) a right to occupy the dwelling under a statutory tenancy under the Rent (Scotland) Act 1984[36];

(iii) a right to occupy the dwelling under a contract to which Part VII of that Act applies or would apply if the contract or dwelling were not excluded by s.63(3)—(5) or under section 64(3) of that Act; and

(iv) a right of occupation under a contract of employment.[37]

If two or more persons are entitled to make a claim to a home loss payment in respect of the same dwelling, the payment to be made on

---

[32] Planning and Compensation Act 1991, s.71(2).

[33] 1973 Act, s.27(2) substituted by the Planning and Compensation Act 1991, s.71(1).

[34] 1973 Act, s.29(3) as substituted by the Planning and Compensation Act 1991, s.71(4).

[35] Section 27(6) refers to different "dwellings" being dwellings consisting of a room or rooms not constructed or adapted for use as a separate dwelling.

[36] s.117(1) and 1984 Act, Sch.8, Pt I.

[37] 1973 Act, s.27(4) as substituted in part by the Planning and Compensation Act 1991, Sch.17, para.20(3). As regards the occupation of a dwelling by a person beneficially entitled under a trust, see s.27(8) of the 1973 Act.

each claim will equal the whole amount of the home loss payment divided by the number of such persons (s.27(6)). An entitlement to an occupant's home loss payment is conferred on a spouse having occupancy rights in the matrimonial home.[38]

If a person entitled to a home loss payment dies without having claimed it, a claim may be made by any person, aged 18 or over, who throughout a period of not less than five years ending with the date of displacement of the deceased, resided in the dwelling or a substantial part of it as his only or main residence. That person must, however, be entitled to benefit by virtue of a testamentary disposition or other deed with testamentary effect taking effect on, or the operation of the law of intestacy as applied to, the death of the deceased (s.29(4)).[39]

The basis for assessing the home loss payment has been a matter of continuing debate. The Urban Motorways Committee considered whether such payments should be tailored to individual circumstances or whether they should be calculated on the basis of a generalised formula. Their conclusion was that the former would give rise to very considerable complexity.[40]

Section 28(1), therefore, initially adopted a generalised formula. The amount of a home loss payment was to be equal to the rateable value of the dwelling multiplied by a multiplier prescribed from time to time by the Secretary of State. The maximum amount of a payment was fixed at £1,500 and the minimum at £150. The adoption of the formula meant that, as Farrier and McAuslan pointed out,[41] the payment "bears no relationship at all to the value placed by this person on his house". It also seemed unfair that those displaced from dwellings with higher rateable values got more than those from dwellings with lower rateable values.

Following the abolition of domestic rateable values by the Abolition of Domestic Rates Etc. (Scotland) Act 1987, the government adopted the former maximum of £1,500 as a flat rate home loss payment with effect from April 1, 1989.[42]

In the same year the Royal Institution of Chartered Surveyors, in a report reviewing the compensation code, concluded that the time had come to pay an individual allowance in all cases of compulsory acquisition (not just dwellings), partly in recognition of the compulsory nature of the sale and partly to reflect personal loss and inconvenience. Publication of the report coincided with massive and strident opposition to a proposal by British Rail to build a high-speed rail link through Kent from the Channel Tunnel to Kings Cross. A consultation paper was issued by the government which invited comments on whether some

---

[38] 1973 Act, s.27A, added by the Planning and Compensation Act 1991, s.72.

[39] A person may also be entitled to benefit by virtue of a right to *jus relicti, jus relictae* or legitim out of the deceased's estate.

[40] *New Roads in Towns, supra,* para.12.19. But see the *Final Report of the RCommission on the Third London Airport, supra,* which attempted to quantify what it referred to as "consumer surplus".

[41] See "Compensation, Participation and the Compulsory Acquisition of 'Homes'," in *Compensation for Compulsory Acquisition,* J. F. Garner (ed), *supra.*

[42] See the Home Loss Payment (Specification of Amount) (Scotland) Regulations 1989, SI 1989/47.

further provision, apart from the home loss payment, would be appropriate for owner-occupiers displaced as a result of compulsory purchase.[43] In the end the government decided not to enlarge the scope of the payment but simply to increase its amount and its availability for persons displaced from dwellings.

The outcome was reflected in the Planning and Compensation Act **12–04** 1991 which, for occupiers, moved away from the flat rate payment back to a generalised formula. For an owner-occupier displaced from a dwelling, the amount of the home loss payment is now ten per cent of the market value of the interest subject to a maximum of £15,000 and a minimum of £1,500.[44] In any other case, for example a displaced tenant, the amount of the home loss payment is now a flat rate payment of £1,500.[45] These figures may be altered from time to time by the Scottish Ministers.[46]

The debate about the basis for assessing the home loss payment continues. On the one hand, it is not evident that people with cheaper homes necessarily experience a lesser degree of home loss than people with more expensive homes. On the other hand, the maximum of £15,000 could be seen as unfairly penalising those living in high value regions or in more substantial properties. CPPRAG noted the divergent views but was unable to reach unanimity on the way forward which it felt, in any event, was a policy matter for ministers.[47] They did, however, stress the importance of regular reviews of the amount payable in line with general movements in property prices.[48]

A claim for a home loss payment must be made in writing accompanied by such particulars as may be required to enable the responsible authority to determine both the entitlement to and the amount of the payment (s.29(1)).[49] The payment must be made on or before the latest of the following dates:

(a) the date of displacement;

(b) the last day of the period of three months beginning with the making of the claim; and

(c) where the amount of the payment is to be determined in accordance with s.28(1) (*i.e.* payment for an owner-occupier), the day on which the market value of the interest in question is agreed or finally determined.[50]

No reduction in the amount of compensation payable in respect of the compulsory acquisition of an interest is to be made on account of such

---

[43] "Land Compensation and Compulsory Purchase" SDD, 1989.

[44] 1973 Act, s.28(1) as substituted by the Planning and Compensation Act 1991, s.71(3).

[45] 1973 Act, s.28(2) as substituted by the Planning and Compensation Act 1991, s.71(3).

[46] 1973 Act, s.28(5) as substituted by the Planning and Compensation Act 1991, s.71(3).

[47] *Fundamental review of the laws and procedures relating to compulsory purchase and compensation: final report*, (2000) DETR paras.91–94.

[48] The Office of the Deputy Prime Minister has now issued a consultation paper reviewing the present thresholds ("Revision of Home-Loss Payments under the Land Compensation Act 1973" (2002)).

[49] As substituted by the Planning and Compensation Act 1991, s.71(4).

[50] 1973 Act, s.29(2) as substituted by the Planning and Compensation Act 1991, s.71(4).

payment (s.46(1) and (3)). Section 6 of the Prescription and Limitation (Scotland) Act 1973 applies to an obligation to make a home loss payment so as to extinguish the obligation in the absence of a claim at the expiration of five years from the date of displacement (s.29 (7A)).[51]

Where the claimant is an owner-occupier, the acquiring authority may at any time make an advance payment on the home loss payment (s.29(2A)(a)).[52] Such an advance must be made if the market value of the owner's interest has not been agreed or determined by the date of displacement or by the end of the period of three months beginning with the making of the claim, whichever is the later (s.29(2A)(b)). The amount of the advance is to be either the maximum prescribed amount for a home loss payment or ten per cent of the agreed value of the owner's interest or, failing agreement, ten per cent of the acquiring authority's estimate (whichever is less) (s.29(2B)). Provision is made for the subsequent payment or recovery of any shortfall or excess (s.29(2C)).

No entitlement to a home loss payment arises when an authority possessing compulsory purchase powers acquire an interest in a dwelling by agreement. However, in such circumstances, the authority have a discretion to make to the person from whom the interest is acquired a payment corresponding to a home loss payment or discretionary payment (s.29(7)).[53] SDD Circular 84/1973 indicates that this provision is intended for use only where there is an element of compulsion in the transaction. The effect of the provision, as McAuslan has pointed out, may be to penalise the cooperative person. By cooperating with the public authority, the person loses the statutory right to a home loss payment and has to rely on their discretion.[54]

Section 30 adapts the provisions for home loss payments and discretionary payments to the circumstances of a person residing in a caravan who is displaced from a caravan site[55] and for whom no suitable alternative site for stationing a caravan is available on reasonable terms.

The home loss payment is a move back towards the pre-1919 position where a supplement was paid to claimants on account of the compulsory nature of the acquisition (see Chapter 4). The Royal Institution of Chartered Surveyors recommended that the time had come to amend rule (1) of the Land Compensation Act rules which provides that no allowance shall be made on account of the acquisition being compulsory and that an additional allowance should be payable to *all* claimants to compensate for the factor of compulsion and in recognition that the

---

[51] Inserted by the Local Government, Planning and Land Act 1980, s.114(5)(6).

[52] Added by the Planning and Compensation Act 1991, s.71(4).

[53] As amended by the Planning and Compensation Act 1991, s.71(7). See s.27(6) (above) as regards the position of a tenant where the landlord's interest is acquired by agreement. See, too, s.29 (7AA) added by the Housing (Scotland) Act 1986, s.20 and subsequently amended by the Housing (Scotland) Act 1987, Sch.23, para.19.

[54] P. McAuslan, *Ideologies of Planning Law, supra*, p.115. And see the consultation paper *Land Compensation and Compulsory Purchase Legislation* (Scottish Development Department, 1989) para.9.

[55] "Caravan site" means land on which a caravan is stationed for the purpose of human habitation and land which is used in conjunction with land on which a caravan is so stationed (s.30(7)).

claimant is an unwilling seller.[56] CPPRAG accepted the case for a business-loss payment in terms of parity with residential occupiers but skewed in favour of small businesses[57] and this recommendation has received sympathetic consideration from the DTLR (see p.101 above).[58]

DISTURBANCE PAYMENTS

When premises are subject to a tenancy, an acquiring authority may, as **12–05** mentioned earlier (see p.254), purchase the landlord's interest and leave the tenancy to expire when possession is required by effluxion of time. In that event, the tenant has no entitlement to compensation for there has been neither a compulsory acquisition, nor a compulsory extinguishment of the interest; merely a termination under the contractual terms of the tenancy. Yet in practice the disturbance suffered by the tenant in these circumstances may be very similar to that experienced upon compulsory acquisition. He may incur removal expenses and other business losses.

The potential hardship arising from this "notorious defect in compensation law"[59] was recognised in section 38 of the Land Compensation (Scotland) Act 1963 which conferred a discretionary power upon acquiring authorities to pay to a person displaced from premises in such circumstances a reasonable allowance towards expenses in removing and towards disturbance of any trade or business being carried on by him in the premises. It is in the nature of discretionary powers that their application tends to be uneven and JUSTICE, in their review of the compensation provisions for compulsory purchase, suggested that "[i]f justice requires that it be paid, it should be paid as a matter of right".[60] This suggestion was taken up in the subsequent White Paper *Development and Compensation—Putting People First*[61] and the entitlement to what is described as a "disturbance payment" was conferred by sections 34 and 35 of the 1973 Act.

The sections provide that where a person suffers loss and expense because of displacement from any land, other than land used for the purposes of agriculture (s.34 (6)), in consequence of specified public sector actions (below), he will be entitled to receive a disturbance payment from the appropriate authority.[62] The specified actions are similar to those which may trigger a home loss payment (above)

---

[56] "Compensation for Compulsory Acquisition" 1995, paras 1.4–1.15. See too City University Business School, "The Operation of Compulsory Purchase Orders" (1996) *Department of the Environment* paras.6.3–6.7; and J Rowan Robinson and N Hutchison, "Compensation for the compulsory acquisition of business interests: satisfaction or sacrifice" 1995 *Journal of Property Valuation and Investment* 13(1), p.44.

[57] "Fundamental review of the laws and procedures relating to compulsory purchase and compensation: final report" (2000) DETR paras 95–97.

[58] "Compulsory purchase and compensation: delivering a fundamental change" (2001) paras 3.16–3.19.

[59] Lands Tribunal for Scotland in *Woolfson v Strathclyde Regional Council*, 1976 S.L.T. (Lands Tr.) 5.

[60] "Compensation for Compulsory Acquisition and Remedies for Planning Restrictions together with a Supplemental Report" (1973) *Stevens* para.113.

[61] (1972) HMSO paras 47 and 50 (Cmnd. 5124).

[62] Defined in s.34(1).

although in this case they may be directed not just at dwellings but at other buildings. They are:

(i) the acquisition of the land by an authority possessing compulsory purchase powers[63];

(ii) the making, passing or acceptance in respect of a house or building on the land of—

- a demolition or closing order under Part VI of the Housing (Scotland) Act 1987 or an order under section 88 of that Act or,
- a resolution under section 125 of the 1987 Act or,
- a final resolution under Part I of Schedule 8 to the 1987 Act (s.34(1)(b))[64];

(iii) the carrying out of any improvement to a house or building on the land,[65] or of redevelopment on the land[66] where the land has previously been acquired by an authority possessing compulsory purchase powers or appropriated by a local authority and is for the time being held by the authority for the purposes for which it was acquired or appropriated (s.34(1)(c))[67];

(iv) the carrying out of any improvement to a house or building on the land or of redevelopment on the land by a housing association which has previously acquired the land and at the date of displacement is registered (s.34(1)(d))[68];

(v) a requirement to remove from a building on the land as a result of action being taken in respect of a dangerous building under section 13 of the Building (Scotland) Act 1959 or any other enactment which requires the demolition of the building on account of its condition (s.34(1)(e)).[69]

---

[63] In *Smith & Waverley Tailoring Co. v Edinburgh District Council (No. 2)*, 1977 S.L.T. (Lands Tr.) 29, the Lands Tribunal for Scotland were prepared to treat a claimant as displaced in consequence of the acquisition of land even though the claimant was allowed to remain in occupation for several years following acquisition. The acquisition was the real cause of ultimate displacement.

[64] See ss.27(7) and 34(8) of the 1973 Act as amended first by the Housing (Scotland) Act 1974, Sch.3, para.48 and then by the Housing (Scotland) Act 1987, s.339 and Sch.23, para.19.

[65] See the Housing Act 1974, s.130 and Sch.13, para.43(1)(a). The displacement must be permanent (s.34(3)).

[66] "Improvement" includes alteration and enlargement and "redevelopment" includes a change of use (ss.27(7A) and 34(8) of the 1973 Act added by the Housing Act 1974, s.130 and Sch.13, para.42). See *R. v Corby District Council, ex p. McLean* [1975] 1 W.L.R. 735; *Greater London Council v Holmes* [1986] 1 All E.R. 739; and *Follows v Peabody Trust* (1983) 10 H.L.R. 62.

[67] See *Greater London Council v Holmes* [1980] 1 All E.R. 735.

[68] Substituted by the Housing Rents and Subsidies (Scotland) Act 1975, Sch.3, para.10(1).

[69] Added by the Housing (Financial Provisions) (Scotland) Act 1978, Sch.2, para.13(a)(i). The displacement must be permanent (s.34(3)). From the date on which it comes into force, the Building (Scotland) Act 2003 will replace the 1959 Act.

In *Prasad v Wolverhampton Borough Council*[70] the Court of Appeal held that the words "displaced from any land in consequence of" were to be construed causatively rather than temporally so that where a person threatened with inevitable dispossession because of compulsory purchase acted reasonably in moving to other accommodation before he was given notice to treat, or before his land was actually acquired by compulsory purchase, he was displaced in consequence of the acquisition within the meaning of the corresponding English legislation.[71] In *Millar v Strath-clyde Regional Council*[72] the Lands Tribunal for Scotland concluded that a similar causal connection existed between the acquisition and prior displacement so as to entitle the claimants in that case to a disturbance payment.

In *Hyland v Castlemilk East Housing Co-operative Ltd*[73] the Lands Tribunal for Scotland held that a claimant, who was decanted temporarily from her house during the carrying out of repairs and improvements and who chose to move permanently to another part of Glasgow, had not established that her move was a consequence of displacement so that there was no entitlement to a disturbance payment. On the other hand, in *Beattie v Monklands District Council*[74] a claimant, who was displaced from her council house and who arranged with another tenant to exchange her offered replacement house for one she preferred, was held to have been displaced to the preferred house and entitled to a disturbance payment.

To qualify for a disturbance payment a claimant must show that he was in lawful possession of the land from which he was displaced (s.34(2)(a)).

In *Wrexham Maelor Borough Council v Macdougall*[74a] the Court of Appeal held that the word 'lawful' in the corresponding English provision imported no more than that possession should not be unlawful; and the word 'possession' was not based on an interest in the land but meant physical occupation with the intention to exclude unauthorised intruders. And in *Smith and Waverley Tailoring Co. v Edinburgh District Council (No. 2)*[75] the Lands Tribunal for Scotland similarly took the view that a person who occupies premises with the consent of the proprietor of the premises is in "lawful possession" of them even though he has no legal title beyond the proprietor's consent. In *Prasad* Stephenson L.J.

---

[70] (1983) 265 E.G. 1073. Stephenson L.J., with whom Fox L.J. and Kerr L.J. agreed, was strongly influenced in his conclusion by the decisions of the Lands Tribunal for Scotland in *Smith v Strathclyde Regional Council*, 1982 S.L.T. (Lands Tr.) 2 and of the Court of Session in *Sim v Aberdeen District Council*, 1983 S.L.T. 250 on the scope of disturbance compensation which he regarded "as of high persuasive authority on a point of law which affects many inhabitants on each side of the Border" (see Ch.10). See too *Paul v Newham London Borough Council* (1991) 61 P. & C.R. 126.

[71] For a discussion of the decision in *Prasad* see W. A. Leach, "Disturbance—the 'Prasad' case" (1983) 267 E.G. 669.

[72] 1988 S.L.T. (Lands Tr.) 9.

[73] Lands Tribunal for Scotland, unreported, May 5, 1993, (but see (1993) 40 S.P.E.L. 85).

[74] Lands Tribunal for Scotland, unreported, May 15, 1992, (but see (1992) 37 S.P.L.P. 82).

[74a] (1995) 69 P. & C.R. 109.

[75] 1977 S.L.T. (Lands Tr.) 29. See, too, *Millar v Strathclyde Regional Council*, 1988 S.L.T. (Lands Tr.) 9.

referring to the use of the word "displaced" in the corresponding English legislation observed that "[i]f its use instead of 'dispossessed' has any significance, it is to get rid of the notion which 'dispossessed' might convey, that what is being considered is the termination of legal possession as opposed to actual possession, the ending of rights and interests in the land as opposed to occupation of it".[76]

Where a person is displaced in consequence of the acquisition of land he must show in order to qualify for a payment that he has no interest in the land for the acquisition or extinguishment of which he would be entitled to compensation under any other enactment (s.34(2)(b)).[77] Alternatively, if he has such an interest, it must be one for which compensation is subject to a site value provision and he must not be entitled to an owner-occupier's supplement (see Chap.10). Similarly, where the displacement is in consequence of the making, passing or acceptance of a housing order, resolution or undertaking, there must be no entitlement to an owner-occupier's supplement (see Chap.10).

12–06   In the case of displacement in the circumstances set out in section 34(1)(a), (c) or (d), a claimant must also show, in the case of land acquired under a compulsory purchase order, that he was in lawful possession not only at the date of displacement but at the time when notice of the *making* of the order was first published or, if it is an order which does not require confirmation, at the time of the preparation of the order in draft.[78] In the case of land acquired by agreement the relevant time is when the agreement was made (s.34(3)). In *R. v Islington London Borough Council, ex p. Knight*[79] a claimant who surrendered her secure tenancy on the allocation of a new house by the local authority was held not to be entitled to a disturbance payment. The surrender of the tenancy extinguished her interest; there was no acquisition by agreement. In the case of displacement under section 34(1)(b) or (e), the claimant must have been in lawful possession at the time when the order was made, the resolution was passed, the undertaking was accepted or he was required to move (s.34(3)).

Where a person is displaced from any land in the circumstances mentioned in section 34(1) but has no entitlement to a disturbance payment or to compensation for disturbance under any other Act the authority responsible for displacement may make a discretionary disturbance payment (s.34(4)). If the authority decide to make such a payment, the amount is determined in accordance with the provisions of section 35(1) to (3) (below).[80]

---

[76] (1983) 265 E.G. 1073 at p.1078.

[77] See *Smith & Waverley Tailoring Co. v Edinburgh District Council (No.2)*, 1977 S.L.T. (Lands Tr.) 29.

[78] In the case of land acquired under an Act specifying the land as subject to compulsory acquisition, the relevant time is when the provisions of the Bill for that Act were first published (s.34(3)(b)).

[79] [1984] 1 All E.R. 154.

[80] 1973 Act, s.34(4). Any dispute as to the amount of a discretionary payment is not a matter which falls within the jurisdiction of the Lands Tribunal for Scotland (*City of Glasgow District Council v Mackie*, 1993 S.L.T. 213, IH disagreeing with the Court of Appeal in *Gozra v Hackney London Borough* (1988) 46 E.G. 87).

The amount of a disturbance payment is to be equal to the reasonable expenses of the person incurred in removing from the land (s.35(1)(a))[81]; and, if the person was carrying on a trade or business on the land, the loss that will be sustained as a result of the disturbance of that trade or business consequent on having to quit the land (s.35(1)(b)). In estimating trade or business loss, regard must be had to the period for which the land might reasonably have been expected to be available for that purpose and to the availability of other land suitable for that purpose (s.35(2)).[82]

In *Glasgow Corporation v Anderson*[83] the First Division held that the term "expenses in removing" in section 35(1)(a) was to be construed more generously than "any expenses in the removal". In that case a tenant was displaced from a house in good decorative condition. The local authority flat to which she moved required a certain amount of necessary decoration. In addition as the flat was all electric, she had to buy and instal a small electric cooker. Her claim for removal expenses, the cost of reconnecting the telephone and of lifting, removing and refitting carpets was accepted by the corporation. Her claim in respect of redecoration, curtain rails, new plugs and the electric cooker was rejected. These items were allowed, although the amount for the cooker was reduced, by the Lands Tribunal for Scotland whose decision was subsequently affirmed by the First Division. Lord President Emslie said:

> "In all these circumstances, it is not unreasonable, when one comes to construe section 35(1)(a) in a common sense way, in the context in which it is set, to conclude that a disturbance payment may include reasonable expenses, reasonably incurred as a direct and natural consequence of and in, the compulsory removing, in addition to the expenses strictly referable to 'the removal' itself. In applying the subsection, the question of whether a particular expense claimed is or is not within the ambit of the disturbance payment will be one of circumstance and degree."[84]

And Lord Cameron observed that the payment "should in a true sense be a 'disturbance payment' and not the mere cost of the removal operation". The decision of the First Division was cited by the English Lands Tribunal in *Nolan v Sheffield Metropolitan District Council* in reaching a similar conclusion about the scope of "expenses . . . in removing".[85] And in *Evans v Glasgow District Council*[86] the Lands

---

[81] It must be doubtful whether the provision is wide enough to cover the cost of any structural modifications to the new accommodation (*Glasgow Corporation v Anderson,* 1976 S.L.T. 225; *Nolan v Sheffield Metropolitan District Council* (1979) 38 P. & C.R. 741); and *Cahill v Monklands District Council,* unreported, May 15, 1992 Lands Tribunal for Scotland (but see (1992) 37 S.P.L.P. 82).

[82] As regards a disturbance payment where a business is carried on by a person over the age of 60—see 1973 Act, s.43(7).

[83] 1976 S.L.T. 225.

[84] See above at p.229. See, too, Lord Cameron at p.230. In *Bryson v Glasgow District Council,* Lands Tribunal for Scotland, unreported, April 24, 1992, (but see (1992) 37 S.P.L.P. 82) a claimant was held to be entitled to claim for replacement carpets because the old carpets were damaged as a consequence of removal.

[85] (1979) 38 P. & C.R. 741.

[86] 1978 S.L.T. (Lands Tr.) 5.

Tribunal for Scotland held that Lord Emslie's broad approach was also applicable in construing the other head of a disturbance payment—trade or business loss under section 35(1)(b) of the 1973 Act. The general approach in assessing this form of disturbance payment was the same as for a rule (6) claim (see Chap.10) and the remoteness test considered in *Harvey v Crawley Development Corporation*[87] and in *Anderson* applied. The tribunal cautioned, however, that the precise wording of section 35 might operate more restrictively in some cases than the general nature of the test in *Harvey*. "[I]t would be unwise," said the tribunal, "to commit ourselves in this particular case to any general proposition that disturbance claims under rule (6) and disturbance payments under section 35, following upon compulsory dispossession, are in all respects identical when it comes to assessing quantum".

When displacement is from a dwelling to which structural modifications have been made to meet the needs of a disabled person[88] and a local authority having duties under section 12 of the Social Work (Scotland) Act 1968 provided assistance in such modifications, or would have done so if an application had been made, the amount of the disturbance payment is to include an amount equal to the reasonable expenses incurred by the claimant in making comparable modifications to the dwelling to which the disabled person removes (s.35(3)).

A disturbance payment will carry interest at the rate for the time being prescribed under section 40 of the 1963 Act from the date of displacement until payment (s.34(5)).

Any dispute as to the amount of a disturbance payment is to be referred to and determined by the Lands Tribunal for Scotland (s.35(4)).

REHOUSING

12–07   Section 36 of the 1973 Act provides that where, in the circumstances described below, a person[89] is displaced from residential accommodation on any land and suitable residential accommodation on reasonable terms is not otherwise available to that person then the local housing authority[90] have a duty to secure the provision of such accommodation.[91] The duty arises where a person is displaced[92] in consequence of:

---

[87] [1957] 1 Q.B. 485.

[88] Whether or not this is the person entitled to the disturbance payment.

[89] The provision does not apply to a person trespassing on the land or who has been permitted to reside in a house or building pending its improvement or demolition (s.36(3) of the 1973 Act, as amended by the Housing Act 1974, s.130 and Sch.13, para.44).

[90] Defined in s.36(7), as amended by the Housing (Scotland) Act 1987, s.339 and Sch.23, para.19 and the Local Government etc (Scotland) Act 1994, s.183.

[91] In *R. v Bristol Corporation, ex p. Hendy* [1974] 1 All E.R. 1047 the Court of Appeal took the view that the duty in the corresponding provision in the English legislation was a duty to act reasonably and to do their best as soon as practicable to provide suitable alternative accommodation. In the meantime, the authority discharged their obligation under the legislation by providing temporary accommodation. See E. Young, "Rehousing Displaced Householders", 1979 *SCOLAG* 76.

[92] In *Glasgow District Council v Douglas*, unreported, November 16, 1978, Glasgow Sheriff Court, Sheriff Irvine Smith took the view that the rehousing obligation did not arise prior to displacement but only when the local authority obtained possession of the house. See E. Young, "Rehousing Displaced Householders," 1979 *SCOLAG* 76.

(a) the acquisition of the land by an authority possessing compulsory purchase powers (s.36(1)(a));

(b) the making, passing or acceptance of: (i) a demolition or closing order under Part VI of the Housing (Scotland) Act 1987 or an order under section 88 of that Act; (ii) a resolution under section 125 of the 1987 Act; (iii) an undertaking accepted under section 117(2)(a) of the 1987 Act; or (iv) a final resolution under Part I of Schedule 8 to the 1987 Act (s.36(1)(b))[93];

(c) the carrying out of any improvement to a house or building on the land or of redevelopment on the land[94] previously acquired by an authority possessing compulsory purchase powers or appropriated by a local authority and held for the time being for the purpose for which it was acquired or appropriated (s.36(1)(c));

(d) a requirement to remove the building containing the residential accommodation in pursuance of section 13 of the Building (Scotland) Act 1959 or any other enactment which requires the demolition of the building on account of its condition (s.36(1)(d)).[95]

In an area designated as the site of a new town the rehousing obligation falls upon the development corporation for displacement arising from the acquisition of land by the corporation or the redevelopment of land held by it (s.36(8)).[96]

The duty to rehouse does not arise where the acquisition is in pursuance of a blight notice served under section 101 of the Town and Country Planning (Scotland) Act 1997 (s.36(2)).[97] Nor does it extend to a person who has been displaced in the circumstances described and to whom money has been advanced either under section 38 of the 1973 Act (see below) to acquire or construct a substitute dwelling or under the Small Dwellings Acquisition (Scotland) Acts 1899 to 1923 or section 214 of the Housing (Scotland) Act 1987[98] or by a development corporation otherwise than under section 38 of the 1973 Act.[99]

A person is not to be treated as displaced in consequence of any such acquisition, improvement or redevelopment as is mentioned in section

---

[93] Defined in s.27(7) of the 1973 Act, as amended first by the Housing (Scotland) Act 1974, Sch.3, para.48 and then by the Housing (Scotland) Act 1987, s.339 and Sch.23, para.19.

[94] "Improvement" includes alteration and enlargement and "redevelopment" includes a change of use (s.27(7A) of the 1973 Act added by the Housing Act 1974, s.130 and Sch.13, para.42).

[95] Section 13 of the Building (Scotland) Act 1959 makes provision for action to be taken in respect of buildings found to be dangerous. From the date on which it comes into force the Building (Scotland) Act 2003 will replace the 1959 Act.

[96] Note that the new town development corporations were all wound up and dissolved under the provisions of the Enterprise and New Towns (Scotland) Act 1990, Pt II.

[97] See Chap.14.

[98] Added by the Housing (Scotland) Act 1987, s.339 and Sch.23, para.19 and amended by the Housing (Scotland) Act 2001, s.112 and Sch.10, para.13.

[99] Section 36(4) of the 1973 Act. There are now no development corporations.

36(1)(a) or (c) (above) unless he was residing in the accommodation in question: (a) in the case of land acquired under a compulsory purchase order, at the time when notice of the making or preparation in draft, as the case may be, of the order was first published (s.36(6)(a)); (b) in the case of land acquired under an Act specifying the land as subject to compulsory acquisition, at the time when the provisions of the Bill for the Act specifying the land were first published (s.36(6)(b)); (c) in the case of land acquired by agreement, at the time the agreement was made (s.36(6)(c)).

Neither is a person to be treated as displaced in consequence of an order, resolution, undertaking or requirement mentioned in s.36(1)(b) or (d) (above) unless he was residing in the accommodation at the time the order was made, the resolution was passed, the undertaking was given, or he was required to move.[1]

Section 37 of the 1973 Act imposes on local housing authorities a similar rehousing obligation in relation to a person displaced from a residential caravan on a caravan site[2] for whom neither suitable residential accommodation nor a suitable alternative site for stationing a caravan is available on reasonable terms.

SDD Circular 84/1973 recognises that many local authorities already voluntarily accept responsibility for rehousing in circumstances which go beyond the statutory requirements in the Act or in earlier legislation. The circular states that the Scottish Ministers: "would not wish the introduction of the new obligations to lead these authorities to adopt less generous practices. He is sure that all authorities will adopt as sympathetic an attitude as possible, bearing in mind the housing situation in their particular area, to the difficulties of displaced occupiers falling outside the scope of section 36."[3]

Section 38 of the 1973 Act enables the local housing authority, subject to such conditions as may be approved by the Scottish Ministers, to satisfy the rehousing obligation by making advances repayable on maturity to displaced residential owner-occupiers. Such an advance may be made where an owner-occupier[4] of a dwelling is displaced from it in any of the circumstances mentioned in section 36(1)(a), (b) or (c) (above) and wishes to acquire or construct another dwelling in substitution for the one from which he has been displaced. The advance will be made on terms providing for the repayment of the principal at the end of a fixed period which may be extended by the authority or upon notice given by the authority, subject in either case to provision for earlier repayment on the happening of a specified event, for example, the sale of the property or the death of the borrower. An advance may be made on such other terms as the authority think fit having regard to all the circumstances. SDD Circular 84/1973 suggests that this would, for example, permit an authority to transfer the advance, as secured, to a spouse or other adult member of the household on the death of the

---

[1] Section 36(6) as amended by the Housing (Financial provisions) (Scotland) Act 1978, Sch.2, para.14(b).

[2] As defined in s.30(7) of the 1973 Act.

[3] Para.34.

[4] Defined in s.38(9) of the 1973 Act.

borrower. An advance for the construction of a dwelling may be made by instalments linked to progress with the work.

The principal of the advance, together with the interest on it, is to be secured by way of a heritable security on the borrower's interest in the dwelling. The amount of the principal is not to exceed the value of the borrower's interest or, as the case may be, the value when the dwelling has been constructed. The authority must satisfy themselves that the dwelling to be acquired meets or will meet the tolerable standard.[5]

Where the displacing authority and the rehousing authority are not one and the same, section 39 of the 1973 Act provides for the former to indemnify the latter against any net loss incurred[6] in providing or securing the provision of accommodation for any person in pursuance of section 36(1)(a) or (c) of the Act. Similar provision is made for indemnifying a net loss incurred[7] in respect of an advance made under section 38 of the Act.

Section 40 provides that where a person displaced from a dwelling[8] in consequence of any of the events specified in section 36(1)(a) to (c) has no interest in the dwelling or no greater interest than as tenant for a year or from year to year and that person wishes to acquire another dwelling as a substitute, the displacing authority may pay any reasonable expenses incurred in connection with the acquisition, other than the purchase price. The substitute dwelling must be acquired[9] not later than one year after displacement and must be reasonably comparable with that from which the person has been displaced. SDD Circular 84/1973 suggests that such expenses might include legal and removal expenses, a contribution towards the cost of alterations to furnishings, etc., to fit the new house and telephone reconnection costs.

Section 46(1) of the 1973 Act prohibits the reduction of compensation payable in respect of the compulsory acquisition of an interest in land on account of the provision or the securing of provision by the acquiring authority of alternative residential accommodation for the person entitled to the compensation.

AGRICULTURAL LAND

Although compensation claims by owners and occupiers of agricultural **12–08** land are determined in accordance with the rules described earlier in this book, there are a number of special provisions relating to such claims which, for convenience, are drawn together in this section.[10]

1. An owner-occupier

An owner-occupier of agricultural land will be entitled to claim under **12–09** section 61 of the 1845 Act for the value of the land taken measured according to rule (2), for disturbance and, where appropriate, for

---

[5] As defined in the Housing (Scotland) Act 1987, s.86 as amended by the Housing Act 2001, s.102(1).
[6] Defined in s.39(2) of the 1973 Act.
[7] Defined in s.39(4) of the 1973 Act.
[8] As regards displacement, see s.36(3) and (6) as applied by s.40(4) of the 1973 Act.
[9] A dwelling acquired pursuant to a contract is to be treated as acquired when the contract is made (s.40(3)).
[10] See, generally, R. N. D. Hamilton, *Compensation for Compulsory Acquisition of Agricultural Land* (3rd ed., RICS, 1980).

severance and other injurious affection. He may also be entitled to a home loss payment (above). In addition, he may be entitled to what is called a "farm loss payment."

The White Paper *Development and Compensation—Putting People First*[11] acknowledged that "because of the long time-scale of agricultural production, its peculiar dependence on land and the complex effects of climatic and other factors on yield, owner-occupiers who lose the whole of their farms and have to move to unfamiliar land may be faced with temporary unavoidable losses". To meet this difficulty a payment, in addition to compensation, was proposed for persons displaced from agricultural land. The provisions for what are called "farm loss payments" were introduced in sections 31 to 33 of the 1973 Act.

Section 31 provides that an owner-occupier[12] of land constituted or included in an agricultural unit[13] will be entitled to a farm loss payment from the acquiring authority if, in consequence of the compulsory acquisition of his interest in the whole or a sufficient part[14] of that land, he is displaced from the land acquired[15] and not more than three years after the date of displacement he begins to farm another agricultural unit elsewhere in Great Britain (s.31(1)).[16] An "owner's interest" means the interest of an owner or a lessee under a lease where his interest is as a lessee for a year or from year to year or a greater interest, or the interest of a crofter or landholder (s.31(2)).[17]

A person is to be treated as displaced from land if, and only if, he gives up possession either on being required to do so by the acquiring authority or on any date after the making or confirmation of the compulsory purchase order but before being required to do so by the acquiring authority, on completion of the acquisition or, where the acquiring authority permit him to continue temporarily in possession, either under a lease of a kind not making him a tenant as defined in the Agricultural Holdings (Scotland) Act 1991 or under a right or permission not amounting to an estate or interest in the land, on the expiration of that lease, right or permission (s.31(3)).[18] There is no entitlement to a farm loss payment if he acquired the interest in or the lease of the new

---

[11] (1972) HMSO para.55 (Cmnd. 5124).

[12] Where the agricultural unit containing the land is occupied for the purposes of a partnership, see s.33(2).

[13] As defined in s.122(1) of the Town and Country Planning (Scotland) Act 1997.

[14] A "sufficient part" means not less than 0.5 ha or such other area as the Scottish Ministers may specify (Planning and Compensation Act 1991, Sch.17, para.14(3)(b)).

[15] 1973 Act, s.31(1)(a) as substituted by the Planning and Compensation Act 1991, Sch.17, para.14(2).

[16] On the date on which he begins to farm the new unit he must be in occupation of the *whole* of that unit as owner or as lessee but the interest in the new unit does not have to correspond with that which he enjoyed in that unit from which he has been displaced; it would be sufficient, it seems, to have no more than a yearly tenancy of the new unit (s.31(4)).

[17] As amended by the Planning and Compensation Act 1991, Sch.17, para.14(3)(a). For the definitions of "crofter" and "landholder" see s.80(1). A short term tenant of an agricultural holding may be entitled to a "reorganisation payment" (see p.278).

[18] As amended by the Planning and Compensation Act 1991, Sch.17, para.14(5). A farmer whose interest is acquired following the service of an effective blight notice is entitled to a farm loss payment if the other criteria are satisfied (1991 Act, Sch.17, para.14(6) repealing the 1973 Act, s.31(6)).

unit before the date on which the acquisition of his original unit was authorised (s.31(4)).

No farm loss payment is to be made as a result of displacement from land of a person who is entitled to a payment under section 56 of the Agricultural Holdings (Scotland) Act 1991.[19]

The formula for calculating the farm loss payment is set out in section 32. The payment is to equal the average annual profit derived from the use for agricultural purposes of the agricultural land comprised in the land acquired. The average is to be computed by reference to the profits for the three years ending with the date of displacement or for the period during which the person displaced was in occupation, whichever is the shorter (s.32(1)).[20] Where a person has been permitted by the acquiring authority to continue temporarily in possession of the original unit and on the date of eventual displacement he has been in occupation of that unit for more than three years, he may elect to compute the annual average profit by reference to the profits, not for the last three years, but for any 3 consecutive periods of 12 months during which he was in occupation and for which accounts have been made up, the last of which ends on or after the date of completion of the acquisition; or, if there are no such periods, by reference to the profits for any three consecutive years for which he has been in occupation, the last of which ends as before (s.32(3)).

In calculating the profits, there is to be deducted a sum equal to the **12–10** notional rent that might reasonably be expected to be payable in respect of the agricultural land comprised in the land acquired if it was let for agricultural purposes to a tenant responsible for rates, repairs and other outgoings. The deduction is to be made whether or not the land is in fact let; and if it is let, no deduction is to be made for the rent actually payable (s.32(4)). There must also be left out of account loss of profits from any activity in respect of which an item would fall to be included in the compensation for disturbance; such loss of profits cannot be counted for both the disturbance claim and for the farm loss payment (s.32(5)).

If the value of the agricultural land comprised in the original unit exceeds the value of such land in the new unit, the farm loss payment is to be proportionately reduced (s.32(6)). When comparing values, the assessment is to be made on the basis of an owner's interest with vacant possession in the land valued solely for agriculture purposes. Account must also be taken of the condition of the land and its surroundings and to prices current, as regards the land comprised in the land acquired, on the date of displacement and, as regards land comprised in the new unit, on the date on which the person concerned begins to farm the new unit. Rules (2) to (4) of section 12 of the 1963 Act (see Chap.6) apply. And the valuation is to be made without regard to the principal dwelling, if any, comprised in the same agricultural unit (s.32(7)).

---

[19] Section 56 of the 1991 Act makes provision for a "reorganisation payment" to be made where an acquiring authority acquire the interest in the whole or part of an agricultural holding of the tenant or take possession of the whole or part of the holding (see p.278).

[20] If the claimant's 12 months' accounting period ends not more than one year before the date of displacement, the date on which that period ends is to be treated as the date of displacement for the purposes of s.32(1).

An upper limit is placed on the amount of a farm loss payment. Section 32(8) provides that it is not to be greater than the amount by which the payment together with compensation for the acquisition of the interest acquired assessed on the basis of the assumptions referred to in section 5(2) to (4) of the 1973 Act[21] (including any sum for disturbance) exceeds the compensation actually payable for the acquisition of the interest. In other words, where the farm loss payment together with compensation assessed on the value of the land put to its existing use (plus disturbance) exceeds the compensation assessed on the basis of the open market value of the land, the payment is limited to the difference.

Any dispute as to the amount of a farm loss payment is to be determined by the Lands Tribunal for Scotland (s.32(9)).

A claim for such a payment, which may include any reasonable valuation or legal expenses incurred in preparing and prosecuting the claim (s.33(5)), must be lodged by the person entitled[22] in writing within a year of the date on which he began to farm the new unit (s.33(1)). The claim is to be accompanied by sufficient information to enable the acquiring authority to determine both entitlement and amount. A farm loss payment will carry interest at the prescribed rate (see p.283) from the date on which the claimant begins to farm the new unit until payment (s.33(6)).

Where an interest in land is acquired by agreement by an authority possessing compulsory purchase powers there is no entitlement to a farm loss payment but the authority have a discretion to make a corresponding payment (s.33(4)). The vendor should seek to ensure at the time of acquisition that such a payment will be made if he begins farming a new unit within the stipulated three year period.

CPPRAG received evidence that the farm loss provisions are used infrequently because the tight criteria which have to be fulfilled ignore modern farming practice. The Group expressed considerable sympathy with the concerns expressed but considered that the remedy lay, not in the reform of the farm loss payment, but in their proposal for a business loss payment (see p.101), which would include agriculturally based businesses, and in the proposed statutory but flexible right to disturbance compensation (see p.205).[23]

2. A Landlord

12–11   Where agricultural land is let, the landlord will be entitled upon the compulsory acquisition of his interest to compensation under section 61 of the 1845 Act for the value of his interest in the land taken assessed in

---

[21] The effect of s.5(2)–(4) of the 1973 Act, as amended by the Planning and Compensation Act 1991, Sch.13, para.32, is that planning permission may only be assumed for the classes of development specified in what is now Schedule 11 to the Town and Country Planning (Scotland) Act 1997. It may not be assumed that planning permission for Schedule 11 development would be granted where such development is the subject of a discontinuance order made under section 71 of the 1997 Act in respect of which compensation has become payable. If planning permission has in fact been granted for development other than Schedule 11 development, it is to be assumed that no such permission has been granted for development that has not been carried out.

[22] Where a person, who would have been entitled to a farm loss payment, dies before the expiration of the period for making a claim, a claim may be lodged before the expiration of that period by his personal representative (s.33(3)).

[23] "Fundamental review of the laws and procedures relating to compulsory purchase and compensation" (2000) DETR paras.149–150.

accordance with rule (2). As he is not in occupation, he is not entitled to disturbance (see Ch.10); but he may claim under section 17A of the Land Compensation (Scotland) Act 1963 for incidental charges and expenses incurred in acquiring replacement land within the UK.[24] As he is not in occupation, he is not entitled to a home loss payment or a farm loss payment (above). In an appropriate case, he will, however, be entitled to claim in respect of severance and other injurious affection.

In assessing the value of the landlord's interest regard must be had to section 44 of the Land Compensation (Scotland) Act 1973. It provides that the security of tenure which the tenant would enjoy were the land not required for use by the acquiring authority is to be taken into account. The provision reverses the effect of the House of Lords decision in *Rugby Joint Water Board v Shaw-Fox*.[25]

In that case the water board obtained a confirmed compulsory purchase order in respect of a large part of a farm for use as a reservoir. As a result of the water board's proposal the agricultural tenant lost his security because the owner was placed in a position whereby he could serve a notice to quit which could not be contested. Notice to treat was subsequently served on the owner who claimed compensation on the basis that his interest was subject to an unprotected tenancy. The water board contested this on the ground that the scheme had altered the nature of the owner's interest and increased its value. In other words, they said, this was an increase in value due to the scheme underlying the acquisition and fell to be ignored under the rule in *Pointe Gourde* (see Chap.8). The House of Lords, Lord Simon dissenting, held that the *Pointe Gourde* rule applied not to the ascertainment of the interests to be valued but to the value of the interests when ascertained. The change in this case had been to the interest to be ascertained and the owner was awarded compensation on the basis that at the date of the notice to treat his interest was subject to an unprotected tenancy.

To avoid a repetition of the hardship to agricultural tenants arising from the decision in *Shaw-Fox*, section 44 of the 1973 Act was introduced. This provides that, in assessing the compensation payable by an acquiring authority in respect of the acquisition of the interest of the landlord in an agricultural holding there shall be disregarded any right of the landlord to serve a notice to quit, and any notice to quit already served by the landlord, which would not be or would not have been effective if:

(i) in section 22(2)(b) of the Agricultural Holdings (Scotland) Act 1991 (land required for non-agricultural use for which planning permission has been granted) the reference to the land being required did not include a reference to its being required by an acquiring authority; and

(ii) in s.24(1)(e) of the 1991 Act (proposed termination of tenancy for purpose of land being used for non-agricultural use not

---

[24] Added by the Planning and Compensation Act 1991, Sch.17, para.6.

[25] [1973] A.C. 202 affirming the decision of the Court of Appeal in *Minister of Transport v Pettit* (1969) 20 P. & C.R. 344.

falling within section 22(2)(b)) the reference to the land being used did not include a reference to it being used by an acquiring authority (s.44(2)(a)).[26]

There is also to be disregarded any entitlement of the landlord to resume land comprised in the holding by virtue of a stipulation in the lease, and any notice already given in pursuance of such a stipulation which would not be or would not have been effective if the stipulation were construed as not including authority to resume the land for the purpose of its being required by the acquiring authority (s.44(2)(b)). If the tenant has quit the holding or any part of it by reason of a notice to quit which is to be so disregarded, it is to be assumed that he has not done so (s.44(2)(c)). And if land comprised in the holding has been resumed by reason of such an entitlement or notice which is to be so disregarded, that land is to be assumed not to have been so resumed (s.44(2)(d)).

Section 45 of the 1973 Act makes corresponding provision where the acquiring authority acquire the interest of the landlord in an agricultural holding which is a croft or take possession of a croft. Section 45 applies also to the holding or part of a holding of a landholder or a statutory small tenant.[27]

3. A Tenant

12–12   A tenant for a term of years is entitled to a notice to treat and may claim under section 61 of the 1845 Act in respect of the value of his interest, for disturbance and, where appropriate, for severance and other injurious affection.[28] He may also be entitled to home loss and farm loss payments. However, tenancies of agricultural land are sometimes on a yearly basis and, as indicated in the discussion of "short tenancies" (above), dispossession may occur in one of two ways. First of all, the acquiring authority may persuade the landlord to serve a notice to quit or, having purchased the landlord's interest, may themselves serve a notice to quit. In such a case the tenant is entitled to compensation not for compulsory acquisition but as between landlord and tenant under the Agricultural Holdings (Scotland) Act 1991. There are three heads of compensation:

(i) Compensation for disturbance equal to one year's rent of the holding. With proof of loss the tenant may be able to claim an amount up to a maximum of two years' rent of the holding;

(ii) Compensation for improvements, generally referred to as "tenant right". This would include such matters as the unexhausted value of fertilisers and loss of growing crops;

---

[26] See, for example, *Anderson v Moray District Council*, 1978 S.L.T. (Lands Tr.) 37.

[27] For the definition of "croft," "landholder" and "statutory small tenant" see the 1973 Act, s.80(1).

[28] From the date on which it comes into force the Agricultural Holdings (Scotland) Act 2003, s.54, will make special provision for compensation where an acquiring authority compulsorily acquires the interest of a tenant under, or takes possession of land comprised in a lease constituting, a short limited duration tenancy or a limited duration tenancy.

(iii) A reorganisation payment under the Agricultural Holdings (Scotland) Act 1991, section 56. This is a payment equal to four times the annual rent of the holding and is intended to help the tenant in the reorganisation of his affairs.

Where dispossession is from part only of the holding, provision is made for an abatement of the rent.

Alternatively, where an acquiring authority is unable to wait for a notice to quit to run its course they may serve a notice of entry and, after the expiration of 14 days, enter on the land and extinguish the tenant's interest.[29] When a general vesting declaration has been employed, the authority must first serve a notice to treat on a short tenant before serving a notice of entry and taking possession.[30] The tenant is entitled to compensation under section 114 of the 1845 Act for the extinguishment of that interest (see p.254).

There are four heads of claim under section 114:

(i) The value of the unexpired term or interest in the land: In *Wakerley v St Edmundsbury Borough Council*[31] Sir David Cairns indicated (in his dissenting judgment) that the value of the unexpired term was to be assessed in accordance with rule (2). As with the landlord's interest, section 44(3) of the Land Compensation (Scotland) Act 1973, reversing the effect of the decision in *Rugby Joint Water Board v Shaw-Fox*[32] (above), provides that in making such assessment no account is to be taken of the consequences of the acquiring authority's scheme on the nature of the interest being extinguished. There is to be disregarded any right of the landlord to serve a notice to quit, and any notice to quit already served by the landlord, which would not be or would not have been effective if the appropriate grounds for possession in the Agricultural Holdings (Scotland) Act 1991 (ss.22(2)(b) and 24(1)(e)) were construed as not including a reference to the land being required or used by an acquiring authority.[33] There is also to be disregarded any entitlement of the landlord to resume land comprised in the holding by virtue of a stipulation in the lease, and any notice already given in pursuance of such a stipulation which would not be or would not have been effective if the stipulation were construed as not including authority to resume land for the purpose of its being required by the acquiring authority (s.44(3)(b))[34];

(ii) Any just allowance which ought to be made to him by an incoming tenant: In *Anderson v Moray District Council*,[35] for

---

[29] Acquisition of Land (Authorisation Procedure) (Scotland) Act 1947, Sch.2, para.3.
[30] Town and Country Planning (Scotland) Act 1997, Sch.15, para.8.
[31] (1979) 38 P. & C.R. 551.
[32] [1973] A.C. 202.
[33] See *Anderson v Moray District Council*, 1978 S.L.T. (Lands Tr.) 37, *Wakerley v St Edmundsbury Borough Council* (1979) 38 P. & C.R. 551, CA.; *Dawson v Norwich City Council* (1979) 250 E.G. 1297.
[34] See s.45 as regards the position of a crofter, a landholder and a statutory small tenant.
[35] 1978 S.L.T. (Lands Tr.) 37.

example, an allowance was made under this head for tenant's improvements for grass seed sown with the waygoing white crop, and for unexhausted fertility;

(iii) Any loss or injury: In *Minister of Transport v Pettit*[36] the Court of Appeal were of the opinion that the corresponding words in section 20(1) of the Compulsory Purchase Act 1965 were not confined simply to financial loss or injury. In *Anderson*, for example, the Lands Tribunal for Scotland awarded sums under this head in respect of loss on forced sale of stock, removal expenses, fees and own time and expenses;

(iv) Where appropriate, compensation for damage arising from severance and other injurious affection: In *Worlock v Sodbury R.D.C.*[37] the corresponding provision in the English legislation was construed as limiting the severance claim to 'damage done to him in his tenancy'; it did not extend to damage to other land in which the claimant had a tenancy. The effect of that decision has been overturned by the Planning and Compensation Act 1991 which has amended s.114 so that it now refers to "damage done to him by severing lands held by him . . ."[38]

12–13   In addition to these four heads of claim, provision is made for a reorganisation payment. Section 56 of the Agricultural Holdings (Scotland) Act 1991 provides that the tenant will be entitled to the tax-free reorganisation payment for which provision is made in section 54 of the Act equal to four times the annual rent of the holding to help in the reorganisation of his affairs. Section 44(4) of the Land Compensation (Scotland) Act 1973, however, provides that the tenant's compensation is to be reduced by an amount equal to the reorganisation payment. Hamilton points out that the reorganisation payment was introduced on the assumption that the tenant had not got a protected tenancy, so that it is reasonable that he should not get both the payment and the enhanced compensation on the protected tenancy basis.[39] The reason for dealing with the payment "in this rather circuitous way of addition and subtraction" is apparently to enable the tenant to continue to enjoy the tax-free advantages of the 1991 Act payment.

Section 44(5) of the 1973 Act goes on to provide that if the tenant's compensation determined on the basis of a protected tenancy but with deduction of the reorganisation payment is less than it would have been before these provisions were introduced, it is to be increased by the amount of the deficiency. In other words, the tenant can be no worse off as a result of these provisions and, in some cases, he will be better off.

As a result of an amendment introduced by the Planning and Compensation Act 1991, a yearly tenant, like other tenants, may now qualify for both a home loss payment and farm loss payment on the extinguishment of his interest.[40]

---

[36] (1969) 20 P. & C.R. 344.
[37] (1961) 12 P. & C.R. 315.
[38] See Sch.17, para.1.
[39] R. N. D. Hamilton, *Compensation for Compulsory Acquisition of Agricultural Land* (3rd ed., RICS, 1980) para.95.
[40] Land Compensation (Scotland) Act 1973, s.31(2) as amended by the Planning and Compensation Act 1991, Sch.17, para.14(3)(a)).

There will be occasions where the compensation available upon extinguishment of the interest is more generous than that available under a notice to quit. Section 55 of the 1973 Act accordingly allows a tenant served with a notice to quit either by the landlord or by the acquiring authority after they have acquired the landlord's interest[41] to elect for notice of entry compensation. If the tenant served with a notice to quit opts for notice of entry compensation and gives up possession of the holding to the acquiring authority on or before the date on which the tenancy terminates under the notice to quit, he is entitled to have compensation assessed under section 114 of the 1845 Act as if the notice to quit had not been served and the acquiring authority had taken possession of the holding pursuant to a notice of entry on the day before that on which the tenancy terminates under the notice to quit. An election must be made by notice in writing served on the acquiring authority not later than the date on which possession of the holding is given up (1973 Act, s.55(4)). The right to opt for notice of entry compensation applies also in cases where a notice of resumption is given under a stipulation in a lease entitling the landlord to resume the land for non-agricultural purposes (1973 Act, s.55(8)).

Section 56 of the 1973 Act confers a similar right of election on a crofter, a landholder or a statutory small tenant who is required to surrender his holding by an order of the Scottish Land Court authorising its resumption.

It should be noted that a person served with notice to quit part of an agricultural holding is not entitled both to make an election under section 55 of the 1973 Act and to give a counter-notice under section 30 of the Agricultural Holdings (Scotland) Act 1991 treating the notice to quit part of the holding as notice to quit the entire holding (1973 Act, s.55(6)). He may, however, elect for notice of entry compensation within two months of the date of the notice to quit, or, if later, the decision of the Scottish Land Court, and then by notice served on the acquiring authority within the same period claim that the remainder of the holding is not reasonably capable of being farmed, either by itself or in conjunction with other relevant land, as a separate agricultural unit (1973 Act, s.57(1)). Any dispute over the validity of such a notice may be referred to the Lands Tribunal for Scotland. If the notice takes effect and the claimant within 12 months gives up possession of the part of the holding to which it relates, compensation under section 114 of the 1845 Act will be payable in respect of the whole (1973 Act, s.57(3)).[42]

Section 58 of the 1973 Act makes similar provision for crofters, landholders and statutory small tenants.

ADVANCE PAYMENT

Section 48 of the Land Compensation (Scotland) Act 1973 confers a **12–14** right upon dispossessed proprietors to an advance payment on account of compensation for the compulsory acquisition of their interest.[43] The

---

[41] *Dawson v Norwich City Council* (1979) 250 E.G. 1297.

[42] Sections 51(2)–(4) and s.52(3) are applied in relation to s.57 (1)–(3) by s.57 (5). And see s.51(3) for the meaning of "other relevant land".

[43] It is questionable whether this entitlement extends to persons having no greater interest in land than as tenants for a year or from year to year who are required to give up possession before the expiration of their term.

entitlement arises where an acquiring authority have taken possession of any land,[44] although it would seem that a request for such payment may anticipate possession. The wide discretionary power in section 80(2) of the Planning and Compensation Act 1991 to make a payment on account of compensation would seem not to apply to an advance payment of compensation prior to possession. CPPRAG recommended that advance payments should be available in respect of costs incurred from the time a compulsory purchase order becomes operative.[45] The DTLR have indicated a reluctance to introduce an earlier entitlement to an advance payment but have proposed instead for a discretionary power to make earlier payments.[46]

A request for an advance payment is to be made in writing to the acquiring authority giving particulars of the claimant's interest in the land if this has not already been given in response to a notice to treat. In practice, satisfactory evidence of title will also be required. Such other particulars as will enable the authority to estimate the compensation in respect of which the advance payment is to be made must be provided.

The amount of any advance payment will be equal to 90 per cent of the compensation agreed between the claimant and the acquiring authority; or, if agreement has not yet been reached, 90 per cent of the authority's estimate of the compensation (s.48(3)). However, no such payment will be made in respect of any land which is subject to a heritable security, the principal of which exceeds 90 per cent of such an amount. Where the principal does not exceed 90 per cent, the advance payment will be reduced by the sum which the acquiring authority consider is required by them to secure the release of the interest of the heritable creditor (s.48(6)).

The payment is to be made not later than three months after the date of the request or on possession, whichever is the later.[47] Notice of the payment is to be recorded in the Register of Sasines or the Land Register for Scotland, as appropriate, and a copy of the notice is to be sent to the planning authority. The acceptance of an advance payment does not prejudice the claimant's ability to dispute the amount of compensation ultimately payable.

Where, at any time after an advance payment has been made on the basis of the acquiring authority's estimate, it appears to the authority that their estimate is too low, they must if requested by the claimant, pay the balance of the amount of the advance payment as calculated at that time.[48] The use of the words 'at any time' suggests that successive supplementary payments should be made in appropriate cases. If, on the other hand, the amount of the advance payment exceeds the amount of

---

[44] Or have first entered land for the purpose of exercising a right which has been compulsorily acquired (1973 Act, s.48(10)).

[45] "Fundamental review of the laws and procedures relating to compulsory purchase and compensation: final report" (2000) DETR paras 180–184.

[46] "Compulsory purchase and compensation: delivering a fundamental change" (2001) DTLR para.3.70.

[47] See H. St. John, "Why advance payments should be claimed promptly" (1980) *Chartered Surveyor* p.208.

[48] 1973 Act, s.48(4A) added by the Planning and Compensation Act 1991, s.73.

the compensation as finally agreed or determined, any excess is to be repaid.[49]

Although there is no entitlement to an advance payment prior to the taking of possession, authorities have a discretion to make a payment of up to 90 per cent before entry. The Scottish Development Department expressed the hope that authorities will do this where claimants need money to reinstate themselves prior to giving up possession.[50]

Some concern has been expressed about the way in which the advance payment provisions work in practice.[51] CPPRAG noted that, where an acquiring authority was unacceptably slow in responding to or unreasonably failed to comply with a request for such a payment, no penalties applied and claimants had no means of enforcing their entitlement.[52] The Group recommended the imposition of an enforceable duty and the government have responded sympathetically to this.[53]

INTEREST

Section 18 of the Law Reform (Miscellaneous Provisions) (Scotland) Act **12–15** 1980 provides that a sum awarded as compensation by the Lands Tribunal for Scotland may, if the tribunal so determine, carry interest as from the date of the award at the same rate as is applicable in the case of a Court of Session decree. The right to interest in respect of a period prior to the award will depend on the existence of other statutory authority.[54] The following provisions relevant to the matters discussed in this book exist:

1. Where, following service of a notice of entry,[55] possession is taken of land before the payment of compensation, provision is made for the payment of interest on the compensation from the date of possession to the date of payment.[56]

   In *Chilton v Telford Corporation*[57] where, following service of a notice of entry physical possession of the land described in the notice (67.87 acres) was taken in eight separate parcels

---

[49] 1973 Act, s.48(5) as substituted by the Planning and Compensation Act 1991, s.73.

[50] SDD Circular 84/1 973, para.50. See, too, "Development and Compensation—Putting People First" (1972) Cmnd. 5124, para.35.

[51] See, for example, "Compensation for Compulsory Acquisition" (1995) RICS, Chap.5; and J. Rowan Robinson and N. Hutchison, "Compensation for the compulsory acquisition of business interests: satisfaction or sacrifice" (1995) *Journal of Property Valuation and Investment* Vol.13(1), p.44.

[52] "Fundamental review of the laws and procedures relating to compulsory purchase and compensation: final report" (2000) DETR paras 180–184.

[53] "Compulsory purchase and compensation: delivering a fundamental change" (2001) DTLR, para.3.67.

[54] Section 80(1) of the Planning and Compensation Act 1991 has substantially enlarged the situations in which compensation will carry interest although they are not relevant for the purposes of this book.

[55] See p.70.

[56] Acquisition of Land (Authorisation Procedure) (Scotland) Act 1947, s.1(3) and Sch.2, para.3(1) applying the Lands Clauses Consolidation (Scotland) Act 1845, s.84.

[57] [1987] 1 W.L.R. 872.

spread over more than two years, the Court of Appeal held that first entry on any part of the land described in the notice constituted entry on the whole. Accordingly, interest on the compensation for the whole land was to be calculated from the date of first entry.

2. Where, as a result of a general vesting declaration, land is vested in an acquiring authority in advance of the payment of compensation,[58] interest is payable on the compensation from the date of vesting to the date of payment.[59]

   In *Birrell Ltd v Edinburgh District Council*[60] premises vested in the acquiring authority in September 1969 under the procedure for expedited completion of title set out in the Town and Country Planning (Scotland) Act 1945, as amended. Entry on the land was postponed until May 1970 during which time the claimants continued to carry on their business in the premises paying rates but no rent to the authority. Agreement was reached on the amount of compensation but not on the date from which the interest on the compensation should run. The owners agreed that interest was due from the date of vesting. The acquiring authority contended that no interest was payable in respect of any period prior to physical entry. The obligation under the expedited procedure was to pay such compensation and interest as would have been required to be paid if the provisions of the 1845 Act and in particular sections 83 to 88 had been complied with. Lord Fraser of Tullybelton, giving judgment for the House of Lords, observed that although the 1845 Act proceeded on the assumption that interest was payable, the date from which it was due was not defined. He concluded that it was reasonable to assume that the draftsman of the 1845 Act had had the common law rule in mind which required a purchaser, who acquired land before he paid the price, to pay the seller interest on the price from the date of purchase. Accordingly, the effect of the provisions of the 1845 Act was that interest on the compensation was due to the claimants from the date of vesting.

3. Section 59 of the 1973 Act provides that compensation awarded under section 6 of the Railways Clauses Consolidation (Scotland) Act 1845, in respect of injurious affection suffered by neighbouring land not held together with land acquired for the scheme of works (see Chap.14)[61] and arising from the *construction* of the works, shall carry interest from the date of claim until payment.[62]

---

[58] See Chap.4.

[59] Town and Country Planning (Scotland) Act 1997, Sch.15, para.30.

[60] 1982 S.C. (H.L.) 75; 1982 S.L.T. 363.

[61] Compensation awarded for injurious affection suffered by land held together with land acquired for the scheme is part of the global sum awarded under s.61 of the 1845 Act and carries interest in the circumstances described above.

[62] See, for example, *Loch Ryan Oyster Fisheries Ltd v British Railways Board*, unreported, December 12, 1985, Court of Session (Outer House), (see note at (1986) 19 S.P.L.P. 81).

4. Similarly, section 16 of the 1973 Act[63] states that an award of compensation under Part I of that Act for damage caused to neighbouring land by the *use* of works shall carry interest at the same rate from the date of service of the notice of claim (or if that date precedes the first claim day—from the first claim day) until payment.

5. Section 34(5) of the 1973 Act provides that a disturbance payment (see page 263) shall carry interest from the date of displacement until payment.

6. Section 33(6) of the 1973 Act provides for farm loss payments to carry interest from the date specified in section 33(1) until payment.

7. Section 48A of the 1973 Act[64] provides that where an advance payment on account of compensation is made, the payment must carry accrued interest from the date of entry. Any top-up payments must also include an appropriate amount for interest; and further payments must be made at yearly intervals where the accrued interest on the unpaid balance of compensation exceeds £1,000, with the final payment of interest being made on the eventual payment of the balance of the compensation.

8. Section 78(5) of the Planning and Compensation Act 1991 provides for the payment of interest on compensation for any consequential loss arising from the promotion of a compulsory purchase order where the notice to treat ceases to have effect. Interest accrues from the time that the claimant was entitled to be informed that notice to treat had ceased to have effect until payment.

9. Section 31(5) of the 1973 Act[65] provides that additional compensation arising from a planning decision made after the compulsory acquisition will carry interest from the date of the decision until payment.

The rate of interest in the nine circumstances referred to above is prescribed by regulations made from time to time under section 40 of the 1963 Act. It is set on a quarterly basis at 0.5 per cent below base rate and is calculated on simple rather than compound interest. Section 80(2) of the Planning and Compensation Act 1991 confers a discretion to make advance payments on account of interest. In the absence of statutory provision, it would seem that the Lands Tribunal for Scotland has no power to award interest in respect of a period antecedent to the date of the award.[66]

It has for some time been a bone of contention that simple, not compound, interest is paid and then only when the compensation itself is

---

[63] As amended by the Local Government, Planning and Land Act 1980, s.112(4).
[64] Added by the Planning and Compensation Act 1991, s.73(2).
[65] Added by the Planning and Compensation Act 1991, s.77 and Sch.16.
[66] See, for example, *Hobbs (Quarries) Ltd v Somerset County Council* (1975) 30 P. & C.R. 286; and *Burlin v Manchester City Council* (1976) 32 P. & C.R. 115.

fixed.[67] It is, of course, not possible to make any precise calculation of
the interest until the principal is known. CPPRAG accepted that the
present interest rates amount, in effect, to a penalty on the claimant for
the late payment of compensation by the acquiring authority and
recommended that ministers give serious consideration to imposing a
requirement that compound interest should be payable on all outstanding compensation due to a claimant.[68] The Group also felt, that where
there has been an advance payment based on the acquiring authority's
estimate, there was a case for removing the minimum threshold for
annual interest payments. The DTLR have deferred any decision on
these recommendations until the Law Commission have completed their
review of the power of the courts to award compound interest.[69]

THE TAXATION OF COMPENSATION

12–16   To what extent, if at all, should the incidence of taxation be taken into
account in an award of compensation? Compensation for the compulsory acquisition of land is a capital sum realised on the disposal of an
asset. Should the compensation be paid net of tax? A disturbance claim
may include an item for loss of earnings or loss of profits which would
have been taxable in the hands of the recipient. If the incidence of
taxation is not taken into account, a claimant will arguably be compensated for more than his real loss.

The question of what to do about the incidence of taxation first arose,
not surprisingly, in the context of disturbance. In *West Suffolk County
Council v W. Rought Ltd.*,[70] the local authority compulsorily acquired the
leasehold interest of a company in factory premises. The company
claimed disturbance compensation for temporary loss of profits for the
period which elapsed between the date when the local authority took
possession and the date when the company was able to recommence
operations in alternative accommodation. The House of Lords, applying
the decision in *British Transport Commission v Gourlay*[71] relating to the
taxation of an award of damages for loss of earnings, held that the Lands
Tribunal should have reduced the award by the amount of the additional
taxation which the company would have had to bear if it had actually
earned the amount which the acquiring authority's action prevented it
from earning. In reaching this decision their Lordships were influenced
by a statement from the Inland Revenue that the compensation award
would not itself be subject to tax. Had it been, the claimant would have
been subjected to double taxation. As it was, the company was simply
denied an undeserved tax bonus.

The decision in *W. Rought Ltd.*, is difficult to reconcile with the legal
fiction that disturbance is part of the value of the land (see Chap.10). In

---

[67] See, for example, "Compensation for Compulsory Acquisition" (1995) RICS, Chap.5.
[68] "Fundamental review of the laws and procedures relating to compulsory purchase and
compensation: final report" (2000) DETR paras.175–179.
[69] "Compulsory purchase and compensation: delivering a fundamental change" (2001)
DTLR para.3.74.
[70] [1957] A.C. 403.
[71] [1956] A.C. 185.

other words, although disturbance items such as temporary loss of profits are income, they are treated for compensation purposes as capital. At a time when income was taxable but capital was not, or not to the same extent, the distinction was important. It was not a distinction that troubled the House of Lords.

As Lord Keith observed:

> "In assessing the loss under this head, liability to tax cannot, in my opinion, be ignored merely because the amount of the loss goes to make up the total compensation or purchase price for the acquisition of a capital asset."[72]

Subsequently in *Rosenberg and Son (Tinware) Ltd v Manchester Corporation*[73] the approach adopted in *W. Rought Ltd* was taken a step further when the Lands Tribunal permitted a deduction for tax from disturbance compensation in respect of a claim for removal expenses. It was thought by the tribunal that such expenses were allowable in the circumstance of compulsory acquisition as an income tax deduction.

The decision in *W. Rought Ltd* was, in due course, reviewed by the Court of Appeal in *Stoke-on-Trent City Council v Wood Mitchell and Co. Ltd*[74] At issue was the amount payable for disturbance under the heading of temporary loss of profits while the respondents' offices and warehouse were being re-established and the question turned on whether the amount should be adjusted to take account of corporation tax. The respondent's contention was that since the decision in *W. Rought Ltd* circumstances had changed and they were now liable for either or both corporation income tax and corporation capital gains tax on the compensation; accordingly the principle laid down in *W. Rought Ltd* no longer applied. Roskill L.J., giving judgment for the court, concluded that "the principles laid down in *Rought's* case can only be applied if after examination of the relevant statutory provisions it is clear beyond peradventure that the sum in question would not be taxable in the hands of the respondents". An examination of the relevant statutory provisions[75] showed that since the decision in *W. Rought Ltd* a liability for capital gains tax on compensation for compulsory acquisition had been introduced on the basis that such compensation is a capital sum received on the disposal of an asset. The provisions furthermore permitted a breakdown of that compensation into its component parts so as to apportion capital and income elements and to exclude from the computation of the capital gain any money charged to income tax as the income of the person making the disposal. The effect of this was to free the compensation for temporary loss of profits of its capital nature and enable it to be treated as a trading receipt. The situation was clearly distinguishable from that in *W. Rought Ltd* and it was held that the

---

[72] [1957] A.C. 403 at p.416.

[73] (1971) 23 P. & C.R. 68.

[74] (1978) 248 E.G. 871. And see *Pennine Raceway Ltd v Kirklees Metropolitan Borough Council*, unreported, 1988 E.G.C.S. 168.

[75] At that time the Finance Act 1965, s.22 and the Finance Act 1969, Sch.19, para.11. See now the Taxation of Chargeable Gains Act 1992, ss.245–248.

compensation should not be adjusted by the acquiring authority to take account of corporation tax.

The Inland Revenue have since indicated that they will follow the decision of the Court of Appeal in *Wood Mitchell & Co. Ltd* In a statement of practice SP 8/1979, issued in June 1979, the Inland Revenue indicate that any element of compensation received for temporary loss of profits for the acquisition by an authority possessing compulsory purchase powers of property used for the purposes of a trade or profession "falls to be included as a receipt taxable under Case I and II of Schedule D. Compensation for losses on trading stock and to reimburse revenue expenditure, such as removal expenses and interest, will be treated in the same way for tax purposes." The statement goes on to indicate that this practice will also apply to compensation cases where no interest is acquired *(e.g.* compensation due for damage, injury or exploitation of land, or to the exercise of planning control).

The statement of practice clarifies the position as regards disturbance items which represent income. Compensation for loss of goodwill, like compensation for the land taken and for severance and other injurious affection, represents capital and will be subject to capital gains tax in the normal way.[76]

Compensation is thus taxable both as capital and as income in respect of its different components. As *The Estates Gazette* aptly observed "the one-time windfall is taken back out of the hands of the acquiring authority into those of the claimant, and thence into the hands of the Inland Revenue, where it disappears".[77]

The recent Law Commission Consultation Paper neatly summarises the present position:

> "[I]t seems that, where the tax position is clear, and the Tribunal can identify a specific increase or reduction in tax liability resulting from the compulsory purchase, compensation will be adjusted accordingly. Otherwise, compensation will be assessed without reference to potential tax liability, which will be a matter to be resolved with the Revenue in due course".[78]

---

[76] See the Taxation of Chargeable Gains Act 1992, s.245(1); and see s.247 as regards roll over relief.

[77] (1978) 248 E.G. 53, Legal Notes. Note, however, the decision of the English Lands Tribunal in *Alfred Golightly & Sons Ltd v Durham County Council* (1981) 260 E.G. 1045, 1135 and 1199 which allowed, as part of a disturbance claim, an item representing the claimant's increased liability to tax (in that case development land tax) which would not have arisen but for the acquisition by the local authority. On the other hand, in *Harris v Welsh Development Agency* [1999] 3 E.G.L.R. 207 the Lands Tribunal rejected a rule (6) disturbance claim for capital gains tax liability arising on the disposal to the local authority on the grounds that, surprisingly, the tax liability was a matter directly based on the value of the land so that rule (6) had no application and that, in any event, the tests of causation and remoteness had not been satisfied. *Golightly* was distinguished on the ground that it involved a liability to tax that would not have been incurred. In *Harris* the effect of the compulsory acquisition was to transform a contingent liability to tax into an actual liability.

[78] "Towards a compulsory purchase code: (1) Compensation" (2002) *Consultation Paper No 165*, para.8.61.

THE LANDS TRIBUNAL FOR SCOTLAND[79]

The Lands Clauses Consolidation (Scotland) Act 1845 made provision **12–17** for the determination of compensation disputes in a variety of ways. Under section 20 the parties could refer disputes to arbitration. However, if the disputed claim did not exceed £50, it was to be settled by the sheriff unless both parties elected for arbitration. For claims in excess of £50 the parties, unless they had elected for arbitration, could petition the sheriff to summon a jury to determine the compensation. At a time when compulsory purchase was linked with the entrepreneurial activity of the industrial revolution carried on for profit as much as for the public good, it seems there was a tendency for juries to sympathise with claimants.[80] In the period of reconstruction that followed the First World War, this generosity to claimants was considered to be misplaced. To curb excesses and to introduce "realism" into awards, the Acquisition of Land (Assessment of Compensation) Act 1919 provided for disputed claims to be determined by official arbiters appointed because of their expertise in valuation.[81]

The system operated reasonably well until the aftermath of the Second World War. The advent of comprehensive planning control introduced very considerable legal complexity into land valuation and the government of the day concluded that the system would have to be changed to accommodate this. "The main defect under the existing machinery," observed the Attorney-General, "is that the official arbitrators, qualified only as surveyors and valuers, have no means of providing themselves with legal advice or assistance in regard to matters of law, or indeed of securing close coordination and consistency of decisions with each other".[82] The Lands Tribunal Act 1949 accordingly made provision for the setting up of a Lands Tribunal for Scotland and one for England and Wales. The tribunals were to bring both legal and surveying expertise to bear on disputes over land valuation.

The Lands Tribunal for England and Wales came into existence on January 1, 1950. However, the limited volume of work in Scotland was thought not to warrant the expense of establishing a Scottish tribunal at that time[83] and the panel of official arbiters continued to operate for a further 20 years. To cope with the legal complexities of valuation, arbiters appointed legal clerks to advise them. The bringing into operation of Part I of the Conveyancing and Feudal Reform (Scotland) Act 1970 provided the trigger for setting up the Lands Tribunal for Scotland. The 1970 Act required the appointment of a body to adjudicate upon applications to vary or discharge land obligations. Differing

---

[79] See generally *Stair Memorial Encyclopaedia, Courts and Competency*, "The Lands Tribunal for Scotland" (Law Society of Scotland/Butterworths), Vol 6.

[80] "Second Report of the Committee Dealing with the Law and Practice Relating to the Acquisition and Valuation of Land for Public Purposes" (the Scott Committee), (1919) HMSO para 8 (Cmnd. 9229).

[81] s.2.

[82] H.C. Deb., 1948–49, Vol. 462, col. 43.

[83] W. A. Elliot, Q.C., "Lands Tribunal Jurisdiction and Procedure" (1977) *Law Society for Scotland* (paper given to a conference organised by the Law Society on compulsory purchase and compensation).

from the recommendation of the Halliday Committee on *Conveyancing Legislation and Practice*,[84] the government conferred this function upon the Lands Tribunal for Scotland which was established with effect from March 1, 1971.[85]

The tribunal exercises a number of separate functions. The common factor which, for the most part, unites these functions is that they are concerned with settling disputes in connection with the valuation of land. For the purposes of this chapter it is sufficient to say that the jurisdiction of the tribunal extends to:

1. The determination of disputes over compensation where land is authorised to be acquired compulsorily; and, where any part of the land to be acquired is subject to a lease which also comprises land not to be acquired, the resolution of questions as to the apportionment of the rent payable under the lease.[86]

2. Any other question of disputed compensation under the Lands Clauses Acts, where the claim is for the injurious affection of any land.[87]

3. The determination of disputed compensation under Part I of the Land Compensation (Scotland) Act 1973.[88]

4. The determination of disputes over other payments under the Land Compensation (Scotland) Act 1973 such as disturbance and farm loss payments.[89]

5. Determining the price under a voluntary reference where the acquisition of land by a public authority is proceeding not by compulsory purchase but by negotiation.[90]

12–18   As indicated in other chapters, the tribunal also has a role to play in resolving disputes over notices of objection to severance[91] and blight notices.[92]

The tribunal comprises a president and such other members as the Lord President of the Court of Session may determine. The president of the tribunal is to be a person suitably qualified by the holding of judicial office or by experience as an advocate or solicitor. The other members are to be persons similarly qualified or persons having experience in the valuation of land appointed after consultation with the Chairman of the Scottish Branch of the Royal Institution of Chartered Surveyors. Appointments are for such period as the Lord President may determine.[93]

---

[84] "Conveyancing Legislation and Practice, (1966) HMSO para.27 (Cmnd. 3118).
[85] The Lands Tribunal Act 1949 (Appointed Day) (Scotland) Order 1971.
[86] Land Compensation (Scotland) Act 1963, s.8.
[87] Lands Tribunal Act 1949, s.1(3).
[88] Land Compensation (Scotland) Act 1973, s.14.
[89] Land Compensation (Scotland) Act 1973, ss.32(9) and 35(4).
[90] Lands Tribunal Act 1949, s.1(5).
[91] See p.65.
[92] See p.328.
[93] Lands Tribunal Act 1949, ss.2–3. At the time of writing the Lands Tribunal for Scotland comprises, in addition to the President, one part-time legal member and one full-time and two part-time surveyor members.

The jurisdiction of the tribunal may be exercised by any one or more of its members.[94] Compensation claims where no legal issues arise are generally determined by one member sitting alone. In most other cases, the tribunal will sit with two members, one a lawyer and the other a surveyor with the former presiding, to obtain the benefits of combined expertise referred to above. Exceptionally, where cases raise matters of particular importance the tribunal may sit with additional members. Where a case is dealt with by two or more members, the decision will be that of the majority. In the event of equality, the member presiding will have a second or casting vote.[95] Where any case before the tribunal calls for special knowledge, the president may direct that the tribunal will be assisted by one or more assessors.[96]

The Lands Tribunal for Scotland has its own permanent staff. Its offices and court room are situated at 1 Grosvenor Crescent, Edinburgh, EH12 5ER. The tribunal is peripatetic but, as in practice the major cases tend to involve advocates, the parties often express a preference for a sitting in Edinburgh to save expense.[97]

Rules may be made for regulating the proceedings of the tribunal and as regards fees. The principal rules at the present time are the Lands Tribunal for Scotland Rules 1971.[98]

No application for the determination of any question of disputed compensation may be made before the expiration of 30 days from the date of service or constructive service of a notice to treat or (where no notice to treat is served or deemed to be served) of notice of claim.[99] A person, whether the claimant or the acquiring authority, requiring to have a question or dispute determined must submit an application to the tribunal in accordance with Form 3.[1]

A copy of the notice to treat (if such notice has been served) and of any notice of claim should accompany an application relating to the compensation payable on the compulsory acquisition of land. In any other case, a copy of the order, direction, notice, decision, authorisation or other document which is evidence of the proceedings giving rise to compensation should be submitted. The tribunal will send copies of the application to the other parties to the question or dispute.

The tribunal is to a considerable extent the master of its own procedure.[2] On the motion of any party to the proceedings or *ex proprio motu* it may: require a party to furnish in writing further particulars of his case; order a record to be made up; grant to a party such recovery of documents as might be granted by the Court of Session; and require the attendance of any person as a witness or require the production of any

---

[94] Lands Tribunal Act 1949, s.3(1).

[95] See above, s.3(3).

[96] The Lands Tribunal for Scotland Rules 1971, r.29.

[97] See W. A. Elliott, *supra.*

[98] As amended by the Lands Tribunal for Scotland (Amendment) Rules 1977 and the Lands Tribunal for Scotland (Amendment) Rules 1985. At the time of writing, the latest rules dealing with fees are the Lands Tribunal for Scotland (Amendment) (Fees) Rules 1996.

[99] The Lands Tribunal for Scotland Rules 1971, r.11(3).

[1] See above, r.11(1). See the Lands Tribunal for Scotland (Amendment) (Fees) Rules 1996 for the appropriate fees.

[2] The Lands Tribunal for Scotland Rules 1971, r.20.

document relating to the question to be determined; and may appoint a time at or within which and place at which such action is to be taken.[3] Small claims, however, are likely to be dealt with informally with next to no pleadings.

With the consent of all parties the tribunal may dispose of any application before it without a hearing.[4] Where a hearing is to be held, not less than 21 days' notice in writing must be given by the tribunal of the date, time and place unless the parties agree to a shorter period.[5] To avoid surprises, parties to a hearing will be ordered to produce a list of any comparable properties to which reference is to be made at least one month in advance. The tribunal will sit in public except that when it is acting as arbiter under a reference by consent the proceedings shall be heard in private if the parties to the reference so request.[6]

12–19   Any party to the proceedings before the tribunal may appear and be heard in person or be represented by counsel or solicitor, or with the leave of the tribunal, by any other person. The tribunal considers there are serious objections to a surveyor also acting as his client's advocate.[7] As Emlyn Jones observes: "combining the role of advocate and expert witness puts an undue strain on an individual. In giving evidence he is under oath to tell the truth; as an advocate he can with complete propriety put forward arguments and submissions based on inference or interpretation".[8] Nevertheless, in small cases a combination of roles is sometimes permitted to keep down expense.

The proceedings before the tribunal are conducted generally in accordance with the rules of evidence. Evidence may be given on oath and will be subject to cross examination. If the parties to the proceedings consent or the tribunal so orders evidence may be given by affidavit but the tribunal may at any stage of the proceedings require the personal attendance of any deponent for examination and cross examination.[9]

Strict rules of evidence such as the requirement of corroboration and the rule against hearsay are not, however, applied. The tribunal must remain accessible to the parties. Nonetheless, it seems that the principle behind the rule against hearsay is still observed. Factual evidence by a valuer about transactions of which he has no direct knowledge and which cannot, therefore, be tested by cross examination is likely to be rejected.[10]

---

[3] See above r.25. The tribunal may not, however, require any person to produce any book or document or to answer any question which he would be entitled, on the ground of privilege or confidentiality, to refuse to produce or to answer if the proceedings were proceedings in a court of law. See, too, *R. v Lands Tribunal, ex p. City of London Corporation* [1982] 1 W.L.R. 258 on the interpretation of the word "decision" in the Lands Tribunal Act 1949, s.3(4) (but note that s.3(4) does not apply to Scotland).

[4] The Lands Tribunal for Scotland Rules 1971, r.31.

[5] See above r.21(1).

[6] Land Compensation (Scotland) Act 1963, s.9(2) as amended by the Local Government, Planning and Land Act 1980, s.193 and Sch.33, para.7; and see also the Lands Tribunal for Scotland Rules 1971, r.21(2).

[7] W. A. Elliott, *supra.*

[8] J. H. Emlyn Jones, *The Lands Tribunal—A Practitioners Guide* (Herbert Bewlay Fund, 1982) p.17.

[9] Lands Tribunal for Scotland (Amendment) Rules 1985, r.5 adding a new r.24A to the principal rules.

[10] W. A. Elliott, *supra.* See, too, *English Exporters v Eldonwall Ltd* [1973] 1 Ch. 415, *per* Megany J. at p.420.

Not more than one expert witness on either side may be heard unless the tribunal otherwise directs.[11] An additional expert witness may, however, be permitted, for example, to support a disturbance claim or to give evidence on planning matters. The tribunal is required to determine disputed compensation claims referred to it[12] so that it has what has been described as an "investigatory" role.[13] The significance of this is that the tribunal "is unable to retire like a judge behind the shield of onus of proof and merely dismiss a claim for want of proof".[14] In the absence of one party, the other party are not automatically entitled to a determination in accordance with their calculations but must lead evidence to support them.

Previous decisions on matters of valuation do not constitute binding precedents. "Valuation is an exercise in determining facts and each case must be decided on the evidence adduced at the hearing of that case".[15] Nor is the tribunal bound by its previous decisions on matters of law although such decisions may be very persuasive.[16] The decision of the tribunal in any proceedings must be given in writing and must include a statement of the reasons for the decision.[17] Where an amount awarded or value determined by the tribunal is dependent upon the decision of the tribunal on a question of law which is in dispute in the proceedings, the tribunal must ascertain and state in its decision the alternative amount or value (if any) which it would have awarded or determined if it had decided otherwise on the question of law.[18] This may avoid the necessity of a further hearing before the tribunal in the event of its original decision on the question of law being subsequently overturned by the Court of Session.

A person dissatisfied with the tribunal's decision on a point of law may either appeal within 21 days to the Court of Session or require the tribunal within 14 days to state a case for the court's decision.[19] The decision of the tribunal is, however, final as to matters of valuation.

Where the acquiring authority have made an unconditional offer in **12–20** writing to a claimant of any sum as compensation and the sum awarded by the tribunal to the claimant does not exceed the sum offered, the tribunal must, unless for some special reason it is considered inappropriate to do so, order the claimant to bear his own expenses and to pay the

---

[11] Land Compensation (Scotland) Act 1963, s.9(3).

[12] See above, s.8.

[13] W. A. Elliott, *supra.*

[14] See above.

[15] Douglas Frank, Q.C., "Lands Tribunal Problems" (1975) *Journal of Planning and Environment Law Occasional Paper* (Sweet & Maxwell), Compensation for Compulsory Purchase.

[16] See *West Midlands Baptist (Trust) Association v Birmingham City Council* [1968] 1 All E.R. 205. CA., *per* Salmon L.J. at p.213 and Sachs L.J. at p.222.

[17] Tribunals and Inquiries Act 1992, s.10(1), Sch.1, para.39; Lands Tribunal for Scotland Rules 1971, r.32(1). In *R. A. Vine (Engineering) Ltd v Havant Borough Council* (1989) 39 E.G. 164, Glidewell L.J. in the Court of Appeal, applying the judgment of Megaw J. in *Re Poyser and Mills' Arbitration* [1964] 2 Q.B. 467 and of Sir John Donaldson (as he then was) in *Norton Tool Co. Ltd v Tewson* [1973] 1 All E.R. 183, observed that such reasons must be proper, adequate and intelligible.

[18] Lands Tribunal for Scotland Rules 1971, r.32.

[19] Tribunals and Inquiries Act 1992, s.11(7)(a)–(d), Sch.1.

expenses of the acquiring authority so far as they were incurred after the offer was made.[20] Similarly, if the tribunal is satisfied that a claimant has failed to deliver to the acquiring authority, in time to enable them to make a proper offer, a notice in writing of the amount claimed by him containing the required particulars[21] it must, unless special reasons exist, order the claimant to bear his own expenses and to pay the expenses of the acquiring authority so far as they were incurred after the time when, in the tribunal's opinion, the notice should have been delivered.[22]

Conversely, where a claimant has delivered to the acquiring authority a notice of claim containing the appropriate particulars and has made an unconditional offer in writing to accept any sum as compensation, then, if the sum awarded to him by the tribunal is equal to or exceeds that sum, the tribunal must, unless for some special reason it is considered inappropriate to do so, order the acquiring authority to bear their own expenses and to pay the expenses of the claimant so far as they were incurred after his offer was made.[23]

In practice, unconditional offers by the acquiring authority or by the claimant, after being communicated to and rejected by the other party, are sealed and lodged with the tribunal and are not disclosed to the tribunal during the hearing. Having reached a determination on the disputed claim, the tribunal will open the sealed offer and make an order as to expenses according to the content.

Apart from the circumstances described above expenses are at the discretion of the tribunal.[24] The normal principle is that expenses follow success and success is generally measured by an award larger than the acquiring authority's offer.[25] The principle may not be applied in a case where the tribunal take the view that success is divided. In *Pepys v London Transport Executive*[26] it was held that where there was a departure from the usual rule, the reasons for that departure must be given; the discretion with regard to expenses had to be exercised judicially.

In default of agreement between the parties as to the amount of expenses, the expenses will be taxed, in the tribunal's discretion, either by the Auditor of the Court of Session according to the fees payable in the Court of Session or by the Auditor of the Sheriff Court specified by the tribunal according to the Sheriff Court Table of Fees.[27]

Counsel's fees and fees for instruction of counsel will be allowed as an item of party's expenses only where the tribunal has sanctioned the employment of counsel.[28] Similarly, additional expenses at such rate as the auditor taxing the expenses considers fair and reasonable shall be

---

[20] Land Compensation (Scotland) Act 1963, s.11(1).

[21] See the 1963 Act, s.11(2).

[22] See above s.11(1).

[23] See above s.11(3).

[24] Lands Tribunal for Scotland Rules 1971, r.33. See *McLaren's Trustee v Secretary of State for Scotland*, 1989 S.L.T. 83, IH; and *City of Aberdeen District Council v Emslie & Simpson*, 1995 S.C.L.R. 317, IH.

[25] See W. A. Elliott, *supra*.

[26] [1975] 1 W.L.R. 234.

[27] Lands Tribunal for Scotland Rules 1971, r.33(3).

[28] Land Compensation (Scotland) Act 1963, s.11(4); Lands Tribunal for Scotland Rules 1971, r.33(4).

allowed for the employment of expert witnesses only where the tribunal has certified the employment of such expert witnesses.[29]

Where the tribunal orders the claimant to pay the expenses, or any **12–21** part of the expenses, of the acquiring authority, the acquiring authority may deduct the amount so payable by the claimant from the amount of the compensation, if any, payable to him.[30]

Legal aid is available in appropriate cases under the terms of the Legal Aid (Scotland) Act 1986 in relation to proceedings in the Lands Tribunal for Scotland.[31]

CPPRAG suggest that considerable time and money might be saved in some cases by the use of alternative dispute resolution techniques as a first step in resolving disputes over compensation claims.[32] In particular, the Group consider that 'early neutral evaluation' could have a role to play. The technique adopts an essentially inquisitorial approach to the issue. The parties agree to seek a written opinion from an appropriate expert assessing their respective prospects if the matter were to be pursued formally. The parties may accept the opinion outright or use it as a basis for further negotiation with the prospect of a formal reference to the tribunal for a final determination in the event of a failure to agree.

---

[29] Lands Tribunal for Scotland Rules 1971, r.33(5).

[30] Land Compensation (Scotland) Act 1963, s.11(5).

[31] Legal Aid (Scotland) Act 1986, Pt III and Sch.2, Part I, as amended by the Law Reform (Miscellaneous Provisions) (Scotland) Act 1990, s.74 and Schs 8 and 9; and by the Convention Rights (Compliance) (Scotland) Act 2001, s.6. And see the comment in W. A. Elliott, *supra.*

[32] "Fundamental review of the laws and procedures relating to compulsory purchase and compensation: final report" (2000) DETR para.70.

PART 3

COMPENSATION FOR REGULATION AND BLIGHT

CHAPTER 13

COMPENSATION FOR REGULATION

INTRODUCTION

13–01 In Chapter 4, reference was made to the well-established judicial presumption that an intention to take away the property of a subject without giving him a legal right to compensation for the loss of it is not to be imputed to the legislature unless that intention is expressed in unequivocal terms. The cases which support this presumption[1] all turn on instances where ownership or, at least, possession or use of property has been taken over by the state.

So far in this book the focus has been on the entitlement to compensation following from the compulsory acquisition of land. The question which is examined in this chapter is the extent to which interference by the state in rights in heritable property falling short of "taking" as defined above may be the subject of compensation. For example, should the proprietor of a factory be expected to bear the cost of installing insulation to prevent noise from disturbing neighbouring residential property? Would it make any difference if the factory had been in operation long before the houses were built? Should the operator of a quarry be expected to bear the cost of making the land suitable for some alternative use upon completion of mineral operations? Who should bear the loss of development value when land which is ripe for development is zoned in the development plan as green belt so that planning permission for development is refused? Who should bear the burden when plans for the conversion of a building are blocked following its listing as a building of special architectural or historic interest? Where should the loss fall when plans for afforestation of land are thwarted because of its nature conservation interest? These questions are of some importance because over the last 150 years owners and occupiers of land have had increasingly to face up to regulation of their activities in the name of public health, safety, amenity and conservation. Compliance with such regulation is regarded as essential in the interests

---

[1] *Burmah Oil Co. (Burma Trading) Ltd v Lord Advocate*, 1964 S.C. (HL) 117; 1964 S.L.T. 218; *Tiverton and North Devon Railway Co. v Loosemore* (1884) 9 App.Cas. 480, HL; *Attorney General v Horner* (1884) 14 Q.B.D. 245; *Cannon Brewery Co. Ltd v Gas Light and Coke Co.* [1904] A.C. 331, HL; *Colonial Sugar Refining Co. Ltd v Melbourne Harbour Trust Commissioners* [1927] A.C. 343, PC; *Bond v Nottingham Corporation* [1940] 1 Ch. 429.

of the wider community. The essence of the compensation problem is whether the cost of compliance should fall upon the heritable proprietor or whether it should be shared amongst the wider community who are benefiting from the regulation.

Although there is in such cases what might be described as an expropriation of[2] or at least an abridgement of[3] rights in property, the judicial eye has been reluctant to discern an entitlement to compensation in the absence of an express provision in the statute. "A mere negative prohibition," said Wright J. in *France Fenwick & Co. v The King*[4] "though it involves interference with an owner's enjoyment of property, does not, I think, merely because it is obeyed, carry with it at common law any right to compensation. A subject cannot at common law claim compensation merely because he obeys a lawful order of the state".

In *Belfast Corporation v O.D. Cars Ltd.*,[5] for example, planning permission was refused for the construction of industrial and commercial buildings on land in Belfast. The proposed industrial buildings were regarded as incompatible with the residential zoning of that part of the site; and the height and character of the proposed commercial buildings were considered not to be in accordance with the requirements for their part of the site. A claim for compensation for "injurious affection" under the Planning (Interim Development) (Northern Ireland) Act 1944 was rejected as it fell, because of the grounds of refusal, within the exceptions to the specific compensation entitlement in the Act. It was argued for the claimants that the exceptions in the legislation were contrary to section 5 of the Government of Ireland Act 1920 which provides that Parliament shall not make a law "to take away property without compensation". This argument was rejected by the House of Lords. Lord Radcliffe pointed out that interference with rights of development and use of land were not treated in the 1944 Act as a "taking" of property. The compensation entitlement in the Act was provided not on the basis that property or property rights had been "taken" but on the basis that property, itself retained, had been "injuriously affected".

And in *Westminster Bank Ltd. v Minister of Housing and Local Government*[6] an application for planning permission to extend bank premises by the construction of a strong room was refused on the ground that it would prejudice the future widening of the road onto which the premises fronted. An appeal was dismissed. The local authority, who were both the highway and the planning authority, had not, however, prescribed an improvement line under the Highways Act 1959 which would have entitled a person whose property was adversely affected by the line to claim compensation. The question to be determined was whether the planning authority could defeat a claim for compensation by refusing planning permission without an improvement line having been

[2] *Belfast Corporation v O.D. Cars Ltd.* [1960] A.C. 490, *per* Lord Radcliffe at p.524.
[3] *Belfast Corporation v O. D. Cars Ltd., per* Viscount Simonds at p.519 citing Brandeis J. in *Pennsylvania Coal Co. v Mahon* (1922), 260 U.S. 393 at p.417.
[4] [1927] 1 K.B. 458.
[5] [1960] A.C. 490.
[6] [1971] A.C. 508.

prescribed. The House of Lords held that local authorities could choose which course to pursue to safeguard land for road widening, even where the course chosen avoided the payment of compensation. In this case, the course chosen had been the refusal of planning permission and it was clear from the legislation that there was no general right to compensation for an adverse decision.

However, simple and attractive as the distinction between the "taking" of property and the regulation of property may seem at first sight, there is no doubt that sustaining the distinction in practice presents considerable difficulty. The Uthwatt Committee, having drawn the conventional distinction, went on to acknowledge that "it will always be a matter of difficulty to draw the line with any satisfactory logic, *i.e.* to determine the point at which the accepted obligations of neighbourliness or citizenship are exceeded and an expropriation is suffered".[7] In *Westminster Bank Ltd*, Lord Reid described the distinction as "too meticulous".[8] Michelman in a wide ranging review of the criteria developed by the American courts for determining when a particular injurious result of government activity should be classed as a "taking" and thus compensatable shows "that none of the standard criteria yields a solid and self-sufficient rule of decision—that each of them, when attempts are made to erect it into a general principle, is either seriously misguided, ruinously incomplete, or uselessly overbroad".[9] And in *Belfast Corporation* Lord Radcliffe recognised that it was not "out of the question that, on a particular occasion, there might not be a restriction of user so extreme in substance, though not in form, it amounted to a 'taking' of the land for the benefit of the public".[10]

13–02   An illustration of the difficulty of drawing the line between regulation and expropriation is provided by a series of decisions on the validity of conditions imposed on grants of planning permission. Section 37(1) of the Town and Country Planning (Scotland) Act 1997 empowers a planning authority to impose "such conditions as they think fit" on a grant of permission.[11] The corresponding English legislation is in identical terms. In *Hall & Co. v Shoreham-by-Sea UDC*[12] conditions were imposed on a permission for industrial development requiring the developers to construct at their own expense a service road along the

---

[7] "Final Report of the Expert Committee on Compensation and Betterment" (1942) HMSO para.32 (Cmnd. 6386).

[8] [1971] A.C. 508 at p.529.

[9] F. I. Michelman, "Property, Utility, and Fairness: Comments on the Ethical Foundations of 'Just Compensation' Law" (1967) 80 Harv. L.R. 1165. See, too, J. Sax, "Takings, Private Property and Public Rights" (1971) 81 Yale L.J. 149; R. A. Epstein, *Takings, Private Property and the Power of Eminent Domain* (Harvard University Press, 1985); F Michelman, "Takings" (1987) 88 Colum. L. Review, 1600; J. Sax, "Property Rights and the Economy of Nature: Understanding *Lucas v South Carolina Coastal Council*" (1993) 45 *Stanford Law Review* 1433; and M. Purdue, "When a regulation of land becomes a taking of land—a look at two recent decisions of the United States Supreme Court" [1995] J.P.L. 279.

[10] [1960] A.C. 490 at p.525.

[11] For a discussion of the restrictions woven by the courts around this seemingly very wide power see: J. Rowan Robinson, E. Young, M. Purdue and E. Farquharson-Black, *Scottish Planning Law and Procedure* (W. Green & Son Ltd., 2001), Chap.9.

[12] [1964] 1 W.L.R. 240.

frontage of the site and to give a right of passage over the road to and from adjoining sites. The Court of Appeal held the conditions to be unreasonable. Wilmer L.J. said, "I can certainly find no clear and unambiguous words in the Town and Country Planning Act 1947, authorising the defendants in effect to take away the plaintiffs' rights of property without compensation by the imposition of conditions such as those sought to be imposed."[13] In somewhat similar vein, Lord Widgery C.J. in *R. v London Borough of Hillingdon, ex p. Royco Homes Ltd*[14] categorised as a "fundamental departure from the rights of ownership and unreasonable" conditions which required the first occupiers of a scheme of residential development to be drawn from the local authority's housing waiting list and which provided for such persons to have security of tenure for 10 years. In *M. J. Shanley Ltd. (in liquidation) v Secretary of State for the Environment*[15] Woolf J., relying on *Hall and Co.*, held that a condition requiring the provision of 40 acres of open space for public use was unreasonable. In *Westminster Renslade Ltd. v Secretary of State for the Environment*,[16] Forbes J. relying on *London Borough of Hillingdon* held that it was wrong to refuse planning permission because the application did not contain provision for an increase in the proportion of parking spaces subject to public control. It was, he said, "perfectly simple to provide off street car parking which was under public control; the local authority could acquire the land to do so. But it was wholly illegitimate to try to seek to do that by imposing conditions on the planning consent." And in *City of Bradford Metropolitan Council v Secretary of State for the Environment*,[17] Lloyd L.J. giving judgement for the Court of Appeal held that a condition on a planning permission for residential development which required improvements to a public road to be undertaken on land which was not owned or controlled by the developers was unreasonable. He could see no relevant distinction between that case and the decision in *Hall & Co.* It would seem to be implicit in all these decisions (and it is made explicit in *Hall & Co.*) that the conditions in question effectively overstepped the mark between mere regulation and the expropriation of land for public purposes without compensation.

On the other hand, in *Brittania (Cheltenham) Ltd. v Secretary of State for the Environment*[18] Sir Douglas Frank was prepared to accept as valid a condition which required the provision of public open space in association with a scheme of residential development. The factor which appeared to distinguish the circumstances in this case from those in *M. J. Shanley Ltd. (in liquidation)* was that the condition did not require land to be dedicated to the public. Yet curiously, the economic loss imposed on the developer would be likely to be heavier in the circumstances of

[13] See above at p.251. See, too, Pearson L.J. at p.260.
[14] [1974] Q.B. 720. See, too, *David Lowe and Sons Ltd. v Musselburgh Town Council*, 1973 S.C. 130; 1974 S.L.T. 5.
[15] [1982] J.P.L. 380.
[16] (1984) 48 P. & C.R. 255; [1983] J.P.L. 454.
[17] [1986] J.P.L. 598.
[18] [1978] J.P.L. 554 (subsequently quashed by the Court of Appeal on other grounds [1979] J.P.L. 534). And see also *R. v Gillingham Borough Council, ex p. F. Parham Ltd.* [1988] J.P.L. 336.

the *Brittania* case in view of the continuing maintenance burden. Once dedicated, the burden of maintaining open space generally passes to the local authority.[19]

And in *Tesco Stores v Secretary of State for the Environment*[20] Lord Hoffman observed that:

> "[T]he test of *Wednesbury* unreasonableness applied in *Hall & Co Ltd v Shoreham-by-Sea UDC* to conditions is quite inconsistent with the modern practice in relation to planning obligations which has been encouraged by the Secretary of State in Circular 6/91 and by Parliament in the new section 106 of the Town and Country Planning Act 1990 and the new section 278 of the Highways Act 1980 and approved by the Court of Appeal in *R v South Northamptonshire DC, ex parte Crest Homes plc*, October 13, 1994".[21]

Although planning obligations have not been introduced into Scotland, encouragement to use planning agreements for much the same sort of purposes is given in SDD Circular 12/1996. Lord Hoffman's observation in *Tesco* inevitably raises some doubt about the sort of line between regulation and expropriation which the Court of Appeal was attempting to draw in *Hall*.

However, profitable though it may sometimes be to challenge a restriction *ad hoc* in the courts on the ground that it is not within the scope of the enabling legislation and is in substance a "taking," it would seem that the courts are reluctant to discern any general entitlement to compensation for regulation in the absence of explicit provision in the statute. This is in marked contrast to the position with compulsory purchase legislation. To establish where the cost of complying with regulation falls it is therefore necessary to refer to the relevant legislation.

It would, of course, be impossible in a book such as this to canvas every code of regulation. The size of such a task is underlined by the comment in a white paper that "there is no readily available measure of the number of regulations, but these run into thousands of pages of statutes".[22] The Uthwatt Committee in their report in 1942, however, summarised the general position. After describing the history of the growth of regulation, the report continued:

> "the essence of the compensation problem as regards the imposition of restrictions appears to be this—at what point does the public interest become such that a private individual ought to be called on to comply, at his own cost, with a restriction or requirement designed to secure that public interest? The history of the imposi-

---

[19] It should, however, be noted that local authorities are increasingly looking for capitalised maintenance payments to accompany the dedication of open space—see J. Rowan Robinson and M. G. Lloyd, *Land Development and the Infrastructure Lottery* (T. & T. Clark, 1988) Ch.4.

[20] [1995] 1 W.L.R. 759.

[21] See above at p.779.

[22] "Building Businesses . . . Not Barriers" (1986) HMSO para.3.7 (Cmnd. 9794).

tion of obligations without compensation has been to push that point progressively further on and to add to the list of requirements considered to be essential to the well-being of the community."[23]

Although the 1980s and the first half of the 1990s witnessed a movement towards deregulation of some sectors of the economy and an increasing interest in self-regulation as opposed to formal regulation, this did not alter the general position as regards compensation. Where formal regulation exists the point has been reached where legislation providing for the regulation of heritable property does not, as a general rule, confer an entitlement to compensation. In other words, the cost of complying with regulations relating to the control of pollution, fire precautions, health and safety at work, building control and so on tends to lie where it falls—upon the proprietor. There are, of course, a number of exceptions to the general statement and some of these are discussed below. It may also be open to a proprietor to alter the initial distribution of cost by passing the burden to other sectors of the community, for example, through higher product prices or through deduction from taxation.

The remainder of this chapter is given over to an assessment of three areas where the distribution of the cost of complying with restrictions on the use, development and management of land have been the subject of recent scrutiny. These are development control, mineral operations and nature conservation. These areas are now considered in turn.

"MAINSTREAM" PLANNING CONTROL

"Mainstream" planning control refers to the general development **13–03** control functions of planning authorities under Part III of the Town and Country Planning (Scotland) Act 1997, as amended, and in particular to their ability to regulate the development of land. Although mineral operations are subject to control under Part III of the 1997 Act like other forms of development, there are a number of special features about the regulation of such development which deserve separate consideration. Mineral operations are, accordingly, the subject of a separate section in this chapter. The 1997 Act in Part VII also provides for additional controls in special cases. These include trees and advertisements. Furthermore, the Planning (Listed Buildings and Buildings in Conservation Areas) (Scotland) Act 1997 provides for the special control of buildings of architectural or historic interest. The operation of these additional controls will in certain circumstances confer an entitlement to compensation but these controls are not a part of mainstream planning control and are beyond the scope of this section of the chapter.[24]

In a report in 1973, JUSTICE aptly observed that "[t]he ability or otherwise of an owner of an interest in land to claim compensation in

---

[23] "Final Report of the Expert Committee on Compensation and Betterment" *supra*, para.33.

[24] For an explanation of the entitlement to compensation in respect of the operation of these additional controls see J. Rowan Robinson, E. Young, M. Purdue and E. Farquharson-Black, *Scottish Planning Law and Procedure, supra*, Chaps 17–19.

respect of any loss he has suffered as a result of the exercise by a local planning authority of its power to control the development of land, can be explained historically but not logically."[25] It would therefore seem appropriate to devote some space to tracing the history of the compensation provisions for regulating the development of land. At the outset, however, it is desirable to make a distinction between the regulation of proposals for new development and the regulation of the existing use of land. New development is not a technical term[26]; it simply refers to new operations on land or to a change to a new use. For the purposes of this chapter the existing use of land is taken to refer not only to the activity presently being carried on but also to activity for which permission exists but has not yet been implemented. The general scheme of the 1997 Act is that the regulation of new development does not, except where a purchase notice takes effect, give rise to an entitlement to compensation. It, therefore, conforms to the general pattern described above. The regulation of the existing use of land, however, does entitle a landowner to compensation. It is convenient to deal with the position relating to new development and to the existing use of land in turn.

1. Regulating new development

13–04   Although, as stated above, the compensation implications of regulating new development are straightforward, the evolution of the legislation to this point has been tortuous. What follows is an historical summary of the evolution of the complex financial provisions of the planning legislation. The purpose of the summary is to explain how and why the present position has been arrived at.

Planning control developed from the public health and housing legislation of the nineteenth century. The first planning Act, the Housing, Town Planning, etc. Act 1909 enabled local authorities to prepare "schemes" for controlling the development of new housing areas so as to secure "proper sanitary conditions, amenity and convenience". The Act gave owners a right, subject to certain exceptions, to claim compensation where their property was injuriously affected by the making of a scheme. Conversely, authorities could recover betterment from a person whose property was increased in value by the operation of a scheme. It is not clear why a compensation entitlement was included in the legislation; Lord Radcliffe in *Belfast Corporation* suggested that it may have had something to do with the shift in emphasis from "consideration of public health to the wider and more debatable ground of public amenity."[27]

The next significant step was the Town and Country Planning (Scotland) Act 1932 which enabled local authorities to make planning schemes, effectively a form of zoning plan, for almost any type of land

---

[25] JUSTICE, "Compensation for Compulsory Acquisition and Remedies for Planning Restrictions together with a Supplemental Report" (Stevens & Sons Ltd, 1973) para.64.

[26] The Town and Country Planning (Scotland) Act 1972 in s.19(5) defined "new development" as development other than that described in Schedule 6 to that Act. However, much of Schedule 6 was repealed by the Planning and Compensation Act 1991 and the statutory definition of 'new development' was repealed at the same time (but see the 1997 Act, Sch.11).

[27] [1960] A.C. 490 at p.524.

whether built-up or undeveloped. The 1932 Act made no fundamental change in the basis of the compensation provisions but added to the list of restrictions in respect of which compensation might be excluded. The result was that compensation could be excluded, for example, in respect of a provision limiting the density of development but not in respect of a provision forbidding building altogether. The Uthwatt Committee in attempting to explain the distinction appeared to regard the outright prohibition of development as amounting almost to an expropriation of a proprietary right or interest. "The difference in treatment as regards compensation may be rested on the difference between expropriation of property on the one hand and restriction on user while leaving ownership and possession undisturbed on the other."[28]

The report of the Royal Commission on the Distribution of Industrial Population in 1940 expressed serious misgivings about the effect of the compensation provision. "Evidence has been placed before the Commission that the difficulties that are encountered by planning authorities under these provisions are so great as seriously to hamper the progress of planning throughout the country".[29] The burden of compensation where planning considerations dictated a prohibition on development was often far too great for local authorities to bear. The result was that planning authorities were unwilling to risk the preparation of a really strong scheme. The commission considered a proposal for the acquisition by the state of the development rights in undeveloped land but because of the important issues of finance and policy involved they recommended the appointment of a body of experts to examine the whole question of compensation, betterment and development.

Such a committee (the Uthwatt Committee) was duly appointed and reported in 1942.[30] The committee concluded that if planning control was to operate effectively, local authorities should be able to make decisions free from the shadow of compensation claims.[31] "It is clear that under a system of well-conceived planning the resolution of competing claims and the allocation of land for the various requirements must proceed on the basis of selecting the most suitable land for the particular purpose, irrespective of the existing value which may attach to the individual parcels of land."[32] As regards undeveloped land the committee recommended the immediate vesting in the state of the rights of development on payment of fair compensation, such vesting to be secured by the imposition of a prohibition against development otherwise than with the consent of the state.[33] The recommendations as regards developed land were more complex but it is unnecessary to go into these as it was the proposals for undeveloped land upon which the subsequent legislation was built.[34]

---

[28] "Final Report of the Expert Committee on Compensation and Betterment", *supra*, para.35.

[29] HMSO para.248 (Cmnd. 6153).

[30] "Final Report of the Expert Committee on Compensation and Betterment", *supra*.

[31] See above para.25.

[32] See above para.22.

[33] See above para.56.

[34] For a detailed discussion of the events leading up to the 1947 planning legislation see J. B. Cullingworth, "Environmental Planning" (1975) HMSO Vol. 1.

The Town and Country Planning (Scotland) Act 1947, introduced by the post-war Labour Government with effect from July 1, 1948, vested in the state the right to develop land. From that time forward, development could only take place upon obtaining the consent of the planning authority. The 1947 Act provided for the payment of a charge on obtaining consent, subject to certain exceptions, to be levied by the Central Land Board. The charge, which was levied at an amount equal to the value by which the land was estimated to have increased as a result of the consent, was intended to secure the recovery of increases in value created by the efforts of the community as a whole. Differing from Uthwatt, the government took the view that owners who were unable to realise development value as a result of the operation of the legislation were not on that account entitled to compensation. Indeed, it would have been logically inconsistent to have provided compensation for a refusal of planning permission given that any increase in value arising from a grant of planning permission was recovered by the state through the development charge. However, it was recognised that the legislation would cause hardship in many cases where land had been acquired prior to the Act in the expectation that it might be developed. Accordingly, claims were invited against a global fund set up for Britain as a whole of £300 million from landowners who could show that their land had development value on the day the legislation came into force that prevented them from realising it. It was intended that payment of established claims would be made on a once and for all basis in 1953.

13–05 However, the incoming Conservative administration in 1951 decided to abolish the development charge thus restoring development value in land to the landowner in the event of planning permission for development being obtained.[35] It followed from this that there would no longer be any necessity to compensate people out of the global fund for hardship caused by loss of development value. The Town and Country Planning Act 1953 accordingly abolished the levy of a development charge on future development and repealed the provisions in the 1947 Act dealing with the distribution of the £300 million fund before any payments were made.

At this point, the government encountered a problem.[36] There were a considerable number of existing owners of land which was ripe for development who had purchased the land at a price which reflected that expectation but who would not for whatever good planning reason obtain permission for its development. Under the financial provisions of the 1947 Act they would have been in a position to claim against the global fund. Now they could not. As development value had been restored to landowners in the event of planning permission being obtained, their failure to realise development value following upon a refusal of permission would be particularly galling. Having restored

---

[35] The arrangements for dealing with development value have varied over the intervening years but as they have not been linked directly to the question of compensation for the regulation of land they are not described here.

[36] For a detailed discussion of the events surrounding the unscrambling of the financial provisions of the 1947 Act see J. B. Cullingworth, "Environmental Planning" (1980) HMSO Vol. IV.

development value to landowners on a grant of permission, the logical step would have been to pay compensation upon a refusal of permission. However, the government would not contemplate the cost of such an exercise; in any event, the experience of the 1932 Act suggested that such an approach would be anathema to effective planning control. The problem was seen essentially as of a transitional nature. New acquisitions of land for development would depend on the availability of planning permission and the price paid would reflect the outcome of the application.

To meet the problem, the Town and Country Planning (Scotland) Act 1954 made provision for compensation to be paid, subject to certain exceptions, following an adverse planning decision on an application for new development of land in respect of which a claim had been lodged and accepted against the now defunct global fund. In other words, compensation in such cases, was to be only for loss of development value which had accrued in the past up to the point at which the 1947 Act took effect. No compensation was to be paid for loss of development value which accrued in the future. Any such established claim, together with an additional sum in lieu of interest amounting to one seventh of the amount of the claim, was converted on January 1, 1955 into the "original unexpended balance of established development value" attaching to the land. Compensation was payable by the Secretary of State in the event of an adverse planning decision relating to land in respect of which there remained an unexpended balance of established development value. The provisions were set out in Part VII of the Town and Country Planning (Scotland) Act 1972. The balance could be reduced or wholly expended in several ways but principally by the payment of compensation following upon such a decision or by deduction of development value realised following a grant of planning permission in respect of the land.

An entitlement to compensation in respect of an unexpended balance of established development was rarely encountered in practice during the 1970s and 1980s. This was because over the intervening years, planning permission for the development of such land (which was considered ripe for development as long ago as 1948) would have been either persistently refused for whatever good planning reasons or granted. In the former case, the balance would have been extinguished following the payment of compensation; in the latter, it would have been extinguished by deduction of the development value realised. For those very few cases where an unexpended balance remained, the compensation payable for a refusal of planning permission was unlikely, based as it was on 1948 development values, to bear any relation to the development value foregone at the time of refusal.[37] It remained, however, the only circumstance in which compensation was payable for the regulation of new development. "It may well be," said the JUSTICE report in 1973, "that the real anomaly in this area of law is not that many people receive no compensation, but that a few people receive some in the shape of the 'unexpended balance of established development value' attached to their

---

[37] The extensive and somewhat cumbersome provisions relating to unexpended balances of established development value were set out in Part VII of the Town and Country Planning (Scotland) Act 1972.

land . . . We believe that the community has now accepted that there should in general be no payment of compensation for such restrictions."[38] It was not, however, until 1991 that this anomaly was eventually disposed of. Section 60(1) of the Planning and Compensation Act 1991 repealed the provisions of Part VII of the 1972 Act. The position now, as Lord Reid observed in *Westminster Bank Ltd. v Minister of Housing and Local Government*, is that "when planning permission is refused the general rule is that the unsuccessful applicant does not receive any compensation".[39]

13–06   Reference was made in the introduction to the comment of Lord Radcliffe in *Belfast Corporation v O. D. Cars Ltd.*[40] that it was not "out of the question that, on a particular occasion, there might not be a restriction of user so extreme in substance, though not in form, it amounted to a 'taking of the land for the benefit of the public'." The 1997 Act effectively acknowledges that the outcome of an adverse decision on an application for development may in certain circumstances be so severe as to amount to an expropriation of land by enabling an owner or lessee of land to serve what is known as a "purchase notice" on the planning authority requiring them to purchase the land at its market value. It is a form of inverse compulsory purchase.[41]

Section 88 of the 1997 Act provides where planning permission is refused or is granted subject to conditions, and the owner or lessee believes that:

(i) the land has become incapable of reasonably beneficial use in its existing state; and

(ii) in a case where planning permission was granted subject to conditions, the land cannot be rendered capable of reasonably beneficial use by the carrying out of the permitted development in accordance with these conditions; and

(iii) in any case, that the land cannot be rendered capable of reasonably beneficial use by the carrying out of any other development for which planning permission has been granted or for which the planning authority or the Scottish Ministers have undertaken to grant planning permission; he may serve a purchase notice on the planning authority requiring them to purchase his interest in the land.

There is no prescribed form of notice but it should be served within 12 months of the adverse decision.[42] Within three months of service of the

---

[38] "Compensation for Compulsory Acquisition and Remedies for Planning Restrictions together with a Supplemental Report", *supra*, para.66.

[39] [1971] A.C. 508 at p.529.

[40] [1960] A.C. 490.

[41] See, generally, on purchase notices, J. Rowan Robinson, E. Young, M. Purdue and E. Farquharson-Black, *Scottish Planning Law and Procedure*, *supra*, Chap.13; also E. Young, 'Purchase Notices in Practice" 1987 S.L.T. 269.

[42] Section 88(2). In the event of an appeal, the 12 months' runs from the date of the appeal decision (*Reside v North Ayrshire Council*, 2001 S.L.T. 6, OH). And see the Town and Country Planning (General) (Scotland) Regulations 1976, reg.4(2). A model form is annexed to D.H.S. Circular 74/1959.

notice, the planning authority should respond indicating either that they or some other public body is willing to comply with the notice or that they are not willing to comply with it, stating the reason, and have referred a copy to the Scottish Ministers for a decision (s.90(1)). If the authority or some other public body are willing to comply with the notice, they are deemed to be authorised to acquire the interest compulsorily and to have served a notice to treat on the date of their response (s.90(3)). Compensation is to be assessed as for compulsory purchase.

In the event of the notice being referred to the Scottish Ministers, they may confirm the notice and in doing so may substitute some other body for the planning authority on whom it was served. Alternatively, they may, in lieu of confirming the notice, grant planning permission for the development which was refused or, if permission was granted subject to conditions, revoke or amend the conditions. Or they may direct that planning permission be granted for some alternative development in the event of an application being made in that behalf (s.92).[43]

The Scottish Ministers may refuse to confirm a purchase notice, even though they are satisfied that the land has become incapable of reasonably beneficial use, if the land has a restricted use by virtue of a previous planning permission and it appears to the Ministers that the land should continue to be allocated for that restricted use. Land is to be treated as having a restricted use if it is part of a larger area in respect of which planning permission was previously granted and either the application contemplated, or a condition on the permission required, that the land should remain undeveloped or be preserved or laid out as amenity land in relation to the remainder of the land (s.93).[44]

The key to the purchase notice provisions is the phrase "incapable of reasonably beneficial use". It is not enough to show that land will be of less use or value as a result of the refusal or conditions than it would have been if the full development potential could be realised.[45] That is generally the effect of an adverse planning decision. What has to be shown is that the land has become incapable of reasonably beneficial use in its existing state.[46]

2. Regulating the existing use of land

The system of planning control, observed Davies, "rests on the **13–07** assumption that the existing use of land—and the value of that use—is the owner's."[47] This is in contrast to the prospect of the development of

---

[43] See E. Young, "Purchase Notices and the Minister's Discretion" 1987 S.L.T. 273.

[44] *Strathclyde Regional Council v Secretary of State for Scotland*, 1987 S.L.T. 724.

[45] *R. v Minister of Housing and Local Government, ex p. Chichester R.D.C.* [1960] 1 W.L.R. 587.

[46] See D.H.S. Circular 74/1959; also *Adams & Wade Ltd. v Minister of Housing and Local Government* (1965) 18 P. & C.R. 60; *Wain v Secretary of State for the Environment* (1981) 44 P. & C.R. 289; *Purbeck District Council v Secretary of State for the Environment* (1982) 263 E.G. 261; *Balco Transport Services Ltd. v Secretary of State for the Environment (No 2)* [1986] 1 W.L.R. 88; and *Whiston v Secretary of State for the Environment* [1989] J.P.L. 178; also the appeal decisions noted at [1976] J.P.L. 649; [1977] J.P.L. 256; [1980] J.P.L. 194; [1982] J.P.L. 257; [1986] J.P.L. 374; [1988] J.P.L. 51; [1991] J.P.L. 774 and 978; and [1992] J.P.L. 286 and 386. See, too, E. Young, "Purchase Notices in Practice" 1987 S.L.T. 269.

[47] K. Davies, *Law of Compulsory Purchase and Compensation* (4th ed., Butterworths), p.271.

land which as a result of the 1947 legislation belongs to the community. The scheme of the legislation is that any proposal to regulate the existing use *will* give rise to an entitlement to compensation.

Regulation of the existing use of land may arise in one of two ways.[48] First of all, a planning authority may take action to secure the discontinuance of a use currently being carried on. Secondly, an authority may revoke or modify an existing but unimplemented planning permission for development.

Until 1991 there was a third situation in which the regulation of the existing use of land could give rise to an entitlement to compensation. Schedule 6 to the Town and Country Planning (Scotland) Act 1972 listed nine categories of development which were not treated as new development. A refusal or conditional grant of planning permission by the Secretary of State for the development of land for any of the purposes in Part II of Schedule 6 to the 1972 Act, as amended, entitled a person with an interest in the land to compensation from the planning authority if it could be shown that the interest was of less value than it would have been if the permission had been granted or granted unconditionally.

The categories of development listed in Part II of Schedule 6 were a hangover from the financial provisions of the 1947 legislation. When planning permission was granted under that Act, a development charge was, until 1953, imposed equal to the amount of any development value arising from the permission. However, certain categories of development listed in the Third Schedule to that Act were considered to be so closely related to the existing use of the land that, as a concession to landowners, they were treated for the purposes of the legislation as part of the existing use value and thus not subject to the development charge which was only levied in respect of planning permission for new development. The converse position was that a refusal of planning permission or the imposition of onerous conditions for such categories of development were treated as a derogation of existing use rights and thus eligible for compensation, at least as regards the categories of development in Part II of Schedule 6. Those categories of development were treated as forming part of the existing use value of the land to the landowner so that under the general scheme of the 1972 Act an adverse decision qualified for compensation.

The SDD consultation paper (1986) on proposed modifications to the compensation provisions relating to the regulation of development commented, of the entitlement in the 1972 Act, that "at a time when local authority expenditure is severely constrained, many planning authorities are unwilling to refuse planning permission because that may lead to a liability to pay compensation if the Secretary of State confirms that decision on appeal," a remark reminiscent of the criticism by the Royal Commission on the Distribution of Industrial Population of the

---

[48] It would seem that the existing use of land may also, in certain circumstances, be regulated without payment of compensation by way of a condition on a grant of planning permission for new development (*Kingston-upon-Thames Royal London Borough Council v Secretary of State for the Environment* [1973] 1 W.L.R. 1549; *British Airports Authority v Secretary of State for Scotland*, 1979 S.C. 200; 1979 S.L.T. 197).

compensation provisions in the Town and Country Planning (Scotland) Act 1932. The paper went on to point out that the entitlement was open to abuse by an unscrupulous applicant who could submit an outrageous proposal simply in the hope of provoking a refusal thus opening the way to a compensation claim. The paper accordingly invited comment on a proposal that the entitlement to compensation for a refusal of planning permission for Schedule 6 (Part II) development should be repealed. It was eventually repealed by section 60(2) of the Planning and Compensation Act 1991.

The two circumstances in which the regulation of the existing use of land may arise and may trigger a compensation entitlement are now summarised in turn.

1. Discontinuance:

A planning authority may, because, for example, of a change in policy **13–08** or because of a change in the character of an area, conclude that a particular use of land should be discontinued, that conditions should be imposed on the continuance of a use or that a building should be altered or removed. They may secure this by way of an order under section 71 of the 1997 Act.[49] Such an order is of no effect unless it is confirmed by the Scottish Ministers. When an order is submitted to the Ministers for confirmation, notice must be served on the owner and on any lessee, occupier or other person who may be affected. There is a minimum period of 28 days for objection and the Ministers must, before confirming the order, grant a hearing to any such person if so requested.

If such an order is confirmed, any person who can show that they have suffered damage by depreciation of the value of an interest in land or by being disturbed in the enjoyment of land is entitled to compensation from the authority (s.83(1)(2)). Such a claim may include any cost reasonably incurred in carrying out any works required by the order. A claim should be lodged within six months of the making of the order or such longer period as the Scottish Ministers may allow.[50] Failure to comply with such an order is an offence (s.148(1)).

2. Revocation or modification:

Under section 65 of the 1997 Act, a planning authority may, if they **13–09** consider it expedient to do so, by order revoke or modify any planning permission granted under Part III of the Act.[51] The power may be exercised in respect of building or other operations, at any time before they have been completed and in respect of a change of use, at any time before the change of use has taken place. Once operations have been completed or a change of use has occurred the planning authority would have to have recourse to a discontinuance order under section 71 of the Act to regulate the existing use (above).

---

[49] See, generally, on discontinuance orders, J. Rowan Robinson, E. Young, M. Purdue and E. Farquharson-Black, *Scottish Planning Law and Procedure, supra*, Ch.14.

[50] Town and Country Planning (General) (Scotland) Regulations 1976, reg.4.

[51] See, generally, on revocation orders, *Scottish Planning Law and Procedure, supra*, Ch.14.

A revocation or modification order will not generally take effect unless it is confirmed by the Scottish Ministers although provision is made under section 67 for an expedited procedure which does not require the Ministers' confirmation where the owner and any lessee, occupier and other affected persons have stated that they have no objection. Such procedure might be employed when a substitute planning permission is to be granted and no compensation entitlement will arise. When submitting an order to the Ministers for confirmation, the planning authority must notify the owner and any lessee, occupier and other affected persons, and any such person has a right to be heard by a person appointed by the Scottish Ministers before a decision is made regarding confirmation of the order.

Where such an order is confirmed, any person having an interest in the land who can show that he has incurred expenditure in carrying out work which is rendered abortive by the order or has otherwise sustained loss or damage, including depreciation in the value of the interest, directly attributable to the order is entitled to be compensated by the authority (s.76(1)). A claim for compensation should be submitted to the planning authority within six months of the date of the order although this period may be extended by the Scottish Ministers.[52]

It should be noted that planning permission may be granted, not only in response to an application under Part III of the 1997 Act, but by way of a development order (s.30). In particular, Article 3 of the Town and Country Planning (General Permitted Development) (Scotland) Order 1992, as amended, grants planning permission for the classes of development specified in Schedule 1. However, the Scottish Ministers or a planning authority may, if they consider it expedient that any such development should not be carried out, except in response to an application for permission made in the normal way, withdraw the permission at any time before it is implemented by way of a direction under Article 4 of the order.

The direction may apply to: (i) all or any development of all or any of the classes in the Schedule in any particular specified area; or (ii) any particular specified development falling within any of the classes in the Schedule.

A direction by the planning authority generally requires the approval of the Scottish Ministers. There is no right of appeal. The consequence of a direction is that the specified development no longer has permission and an application for permission must be submitted to the planning authority and approved in the normal way before it can commence. The significance of this for the purposes of this chapter is that, if such an application is refused or subjected to conditions more onerous than those originally imposed by the development order, a claim for compensation may be lodged with the planning authority under section 77 of the Act and compensation is assessed as for a revocation order.

A claim under section 77 may also be made where planning permission for development granted by a development order is withdrawn following the revocation or amendment of the order by the Scottish Ministers and where a subsequent application under Part III for

---

[52] Town and Country Planning (General) (Scotland) Regulations 1976, reg.4.

planning permission for the development in question is refused or onerously conditioned. However, a claim may only be made in these circumstances if the subsequent application for planning permission is made within a year of the revocation or amendment of the order.[53]

3. Conclusion

One of the interesting features of the history of the compensation **13–10** provisions for mainstream planning control is the reverse of the compensation entitlement. A general right to compensation, such as existed prior to and under the 1932 Act is not, it seems, consistent with an effective system of regulation.

It is probable that most people today would regard as reasonable the provisions whereby compensation is payable for action initiated by a planning authority to discontinue an existing use of land or to revoke a planning permission. The value of that use or permission belongs to the landowner. Such provisions, however, are not often invoked in practice because, as Grant observes, "[l]ocal authorities have rarely been in a position to buy environmental improvements by using the powers of direct intervention".[54]

MINERAL OPERATIONS

Mineral operations are "development" within the meaning of section **13–11** 26(1) of the Town and Country Planning (Scotland) Act 1997 and consequently require planning permission in the normal way. As with other forms of development, the general rule is that a refusal of permission or the imposition of conditions on a grant of permission will not give rise to a claim for compensation. It is in the context of the regulation of existing operations that the regime governing the winning and working of minerals departs in certain important respects from the general scheme of the planning legislation.

As mentioned above, the position under the 1997 Act is that proposals to restrict or take away an established right to use or develop land will generally entitle the landowner to compensation. That entitlement was modified by the Town and Country Planning (Minerals) Act 1981 in respect of existing mineral operations. The 1981 Act was the progeny of the report of the Stevens Committee on *Planning Control over Mineral Working*.[55] Stevens recognised that the winning and working of minerals could be distinguished from other operations in a number of important respects.[56] Most operations are transitory; they are simply a means to an end in that they fit land for some alternative use. Mineral operations, on the other hand, are an end in themselves; and, although not permanent, they may be carried on for a great many years. They do not fit land for

---

[53] 1997 Act, s.77(2).

[54] M. Grant, *Urban Planning Law* (Sweet & Maxwell, 1982) First Supplement (1986) p.646.

[55] Report of the Committee under the chairmanship of Sir Roger Stevens (1976) HMSO.

[56] See above, Chap.3.

some other use; indeed, they are essentially destructive of land. Further-more, there is little scope for locational choice; such operations must, of course, locate where the minerals exist. As mineral deposits tend to coincide with some of our most interesting and beautiful landscapes, proposals for their extraction are often attended by considerable contro-versy. Mainstream planning control, geared as it is to once and for all decisions, has proved to be incapable of adequately safeguarding the environment over the life of the mineral operations. Conditions imposed at the outset may become less relevant and effective as time goes by. Because of these characteristics, Stevens recommended that certain additional controls should be applied to the winning and working of minerals. The 1981 Act implemented these recommendations in modi-fied form. Broadly, the effect of the 1981 Act was to increase the burden of regulation on operators without compensation.

In particular, the 1981 Act imposed a duty on planning authorities to review mineral sites in their area from time to time with a view to making any changes to the terms of the planning permission which circumstances might require (below). It was recognised, however, the conventional powers to make revocation and discontinuance orders were unlikely to achieve the changes required, partly because they did not address some of the difficulties arising from mineral working and partly because the obligation to pay compensation was a disincentive. To overcome these problems, the 1981 Act introduced additional mecha-nisms for tackling some of the problems arising from existing mineral sites and also conferred power on the Secretary of State to make regulations modifying the normal compensation entitlement.

The new powers did not work as well as intended and, following a review,[57] the government introduced further measures in the Planning and Compensation Act 1991 directed at the oldest extant mineral consents.[58] Further reforms directed at strengthening control over more recent consents were brought forward in the Environment Act 1995.[59] All these provisions for regulating existing mineral sites are now to be found in the 1997 Act.

The provisions are complex and what follows is no more than a summary of their effect.[60] Their relevance to this chapter is that they provide an illustration of a political decision to redistribute the cost of complying with regulation from the community to the individual land-owner (or in this case the mineral operator). The provisions revolve around four changes in the normal approach under the planning legislation to the regulation of existing activity.

Aftercare conditions: First of all, section 41(6) and Schedule 3 of the 1997 Act enables a planning authority to impose an "aftercare" condi-tion where planning permission for mineral working is granted subject to a condition requiring restoration of the site. Stevens considered that

[57] *The Reform of Old Mineral Permissions 1948–1981*, Department of the Environment, 1994.
[58] 1991 Act, s.52.
[59] 1995 Act, s.96 and Sch.13 and 14.
[60] For a detailed discussion of these provisions see J. Rowan Robinson, E. Young, M. Purdue and E. Farquharson Black, *Scottish Planning Law and Procedure*, Chap.19.

restoration conditions tended to lack any clear objective. Now they may be coupled with an "aftercare condition" requiring the land to be planted, cultivated, fertilised, watered, drained or otherwise treated on completion of restoration for a specified period so as to fit the land for use for agriculture, forestry or amenity, a condition which will clearly have cost implications for the mineral operator.[61]

Defined life: Secondly, section 41(6) and Schedule 3 to the 1997 Act **13–12** subjects every planning permission for mineral working to a defined life which unless otherwise specified is to be 60 years from February 22, 1982[62] for consents granted before that date or 60 years from the date of the consent for a consent granted after that date. Stevens thought it important that there should be no doubt about the time for commencement of restoration. The committee also felt that future generations should be allowed an opportunity to review the position.[63]

Periodic review: Thirdly, and most importantly for compensation purposes, planning authorities are required to review mineral permissions from time to time. The procedures for review differ according to the date of the relevant consent. Consents granted between 1943 and 1948 by way of Interim Development Order were required to be registered during 1992 as 'old mining permissions'.[64] Following registration there was a procedure for determining the conditions which should be imposed on the continuation of such permissions. No compensation liability arose from the imposition of such conditions.

Section 74 and Schedule 9 to the 1997 Act, make provision for the first review of consents granted after June 30, 1948 and before February 22, 1982. The reviews were carried out in two phases: Phase 1 sites were those granted permission before December 8 together with later consents for mineral sites in sensitive locations.[65] Consents granted after December 7, 1969 are designated Phase II sites. The legislation distinguishes between 'active' and 'dormant' sites according to when they were last worked.[66] It was not lawful to carry on working a dormant site unless and until the planning authority approved modern conditions for it following a review in accordance with a statutory timetable[67]; active sites could continue in operation while the review process was underway. The review process involved the listing of sites by the planning authority followed by phased applications for the determination of new conditions for the sites. The great majority of the determinations of new conditions for Phase I sites are likely to have been completed. The determination of conditions for Phase II sites will still be underway in some cases. Failure to apply for the determination of new conditions within the appropriate

---

[61] See SDD Circular 5/1982 "Town and Country Planning (Minerals) Act 1981." Such a condition may be added to an existing permission by way of orders under the 1997 Act, ss.65, 71 and Sch.8, as appropriate (see below), subject to the payment of compensation. The compensation entitlement may, however, be reduced in certain circumstances (below).

[62] The date on which the Town and Country Planning (Minerals) Act 1981 came into force.

[63] *Planning Control over Mineral Working* (1976) HMSO para.7.16.

[64] Section 49H and Schedule 9 to the Town and Country Planning (Scotland) Act 1972.

[65] *i.e.*, national scenic areas, natural heritage areas and sites of special scientific interest.

[66] A dormant site is a Phase I or II site in which no mineral development was carried out to any substantial extent between February 22, 1982 and June 6, 1995.

[67] 1997 Act, Sch.9, para.12.

timescale for a Phase I, Phase II or dormant site meant that the consent will have ceased to have effect except in so far as it contains a restoration or aftercare condition.[68] There was a right of appeal to the Scottish Ministers against the imposition of conditions different from those set out in the application. Detailed guidance on such conditions is to be found in SODD Circular 34/1996.

The outcome of the first review for post June 1948 consents may well be the imposition of some new or upgraded conditions. The legislation provides that conditions dealing with environmental and amenity aspects of the site should not attract compensation; conditions restricting working rights "such as to prejudice adversely to an unreasonable degree (i) the economic viability of operating the site, or (ii) the asset value of the site"[69] will give rise to an entitlement and provision is made for determining which is which.[70] New or modified conditions that adversely affect to an unreasonable degree the economic viability of operating the site or the asset value of the site will be treated as though an order has been made under section 65 of the 1997 Act modifying the planning consent[71] thus giving rise to an entitlement to compensation under section 76.

So much for the *first* reviews of mineral permissions granted prior to February 22, 1982. Section 74 and Schedule 10 to the 1997 Act place a duty on planning authorities periodically thereafter to review *all* mineral permissions. Broadly, the first such review must be commenced not later than 15 years from the date of the determination of the conditions for an IDO site or a Phase I or II site or from the date of the grant of planning permission if permission was granted after February 22, 1982. The review process is modelled on that for the first reviews of Phase I and II sites involving an application for the determination of conditions with a right of appeal to the Scottish Ministers. The outcome of such a review may be the imposition of more stringent conditions that restrict working rights in respect of the site.[72] New or modified conditions that restrict working rights will be treated as though an order had been made under section 65 of the 1997 Act modifying the planning consent[73] thus giving rise to a compensation entitlement under section 76.

Revocation, discontinuance, suspension and prohibition orders: Simply altering the conditions attached to a consent for mineral workings may be insufficient to achieve the objectives of a review. It may be necessary to go further and alter the terms of the consent itself. The power in section 65 of the 1997 Act to revoke or modify the terms of a consent applies also to planning permissions for mineral development. The power in section 71 to make a discontinuance order, however, does not apply as it extends only to discontinuing a "use" of land and not an "operation". Mineral workings are classed as "operations" under the planning legislation so, to circumvent this difficulty, Schedule 8, para-

---

[68] See above.

[69] 1997 Act, Sch.9, paras 10(2)(d) and 15.

[70] 1997 Act, Sch.9, para.11.

[71] 1997 Act, Sch.9, para.15.

[72] Working rights are restricted in the circumstances set out in the 1997 Act, Sch.10, para.13(3).

[73] 1997 Act, Sch.10, para.13(4).

graph 1 of the 1997 Act confers a similar power directed at the use of land for the winning and working of minerals, at the alteration and removal of buildings on land so used and at the alteration or removal of plant and machinery. Orders under section 65 or Schedule 8 may provide for the imposition of a restoration condition and, if so, an aftercare condition may also be imposed.

Reference was made during the discussion of "mainstream planning **13–13** control" (above) to the limited use made by planning authorities of the power to make revocation and discontinuance orders because of the compensation entitlement. Planning authorities in their representations to the Stevens Committee made it clear that a system of review would only be effective if the compensation entitlement was modified. This could be justified, they argued, on the ground that the permissions requiring change would be likely to be those where operations had been carried on over a number of years under what, by comparison with present controls, was a relatively relaxed regime of conditions. The change would simply bring further operations on such sites into line with the position on other sites governed by modern permissions. The minerals industry accepted that these arguments had some force in relation to changes in conditions which gave rise to no more than reasonable additional costs. Stevens accordingly concluded that:

> "a mineral operator should be required to bear reasonable costs arising from a review of conditions. We are also satisfied that to require him to bear all costs in every case might often expose him to the risk of an unjustifiable derogation from his existing rights to use or develop his land. We are consequently faced with the task of drawing a line which separates reasonable costs, which the operator will bear, from unreasonable costs, for which he should be compensated. The difficulties of drawing such a line are formidable."[74]

The 1997 Act in section 84 and Schedule 13 make provision for drawing this line. They provide planning authorities with an incentive to use these powers following a review of mineral operations by enabling the Scottish Ministers to make regulations modifying the normal compensation entitlement. The current regulations are the Town and Country Planning (Compensation for Restrictions on Mineral Working and Mineral Waste Depositing) (Scotland) Regulations 1998. These broadly bring the compensation provisions for revocation and discontinuance orders for mineral working in line with the compensation entitlement for new conditions (above) so that, provided the conditions of Regulations 3 or 4, as the case may be, are met, no compensation liability will arise unless the order imposes, modifies or replaces a restriction on working rights.[75]

In addition to revocation and discontinuance orders, planning authorities are given power to make two new types of order in recognition of the environmental problems that can arise from the intermittent nature of mineral operations, problems which may become apparent during a

---

[74] *Planning Control over Mineral Working, supra*, para.8.18.
[75] As defined in Reg.2(1).

review. First of all, a planning authority may, through a 'prohibition order', prohibit the resumption of mineral working where no work has been carried out at a site for at least two years and it appears that the resumption of work is unlikely.[76] Such an order can require steps to be taken to tidy up the site. Such an order requires confirmation by the Scottish Ministers and the procedure is modelled on that for revocation and discontinuance orders. Providing certain conditions are satisfied,[77] the 1998 Regulations apply to modify the compensation entitlement which might be expected to arise from the making of such an order.[78] Where applicable, compensation is payable in respect of expenditure rendered abortive by the order and for other loss or damage directly attributable to the order[79] but no account is to be taken when calculating that loss or damage to the value of any mineral which cannot be won or worked in consequence of the order or to the cost of complying with any restoration or aftercare condition that may be imposed.[80] Regulation 5(1)(b) further provides for the abatement of the sum assessed in accordance with sections 83 (as modified) and 87 of the 1997 Act.[81]

The second new order available to a planning authority is a "suspension order". Where no development has been carried out at a mineral site to any substantial extent for a period of at least twelve months but it appears that resumption is likely, a planning authority may, by way of a "suspension order", require interim steps to be taken for preserving the environment.[82] Such an order requires confirmation by the Scottish Ministers and the procedure is modelled on that for revocation and discontinuance orders. Regulation 6 of the 1998 Compensation Regulations provides for modification of the normal compensation entitlement under section 83 of the 1997 Act. Compensation is payable in respect of expenditure rendered abortive by the making of the order and for other loss or damage directly attributable to the order[83] but no account is to be taken, when calculating that loss or damage, to the value of any mineral that cannot be won or worked in consequence of the order.[84] As with a prohibition order, Reg.6(2) further provides for the abatement of the sum assessed in accordance with sections 83 (as modified) and 87 of the 1997 Act.[85]

Nature Conservation

13–14 Nature conservation is concerned with safeguarding flora, fauna and geological or physiographical features. Although it is concerned with both species and habitats, this part of the chapter is concerned with the

---

[76] 1997 Act, Sch.8, para.3.
[77] Set out in Reg.5(2) of the 1998 Regulations.
[78] Reg.5 modifies the effect of s.83 of the 1997 Act.
[79] Reg.5(3).
[80] Reg.5(3).
[81] The sum is abated by the appropriate portion (as defined in Reg.7) of the sum of £8,1000.
[82] 1997 Act, Sch.8, para.5.
[83] Reg.6(2).
[84] See above.
[85] The sum assessed is to be abated by the appropriate portion (see Reg.7) of the sum of £8,100.

protection of habitats. The question at the heart of this chapter is the extent to which interference by the state in rights in heritable property falling short of "taking" may be the subject of compensation. The picture which emerges from the study of mainstream planning control and mineral operations is one of the state progressively pushing forward the point at which obligations may be imposed without compensation. Nature conservation has been selected for consideration because, at present, it offers a markedly different picture, although that is likely to change (see below). The general position here is that obligations may only be imposed upon payment of compensation.

The focus of this chapter is on the land compensation implications of regulations rather then on the detail of the regulations themselves. This section of the chapter accordingly does no more than outline the regime for safeguarding nature conservation in so far as this is necessary for an understanding of the compensation arrangements.[86]

Responsibility for safeguarding habitats in Scotland rests largely, but not wholly, with Scottish Natural Heritage (SNH).[87] One of the key mechanisms employed by SNH for promoting nature conservation is the designation of sites to which a special safeguarding regime is to be applied. Three principal designations are employed to this end: nature reserves, sites of special scientific interest (SSSIs) and European sites.

Nature reserves may be dealt with shortly. The essential feature of a nature reserve is that it is managed primarily in the interests of nature conservation. "Nature reserves" are defined in section 15 of the National Parks and Access to the Countryside Act 1949 as land managed for the purpose of preserving flora, fauna, or geological or physiographical features and for providing special opportunities for the study of and for research into such matters. Nature reserves are "declared" by SNH under section 19 of the 1949 Act and safeguarded through acquisition or leasing or through negotiation of management agreements with the landowners under section 16 of the 1949 Act. It is through ownership, possession or agreement that the primacy of nature is achieved rather than through regulation.[88] The Wildlife and Countryside Act 1981 (s.35(1)) provides for the declaration by SNH that nature reserves of national importance, held or managed by them under an agreement or held by an approved body, are "national nature reserves", although the term "national nature reserve" was in use before that time. Local authorities may also establish local nature reserves. If SNH wishes to acquire or lease land as a nature reserve or to manage it as a reserve by means of a section 16 agreement, the terms of such acquisition, lease or agreement will reflect the value of the land for any alternative more profitable use. Many national nature reserves are also designated at sites of special scientific interest (below).

SSSIs and European sites are best considered together because it has been government policy to underpin a European site designation in

---

[86] For a detailed account of the regime see C. T. Reid, *Nature Conservation Law* (2nd ed., W. Green & Son Ltd, 2002); and J. Rowan Robinson, C. Philp and M. de la Torre, "The Protection of Habitats" in *Countryside Law in Scotland* (T&T Clark, 2000) Chap.11 (J. Rowan Robinson and D. McKenzie Skene, eds).

[87] A planning application for development in a designated site is dealt with by the appropriate planning authority; SNH is simply a consultee in such a case.

[88] Although bylaws may be made for national nature reserves.

nearly all cases with an SSSI designation. European sites essentially comprise special areas of conservation (SACs) designated under Directive 92/43 on the conservation of natural habitats and of wild fauna and flora (the "Habitats Directive") and special protection areas for birds (SPAs) classified under Directive 79/409 on the conservation of wild birds (the "Birds Directive"). The objective of the Directives is to establish, maintain and, where appropriate, restore, at a favourable conservation status, a coherent European ecological network of natural habitat types and species' habitats. The Habitats Directive has been given effect within the UK through the Conservation (Natural Habitats etc) Regulations 1994. The 1994 Regulations have important application also to sites classified as SPAs under the Birds Directive. As at March 31, 2002, 132 sites covering a total of 520,026 ha had been classified in Scotland as SPAs with more still to come; 222 sites covering a total of 839,739 ha (in some cases overlapping with SPAs) had been submitted to the European Commission as candidate SACs with more still to come.[89]

The UK government is relying on a combination of the SSSI regime and the 1994 Regulations to achieve the necessary protection for European sites. It is appropriate, therefore, to turn at this point to the SSSI regime. The extent to which the 1994 Regulations alter the system of regulation for European sites will be considered at the appropriate points.

13–15   With sites notified as SSSIs, the nature conservation interest has, unlike nature reserves, to fit in with other land management objectives. The legislative provisions for SSSIs are built around a reciprocal notification procedure set out in Part II of the Wildlife and Countryside Act 1981. Section 28 of the Act imposes a duty on SNH, where they are of the opinion that an area of land is of special scientific interest, to notify the fact to the planning authority, to every owner and occupier of the land and to the Scottish Ministers. SNH have no discretion with regard to notification if they consider a site to be of scientific interest—it must be notified. The notification to owners and occupiers will specify the features of scientific interest and list operations which appear to SNH to be likely to damage those features. As at March 31, 2002 1,447 sites covering 1,007,260 ha (approx 13 per cent of Scotland's land area) had been notified as SSSIs in Scotland.[90] Many of these have also subsequently been classified as SPAs or designated as candidate SACs

Provision is made for representations or objections to be made to SNH within a minimum period of three months from notification of a site as an SSSI. Any such representations or objections which are not withdrawn must be referred to the Advisory Committee on SSSIs who provide an independent review of the scientific case for notification. Where there is such a reference, SNH will take account of the views of the Advisory Committee (s.28(2)) and have nine months from the original notification to decide whether to confirm the notification.

The SSSI is, however, safeguarded from the date of original notification. The consequence is that an owner or occupier who wishes to carry out one of the listed operations (referred to as "potentially damaging

[89] *Facts & Figures 2001/02*, SNH, 2002.
[90] *Facts & Figures 2001/02*, SNH, 2002.

operations" (PDO)) must notify SNH (the reciprocal notification). The operation may not be carried out unless: (i) SNH give their consent; or (ii) the operation is carried out in accordance with the terms of an agreement entered into under section 16 of the 1949 Act (a nature reserve agreement) or section 15 of the Countryside Act 1968 (an SSSI agreement); or (iii) four months have elapsed since SNH were notified without consent being given or an agreement being entered into (section 28(5)(6)).

A person who, without reasonable excuse, carries out a P.D.O. without satisfying these requirements commits a criminal offence. It is a reasonable excuse to carry out an operation if it was authorised by a planning permission granted under Part III of the Town and Country Planning (Scotland) Act 1997.

Part II of the 1981 Act regulates land use only in so far as it imposes a temporary restraint on the activities of owners and occupiers. The temporary restraint gives SNH an opportunity to assess the impact of what is proposed on the nature conservation interest and, where the impact is adverse, to attempt to persuade the owner or occupier to desist or to negotiate an agreement to safeguard that interest. The process under the 1981 Act is, however, voluntary. Owners and occupiers of SSSIs are under no obligation to fall in with the wishes of SNH and may persist in proceeding with their activity at the end of the period of restraint.

The government, nonetheless, originally believed that "the best guarantee of the future of Britain's landscape lies in the natural feel for it possessed by those who live and work in it. This is why the heart of the Wildlife and Countryside Act is fashioned from a policy of consent."[91] Those who live and work on the land were thus seen as stewards of the nature conservation interest on behalf of the nation. The regime under Part II is, at present, effectively one of self- regulation; this is manifested in the Code of Guidance issued by the government in 1982 (subsequently withdrawn) which emphasised that the conservation and proper management of SSSIs is vital to the maintenance of Britain's wildlife and urged owners and occupiers to co-operate.[92] However, in order to achieve their nature conservation objectives, the government have not relied solely on the 'natural feel' of those who live and work on the land. There is, as will be explained in a moment, a financial incentive to fall in with SNH's wishes.

Where SNH encounter difficulties in persuading an owner or occupier to fall in with their wishes, provision is made under section 29 of the 1981 Act for an extended period of protection beyond four months to be given by order of the Scottish Ministers to certain SSSIs of national importance. Experience shows that such orders are made *ad hoc* by the Ministers, if they consider it appropriate, in response to a request from SNH.

---

[91] "Operation and Effectiveness of Part II of the Wildlife and Countryside Act 1981: The Government's Reply to the First Report from the Environment Committee" (May 1985) HMSO Cmnd. 9522.

[92] "Code of Guidance for Sites of Special Scientific Interest" (1988) D.of E., M.A.F.F. Scottish Office and Welsh Office.

However, an extended period of protection may not be sufficient to comply with the Habitats Directive and with the 1994 Regulations so far as European sites are concerned. The Directive and the Regulations provide that if a plan or proposal the subject of a PDO notice is likely to have a significant effect on a European site, SNH must assess the implications of what is proposed for the site and if they conclude that it will affect the integrity of the site, consent cannot be given unless there are imperative reasons of overriding public interest (Art.6(3)(4); Regs 20(1)(2) and 24(6)). In other words, the Birds and Habitats Directives and the 1994 Regulations are more prescriptive in their application to European sites than the 1981 Act is to SSSIs. To ensure compliance with European law, SNH, where they experience difficulty in persuading an owner or occupier to fall in with their wishes, will seek a Special Nature Conservation Order from the Scottish Ministers, the effect of which will be to suspend the planned activity indefinitely unless agreement is reached with SNH. Ultimately, SNH have power to promote a compulsory purchase order to secure their objectives (Reg.32(1)).

As mentioned earlier, the SSSI regime provides a considerable incentive for owners and occupiers to co-operate with SNH. The outcome of negotiations following a PDO notice to which SNH cannot consent (whether just for an SSSI or for an SSSI which is also an SPA or a candidate SAC) will in most cases be embodied in a formal agreement. An agreement under section 16 of the 1949 Act or section 15 of the 1968 Act may provide for payments to be made in accordance with guidelines provided by the government.[93] Indeed, section 32(2) of the 1981 Act goes so far as to provide that where an application for a farm capital grant has been made under section 29 of the Agriculture Act 1970 in respect of expenditure incurred or to be incurred for the purposes of activities notified to SNH under sections 28 or 29 of the Act, and the Ministers refuse to make a grant in consequence of an objection from SNH, SNH *must* offer to enter into an agreement imposing restrictions on such activities and providing for the making of payments to the applicant in accordance with the guidelines. And SNH have indicated that they will voluntarily apply the provisions of section 32(2) to applications made for all types of farm capital grant and, until 1989, for grants or felling permission under forestry legislation.[94]

Financial guidelines for management agreements were issued by the government in 1983.[95] Their objective was to establish a means by which a fair balance could be struck which did not place the land user at a financial disadvantage while at the same time ensuring that the interests of the community at large who foot the bill were properly protected.[96] Owners and occupiers may choose between a lump sum or annual payments; tenants are eligible for annual payments only. For agreements, other than those relating to forestry operations, the lump sum

---

[93] The financial regime of Part II of the 1981 Act was based on the compensation guidelines developed to promote moorland preservation on Exmoor.

[94] "Wildlife and Countryside Act 1981—Financial Guidelines for Management Agreements" (1983) *D. of E. Circular 4/83*, para.4.

[95] See above.

[96] "Wildlife and Countryside Act 1981—Review of Financial Guidelines," (April 1987) *D. of E. Consultation Paper*, para.2.

payment represents the difference between the restricted and unre-stricted value of the claimant's interest calculated having regard to the rules set out in section 12 of the Land Compensation (Scotland) Act 1963. Annual payments reflect the net profits foregone because of the agreement. As regards agricultural operations, it is to be assumed in calculating the payment that farm capital grant would have been payable. For agreements relating to forestry operations, lump sum payments are to be determined by individual assessments of net revenue foregone based generally on a comparison of discounted streams of expenditure and income over the period of the agreement and calculated (a) with, and (b) without, the constraints imposed by the particular management agreement. The claimant may, alternatively, elect to receive payment based on the depreciation in value of the land or woodlands concerned assessed according to the rules in section 12 of the 1963 Act. Where annual payments are to be made, these are to be derived from the lump sum calculated as above and amortised to produce a flow of annual payments based on an estimate of current market rates of interest over the period of the agreement. If forestry grant would have been payable, this should be taken into account in assessing the appropriate payment. During the financial year 2001/2002, SNH paid out £1,913,000 on SSSI agreements.[97]

Experience of the guidelines in operation led to criticism that they were complex, imprecise and overgenerous.[98] Consultants were commissioned to examine the operation and effectiveness of the guidelines and they reported in September 1985.[99] Although for a while it seemed likely that the guidelines would be amended, any amendment has now been overtaken by proposals to switch from a system of self-regulation to one of formal regulation with no compensation (see below).

It should be noted that where a Nature Conservation Order has been made under section 29 of the 1981 Act (above), and a PDO notice has been submitted and an agreement has not been concluded, a person having an interest in land comprising an agricultural unit, who can show that the value of his interest is less than it would have been if the order had not been made, will be entitled to compensation from SNH (1981 Act, section 30(2)). Similar provision is made in the 1994 Regulations for a Special Nature Conservation Order (Reg.25). Compensation may also be payable to any person having an interest in land to which a Nature Conservation Order relates who can show that he has incurred abortive expenditure or has incurred other loss or damage (other than a reduction in the value of the interest) as a direct result of the extended period of negotiation resulting from Order.

The compensation provisions relating to the operation of Part II of the 1981 Act could be viewed as in accord with the general scheme for

---

[97] *Annual Report 2001/02*, SNH, 2002. It is not possible to disaggregate the figure for compensation from payments made for work undertaken in SSSIs.

[98] See the arguments rehearsed in the First Report from the Environment Committee of the House of Commons, "Operation and Effectiveness of Part II of the Wildlife and Countryside Act", Session 1984–85 (1985) HMSO Vol.1.

[99] Final Report by Laurence Gould Consultants Ltd, "Wildlife and Countryside Act 1981: Financial Guidelines for Management Agreements" (September 1985) *D.of E. Circular.*

compensating landowners under the planning legislation for restrictions on the existing use of land. The use of land for agriculture and forestry is excluded from the definition of "development" under the Town and Country Planning (Scotland) Act 1997;[1] the right to undertake such activity was not vested in the state under the 1947 planning legislation. The value of such activity belongs to the landowner; any restriction on the realisation of that value as a result of a nature conservation designation is properly the subject of compensation.

However, such a view, to borrow Lord Reid's words, is arguably "too meticulous."[2] The mere fact that the value of an activity belongs to a landowner has not prevented successive governments from imposing restrictions on the activity without compensation. As the Uthwatt Committee observed, the trend has been to push the point at which obligations may be imposed without compensation progressively further forward. Examples of this may be seen, as mentioned earlier, in the fields of building control, health and safety at work, fire precautions and the control of pollution. The decision to couple compensation to an exercise of self-regulation reflects a political decision to employ subsidy rather than formal regulation to promote behavioural change.

This is not, of itself, a cause for criticism. There is a case to be made for the use of economic incentives rather than formal regulation as a mechanism for securing behavioural change.[3] The government have extended the role of such incentives in the countryside in the form of payments to farmers under the Rural Stewardship Scheme for continuing with or adopting farming methods which are environmentally benign; and SNH are providing financial assistance through their Natural Care programme to estate owners who manage land designated as a European site in a manner which supports the objectives of the designation.

However, experience with the compensation provisions of the Town and Country Planning (Scotland) Act 1932 (above) suggests that public bodies are not generally well-placed to buy control and that, if conservation is not to be compromised, the employment of economic incentives must be coupled with a commitment of resources.

13–16 The financial arrangements for safeguarding nature conservation have been the subject of continued criticism. The Environment Committee of the House of Commons, for example, commented that: "[t]he illogicality of one part of government offering financial inducement to someone to do something which another part of government then has to pay him not to, is clear."[4] The arrangements have also been criticised as giving legal expression "to the surprising notion that a farmer has a right to grant aid from the tax-payer: if he is denied it in the wider public interest, he must be compensated for the resulting, entirely hypothetical losses."[5] The

[1] 1997 Act, s.26(2)(e).

[2] *Westminster Bank Ltd. v Minister of Housing and Local Government* [1971] A.C. 508.

[3] J. K. Bowers and P. Cheshire, *Agriculture, The Countryside and Land Use: an Economic Critique* (Methuen, 1983) p.143.

[4] "Operation and Effectiveness of Part II of the Wildlife and Countryside Act", *supra*, para.46.

[5] Letter from the Director of the Council for the Preservation of Rural England to *The Times* cited in P. Lowe, G. Cox, M. MacEwen, T. O'Riordan and M. Winter, *Countryside Conflicts*, (Gower/Maurice Temple Smith, 1986), p.147. But see in this connection *Palatine Graphic Arts Co. Ltd. v Liverpool City Council* (1986) 56 P. & C.R. 308, a case which turned on the question whether the payment of a discretionary regional development grant should be deducted from disturbance compensation.

government's explanation of this "surprising notion" is that it would be unfair to put the particular farmer who happens to be in a conservation area at a disadvantage just because of that reason, as opposed to the farmer next door who might be getting the grant.[6] The explanation is unconvincing. The government have not shown themselves so sensitive to the plight of the developer who is refused planning permission for development because land is designated as a green belt or as a conservation area.

One of the most serious criticisms was that payments were made to owners and occupiers who threatened to damage sites of nature conservation interest while those who voluntarily managed their sites in accordance with that interest received nothing.[7] The Environment Committee recommended that the legislation should be amended to allow for positive conservation measures to be included in agreements. The government response was that it was misreading the 1981 Act to construe it in a way which discouraged the possibility of positive conservation operations. In fact it seems that the existing powers are being interpreted by nature conservation agencies in this more positive way in practice. Rogers and Bishop note in a recent and comprehensive review of the use of management agreements to promote nature conservation in England and Wales that the trend over the last 15 years has been towards the adoption of proactive conservation measures.[8] The same is true of Scotland as well.

These criticisms have had an effect. In a consultation paper issued in 1998 the Scottish Office questioned whether the time had come to bring the SSSI regime into line with planning control by removing the compensation entitlement.[9] Subsequently, a policy statement issued by the Scottish Executive proposed a move towards a position very much in line with the planning legislation[10]; the regulation of existing activity in the interests of nature conservation would give rise to a compensation entitlement but the regulation of new activity would not. This is now the position in England and Wales. Legislation has been promised for Scotland and a draft Nature Conservation (Scotland) Bill was published for consultation in March 2003.

CONCLUSION

In the introduction to this chapter, attention was drawn to the question **13–17** raised by the Uthwatt Committee—at what point does the public interest become such that a private individual ought to be called on to comply, at

---

[6] Hon. W. Waldegrave M.P., cited in the First Report of the Environment Committee of the House of Commons, "Operation and Effectiveness of Part II of the Wildlife and Countryside Act", *supra*, para.14.

[7] See L. Livingstone, J. Rowan Robinson and R. Cunningham, "Management Agreements for Nature Conservation" (1990) *Department of Land Economy Occasional Paper, Aberdeen University*.

[8] C. Rodgers and J. Bishop, "Management Agreements for Promoting Nature Conservation" (1998) RICS.

[9] *People and Nature.*

[10] "The Nature of Scotland" (2001) Annex A para.A3.12.

his own cost, with a restriction or requirement? This chapter shows that there is no clear cut answer. Although the trend has been towards placing the whole cost of compliance on the individual, the trend is by no means consistent. There are differences, as will be apparent from the sections on mainstream planning control and on mineral operations, in the distribution of the burden between the individual and the wider community; and the section on nature conservation provides an example of a code where the cost of compliance is borne entirely by the community. The decision whether or not to compensate for the imposition of restrictions is, at the end of the day, a political one[11] and it is necessary in any given case to refer to the relevant legislation to determine the outcome. The factors which have influenced political choice, although touched on in places, are beyond the scope of this book.[12]

---

[11] But see possible models for determining this question discussed in F. I. Michelman, "Property, Utility and Fairness: Comments on the Ethical Foundations of 'Just Compensation' Law" (1967) 80 Harv. L.R. 1165; J. Sax, "Takings and the Police Power," (1964) 74 Yale L.J. 36; and R. A. Epstein, *Takings, Private Property and the Power of Eminent Domain* (Harvard University Press, 1985).

[12] For an insight into these factors as regards mainstream planning control, see J. B. Cullingworth, *Environmental Planning* (1975) HMSO Vol. I and (1980) HMSO Vol. IV; and as regards nature conservation, P. Lowe *et al.*, *Countryside Conflicts, supra*.

CHAPTER 14

BLIGHT

INTRODUCTION

"Blight" is a term which means different things to different people. **14–01**
There are, as the Interdepartmental Working Group on Blight (IWGB)
pointed out, a great many factors, both natural and man-made, which
may have a "blighting" effect on property values.[1] Natural factors
include coastal erosion and natural emissions of noxious substances from
the ground; man-made factors include the vast spectrum of development
projects—from a major industrial complex to the unsympathetic
redevelopment of an adjoining house. In this chapter "blight" is taken to
refer to the depressing effect on property values of *public* sector actions
and decisions. A nuclear power station or a major road, for example,
may have a depressing effect on the value of land required for or located
near to the works. This depressing effect is sometimes referred to
alternatively as "injurious affection" or "worsenment".

Of course not all public sector actions and decisions serve to depress
the value of land. Some may have the reverse effect. Land allocated for
industrial use or for a hotel, for example, may increase in value if the
public road network serving the site is significantly improved. This
increase in value is generally referred to as "betterment". The way in
which betterment is dealt with in the context of compulsory acquisition
was considered in Chapters 8 and 11.

There would seem to be something to be said for looking at the topics
of betterment and worsenment in the round. In Chapter 11 reference
was made to the opinion of the Scott Committee that "the principle of
Betterment, *i.e.* the principle that persons whose property has clearly
been increased in market value by an improvement should specially
contribute to the cost of such an improvement, and the principle of
Injurious Affection, *i.e.* the principle that persons whose properties are
damaged by the construction or user of the promoters' works shall be
entitled to receive compensation are correlative".[2] This is not, however,
the way in which these topics have been treated by the legislation in this
field.

What, if anything, should be done about blight generated by public
sector actions and decisions is a question which has troubled successive

---

[1] *Final report* (1997) DETR para.2.1.
[2] "The Second Report of the Committee dealing with the Law and Practice relating to
the Acquisition and Valuation of Land for Public Purposes" (1918) HMSO para.32
(Cmnd. 9229); also the IWGB, *Final report* (1997) DETR.

governments for many years. On the one hand, it may be argued that blight should be regarded as one of the risks of land ownership and that there is no case for remedial measures.[3] As IWGB observed: "It is axiomatic to say that when one buys property one buys into a risk".[4] On the other hand, it may be argued that fairness requires that the loss should be shared among the wider community who benefit from the actions and decisions giving rise to blight. There is, indeed, as McAuslan suggests, a strong public interest incentive in alleviating the hardship.[5] By way of example, he cites the Minister of Local Government and Development in the context of the debate in 1972 on the Land Compensation Bill which introduced proposals for improving the compensation entitlement where land is depreciated by public works. "I believe," said the Minister, that the proposals will have "the beneficial effect of speeding up the administration of development projects. There will I believe be less incentive for those affected to obstruct good public schemes by using every legal means at their command."[6]

In the discussion in Chapter 13 on "Compensation for Regulation" it was suggested that the essence of the compensation problem is whether the cost of regulation should fall upon the heritable proprietor or whether it should be shared amongst the wider community who are benefiting from the regulation. The conclusion was that, although the pattern is by no means consistent, the history of the imposition of regulation has been to push the point at which the wider community are expected to share the burden progressively further away.

The essence of the problem of blight may be presented in similar terms. Should the injury fall upon the heritable proprietor or should it be shared amongst the wider community who are benefiting from the public works giving rise to the blight? The history of the involvement by the state in alleviating blight suggests that, unlike regulation, the burden on the wider community has steadily increased over the years. In reality, the question has not been whether something should be done but where the line should be drawn; how far the state should go in granting relief from blight.

The extent of the relief is considered below; but, inevitably, given the tension created by an attempt to strike a balance between the community good and private rights, the recent incorporation of the European Convention on Human Rights into domestic law has raised the question whether the line should be redrawn.[7] Consideration has already been given earlier in this book to the consequences of Convention rights

---

[3] See, for example, the discussion of this by the government's inter-departmental working party on blight cited in J. B. Cullingworth, "Environmental Planning" (1980) HMSO Vol.IV, p.209.

[4] *Final report*, para.2.1.

[5] P. McAuslan, *Ideologies of Planning Law* (Pergamon Press, 1980) Chap.4.

[6] H.C. Deb., vol.847, col. 39. See, too, the recommendation in the Fifth Report from the Environment Committee, "Planning: Appeals, Call-In and Major Public Inquiries" (1986) HMSO para.167, that "the Department of the Environment undertake a cost-benefit analysis of paying realistic compensation to those financially disadvantaged by the consequences of proposals which are the subject of major inquiries as against the costs to the national economy of such inquiries".

[7] See M. Redman, "Compulsory Purchase, Compensation and Human Rights" [1999] J.P.L. 315.

for compulsory purchase and compulsory purchase procedure (see pp.13 and 45). There are two provisions of the Convention of particular relevance to blight: Article 8 and the First Protocol, Article 1. These are considered briefly in turn.

Article 8 provides that:

> "1. Everyone has the right to respect for his private and family life, his home and his correspondence.
>
> 2. There shall be no interference by a public authority with the exercise of this right except such as is in accordance with the law and is necessary in a democratic society in the interests of national security, public safety or the economic well-being of the country, for the prevention of disorder or crime, for the protection of health or morals, or for the protection of the rights and freedoms of others."

In *Powell and Rayner v United Kingdom*[8] the applicants owned property near Heathrow Airport and complained of excessive noise from its operation. The ECHR accepted that Article 8 was material given that "the quality of the applicant's private life and the scope for enjoying the amenities of his home had been adversely affected by noise generated by aircraft using the airport." It went on to hold, however, that the importance of the airport to the economy justified the interference with private rights in terms of Article 8(2). Furthermore, the noise abatement measures that had been introduced meant that the interference was not disproportionate.

A different view was taken in *Hatton v United Kingdom*[9] which also **14–02** involved a complaint about noise from aircraft using Heathrow Airport. The applicants argued that night time noise levels were well in excess of acceptable levels and that changes to night flying arrangements at the airport made sleeping difficult for those living nearby. The government relied on the noise mitigation and the abatement measures which had been introduced and on the consequences for the economy of prohibiting night flying. It argued that the balance it had struck was within the margin of appreciation enjoyed by States in ensuring compliance with the Convention. The ECHR accepted that there had been no direct interference by the government in the private or family life of the applicants (it did not own or operate the airport or the aeroplanes) but the State, nonetheless, had a positive duty to take responsible and appropriate measures to secure the applicants' rights under Article 8(1). The ECHR interpreted this as meaning that "States are required to minimise, as far as possible, the interference with these rights, by trying to find alternative solutions and by generally seeking to achieve their aims in the least onerous way as regards human rights". In this case, the government had not undertaken a critical assessment of the importance of night flying to the economy; and the research undertaken into sleep disturbance had been inadequate. The government had, accordingly,

---

[8] (1990) 23 E.H.R.R. 355.
[9] 36022/97, *The Times*, October 8, 2001, ECHR.

failed in its duty to secure the applicants' rights. As Layard observes, "what the majority of the Court clearly held was that if infringements were to comply with Article 8(2), governments would need to rely on more than asserted 'self-evident' facts".[10]

If it stands, the decision in *Hatton* on the operation of Article 8 may well require a re-appraisal of where the line should be drawn in the relief of some categories of blight. At the time of writing, the case has been referred to the Grand Chamber of the Court for review.

The First Protocol, Article 1 provides that:

> "Every natural or legal person is entitled to the peaceful enjoyment of his possessions. No one shall be deprived of his possessions except in the public interest and subject to the conditions provided for by law and the general principles of international law.
>
> The preceding provisions shall not, however, in any way impair the right of a State to enforce such laws as it deems necessary to control the use of property in accordance with the general interest or to secure the payment of taxes or other contributions or penalties".

There has been insufficient case law at present to determine what effect this provision could have on the line to be drawn in relieving blight. However, the decision of the ECHR in *Sporrong and Lonnroth v Sweden*[11] suggests that it could have relevance. In that case the court held there had been a violation of the First Protocol, Article 1 of the Convention arising from expropriation permits and construction prohibitions which had blighted two areas of land for many years before they had been revoked.

Blight manifests itself in different ways. Some of these manifestations have already been considered in earlier chapters in this book. In Chapter 8 the interrelation between section 13 of the Land Compensation (Scotland) Act 1963 and the *Pointe Gourde* principle was discussed, both of which require that in assessing compensation for the compulsory acquisition of land no account is to be taken of any decrease in the value of that land due to the scheme. Reference was also made to section 16 of the 1963 Act which requires any depreciation in the value of land due to an indication that it is likely to be acquired for public purposes to be ignored when assessing compensation upon its eventual acquisition. And in Chapter 11 the entitlement to compensation for depreciation in the value of land "held together with" land taken for the scheme was examined.[12] These are all forms of blight.

There are, however, other manifestations and these are the subject of this chapter. Its concern is with depreciation in the value of land which has not, or which has not yet, been acquired for or "held together with" land acquired for the scheme.

---

[10] A Layard, "Night flights: A surprising victory" (2002) *Environmental Law Review* Vol.4, p.51.

[11] (1983) 53 E.H.R.R. 35.

[12] See, too, the provisions for serving a "notice of objection to severance" discussed in Chap.3.

The chapter is divided into three parts. In the first part attention focuses on the topic of "planning blight". For more than thirty years now the state has given relief to owners of land blighted by its earmarking for eventual acquisition for public purposes. Subject to certain qualifications, such an owner may serve a "blight notice" requiring the public authority responsible for the blight to purchase the land at a price which ignores the blighting effect of the scheme. It is a form of inverse compulsory purchase.

In a discussion paper in 1995, the Royal Institution of Chartered Surveyors recommended that the right to require a public authority to buy land should be extended to cases where land which is not earmarked for eventual acquisition is nonetheless adversely affected to a material degree as a result of the execution or use of works on neighbouring land.[13] It could be argued that this is the logical extension of section 54(1) of the Land Compensation (Scotland) Act 1973 (see p.65) which provides that in assessing material detriment to a "house, building or manufactory" in the context of a notice of objection to severance, regard may be had to the consequences of the use of the land acquired and of other land for public purposes. In other words, why should one landowner be in a better position to serve what amounts to a "blight notice" (see below) than another when faced with the same form of material detriment simply because of the coincidence that some of his land has been acquired for the public works?

The question might be extended further by asking why the blight notice provisions are not available to anyone whose land is substantially depreciated in value regardless of whether the land is earmarked for eventual acquisition and regardless of whether the level of depreciation is such as to amount to "material detriment".[14] The answer advanced by the government interdepartmental working party on blight which preceded the 1959 planning legislation[15] was that there is a qualitative distinction between blight arising from the earmarking of land for public purposes and blight caused to neighbouring land by the use of the earmarked land for public purposes. The latter, concluded that committee, may be regarded as one of the risks of ownership; the former is not. A similar distinction was drawn by the IWGB between "statutory blight" (where land is earmarked for public acquisition) and "generalised blight" (depreciation attributable to an infrastructure scheme).[16] Although there is some substance in this distinction, it simply focuses on different aspects of the same problem—the problem of hardship resulting from depreciation caused by proposed or implemented public works. A more pragmatic answer is that a balance has to be maintained between alleviating hardship to heritable proprietors and imposing too great a burden on public authorities. The blight notice provisions discussed in the first section of this chapter are directed towards giving relief in the most serious cases of hardship.

---

[13] "Compensation for Compulsory Acquisition" (1995) RICS para.8.22.
[14] See, for example, P. Cooke-Priest, "Improving Compensation Provisions" (1988) 8807 E.G. 66.
[15] See J. B. Cullingworth, "Environmental Planning" Vol.IV, *supra*, p.209.
[16] *Final report*, (1997) pp.6–7.

The government, however, has not been allowed to ignore the plight of owners of land adjoining public works. The need to make some provision for compensating for damage to neighbouring land caused by major works carried out under statutory authority was particularly apparent during the railway building era of the nineteenth century. During the late 1960s, the urban motorway building programme and proposals for a third London airport again focussed attention on the hardship suffered by neighbouring proprietors. Most recently, the planning and development of the high speed rail link between the Channel Tunnel and London has caused a very vocal revival of interest in the plight of adjoining owners. The second part of this chapter examines the complex provisions for compensating such proprietors in respect of this form of blight.

The payment of compensation does not, of course, remove the cause of depreciation. The promoter of the scheme effectively buys the right to continue the nuisance indefinitely. Those affected may well prefer that steps should be taken to reduce the nuisance so far as practicable. The third part of this chapter describes the provisions for mitigating the injurious effects of public works.

These three approaches to tackling blight are now considered in turn.

Planning Blight

14–03 The Planning Advisory Group in their report on *The Future of Development Plans*[17] defined planning blight as "the depressing effect on existing property of proposals which imply public acquisition and disturbance of the existing use". The earmarking of land in a development plan for future public purposes is likely, for example, to have an adverse effect on its marketability. The uncertainty surrounding its future will deter investment and a landowner will only be able to sell, if at all, at a significantly reduced price.

The massive programme of public works planned in the aftermath of the Second World War, coupled with the requirement that development plans should designate as land subject to compulsory acquisition any land allocated for public purposes,[18] gave rise to very considerable planning blight and, to that extent, modified the general scheme of the post-war planning legislation which was to leave the existing use value of land in the hands of landowners.[19] In some cases of blight, a landowner could implement the purchase notice provisions in section 17 of the Town and Country Planning (Scotland) Act 1947. In such cases, the local authority would be required to purchase the property at a price which ignored the effects of blight. However, the provisions in section 17 could only be implemented where it could be shown that the land had become incapable of reasonably beneficial use. In many cases where property was blighted there was nothing to prevent the existing beneficial use continu-

---

[17] (1965) HMSO.

[18] Town and Country Planning (Scotland) Act 1947, s.3(2).

[19] See, generally, J. B. Cullingworth, Environmental Planning (1980) HMSO Vol.IV p.207 *et seq.*

ing until such time, if ever, as the property was eventually compulsorily acquired for the public works.

If the owner of blighted property can hold on until it is eventually acquired for public purposes there will be no problem. The price paid upon acquisition will be that which would have been realised on a sale in the open market by a willing seller ignoring the blighting effects of the scheme. However, the lead time for finalising and implementing schemes of public works is commonly a matter of years. IWGB noted, for example, that a major road is seldom completed in less than twelve years from inception to first use.[20] An owner, for reasons beyond his control, may have to place the property on the market in the interim. In these circumstances, the blighting effects of a scheme may give rise to very considerable hardship.

Increasing concern about the effects of blight led to the setting up by the government in the mid 1950s of an interdepartmental working party. Its terms of reference were to consider ways of reducing hardship to landowners occasioned by the publication of proposals foreshadowing the public acquisition of their property at some future time.[21] It was apparent to the working party that the blighting effects of a proposal were not necessarily confined solely to land earmarked for eventual acquisition. A proposed scheme of public works might also affect the value of other property in the vicinity. Nonetheless, as already mentioned, the working party felt that a distinction could be drawn between blight caused by the prospect of compulsory acquisition and blight caused by the prospect of an alteration by a scheme of public works to the character of an area and that the former justified separate treatment. The solution proposed, which was modelled on the purchase notice provisions, was the introduction of a right to require the advance purchase of blighted property. The solution was given legislative effect in Part IV of the Town and Country Planning (Scotland) Act 1959.

Subsequently, the requirement that development plans should designate for compulsory acquisition land required at some future time for public purposes was repealed.[22] This has served to alleviate the impact of blight on land which would otherwise have been so designated. Nonetheless, the publicity which attaches to public sector proposals signalled in development and other plans will still have some blighting effect which, in the absence of a precise location, may now be distributed more widely.

The power to serve a blight notice is contained, in amended form, in Part V, Chapter II of the Town and Country Planning (Scotland) Act 1997. It arises where a person with an interest in land qualifying for protection has made reasonable endeavours to sell that interest but has been unable to do so except at a much reduced price because the land has been identified as likely to be affected by public works (1997 Act, s.101(1)).[23] A person seeking to take advantage of the provision must, therefore, satisfy three requirements:

[20] *Final report*, para.7.2.2. See too City University Business School, "The Operation of Compulsory Purchase Orders" (1996) Department of the Environment Chap.2.

[21] J. B. Cullingworth, "Environmental Planning", *supra*.

[22] See the White Paper, "Town and Country Planning" (1967) para.26, Cmnd. 3333.

[23] See, generally, on blight notices J. Rowan Robinson, E. Young, M. Purdue and E. Farquharson-Black, *Scottish Planning Law and Procedure* (W. Green & Son Ltd., 2001), Chap.16B.

1. Qualifying interest

14–04   The person serving the blight notice[24] must show that on the date of service of the blight notice he is: (a) the resident owner-occupier of the whole or part of a hereditament[25]; (b) the owner-occupier of the whole or part of a non-residential hereditament, for example a shop or office, the annual value[26] of which does not exceed an amount prescribed by order made by the Scottish Ministers[27]; (c) the owner-occupier of the whole or part of an agricultural unit.[28]

The reference to an "owner's" interest includes the interest of a lessee under a lease, the unexpired portion of which on the date of service of the blight notice is not less than three years, and the interest of a crofter or cottar.[29] The term "owner-occupier" bears a somewhat specialised meaning. The "owner-occupier" of a hereditament means a person who occupies the whole or a substantial part of the hereditament as owner and who has done so for the six months preceding the date of service of the blight notice; or a person who has occupied the whole or a substantial part of a hereditament as owner for a period of six months ending not more than 12 months before the service of the notice, the hereditament or part having been unoccupied since the end of that period (s.119(1)). "Owner-occupier" in relation to an agricultural unit refers to a person who owns the whole or part of the unit and who either occupies the whole of the unit at the date of service of the notice and has done so during the preceding six months or has occupied the whole of the unit during a period of six months ending not more than 12 months before the service of the blight notice (s.119 (2)). And the term "resident owner-occupier" in relation to a hereditament refers to a person who either occupies as owner the whole or a substantial part of the hereditament as a private dwelling and has so occupied it for the six months preceding the date of service of the blight notice; or occupies as owner the whole or a substantial part of the hereditament as a private dwelling for a period of six months ending not more than 12 months before the date of service of the notice, the hereditament or part having been unoccupied since the end of that period (s.119(3)).

These somewhat complex provisions are designed to limit public liability by admitting only certain classes of property owners to the right

---

[24] As to the power of a heritable creditor to serve a blight notice, see s.113.

[25] Defined as the aggregate of the lands and heritages which form the subject of a single entry in the valuation role for the time being in force for a valuation area (s.122(1)–(4)). For the transitional provisions consequent on the abolition of domestic rates see the Abolition of Domestic Rates Etc. (Scotland) Act 1987, s.5.

[26] Defined in s.122(1) as the value which, on the date of service, is shown in the valuation role as the rateable value of that hereditament. Where, however, the rateable value differs from the net annual value, the reference is to the net annual value.

[27] Presently £24,725 (Town and Country Planning (Limit of Annual Value) (Scotland) Order 2001). The Royal Institution of Chartered Surveyors recommended that the rateable value limit should be removed in the case of owner occupier property and that, in certain cases, investment owners should qualify for the serving of a blight notice but subject to a rateable value limit ("Compensation for Compulsory Acquisition" 1995 RICS paras 8.4 and 8.8).

[28] Defined in s.122(1) as land occupied as a unit for agricultural purposes, including a dwelling-house or other building occupied by the same person for the purpose of farming the land.

[29] See ss.101(5) and 122(1).

of advance purchase. In particular, they reflect the belief that large businesses and investment owners are better able to absorb the hardship created by blight. These limitations have not gone unchallenged.[30]

2. Qualifying Land

Blight may arise from the point in time at which the prospect of land **14–05** being required for public purposes first becomes public knowledge. That prospect may, however, never become a reality; and, even if it does, it may be some considerable time, perhaps a matter of years, before the prospect takes any concrete form. Determining the point in time at which a right of advance purchase should come into operation which is fair both to the public authority and to the landowner raises issues which JUSTICE acknowledged to be both complex and intractable.[31] The legislation in this area has tended to move cautiously by postponing the right of advance purchase to the point at which compulsory purchase is foreshadowed or has begun. This point is differently defined according to the public purpose for which the land is required. The blight notice provisions may be operated by a person with a qualifying interest from the point in time at which the land can be shown to fall within one of the descriptions of "blighted land" (below). Experience indicated that, in some respects, these descriptions were at first too narrowly drawn. The government responded to pressure for change[32] by enlarging the descriptions somewhat in the Land Compensation (Scotland) Act 1973.[33]

Section 101(1) of the 1997 Act provides that a blight notice may be served only where the whole or a part of a hereditament or agricultural unit is comprised in "blighted land". The descriptions of "blighted land" are set out in Schedule 14 to the 1997 Act and are grouped under five headings. These are as follows:

1. Land allocated for public authority functions in development plans etc:

(a) Land indicated in a structure plan in force for the area in **14–06** question as land which may be required for the purposes of any functions of a government department, local authority or statutory undertaker or for the purposes of the establishment or running by a public telecommunications operator of a telecommunications system or as land which may be included in an action area (Sch.14, para.1(1)).[34] This provision also applies to land so indicated in a structure plan which has been submitted

---

[30] See "Compensation for Compulsory Acquisition and Planning Restrictions" (1968) *Chartered Land Societies Committee* paras 75–78; also JUSTICE, *Compensation for Compulsory Acquisition and Remedies for Planning Restrictions together with a Supplemental Report* (Stevens, 1973) paras 74–84 and 126–132; the "Compensation for Compulsory Acquisition" (1995) RICS paras 8.2–8.8; and J. Rowan Robinson and N. Hutchison, "Compensation for the compulsory acquisition of business interests: satisfaction or sacrifice?" *Journal of Property Valuation and Investment* Vol.13(1), p.44.

[31] See above, para.79.

[32] See Chartered Land Societies Committee and JUSTICE, *supra.*

[33] See the White Paper, *Development and Compensation—Putting People First* (1972) HMSO paras 57–64 and Appendix.

[34] See 1997 Act, s.11(6).

to the Scottish Ministers for approval, or in proposals submitted to the Ministers for the alteration of a structure plan, or in modifications proposed to be made by the Ministers to any such submitted plan or proposals. The provision does not, however, apply if a local plan is in force which already allocates or defines land in the area for such purposes (para.1(2)).

(b) Land indicated for the purposes of any such functions as are mentioned in (a) above in an adopted local plan or land defined in such a plan as the site of proposed development for the purposes of any such function (para.2(1)). This provision applies also to land so indicated or defined in a local plan which has been made available for inspection prior to adoption or approval, or in proposals for alterations to a local plan which have similarly been made available for inspection, or in modifications proposed to be made by the planning authority or the Scottish Ministers to any such plan prior to adoption or approval (para.2(2)).

(c) Land indicated in a plan (other than a development plan) approved by a resolution of the planning authority for the purpose of the exercise of their development control powers as land which may be required for the purposes of any function of a government department, local authority or statutory undertaker (para.2(3)) or land which the planning authority have resolved or have been directed by the Scottish Ministers to take action to safeguard for development by such bodies (para.2(4)).

2. New towns and urban development areas:

14–07

(a) Land described as a site of a proposed new town in a draft order, notice of which has been published as required by Schedule 1, paragraph 2 to the New Towns (Scotland) Act 1968 (para.5) or land designated as the site of a proposed new town by an order under section 1 of the 1968 Act (para.6).

(b) Land within an area intended to be designated, or which has been designated, as an urban development area under section 134 of the Local Government, Planning and Land Act 1980 (para.7)).

3. Housing action areas

14–08 Land within, surrounded by or adjoining an area declared to be a housing action area by resolution under sections 89, 90 or 91 of the Housing (Scotland) Act 1987 (paras 8 and 9)

4. Roads

14–09

(a) Land indicated in a development plan for the construction, improvement or alteration of a road (para.10).

(b) Land on or adjacent to the line of a road proposed to be constructed, improved or altered as indicated in a proposed or operative order or scheme under Schedule 1 to the Roads (Scotland) Act 1984 being land in relation to which a power of compulsory acquisition may become exercisable for the purposes of construction, improvement or alteration as indicated in the order or scheme (para.11) and land required for the purpose of mitigating the adverse effect which the existence or use of a new or improved road may have on its surroundings.[35]

(c) Land shown on plans approved[36] by resolution of a roads authority as land comprised in the site of a road as proposed to be constructed, improved or altered by that authority (para.12) or for the mitigation of a new or improved road.[37]

(d) Land comprised in the site of a road as proposed to be constructed, improved or altered by the Scottish Ministers or land proposed to be acquired for the mitigation of the adverse effects of such a road[38] if the Ministers have given written notice of the proposal, together with maps or plans sufficient to identify the land in question, to the planning authority (para.13).

5. Compulsory purchase

(a) Land authorised for compulsory acquisition in a special Act (para.14).[39]   **14–10**

(b) Land in respect of which a compulsory purchase order has been submitted for confirmation to, or been prepared in draft by, the Scottish Ministers or is in force but notice to treat has not yet been served (para.15). Similar provision is made in respect of land affected by a compulsory purchase order providing for the acquisition of a right in or over land.

It would seem that the onus is upon the person serving the blight notice—the claimant—to show that the land falls clearly within one of the categories of 'blighted land'. In *Bolton Corporation v Owen*,[40] where land, including the subject land, had been earmarked in a development plan for clearance and redevelopment for residential purposes, the Court of Appeal declined to speculate on the probability or otherwise of all or part of the redevelopment being carried out by the local authority rather than by private enterprise. The claimant had not discharged the onus of showing that the land was allocated in a development plan for the purposes of any functions of a local authority. However, where in the

[35] Roads (Scotland) Act 1984, s.106(7).
[36] As to the meaning of "approval" see *Fogg v Birkenhead County Borough Council* (1971) 22 P. & C.R. 208; *Page v Borough of Gillingham* (1970) 21 P. & C.R. 973.
[37] Roads (Scotland) Act 1984, s.106(8).
[38] *See above.*
[39] Defined in s.122(1).
[40] [1962] 1 Q.B. 470. See, too, *Ellick v Sedgemoor District Council* (1976) 32 P. & C.R. 134; *Broderick v Erewash Borough Council* (1976) 34 P. & C.R. 214; *Elcock and Elcock v Newham BC* (1995) 71 P. & C.R. 575.

descriptions of "blighted land" reference is made to an "indication" in a plan, it would seem that a diagrammatic representation will be enough. The word "indicated" said the Lands Tribunal in *Bowling v Leeds County Borough Council*[41] is a word "of simple meaning which does not import any requirement of resolution by the Council or programming by it or allocation of money by it".

There will, inevitably, be cases where land is blighted which does not fall within one of the descriptions of "blighted land". Local authorities have been given some encouragement to consider alleviating hardship in such cases where eventual acquisition is likely by exercising their powers to acquire land in advance of requirements.[42]

3. Reasonable endeavours to sell

14–11   It is not enough for a claimant to show that he has a qualifying interest in land falling within one of the descriptions of "blighted land". He must also show that he has made reasonable endeavours to sell that interest but has been unable to do so except at a much reduced price because the land has been identified as required or likely to be required for public purposes (s.101(1)(b)). This requirement does not apply where the land falls within the categories of "blighted land" in Schedule 14, paras 14 and 15 (s.101(1)(b)). The onus is upon the claimant to show that this requirement has been satisfied by a sufficiency of evidence.[43]

In *Malcolm Campbell v Glasgow Corporation*[44] a blight notice was served in respect of a shop shown in a development plan to be affected by a road widening proposal. The corporation objected on the ground that the claimant had not shown that he had made reasonable endeavours to sell but had been unable to do so except at a much reduced price because of the road proposal. There were, argued the corporation, other factors which had had a significant effect on the value of the shop including the proximity of a new shopping arcade, an abundance of older shops in the vicinity which had been left vacant as a result of traders moving to the new arcade, and the introduction of traffic restrictions. On a reference of the objection to the Lands Tribunal for Scotland, the claimant invited the tribunal to adopt the simple view that at the very least there must have been some element of prejudice attributable to the road widening proposal and this was enough to discharge the onus of proof. The tribunal declined to adopt the simple view. The onus was on the claimant to establish what price the property would have realised having regard to the other factors referred to by the corporation but disregarding the effects of the road proposal and then to show that because of the road proposal that price could not be realised. The claimant had not disentangled the effects of the road proposal from the

---

[41] (1974) 27 P. & C.R. 531; also *Williams v Cheadle and Gately U.D.C.* (1965) 17 P. & C.R. 153. But see *Comley and Comley v Kent County Council* (1977) 34 P. & C.R. 218.

[42] DHS Circular 66/1959; SDD Circular 89/1971; SDD Memorandum 85/1973; and SDD Circular 42/1976.

[43] Section 104(3). The Royal Institution of Chartered Surveyors recommended that the requirement to have made efforts to sell the property should be removed for owner occupiers (*Compensation for Compulsory Acquisition*, 1995, para.8.13).

[44] 1972 S.L.T. (Lands Tr.) 8.

other effects. There was an insufficiency of evidence to establish that the objection was not well-founded and the blight notice failed. In *Bowling v Leeds County Borough Council*,[45] on the other hand, the claimants were held to have discharged the onus of proof upon them to show that the diminution in the value of their shops was partly due to a road widening scheme and not wholly due to other factors such as the clearance of houses in the neighbourhood.

What is meant by "reasonable endeavours to sell" will turn very much on the particular circumstances of each case.[46] It seems, however, that an actual attempt to sell must be made. In *Perkins v West Wiltshire District Council*[47] the Lands Tribunal held that it was not enough to instruct an estate agent to sell and then accept his advice that a sale would be impossible because any purchaser would lose interest on being informed that the land was allocated for public purposes. In *Lade & Lade v Brighton Corporation*[48] the tribunal member, while accepting that in general the normal procedure for sale should be carried out, held that in the particular circumstances which involved a shop selling antiques and bric-a-brac it was sufficient to put a notice to the window of the shop and to inform visiting dealers. In *Mancini v Coventry City Council*[49] a blight notice was served in respect of two dwelling-houses converted for use as one, with office accommodation and a detached workshop at the rear used for the manufacture of ice-cream. In an effort to sell the premises, the claimant had advertised in the press, informed various business acquaintances, and instructed a local estate agent. The council argued that in view of the specialised nature of the property a more forceful selling programme was required involving wide circulation among agents specialising in business transfers and advertisements in nationally distributed trade journals. The tribunal held that, as the claimant was endeavouring to sell the premises, not the business, and as the principal value of the premises arose from their residential and not their manufacturing use, putting the premises in the hands of an estate agent was sufficient.

4. Counter-notice

If a person has a qualifying interest in land which falls within one of 14–12 the descriptions of "blighted land" and has been unsuccessful in his endeavours to sell that interest he may serve a blight notice in the prescribed form[50] on the authority responsible for the blight[51] requiring the acquisition of his interest.[52]

---

[45] (1974) 27 P. & C.R. 531; also *Stubbs v West Hartlepool Corporation* (1961) 12 P. & C.R. 365.
[46] See, for example, decisions of official arbiters Ref. Nos 5/1962, 1/1969, 3/1969. See, too, *Trustees of St John's Church, Galashiels v Borders Regional Council*, 1976 S.L.T. (Lands Tr.) 39.
[47] (1975) 31 P. & C.R. 427.
[48] (1971) 22 P. & C.R. 737.
[49] (1982) 44 P. & C.R. 114, LT; (1983) 49 P. & C.R. 127, CA.
[50] See the Town and Country Planning (General) (Scotland) Regulations 1976, Reg.3 and Sch.1.
[51] Referred to as the "appropriate authority," a term which is defined in s.120. In the event of a dispute as to which is the appropriate authority the matter will be resolved by the Scottish Ministers.
[52] Such a notice may subsequently be withdrawn within the time specified in s.107.

Within two months, the appropriate authority may serve a counter-notice on the claimant in the prescribed form[53] objecting to the blight notice (s.102(1)). The seven grounds upon which objection may be made are as follows:

1. That no part of the hereditament or agricultural unit to which the notice relates is comprised in "blighted land" (s.102(4)(a)).

2. That the appropriate authority do not propose to acquire any part of the hereditament or any part of the affected area of an agricultural unit consisting of "blighted land" (s.102(4)(b)).[54]

3. That the appropriate authority propose to acquire only that part of the hereditament or of the affected area of an agricultural unit specified in the counter-notice (s.102(4)(c)).[55]

4. That in the case of land falling within paragraphs 1 or 10 but not 11, 12 or 13 of Schedule 14 to the 1997 Act (corresponding to paras 1(a) and 4(a) but not 4(b)–(d) above), the appropriate authority do not propose to acquire any part of the hereditament or of the affected area of an agricultural unit during the period of 15 years from the date of the counter-notice or such longer period from that date as may be specified in the counter-notice (s.102(4)(d)).

5. That on the date of service of the blight notice the claimant was not entitled to an interest in any part of the hereditament or agricultural unit to which the notice relates (s.102(4)(e)).

6. That, for the reasons specified in the counter-notice, the interest of the claimant is not one which qualifies for protection (s.102(4)(f)).

7. That the claimant has not made reasonable endeavours to sell his interest and cannot show an injury to that interest as required by section 101(1)(b) and (c) (above) (s.102(4)(g)).

The counter-notice must specify the grounds upon which objection is made (s.102(3)).[56]

---

[53] Town and Country Planning (General) (Scotland) Regulations 1976, Sch.1. The Lands Tribunal for Scotland would appear to have no jurisdiction to entertain an objection not made within the prescribed period *(Essex Incorporated Congregational Church Union v Essex County Council* [1963] A.C. 808; *Church of Scotland General Trs v Helensburgh Town Council*, 1973 S.L.T. (Lands Tr.) 21; *Ibbotson v Tayside Regional Council*, 1978 S.L.T. (Lands Tr.) 25).

[54] For the meaning of "affected area" see s.122(1).

[55] But note the possibility of the service by the claimant of a notice of objection to severance (p.65).

[56] It would seem that a new ground of objection may not subsequently be introduced (see *Ibbotson v Tayside Regional Council*, 1978 S.L.T. (Lands Tr.) 25; *Church of Scotland General Trs. v Helensburgh Town Council* 1993, S.L.T. (Lands Tr.) 21; *Essex County Council v Essex Incorporated Congregational Church Union* [1963] A.C. 808; and see, too, *Bins v Secretary of State for Transport* (1985) 50 P. & C.R. 468); *McGingle v Renfrew District Council*, 1992 S.L.T. (Lands Tr.) 97; and *Burn v North Yorkshire County Council* (1991) 63 P. & C.R. 81.

An authority may not, however, object to a blight notice on the ground that they have no intention of acquiring the interest in the next 15 years (s.102(4)(d)) if, in fact, they have no present intention of acquiring it at all. They should in these circumstances employ section 102(4)(b). And where land the subject of a blight notice is within a housing action area[57] or is surrounded by or adjoins such an area, an authority may not object to the notice on the ground that they do not intend to acquire the land (s.102(4)(b)) or intend only to acquire part (s.102(4)(c)).[58]

The ability of the appropriate authority to object to a blight notice under section 102(2)(c) on the ground that they intend only to acquire part of a hereditament or, in the case of an agricultural unit, part of an affected area, does not affect the right of a claimant under normal compulsory purchase legislation to object to severance and, in prescribed circumstances, to insist on selling the whole (s.117) (see p.65). With this possibility in mind the Lands Tribunal for Scotland are required when determining an objection relating to a hereditament under section 102(4)(c) (in addition to the other matters to which they should have regard) to apply the same tests as for a notice of objection to severance. They must consider whether: (a) in the case of a house, building or factory, the part may be taken without material detriment to the whole; or (b) in the case of a park or garden belonging to a house, the part can be taken without seriously affecting the amenity or convenience of the house.[59]

Where a blight notice is served in respect of an interest in the whole or part of an agricultural unit and that unit or part contains land which is not "blighted land" (the unaffected area) the claimant may include in the notice a claim that the unaffected area is not reasonably capable of being farmed, either by itself or in conjunction with other "relevant land"[60] as a separate agricultural unit. Where such a claim is made the appropriate authority may object to the blight notice on the ground that it is not justified (s.110(1)). Indeed, such an objection must be taken where the authority are also seeking to rely on s.102(4)(c) (1997 Act, s.110(3)). Where such a claim succeeds the authority are required to purchase the claimants' interest in the whole unit (1997 Act, s.111).

Where a counter-notice has been served, the claimant may, within two **14–13** months, require the objection to be referred to the Lands Tribunal for Scotland (s.104(1)(2)). On any such reference, the tribunal must uphold the objection unless the claimant shows that it is not well-founded (s.104(3)).[61] Exceptionally, where objection is made on the grounds set out in section 104(b)(c) or (d), the onus rests upon the appropriate authority to show that it is well-founded (s.104(4)).[62] In *Sabey and Sabey*

---

[57] Designated under the Housing (Scotland) Act 1987, Part IV.

[58] 1997 Act, s.102(7).

[59] 1997 Act, s.117(2). See *McMillan v Strathclyde Regional Council*, 1984 S.L.T. (Lands Tr.) 25.

[60] Defined in s.109(3).

[61] See *Malcolm Campbell v Glasgow Corporation*, 1972 S.L.T. (Lands Tr.) 8. The hardship faced by the claimant and the prospect of alleviating that hardship are irrelevant to the question of whether objections are well-founded (*Mancini v Coventry City Council* (1985) 49 P. & C.R. 127).

[62] See *Trustees of St John's Church, Galashiels v Borders Regional Council*, 1976 S.L.T. (Lands Tr.) 39.

v Hartlepool County Borough Council[63] a blight notice was served in respect of a house included in an area allocated in the development plan for civic, cultural and other special uses. The Lands Tribunal declined to accept that an objection, based on the ground that the local authority had no intention of acquiring the land, was well-founded. The house was still earmarked in the development plan. As the tribunal observed: "[i]f all that be required in order to avoid the consequences of a purchase notice is a statement by the local authority of its intentions, as expressed in this case, it is difficult to see the purpose of [section 104(4)]. It seems to me that in placing the onus on a local authority to show that an objection of this kind is well-founded, Parliament must have intended the Lands Tribunal to look at all the facts of the case and to dismiss the objection unless satisfied that an effective protection against 'blight' is provided."[64]

In *Mancini v Coventry City Council*[65] the Court of Appeal held that the material date for determining whether an objection can be established was the date of the counter-notice rather than the date of the blight notice. Purchas L.J. went on to say, *obiter,* that nothing in his judgment should be taken to preclude the possibility of contending in an appropriate case that the material date might even be postponed to the date of the hearing by the tribunal. In *Sinclair v Secretary of State for Transport*[66] the Lands Tribunal held that where an objection is taken on the ground that no part of the land is blighted (see s.102(4)(a) above) the material date for determining whether or not that objection is well-founded and the land is blighted is the date of the service of the counter-notice. The tribunal went on to observe that some doubt remained as to the relevant date for determining whether or not an objection is well-founded where that objection is based on the English equivalent of section 102(4)(b)(c) and (d). In such cases there may an argument for testing the authority's intentions at a date subsequent to the service of the counter-notice. Indeed, in *Kayworth v Highways Agency*[67] the Lands Tribunal considered facts subsequent to the counter-notice in order to determine whether an objection to a blight notice on the ground that the responsible authority did not propose to acquire any part of the hereditament was well-founded.

If an objection on the ground that the authority have no intention of acquiring the interest at all (s.102(4)(b)) or within the next 15 years (s.102(4)(d)) is upheld, any power compulsorily to acquire that interest will cease to have effect (s.106(1)(2)). And similar provision operates where objection is successfully made on the ground in section 102(4)(c)

---

[63] (1970) 21 P. & C.R. 448.

[64] See, too, *Duke of Wellington Social Club v Blyth Borough Council* (1964) 15 P. & C.R. 212; *Louiseville Investments Ltd v Basingstoke District Council* (1976) 32 P. & C.R. 419; *Charman v Dorset County Council* (1986) 52 P. & C.R. 88.

[65] (1983) 270 E.G. 419 (Lands Tr.); (1983) 49 P. & C.R. 127, CA. See, too, *Cedar Holdings Ltd v Walsall Metropolitan Borough Council* (1979) 38 P. & C.R. 715; *Sinclair v Secretary of State for Transport* (1997) 75 P. & C.R. 48; and *Kayworth v Coventry City Council* (1996) 72 P. & C.R. 433.

[66] (1997) 75 P. & C.R. 48.

[67] (1996) 72 P. & C.R. 433. See too *Charman v Dorset County Council* (1986) 52 P. & C.R. 88.

that the authority intend to acquire only part of an interest in land. Any power to acquire compulsorily the remainder of the land will cease to have effect (s.106(3)(4)). Where the tribunal decides not to uphold an objection it will declare the blight notice valid.[68]

Where a blight notice has been served and either no counter-notice is served or a counter notice is served but the objection is subsequently withdrawn or is not upheld by the tribunal, the appropriate authority is deemed to be authorised to acquire the interest compulsorily and to have served a notice to treat (s.105(1)(2)).[69] The power conferred by section 39 of the Land Compensation (Scotland) Act 1963 on authorities to withdraw a notice to treat does not apply in these instances (s.118).

Compensation is assessed as for compulsory acquisition.[70] The effects of blight resulting from the land falling within one of the categories of "blighted land" are, therefore, to be ignored.[71] The provisions relating to "home loss" and "farm loss" payments apply.[72]

COMPENSATION FOR INJURIOUS AFFECTION

There is an alternative way of alleviating hardship resulting from **14–14** depreciation in the value of land arising from public works which imposes less of a burden on public authorities than an obligation to buy the land. Compensation may be paid. In Chapter 11 it was suggested that where a body carrying out a scheme of public works is rendered immune by statutory authority from an action at common law in respect of the consequences of the scheme, it is reasonable to expect that Parliament will make provision for compensation in lieu (see p.238). That expectation is satisfied as regards injury to land formerly held together with land acquired for the scheme.

The blighting effects of a scheme do not, however, discriminate between those who have had some of their land acquired for the scheme and those who have not. The question which is addressed in this part of this chapter is the extent to which this expectation of compensation is satisfied as regards proprietors who have had no land acquired for the scheme.[73]

In Chapter 4 it was pointed out that the entitlement to compensation for expropriation depends upon statutory authority (p.82) but that "there is a natural leaning in favour of compensation in the construction of a

---

[68] Where an objection is upheld under s.102(4)(c), the notice will be declared valid as regards the remaining part (s.104(6)).

[69] The date of the notice to treat will be the date specified in a direction given by the tribunal following the reference of an objection or, in any other case, two months from the date of service of the blight notice (s.105(3)).

[70] But see the 1997 Act, s.108 as regards two circumstances in which special rules apply.

[71] Land Compensation (Scotland) Act 1963, s.16.

[72] Planning and Compensation Act 1991, s.71(2) repealing s.27(5) of the Land Compensation (Scotland) Act 1973 Act (home loss payment) and the 1991 Act, Sch.17, para.14(6) repealing s.31(6) of the 1973 Act (farm loss payment).

[73] The same question also arises with regard to the proprietors of remaining land which was not "held together" with land acquired for the scheme (see *City of Glasgow Union Railway v Hunter* (1870) 8 M. (H.L.) 156).

statute".[74] The entitlement to compensation for injurious affection in the absence of expropriation also depends upon statutory authority and it is now appropriate to consider such authority and the way in which the courts have "leaned" in the construction of such authority.

Prior to the decision of the House of Lords in *Metropolitan Board of Works v McCarthy*[75] (below) the courts took the view that the Lands Clauses Acts in both England and Scotland made no provision for compensating injurious affection except where the land in question had been held together with land acquired for the scheme of works.[76] Owners, none of whose land had been acquired, had to rely on provisions, relating to injurious affection, if any, in other legislation[77] authorising the particular undertaking. As many of the claims for injurious affection during the nineteenth century arose from the construction of the railways, particular reliance was placed on sections 6 and 16 of the Railways Clauses Consolidation (Scotland) Act 1845.[78]

Section 6 provides that:

> "The Company shall make to the owner and occupier of and all other parties interested in any lands taken or used for the purposes of the railway or injuriously affected by the construction thereof, full compensation for the value of the lands so taken or used, and for all damage sustained by such owners, occupiers, and other parties by reason of the exercise as regards such lands of the powers of this, or the Special Act, or any Act incorporated therewith, vested in the Company."

And section 16 requires the Company to make "full satisfaction to all parties interested" for all damage resulting from the carrying out of various works connected with the construction of the railway.

In *Metropolitan Board of Works v McCarthy*,[79] section 68 of the English Lands Clauses Act was "benevolently misinterpreted" by the House of Lords so as to enable a person, none of whose land had been acquired for the scheme, to claim compensation for injurious affection. The decision has been described by Davies[80] as a "misinterpretation" because the section appears in that part of the Act concerned with the purchase and taking of land otherwise than by agreement and appears to be directed at laying down a procedure for settling compensation where land has been taken in advance of payment. Davies regards the

---

[74] *Burmah Oil Company (Burma Trading) Ltd v Lord Advocate*, 1964 S.C. (H.L.) 117, *per* Lord Hodson at p.154.

[75] (1874) L.R. (H.L.) 243.

[76] *Hammersmith and City Rail Co. v Brand* (1869) L.R. 4 H.L. 171; *City of Glasgow Union Railway Co. v Hunter* (1870) 8 M. (H.L.) 156.

[77] See, for example, the Railways Clauses Consolidation (Scotland) Act 1845, s.6; and the Market and Fairs Clauses Act 1847, s.6. And the Roads (Scotland) Act 1984, s.116, currently provides for the payment of compensation for damage caused by reason of the execution of works under certain sections in that Act.

[78] J. C. Irons and R. D. Melville, *Law of Arbitration in Scotland* (W. Green & Son, 1903), p.300.

[79] (1874) L.R. (H.L.) 243.

[80] K. Davies, " 'Injurious Affection' and the Land Compensation Act 1973" (1974) 90 L.Q.R. 361.

misinterpretation as "benevolent" because it can be construed as a "lamentably clumsy attempt" to mitigate the consequences of a previous much criticised decision.[81] The Scottish Lands Clauses Act, however, contains no provision corresponding to section 68 of the English Act, so that the decision in *McCarthy* was of no assistance to claimants in Scotland.[82]

The anomaly was eventually remedied by section 1 and paragraph 1 of the Second Schedule to the Acquisition of Land (Authorisation Procedure) (Scotland) Act 1947 which provides that in relation to any compulsory purchase to which the provisions of the First Schedule apply, section 6 of the Railways Clauses Act is incorporated with the enactment under which the purchase is authorised. Section 6, as incorporated by the 1947 Act, accordingly, provides statutory authority for a claim for compensation for injurious affection where no land has been taken.

Interpretation of section 6 and of its English counterpart by the courts during the second half of the nineteenth century has given rise to very considerable complexity[83] which unfortunately remains with us today. The following propositions appear to have been established by judicial authority:

1. The injury complained of must arise from the legitimate exercise of statutory powers;

2. The injury must be such that but for the statutory powers, it would have grounded an action at law;

3. The injury must be one affecting the value of land; and

4. The injury must arise from the construction of the public works and not from their subsequent use.

These propositions[84] are now examined in turn.

1. The injury complained of must arise from the legitimate exercise of statutory powers

In Chapter 11, mention was made, in the context of the entitlement to **14–15** compensation for injurious affection where land has been acquired, that for anything done in excess of or contrary to statutory powers, the common law remedy remains (see p.237). Compensation may only be claimed under section 6 of the Railways Clauses Act in respect of losses sustained in consequence of what the promoter may lawfully do under the powers conferred by Parliament. It is well established that "for anything done in excess of these powers, or contrary to what the

[81] See the discussion on p.346 of the decision in *Hammersmith and City Rail Co. v Brand* (1869) L.R. 4 H.L. 171.
[82] But see the arguments advanced in *Stone v Corporation of Yeovil* (1876) 1 C.P.D. 691; aff. 2 C.P.D. 99 regarding the interpretation of s.9 of the English Lands Clauses Act.
[83] For a full discussion of this complexity see F. Deas, *The Law of Railways Applicable to Scotland*, as revised by James Ferguson (W. Green & Son, 1897) Part IV, Chap.2.
[84] These propositions are often referred to as the "McCarthy Rules" after the decision of the House of Lords in *Metropolitan Board of Works v McCarthy* (1874) L.R. (H.L.) 243.

Legislature, in conferring these powers, has commanded, the proper remedy is a common law action in the Common Law Courts".[85] Thus in *Samuel v Edinburgh and Glasgow Railway Company*[86] an action was brought against the railway company in respect of damage to the pursuer's farm alleged to have been caused by the inadequacy of the arrangements for carrying off surface water during the formation of the railway. The defender argued that the action was incompetent, statute having made provision for determining questions of damage arising from the construction of the railway. It was held that the provisions of the statute applied to the original construction of the railway but not to questions of damage which might subsequently occur arising from the insufficiency of the works.

2. The injury must be such that but for the statutory powers, it would have grounded an action at law

14–16   This proposition derives from the decision of the House of Lords in *Caledonian Railway v Ogilvy*.[87] A proprietor claimed £300 by way of compensation for injurious affection for the "very material injury done to the place as a residence, and deterioration to the amenity and value of the house and policy" resulting from the inconvenience, interruption and delay caused by the placing by the railway company of a level crossing on a public road some 50–60 yards from the entrance to the property. In the course of his judgment Lord Chancellor Cranworth stated:

> "the construction that is put upon this expression, 'injuriously affected', in the clauses in an Act of Parliament which gives compensation for injuriously affecting lands, certainly does not entitle the owner of lands which he alleges to be injuriously affected, to any compensation in respect of any act which, if done by the Railway Company without the authority of Parliament, would not have entitled him to bring an action against them."[88]

An illustration of this test is provided by the decision in *Re Penny and the South-Eastern Railway Co.*[89] where the question arose whether the English Lands Clauses Act enabled compensation to be claimed following the construction of a railway for annoyance caused by persons standing on the bank of the railway and overlooking the claimant's premises, no land having been acquired from the claimant for the railway. The court held that it did not. Lord Campbell C.J. said:

> "The test is, whether, before the railway Act passed authorising the company to do what has been done here, an action would have lain

---

[85] *Caledonian Railway Co. v Colt* (1860) 3 Macq. 833, *per* Lord Chancellor Campbell at para.839. See too F. Deas, *The Law of Railways Applicable to Scotland*, *supra*, p.307.
[86] (1849) 11 D. 968.
[87] (1856) 2 Macq. 229. See, too, *Re Penny and South Eastern Railway Co.* (1857) 7 E. and B. 660; *Ricket v Metropolitan Railway Co.* (1867) L.R. 2 H.L. 175; *Metropolitan Board of Works v McCarthy* (1874) L.R. (H.L.) 243; and *Caledonian Railway Co. v Walker's Trustees* (1882) 9 R. (H.L.) 19.
[88] See above para.235.
[89] (1857) 7 E. & B. 660.

at common law for what has been done, and for which compensation has been claimed . . . if the land is not taken and nothing is done which would have afforded a cause of action before the act passed, then, although it may produce a deterioration of the property, it does not injuriously affect the land and constitute a ground for compensation."

In this case an action would not have lain in the absence of statutory authority for the construction of the railway for the claimant's grounds being overlooked and his privacy being disturbed.

These decisions indicate that the basis of the claim for compensation for injurious affection where no land has been taken is *damnum cum injuria*. The inference drawn from the legislation was that Parliament simply intended to confer on landowners a compensation entitlement co-extensive with the right of action removed by statute.[90] This contrasts with cases where the affected land was held together with land taken for the scheme (see Chapter 11). The entitlement there, following the decisions in *Re Stockport, Timperley and Altrincham Railway Co.*[91] and *Cowper Essex v Acton Local Board*[92] would appear to rest upon *damnum* alone. Crompton J. in *Re Stockport, etc.* explained the distinction in this way:

> "where, however, the mischief is caused by what is done on the land taken, the party seeking compensation has a right to say, 'it is by the Act of Parliament, and the Act of Parliament only, that you have done the acts which have caused damage; without the Act of Parliament, everything you have done, and are about to do, in making and using the railway, would have been illegal and action-able, and is, therefore, matter for compensation according to the rule in question'."[93]

Whilst this may be a ground for awarding some special element in the compensation for the land taken, it would seem to have very little to do with injury to the land retained. While reservations were subsequently expressed about the requirement to establish that the injury would have been actionable but for the statute,[94] it remains a prerequisite for a claim

---

[90] CPPRAG suggest that in some instances the right to be compensated is inferior to common law rights ("Fundamental review of the laws and procedures relating to compulsory purchase and compensation: final report" (2000) DETR para.196; and see the (2002) Law Commission Consultation Paper No 165 paras 9.17–9.21). See too *Wildtrees Hotels Ltd v Harrow London Borough Council* [2001] 2 A.C. 1, HL. Contrast *Clift v Welsh Office* (1999) 78 P. & C.R. 32, CA. It should be noted that the measure of compensation may not, however, equate with an award of damages (*Wrotham Park Settled Estates v Hertsmere Borough Council* (1993) 27 E.G. 124, CA).

[91] (1864) 33 L.J.Q.B. 251.

[92] (1889) 14 App.Cas. 153, HL. See, too, *Duke of Buccleuch v Metropolitan Board of Works* (1872) L.R. 5 H.L. 418.

[93] Page 253. See, too, *Duke of Buccleuch, supra, per* Mr Justice Hannen at p.445.

[94] See, for example, *Ricket v Metropolitan Railways Co.* (1867) L.R. 2 H.L. 175, *per* Lord Westbury at p.202; *Metropolitan Board of Works v McCarthy* (1874) L.R. 7 H.L. 243, *per* Lord Chancellor Cairns at p.252 and Lord O'Hagan at p.266; and *Caledonian Railway Co. v Walker's Trustees* (1882) 9 R. (H.L.) 19, *per* Lord Selborne at p.23.

for injurious affection where the affected land was not held together with land taken for the scheme.

3. *The injury must be one affecting the value of the land*

14–17   An owner, says Cripps, is only entitled to compensation "for loss caused by interference with an interest in lands, and not for damage to his trade or business, or for damages resulting in personal loss or inconvenience, unless such damage is reflected in the depreciation in the value of the land".[95] Thus in *Caledonian Railway v Ogilvy*[96] (above) the House of Lords considered that the injury suffered by the location of a level crossing on a public road at a distance of some 50–60 yards from the entrance to a property was not an injury to the property but in the nature of personal inconvenience:

> "for all attempts at arguing that this is a damage to the estate is a mere play upon words. It is no damage at all to the estate, except that the owner of that estate would oftener have a right of action from time to time than any other person, inasmuch as he would traverse the spot oftener than other people would traverse it."[97]

It was in the context of temporary or permanent obstruction of access to premises that this proposition gave rise to particular difficulty. In *Ricket v Metropolitan Railway Co.*[98] the occupier of a public house experienced temporary loss of trade while the usual (public) access to his premises was obstructed during the construction of the Metropolitan Railway. His claim in respect of this loss under section 16 of the English Railways Clauses Act was rejected by the House of Lords, Lord Westbury dissenting. Lord Chancellor Chelmsford, after an extensive review of the decisions in this field, considered, *inter alia*, that the injury was too remote from the mischief to which the section was directed. Lord Cranworth concluded that no damage had been occasioned to the land. "Both principle and authority seem to me to show that no case comes within the provisions of the statute, unless where some damage has been occasioned to the land itself, as by loosening the foundation of the buildings on it, obstructing its lights or its drains, making it inaccessible by lowering or raising the ground immediately in front of it, or by some such physical deterioration."

Lord Cranworth's catalogue would seem to be incomplete in so far as it is directed at physical deterioration in the land itself. The decision of the House of Lords in *Metropolitan Board of Works v McCarthy*[99] established that depreciation resulting from interference with any right, public or private, which owners and occupiers are entitled to use in connection with property and which gives an additional market value to the property, apart from the uses to which any particular owner might

---

[95] H. Parrish, *Cripps on Compulsory Acquisition of Land* (11th ed., Stevens & Sons Ltd) para.5–0322.
[96] (1856) 2 Macq. 229.
[97] *Per* Lord Chancellor Cranworth at paras 236–237.
[98] (1867) L.R 2 H.L. 175.
[99] (1874) L.R. 7 H.L. 243.

put it, could found a claim for compensation. As Deas asserts,[1] though the injury is to the land, it need not be upon the land provided the premises suffer special damage. This point is well illustrated by the decision in *Caledonian Railway Co. v Walkers' Trustees*.[2] The trustees owned a mill and related buildings located to the west of Eglinton Street, one of the main thoroughfares in Glasgow. Access to Eglinton Street was by either of two roads contiguous to and to the north and south of the premises. The operations of the railway company effectively blocked such access. The only alternative access involved a considerable detour and a steeper gradient. The trustees' claim under section 6 of the Railways Clauses Act in respect of the diminution in the value of their premises was upheld in the House of Lords. Lord Watson said:

"When an access to private property by a public highway is interfered with, the owner can have no action of damages for any personal inconvenience which he may suffer in common with the rest of the lieges. But, should the value of the property, irrespective of any particular uses which may be made of it, be so dependent upon the existence of that access as to be substantially diminished by its obstruction, then I conceive that the owner has, in respect of any works causing such obstruction, a right of action if these works are unauthorised by Act of Parliament, and a title to compensation under the Railway Acts if they are constructed under statutory powers."[3]

The question of compensation for temporary interference with a business, which had produced such an inequitable result in *Ricket*, raised its head again in *Wildtree Hotels Ltd v Harrow London Borough Council*.[4] The circumstances were similar. A complex road improvement scheme created temporary problems for customers taking access to a hotel. This was partly because hoardings were erected which obscured the hotel and the roads and pavements giving access to it were obstructed. The interference was detrimental to the hotel business. As no land had been acquired from the hotel for the scheme, an injurious affection claim was lodged under section 10 of the Compulsory Purchase Act 1965. The claim was upheld by the Lands Tribunal but rejected by the Court of Appeal. Ralph Gibson L.J., in dismissing the claim, said he could not understand "how a temporary loss of value which would have been observable at earlier dates but which was no longer obtaining at the agreed date of assessment can give rise to a claim for compensation".[5]

The House of Lords took a different view. Giving judgement for the House, Lord Hoffmann, after a full review of the cases and, in particular the decision in *Ricket*, held that compensation under section 10 was not only to be assessed by considering the capital value of the claimants' land at a given date and deducting from it an estimate of what its value would

[1] F. Deas, *The Law of Railways Applicable to Scotland, supra*, p.335.
[2] (1882) 9 R. H.L. 19.
[3] See above at p.38.
[4] [2001] 2 A.C. 1.
[5] [1999] Q.B. 634 at pp.672–673.

have been if the land had not been injuriously affected. The claimants were simply entitled to compensation for the damage to their land. While it might be sensible with permanent or long term damage to land to take a valuation date and capitalise the value of the future loss at that date, there was no reason why, with damage that has occurred in the past, one should not calculate the effect on the value of the land by reference to the reduction in its letting value in the open market while the damage continued. The claim for compensation for temporary interference was upheld.

4. The injury must arise from the construction of the public works and not from their subsequent use

14–18   Sections 6 and 16 of the Railways Clauses Act refer to damage caused by the *construction* of the works. In *Hammersmith and City Rail Co. v Brand*[6] the House of Lords concluded that the corresponding provisions in the English legislation did not entitle a claimant to compensation for injurious affection arising, not from the *construction* of the works, but from their subsequent *use*. The claimants owned a house adjoining the defendant's railway. No part of their land had been acquired for the construction of the railway. They claimed compensation, *inter alia*, for depreciation in the value of their property resulting from vibration, arising from the proper and ordinary use of the railway by trains. In the House of Lords it was accepted that the use of the railway had, indeed, depreciated the value of the property. Lord Chelmsford said "The plaintiff's remedy by action being taken away, the question remains, whether they are entitled to receive compensation from the company for the injury done to their house—a question which must be decided entirely by the provision of the Acts of Parliament relating to the subject". After an examination of these provisions he concluded "it is not that the Legislature has excluded compensation for injury arising as the necessary consequence of using the railway, but that it has not, as far as I can discover, given any right to claim compensation for this species of injury".[7]

The House of Lords reached a similar conclusion the following year in *City of Glasgow Union Railway Co. v Hunter*.[8] A proprietor of a block of tenement houses and shops which were adversely affected by the use by trains of a new railway bridge constructed near the property claimed compensation for injurious affection. The claimant sought to distinguish *Brand* on two grounds. First of all, it was argued, he was entitled to all loss arising from the construction and use of the railway as part of his

---

[6] (1869) L.R. 4 H.L. 171.

[7] See above at pp.202–203. In *Allen v Gulf Oil Refining Ltd* [1979] 3 W.L.R. 523, the Court of Appeal adopted somewhat similar reasoning to very different effect. An examination of the private Act authorising the compulsory acquisition of land at Milford Haven for the construction of an oil refinery revealed that the Act specifically authorised its construction but did not specifically authorise its use. Therefore, said the court, the right of a neighbour to sue the promoters at common law for nuisance caused by the use of the refinery was retained. It was left to the House of Lords ([1981] 1 All E.R. 353) to point out the "remarkable consequences" of such a proposition and to hold that "construction" in the private Act implied "use" as well.

[8] (1870) 8 M. H.L. 156.

land had been acquired for its construction (see Ch.11). This argument was rejected on the ground that the claim did not arise in connection with anything done on the land taken (see p.244); and, furthermore, that the land taken for the scheme, although adjoining the tenement and held under the same title, had not been "held together" with it (see p.241). The claimant was, therefore, in the same position as regards a claim for injurious affection as a person who had had none of his land acquired for the scheme. Secondly, it was evident that if sections 6 and 16 of the Railways Clauses Act governed his claim, his position was indistinguishable from that in *Brand*. Mr Hunter, accordingly, founded his claim on sections 17 and 48 of the Lands Clauses Act, particularly the latter. The claim was rejected by their Lordships who considered that the provisions in question were concerned with the respective rights of the promoter of the undertaking and the owners of land acquired in order to carry out the work.

It would seem from the four propositions described above that the attitude of the courts to claims for injurious affection compensation where no land is taken is somewhat different to their approach to such claims where expropriation has occurred. Reference was made earlier, in the context of expropriation, to the "natural leaning in favour of compensation in the construction of a statute". The courts appear, at least in the heyday of injurious affection claims in the second half of the nineteenth century, to have leaned the other way where no land was taken. "It is not," said Lord Chelmsford in *Brand*, "that the Legislature has excluded compensation for injury arising as the necessary consequence of using the railway, but that it has not, as far as I can discover, given any right to claim compensation for this species of injury."[9] Yet the logic of this distinction is questionable as the injurious effects of public works do not discriminate between those who have had land acquired for the works and those who have not.

5. Compensation for injury arising from the use of the public works

The considerable hardship arising from the decision in *Brand* that **14–19** compensation could only be recovered for injurious affection arising from the construction and not the use of works was somewhat alleviated in England by the decision in *Re Simeon and Isle of Wight Rural District Council*[10] on the meaning of the words "execution of the works" in section 68 of the English Lands Clauses Act. Section 68 had been construed in *McCarthy* as entitling a person, none of whose land had been acquired for the works, to claim compensation for injurious affection arising from the "execution of the works" (see p.340). In *Re Simeon and Isle of Wight Rural District Council*, Luxmoor J. interpreted these words as having a wider compass than "construction of the works," the term used in section 6 of the Scottish Railways Clauses Act. They include, he said, "the exercise, that is, the carrying out and the execution, of the appropriate statutory powers".[11] Cripps suggests that, as a result,

---

[9] (1869) L.R. 4 H.L. 171 at p.203.
[10] [1937] Chap. 525.
[11] At p.539.

where the statutory works include construction and maintenance or user, "then compensation may be claimed for injury by construction or user but only in respect of injury to land".[12]

The Scottish Lands Clauses Act, however, as mentioned earlier, contains no provision corresponding to section 68 of the English Act and it was not until 1973 that legislation was passed to make it clear that the reference to "construction" of a railway in section 6 of the Railways Clauses Act was to be interpreted as including a reference to the execution of works in connection therewith.[13]

The same legislation, however, made an altogether more far-reaching change to the entitlement to compensation for injurious affection where no land is taken. The urban motorways programme of the 1960s and the proposal for a third London Airport served to focus attention on the anomalous distinction drawn by the courts between injury caused by the construction of the public works and that resulting from their use. Householders affected by urban motorways might be exposed to considerable disturbance from a substantial volume of traffic passing close to their houses, in some places at first floor level, at all hours of the day and night without compensation unless some part of the land had been acquired for the road. "We believe it to be a sad commentary on the present law," observed the JUSTICE report, "that an owner of land in an area through which a motorway is to be constructed should prefer that the motorway takes the whole of his property than go near to it".[14] McAuslan suggests that the JUSTICE report was instrumental in creating "an informed climate of opinion amongst policy-makers about compensation and its inadequacies".[15] Other reports around the same time[16] culminating in the report of the Urban Motorways Committee[17] commented on shortcomings in the compensation arrangements. The Urban Motorways Committee recommended that "compensation for injurious affection should be extended generally to cases where no land is taken but where property suffers loss of value because of the effects of the road".[18]

In a white paper in 1972[19] the government acknowledged that the time had come to redistribute the burden of cost arising from public developments so that more would be borne by the community at large in the form of improvements in the arrangements for compensating those most affected by such developments.[20] These improvements were intro-

---

[12] H. Parrish, *Cripps on Compulsory Acquisition of Land, supra,* para.5–031.

[13] Land Compensation (Scotland) Act 1973, s.61 adding a new subsection (2) to section 6 of the Railways Clauses Consolidation (Scotland) Act 1845. Note that section 116 of the Roads (Scotland) Act 1984 currently provides for the payment of compensation in respect of damage caused by the execution of works under certain sections of that Act.

[14] JUSTICE, *Compensation for Compulsory Acquisition and Remedies for Planning Restrictions* (1969) *together with a Supplemental Report* (Stevens, 1973) para.55.

[15] P. McAuslan, *The Ideologies of Planning Law* (Pergamon Press, 1980) p.107.

[16] Chartered Land Societies Committee, "Compensation for Compulsory Acquisition and Planning Restrictions (1968); the Report of the Commission on the Third London Airport" (1971) HMSO.

[17] "New Roads in Towns" (1972) HMSO.

[18] See above para.12.7.

[19] "Development and Compensation—Putting People First" (1972) HMSO Cmnd. 5124.

[20] See above, paras 5, 6 and 9.

duced in Part I of the Land Compensation Act 1973 and subsequently re-enacted for Scotland in Part I of the Land Compensation (Scotland) Act 1973.[21] The provisions of Part I do not alter the present arrangements described above for compensating loss resulting from the *construction* of public works where no land has been taken.[22] They simply confer an additional entitlement to compensation for depreciation caused by the *use* of the works.[23]

Section 1 of the 1973 Act provides that if the value of a qualifying interest in land is depreciated by physical factors caused by the use of public works, the responsible authority will pay compensation for that depreciation in response to a claim made by the person entitled to that interest. "Qualifying interest," "physical factors," "public works" and "responsible authority" all require definition.

An interest qualifies for compensation under Part I if it was acquired[24] by the claimant before the "relevant date" (below) and the following requirements are satisfied on the date of service of the notice of claim (s.2(1)): (i) as regards a dwelling-house, the interest is an owner's interest; and if the interest carries the right to occupy the dwelling, the claimant is in occupation in right of that interest (s.2(2)); (ii) as regards other land, the interest is that of an owner-occupier and the land is or forms part of either an agricultural unit or a hereditament the annual value of which does not exceed an amount prescribed by regulations made by the Scottish Ministers (s.2(3)).[25]

An "owner's interest"[26] includes the interest of a lessee under a lease, the unexpired period of which on the date of service of the notice of claim is not less than three years (s.2(4)(a))[27] and the interest of a crofter, a landholder, a statutory small tenant and a cottar.[28] "Owner-occupier" in relation to land in an agricultural unit means a person who occupies the whole of that unit and is entitled while so occupying it to an owner's interest in the whole or any part of that land. In relation to land in a hereditament, the term refers to a person who occupies the whole or a substantial part of the land in right of an owner's interest therein (s.2(5)).[29]

---

[21] For a discussion of these provisions see, generally, P. McAuslan, *The Ideologies of Planning Law, supra.*, Chap.4; K. Davies, " 'Injurious Affection' and the Land Compensation Act 1973" (1974) 90 L.Q.R. 361; R.N.D. Hamilton, "Land Compensation Act 1973–I and II" (1973) 117 S.J. 514 and 538; Alec Samuels, "The Land Compensation Act 1973" (1973) 123 N.L.J. 556.

[22] But see section 61 which declares that the reference to "construction" in section 6 of the Railways Clauses Act 1845 is to include a reference to "the execution of works in connection therewith". For the position regarding land "held together with" land acquired for public works see Chap.11; also the 1973 Act, s.8(2) and (5).

[23] For an explanation of these provisions see SDD Circular 84/1973.

[24] For the position where an interest is acquired by inheritance, see the 1973 Act, s.11.

[25] At the time of writing the amount prescribed is £24,725 (the Town and Country Planning (Limit of Annual Value) (Scotland) Order 2001).

[26] For the position of heritable creditors and other restricted interests in land, see the 1973 Act, s.10.

[27] The Royal Institution of Chartered Surveyors proposed that compensation should be payable under Part I to any claimant who has a legal interest in the land (Compensation for Compulsory Acquisition (1995) para.3.14).

[28] For the meaning of "crofter", "land holder", "statutory small tenant" and "cottar," see the 1973 Act, s.80(1).

[29] For the position of trustees, see the 1973 Act, s.10(3).

The physical factors which may trigger a claim in respect of depreciation are defined in s.1(2) of the 1972 Act. They are: (i) noise; (ii) vibration; (iii) smell; (iv) fumes; (v) smoke; (vi) artificial lighting[30]; (vii) discharge on to the land in respect of which the claim is made of any solid or liquid substance.

The source of the "physical factor" or factors giving rise to the claim must be situated on or in the public works in question. Exceptionally, depreciation resulting from aircraft arriving at or departing from an aerodrome[31] is to be treated as caused by the use of the aerodrome, whether or not the aircraft are within the boundaries of the aerodrome (s.1(5)).

The "public works," the use of which has given rise to physical factors causing depreciation, are defined in s.1(3). They are: (i) any road[32]; (ii) any aerodrome; and (iii) any works or land (not being a road or aerodrome) provided or used in exercise of statutory powers.

14–20 The compensation entitlement is not confined solely to depreciation arising from the bringing into use of new public works but extends also to depreciation arising from alterations to existing roads, the reconstruction, extension or alteration of other existing public works or from a change in the use of any existing public works[33] other than a road or aerodrome. Alterations to an existing aerodrome will only give rise to an entitlement if they take the form of alterations to existing runways or aprons (s.9(3)).[34] And the carriageway of a road may be considered to be altered if, but only if, the location, width or level of the existing carriageway is altered (otherwise than by resurfacing), or an additional carriageway is provided for the road beside, above or below an existing one (s.9(5)); the entitlement will then lie in respect of depreciation arising from physical factors caused by the use of, and the source of which is situated on, the length of carriageway as so altered or the additional carriageway and the corresponding length of the existing one as the case may be.

The authority responsible for compensating a claimant is, in relation to a road, the appropriate roads authority,[35] and in relation to other public works, the person managing those works.

Compensation is not payable under the provisions of Part I in respect of the use of any public works, other than a road, unless the legislation relating to those works confers immunity from actions for nuisance in respect of that use, either expressly or by implication (s.1(6))[36]; neither is it payable in respect of aerodromes and physical factors caused by

---

[30] A term which would seem to encompass both street lights and vehicle lights.

[31] For the meaning of "aerodrome," see the Civil Aviation Act 1982, s.105(1).

[32] "Road" has the same meaning as in the Roads (Scotland) Act 1984 (see the Roads (Scotland) Act 1984, s.156(1) and Sch.9).

[33] References in the 1973 Act, s.9 to "a change of use" do not include references to the intensification of an existing use (s.9(7)).

[34] As defined in the 1973 Act, s.9(6). See *R v Secretary of State for the Environment, Transport and the Regions and Thomas, ex parte Plymouth City Airport Ltd.* (2001) 82 P. & C.R. 265, CA.

[35] As defined in the Roads (Scotland) Act 1984 (see the Roads (Scotland) Act 1984, s.156(1) and Sch.9).

[36] But see the 1973 Act, s.16. See too *Marsh v Powys County Council* (1997) 33 E.G. 100, Lands Tr.

aircraft unless the aerodrome is one to which section 77(2) of the Civil Aviation Act 1982 applies (which confers immunity from actions for nuisance). And no compensation is payable in respect of physical factors caused by accidents involving vehicles on a road or accidents involving aircraft (s.1(7)).

The procedure for a claim is set out in section 3. A claim under Part I **14–21** is made by serving a notice on the responsible authority containing the particulars referred to in section 3(1) of the 1973 Act.[37] Subject to the one exception referred to below, no claim may be made before the expiration of 12 months from the "relevant date" (s.3(2)). The day following the expiration of the 12 month period is referred to as "the first claim day". The "relevant date" is defined, as regards a road, as the date on which it was first opened to public traffic[38] and as regards other public works the date on which they were first used after completion (section 1(9)).[39] With regard to claims arising from alterations to carriageways, the relevant date is the date on which the road was first open to public traffic after completion of the alterations; and with regard to claims arising from alterations to other public works, the relevant date is to be that on which the works were first used after completion of the alterations. The relevant date in respect of a change in the use of any public works, other than a road or aerodrome, is to be the date of the change of use (s.9(2)). The responsible authority is required to keep a record of the appropriate relevant date and to furnish information about it on request (s.13(1)). A certificate from the Scottish Ministers as to the relevant date in respect of runway or apron alterations at an aerodrome is to be taken as conclusive (s.13(2)). The time limits, observed the Lands Tribunal for Scotland in *Inglis v British Airports Authority*[40] "appear designed to ensure that land valuations have had time, following first use on the relevant date, to settle down and show the full extent of any depreciation".

The only circumstance in which a claim may be lodged prior to the "first claim day" is where the claimant during the 12 months preceding that day has contracted to dispose of his interest or to grant a tenancy of the land (provided the land does not comprise a dwelling) and the claim is made prior to the disposal of the interest or the grant of the tenancy (s.3(3)). In *Inglis v British Airports Authority* the Lands Tribunal for Scotland held that "disposal of the interest" referred to actual disposal and not to a contract for its disposal.[41] Even then, compensation in respect of such a claim is not payable before the "first claim day".

A claim must be lodged within five years of the "first claim day" (s.17(2A)).[42]

---

[37] See, too, the 1973 Act, s.9(4).

[38] But see the 1973 Act, s.17(3).

[39] See *Davies v Mid-Glamorgan County Council* (1979) 38 P. & C.R. 727; and *Shepherd and Shepherd v Lancashire County Council* (1976) 33 P. & C.R. 296.

[40] 1978 S.L.T. (Lands Tr.) 30.

[41] 1978 S.L.T. (Lands Tr.) 30.

[42] Added by the Local Government, Planning and Land Act 1980, ss.112(7) and (9) applying section 6 of the Prescription and Limitation (Scotland) Act 1973.

The compensation is to be assessed having regard to the following matters.[43] It is to be assessed by reference to prices current on the "first claim day" (s.4(1)).[44] Depreciation is to be estimated by reference to the level of use of the public works on the "first claim day" but having regard to any intensification that may then reasonably be expected (s.4(2)). In *Dhenin v Department of Transport*,[45] the Lands Tribunal stated that compensation under Part I has to be ascertained at a specific date, on the facts at that date, on the prices current at that date and on any intensification of the depreciation which could be anticipated at that date. In other words, the principle in *Bwlfa and Merthyr Dare Steam Collieries (1891) Ltd v Pontypridd Waterworks Company*[46] (see p.251) has no application. Account is to be taken of the benefit of any sound-proofing works which could be or could have been carried out, or in respect of which a grant could be or could have been given, under this or other legislation (see p.355) and of any mitigating works carried out under section 25 of the 1973 Act or section 52 of the Roads (Scotland) Act 1984 (see p.356) (s.4(3)). An interest is to be valued by reference to the nature of the interest and the condition of the land as it subsisted at the date of service of notice of the claim (s.4(4)(a)); and in accordance with rules (2) and (4) of section 12 of the Land Compensation (Scotland) Act 1963 (see c.6) (s.4(4)(b)). In *Inglis v British Airports Authority (No. 2)*[47] the Lands Tribunal for Scotland described the claim as "akin to one for injurious affection on a before and after basis". The proper valuation approach, observed the tribunal, in respect of a claim for depreciation to a dwelling-house caused by physical factors arising from the bringing into operation of a new runway,[48] "was to assess the open market value of the house as at April 7, 1977 with no runway and, second, the market value taking into account the use of the runway as at that date and any intensification of usage which might then reasonably be expected". In *Brown v Central Regional Council*[49] the tribunal said there were two established methods of assessing the effect on value of physical factors (in that case noise and light). The first is to value the affected property with the public works in place, but net of the effect of the physical factors. The second, more common approach, is to value the affected property before the public works are undertaken and then to compare that value with the value of the property with the public works in place and in use. The gross difference in value attributable to both compensatable and non-compensatable factors is then adjusted by apportioning the effect of the compensatable and non-compensatable factors.

---

[43] See, generally, B. Sparks, "Land Compensation Act 1973: A Practical Approach to Part 1 Claims" (1986) 278 E.G. 1464. Also P. Cooke-Priest, "Improving Compensation Provisions" (1988) 8807 E.G. 66.

[44] See *Fallows v Gateshead Metropolitan Borough Council* (1993) 66 P. & C.R. 460.

[45] (1990) 60 P. & C.R. 349, Lands Tr.

[46] [1903] A.C. 426. The principle is to the effect that in assessing damages it is unnecessary to speculate on what might be the measure of loss if at the time of the trial the true loss has become a fact.

[47] 1979 S.L.T. (Lands Tr.) 10.

[48] See, too, *Stuart v British Airports Authority*, 1983 S.L.T. (Lands Tr.) 42.

[49] unreported, November 22, 1993, Lands Tribunal for Scotland.

No account is to be taken of a heritable security, missives of sale or a contract made after the relevant date for the grant of a tenancy (s.4(4)(c)). Neither is account to be taken of any value attributable to any building, or to any improvement or extension of a building, if it was first occupied after the relevant date; nor of any value attributable to a change in the use of the land made after that date (s.4(5)).

The only planning assumption that may be made in assessing the value of the interest in respect of which a claim is made is that planning permission would be granted for the categories of development listed in Schedule 11 to the 1997 Act.[50] Otherwise it is to be assumed that planning permission would not be granted for development; and if planning permission has been granted for the development of the whole or a part of the relevant land which does not fall within one of the categories of development in Schedule 11, it is to be assumed that no such permission has been granted in so far as the permission relates to development that has not been carried out (s.5(4)).

Betterment arising from the scheme is to be set-off. Any increase in the value of the claimant's interest in the land in respect of which the claim is made,[51] and any increase in the value of any interest in other land contiguous or adjacent to that land to which the claimant is entitled in the same capacity[52] at the relevant date, which is attributable to the existence of or the use or prospective use of the public works to which the claim relates, is to be set-off against any compensation which is payable (s.6(1)).[53] The onus is on the responsible authority to show that any compensation which would otherwise have been due in respect of physical factors should be reduced or extinguished by set-off.[54] Section 6(3) and (4) prevents the operation of double set-off in the event of the subsequent acquisition of the interest in such other contiguous or adjacent land, the increased value of which has already been taken into account.

Five other restrictions on a Part I claim deserve mention. First of all, **14–22** compensation is not payable on any claim unless the compensation exceeds £50 (s.7).[55] Secondly, a claim is to be made once and for all. Where compensation has been paid or is payable under Part I in respect of depreciation in the value of an interest in land caused by the use of any public works, no subsequent claim will be entertained in respect of the same works and the same land (s.8(1)).[56] Thirdly, compensation is not payable under Part I in respect of land "held together with" land acquired for the public works whether or not compensation for injurious affection in respect of the retained land is paid under section 61 of the

---

[50] 1973 Act, s.5(2), as amended by the Planning and Compensation Act 1991, Sch.12, para.5.

[51] In assessing any such increase in value, the provisions of sections 4 and 5 of the 1973 Act do not apply (s.6(2)).

[52] For the meaning of this see the 1973 Act, s.6(5).

[53] As to the inter-relation between the section 1 valuation and set-off see *Dobbie v Fife Council*, unreported, January 14, 1998, Lands Tribunal for Scotland.

[54] *Dobbie v Fife Council*, see above.

[55] The Royal Institution of Chartered Surveyors suggested that this figure is overdue for revision (*Compensation for compulsory acquisition*, 1995 RICS para.3.14).

[56] Although this does not preclude a claim in respect of a dwelling by both the owner and a tenant.

1845 Act (s.8(2)). It is unlikely that such a duplication of claims will arise as the notice to treat in respect of the land to be acquired will generally precede the opportunity to claim under Part I. Furthermore, the compensation entitlement under section 61 may, in some respects, be more generous (see Ch.11). Fourthly, where after a claim has been lodged under Part I in respect of depreciation in the value of an interest in land the whole or a part of the land in which that interest subsists is compulsorily acquired, then if the depreciation is established but the compensation for the compulsory acquisition falls to be assessed without regard to the depreciation, the compensation for the acquisition is to be reduced by an amount equal to the compensation paid or payable on the Part I claim (s.8(6)). Finally, where a compensation entitlement under Part I is duplicated in other legislation, compensation will not be payable twice in respect of the same depreciation (s.8(7)).

Any question of disputed compensation under Part I is to be referred to and determined by the Lands Tribunal for Scotland although no question arising out of a claim may be referred before the "first claim day" (s.14). Compensation will carry interest at the prescribed rate[57] from the date of service of the notice of claim or from the "first claim day," whichever is the later, until payment (s.16). The responsible authority will also pay, in addition to the compensation, any reasonable valuation and legal expenses incurred by the claimant in preparing and prosecuting the claim (s.3(5)).[58]

The provisions for Part I which are described above do not entirely close the gap as regards an injurious affection claim between a person who has had land acquired for the scheme and one who has not. The provisions of Part I appear to be co-extensive with and a substitute for an action for nuisance.[59] "We are putting the public authority in the same position of liability," said the Minister for Local Government and Development during the committee stage of the Land Compensation Bill, "as is the private individual so far as permanent depreciation to the property is concerned. There is no justification for placing on the public authority a greater liability than the law places upon the private citizen."[60] Thus, no claim arises under Part I in respect of depreciation caused by loss of a view or loss of privacy. These are not among the factors listed in section 1(5).[61]

The provisions may also been criticised on other grounds. The limitation on the right to claim for physical factors arising from public works (as defined) rules out any claim for depreciation resulting from a mere intensification in the use of public works, for example, an intensification of the use of existing roads feeding a new motorway. Furthermore, as with planning blight (above), the definition of interests qualifying for compensation excludes those with an interest in land,

---

[57] Prescribed under the Land Compensation (Scotland) Act 1963, s.40.

[58] But without prejudice to the powers of the Lands Tribunal for Scotland in respect of the expenses of proceedings before the tribunal by virtue of the 1973 Act, s.14.

[59] Contrast the position as regards a claim for injurious affection in respect of land "held together with" land acquired for the public works (see p.244).

[60] Standing Committee A, December 5, 1972, col.16.

[61] And see *Shepherd and Shepherd v Lancashire County Council* (1976) 33 P. & C.R. 296; and *Hickmott v Dorset County Council* (1977)35 P. & C.R. 195.

other than a dwelling, comprising a hereditament the annual value of which exceeds a prescribed amount. And the provision for setting-off betterment arising from the works operates, as Davies[62] points out, regardless of the fact that any increase in the value of some other owner's land goes scot-free if he does not happen to suffer depreciation.

There is no doubt that Part I seeks to strike a balance between compensating those who are most seriously affected by public works and containing the burden of compensation imposed on public authorities. Notwithstanding the criticisms voiced above, the provisions go a long way towards remedying the difficulty created by the distinction between injury arising from the construction of works and that from their use drawn by the House of Lords in *Brand* and *Hunter*.

MITIGATION

In the introduction to this chapter it was suggested that those likely to be **14–23** injuriously affected by the bringing into use of a scheme of public works might prefer the injurious effect to be abated rather than receive compensation. The Urban Motorways Committee in their report *New Roads in Towns*[63] recognised that much could be done during the design and implementation of major roads to alleviate the adverse effects of the use of such roads on neighbouring land. The committee recommended that roads authorities should be given appropriate powers to mitigate the impact of roads on the environment of adjacent areas and to enable works to be carried out to fit roads more satisfactorily into their surroundings. They further recommended that roads authorities should be required to pay for sound insulation. In the White Paper *Development and Compensation—Putting People First*,[64] the government accepted these recommendations, suggested that the same approach could be applied to other public works and announced their intention to introduce the necessary legislation. Provisions for mitigating the injurious effects of public works are contained in Part II of the 1973 Act as amended.[65] These are considered under three headings.

1. Noise insulation

Section 18 deals with noise insulation. It enables the Scottish Ministers **14–24** to make regulations imposing a duty or conferring a power on responsible authorities to insulate buildings against noise caused or expected to be caused by the construction or use of public works.[66] Such regulations

---

[62] K. Davies, "Injurious Affection'; and the Land Compensation Act 1973" (1974) 90 L.Q.R. 361.

[63] (1972) HMSO.

[64] (1972) HMSO (Cmnd. 5124).

[65] The provisions in the 1973 Act, ss.20–23, were repealed and replaced by the Roads (Scotland) Act 1984, ss.52, 53 and 106 of; and new subsections (2A)–(2C) were added to the 1973 Act, s.24, by the Planning and Compensation Act 1991, s.76(1).

[66] "Public works" and "responsible authority" in s.18 bear the same meaning as in the 1973 Act, s.1 except that "public works" does not include an aerodrome, and "responsible authority" in respect of a road includes an authority empowered to make a traffic regulation order under the Road Traffic Regulation Act 1984, s.1.

may also provide for the making of grants in respect of the cost of insulation. It should be remembered that, in assessing a claim for compensation under Part I of the 1973 Act, it will be assumed that any entitlement under section 18 has been exercised (see p.352).

The Noise Insulation (Scotland) Regulations 1975,[67] made under section 18, provide for the insulation of buildings against noise caused or expected to be caused by traffic using new roads and certain altered roads. Regulation 3 imposes a *duty* on the appropriate roads authority to carry out sound insulation or to make a grant in respect of the cost of such insulation where the use of a road to which the regulation applies causes or is expected to cause noise at a level not less than the specified level which affects an "eligible building". The regulation applies to new roads and existing roads for which an additional carriageway has been or is to be constructed. To qualify, the noise level, which is to be calculated in accordance with advice and instructions issued by the Minister, must be greater by at least ldB(a) than the prevailing level immediately before works began and must be not less than the specified level (Regulation 6). "Eligible buildings" comprise dwelling-houses and other buildings used for residential purposes (Regulation 7). The roads authority must prepare and publish a map or list identifying eligible buildings having a facade in respect of which the noise level is greater than the specified level. Provision is made for offer and acceptance of insulation work or grant, for establishing the nature and extent of the work to be under-taken and for determining the amount of grant.

Regulation 4 also gives roads authorities a *discretion* to carry out insulation works or to make a grant in respect of noise caused or expected to be caused by alterations to an existing road and in other prescribed circumstances.

Similar power to that set out in section 18 of the 1973 Act is conferred on the Scottish Ministers by section 79 of the Civil Aviation Act 1982. If it appears to the Scottish Ministers that buildings near to an aerodrome designated by the Ministers require protection from noise and vibration attributable to the use of the aerodrome, they may make a scheme requiring the person for the time being managing the aerodrome to make grants towards the cost of insulating such buildings against noise. Such a scheme is limited to a particular aerodrome and its locality.

2. Mitigating works

14–25   Section 106 of the 1984 Act[68] enables a roads authority to acquire land, compulsorily or by agreement, for the purpose of mitigating any adverse effect which the existence or use of a road constructed or improved by them[69] (or proposed to be constructed or approved by them) will have on the surroundings of the road (section 106(1)). The authority may also acquire, but only by agreement, land the enjoyment

---

[67] SI 1975/460.

[68] Sections 52, 53 and 106 of the Roads (Scotland) Act 1984 replaced sections 20–23 of the 1973 Act (which were repealed by section 156(3) and Schedule 11 to the 1984 Act).

[69] References to the construction or improvement of a road in section 106 of the 1984 Act include references to the construction or improvement of a road under an order made under sections 9 or 12 of that Act (s.106(6)).

of which is seriously affected by the construction or improvement of a road (s.106(2)(a)) or by the subsequent use of the road (s.106(2)(b)). The interest of the seller of such land must however fall within the definition of a "qualifying interest" for the purposes of the planning blight provisions.[70] The powers under section 106(1) and (2)(a) may not be exercised unless the acquisition is begun before the date on which the road, or the improved road, as the case may be, is opened to public traffic, and the powers conferred by section 106(2)(b) may not be exercised unless the acquisition is begun before the end of one year after that date (s.106(3))[71] Section 106(2A) allows the discretionary power of acquisition to be exercised from an early stage in the life of the works.[72]

Section 52 of the 1984 Act empowers a roads authority to carry out on land acquired under section 106 or on other land belonging to them[73] works for mitigating any adverse effect which the construction, improvement, existence or use of any road has or will have on its surroundings. These works may include the planting of trees, shrubs or plants and the laying out of any area as grassland (s.52(2)). The authority may also develop or redevelop such land for the purpose of improving the surroundings.

A roads authority may also negotiate an agreement with any person having an interest in land adjoining or in the vicinity of a road, or proposed road, with a view to restricting or regulating the use of the land permanently or for a specified period so as to mitigate the adverse effect generated by the construction, improvement, existence or use of such road. The agreement may provide for the planting and maintenance of trees, shrubs or plants and for restricting the lopping or removal of trees, shrubs or plants. If recorded in the Register of Sasines or in the Land Register of Scotland, as appropriate, such an agreement will be enforceable against singular successors (s.53(3) and (4)).

Somewhat similar powers to acquire land by agreement and to carry out works for the purpose of mitigating the adverse effects of public works on their surroundings are conferred on the "responsible authority"[74] by sections 24 and 25 of the 1973 Act.[75]

3. Expenses of temporary removal

A roads authority, in respect of the construction and improvement of **14–26** a road, and a "responsible authority" in respect of the construction or alteration of other public works, are empowered to pay the reasonable

---

[70] The reference to the date of service of a notice under section 101 of the 1997 Act is to be taken as a reference to the date on which a purchase agreement is made under the 1984 Act, s.106(2).

[71] The circumstances in which an acquisition is to be treated as begun for the purposes of s.106(3) are defined in subs.(4).

[72] Added to section 106 of the 1984 Act by the Planning and Compensation Act 1991, s.76(2).

[73] Such works may also be carried out by the roads authority on a road for which they are the responsible authority and on a road which they have been authorised to improve or construct by an order under sections 9 or 12 of the 1984 Act (s.52(1)(c) and (d)).

[74] "Public works" and "responsible authority" are defined in s.24(6) by reference to the 1973 Act, s.1 except that "public works" does not include a road or any works forming part of a statutory undertaking as defined in section 214(1) of the 1997 Act.

[75] Section 24 was amended by the Planning and Compensation Act 1991, s.76(1) by the addition of subsections (2A)–(2C) which allow the exercise of the power of discretionary acquisition from a much earlier stage in the life of the works.

expenses of the occupier of a dwelling adjacent to the works who is required temporarily to find and move to suitable alternative accommodation because the carrying on of the works affects the enjoyment of the dwelling to such an extent that continued occupation is not reasonably practicable (section 26 of the 1973 Act).

PART 4

THE ACQUISITION OF NEW RIGHTS IN LAND FALLING SHORT OF OWNERSHIP

CHAPTER 15

UTILITY "WAYLEAVES"[1]

INTRODUCTION

In order to bring services such as water, sewerage, electricity, gas and **15–01** telecommunications to the consumer, it is necessary to install a network of pipes, cables, poles, pylons and masts, together with supporting facilities. Ready access to such services is considered to be in the public interest and Parliament has conferred statutory powers on the suppliers, including where necessary the use of compulsion, to secure the installation, maintenance, repair, improvement and replacement of the necessary infrastructure. These powers typically provide for the creation of a "wayleave"[2] or, where a more formal arrangement is required, something akin to a servitude (below).

This is a relatively neglected area of academic and professional literature.[3] This is surprising given the extensive network of pipes, cables and so on in existence at the present time, given the large number of "wayleaves" that are negotiated each year and given the anticipated growth in the level of services to be supplied by cable and telephone during the next decade.

The exercise of powers of compulsion in this context differs from the powers described earlier in this book in that some of these services are

---

[1] This chapter is derived from, and in some places makes use of, earlier work undertaken by N. Hutchison and the author with the support of the RICS Education Trust and published as *Utility Wayleaves: A Legislative Lottery* (2002) RICS *Research Paper* Vol.3, No.10. See too J. Rowan Robinson and N. Hutchison, "Utility Wayleaves: Time for Reform" [2001] J.P.L. 1247; and N. Hutchison and J. Rowan Robinson, "Utility Wayleaves: A Compensation Lottery?" (2002) *Journal of Property Investment & Finance* Vol.20, No.2, p.159.

[2] The term "wayleave" seems to have been imported into Scots Law from England where it originally referred to a money payment in exchange for the use of land for the extraction of minerals. It has come to apply to any arrangement under which a person is granted a licence to use land, often for running pipe-lines, cables and so on, in return for a money payment.

[3] But see, in addition to the articles cited above, D. Cusine and R. Paisley, *Servitudes and Rights of Way* (W. Green & Son, 1998) Chap.26; H. W. Wilkinson, *Pipes, Mains, Cables and Sewers* (6th ed., FT Law & Tax, 1995); and B. Denyer-Green, "Specific Purposes, Specific Powers: the Powers of the Privatised Utilities", in Proceedings of the National Symposium *Compulsory Purchase: An Appropriate Power for the 21st Century?* (1999) DETR.

now provided by the private sector. There is nothing very new about this; it may be seen as a move back towards the approach adopted in the ninetenth century when many of the utilities were in the private sector and operated with the benefit of compulsory powers. When the utilities were brought into the public sector, procedures were streamlined and compensation was pegged to the fair market value. When some of them were returned again to the private sector during the 1980s,[4] they took with them the compulsory powers accompanied, for the most part, by the streamlined procedures and fair market value compensation. There was no significant adjustment in procedure or compensation to reflect the new status of the utilities as profit-seeking bodies. This lack of adjustment has not gone unchallenged. McAuslan and McEldowney observed:

> " . . . the whole law of compulsory acquisition and compensation is based on the assumption that a public agency is acquiring land in the public interest and it is permissible in the circumstances that a legal framework is created which ensures that an even hand is held between the interests of the tax-payer and the private land-owner. It must be open to question whether the same basic framework is wholly appropriate where a commercial organisation wishes to purchase land for its commercial purposes".[5]

And Barry Denyer-Green commented that:

> "When these powers were exercised by public authorities and publicly owned industries, there was probably a degree of grudging acceptance that expropriation was being carried out for the public benefit. Now that powers are frequently exercised in connection with commercial activities, property owners cannot be expected to accept that there is public benefit. They want a share of the commercial advantage and an appropriate price for the right taken through the land".[6]

The justification for conferring powers of compulsion to secure the provision of these services rests on the premise that the appropriate body, public or private, is carrying on functions having a public purpose. For example, under the Gas Act 1986, Transco, as a public gas transporter, is under a duty to develop and maintain an efficient and economical pipe-line system for the conveyance of gas[7]; and under the Electricity Act 1989 there is a duty on public electricity suppliers to develop and maintain an efficient, co-ordinated and economical system of electricity supply.[8] Although research suggests that, in practice, it is

---

[4] Unlike the position in England and Wales, water supply and sewage disposal have remained public sector functions in Scotland.

[5] "Electricity Act 1989", *Current Law Statutes Annotated*, Chap.29, annotations by P. McAuslan and L. McEldowney.

[6] B. Denyer-Green, "Specific Purposes, Specific Powers: The Powers of Privatised Utilities", *supra.*

[7] Gas Act 1986, s.9, as substituted by the Gas Act 1995, Sch.3, para.3.

[8] s.9(1).

rarely necessary for the utilities to resort to compulsory powers, it seems that the existence of such powers in the background is an important factor in securing agreement.[9] Many of the services are also provided in linear form so that landowners along the line enjoy something of a monopoly position and there is a fear that, in the absence of fall-back powers of compulsion, the market would not operate efficiently. The public purpose underlying the exercise of powers suggests that, if there is to be an adjustment to reflect the change in status of some of the utilities, this should focus, not on powers, but on procedures and compensation. This matter is currently under review.[10]

As mentioned at the beginning of this book (p.12), an acquiring **15–02** authority has no rights beyond those expressly conferred by Parliament. A power to acquire land compulsorily cannot be relied on as the basis for creating *new* rights in land falling short of ownership unless this is expressly stipulated for in the legislation.[11] If a public authority does not need to acquire the ownership of land but requires a lesser right in the land, for example a right to lay and maintain a pipe-line, it must be able to point to express statutory authority to create such a right. Such a power cannot be implied. There are, however, numerous Acts providing in one way or another for the creation of a 'wayleave' or something akin to a servitude[12]; indeed, so numerous are these provisions that it is not possible in this book to deal comprehensively with them. Attention is, therefore, focused in this chapter on the provisions relating to what are generally regarded as the most important of the services: gas, electricity, telecommunications, water and sewerage. Reference is also made to the procedure whereby a private pipe-line promoter can obtain a compulsory rights order.

The instrument created by these provisions has been referred to so far as a 'wayleave' or a right akin to a servitude. The terminology can, however, be confusing and it is sometimes difficult in practice to distinguish the one from the other. Before examining the relevant provisions, it is appropriate, therefore, to say something about the nature of these instruments—to use a neutral term.

The legislation quite often makes provision for the creation of two different instruments. First of all, the power to acquire land compulsorily will sometimes expressly include acquisition by the creation of a new right. This right is sometimes referred to in practice as a servitude but this is not a term generally employed in the legislation[13] and the right does not altogether conform to the requirements of a servitude at common law.[14] In particular, there is no dominant tenement and some of

---

[9] N. Hutchison and J. Rowan Robinson, "Utility Wayleaves: A Legislative Lottery" (2002) RICS *Research Paper* Vol.3, No.10.

[10] See the Law Commission Consultation, "Towards a compulsory purchase code: (1) Compensation" *Paper No 165*, para.8.11.

[11] *Sovmots Investments Ltd v Secretary of State for the Environment* [1977] 1 Q.B. 411. It will generally be sufficient to acquire *existing* rights.

[12] For a list of the more obvious powers, see N. Hutchison and J. Rowan Robinson, *supra*, n.9, App.1.

[13] Exceptionally, the Telecommunications Act 1984, s.34(1) specifically refers to the creation of an easement or other right.

[14] For a comprehensive discussion of these requirements see D. Cusine and R. Paisley, *supra*, n.3, Chap.2.

the ancillary rights to install fixtures go beyond what could be achieved with a servitude. Indeed, research suggests that the new right is sometimes constituted in practice as a lease which, in some cases, might be said to more properly reflect the nature of the relationship between the parties[15]; and leases are quite often used for pipe-lines.

Secondly, the same legislation may also provide for the creation of what is generally referred to as a wayleave, although the legislation does not always use this term. The term is loosely applied to a statutory right conferred on utilities to install, maintain, repair and replace their infrastructure in private land. The purpose of the provision would seem to be to provide a less formal option for dealing with short term arrangements.

Normally, a wayleave would be regarded as a form of licence which is personal to the parties and precarious or terminable after an agreed period. It will not run with the land so as to bind successors in title. Because of this, the price for a wayleave is often paid by way of annual payments. Servitudes, on the other hand, if properly constituted, constitute a real right in land, they are annexed to identifiable land, they may be of indefinite duration and the benefit and burden run with the respective dominant and servient tenements so as to be enforceable by and against singular successors. Because of this, payment for the grant of a servitude is likely to be by way of a capital sum.

The problem with the statutory versions of these two instruments is that, when employed in practice, they may not conform to either model; the distinctions become blurred. The benefit of these statutory 'servitudes' is not annexed to identifiable land; and statutory wayleaves often run for a considerable period, sometimes indefinitely; indeed, some of the statutory provisions stipulate that they will bind anyone who is at any time an owner or occupier of the land so that to all intents and purposes they serve the same purpose as the right akin to a servitude. It may therefore be difficult to know just what has been created under these statutory powers and how far, if at all, the general law may be applicable. They are creatures of statute and their creation, extent and consequence depend on the relevant statute.

The purpose of this chapter is to describe the procedures and the compensation provisions applicable to these instruments in securing the installation of these services in and through private land.[16] It should be noted that the rights described are generally supplemented in statute by other provisions such as the right of entry to inspect, maintain, repair and replace the infrastructure. As these rights differ in some respects from one service to another, the key services are now considered in turn.

GAS

15–03 The Gas Act 1986 imposes a duty on a gas transporter to develop and maintain an efficient and economical pipe-line system for the conveyance of gas.[17] A gas transporter is responsible for providing and

---

[15] See N. Hutchison and J. Rowan Robinson, *supra*, n.9.
[16] It does not deal with the provisions for taking services through public roads and streets.
[17] s.9, as substituted by the Gas Act 1995, Sch.3, para.3.

operating the pipe-line system through which gas is delivered. To assist in the discharge of this duty, gas transporters, at the moment principally Transco, are given power in the 1986 Act to acquire land compulsorily and this power expressly includes the acquisition of rights by the creation of new rights.[18] The exercise of the right requires the authorisation of the Secretary of State for Trade and Industry.[19] The 1986 Act applies the procedure in the Acquisition of Land (Authorisation Procedure) (Scotland) Act 1947 to the creation of such rights.[20] The procedure mirrors that for compulsory purchase order procedure (see Chapter 2) with slight adaptations. The procedure involves the following steps:

- preparation of order;
- notice to owners, lessees and occupiers of the making of the order;
- public advertisement of the making of the order;
- submission of the order for authorisation to the appropriate Minister;
- opportunity for objection;
- right to be heard in support of objections;
- notice to owners, lessees and occupiers of the decision of the confirming authority; and
- public notice of the decision.

The 1986 Act makes provision for compensation for the creation of the new right. It applies section 61 of the Lands Clauses Consolidation (Scotland) Act 1845, as amended.[21] In its amended form it reads:

"In estimating the purchase money or compensation to be paid by the promoters of the undertaking in the Special Act, in any of the cases aforesaid, regard shall be had not only to the extent (if any) to which the value of the land over which the right is to be acquired is depreciated by the acquisition of the right, but also to the damage (if any) to be sustained by the owner of the land by reason of its severance from other land of his, or injuriously affecting that other land by the exercise of the powers conferred by this or the Special Act".

As Denyer-Green points out,[22] this identifies two heads of claim: depreciation in the value of the land in, on or over which the apparatus

---

[18] s.9(3) and Sch.3, Pt I, para.1(2), as amended by the Gas Act 1995, Sch.3, para.56.
[19] Gas Act 1986, Sch.3, para.1.
[20] Sch.3, Pt III, para.14–22, as amended by the Gas Act 1995, Sch.3, para.56.
[21] Gas Act 1986, Sch.3, para.24, as amended by the Gas Act 1995, Sch.4, para.56.
[22] B. Denyer-Green, "Specific Purposes, Specific Powers: The Powers of Privatised Utilities" in Proceedings of the National Symposium on *Compulsory Purchase: An Appropriate Power for the 21st Century?* (1999) DETR.

is to be laid, including any lost development potential; and severance and other injurious affection. Any value attributable to the scheme of the gas transporter would be ignored on the basis of the rule in *Pointe Gourde* (see ch.8).[23] The Land Compensation Act rules are indirectly applied via the application of section 1(3) of the 1947 Act. Disturbance would seem to be payable, if any, on the basis that disturbance is part of the value of the land to the owner (see chapter 10). Unresolved disputes over compensation are referred to the Lands Tribunal for Scotland.[24]

Curiously, there is no provision in the Gas Acts of 1986 and 1995 for the compulsory creation of wayleaves for the benefit of gas transporters. The practical result is that where Transco need to rely on statutory powers, they will use the more formal right akin to a servitude.

ELECTRICITY

15–04 The Electricity Act 1989 imposes a duty on public electricity suppliers to develop and maintain an efficient, co-ordinated and economical system of electricity supply.[25] To assist in the discharge of this duty, suppliers are given power to acquire land compulsorily including the acquisition of rights by the creation of new rights.[26] The 1989 Act applies the procedure in the Acquisition of Land (Authorisation Procedure) (Scotland) Act 1947 to the exercise of this power.[27] The procedure is slightly adapted for the creation of a new right. The steps in the procedure are the same as those described above for creation of a new right for gas transporters.

The 1989 Act makes provision for the payment of compensation for the creation of a new right.[28] It applies section 61 of the Lands Clauses Consolidation (Scotland) Act 1845, as amended. In its amended form it reads:

> "In estimating the purchase money or compensation to be paid by the licence holder under the Special Act, in any of the cases aforesaid, regard shall be had not only to the extent (if any) to which the value of the land over which the right is to be acquired is depreciated by the acquisition of the right, but also to the damage (if any) to be sustained by the owner of the land by reason of its severance from other land of his, or injuriously affecting that other land by the exercise of the powers conferred by this or the Special Act".

As with the Gas Acts, the provision identifies two heads of claim: depreciation in the value of land and severance and injurious affection.

---

[23] *Pointe Gourde Quarrying and Transport Co v Sub-Intendent of Crown Lands* [1947] A.C. 565.
[24] Land Compensation (Scotland) Act 1963, s.8.
[25] s.9(1).
[26] 1989 Act, s.10 and Sch.3, para.1(1)(2).
[27] 1989 Act, s.10(1) and Sch.3, Pt III, para.16.
[28] 1989 Act, Sch.3, Pt III, paras 25–29. See too N. Hutchison, A. Cameron and J. Rowan Robinson, "Assessing the compensation for electricity wayleaves" (1999) *Journal of Property Investment and Finance* Vol.17, No.2, p.176.

Any value attributable to the scheme of the electricity supplier would be ignored on the basis of the rule in *Pointe Gourde* (see ch.8). The Land Compensation Act rules are applied.[29] Disturbance would seem to be payable, if incurred, on the basis that disturbance is part of the value of the land to the owner (see ch.10). Unresolved disputes over compensation are referred to the Lands Tribunal for Scotland.[30]

In the discharge of their duties under the Electricity Act 1989 suppliers are also given power to make application to the Secretary of State for Trade and Industry for the grant of a wayleave to install and keep an electric line on, under or over land where this cannot be secured by agreement.[31] The following procedural steps are prescribed:

- the electricity supplier must be satisfied that it is necessary or expedient to install and keep installed an electric line on, over, under, etc land;
- the owner or occupier of the land must be given notice requesting the grant of a wayleave in appropriate terms within a specified period (minimum 21 days);
- the owner or occupier must fail to grant the wayleave or must grant it subject to terms and conditions which are not acceptable to the electricity supplier;
- the electricity supplier applies to the Minister for the grant of the necessary wayleave on acceptable terms and conditions[32];
- the Minister will afford the owner and occupier an opportunity of being heard in connection with the application;
- the Minister will make a decision on the application;
- if granted, the wayleave will run for whatever period is stipulated.

Such a wayleave can confer wide powers on an electricity supplier. These include power to install, maintain, adjust, repair, alter, replace and remove a line together with power to place support for a line. A wayleave granted by the Minister will, for its duration, bind any person who is at any time the owner or occupier of the land.[33]

The 1989 Act provides for the payment of compensation to the occupier of the land (and to the owner where the owner is not in occupation) for the grant by the Minister of a wayleave.[34] In addition, compensation is payable for any damage to land or moveables and for disturbance.[35] The onus is on a claimant to substantiate his claim and the claim is usually made once and for all at the valuation date.[36] Compensa-

---

[29] 1989 Act, Sch.3, para.29.
[30] Land Compensation (Scotland) Act 1963, s.8.
[31] 1989 Act, s.10 and Sch.4, para.6.
[32] No application may be made in respect of land covered by a dwelling.
[33] 1989 Act, s.10(1) and Sch.4, para.6(6)(b).
[34] See above, para.7(1).
[35] See above, para.7(2).
[36] *Christian Salvesan (Properties) Ltd. v Central Electricity Generating Board* (1984) 48 P. & C.R. 465. There is, however, nothing to prevent the parties from stipulating in the wayleave for a review of compensation in the event of a defined future event, *e.g.*, a refusal of planning permission because of the existence of the structures. The valuation date will be the earlier of the date of entry on the land or the date of assessment of compensation.

tion may be paid as a lump sum or as a periodical payment or partly one way and partly the other. Unresolved disputes are referred to the Lands Tribunal for Scotland.[37] No further assistance is gained from the Act as to what is meant by "compensation for the grant". Is it to be measured by the loss to the claimant or is an element of consideration to be paid?[38] And if it is limited to loss to the claimant, what losses are contemplated? Unlike wayleaves for pipe-lines, electricity wayleaves may result in structures on land which have a serious effect on the view and a corresponding depreciating effect on the value of 'retained' land. Not only that, but the safety requirements of grid lines can sterilise not only the strip of land below the wires but also adjoining land. Does compensation for the grant encompass compensation for injurious affection? In practice such compensation is paid. However, the Land Compensation Act rules are not applied and the result, as Denyer-Green points out, is that the measure of compensation remains unclear.[39]

To overcome these uncertainties, the electricity suppliers have negotiated rates of payment for wayleaves with the Scottish Landowners Federation and the National Farmers Union for Scotland, representing the people most affected by the installation of electricity apparatus. These guideline rates, although not binding, are widely applied in practice.

TELECOMMUNICATIONS

15–05   The Telecommunications Act 1984 provides for the operation of telecommunications systems by licensed public telecommunications operators. The Act imposes no specific public duty on operators but access to telecommunications systems is considered to be a matter of public interest; indeed, the Telecommunications Code in Schedule 2 to the Act refers to the "principle" that no person should be unreasonably denied access to a telecommunications system.[40]

Public telecommunications operators are given power to acquire land compulsorily in discharge of their functions and this power includes the acquisition of servitude or other rights by the creation of new rights.[41] The procedure set out in the Acquisition of Land (Authorisation Procedure) (Scotland) Act 1947 is applied to the creation of such rights[42] and the principal steps are set out in the section dealing with *Gas* (above). The 1947 Act incorporates the provisions of the Lands Clauses Consolidation (Scotland) Act 1845, including the compensation provisions so that compensation is payable under section 61 of the 1845 Act for depreciation in the value of land and for severance and injurious affection. The Land Compensation Act rules are applied indirectly

---

[37] 1989 Act, s.10(1) and Sch.4, para.7(4).
[38] There is some evidence that the Lands Tribunal have taken as the measure of compensation the effect on the market value of the land (see *Clouds Estates Trs. v Southern Electricity Board* (1983) 268 E.G. 367 and 451).
[39] B Denyer-Green, *supra*, n.3.
[40] para.5(3).
[41] Telecommunications Act 1984, s.35(3).
[42] 1984 Act, s.35(1).

through the section 1(3) of the 1947 Act. Disturbance would seem to be payable, if incurred, on the basis that it is part of the value of the land to the claimant (see ch.10). Unresolved disputes are referred to the Lands Tribunal for Scotland.[43]

The 1984 Act also makes provision for something akin to wayleaves. The Telecommunications Code deals with the arrangements for the execution of works on private land by operators in discharge of their functions. Paragraph 2 of the Code provides that an operator must obtain the agreement in writing of the occupier of the land to confer a right to carry out works for telecommunications purposes on the land. The right includes the right to install lines to connect to telecommunications apparatus (para.10). Paragraph 2 also deals with the extent to which the owner is bound by such an agreement if the owner is not the occupier. It will be for the parties to agree the terms and conditions, including financial provisions, that will apply to such an agreement.[44] However, paragraph 4(4) of the Code protects the position of owners not currently in occupation by providing for compensation to be paid equal to any depreciation in the value of the claimant's interest in the land which will result from the constraints on removal of the works from the land. The Land Compensation Act rules are applied to the determination of depreciation. Unresolved disputes are to be referred to the Lands Tribunal for Scotland.

Where the agreement of any person is required to the conferring of such a right and this cannot be obtained, the operator may give notice under paragraph 5 of the Code to that person of the right and the agreement required. If after 28 days the required agreement in writing has not been forthcoming, the operator may apply to the sheriff for an order conferring the proposed right and dispensing with the need for the agreement of the person (para.5). A sheriff is to make such an order only if he is satisfied that any prejudice caused by an order is: (a) capable of being adequately compensated for by money (below); or (b) the prejudice is outweighed by the benefit accruing from the order to the persons whose access to a telecommunications system will be secured by the order. The Code provides that, in determining the extent of prejudice, the sheriff is to have regard to all the circumstances and to the principle (referred to above) that no person should unreasonably be denied access to a telecommunications system. The order may include such terms and conditions as appear to the sheriff appropriate for ensuring that the least possible loss and damage is caused by the exercise of the right.

Where agreement of the occupier is dispensed with, the sheriff will fix the terms and conditions governing the right, including the financial terms. The financial terms will include such payment, reflecting consideration for the 'agreement' or the exercise of rights, as appears "would have been fair and reasonable if the agreement had been given willingly" (para.7(1)). This test was considered in *Mercury Communications Ltd v London and India Dock Investments Ltd.*[45] in which the court held that

---

[43] Land Compensation (Scotland) Act 1963, s.8.
[44] But see the discussion below regarding the financial conditions that will apply where the agreement of any person is dispensed with.
[45] (1994) 69 P. & C.R. 135.

what was fair and reasonable involved an element of subjective judgement and that the phrase should be interpreted without regard to
compulsory purchase principles.[46] The *Pointe Gourde* rule therefore had
no application. The court considered that wayleave payments for rights
granted under the Act should normally reflect the use made of the right
granted and its importance to the grantee. However, that was considered
inappropriate in this case which was essentially a right of way case. In
the end, a fair and reasonable consideration was determined by reference to settlements under two earlier agreements negotiated in the area.

The compensation will also include recompense for any loss or
damage sustained in consequence of the exercise of the right (para.7(1)).
In addition, regard is to be had to the prejudicial effect, if any, of the
order or the exercise of the right on the claimant's enjoyment of land
other than that in relation to which the right is conferred (para.7(2)).

WATER SUPPLY

15–06 Unlike England and Wales, water supply remains a public sector
function in Scotland. Until 1994 it was a local authority function. It was
removed from local authority control by the Local Government etc
(Scotland) Act 1994 and given to three appointed water authorities.
Subsequently, as a result of the Water Industry (Scotland) Act 2002 it
became the responsibility of Scottish Water.

Section 6 of the Water (Scotland) Act 1980 requires Scottish Water to
provide a supply of wholesome water to every part of its limits of supply
where a supply of water is required for domestic purposes and can be
provided at a reasonable cost. Section 9 of the Act deals with the supply
for non-domestic purposes.

To discharge these duties, Scottish Water is given power to acquire
land compulsorily subject to confirmation by the Scottish Ministers.[47]
However, no mention is made of acquiring a right by the creation of a
new right and such a power cannot be implied.[48] There is, therefore, no
provision for the creation of a new right akin to a servitude.

However, under section 23 of the 1980 Act, Scottish Water is given
power to lay a water main in private land after first giving notice to the
owner and occupier. Section 23(1A) of the 1980 Act[49] provides that, if
within two months of giving notice, the owner or occupier objects, the
authority cannot proceed but must refer the matter by summary
application to the sheriff whose decision on the matter will be final. In
Central Regional Council v Ferns[50] Lord Kincraig described the right to
lay and maintain a water main as "similar to, if not identical with, those
of a servitude of *aquaeductus* in which the Board is the dominant owner
and the proprietors of the land the owners of the servient tenement".

---

[46] Contrast the decisions in *Re Naylor Benzon Mining Co Ltd* [1950] Ch. 567; and *BP
Petroleum Developments Ltd v Ryder* [1987] R.V.R. 211, both of which turned on similar
wording in the Mines (Working Facilities and Support) Acts 1923 and 1966.
[47] Water Industry (Scotland) Act 2002, s.47. Separate provision is made for the
acquisition of water rights.
[48] *Sovmots Investments Ltd v Secretary of State for the Environment* [1977] 1 Q.B. 411.
[49] Added by the Local Government, etc (Scotland) Act 1994, s.109.
[50] 1979 S.C. 136.

Section 23(2) makes provision for compensation for any damage done to or injurious affection of the land resulting from the laying of the main. The Land Compensation Act rules are not applied. Disputes are to be settled by arbitration.

SEWAGE DISPOSAL

Like water supply, sewage disposal remains a public sector function in **15–07** Scotland and is the responsibility of Scottish Water. Section 1 of the Sewerage (Scotland) Act 1968 imposes a general duty on Scottish Water to provide such public sewers as may be necessary to effectively drain its area of domestic sewage, surface water and trade effluent. To assist in the discharge of this function the authority is given power in section 47 of the Water Industry (Scotland) Act 2002 to acquire land compulsorily subject to confirmation by the Scottish Ministers. However, this power does not include a power to acquire a right by the creation of a new right and no such right can be implied.[51]

Section 3 of the 1968 Act does, however, confer a power to lay a public sewer in private land. Prior notice must be given to the owner and occupier. Section 3A of the Act allows the authority to authorise some other person to exercise the power.[52] In both cases there is an opportunity to object (within two months of the giving of the notice) to the laying of the pipe and the authority must obtain the consent of the sheriff before proceeding.

Section 20 of the 1968 Act makes provision for compensation for any loss, injury or damage sustained by any person by reason of the exercise of this power. The Land Compensation Act rules are not applied. Any disputes are to be settled by arbitration.

PIPE-LINES

So far in this chapter, attention has focused on rights granted by **15–08** Parliament to public and private bodies to enable them to exercise public functions. Private bodies exercising private functions will normally have to rely on negotiation if they wish to acquire rights over someone else's land. However, it has been recognised that there will sometimes be a public interest in the efficient discharge of private functions. For example, there is a public interest in access to the nation's mineral resources. This is recognised in the Mines (Working Facilities and Support) Acts 1966 and 1974 which make provision for the granting of compulsory rights orders giving access to such resources where this is considered to be expedient in the national interest. This provision is not often employed in practice.

Another example is oil and chemical companies wishing to convey liquids, commercial gases and slurries by pipe-line. The efficient distribu-

---

[51] *Sovmots Investments Ltd v Secretary of State for the Environment* [1977] 1 Q.B. 411.
[52] Added by the Local Government (Scotland) Act 1994, s.101.

tion of oil by pipe-line throughout Great Britain would seem to be as much in the public interest as the efficient distribution of gas. This is recognised in the Pipe-lines Act 1962 which allows a private pipe-line promoter to obtain a compulsory rights order to install a commercial pipe-line in private land. The Act does not apply to the installation of drains and sewers; nor does it apply to pipe-lines operated by gas transporters. There is an extensive network of commercial pipe-lines in the UK and the development of the offshore oil industry has resulted in considerable onshore pipe-line construction activity in Scotland over the years.[53] Because of this the procedure for acquiring the necessary rights to install a pipe-line in private land is outlined here.

The 1962 Act distinguishes the authorisation procedure for the construction of a "cross-country"[54] pipe-line along a defined route[55] from the procedure for acquiring the necessary rights to install a pipe-line in private land. The purpose of the authorisation procedure is to consider the case for the installation of the pipe-line, the route to be followed and the specification. The acquisition of the necessary rights to install the pipe-line is initially a matter for private negotiation. However, in recognition of the difficulties that may be encountered in securing such rights, the 1962 Act provides for an application by the promoter to the appropriate Minister for a compulsory purchase order[56] or a compulsory rights order.[57]

The 1962 Act sets out its own procedure for the application by a promoter for the grant of a compulsory purchase order and for the making of the order by the Minister.[58] The Land Compensation Act rules apply to the assessment of compensation.[59]

A compulsory rights order confers power on the promoter to install and use the pipe-line[60] together with ancillary rights. The procedure for the making of such an order is modelled on that for a compulsory purchase order but with adaptations.[61] If such an order is granted and implemented, a person having an interest in the subject land is entitled to compensation for any depreciation in the value of the interest and for any damage or disturbance resulting from the exercise of the rights granted by the order.[62]

Compulsory powers are not often employed in respect of pipe-lines but their existence in the background has facilitated negotiations for leases, servitudes or wayleaves, as appropriate.

---

[53] See Planning Advice Note 25: Commercial Pipelines.

[54] The Act sets out an authorisation procedure for pipe-lines exceeding 16 km in length. Shorter "local" pipe-lines are subject to planning control in the normal way.

[55] For a discussion of the issues arising in the authorisation process, see Planning Advice Note 25: Commercial Pipelines.

[56] 1962 Act, s.11. There is no power to promote a compulsory purchase order to acquire a right by the creation of a new right, presumably because of the power in s.12 to promote a compulsory rights order.

[57] See above, s.12.

[58] See above, Second Schedule.

[59] See above, s.11(4)(6) and the Third Schedule.

[60] See above, s.12(1) and the Fourth Schedule.

[61] See above, s.12(3) and the Second Schedule.

[62] See above, s.14.

CONCLUSION

The provisions whereby the different services described in this chapter **15–09** are provided are unnecessarily complex and confusing. They have evolved in a piecemeal way. Not only do the procedures differ, so too do the measures of compensation—and for no obvious reason. As one commentator aptly observed, "the only principle of general application is that compensation is payable for land or rights acquired. Beyond that, the compensation regime is industry specific.[63] Denyer-Green saw no reason why there should not be consistency across all utility services.[64] There would seem to be much to be said for introducing a standard procedure for wayleaves in much the same way as there is a standard procedure for compulsory purchase; and the opportunity could be taken at the same time to standardise the measure and scope of the compensation claim. This is currently under consideration.[65]

---

[63] T. Smithers, "Utilities and land rights" (February 13, 1999) *Estates Gazette* p.172.

[64] "Specific Purposes, Specific Powers: the Powers of Privatised Utilities" in Proceedings of the National Symposium *"Compulsory Purchase: An Appropriate Power for the 21st Century,* (1999) DETR. See, too, J. Rowan Robinson and N. Hutchison, "Utility Wayleaves: Time for Reform" [2001] J.P.L. 1247; and N. Hutchison and J. Rowan Robinson, "Utility wayleaves: a compensation lottery" (2002) *Journal of Property Investment and Finance* Vol.20, No.2, p.159.

[65] See the Law Commission Consultation, "Towards a compulsory purchase code: (1) Compensation" *Paper No 165*, para.8.11.

INDEX